HISTORY OF THE

COLD WAR

..

FROM THE KOREAN WAR

TO THE PRESENT

ALSO BY ANDRÉ FONTAINE

HISTORY OF THE COLD WAR

FROM THE OCTOBER REVOLUTION

TO THE KOREAN WAR

A DIVISION OF RANDOM HOUSE *NEW YORK*

ANDRÉ FONTAINE

HISTORY

OF THE

COLD

WAR

FROM THE KOREAN WAR

TO THE PRESENT

· ·

TRANSLATED FROM THE FRENCH BY

RENAUD BRUCE

PANTHEON BOOKS

CONTENTS

PART TWO

CHINA TAKES UP THE TORCH

LIST OF MAPS

LIST OF
ABBREVIATIONS

A.I.O.C.—Anglo-Iranian Oil Company

ANZUS—Treaty between the United States, Australia and New Zealand

Comecon—Organization of Mutual Cooperation of the European socialist countries

Cominform—Information Bureau of the National Workers' Parties

C.P.S.U.—Communist Party of the Soviet Union

Ex-Com—Executive Committee (of the National Security Council of the United States during the Cuban crisis)

G.D.R.—East German Democratic Republic

NASA—National Aeronautics and Space Administration

N.E.P.—New Economic Policy

N.I.O.C.—National Iranian Oil Company

O.A.S.—Organization of the Secret Army (in Algeria)

O.A.S.—Organization of American States

NATO—North Atlantic Treaty Organization

SEATO—Southeast Asia Treaty Organization

U.A.R.—United Arab Republic

HISTORY OF THE
COLD WAR

. .

FROM THE KOREAN WAR
TO THE PRESENT

INTRODUCTION

FIFTY YEARS AFTER THE BOLSHEVIK REVOLUTION, HAS the Cold War, its illegitimate offspring, finally come to an end? It would be premature to give a positive answer to that question while its most sinister symbol, the Berlin Wall, still stands in the heart of Europe, while Czechoslovakia is occupied by the troops of a bloc she is forbidden to leave, and while tens of thousands of Marxist guerrillas still clash with the superbly equipped gendarmes of the affluent society in Viet Nam. Moscow and Washington continue to invest a wealth of technological genius and fantastic amounts of money in the search for miracle weapons, for protective shields against those weapons and for the means of foiling those defenses. But every day, also, the two superpowers of the modern world are more clearly convinced that, in the nuclear age, force is incapable of resolving the differences over which, several times, they have come within inches of annihilating humanity.

This second volume of the *History of the Cold War,* which opens with the Korean War—the climax of the confrontation between the Soviet bloc and the bourgeois world—is, like the first, an attempt to analyze those differences and to retrace the chain of numerous resulting tests of strength. The last one goes back to 1962. That year, Kennedy and Khrushchev found themselves engaged in a dramatic confrontation over Cuba, when the least false step could have brought about a catastrophe. But having faced each other "eyeball to eyeball" during a long October week, they resolved that they would do everything possible to avoid the recurrence of such adventures, and less than a year later, in August 1963, their foreign ministers signed a treaty on the cessation of nuclear tests in the atmosphere.

It has been said repeatedly that the technological significance of that accord was minor, and no one denies it, but its political significance was immense, as it coincided with the first denunciation of Mao's heresy by the Kremlin.

For the first time in its history the country of the October Revolution placed the conclusion of an accord with "imperialism" before the maintenance of the unity in the socialistic bloc. Contrary to what the Communists had believed for years, it was clear that in their camp as well, competition between national interests could be stronger than ideological solidarity and the similarity of social systems. It is too early, of course, to speak of a reversal of alliances, but when one faces two enemies fighting each other, one cannot long refuse to choose between them. In any case the Chinese, for their part, have already decided that the Soviet "revisionists" have "effectively" become the allies of the Americans.

The turning point in the summer of 1963, which neither Kennedy's subsequent assassination nor Khrushchev's sudden fall really changed, marks the provisional termination of a "cold war" which historians will probably see more and more as the Third World War; a war in which it has been possible to localize the recourse to arms, but whose extreme severity was relative to its stakes—the triumph, on a world scale, of one or the other of two apparently irreconcilable social conceptions of life. In reality the Moscow treaty has confirmed the failure of the claims of each of them. The game that started immediately following the defeat of the Reich ended in a draw, in an armistice without victor or vanquished. One already wonders whether the Fourth World War, in which China will be one of the belligerents, will see it opposed either to the United States or to the U.S.S.R., or to both at the same time, and whether or not it will remain cold. Unless, of course, an unforeseen reversal brings back to power in Peking friends of the Moscow "revisionists"—which does not mean, however, that the Soviet bloc would thereby regain the conquering dynamism which earned it so many admirers and so many enemies twenty years ago.

Such speculations remain beyond the scope of this book. The author has attempted to take his revenge on time-serving journalism in doing the work of a historian. Has he succeeded? Of all the readers who have been willing to share with him their feelings on the first volume of this work, only one—not, however, the least—thought it was premature to write the history of the Cold War. It is tempting to rebut him with Pascal, for whom "any history which is not contemporary is suspect." As for me, I am rather tempted to believe that meeting the protagonists and knowing the places where events took place are no less necessary than a knowledge of the archives when trying to understand an epoch. Yet while the historian may not have at his disposal all the documents—who will ever have them, and who in our paper-consuming time could ever examine them?—at least he must not ignore whole segments of reality which, at the moment, are not perceptible. Alfred Fabre-Luce is correct in citing, in his brilliant *Histoire démaquillée,* the words of Jules Isaac, one of the most impartial historians in this century: "It is later, always later, that the disquieting visage of reality appears."

Reality: that is precisely what I have tried to find in this book; the reality that the revelations of destalinization and the publication of the principal elements in the Sino-Soviet dispute have greatly helped to discover, in retrospect. Unfortunately, one of the sources has dried up since Khrushchev's fall. And, also, for the history of American diplomacy since Kennedy's death, we do not have at our disposal the unrivaled documents such as those that three of his close advisers—Ted Sorensen, Arthur Schlesinger and Pierre Salinger —have devoted to his presidency. In particular everything concerning Viet Nam remains too controversial and insufficiently known to be talked about with the necessary serenity and objectivity.

Those two reasons—the importance of the turning point of 1963 and the insufficiency of information on the subsequent period—made me end the story of the Cold War there. For what followed, I have limited myself to an epilogue whose conclusions will probably have to be revised.

It remains for me to express my deep gratitude to the politicians and the diplomats who have been willing to search their memories for me or to discuss certain aspects of the events I am reporting; to my friends on *Le Monde,* without whose archives and advice the number of inevitable errors and omissions in such a book would certainly be much greater; to the readers—known and unknown— who have encouraged me to continue; and finally to the critics from all sides, who agreed in recognizing the honesty of my approach. Will

INTRODUCTION

they say as much of the second volume? This one reports events which
I have followed too closely not to have been passionately involved in.
However, my readers can be sure that, as with the first volume, it has
been written dispassionately and with the single aim of presenting, as
jurists say, the facts of the case.

A.F.

PART ONE

LEARNING THE FACTS OF COEXISTENCE

God wanted to stop their continual quarreling, and when he found that it was impossible, he fastened their heads together . . .

—Plato, *Phaedo*

· CHAPTER 1 ·

WAR IN THE

NAME OF PEACE

Being the strongest, he does not consider himself the
aggressor, and he defines his intention to invade the
lands of free peoples as self-defense.

—Bossuet, *Political Principles Drawn
from Holy Scripture*

AT DAWN ON SUNDAY, JUNE 29, 1950, NORTH KOREAN
troops crossed in force the narrow demarcation line which, at the
38th Parallel, divided the people's democracy from the pro-Western
regime of the aging Syngman Rhee. The Cold War was becoming a
hot war.

The news seemed so unbelievable, in spite of warnings which
American intelligence had been sending out for weeks, that at
first, people refused to take it seriously. A journalist passing
through Tokyo asked MacArthur if it was advisable for him to delay
his return to the United States. The hero of the Pacific war, now the
American proconsul in Japan, advised him not to be concerned over
such a trifle. Soon, however, the evidence had to be accepted. The
North Koreans had committed almost the whole of their small, Rus-
sian-equipped army—four divisions and three brigades of militia.
The attack was launched at four different points and was combined
with amphibious operations. In order to justify itself, the government of Pyongyang—the Communist capital—maintained, in an
order of the day, that the South Korean Government, after having
rejected all offers for the unification of the country, had invaded the

North. Under those circumstances their own action was no more than simple retaliation. This contention, which every Communist party the world over was to obstinately uphold for years, doesn't really stand up. The evident disproportion of forces involved, the need for extensive preparation, the speed with which they achieved their gains, all prove that the North Koreans had long premeditated their attack.

Who made the decision? Even today on this side of the Iron Curtain no one knows with certainty. Khrushchev's secret report on the crimes of Stalin is silent on the subject. However, it is improbable that the dictator had not, at least, approved the attack. From the day the war began, the Moscow press upheld Pyongyang's explanation without any reservations. If the Soviet leaders had not been informed of the plans of their Korean protégés, they would have needed time to formulate their position. On the other hand, the Chinese newspapers waited to learn the Russian attitude before falling into line.

Whether it was Russia or North Korea who first conceived the attack is of only secondary importance. What is clear is that no one in the Communist bloc had foreseen its repercussions. Once before, when he hurled his troops against Finland in 1939, Stalin had believed that the affair would be settled in a few days and at little cost. He had been mistaken and was, consequently, more prudent from then on. But this time an unfortunate statement by the American Secretary of State, Dean Acheson, had probably convinced him there was no risk. On January 12, 1950, speaking before the National Press Club, Acheson had declared that the "defensive perimeter" of the United States extended from the Aleutians to Japan, and from there to the Ryukyu Islands and the Philippines, which clearly excluded Korea. And he had added: ". . . so far as the military security of other areas in the Pacific is concerned, it must be clear that no person can guarantee these areas against military attack. . . ."[1]

MacArthur himself, in an interview given to a British journalist March 1, 1949, had expressed the same opinion.

Obviously, this was almost an invitation to invasion. Besides, how could anyone believe that America, which had not intervened while the Communists took over the whole of China, would fight for a small piece of Korea which its troops had evacuated the year before? Dean Acheson's declaration seemed to herald the adoption of a peripheral strategy, perfectly understandable on the part of a country possessing powerful atomic weapons but very poor in "conventional" means of waging war.

Stalin could not have known that in April 1950 the National Security Council of the United States, in a session presided over by Truman, had completely abandoned that strategy and determined to rebuild its armed forces and put the country in a position to meet any challenge. Starting with the premise that there existed between the Communist and democratic ideologies a fundamental incompatibility which would keep them in conflict for a long time, the report adopted by the Security Council, known as N.S.C. 68, provided for the allocation of some 20 percent of the government's income to military expenses, and for an increase in the defense budget from $13 to $50 billion. If the implementation of that report had not begun immediately, American forces would have been unable to offer serious opposition to the invasion of South Korea.

Another factor may help to explain the attack. Three weeks earlier the elections in South Korea had given a clear majority to the opponents of Syngman Rhee, the unpredictable old man who after thirty-three years in exile had become the first President of the Republic in August 1948. This was despite the fact that he had vigorously repressed, by methods somewhat less than democratic, all reputed Communist activities, imprisoning 14,000 people, including 14 Deputies. The increasing deterioration of the country's economic situation was followed by general unrest. The government was unable to manage its finances, and Washington obliged it to agree to general elections only by threatening to cut off all aid. None of this prevented Rhee from loudly proclaiming his intention to attack the North, which thus had more than one excuse to invoke self-defense and to suppose its troops would be welcomed as liberators.

It is obvious that on June 25, 1950, the day hostilities began, no one in the North or the South believed the division of the country, resurrected from its ashes after the capitulation of Japan, would be permanent.

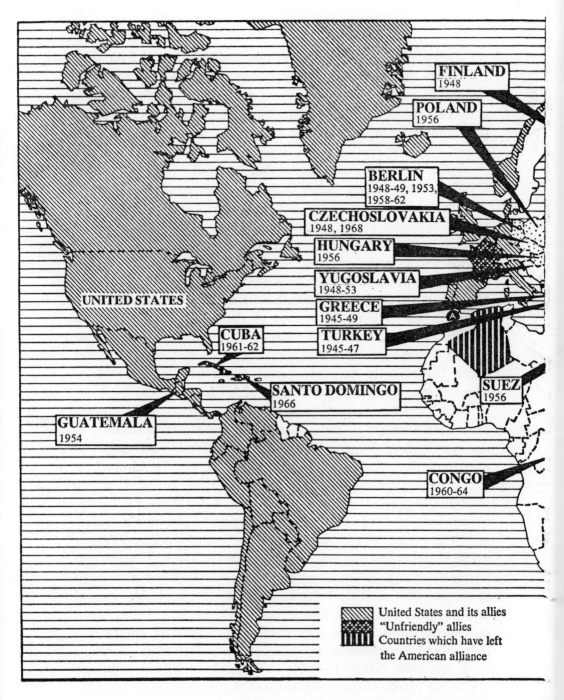

FINLAND
1948

POLAND
1956

BERLIN
1948-49, 1953,
1958-62

CZECHOSLOVAKIA
1948, 1968

HUNGARY
1956

YUGOSLAVIA
1948-53

GREECE
1945-49

TURKEY
1945-47

UNITED STATES

CUBA
1961-62

SANTO DOMINGO
1966

SUEZ
1956

GUATEMALA
1954

CONGO
1960-64

United States and its allies
"Unfriendly" allies
Countries which have left
the American alliance

I THE PRINCIPAL BATTLES

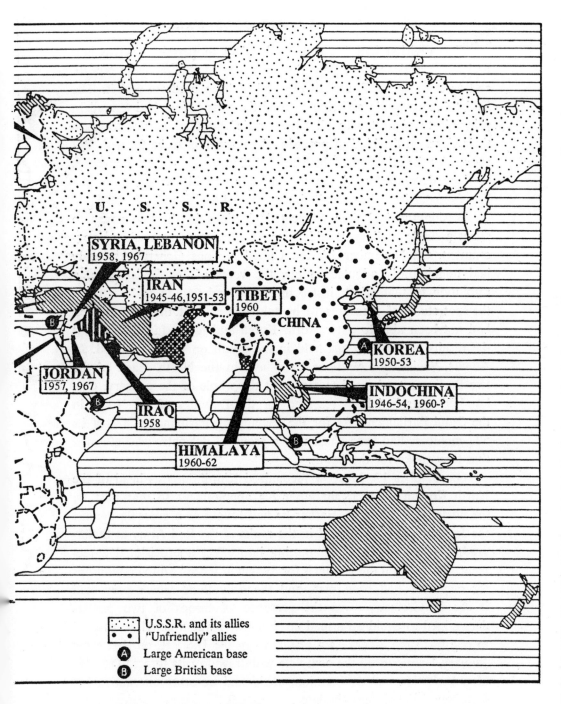

OF THE COLD WAR

That division had been effected solely to permit the Russians and the Americans to accept the surrender of the Japanese troops, and as early as 1947, serious efforts had been made to end it. The Soviet-American Commission created the year before had agreed in principle to consult with all "democratic" political parties to learn their views on the kind of provisional government to be formed. But soon, with the rejection of the Marshall Plan by the Eastern countries, tensions developed, and the Commission, unable to agree on the list of the parties to be consulted, was obliged to disband.

Washington had then advocated elections in the two zones to select a single parliament which would appoint the provisional government. On November 14, the United Nations General Assembly had unanimously adopted, minus the votes of the Soviet bloc, a resolution to that effect, instructing a commission to make an on-the-spot study of measures to be taken later. But that commission had not been able to enter North Korea and had refused to accept the results of the elections held in the South on May 10, 1948. In August, Soviet-style elections were held in the North. Each of the two Parliaments claimed to represent the whole of the country. One hundred seats had been reserved for the Deputies of the North in the Seoul Parliament. As for the Pyongyang Parliament, 360 of its 572 members had been chosen by a group of delegates who affirmed that they spoke for the South.

On October 12, Moscow recognized Kim-il-Sung as head of the North Korean Government, after his appointment to that post by the northern Parliament. Earlier he had fought as a guerrilla against the Japanese and had served in the ranks of the Red Army at Stalingrad. On January 1, 1949, putting into effect a provisional agreement, Washington did as much for Syngman Rhee. All the conditions for civil war had been met, and the only thing which prevented it—as in Germany—was the presence of troops of two powers determined to avoid an armed confrontation which could be as fatal to one as to the other. As a result, when the U.S.S.R. on that same January 1 announced the complete withdrawal of its forces, Truman, after hesitation and deliberation, could find no other alternative but to follow suit—six months later.

The former President, in his *Memoirs*, gives no completely satisfactory explanation for that decision beyond the fact that MacArthur favored it and that the experts regarded the outlook as "favorable as long as it can continue to receive larger scale aid from the U.S." [2] It is apparent that, above all, the decision must be credited to the setback suffered by the United States in China, and to the hostility of the Korean population to the occupying forces, whose chief, General Hodge, had committed blunder after blunder. This soldier's skill and intelligence did not equal his courage, and no one had forgiven him the remark imputed to him on his arrival in Seoul that "Koreans are the same breed of cats as the Japanese," [3] or his decision to retain Japanese functionaries in their posts.

§ § §

Although five hundred American military advisers remained in South Korea to train the 60,000-man army of the young republic, it was soon evident that their efforts were less successful than those of their Soviet counterparts in the north. Twenty-four hours after the beginning of the war, on June 26, 1950, North Korean tanks were in the outskirts of Seoul. Clearly Pyongyang did not have the slightest intention of accepting the Security Council resolution—adopted the day before by a vote of 9 to 0, with one abstention (Yugoslavia)— which requested North Korea to withdraw its troops as quickly as possible to the 38th Parallel.

The vote on that resolution was made possible only by the absence of the U.S.S.R., which on January 13 had made it known that it would not take part in the deliberations of the Security Council "as long as the representative of the Kuomintang group would not be excluded from it" [4]—in other words, as long as the Chinese seat was not assigned to the Peking Government. Because the United Nations Charter states in Article 27 that the Council's decisions on other than procedural questions are to be taken by "an affirmative vote of seven of its members, including the votes of all permanent members" (the United States, Great Britain, the U.S.S.R., France and China), the Soviet Government was in a good position to contest the legality of the resolution.

But it did not expect the Council, taking advantage of its absence and without showing too much concern for the letter of the Charter,

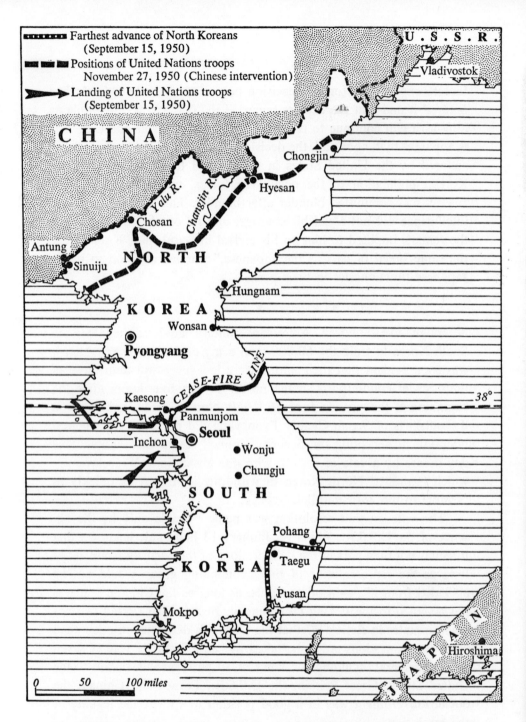

Farthest advance of North Koreans
(September 15, 1950)
Positions of United Nations troops
November 27, 1950 (Chinese intervention)
Landing of United Nations troops
(September 15, 1950)

U.S.S.R.

Vladivostok

CHINA

Chongjin

Hyesan

Yalu R.

Changjin R.

Chosan

Antung

NORTH

Sinuiju

Hungnam

KOREA

Wonsan

Pyongyang

CEASE-FIRE LINE

Kaesong

38°

Panmunjom

Inchon

Seoul

Wonju

Chungju

SOUTH

Kum R.

KOREA

Pohang

Taegu

Pusan

Mokpo

JAPAN

Hiroshima

0   50   100 miles

II THE WAR AND THE ARMISTICE IN KOREA

to adopt on June 27—by a vote of 7 to 1 (Yugoslavia), with two abstentions (India and Egypt)—another resolution submitted by Warren Austin, the United States delegate. This resolution requested the U.N. members "to provide the Republic of Korea with all necessary aid to repel the aggressors." [5]

The American Government did not wait for the vote before taking action. The evening of June 25, Truman, having hastily returned from his home in Independence, Missouri, where he was spending the weekend, gathered together his principal advisers. They were unanimous in recognizing the gravity of the situation and agreed with General Bradley, then Head of the Chiefs of Staff, that "we would have to draw the line somewhere." In his opinion, Russia "was not yet ready for war, but in Korea they were obviously testing us, and the line ought to be drawn now." [6]

The President immediately ordered the Seoul Government to be supplied with all arms needed, and he authorized MacArthur to provide military protection for the delivery of that matériel and for the evacuation of American dependents in Korea. He also "instructed the service chiefs to prepare the necessary orders for the eventual use of American units." The following day he was convinced that "The Republic of Korea needed help at once if it was not to be overrun," [7] which would then endanger Japan, Formosa and the American base of Okinawa.

He saw in this situation a "repetition on a larger scale" of the Berlin blockade and he telephoned MacArthur, ordering him to give immediate naval and air support to the South Korean Army, without, however, crossing the 38th Parallel. At the same time, he decided to station the Seventh Fleet between Formosa and China, as much to prevent the Communists from invading the island as to prevent the Nationalists from attempting raids on the mainland likely to draw Mao's troops into the conflict. It was still a matter of applying the doctrine of "containment" as defined by George Kennan: to resort to force if necessary in order to defend the *status quo,* but to abstain from trying to modify it by force. Truman also ordered the Philippine defenses reinforced and aid to French troops in Indochina increased.

On the 27th, even before the vote of the Security Council, the

President made his decision public in an address to the nation. He also ordered his ambassador to Moscow to ask the Soviet Government, because of "the universally known fact of the close relations between the U.S.S.R. and the North Korean regime," [8] to accept its responsibilities in this affair and to use its influence to persuade the North Koreans to withdraw their forces. The U.S.S.R. replied that the South Koreans were to blame for the invasion and that it was maintaining its policy of nonintervention, the sincerity of which had been demonstrated by the recall of Soviet troops from Korea the year before.

The National Security Council, meeting the next day at the White House, interpreted this reply as signifying that the Kremlin had no intention of intervening directly. However, it pointed out certain statements made by Peking which might indicate an eventual involvement of the Chinese Communists in the conflict. Truman was pleased by the nearly unanimous support of the American people for the prompt action of their President, and by offers of assistance from Canada, Australia, New Zealand and the Netherlands.

Finally, on June 29, in the face of the increasing deterioration of the military situation, Truman decided to send to Korea two divisions of American ground troops based in Japan. He had earlier rejected a proposal from Chiang Kai-shek, encouraged by MacArthur, to put at the latter's disposal 33,000 Nationalist soldiers.

Meanwhile, the U.S.S.R. remained astonishingly passive. Its newspapers gave little space to the Korean situation, devoting most of their columns to the real or alleged successes of the "Partisans for Peace" movement, which was more or less faithfully defending its diplomatic line throughout the entire world. A statement made on July 4 by Gromyko, then Deputy Foreign Minister, reaffirmed the policy of prudence Stalin had decided to follow. While contesting the right of the Security Council to make a decision in the absence of the Soviet representative and accusing the United States of armed intervention in a conflict which he did not hesitate to compare to the American Civil War, Gromyko stated that Moscow would pursue its policy of nonintervention, hoping that the U.N. would persuade Washington to adopt the same attitude. Three days later the Security Council, from which the Soviet delegate was still absent, created a

United Nations Command in Korea, to which MacArthur was assigned the following day. It authorized an expeditionary corps to fight under the U.N.'s light-blue flag emblazoned in white with a stylized globe—a serene image of a world that had never been less "united."

After rejecting Nehru's proposal to seat the People's Republic of China in the U.N. as a way of establishing unofficial "contacts" to study means of restoring peace, the American leaders made it their prime objective to regain the advantage in the field.

On September 15, by which time the North Koreans had conquered practically all of South Korea, MacArthur landed his forces at Inchon, behind their lines, and the situation was reversed overnight. By October 1 his forces had captured half the aggressors and had everywhere reached the 38th Parallel.

Would he stop there? On September 11 the National Security Council ordered the general to "make plans for the occupation of North Korea." [9] At the same time it was decided that no ground operations were to be undertaken above the 38th Parallel, to avoid precipitating Soviet or Chinese intervention. But MacArthur, who believed this a favorable moment for a decisive blow against Communism, took the risk lightly. On September 30 he urged Kim-il-Sung to order his troops, wherever they were, to lay down their arms. The same day, eight nations allied with the United States, including Great Britain, submitted a resolution to the U.N. requesting the General Assembly to "take all appropriate measures to insure a stable situation in the whole of Korea," [10] which implicitly authorized crossing the demarcation line.

According to the United Nations Charter, this type of proposal should have been submitted to the Security Council. But the U.S.S.R., realizing its error in boycotting the international organization, had resumed its seat, determined from that time on to use its right of veto as often as possible.

To circumvent it, the Western Powers conceived the idea of asking the General Assembly—to which, however, the Charter gives no decision-making power—to establish a policy for them. In order to justify this twisting of international law, America, together with six other countries—including Great Britain, France and Canada—

sponsored another resolution, known as the Seven Powers' Resolution, under whose terms, whenever there is a threat to peace or an act of aggression and the Security Council "fails to discharge its principal responsibility" because of a veto, the General Assembly "will immediately study the question in order to make appropriate recommendations to members on collective measures to be taken," including the use of armed force.[11]

Warren Austin and Gromyko engaged in violent exchanges over the first resolution, and John Foster Dulles, who, although a Republican, headed the United States delegation in the name of "bipartisanship," opposed Andrei Vishinsky over the second. The contest between these stars, especially the latter, was dramatic, as both were brilliant lawyers, gifted with exceptional aggressiveness and knowledge of jurisprudence.

Other debaters participated: Lester Pearson of Canada, Frank Soskice of Britain and Benegal Rau of India. But their speeches chiefly served to demonstrate that the Charter—founded on the naive hypothesis of a lasting understanding between the conquerors of the Third Reich—had anticipated everything but situations such as the one which prevailed in Korea. Consequently, to allow the United Nations to intervene there, the Charter had to be manipulated. At this time the African and Asian nations were virtually unrepresented in the U.N., and the United States, thanks to its Latin American clientele, more or less laid down the law. The Eight Powers' Resolution, authorizing the crossing of the 38th Parallel, was thus approved —by a vote of 47 to 5, with 7 abstentions—on October 7, 1950. And the Seven Powers' Resolution, expanding the powers of the General Assembly, was approved—minus the votes of the Soviet bloc and with 5 abstentions—on November 3. Meanwhile, the political and military situation had changed dramatically. By October 2, that is to say, before the U.N. vote, the South Koreans had advanced beyond the 38th Parallel without meeting much resistance. The same day, Chou En-lai, Communist China's premier, summoned the Indian ambassador, Sardar K.M. Pannikar, and told him that if U.N. forces other than the South Koreans penetrated North Korea, his government would send troops into that country. Truman writes in his *Memoirs* that this information was received in Washington with some skepticism, because the Indian diplomat had in the past "played the game of the Chinese Communists fairly regularly." [12] However, the warning was confirmed by diplomatic cables from Moscow, Stockholm and New Delhi and was featured in all the newspapers. The President, without modifying his previous instructions to MacArthur, added a new message which asked him "in the event of the open or covert employment anywhere in Korea of major Chinese Communist units," to continue operations as long as, in his judgment, action by the forces under his command "offers a reasonable chance of success." [13] Lastly, he was forbidden to undertake any action against Chinese territory without the approval of Washington.

That final directive was not superfluous. On July 31, MacArthur had paid a widely publicized visit to Chiang on Formosa and, a few days later in a message to the Veterans of Foreign Wars, had demanded "aggressive, resolute and dynamic leadership" [14] in foreign policy, thus provoking admonition from the Defense Department. He was obviously growing restive under the restrictions imposed by Truman's concern over Peking. To straighten out the situation, the President decided to meet with his fiery proconsul, not overly concerned with the fact that it would merely add to MacArthur's prestige.

The meeting took place October 15 on Wake Island, in the middle of the Pacific. The stenographic zeal of a secretary who had been left alone in an adjoining room was responsible for the publication later of the transcript of an exchange much less tense and dramatic than might have been imagined. MacArthur, after having apologized for his outburst, said that victory in Korea had already been achieved. He stated that the Chinese realized this and knew that if they intervened, they would be faced with a disaster, and that for this reason they would do nothing. He added that all resistance would cease by Thanksgiving.

He couldn't have been more mistaken. However, MacArthur, in an interview given to one of his friends, which was not published until 1964, after his death, maintained that he had never said that the Chinese would not enter the war, and that any allegations to that effect were part of a plan designed to "discredit" him. In the event of their intervention, he said he had advocated bombing the bridges over the Yalu River, which separates Korea from Manchuria, in order to cut the invaders' lines of communications so that they would be doomed "to starve a while before being destroyed." [15] But, still according to MacArthur, the British revealed his plans to the Chinese while pointing out that he would not be permitted to put them into effect, and it was this information that incited Peking to invade Korea. Naturally, Washington and London categorically denied those charges.

In any case, at the very moment that the general was meeting with Truman on Wake, Chinese soldiers were slipping into Korea. This was only revealed ten days later with the capture of the first Chinese prisoners. Still, on November 4, MacArthur minimized the situation, as confirmed by the official version. By the 5th, he decided it was the opportune moment to issue a communiqué denouncing the Chinese action as "one of the acts most contrary to international law" [16] which had ever been recorded. Mao replied immediately that "the entire Chinese people had voluntarily decided to dedicate themselves to the sacred duty of resisting America, helping Korea and defending their homes and lands," [17] thus giving the "volunteer" concept the broadest interpretation imaginable.

The following day, MacArthur at last realized the gravity of the situation and declared that a trap had been set for his troops. Without consulting anyone he ordered ninety Flying Fortresses to attack the bridges on the Yalu. On learning of it, General Marshall, then Secretary of Defense, prohibited the operation three hours before takeoff. It was authorized only two days later, on the express condition that only the Korean side of the river would be bombed, excluding the dams furnishing electric power to Manchuria. The next day, MacArthur pointed out the impossible situation his aviators faced because of the inviolability of the "Manchurian sanctuary." Not only did the enemy have bases in which he could concentrate soldiers and matériel with impunity, but the Communist pilots could seek refuge in a safe sky as soon as the fighting was going against them. He demanded "corrective measures" and "instructions for dealing with this new and threatening development." [18]

Truman was determined to refuse them to him. At all costs he wanted to prevent the Korean War from degenerating into a general conflict. He was equally influenced by the intelligence reports, according to which the Russians wanted to force the United States to engage itself as deeply as possible in Asia, so that they could have a free hand in Europe. The British and the French, for their part, were anxious about the repercussions which an extension of hostilities could have on the American commitments to them.

Washington thus chose to pursue a policy of prudence. While alerting the Security Council, the President, Dean Acheson and Dean Rusk, then Assistant Secretary of State for Far Eastern Affairs, sent out a series of statements designed to reassure Peking's leaders, particularly on the fate of the Yalu hydroelectric plants.

They carefully avoided asking the U.N. to take military sanctions against China. They reiterated their prohibition to MacArthur against violating the Manchurian sanctuary. However, at the same time they let him launch a new offensive, allegedly to determine, as the former President maintains in his *Memoirs,* "the strength and the direction and aim of the Chinese Communist effort." [19]

On November 24, with his usual flamboyance, the general directed one of his aides to announce to the troops they would be home for Christmas. But, by December 3 they were retreating in disorder under the protection of the Turkish contingent, which was cut to pieces in order to save them from disaster. MacArthur sent the Chiefs of Staff a report declaring that the expeditionary corps was in reality fighting "the entire Chinese nation" [20] and unless positive action was immediately taken, no hope of success could be justified.

The crisis was taking a dramatic turn. A report had reached Washington on November 15, according to which a Soviet diplomat had assured Peking that the Russian Air Force would intervene in the event of Manchuria's being bombed. On November 30, in the course of his press conference, Truman made an ambiguous reply to the question of the eventual use of atomic bombs. This sent a wave of panic throughout the world that an official clarification did not succeed in calming. The same day, during a debate in the House of Commons, the Conservative Butler and Churchill himself joined their voices to the Labourite majority in demanding that the march toward war be halted. At the end of the session, Attlee announced that he had decided to go and confer with the President of the United States.

The policy of "calculated risk," so highly thought of in America, had confounded its practitioners.

On December 4, the Prime Minister met with Truman and Acheson. He found them not very optimistic. They told him that they wanted a cease-fire, but that they didn't see why the Chinese would accept it. And although they rejected the idea of a preventive war, which then had many champions in the United States, they did not intend to buy peace through concessions on Formosa or through the admission of Peking to the Security Council. A failure to pursue such a policy would rapidly lead to the collapse of all Western resistance in the Far East. As for abandoning Korea, it could not be considered, they said, unless Chinese intervention assumed such proportions that the U.N. forces were in danger of being overwhelmed.

In the face of such an eventuality, Washington had decided to ask the U.N. to brand Red China the "aggressor," to consider military action against it and to reinforce Japan's "self-defense potential"— in other words, to rearm it. Washington also envisaged a Marshall Plan for Southeast Asia to enable the countries of that region to better resist the Communist contagion. Attlee agreed on the necessity of holding fast in Korea—he was, in fact, going to publicly denounce, before the National Press Club, any policy of "appeasement"—but he maintained, contrary to American opinion, that the Chinese, far from being satellites of the U.S.S.R., were "ripe" for "Titoism" and that they had to be admitted to the U.N. in order to fully exploit all the "contradictions" of the socialist bloc.[21]

The facts hardly seemed to support that judgment. On November 22, Peking's representatives arrived in New York. They had been invited by the U.S.S.R., Great Britain and France to participate in the Security Council's meeting on MacArthur's report on the Chinese intervention. They were headed by General Wu Hsiu-chuan, who had been educated in Moscow and had accompanied Mao there a few months before. At no time did there appear to be the slightest divergence between their position and that of the Soviet delegation, whose secret code, besides, they did not hesitate to use for their communications. The Americans, in their desire to conciliate, had accepted that the agenda of the meeting be called "The American intervention in Formosa and the Chinese intervention in Korea." The Chinese, supported by the U.S.S.R., had countered with a title "American aggression against Taiwan and American intervention in Korea," [22] the deliberately provocative wording of which precluded any possibility of compromise.

In the midst of the talks, a telephone call from the Pentagon was to further increase anxiety: Radar in the far north signaled the approach of a large number of "unidentified airplanes." An hour later the world breathed a sigh of relief. It was nothing more than an atmospheric disturbance. In the end, Truman and Attlee agreed on a long memorandum which, without ignoring their disagreement over the entry of Communist China into the U.N., and while expressing their desire to reach a negotiated solution, dismissed any idea of "rewarding aggression" and insisted on the need to reinforce Western military power. The Prime Minister had gotten from the President a public statement hoping "that world conditions would never call for the use of the atomic bomb." [23] This didn't commit him to much.

In the days following the meeting, the "situation" was actually becoming more and more disturbing. Moscow and Peking scornfully rejected an appeal from thirteen Asiatic nations, led by India, requesting the Chinese and North Korean troops to stop at the 38th Parallel. Persevering in their efforts, these thirteen countries had got the U.N. General Assembly to approve unanimously, less the Communist votes, a resolution empowering a committee of three members to make recommendations leading to a peace settlement. General Wu asserted that such a plan "only served to facilitate acts of aggression from the Anglo-American bloc" [24] and announced that he was returning to China with his delegation.

On December 15, Truman decreed a state of emergency so as to strengthen the nation's defense efforts. His decision was enthusiastically received by a public opinion already overheated and so little aware of the real state of the American armed forces—there was not a single division in reserve in Japan—that it would have approved any kind of ultimatum to the Kremlin. On December 26 the Communists recrossed the 38th Parallel, and on the 29th the Chiefs of Staff cabled MacArthur that the Chinese were capable, "if they chose to," of throwing the U.N. forces out of Korea. And while recognizing that "a successful resistance to . . . aggression at some position in Korea . . . would be of great importance to our national interest, if [it] could be accomplished without incurring serious losses," they would order him "if you are forced back to a position in the vicinity of the Kum River . . . to commence a withdrawal to Japan." [25]

The next day MacArthur replied, proposing to "recognize the state of war imposed by the Chinese authorities" and therefore to have recourse to measures of which he was to give, in two posthumously released interviews, heart-stopping details: "Dropping from 30 to 50 atomic bombs on airbases and other sensitive points" in Manchuria, and landing an amphibious force composed of 500,000 of Chiang Kai-shek's troops, supported by two divisions of marines,[26] at both ends of the Sino-Korean border. This was to be followed "by laying down, after the defeat of the Chinese," [27] a belt of radioactive cobalt all along the Yalu.

It goes without saying that these suggestions were brushed aside. All that was asked of MacArthur was that he try to hold onto a beachhead.

On January 17, Peking rejected the ultraconciliatory proposals made by the committee of three appointed by the U.N. They had even gone so far as to recommend, following the cessation of hostilities, the creation of a body made up of representatives of the United States, Great Britain, the U.S.S.R. and Red China, charged to "succeed . . . in reaching a settlement of the problems of the Far East, including the question of Formosa and the representation of China in the United Nations Organization." [28] But Mao insisted that the discussion of those questions begin before the cessation of hostilities. Two days later, the House of Representatives adopted a resolution requesting the U.N. to declare Red China guilty of aggression. On February 1 the General Assembly fell into line, after having rejected, at the request of the American delegation, a compromise proposal offered by India.

Meanwhile, little by little, a new situation was beginning to emerge. In the field the counteroffensive launched by the U.N. forces on January 25 had, by March, advanced the front line to the vicinity of the 38th Parallel. Perhaps aware of the impossibility of total victory, the Chinese took a cautious step forward by accepting the idea of a truce and allowing the summoning of a Conference of Seven (the United States, the U.S.S.R., Great Britain, Red China, France, India and Egypt) on the problems of the Far East. In the U.S.A. the price of raw materials, which had skyrocketed, began to decline, a sign that the government no longer believed a general war imminent.

At the beginning of March, Truman's advisers came to the conclusion that negotiations should be attempted on the basis of a return to the *status quo ante*. A proposed Presidential declaration was submitted to the Allies, stating that the aggressors having been repulsed, the problem of re-establishing peace had to be settled and that to achieve it there had to exist "a basis . . . which should be acceptable to all nations which sincerely desire peace." [29]

However, before this document was made public, MacArthur took it upon himself, without consulting anyone, to issue a proclamation which had the effect of a thunderbolt. Maintaining that "Even under the inhibitions which now restrict the activity of the United Nations Forces and the corresponding military advantages which accrue to Red China, it has been shown its complete inability to accomplish by force of arms the conquest of Korea. The enemy, therefore, must by now be painfully aware that a decision of the United Nations to depart from its tolerant effort to contain the war to the area of Korea, through an expansion of our military operations to its coastal areas and interior bases, would doom Red China to the risk of imminent military collapse. These basic facts being established, there should be no insuperable difficulty in arriving at decisions on the Korean problem if the issues are resolved on their own merits, without being burdened by extraneous matters not related to Korea, such as Formosa or China's seat in the United Nations." [30]

This text had every appearance of an ultimatum to Peking: Accept the armistice on the 38th Parallel, or we will carry the war into Manchuria. It went directly counter to the efforts of Truman, who was seeking a peace without victors or vanquished, and who wanted above all, to avoid "being stuck" on the continent of Asia. But how was the enemy to be made to understand that MacArthur's views were not those of the American Government? The President was deliberating which course to follow when, on April 5, the Republican Representative Joseph Martin made public a letter which the general had addressed to him March 20. In it he advocated once more the use of Chiang Kai-shek's troops and denounced those who refused to understand that it is in Asia that "the Communist conspirators have elected to make their play for global conquest." He concluded that "There is no substitute for victory." [31] The defiance could not be more clear. On the 11th, after having taken the advice of his principal advisers, the President dismissed the controversial proconsul.

In the climate of patriotic fervor which prevailed in the United States, it was a bold decision. On his return to San Francisco, and later to New York, MacArthur received an unprecedented welcome from millions of people who acclaimed him as the true hero sacrificed to the cowardice of politicians. When Washington's turn came to celebrate the return of the dismissed general, Truman, in order to show his *sang-froid,* went alone to the movies. For weeks the excitement was maintained at fever pitch, through MacArthur's testimony before a commission of inquiry appointed by Congress to evaluate the causes of his removal. He expressed his conviction that if Manchuria had been attacked, the Sino-Soviet Mutual Assistance Treaty of 1950 would not have been invoked. However, he agreed that he had no specific information on that subject. One after the other, the chiefs of the armed forces came and refuted his theories. Bradley summed up their arguments, declaring, in a formula which was to become famous, that a war with China would have been "the wrong war, at the wrong place, at the wrong time, and with the wrong enemy." [32]

In the end, public opinion was shaken by the statements of government representatives. Popular feeling subsided, and little by little MacArthur was forgotten after having quoted in a memorable speech the words "old soldiers never die." He was to be satisfied with the presidency of Remington Rand; at one time it had been thought he could well aim at that of the United States.

The initial Communist reaction to the general's dismissal took the form of a new Chinese offensive on April 22. It was stopped by the Allied forces, by then solidly entrenched on an unbroken front around the 38th Parallel and even reaching, at one point, as far as Pyongyang. On May 18 the U.N., at the request of the United States, voted an embargo on all strategic materials destined for China. Once again it appeared that the world had fallen into the rut of an interminable war. However, the next day a ray of light appeared on the horizon. *Pravda* reproduced *in extenso*—a sure sign of the importance attached to it by Moscow—a proposal by Senator Johnson, the isolationist from Colorado and namesake of the future President, who had campaigned against the Atlantic Pact. He wanted a cease-fire to be proclaimed on June 25, the anniversary of the outbreak of war, along with the withdrawal of both armies to their respective sides of the 38th Parallel.

June 1, the Norwegian Trygve Lie, U.N. Secretary General and *bête noire* of the Russians—who had not forgiven him for having cloaked the Allied intervention in Korea with the U.N.'s blue and white flag—declared that an armistice on such terms would meet the objectives sought by the international organization.

On the 7th, Acheson made a statement to the same effect. On June 22, the Voice of America, quoting Trygve Lie's statements, appealed to Malik, the permanent delegate of the U.S.S.R. to the United Nations, who two years earlier had negotiated the lifting of the Berlin blockade: "There's a wide open door, Mr. Malik. Walk right in." [33] The next day, on the occasion of a U.N. broadcast, "The Price of Peace," the Soviet diplomat replied. Nine-tenths of his speech constituted a virulent attack against the United States and its Allies. But in the remaining tenth was found a short sentence which quickly intrigued the chancelleries: "The Soviet people believe that, as a first step in the settlement of the Korean conflict, the belligerents should start talks in order to establish a cease-fire and an armistice calling for a withdrawal of armed forces on both sides of the 38th Parallel." [34]

There was no mention of political preliminaries. Admiral Kirk, the U.S. ambassador to Moscow, was charged to ask the Kremlin if that omission was fortuitous. It was confirmed that it was not and that Stalin favored a meeting of the emissaries of the two commanders in chief. The meeting took place at Kaesong, on the 38th Parallel, on July 10, although hostilities had not been ended.

They would only end nearly two years later, after interminable talks—so trying and so often broken off that the name of the village of Panmunjom, where they were held, quickly became synonymous with futile parleys. In fact, it took the death of Stalin to make the Communists decide to yield on the question which blocked everything—the fate of the prisoners of war.

BIBLIOGRAPHY AND NOTES

1 Philip Mosely, *The Kremlin and World Politics: Studies in Soviet Policy and Action* (New York: Vintage, 1960), p. 327.

2 Harry S. Truman, *Memoirs* (New York: Doubleday, 1955), II, p. 328.

3 John Gunther, *The Riddle of MacArthur* (New York: Harper, 1951), p. 180.

4 Georges Day, *Le droit de veto dans l'organisation des Nations Unies* (Paris: Pedone, 1952), p. 133.

5 *Le Monde*, June 29, 1950.

6 Truman, *op. cit.*, II, p. 335.

7 *Ibid.*, p. 337.

8 Keesing's Contemporary Archives, 10608 A (hereinafter referred to as Keesing's).

9 Truman, *op. cit.*, II, p. 359.

10 Marc Frankenstein, *L'Organisation des Nations Unies et le conflit coréen* (Paris: Pedone, 1952), p. 346.

11 *Ibid.*, pp. 348–54.

12 Truman, *op. cit.*, II, p. 361.

13 *Ibid.*, p. 362.

14 *Ibid.*, p. 354.

15 *U.S. News and World Report*, April 20, 1964.

16 Frankenstein, *op. cit.*, p. 175.

17 *Ibid.*, p. 176.

18 Truman, *op. cit.*, II, p. 377.

19 *Ibid.*, p. 381.

20 *Ibid.*, p. 392.

21 *Ibid.*, p. 402.

22 Frankenstein, *op. cit.*, p. 200.

23 Truman, *op. cit.*, II, p. 413.

24 Frankenstein, *op. cit.*, p. 252.

25 Courtney Whitney, *MacArthur, His Rendez-vous with History* (New York: Knopf, 1956), pp. 429–30.

26 Interview with Bob Considine in *New York Journal American*, April 8, 1964.

27 *U.S. News and World Report*, April 20, 1964.

28 Frankenstein, *op. cit.*, p. 273.

29 Truman, *op. cit.*, II, p. 439.

30 *Ibid.*, p. 441.

31 *Ibid.*, pp. 445–46.

32 Arthur S. Link, *American Epoch* (New York: Knopf, 1955), p. 691.

33 *The New York Times*, June 23, 1951.

34 Frankenstein, *op. cit.*, p. 312.

· CHAPTER 2 ·

THE APPEAL TO
THE VANQUISHED

Thus the failure to form an alliance of the victors
will mean the formation of alliances between the vanquished and some of the victors.

—Walter Lippmann, *United
States Foreign Policy: Shield
of the Republic*

UNTIL THE KOREAN WAR THE WESTERN LEADERS HAD
always believed that the Russians would employ any means to further
their cause, short of war. Now that signs of the socialist bloc's bellig-
erency were multiplying throughout the world, they had to anticipate
any eventuality. In October 1950 the Chinese Communists not only
intervened in Korea but also invaded Tibet. Six weeks before, Peking
had notified India, which was the heir to certain rights of extrater-
ritoriality previously granted Great Britain, of its intention to settle
the Tibetan question peacefully. When New Delhi protested China's
attack, pointing to the unfortunate effects it might have on Red
China's U.N. candidacy, China replied by accusing Nehru of being
influenced by "foreign influences hostile to China in Tibet." [1] And it
was in that same month that the Viet Minh, recognized as the government of the "Democratic Republic of Viet Nam" (D.R.V.N.) by
Mao—and a few days later by Stalin—inflicted on the French Army
its first irreparable defeat, capturing the two citadels of Cao Bang and
Lang Son on the Chinese frontier. In Lang Son it seized 13 cannons,
940 machine guns and 8,000 rifles. These arms, added to those

· 31 ·

which now poured in from China, permitted General Giap to equip his first sizable units—5 divisions—which launched an assault on Hanoi in the beginning of January 1951. But the arrival of General de Lattre de Tassigny on December 17 had given renewed confidence to the French troops, who now held their own against the enemy's redoubled attacks. In Malaya the efforts of High Commissioner Gurney to put an end to the Communist rebellion through a policy of reforms were a total failure. He was shot down by a rebel after having begun a program of resettlement of certain groups of the population which was completely alien to his own beliefs. His successor, General Templer, who had faith in a hard-line policy, was more successful.

And although no fighting had broken out anywhere in Europe, the situation there was no less disturbing. Incident after incident occurred on Yugoslavia's frontiers. In September 1950 the Austrian Communists had called an insurrectionary general strike, with the open support of the Soviet occupation authorities. It failed only because of determined resistance from the great majority of the Viennese working class. In Poland, Rokossovski, a Russian marshal, who though of Polish origin had almost forgotten his native tongue, had been appointed Minister of War and Commander in Chief of the armed forces. It was learned only much later that Warsaw's leaders had specifically requested his appointment in order to allay Stalin's pathological distrust of them and to have some kind of a protective shield at their disposal. But, at the time, it was difficult to interpret Moscow's action as anything other than the nomination of a gauleiter, whose first mission would be to put Poland on a war footing.

The former satellites of the Reich—now those of the U.S.S.R.—were being hastily rearmed, in violation of the peace treaties, and their armed forces reorganized on the Soviet model, even to their uniforms. Last but not least, the Russians did not hesitate to reinforce the police units which had been recruited since 1945 in their occupation zone of Germany with other armored garrisoned units. Commanded by veterans of the Spanish Civil War, like Heinz Hoffmann, and by former members of the Wehrmacht, like Vincenz Müller and Arno von Lenski, and closely controlled by Russian officers, these forces constituted an actual army. Who could be sure that Moscow would not allow those soldiers to start a "Korean" civil war in the heart of Europe?

The Korean War had dramatized the weakness of the West's military posture. The United States had no more than ten combat-effective divisions. In the spring of 1951 the largest part of its armed forces was engaged in Korea and the remainder was stationed in Germany. In the whole of the continental United States there was no more than one division. A tremendous build-up was imperative.

On January 31, 1950, Truman had announced to the world his decision to undertake the fabrication of a "thermonuclear" bomb, two hundred times more powerful than the one dropped on Hiroshima. Four days previously, the physicist Klaus Fuchs had confessed to the British police that for seven years he had been transmitting vital information to the Kremlin on the military uses of the atom. The President's announcement, along with others, had the result of counteracting the disastrous effect of those revelations on public opinion. But the basic argument in the controversy between those for and those against the H-bomb was stated by General Bradley. According to him, the Russians would secure a decisive strategic advantage if they were allowed to be the first to produce that new weapon. It was in vain that many American scientists, including Fermi, the Nobel Prize winner and the first man before the war to have conceived of the fission of the uranium atom, had asked Truman to publicly renounce his plans to build the H-bomb and to invite the Russians to make a similar pledge.

It was to be two years before the first weapon could be tested. And even then it was not an actual bomb, but rather a complicated apparatus weighing 65 tons, the transportation of which to the test site, Eniwetok Atoll in the Pacific, created all sorts of problems. The test took place at dawn, November 1, 1952, releasing energy equivalent to 3 million tons of T.N.T.—what is today called 3 megatons. For the first time, man had succeeded in producing on earth the fusion of hydrogen atoms—until then the sun's monopoly. Since that time the United States and the U.S.S.R. have built thousands of H-bombs, some several times more powerful than the first, others "miniaturized." Great Britain, France and China joined the race, but no one

HISTORY OF THE COLD WAR

has yet succeeded in harnessing this inexhaustible source of energy for peaceful purposes.

In spite of the fantastic quantitative difference which separated the thermonuclear weapon from the bomb dropped on Hiroshima, its possession was far from ensuring the United States as decisive a superiority as the atomic-bomb monopoly had given it until 1945— a superiority which lasted as long as the Soviet Union did not possess bombers or missiles capable of reaching American territory. In fact, the Russians were to proceed with their first thermonuclear test in August 1953, a few months after Stalin's death and before the American H-bomb had become operational. There could be foreseen a balance of terror in which each country's possession of the same means of massive destruction would dissuade the other from having recourse to the "ultimate" weapon because of the threat of unacceptable retaliation. Knowing that it would soon be deprived of the security granted it by the exclusive possession of atomic arms, the United States felt obliged to give the Western world, as quickly as possible, conventional military protection. It would provide whatever was necessary to deal with either limited "police actions" of the Korean type, or with the general offensive which it feared the U.S.S.R. might launch against western Europe to take advantage of an almost total military vacuum.

America was determined to make a tremendous effort. In August 1950, Congress approved the Defense Production Act, which affirmed America's intention to "oppose acts of aggression and . . . to develop and maintain whatever military and economic strength is found to be necessary to carry out this purpose." [2] Congress raised the military budget by more than $12 billion, voted $5 billion for military aid to friendly nations and decided to increase the nation's armed forces from 1,500,000 to 3,000,000 men within a year. But America could not do everything alone, and it quickly expressed its desire to mobilize all available human and material resources in every country in the world which rejected communism. In September 1950 the Council of Foreign Ministers of the Atlantic Pact gathered in New York and approved the creation, in the soonest possible time, of "an integrated military force, adequate for the defense of freedom in Europe." [3]

There were then, on the continent, scarcely more than 14 divisions available, against Russian divisions estimated at the time—but incorrectly, so states American Intelligence today—at 175. Therefore, the Allies were asked to assess their military potential, and for the first time in peacetime, a military force unified under a central command was created. The first appointee to assume that post was Eisenhower, who had been called out of retirement. He took over his functions in December and set up his general headquarters at Rocquencourt, near Versailles.

The months that followed were filled with interminable discussions between the military and the economists. The former wanted dozens of divisions, the latter maintained that they could not be created without wrecking the economy and productive capacity of western Europe, thus creating the ideal conditions for a Communist takeover. A committee composed of a Frenchman, Jean Monnet, an American, Averell Harriman, and an Englishman, Eric Plowden—the three wise men—was appointed to arbitrate the controversy. The Atlantic Council ratified the committee's proposals during a conference held in Lisbon in February 1952. The number of divisions decided upon was fifty. At that time it was recognized that this goal could not be reached without calling upon Germany.

Actually, Washington had long ago accepted the idea that it must make use of every available resource. Italy had been the first country to benefit from the turnabout of alliances made inevitable by Soviet-American tensions. Already, in the spring of 1948, in order to increase the stability of the centrist government headed by Gaspari—which was faced with general elections that many observers mistakenly expected to result in a Communist victory—the three Western Powers had informed Italy, through Georges Bidault, of their intention to return the territory of Trieste, made into a free city the year before by the peace treaty. They did not suspect that this gesture, which was directed against the U.S.S.R., would affect Yugoslavia, a country on the verge of open rebellion with Russia. In 1949 no one made any objection to Rome's membership in the Atlantic Pact.

Spain, on the other hand, was kept out of the Pact. It was nonetheless made the beneficiary of ever-increasing favors from the United States, where its unofficial representative—later ambassador,

J. F. de Lequerica had cleverly organized a "Franco" lobby particularly effective among conservative circles and the admirals.

On November 5, 1950, the U.N., on the initiative of seven Latin American countries, decided to abrogate the 1946 diplomatic boycott of the Madrid regime. Great Britain and France abstained, but soon followed the example of the United States, whose Dean Acheson had advocated that measure as early as January. The three governments shortly named ambassadors to the Caudillo and in July 1951 he was visited by Admiral Sherman, Chief of Naval Operations in Washington. However, it was to take two years and the coming to power of the Republican Party in the United States before the two countries concluded military agreements.

At the other extreme of the ideological spectrum, Yugoslavia itself was also enrolled in programs designed to resist Stalinist expansion. In June 1951, Kotcha Popovich, Chief of the Yugoslav General Staff, went to Washington to sign an agreement for the purchase of arms. The following month the United States, Great Britain and France decided to extend a loan of £50 million to Marshal Tito "to aid Yugoslavia to maintain its independence in the face of growing Soviet pressure." [4] In any case, in April, Truman had promised him American aid. In January 1953, Belgrade went one step further by signing a treaty of friendship and military, economic and cultural cooperation with Ankara and Athens. This was the "Balkan Pact," which was transformed the next year into an alliance pure and simple. Greece and Turkey having become by then members of the Atlantic Pact, Yugoslavia was thus, so to speak, a sort of associated member. In an interview which he granted me in Istanbul in April 1954, Marshal Tito went so far as to declare himself "in favor of the rearmament of West Germany." [5] On October 5 of the same year, he accepted an accord by which Trieste was returned to Italy in exchange for Yugoslavia's annexation of the territory occupied by its troops. In this way one of the bones of contention which had developed in the aftermath of the war was disposed of.

Not satisfied with defying geography and welcoming Greeks and Turks into the "Atlantic Pact," the Western Powers sought to extend their net of alliances. In October 1951 the United States, Great Britain, France and Turkey proposed that Egypt become a founding member of a "Middle East Command." The Cairo Government curtly refused, saying that it had no intention of entering into negotiations on such a project so long as British troops occupied the Suez Canal zone. The following month, Australia and New Zealand agreed to sign a mutual defense treaty with the United States known as the ANZUS Pact.

§   §   §

Of far greater significance was the signing with Japan, despite Moscow's opposition, of a peace treaty which recognized its right to rearm. As early as 1948 the Kremlin had favored a prompt peace settlement with Tokyo, but Russia and the United States could not agree on procedures. The United States wanted the treaty to be negotiated by the eleven member countries of the Far East Commission, subject to the decisions of a two-thirds majority, which would have deprived Moscow of any possibility of having its way. Russia advocated discussions between the United States, Great Britain, China and itself, with each having the right of veto. But the Americans, who above all wanted to have their right to maintain bases on Japanese soil confirmed, had every reason to believe that Russia would be opposed.

The discussions dragged on until September 14, 1950. At that time Truman, against the advice of his principal military advisers, had the State Department send all interested countries a document enumerating the principles, in his judgment, on which a Japanese peace treaty should be based. The following day, Washington sources reported that the President was prepared to authorize the rearming of Japan. This was a major decision, inasmuch as MacArthur's entire policy in Tokyo had been explicitly directed toward the demilitarization of that nation. He had even inserted in the 1946 constitution, in Article Nine, a statement to the effect that the Empire of the Rising Sun completely renounced war and the use of any threats of force: "The maintenance of land, sea and air forces, as well as other war potential, will never be authorized." [6]

If there is one word that should be used in politics with the greatest possible caution, it is the word "never." In February 1950 the proconsul had advocated Japan's neutralization and hastily assigned to it a role as the Switzerland of the Far East. Four months later the Korean War broke out, and on July 8, MacArthur had to authorize the recruitment of a "reserve national police" of 75,000 men, which was to assume the duties of the American troops which had been rushed to the Land of Morning Calm. The following January 1, he stated: "This concept [the renunciation of recourse to war] represents one of the highest ideals the world has ever known. . . . If, however, international lawlessness continues to threaten the peace . . . it is inherent that this ideal must give way to the overwhelming law of self-preservation. . . ." [7]

On receiving the State Department's *aide-mémoire*, the Russians were astonished, and not without reason, to see negotiations proposed on the fate of Formosa, the Pescadores, Southern Sakhalin and the Kuriles when, to their way of thinking, those matters had been specifically settled at Yalta. They were concerned about American intentions to maintain bases in Japan and to rearm that country. For its part, the Chinese People's Republic, totally involved in the Communist counteroffensive in Korea, demanded to participate in the negotiations. Its request was not even acknowledged. In January 1951, John Foster Dulles arrived in Tokyo to confer with the Japanese Government and to finalize a proposed treaty which wholly ignored the Soviet objections. Moscow protested, bombarding Washington with notes, but nevertheless agreed to send Gromyko to the peace conference, which opened on September 4 in San Francisco, on the initiative of the United States.

The Kremlin's representative submitted a long list of amendments to the American proposal. They asked for the withdrawal of all foreign troops, Peking's participation in the treaty, the interdiction to Japan to enter into coalitions directed against any of the countries with which it had been at war, the limitation of its army to a maximum of 195,000 troops, with no more than 200 tanks and 350 airplanes, and finally, the demilitarization of straits between Japan and other countries, through which only the ships of bordering countries would have free passage. These amendments were not accepted, and the U.S.S.R. and its allies refused to join with the other 48 powers in the treaty which, on September 8, 1951, was concluded with Japan. The same day, Dean Acheson and Yoshida, the head of the Tokyo government, signed a mutual security pact calling for the provisional maintenance of American forces in Japan. Japan's rearmament was accelerated. On October 12, 1952, the "reserve national police" became a "National Security Corps," whose first contingents, entirely American-equipped, were reviewed by the Prime Minister.

Naturally, the Soviet Union protested the remilitarization of the empire and the signing of a separate peace on several occasions. But either because it understood that the game was lost in advance or because it judged the stakes less important, its actions against the rearming of Japan never approached, even when viewed in perspective, the violence of the campaign unleashed against the rearmament of West Germany. It is true that this last was combined with the integration of the Federal Republic into the Western political system, and that Moscow could not with equanimity see the Ruhr's industrial potential added to the already tremendous resources at America's disposal.

§ § §

At the time of the signing of the Atlantic Pact, the possibility of rearming the vanquished countries—which the Potsdam Agreement categorically forbade—had been officially discounted. But what was that promise worth? *Le Monde,* April 6, 1949, did not hesitate to state, under the signature of Sirius: "Germany's rearmament is contained in the Atlantic Pact as the embryo is in the egg." Robert Schuman, then Minister of Foreign Affairs, nevertheless solemnly declared, in the course of debate on the ratification of the Pact in the National Assembly on July 25: "Germany has no army and cannot have one; it has no armaments and it will not have any." [8] Pierre-Henri Teitgen, Minister of Information, expanded on that thought in November, when he said: "The world should realize that France cannot remain a member of a security system that endorses German rearmament." [9]

He made such a statement only because the American and French newspapers were filled with rumors about the possible recruitment of German contingents. Adenauer, questioned on this matter by the correspondent of the *Cleveland Plain Dealer* on December 3, a few days after having received a visit from Acheson, replied that: "Even if the Allies put forth a demand for a German contribution to the security of Europe, I would refuse to establish German armed forces. At the very outside I would be prepared to consider the question of a German contingent in the framework of the army of a European federation." [10] He returned to this argument in speeches delivered the following days in Königswinter and before Parliament. In so doing, he was already significantly moving away from the Petersberg agreement which he had signed on November 22, and in which he had stated his determination to "maintain the demilitarization of the Federal territory" and to endeavor by all means in his power "to prevent re-creation of armed forces of any kind." [11]

Acheson, and later the Secretary of War, Louis Johnson, made it known in explicit statements that Bonn had been asked for nothing. In the wake of these comments, General Clay, the American Commander in Chief in Germany, on May 7, 1950, publicly declared himself in favor of German rearmament. This earned him a sharp retort from Vincent Auriol, then President of the French Republic. The Korean War, which began on June 25, was to give a decisive argument to those who had advocated appealing to yesterday's enemies. On July 23, McCloy, the United States High Commissioner in the Federal Republic, stated that "in case of aggression it would be difficult to refuse the Germans the right and the means to defend their country." [12] On August 17, Adenauer requested that the representatives of the Big Three increase the number of their troops and that he be given the right to raise a force of 150,000 volunteers comparable to the People's Police of East Germany.

This request was studied by the three Western foreign ministers, Acheson, Schuman and Bevin, who met in New York on September 11. The Frenchman and the Englishman strongly supported the request for American reinforcements. But when, on the 12th, the Secretary of State called for "an integrated army comprised not only of Allied troops but also of an as yet undetermined number of German divisions which would serve under a single command—naturally American—with an international general staff," [13] Schuman declared himself unalterably opposed to this proposal, saying that the other allies should be rearmed first. As for the British, the Prime Minister, Clement Attlee, defined their position the same day: "We hold the view that the eventual participation by Germany in the defense of Europe can only be considered within the framework of a common defense of the West. . . . The Federal Chancellor has asked the occupying Powers for authority to raise an armed Federal police force. There are strong reasons for this. . . . What is envisaged is a *gendarmerie* or mobile guard under proper democratic control, and not an embryo army. . . ." [14]

In Paris, as well as in London, a major part of public opinion did not hide its hostility to the rearming of Germany, and besides, it echoed the more or less "neutralist" philosophy favored by many of the intelligentsia. And though the Big Three could easily enough agree on such measures as the acceleration of their own rearmament, the guaranteeing of the security of Germany and of Berlin, and the relaxing of controls and the end of the state of war with the Federal Republic, they separated on the 14th without having come any closer to reconciling their divergent views on the participation of Germany in its own defense.

The next day, they met with the other ministers of the Atlantic Pact, who on the whole were much more disposed to accede to the urgent requests of the United States. The Americans, as Pierre Schneiter, interim representative of the Quai d'Orsay, noted, "have, since their defeat in 1940, more confidence in the German soldiers than in the French soldiers." [15] Other factors also influenced their attitude. They were the size of the Communist electorate in France, the reiterated declarations of Maurice Thorez which maintained that "the French people will never make war against the Soviet Union," [16] and the instability of the Fourth Republic and its constant appeals to the American moneylender. On the 16th, Bevin, knowing he was on the point of death and wanting nothing more than to give the Atlantic Community a sound foundation, came around to Washington's point of view.

Schuman, who had only the support of his Belgian and Luxembourgian colleagues, van Zeeland and Bech, deemed it advisable to modify his stand. Indicating that the French Government "is not at all inclined to make an absolute refusal," he concluded that "the German forces must be made part of an existing organization, so as to be solidly integrated within its structure, and not organized simultaneously with it." [17]

On the 22nd, the Big Three resumed their deliberations, but this time with the help of their defense ministers: General Marshall, whom Truman had just recently brought back once again from retirement in order to entrust him with this heavy responsibility; the British Shinwell, a determined advocate of German rearmament; and Jules Moch, who was categorically opposed to it, and who could invoke the decision made by the French Council of Ministers, on the 20th, to oppose any even eventual rearmament of Germany.

The talks between the Big Three, who had now become six, were lively, and Acheson made the French delegation clearly understand that unless Paris came around within a month, the United States would have "to reconsider its entire proposal and seek another solution." [18] He dismissed any possibility, in the interval, of reinforcing the American or English troops stationed in Europe. Nevertheless, the Big Three ended by agreeing on a text, which was amended to take the French position into account. The Atlantic Council, meeting again on the 26th, ratified it the same day. After having expressed its approval of Germany's being enabled to contribute to the build-up of the defense of Western Europe," the Council ordered its Defense Committee to present, as quickly as possible, recommendations as to the best means to achieve it. [19] A few hours earlier, Jules Moch, having returned to France, had heard from René Pleven, the Prime Minister, the broad outlines of an idea which had been broached to him by Jean Monnet. Designed to forestall the anticipated United States proposals, the plan was to create a European Army under the command of a European Minister of Defense, through the juxtaposition of national divisions none of which would be German, and others in which Germans would be integrated at the battalion level. In other words, Germany would not be rearmed, but German soldiers would be incorporated within the framework of a "European" Army.

This revolutionary concept broke with many traditions. Yet at the same time it did not remove the fears of those who could not accept the idea of a rebirth of German militarism, twice responsible within this century for countless deaths and incalculable destruction. But it was a logical sequel to the endeavor to achieve European unification which France itself had initiated in the spring.

In May 1949 the efforts of the "European movement," created by Churchill to hasten the development of a "United States of Europe," had achieved their first result: the creation by the majority of the democratic governments on the continent of a "European Council," headquartered in Strasbourg and made up of a purely consultative Parliamentary Assembly and a Council of Ministers meeting periodically and acting in unanimity. In August, Churchill, the same man who in 1919 had advocated reconciliation with Germany to meet the Bolshevik peril, now recommended the admission of the Federal Republic into the new organization.

However, before applying for admission, the Bonn Government had to settle its large backlog of differences with France. The principal one concerned the Saar, where Paris intended to preserve a *de facto* protectorate by means of a customs union. In January 1950, Robert Schuman went to confer with Adenauer but could not reach agreement with him. It was to overcome this principal obstacle to Franco-German reconciliation, which he had made the first article of his political credo, that the Chancellor revived the idea he had nurtured twenty five years before—an economic union of the two countries. As early as August 25, 1949, he had written to Schuman proposing to him that, in exchange for halting the dismantling of the Thyssen steel mills, the company's most important plant, in Hamburg, would be put under international control. Adenauer showed how such a plan "could become the starting point for a major international cooperative effort in the area of coal and steel, and, it seemed to him, would be highly desirable in terms of Franco-German understanding." [20]

In interviews in March 1950, he publicly discussed the possibility of an economic union between the two nations. At that time his statements had little impact. But on May 9 he received a letter from the Quai d'Orsay suggesting that "The gathering together of the nations of Europe requires the elimination of the age-old opposition of France and Germany" and that the French Government proposed to "place Franco-German production of coal and steel as a whole under a common higher authority, within the framework of an organization open to the participation of the other countries of Europe." [21] This was the "Schuman Plan," conceived by Jean Monnet together with his colleagues on the planning committee, who had studied its modalities in the greatest secrecy.

From the beginning, the boldness of the proposal was apparent. After four days of deliberations the French Government, then presided over by Georges Bidault, unanimously endorsed it. The creation of a supranational "High Authority", which would have complete charge of organizing European coal and steel production under the jurisdiction of a parliamentary assembly and a court of justice, not only removed from the various nations their unhampered disposition of the physical means of waging war against each other, but also, in the eyes of its sponsors, constituted, in embryo, a federal power whose spheres of influence were to be rapidly extended. Instead of distrust of Germany, which had been the alpha and omega of its diplomacy since liberation, France substituted an offer of cooperation without restrictions or discrimination—a joint effort toward the objective of a United Europe.

Without hesitation, Adenauer grasped the hand extended to him. Alcide de Gasperi's Italy made known its approval immediately. With more or less enthusiasm, the "Benelux" countries followed suit, while Great Britain, despite the favorable reception the project found among many of its ruling class, decided to remain out of it. So far as Britain was concerned, the enterprise—helped by the affinities of Schuman, Adenauer and de Gasperi for the Holy Roman Empire —was too contrary to its insularity, to its antipapism, to its mistrust of institutional machinery (especially any created in Europe), to its desire to preserve, above all, its "special ties" with the United States and to maintain the Commonwealth, and finally, to its belief in its role as a Great Power.

The meeting of the six countries which had accepted the French invitation opened June 20 in the Clock Room of the Quai d'Orsay. Five days later, the Korean War broke out and instantly changed all the perspectives of the Schuman Plan. It had been conceived and welcomed in a climate still dominated by the old dream of a European "Third Force" called upon to intercede between the two superpowers. Now it was to become a means of strengthening the West in its struggle with communism, and one asked whether the method used to overcome the old Franco-German hostility could not be equally effective in allowing Germany to participate in the common defense without awakening the long-held fears of German militarism.

As early as December 1949, Adenauer, in the interview already cited with the *Cleveland Plain Dealer,* had envisaged the incorporation of a "German contingent in the army of a European federation." On Churchill's initiative, the Assembly of the Council of Europe voted—89 to 5—on August 11, 1950, to consider the question. It was on the same day that the delegates of the Federal Republic took their seats around the horseshoe table. The French Government quickly saw in the vote a means of breaking the impasse in which it had been placed by Washington's insistence on rearming the Germans and, at the same time, of taking a giant step toward the building of a United Europe. Wouldn't this goal be more than halfway achieved when, after coal and steel, Europe put its soldiers "in common"?

On October 21, Paris officially approved the project for a European army, which Pleven had presented a month earlier to Jules Moch, who was only "half convinced, but gave up the fight." [22] In the meantime, another trip to the United States had convinced him of American determination to seek German troops at any cost. Besides, the Americans feared that the realization of the Pleven plan, which appealed to them because it led toward the unification of Europe, one of their constant aims, would lose them precious time.

On the 24th, Pleven presented to the General Assembly the broad outline of the plan with which his name was to remain associated: the creation of a common army linked to the political institutions of Europe and directed by a European Minister of Defense, responsible to a European Assembly; a common defense budget; the integration at the lowest possible level of contingents supplied by the member states; the maintenance of overseas forces outside the project. Negotiations were to begin only after ratification of the Schuman Plan, and it was understood that the Federal Republic was to be kept out of the Atlantic Pact.

The Fourth Republic was then going through a particularly turbulent phase of its existence. The news of the fall of Cao Bang and Lang Son had just burst upon France like a bombshell; currency speculation in Indochina and the so-called "affair of the generals" showed the corruption of the regime and its inability to maintain internal security; de Gaulle heightened his attacks on the government in anticipation of the elections, which he expected would ensure the victory of his partisans. Even in Parliament, Communists and nationalists, Gaullists or not, joined in a chorus against the Pleven plan.

However, when the debate ended, the government won by 342 votes to 225. The article prohibiting any rebuilding of a German army or general staff was adopted by 402 votes to 168.

The plan was not well received in Bonn, which, above all, saw implicit in it a distrust of Germany and a denial of the principle of "equality of rights," as dear to the leaders of the Federal Republic as it was once to their predecessors in the Weimar Republic. On the other side of the Atlantic, many were tempted to see the Pleven plan primarily as a way for France to gain time. On October 27, during a meeting of the defense ministers of the Atlantic Pact, the United States sought to have the immediate rearmament of two German divisions tentatively adopted. But Jules Moch unconditionally opposed it. On the other hand, he yielded on the levels of integration. Whereas in the beginning he had advocated integration of the battalion level, he now accepted that it be effected on a "combat-team" basis. A tentative accord on that point was reached in December, at the Brussels meeting of the Atlantic Conference.

§   §   §

It would be almost eighteen months before the treaty creating a "European Defense Community" was signed in Bonn. The French Parliament finally rejected it in August 1954. The first German soldiers were to be incorporated only in the summer of 1955—five years after Washington had asked for the appeal to yesterday's enemy.

From the first, Soviet diplomacy was used extensively to block the treaty, or at least to postpone its ratification. On October 23, 1950, the foreign ministers of the socialist bloc, assembled in Prague under Molotov's presidency, had advocated the signing of a peace treaty with Germany, its demilitarization, and the withdrawal of foreign forces. A Constitutional Council, representing the two German nations on an equal basis, would be invited to make suggestions on unifying the country. On November 3, Moscow proposed a meeting of the Council of Foreign Ministers for the purpose of considering the Prague Resolution. The Council had been created at Potsdam but had not met since the fruitless conference at the Pink Palace in the spring of 1949. In December the Western Powers accepted the proposal but asked that the meeting deal with all the problems which divided East and West. Discord was to appear at the first session of the "Four-Power meeting" which opened with "alternates" on March 2, 1951, at the Château de la Muette. The presence of Philip Jessup and of Jacob Malik, who had negotiated the settlement of the Berlin crisis two years before, seemed a good omen. But on June 21 the participants separated without even having been able to establish a common agenda.

In retrospect their failure to agree on an agenda seems astonishing, for they had arrived at almost identical versions of one when the breakdown occurred over a very minor point. The Russians insisted on a discussion of the Atlantic Pact, and the West refused to let it be considered separately. To understand the collapse of negotiations, two things must be taken into account. First, the climate of exasperation then existing, and secondly, the Americans' fear that the start of negotiations would still further postpone the beginning of German rearmament. For their part, the Russians may have felt that, because of the increasing hesitation, not only in France but also on the banks of the Rhine and the Thames, and because of the climate of relative détente created by the opening of armistice talks in Korea, the issue of German rearmament could be avoided at small cost.

However, the following year they were to make a new effort. It came right after the Lisbon Conference, held in February 1952, at which the leaders of the Atlantic Alliance succeeded in adopting the first concrete proposal for the rearming of Europe, including the Federal Republic. The timing of the Russian move gives weight to the hypothesis that the Kremlin's decisions to make demands were closely dependent on its evaluation of America's chances of achieving its objective.

On March 10 the U.S.S.R. sent a note to the three Western Powers proposing a peace treaty (its draft was appended) with a reunified and neutralized Germany. This was the proposal the United States had made as early as September 1945 through James Byrnes, and which Molotov, after an initially favorable reaction from Stalin, had discarded with somewhat unconvincing arguments. Now the Russians, in accepting the proposal, added new provisions which were evidently intended more for German consumption than for the Allies. Whereas Byrnes, in 1945, had wanted Germany demilitarized for twenty-five years, it would now be authorized to establish the armed forces necessary to its defense and to produce the required war matériel. Civil and political rights would be restored to all officers and to all former Nazis, except those in prison for war crimes.

These changes clearly suggested a return to the policy of Rapallo to which the Soviet republic had nostalgically clung throughout the course of its turbulent history. But this time, in order to win over the German people, the Kremlin would have to pay more. It would have to cease making the acceptance of the Oder-Neisse frontier a preliminary condition for negotiations, and above all, it would have to agree that the new pan-German government be the result of completely free elections. But it had refused to let a U.N. commission enter into the territory occupied by the Red Army. That commission had been appointed by the U.N. the preceding winter to conduct a survey of the political and personal liberties effectively enjoyed by the citizens of the two rival republics. The West was thus in a good position to point out that the conclusion of a German peace treaty implied first of all the forming of a government empowered to sign it, and therefore, before anything else, the holding of general elections had to be agreed upon.

The brutality of the Russian reaction makes one wonder whether Stalin had not deluded himself on his proposal's chances of success. If that was the case, he had completely misunderstood the profound sentiments of the man who, having become the first Chancellor of the German Federal Republic by one vote, was consolidating his power with exceptional determination. "An unarmed, neutralized Germany," he had stated in December 1951 during his first visit to London, ". . . would sooner or later inevitably be drawn into the maelstrom of the Eastern bloc . . . and would be followed by the downfall of the other free nations of Europe as well." [23] Much water had flowed under the Rhine's bridges since the moment in December 1946 when the same Adenauer, as Mayor of Cologne, had remarked, "I believe that the majority of the German people would approve if we were to become neutral like Switzerland." [24] Between the alternatives of integration with the West and Germany's reunification, which he knew would remain incompatible for a long time, "the old man" had chosen the first. He did not have sufficient confidence in his countrymen to calmly accept the return to a situation in which a new

Reich would play off East against West and vice versa. A few months before retiring in 1963, he confided to some people that the unchanging goal of his policies had been to prevent a repetition of the 1939 Soviet-German pact as much as a new Franco-Soviet pact against Germany.

The Russian note, despite the build-up it had, could not overcome Adenauer's determination, which the West German population supported, albeit without enthusiasm. Little by little the U.S.S.R. resigned itself to the existence of the Federal Republic, to its rearmament and to its adherence to the West, even to the point where Marshal Zhukov could remark in 1955 to a French diplomat friend of mine: "You have your Germans and we have ours. Isn't that the best solution?" [25]

It has to be admitted that Stalin's demise during that interval had completely transformed the international climate.

BIBLIOGRAPHY AND NOTES

[1] Keesing's, 11101 A.

[2] Link, *op. cit.*, p. 687.

[3] Keesing's, 10985 A.

[4] *Ibid.*, 11640 A.

[5] *Le Monde*, April 22, 1954.

[6] Keesing's, 7862 A.

[7] *Ibid.*, 11206 B.

[8] Jacques Fauvet, *La IVe République* (Paris: Fayard, 1959), p. 145.

[9] Konrad Adenauer, *Memoirs, 1945–1953* (Chicago: Regnery, 1966), p. 267.

[10] *Ibid.*

[11] Keesing's, 10369 A.

[12] *Le Monde*, July 25, 1960.

[13] Jules Moch, *Histoire du Réarmement allemand depuis 1950* (Paris: Robert Laffont, 1965), pp. 46–47.

[14] Keesing's, 10956 A.

[15] Jacques Dumaine, *Quai d'Orsay* (Paris: Julliard, 1955), p. 525.

[16] Alexander Werth, *France 1940–1955* (New York: Henry Holt, 1956), p. 438.

[17] Moch, *op. cit.*, p. 48.

[18] *Ibid.*, p. 78.

[19] Keesing's, 10985 A.

[20] Alfred Grosser, *La IVe République et sa politique extérieure* (Paris: Armand Colin, 1961), p. 209.

[21] Paul Weymar, *Adenauer: His Authorized Biography* (New York: Dutton, 1957), p. 324.

[22] Moch, *op. cit.*, p. 133.

[23] Weymar, *op. cit.*, pp. 427–28.

[24] Gilbert Badia, *Histoire de l'Allemagne contemporaine* (Paris: Editions sociales, 1962), II, p. 296.

[25] Author's personal notes.

· CHAPTER 3 ·

THE CHANGE OF

COMMAND

Thus it is that one man [Peter the Great] has transformed the greatest empire in the world. What is frightening is that this reformer of men lacked the cardinal virtue: "humanity."

—Voltaire, *History of Charles XII*

BY 1952 THE COLD WAR HAD ESSENTIALLY BECOME A duel between Truman and Stalin. Suddenly, within a few weeks, both camps were to change command.

Already, at the end of 1951, two percent of the British electorate, by abandoning a Labour Party exhausted from six years of uninterrupted governing, had returned Winston Churchill to power. But the lion had aged—he was seventy-seven years old, rather deaf, and had lost much of his proverbial energy. One month before his victory he had confided to his doctor that he no longer completely trusted his own judgment. And during the four years he spent at the same 10 Downing Street from which, a few years earlier, he had seemed to rule the world, he continually reversed himself. Under American pressure he had to accept the eventual withdrawal of British soldiers from Egypt, whereas in the past he had vehemently denounced the abandonment of India and the haste with which the Labourites were liquidating the empire.

He refused to let his country participate in the European Army, although he himself had introduced the idea in Strasbourg while he was the leader of the opposition. Of late he had become concerned with the risk of war, and he pleaded for prudence and conciliation with the same Russians whose actions he had so often denounced. He had gone so far as to say, in a speech at Llandudno, October 9, 1948: "The Western nations will be far more likely to reach a lasting settlement without bloodshed if they formulate their just demands while they have the atomic power and before the Russian Communists have got it, too." [1]

His dream was to re-establish the Anglo-American partnership he had set up with Roosevelt during the war. But circumstances had changed. Heavily in debt to the United States, Great Britain was discovering the price it had to pay for its lonely, long-drawn-out struggle and its exhaustion following victory. Imperial grandeur was no more than a memory; Britain had to choose between leading Europe, which demanded that it become a full-fledged member of an integrated federation, and playing the part of Washington's privileged ally in the hope that it could influence American decisions, or at least their execution. It is the second course that Churchill decided to follow. Britain had not yet realized the scope of Europe's revolution and believed that it was called upon to play vis-à-vis the United States, as Macmillan had once said during the war, the civilizing role which, in the Roman Empire, was that of Greece.

It is always dangerous to reconstruct history from a hypothetical basis. But it is hard to see how Great Britain's foreign policy and that of the Western world in general would have been different if Churchill had not taken the helm again in 1951. Can the same be said of what happened in the United States? In November 1952 a landslide vote had brought to the White House the Commander in Chief of the Allied armies during the war, who had left retirement in 1950 to become the Supreme Commander of the Allied Powers in Europe. However, in spite of the slogan "It's time for a change," the American vote had expressed not so much the desire to alter the conduct of the Cold War as to entrust it, in a critical time, to the most illustrious of the nation's sons.

General Eisenhower was a great man, but a very simple great man. He was extraordinarily similar in his manners and his tastes to the majority of his countrymen. They, knowing his distaste for politics, saw in his rise to power the triumph of his selflessness and patriotism. "Ike" was to be triumphantly re-elected in 1956 and his popularity remained intact. However, for all his dignity, his moral rectitude, his talent as a conciliator and as a staff organizer, Dwight D. Eisenhower—whose army career had not affected a pacifism inherited from his mother, a Jehovah's Witness—does not appear, in the history of East-West relations, as an antagonist of the stature of his predecessor or of his successor, John Kennedy. Therefore, more often than not, he left the conduct of the nation's diplomatic affairs to his Secretary of State, whose death in 1959 was to leave him almost helpless.

§   §   §

The American tradition is that the President be his own foreign minister, but the power of John Foster Dulles represented the exception to that rule. He was a man far more complex than was suggested by the stern-father attitude he adopted, his crooked mouth sometimes trembling with anger, his eyes distrustful behind their gold-rimmed glasses. Authoritarian, hardly using the many talents gathered around him, he was little loved but combined very great qualities with a total fearlessness—which allowed him to withstand the most violent attacks and threats without raising an eyebrow—tactical ability, an exceptional memory and a capacity for work which enabled him to always develop the right argument against the adversary, as well as to uncover the trap hidden in the most tempting offers.

Born into the State Department—his grandfather and uncle had been secretaries of state—at nineteen he had taken part in the international conference at the Hague in 1907. But he had to wait until he was sixty-four years old to take charge of American diplomacy, after having played an important role in it as a Republican consultant to the State Department and negotiator of the peace treaty with Japan. In the meantime he had headed a large law firm in New York and was reputed to be America's highest-paid lawyer. He was, at the same time, the president of the World Council of Churches.

This conservative, unbending in his judgments, had long been a pacifist and isolationist. Like many others, however, he had changed, and his anticommunism gave him a new and heightened awareness of America's world responsibilities. During the campaign which was to lead to Eisenhower's election, he harshly criticized the policy of containment as too passive, and while he advocated the rollback of communism, he did not specify the methods to be used. In fact, one of his first moves after taking office was to go overseas to reassure the European leaders who had been alarmed by his bellicose language and explain to them that there would be no fundamental change in U.S. policy.

§   §   §

On October 26 in Detroit, on the advice of his friend C. D. Jackson, one of the editors of *Life,* Ike had committed himself to bringing the Korean War to "an early and honorable end." "That job," he had continued, "requires a personal trip to Korea. I shall make that trip." [2] That sentence transformed the Republican candidate's expected victory into a triumph. Tired of war, the American people trusted him to get them out of it one way or another. But, as the journalist Samuel Lubell has written, "the election should not be interpreted as a vote for peace at any price. It was more a vote of impatience with the frustrating state of neither war nor peace." [3]

The armistice negotiations begun in June 1951 had promptly reached a deadend. The Communists wanted the cease-fire line to coincide with the 38th Parallel. The Allies wanted it to follow the front line existing on the day of the armistice in order to maintain pressure on the adversary until the last minute. On August 28, using the pretext of a frontier incident in the demilitarized zone, the North Koreans suspended the talks *sine die.* They were reopened in October in Panmunjom, where a month's truce was finally agreed upon. No progress having been made in that time, hostilities resumed. In the meantime the Chinese and North Koreans had fortified their positions in depth, while increasingly savage encounters over Korea pitted one air force against the other.

The question of the demarcation line having finally been settled, negotiations now snagged on the crucial issue of the prisoners of war. Peking and Pyongyang demanded their unconditional repatriation. The Americans wanted to give the 132,000 Communist soldiers in the hands of U.N. troops the right to decide whether or not they would go home. They remembered and regretted the alacrity with which they had returned to the U.S.S.R. the Russian prisoners they had liberated from the Germans in 1945. Many of those former prisoners were sent to forced-labor camps and even executed in the name of the principle that a Soviet patriot does not let himself be captured. "We will not buy an armistice," Truman declared on May 7, 1952, "by turning over human beings for slaughter or slavery." [4]

The Sino-Koreans were able to counter their adversaries' demand with an important legal argument, for the Geneva Convention provides for the repatriation of all war prisoners, without delay, at the termination of hostilities. However, they accepted to exchange lists of prisoners and to let the men be questioned as to their intentions.

Because the Communists, solidly organized in their internment camps, had so many ways of putting pressure on any of their comrades who wanted to "choose freedom," they imagined that consultations would turn to their triumph. On February 18, 1952, a riot resulting in seventy-five deaths among the prisoners erupted in Kobe when the G.I.'s tried to break up their secret political cells. Peking's propaganda promptly exploited the use of such "barbaric methods." But soon, Peking was to launch a campaign of far greater scope, accusing the Americans of resorting to bacteriological warfare.

The real purpose of that campaign has never been completely understood. It ended abruptly after Stalin's death, and since then, Communist leaders have never made the slightest allusion to it. In the beginning, it may have been started to explain the typhus epidemic which had broken out in North Korea and in Manchuria. In any case, the affair very quickly assumed the proportions of a vast collective hallucination, carefully organized and exploited, and mobilizing in the service of their improbable thesis admissions wrested by violence from American airmen who had been shot down, as well as the testimony of naive or obliging foreign observers. Washington proposed that an investigation be made by the International Red Cross, which accepted but was immediately accused by Peking of being under orders from the American Government and therefore disqualified. In any case, the campaign helped rid China of myriads of insects and rats which, since the beginning of time, had menaced it with worse epidemics. Who knows whether this result could have been obtained if the population summoned to an insect-hunt had not believed it was at the same time fighting a completely unscrupulous enemy?

The entire anti-American campaign became so vituperative that the U.N. command, tired of having its representatives insulted at lengthy sessions in Panmunjom, decided in October to suspend armistice talks. While it began massive bombing operations against North Korea, the Communists launched furious and bloody assaults against the Allied positions which, in the end, were always repulsed with heavy losses. It was becoming evident that the war could not much longer be limited to Korea. Truman, a short time before the Presidential election, directed his ambassador in New Delhi to make the Indian Government aware of that danger and to suggest that they act as intermediaries. India then submitted to the U.N. a new plan for the repatriation of prisoners, but Vishinsky rejected it in the most violent terms.

Eisenhower, following his landslide election, kept the promise he had made to go to Korea prior to his move into the White House. From his visit to the front, and from his talks with Syngman Rhee and with military leaders followed by daily conferences on board the cruiser *Helena* with John Foster Dulles and his principal advisers, he came to the conclusion which he outlined December 7, on Wake Island, to the men who were to become his ministers: "We could not tolerate the indefinite continuance of the Korean conflict: the United States would have to prepare to break the stalemate." [5]

But how? A general offensive undertaken with conventional means? It would not achieve the objective. MacArthur, whom the new President met at Dulles' house in New York on December 17, 1952, addressed him melodramatically: "You have in your hands today the power to make the greatest impression on civilization since the crucifixion of Christ. If when you go to the White House you act instantly and dynamically . . . you cannot fail to be remembered in history as a messiah. . . ." Ike had tears in his eyes. He made no reply. It was Dulles who took it upon himself to break the silence by saying to the President-elect: "You know, General MacArthur could be just as wrong in this matter as when he backed Bob Taft against you." [6]

Dulles was haunted by the fear of "miscalculation," a subject he pursued tirelessly during the talks on board the *Helena*. He recalled with complacency the mistake made by Acheson when he stated that Korea was not within the strategic perimeter of the United States. Eisenhower finally accepted a policy by which he would attempt to make the Communists understand that if an agreement was not reached at Panmunjom within a reasonable time, the United States would no longer be bound by the restrictions it had until now imposed upon itself. In other words, that the U.S. could attack targets in Manchuria as well as use tactical atomic weapons on the battle-field.[7]

As a beginning, Eisenhower announced to Congress on February 2, 1953, that he "was issuing instructions that the Seventh Fleet . . . no longer be employed to shield Communist China." [8] That is to say, it would continue to protect Formosa but it would cease to oppose any possible operations on the part of the Chinese Nationalists against the mainland. This "deneutralization" of Formosa greatly disturbed the British and the Indians, but at least it resulted in obliging Peking to shift part of its forces and deploy them along the coast.

At the time it had no effect on the parley, and the Communists left unanswered the appeal addressed to them by General Clark on February 22 to exchange sick and wounded prisoners. However, there was in this issue an obvious means of reopening discussions, and in the end Moscow was to judge it expedient to take advantage of it. But by the time the Sino-Korean command's decision to agree to an exchange had reached the U.N. command, on May 28, an event of incalculable importance had occurred which modified all the perspectives of the war: Stalin was dead. Two months after Truman, his principal adversary, had also left the scene.

§   §   §

While the change of administration in Washington took place without incidents—other than those created by the usual pettiness between rival political parties, in Moscow it was to take place amidst the horrors of classical tragedy.

Svetlana Stalin's defection to the West and the book she published have cleared up most of the mystery which surrounded the death of her father, officially reported as having occurred March 5, 1953, at 9:50 P.M. It took place at an opportune time: Khrushchev in his famous secret report of 1956 formally accused Stalin of having wanted to get rid of all the members of the Politburo, implying that if Stalin had remained at the helm a few months longer,[9] Malenkov and Mikoyan—both accused of imaginary crimes during one of Stalin's appearances before the Central Committee—could very well have fallen under the bullets of some firing squad. A frenzied purge had decimated the cadres of the party in the U.S.S.R. as well as in those democracies called "people's" through a redundancy which underscores its presumptuous irony. Seasoned veterans of international communism, heroes of the Spanish Civil War and of the Resistance, were sent to prison or to the gallows as Hitlerian, Titoist, American or Trotskyite agents. Beginning in 1952 a new accusation, that of "Zionism," had been added to the classic themes of the indictments. It had been first used against Rudolf Slanski, who, until September 1951, was Secretary General of the Czechoslovakian Communist Party and assistant to the Prime Minister. He was arrested with a group of militants, most of them Jews like himself, among them the Foreign Minister, the Finance Minister and the editor in chief of the party's newspaper. After a trial that appealed to the worst racist sentiments, Slanski, the man who had stated in 1949 that "the attitude he holds toward the Soviet Union is the touchstone for every Communist," [10] was hanged on December 3, 1952.

§　　　　　§　　　　　§

Slanski was not rehabilitated until 1963, long after most of the other victims of Stalinism. No explanation has ever been given for the real reasons for his condemnation. The most probable that comes to mind is that the generalissimo, who was notorious for sharing the anti-Semitic prejudices of many of his countrymen, had been offended by the tumultuous welcome extended by many of Moscow's Jews to Golda Meir, the first minister plenipotentiary from the state of Israel; he saw in her coreligionists—once all his other virtual opponents had been eliminated—potential conspirators. From there to gradually persuading himself of the reality of that conspiracy was only a single step, which his sickly, suspicious brain was soon to take.

In January 1953, perhaps fearing that he would be liquidated by them, the dictator ordered the arrest of nine doctors, six of whom were Jews. They were accused of having assassinated Zhdanov, the master ideologist who had died a few months previously, and another party leader, Scherbakov, in collaboration with a charitable Jewish organization, the American Joint Committee—identified for the occasion as a "Zionist espionage organization." The communiqué from TASS stated that "that band of wild beasts," [11] by making false diagnoses and by using counterindicated treatments, had tried to do away with half a dozen leading generals. The Soviet press took advantage of that affair, shortly followed by the arrest of other "plotters," particularly in economic circles, to begin a violent campaign against Zionism. It was further heightened following the explosion of a bomb on February 9 in the compound of the Russian legation at Tel Aviv. Despite the apologies and offers of reparation which the Ben-Gurion government made, the Kremlin decided to break diplomatic relations with Israel. No one can say where this madness would have led had Stalin not opportunely died. What was going to happen now? It soon became evident that even while voicing endless protestations of fidelity to "the inspired continuer of Lenin's work," whose loss was irreparable "to the Party, to the workers of the Soviet Union and to the entire world," whose name "will live forever in the hearts of the Soviet people and of all progressive humanity," [12] his heirs were determined to slow down.

An extraordinary photograph shows them together, carrying on their shoulders the mortal remains of the man who had defeated Hitler, defied America, terrorized the Russians and made their country one of the greatest powers of all time; the man who had, perhaps, inspired more love and more hatred than any national leader remembered by history. They are all there, with vacant eyes and frozen faces: the deceased's son, the debauched Vassily Stalin, who would die of cirrhosis of the liver after having spent a few months in prison, and the three among whom, the consensus was, the struggle for power was going to unfold—Malenkov, his weasel eyes buried in his fat, beardless cheeks; Molotov, narrow-shouldered and prim as usual behind his old-fashioned pince-nez; and Beria, the mastermind of the secret police, more disturbing than ever with his enormous black hat and an oversized overcoat that made him look like the villain in a melodrama. No one noticed the man who had been put in charge of organizing the funeral, Nikita Sergeyevich Khrushchev, whose name was known outside the U.S.S.R. only by Kremlinologists. Nevertheless, a communiqué published the day before had just freed him from his duties as First Secretary to the Moscow Committee in order to permit him to "concentrate on the work of the Central Committee."

Today, there is every reason to believe that in the hours following Stalin's death a violent discussion broke out among his lieutenants on the devolution of his powers. They quickly agreed on the necessity of re-establishing, under another name, the Politburo, which had been suppressed in 1952, and of separating, as in the past—and as it is now—the government's functions from the leadership of the party. It was learned only eight days later that Malenkov, probably too strong a personality for the liking of his peers, had had to give up his duties as Secretary of the Central Committee in order to assume the post of President of the Council, where he was flanked by Molotov as Foreign Minister and Beria as Minister of the Interior. As for the party, the three, accomplices until they became rivals, had thought it expedient to put at its head a man whose strictly limited gifts seemed to prevent his aspiring to the highest power. Nikita Khrushchev was later to tell this story: "Once upon a time, there were three men in prison: a Social Democrat, an anarchist, and a shy Jewish youth named Pinia, not long out of school. The three inmates decided to elect a leader in order to proceed with the distribution of food and tobacco. The anarchist, a powerful guy, was opposed to the election.

"But to show that he respected law and order, he proposed that they elect the little Pinia. This was done. Everything was going fine, until the day they decided to escape and dug a tunnel.

"Knowing that the first one to go through would expose himself to the guards' fire, they asked the anarchist—the biggest and strongest of the three—to go. But he was afraid. Then, the little Jew Pinia got up and said, 'Friends, you have elected me your leader in the most democratic manner. Therefore, I'll go out first.' Do you want to know the moral of this story?" Khrushchev continued. "As modest as a man's beginnings may be, he always reaches the heights to which he was destined." And so that nobody could misunderstand, he added, "The little Pinia, it's me." [13] The stalwart anarchist would have been Marshal Zhukov, whom he had just dismissed after having relied on him for years.

Like Stalin, the little Pinia knew how to methodically seize the levers of power. He prepared for his victory by accumulating arguments and allies against the short-lived successors to Joseph Stalin which later allowed him to overthrow them. But, less distrustful than Stalin had been, one fine morning he found himself evicted by a majority vote from the Central Committee and had to bow out like a common bourgeois politician repudiated by his Parliament.

§   §   §

While waiting for fate to select the man who, after a fierce struggle, would sit in Stalin's chair for seven years, the hierarchy agreed on the following essentials: It was necessary to reassure the Soviet people and the outside world; it was necessary to stop the race toward war in which humanity seemed to be inexorably engaged; it was necessary to prevent the imperialist camp from succumbing to any temptation to profit from the succession crisis by implementing the promises to liberate eastern Europe which the Republican leaders had so often made during the American election campaign.

Actually, Uncle Joe had never been an insatiable conqueror, but this evaluation only came to be accepted later. Capable of anything when it came to getting rid of his rivals, he had shown extreme prudence in foreign policy in his dealings with both Hitler and Truman, to the extent that Khrushchev, talking to Fidel Castro one day, had accused Stalin of "abdication." [14] It was not he who, like Khrushchev in Berlin or Cuba, gambled the fate of the world on a throw of the dice. A chess player—cunning, attentive, patient—he was determined to take advantage of every opportunity that presented itself; and it had happened, in Finland and in Korea, that he had grossly misjudged his adversary's determination. But he never hesitated to retreat, as soon as he judged that he was losing, and he successively counseled moderation to the French, Italian, Chinese, Greek or Yugoslav Communists at times when Western "experts" credited him with the most aggressive intentions.

Was Stalin preparing a new withdrawal at the time of his death? Or had he finally resigned himself to a war with the capitalist world?

Had he lived, the answer would have been quickly known because Eisenhower and Dulles had decided to threaten the atomic bombardment of Manchuria to bring an end to the Korean War.

The facts available today are not decisive in determining the intentions of the dictator. It is a fact that the eastern European countries had been put on a war footing, the length of military service extended, their troops closely integrated into the Soviet military dispositions with the help of Russian officers at all command levels, and their entire economies mobilized for defense. But it is no less true that the "Conference for Peace in Asia and the Pacific," held in Peking in October 1952, had ended without the slightest reference to the necessity of armed conflict, unlike the one that had preceded it. If Stalin in his last article, on "the economic problems of Socialism in the U.S.S.R."—published in September of the same year—had asserted that the "contradictions" between capitalist countries were "theoretically" less strong than those between socialist countries and capitalist countries, he had also added that it was not necessarily so in practice. He prophesied that "in the end capitalist Great Britain and capitalist France would be forced into conflict with the United States in order to remain independent and to secure for themselves enormous profits." Since "it would be fantasy to think that Germany and Japan would not do everything to become independent vis à vis the United States," the situation was the same so far as they were concerned. The result of this, contrary to the opinions of some comrades, was that "wars remained inevitable between capitalist countries." [15] The Georgian was to return to that theme during the final conversation he had with a foreigner, the Indian Saiffudine Kitchlu, to whom he presented the Stalin Peace Prize on February 17, 1953.

At the time, these statements seemed odd to many observers; some wondered if they were not largely an indication of a deranged mind. But they could just as well have foretold a sudden strategic reversal: the substitution for the two-bloc thesis which had been promulgated by Lenin and Zhdanov, of an attempt to utilize the "contradictions of imperialism" by appealing to the nationalism of the good capitalists, or rather the least dangerous, the Europeans, against the most wicked, the Americans.

In any case, Stalin's language did not prepare Soviet public opinion for the idea of imminent world conflict. Besides, at Christmas *The New York Times* published an interview with the generalissimo in which, after having reasserted that war was not inevitable, he declared himself ready to cooperate in an eventual joint diplomatic action "because the U.S.S.R. is interested in ending the war in Korea" [16] and to meet with President Eisenhower. However skeptical he was on the results of such a meeting, Ike had replied on February 25 to a journalist: "I would meet anybody, anywhere, where I thought there was the slightest chance of doing any good, as long as it was in keeping with what the American people expect of their Chief Executive."[17] Stalin's death, ten days later, prompted him to make overtures to the Soviet leaders that might be "at least a start toward the birth of mutual trust founded in cooperative effort." [18]

BIBLIOGRAPHY AND NOTES

[1] *The New York Times,* October 10, 1948.

[2] Link, *op. cit.,* p. 701.

[3] *Saturday Evening Post,* January 10, 1953.

[4] Truman, *op. cit.,* II, p. 460.

[5] Dwight D. Eisenhower, *Mandate for Change: The White House Years 1953–1959* (New York: Doubleday, 1963), I, p. 104.

[6] Interview with Bob Considine in *New York Journal American,* April 8, 1964.

[7] James Shepley, "How Dulles Avoids War," *Life,* January 16, 1956 (article approved by Dulles); cf. Eisenhower, *op. cit.,* I, p. 178.

[8] Eisenhower, *op. cit.,* I, p. 123.

[9] *Le Monde,* June 19, 1956.

[10] François Fejtö, *Histoire des démocraties populaires* (Paris: Editions du Seuil, 1952), p. 267.

[11] Keesing's, 12728 A.

[12] Communiqué of the Central Committee of the C.P.S.U., *Le Monde,* March 7, 1953.

[13] *Le Monde,* October 29, 1957.

[14] Interview with Fidel Castro by Jean Daniel, *L'Express,* December 6, 1963.

[15] *Le Monde,* October 4, 1952.

[16] *The New York Times,* December 25, 1952.

[17] Eisenhower, *op. cit.,* I, p. 143.

[18] *Ibid.,* pp. 144–45.

· CHAPTER 4 ·

THE THAW

With all the nations that Alexander has conquered,
isn't it time, Oh Lord, that he seek friends?

—Racine, *Alexander*

A FEW DAYS BEFORE STALIN'S DEATH, ANTHONY EDEN
summoned Andrei Gromyko, then Russian ambassador to Great
Britain, and asked him to do all he could to obtain the freedom of
the British minister in Seoul and of other British subjects unjustifi-
ably detained by the North Koreans since June 1950. The diplomat
answered him that to the best of his knowledge the Soviet Government bore no responsibility in the matter. Nonetheless, he agreed
to transmit the *aide-mémoire* prepared by Downing Street to Moscow.

March 18, or exactly eleven days after the funeral of the generalissimo, it was the turn of the British ambassador to be summoned to
the Kremlin, where to his astonishment he was shown a list of his
countrymen interned in Korea and was assured that the U.S.S.R.
would do its utmost to secure their release. Although this was only
one tiny swallow, it was still the harbinger of spring, or at least of
the "thaw"—a word Ilya Ehrenburg's novel was soon to popularize.
Two days later, Zhukov, Soviet commander in Germany, proposed
a conference with the West for the purpose of devising a means to
prevent any recurrence of aerial incidents such as those in which, the
preceding week, two Allied planes had been shot down by Russian
Migs.

The annual thaw in western Europe does not amount to much. A
few broken conduits, a ray of sun, a little mud in the sunken roads.
In the east, where it is anticipated for weeks, it is a great event, a

· 63 ·

tremendous upheaval of the ice, with everything caught up and swept along in millions of tons of melting snow. The yoke of ice which has for months imprisoned man and nature finally breaks up. It is a liberation.

On March 28, 1953, a little ahead of time, momentous news announced that liberation to the Soviet people. The new government granted amnesty to most prisoners condemned to less than five years in prison. The same day, the Sino-Korean command agreed to the exchange of sick and wounded prisoners—a proposal made by General Clark on February 22. Kim-il-Sung and P'eng Teh-huai expressed the hope that "a reasonable settlement of this question" would allow "a friendly settlement of the whole question of prisoners of war, leading also to the armistice for which the whole world hopes." [1] In that spirit they offered to reopen the negotiations at Panmunjom immediately. Forty-eight hours later, Chou En-lai, returning from Moscow where he had attended Stalin's funeral, suggested that a neutral country be entrusted with the custody of those prisoners who refused repatriation. On April 22, Molotov, once again Foreign Minister, replacing Vishinsky, who had been named permanent representative to the U.N., seconded that important concession. At the same time the Kremlin, giving up a veto it had maintained for months, agreed to the candidate proposed by France—the Swedish economist Dag Hammarskjöld—for Secretary General of the U.N. The Norwegian, Trygve Lie, whose role in the Korean intervention had earned him so many insults from Moscow, had finally resigned.

On April 4 the alleged "assassins in the white coats" were freed and *Pravda* recognized that their confessions had been obtained through unacceptable methods. Ignatiev, Minister of the Interior at the time the affair had broken, was held responsible for it. He was relieved of all his duties and his former assistant Rioumine, identified as "a despicable adventurer," was arrested.

From then on, almost every week brought good news: lower prices for basic commodities, a reduction in forced loans, a purge of the police, the elimination from non-Russian republics of those groups which had persecuted "bourgeois Nationalists," the renewal of relations with Israel, the abandonment of territorial claims against Turkey, the appointment of an ambassador to Belgrade, the liberation of the American journalist Oatis, condemned in Prague in 1951 to ten years imprisonment, etc.

There was a swift change of tone on the Russian radio, at the U.N.—where Vishinsky unhesitatingly applauded a disarmament appeal made by Henry Cabot Lodge—at the embassy cocktail parties, which the Soviet diplomats again began to attend after years of avoiding them, and even in Berlin, where occasional minor incidents were promptly settled.

On April 11 the exchange of sick and wounded prisoners began at Panmunjom. The moment seemed opportune for Eisenhower, speaking on the 16th before the American Society of Newspaper Editors, to declare that "an era ended with the death of Joseph Stalin." He claimed that the Soviet leadership "now has a precious opportunity to awaken, with the rest of the world, to the point of peril reached and help turn the tide of history." Noting that "recent statements and gestures" showed that "they may recognize this critical moment," he asked them to support his efforts to reduce the arms burden and to demonstrate by concrete actions the sincerity of their desire for peace.[2]

Churchill didn't want to be left out. He was convinced, as he was later to tell Lord Moran, that he could "do something no one else can do," and that he was at the peak of his opportunities. Felled by a stroke a few weeks later, he refused to leave his post as Prime Minister until he had "had a shot at settling this Russian business."[3] On April 20 he revealed his innermost thoughts in the Commons. According to him he hoped that "nothing will be said here or elsewhere which will check or chill the processes of good will which may be at work, and my hope is that they may presently lead to conversations at the highest level, even if informal and private, between some of the principal powers concerned."[4] In a word, he was extremely anxious to meet with Malenkov, and he imagined, a little as Roosevelt once did with Stalin, that by negotiating with him he would be able to decide the fate of the world. *Pravda,* which had published these hints, only answered on the 25th. The tone of its commentary was infinitely less polemical than in Stalin's time. But it still asserted the "continuity" of a foreign policy whose "value has been subsequently proven by international developments." It imputed to the U.S. most of the responsibility for the tension that existed. Obviously, anyone expecting Moscow's public conversion was disappointed. As will soon be seen, the Cold War continued. The only thing left to do was to make it less dangerous and to begin to bring the war in Korea to an end.

§   §   §

Armistice negotiations began again April 27. On May 7 the Sino-Koreans, renouncing their earlier condition that prisoners who refused to go home be transferred to a neutral country, now proposed to entrust their custody to troops supplied by the members of the Repatriation Commission. This was something which India had advocated a few months before, and which had immediately been rejected by Molotov. As some of the commission's members would have been Communist countries, the Allies replied twelve days later, asking that the troops be entirely Indian. It was then that Dulles went to New Delhi to advise Nehru—in accordance with a decision taken by Ike on his return from Korea—that the U.S. had decided to bomb Manchuria or to use tactical atomic weapons on the battlefield if an accord was not reached in the shortest possible time. Was that threat effective? On June 4 the North Koreans and the Chinese agreed that any prisoners who stated before the Repatriation Commission that they refused to go home would be freed and demobilized.

On June 8 the problem which had blocked negotiations for months was finally resolved. The signing of the armistice seemed to be just a few hours away. But an incident occurred which immediately caused the gravest concern. Syngman Rhee, the unpredictable President of South Korea, apprehensively viewed the prospect of an armistice which would confirm, probably for many years, the division of his country. Secretly he sent orders to the commanders of the prison camps to let 25,000 anti-Communist North Koreans escape. The operation, which it is hard to believe American intelligence had no previous knowledge of, had been painstakingly organized with the cooperation of South Korean police who immediately provided the fugitives with civilian clothes and helped them find shelter and food. In many cases they were joyfully welcomed by the South Korean populace.

Ike immediately rushed a telegram to Rhee protesting against an action which, in his own words, put the U.N. command in "an impossible situation" [5] and asked him to immediately find a means of correcting it. The greatest confusion reigned in Washington, where some people feared that the North Koreans would denounce the American double cross and once more break off negotiations. Foster Dulles did not agree with them. While making public a communiqué disavowing any action and asserting that American negotiators would continue to act as before, [6] he delivered an optimistic prognosis to Ike and his advisers saying "if the Communists desired a truce as much as he thought they did, they would overlook Rhee's impetuosity and would be content to sign an agreement, provided they were given proper assurances." [7]

In a way, they were both right. As expected, the Communists broke off negotiations on June 20, but resumed them on July 10, at the same time launching a major offensive. Why that attack, which cost them 25,000 dead? Perhaps it was undertaken to try to obtain a better armistice line, but more probably it was to give dramatic proof of the inefficiency of the South Korean troops against whom the attack had been launched.

On July 24, Ike, who remained dubious that even if an agreement were signed it would have any real significance as long as Syngman Rhee and the Communists continued to express their mutual hostility, discreetly ordered reinforcements to be sent to Korea. But someone in the Kremlin had decided that it was time to call a halt. On July 27, during a ceremony whose chilliness was in contrast to the intense heat, generals Nam Il and Harrison signed the eighteen copies of the armistice agreement without shaking hands or exchanging a single word. The war had lasted 37 months, left almost 2,000,000 dead, of whom four-fifths were civilians, and restored Korea, for all practical purposes, to the *status quo ante*. For the first time in history the Americans, who had lost 54,000 men, ended a war without winning it. They were determined not to let it happen again. However, that would not prevent them, fifteen years later, from again finding themselves entangled in Asia.

§ § §

The cessation of hostilities in Korea served to suppress only one of the many causes of tension existing between the two sides in the Cold War. Of those remaining, the principal one was still the partition of Germany. How principal was soon to become evident. Walter Ulbricht, secretary general of the United Socialist Party of East Germany and actual dictator of the young "German Democratic Republic," for fifteen years a refugee in the U.S.S.R. and a naturalized Soviet citizen, had been brought to power by the Red Army. He had never succeeded in winning the hearts of his countrymen. A rigid doctrinarian, without finesse or eloquence, hampered by his Saxon accent, a goatee and an unprepossessing appearance which made him resemble the wretched Professor Unrath in *The Blue Angel*, he was obedient to Stalin's orders in every situation.

The death of his master caught him unprepared, especially since the Kremlin's new leaders were visibly hesitating over what policy to follow in Germany. Conscious of the unpopularity of the regime established under the protection of the Red Army, they decided that it was necessary to let the German Democratic Republic benefit from a loosening of controls which—following the experience in the U.S.S.R.—most people's democracies were then enjoying. The East German government agencies were asked to admit "certain errors." They were even permitted to put partial blame for them on the Russian control commission, which was immediately dissolved and replaced by a High Commissioner. On June 11 the party and the government announced a series of decrees which together represented the "new course" (*Neue Kurs*), and whose orientation was so greatly in contrast to the one the regime had been following for a whole year that there could be no doubt of its Soviet authorship. It consisted of an amnesty, a relaxing of controls at the demarcation line and a halt to forced collectivization of lands and to the antireligion campaign.

For Ulbricht, these represented the extreme limit of acceptable concessions and in his mind they were, in part, intended to help gain acceptance of the higher production norms (on which wage scales were calculated) in industry. These new norms were promulgated on May 28. But the German workers saw in them proof of the regime's weakness and of its ingratitude. They felt justified in refusing the adjustment, the equivalent of a 10 percent reduction in their salaries.

On June 16 the masons clearing the Stalinallee, which Ulbricht wanted to make Communist Germany's Champs-Elysées, were soon joined by thousands of other workmen and together they would march through the streets demanding the withdrawal of the "Ivans" —the Russian soldiers—and free elections. That evening, the Polit-buro of the party met and denounced the *provocateurs* who were trying to sow discord among the ranks of the proletariat, but, at the same time, abandoned any arbitrary increase in the norms. That concession came too late to appease a city which believed the time had finally come when it could release the anger kindled for so long by the American radio broadcasts. The next day, ignoring the sector's boundaries, hundreds of thousands of Berliners formed an endless procession which passed through the streets demanding the end of the hated order. The People's Police were quickly outflanked. With a restraint in contrast to the brutality of the repression which descended on Hungary in 1956, the Soviet command deployed its armored cars and soldiers and succeeded in restoring order without ever shooting into the crowd, which bombarded them with stones and pieces of scrap iron. A state of siege was proclaimed, a Russian division was rushed in as reinforcement, and the frontier between the two Berlins was closed *manu militari*. Other incidents were reported in several large cities.

The Western Powers duly applauded the demonstration as proof of the unpopularity of the regime imposed on the Berlin workers by the Kremlin. Adenauer, although an alleged "warmonger," nonetheless realized the danger of the situation. On June 17 he asked that "the men and women of Berlin who today ask to be freed from oppression and poverty . . . must not let themselves be led by agitators to resort to actions which could endanger their lives and their freedom. A real change in the life of the Germans of the Soviet Zone," he continued, "can result only from the restoration of German unity." [8] This was a warning to Ulbricht's subjects: They could not count on any outside intervention, in spite of all the claims of Communist propaganda that the uprising had been organized by the Western Powers.

In a few days the Russian commander regained control of the situation. Some arrests were made, and a few executions took place, but the number of victims did not total more than about thirty. On July 11 the state of siege was completely lifted and food distribution was organized. There was no longer any question of raising the norms.

§   §   §

The Soviet hierarchy did not waste any time in learning a lesson from this incident. It proved, first of all, that contrary to the claims of its intelligence service the Communist Party did not have control over the working class, despite the fact that it was supposed to be the party's spearhead. "If the masses no longer understand the party, it is the party's fault and not the masses'," [9] stated the Central Committee of Ulbricht's party on June 21. The situation was not much better in Czechoslovakia, where riots took place at the beginning of the month. But how could the Soviet Union solve the problem?

Only two policies were conceivable: the return to the hard line, or the granting of sufficiently large concessions, so that no one could doubt the sincerity of the spirit which inspired them.

The name of Beria, Stalin's police chief who had become Minister of the Interior on Stalin's death, symbolized the first of these policies. The fact that his fall occurred within ten days of the Berlin uprising suggests that there was a connection between the two events. If in fact his arrest for "criminal activities . . . for the benefit of foreign capital" was only announced July 10 and his execution the following December 25, a document proves that on June 27 he was, if not dead, at least politically liquidated. *Pravda* of the 28th, mentioning the presence of leaders of the party and government at a performance of *The Decembrists,* omitted the names of Beria and his assistant Baguirov without explanation.

What had happened? Did they, as was said, attempt to seize power by force? Had a dispute started, which had suddenly taken a dramatic turn? Had the partisans of "liberalization" become convinced that it would be impossible to achieve it so long as Beria was the head of security operations? Had they decided to sacrifice Stalin's principal accomplice to popular vindictiveness, to clearly demonstrate to the people that they were breaking with the past? Until the spring of 1956, when Khrushchev would directly attack Stalin's memory, it was Beria who served as the scapegoat on all occasions.

Another version of the events should not, however, be completely dismissed. If the former Italian Communist Giulio Seniga is to be believed, a secret meeting of the Cominform took place in the Kremlin, from July 12 to 14, 1953. Italy was represented by Pietro Secchia, whose notes Seniga cites. Malenkov, Molotov and Khrushchev presented a report on Stalin's crimes, which preceded the one that Khrushchev was to submit in 1956 to the Twentieth Congress of the Soviet Communist Party. Afterward, they took up the case of Beria, who had attempted, "through the acts of a treacherous schemer, to destroy the active Leninist core of the party, to increase his personal prestige and to achieve his criminal, antisocialist aims." His proposals on the German question could be "summed up as the abandonment of the building of socialism and the transformation of the German Democratic Republic into a bourgeois state." They also asserted that they had discovered "in the last few days" the criminal projects of the Minister of the Interior, "who had sought to establish, through the use of his agents, personal contact with Tito and Rankovich in Yugoslavia." [10]

Less than two years later the U.S.S.R. would renew "contacts" with Belgrade—compared with which any Beria could have made seem quite innocent. However, it can be wondered whether the former police chief, in the wake of the Berlin uprising, had not advocated a complete revision of Soviet foreign policy in order to reach a real détente with the Western world. The personal organization which he had abroad, thanks to the agents of the secret police, might have allowed him to conclude the détente himself, and thus further his own ambitions.

Whatever the primary reason for Beria's fall, it was immediately followed by a massive purge of the secret police apparatus and by important concessions to public opinion in the field of economics: Malenkov's announcement of a sizable increase of investment in light industries and food production; a report from Khrushchev in September to the Central Committee advocating as a remedy to the disastrous condition of agriculture—publicly recognized for the first time—a decrease of mandatory deliveries from the collective farms and an increase in the prices to be paid by the state; nomination to the head of the Hungarian Government—Rakosi remaining leader of the party—of the "liberal" Imre Nagy, who announced on July 4 many concessions to the peasants, conciliatory measures in Rumania, and an amnesty in Bulgaria.

All these gestures of détente, crowned by the Korean armistice, soon persuaded a portion of Western public opinion, tired of being afraid, that the moment had come to seek an accord with the East which might perhaps obviate the necessity of rearming Germany. This statement was particularly strong in Great Britain, where the Conservative Party had called for a general election in June in order to consolidate the slim majority which had brought it back to power the preceding year. In anticipation of the election, Churchill, on May 11, had renewed the proposal for the "summit" conference he wanted so badly.

In France the Left's opposition to the rearming of yesterday's enemy was reinforced by that of the Gaullists and of many military men opposed to the creation of a European Army into which the French Army would disappear. Signed on May 22, 1952, the treaty creating the European Defense Community had only been put before the National Assembly in January 1953. The René Mayer government had been overthrown on May 21 of that same year, as soon as its leader had voiced his intention of opening the debate on ratification. Four candidates to his post had fallen before the taciturn Joseph Laniel was at last confirmed, on June 27, after having read a ministerial statement of surprising discretion on the subject of the E.D.C. The fact that the Gaullists took posts in his cabinet demonstrated that he had decided to keep "the body hidden in the closet" for the time being. His Foreign Minister, Georges Bidault, had no sympathy whatever with Soviet policies. But he knew that the confirmation of the treaty was impossible so long as the uncompromising attitude of the Kremlin could not be demonstrated, and he was therefore also campaigning for negotiations with the U.S.S.R.

Even Chancellor Adenauer added his voice to the chorus. As a general election was to take place in September in the Federal Republic, his countrymen would not have forgiven him had he not done his utmost—following the East Berlin uprising—to try and bring about national reunification. Had not some of them already accused him of gladly accepting the division which, given the traditional predominance of socialism and of Protestantism in East Germany, could only result in the strengthening of a Christian Democratic government, led by a conservative Catholic in West Germany?

On June 22, 1953, he had written a letter to the Western foreign ministers, gathered in Washington, which was quickly made public. In it he advocated holding a Four-Power conference, at the latest in the fall, to study the German question and to work out, on the basis of the E.D.C., a system "taking into account the security requirements of all European nations, including those of the Russian people." [11]

Dulles would have wanted to begin by ratifying the European Army treaty. However, he had to yield to unanimous pressure from the Allies, and he joined in sending a note to the Kremlin, on July 15, proposing a meeting of limited duration of the four foreign ministers toward the end of September. It contained the following as "subjects for discussion": Before any negotiations on a German peace treaty, there should be a plan for "free elections," implying "the use of fundamental liberties by all Germans," and conditions under which a German Government would be established "possessing complete freedom of action." The signatories of the note also stated "that a definitive agreement on the Austrian treaty would have to be obtained during that first conference." [12]

This was asking the U.S.S.R. to accept what it had rejected the preceding year—namely, the abandonment of East Germany. Indeed, after the East Berlin uprising, no one had any illusions about the way that the inhabitants of the German Democratic Republic would vote if, by chance, they could express themselves freely. Therefore, everything pointed to the rejection of the proposed agenda. On August 5, Moscow expressed its preference for a Five-Power conference, including Red China, at which would be discussed measures intended to reduce international tension, the reunification of Germany and the conclusion of a peace treaty. As to the Austrian problem, its solution would obviously be facilitated, the note continued, by a satisfactory settlement of the German problem. [13]

Three days later, before the Supreme Soviet, Malenkov stated that his country had no intention of capitulating before the demands of the Western "aggressive circles." Never, he exclaimed, had the international position of the U.S.S.R. been more stable. He also revealed to the world that "the United States no longer had the monopoly of the hydrogen bomb." [14] Without mentioning the 1952 Soviet proposal for a neutral and rearmed Germany, he appealed to France, linked to the Kremlin by the 1944 Treaty of Alliance, to return to an independent foreign policy.[15]

On September 2 the Allies proposed a conference of the Big Four for October 15 at Lugano, this time without any conditions whatsoever. Nonetheless, on September 29, Moscow reproached the Western Powers for their silence on German elections, "a question which must be resolved by the German people without any interference from foreign powers," and demanded again a Five-Power conference, even if German affairs were to be discussed only by the Four Powers.[16]

A new exchange of notes only served to confirm each camp's previous position. Washington refused to go along with Paris, which was rather inclined to accept the Five-Power conference. Of course, it would have meant *de facto* recognition of the Peking regime, with which, two months before, the U.S.A. had still been virtually at war. But on November 26, changing its stand, the Kremlin—at the end of a lengthy note largely devoted to denouncing the European Army as a project likely to "cut Europe in two"—stated it would unconditionally accept the West's proposal for a Four-Power meeting, but also expressed its intention of raising at that time the matter of convening "with the briefest delay a Five-Power conference." [17]

Why this turnabout? Perhaps it was to influence the outcome of the debate on foreign policy which had begun on November 17 in the French National Assembly, and during which the opponents of the E.D.C., on the Right as well as on the Left, had vied with each other in eloquence. In any case, on the 27th, the debate ended in utter confusion. Internal political considerations played a determining role in the rejection of a conciliatory resolution, and the final adoption of one which only asked that "the policy of building a united Europe be continued" [18] did not mean much.

However, it can be assumed that the most important reason for the Soviet decision was the impending meeting of Eisenhower, Churchill and Laniel, scheduled to take place in Bermuda from December 4 to 7, in the intimate and comfortable surroundings of a millionaires' club. It had been discussed for a long time. As soon as he assumed the Presidency, Ike had wanted to begin an in-depth dialogue on the international situation with the British Prime Minister. The role played by France in the deliberations on the European Army, as well as in Indochina, apparently made its participation necessary in a discussion whose urgency was underscored by Stalin's death and the changes stemming from it.

At first, it had been decided to hold the talks in June. But the fall of René Mayer's cabinet, and then Churchill's stroke, postponed them to the end of the year. As soon as Laniel arrived on the island, it was his turn to fall ill, leaving to Georges Bidault—from beginning to end—the presentation and defense of France's point of view. It was not an easy task. Although himself a backer of the E.D.C., Bidault was the Foreign Minister of a government which only half-heartedly supported it, and was in conflict with a Parliament that liked it even less. And thus he had to defend against two powerful allies a thesis in which he only partially believed. He took advantage of a moment alone with Ike to explain his position to him. In open session, he outlined several preliminary conditions to France's ratification of the treaty. These were the settlement of the Saar problem and the commitment by Britain and America to maintain in Europe for twenty years as many troops as were presently there. The American President finally lost patience: "What nation does France now regard as a potential enemy," he asked, "Germany or Russia?" [19] At the next meeting, Churchill, a strong advocate of the E.D.C.—on condition, of course, that Britain should not take part in it—was still more insistent. He warned Bidault that if the treaty finally had to be abandoned, he would favor the unilateral rearmament of West Germany. Pierre Mendès-France was to discover, less than a year later, that these were not idle words.

Whatever the harshness of the discussion on the E.D.C., it did not prevent the Big Three from easily agreeing on a reply to the latest Russian note. Dulles did not expect anything to come out of a Four-Power meeting, and it was in vain that Churchill—without, however, the least encouragement from Eden—reiterated, in the hope of being sent to Moscow as the West's spokesman, that the

U.S.S.R. had changed profoundly. The Secretary of State remained completely unresponsive as did his President, who, according to the disappointed Prime Minister, behaved as if he were "no more than a ventriloquist's doll" in the hands of that "bastard." [20] Americans had realized that France would never ratify the European Army treaty until a last attempt at negotiation with the Russians had been made. Therefore they wanted the conference to be held as quickly as possible so that any illusions would be dispelled.

The conference of the Big Four ministers—the first since 1949 —opened in West Berlin on January 25, 1954, in the vast building where the sinister "People's Court," in the last months of Nazism, had sat in judgment on the participants in the plot of July 20, 1944. It had later become the site of the Allied Control Commission and had remained unoccupied ever since that memorable day in March 1948 when Sokolovsky had slammed the door of the meeting hall behind him, never to open it again.

Was the conference going to lead to a resurrection of Four-Power rule? That is what the Russians demanded. They spoke continually of a "return to Potsdam." The Western Powers, for their part, did not entertain the idea for one minute. To combat the efforts of Soviet propaganda, which was going full blast during the conference, the U.S. had launched a two-pronged counteroffensive. First, it intended to convince the peoples of the world that the U.S.S.R. and Churchill's Britain did not have a monopoly on international attempts to achieve détente and peace, and secondly, that the United States would not stand idly by in the event of an ultimate rejection of the E.D.C. by the French Parliament. The "Atoms for Peace" program met the first objective; the menace of an "agonizing reappraisal" of American policies met the second.

In his memoirs, Eisenhower claims the credit for the "Atoms for Peace" program, which had very rapidly taken form. The President had been greatly affected by the explosion of the Soviet's first H-bomb, and he envisioned the abyss into which the arms race threatened one day to hurl humanity. Therefore, he sought a new way of dealing with the problems of weapons of mass destruction, by resolving the impasse created by the Russian refusal to accept any kind of control system.

He wrote that one day the idea came to him that the U.S. could take isotopes from its stockpile (the Soviet Union making an equal contribution) and put them into a common pool devoted to peaceful uses.[21] It led to the speech he made on December 8, 1953, before the U.N. General Assembly, proposing the creation of an international agency of atomic energy which would have as a principal purpose the allocation of a portion of its fissionable materials for the development of energy resources in the least favored nations. The proposal, which Ike had mentioned to his colleagues at the Bermuda meeting, had been subjected to revisions until the last minute. They took into account the objections of Admiral Strauss, head of the Atomic Energy Commission, and of all those who, like him, were hostile to any nuclear cooperation with the U.S.S.R., as well as being designed to counteract as much as possible the conviction of many people that Malenkov was really holding out an olive branch and that the Americans were wrong not to grasp it enthusiastically.

The effect of the proposal on world opinion was considerable. The Russians seemed embarrassed. Too suspicious of "imperialism" to say "yes" and fearing the repercussions of a "no" on their "peace offensive," they tried to gain time by posing questions. In 1955 the proposal finally led to the creation of an International Agency of Atomic Energy, located in Vienna, to which the Soviet Union belonged. That organization would make important contributions in the field of technical cooperation and in the control of reactors used for peaceful purposes in countries without nuclear weapons. But its contribution to international understanding would remain modest and would not affect, in any way, the tempo of the arms race.

§   §   §

The United States, extending both olive branch and lightning bolts —as does the eagle on its national seal—did not want anyone to interpret its good will as an indication of any inclination to abandon the requirements of its security policy. Before the conference in Berlin took place, it wanted to let all interested parties understand its determination to exert the strongest possible pressure to obtain France's rapid ratification of the treaty on the European Army. It is with this in mind that Dulles, at the end of December 1953, warned the members of the Atlantic Council that, in the event of nonratification, he could not guarantee that Congress would continue to maintain a significant American military and economic presence on the continent. A little later he repeated it to reporters summoned to the Palais de Chaillot. They needled him somewhat and witnessed an extraordinary display of anger. The naked threat of an "agonizing reappraisal"—which would lead to the adoption of a "peripheral strategy" abandoning Europe to its fate—was likely to impress governments facing both the internal threat of communism and the external threat of the U.S.S.R. and which would have felt lost without the presence of G.I.'s. But at the same time, it encouraged some of those governments to accept the challenge and led Moscow to offer, as an alternative, an alliance embracing all Europeans from the Atlantic to the Urals and excluding the Americans, who were, according to Russian propaganda, no more than foreigners, "intruders," and the principal obstacle, along with the "revenge-minded" Adenauer, to lasting peace.

The Chancellor had anticipated the Russian move. Receiving Eden in Bonn on December 12, he pointed out that, in his opinion, "the Russians were behaving more intelligently since Stalin's death." [22] Confirming that judgment, Molotov in Berlin on February 10, 1954, pulled out of his briefcase a proposed treaty on collective security for Europe. It had been inspired by the Inter-American pact concluded in 1947 in Rio de Janeiro between all the nations of the Western Hemisphere, with the exception of Canada. Red China and the United States, in recognition of its special responsibilities as a member of the Security Council, were asked to delegate "observers" to the organization to be created by the treaty.

The reaction of the Allies to what Eden termed a "European Monroe Doctrine" was immediate. It's a "bad joke," said Foster Dulles. Georges Bidault, whom the parliamentary basis of the Laniel cabinet compelled to more circumspect language, stated that the Molotov plan was "perfectly possible," but on two conditions. First, "that it culminate in a German peace treaty, and second, that it not prevent other arrangements of a defensive nature." [23] But the Soviet minister's sharp attacks against the Atlantic Pact—which he compared to the anti-Comintern pact of Hitler and Mussolini, and for which he predicted the same fate—did not leave any doubt that his proposal was essentially aimed at rendering NATO as well as the E.D.C. superfluous. Eden, Foreign Minister of a government whose leader had initiated the campaign for renewed contracts with the Kremlin, was the first to advise his government in a memo that "I do not think that we can do any good by discussing Soviet demands for the abolition of NATO in public, and I am more than ever convinced that the sooner this conference ends its discussion of the German side of our affairs the better." [24]

The previous discussions had indeed revealed the complete incompatibility of the positions of the West and the Soviets on the German problem. The Allies had offered an "Eden plan" leading to reunification through the selection, by means of free elections in the two zones, of a pan-German Constituent Assembly. The government to which it would give birth would have complete freedom to determine the orientation of the nation's foreign policy by choosing either alliance to one of the blocs or neutrality. Malenkov's continued objections were based on his fear of seeing that government adhere to the Western bloc.

The U.S.S.R., however, had the means to oblige a reunified Germany to declare itself neutral by making this the *sine qua non* of its troops' withdrawal. The following year it successfully used this method with Austria, but it would have had to pay for such an agreement with the abandonment of East Germany. All its proposals indicate that it was by no means ready to do that. When, on February 11, Molotov proposed the neutralization of Germany, with the withdrawal of occupation forces within six months, he also specified something which robbed his suggestion of any real importance, namely that the troops could return to their respective zones in the event their security was threatened. He did not foresee any other method of reunification outside of an accord between the two German governments, which made it clear that he dismissed any possibility of either one of them disappearing.

In any case, did the Kremlin believe that the Federal Republic would not be rearmed? Or did they decide there were advantages in a rearmament which justified the continued partition of Germany and permitted them to maintain a military beachhead as well as an ideological springboard in the German Democratic Republic? The fact is that at no time in Berlin or later did Molotov make the one gesture—so feared by the Allies and so desired by leftist groups—

which would have blocked Germany's rearmament. It is also rather surprising to observe that it was after the French Parliament had ratified the Paris accords—which, following the failure of the E.D.C., would permit the rearming of Germany within the NATO framework —that the U.S.S.R. decided to grant Austria the concession that, had it been announced earlier, would in all probability have long postponed that ratification.

The negotiations on Austria, which were the other purpose of the Berlin meeting, were no more fruitful, in fact, than those on Germany. Nevertheless, in the weeks following Stalin's death, a series of measures had made one wonder whether the U.S.S.R. had not considered making a gesture which, in the wake of the Korean armistice, would have completely changed the international climate. Successively, Russia had extended amnesty to the Austrian prisoners it was still holding, eliminated controls at the demarcation line as well as censorship and occupation costs, and also replaced its "High Commissioner" with an ambassador. But the hopes of the Foreign Minister of the Vienna Government, Leopold Figl, who had been allowed for the first time to negotiate with the Big Four in Berlin, were soon disappointed. Molotov made two conditions to the signing of the treaty: (1) Austria's neutrality; and (2) the maintenance of Allied garrisons on its soil until the conclusions of a German peace treaty. According to a confidence of Khrushchev's to Bruno Kreisky, then Austrian Foreign Minister, it was Molotov himself who had imposed that second condition—against the advice of Khrushchev and Mikoyan—both of whom were anxious to demonstrate Soviet good will toward the West.

The first condition was more acceptable to the Vienna Government, which had long ago limited its ambition to become a new Switzerland. It well understood that in the context of the Cold War it had no chance of maintaining the country's unity if it adhered to either bloc. Kreisky did not have much trouble in making Dulles admit this. On the other hand, the Austrians, knowing too well that there would not soon be a German peace settlement, forcefully rejected Molotov's second condition. As he was adamant, the negotiations were once more quickly terminated.

As a consequence, the four foreign ministers separated on February 18, 1954, declaring that they had been unable to agree either on Germany or Austria or European security.

Nevertheless, their communiqué did contain one item of agreement: the Big Four had decided to propose that a conference be convened on April 26 in Geneva "to seek a peaceful settlement of the Korean question." Besides their respective countries, Red China, the two Koreas and other nations having taken part in the war would be represented. They suggested that the conference be asked to examine, with the help of other interested states, "the problem of restoring peace in Indo-China." [25] This was a great victory for Georges Bidault, who, in going to Berlin, had as a principal objective the convocation of a conference on Indochina. He did not suspect that the result of the negotiations at that conference would produce one of the most dramatic developments of the postwar period.

BIBLIOGRAPHY AND NOTES

[1] Robert Leckie, *La guerre de Corée* (Paris: Robert Laffont, 1963), p. 438.

[2] Eisenhower, *op. cit.*, pp. 145–46.

[3] Lord Moran, *The Moran Diaries:* "Stricken Churchill Fights a Secret Battle," *The Sunday Times* (London), May 15, 1966.

[4] Keesing's, 12885 A.

[5] Eisenhower, *op. cit.*, pp. 185–86.

[6] Leckie, *op. cit.*, p. 459.

[7] Eisenhower, *op. cit.*, pp. 186–87.

[8] Bernard Winter, *Berlin, enjeu et symbole* (Paris: Calmann-Lévy, 1959), pp. 110–11.

[9] Georges Castellan, *DDR, Allemagne de l'Est* (Paris: Editions du Seuil, 1955), p. 196.

[10] Giulio Seniga, *Togliatti e Stalin* (Milan: Sugar, 1961), pp. 39–43.

[11] Weymar, *op. cit.*, p. 468.

[12] *Le Monde*, July 17, 1953.

[13] *Ibid.*, August 6, 1953.

[14] *The New York Times,* August 9, 1953.

[15] *France Nouvelle*, No. 400, August 1953.

[16] *Le Monde*, October 1, 1953.

[17] *Ibid.*, November 29–30, 1953.

[18] Raymond Aron, Daniel Lerner et al., *La querelle de la CED* (Paris: Armand Colin, 1956), pp. 37–39.

[19] Eisenhower, *op. cit.*, p. 245.

[20] Lord Moran, *op. cit., The Sunday Times* (London), May 22, 1966.

[21] Eisenhower, *op. cit.*, p. 252.

[22] Eden, *Full Circle* (Boston: Houghton Mifflin, 1960), p. 62.

[23] *Le Monde*, February 19, 1954.

[24] Eden, *op. cit.*, p. 82.

[25] Keesing's, 13433 A.

· CHAPTER 5 ·

CUTTING

THEIR LOSSES

What has been accomplished by destroying legions
with fire and sword, but that more legions and
stronger have been brought up?

—Tacitus, *The Histories*, V, 25

ON OCTOBER 19, 1950, A SMALL, DARK, HEAVY-SET MAN
with protruding ears and unruly hair climbed the rostrum of the
French National Assembly. In 1936, Pierre Mendès-France had been
the youngest member of the Popular Front government. A pilot with
the Free French and later Minister of National Economy in Algiers, he
had quickly resigned after the liberation as he had been unable to
get General de Gaulle to accept an austerity program necessary to
prevent inflation. Since then he had held the dual positions of Socialist
Radical Deputy from the Eure department and of financial consultant
representing France at the International Monetary Fund. He was
interested enough in his specialty to be able to relax, at the end of a
long, hard day, in reading John Maynard Keynes as others read
detective stories.

But, on that day, four months after the start of the war in Korea, it
was not economics that the Deputy and Mayor of Louviers wanted to
talk about. Patiently, in his incisive voice, he had come to give a
blunt warning to a government that had resigned itself a little too
easily to the aggravation of the situation in the Far East. "We will
not hold Indochina," he contended, "with only the troops and resources
actually at our disposal over there, even if the most desirable adminis-

trative, military and financial reforms are made. . . . To gain a military solution we need a massive new effort: sufficiently massive, sufficiently rapid, to forestall the already considerable increase of the forces opposing us. The other solution consists of seeking a political agreement, obviously an agreement with those who are fighting us. . . ." [1]

The speaker frankly advocated the second solution, whose "difficult" and perhaps "painful" character he recognized. The only applause he got was from the seats of the Left and the extreme Left, while righteous indignation was manifested from those of the Center and the Right. However, less than four years later the same assembly was, by a large majority, to elect him Prime Minister, and with a program whose first point committed him to seek a prompt peace in Indochina. Between those two dates, how much blood and money was wasted! How many errors were made! How many illusions were lost!

In reality, the fate of the war had already been settled at the moment when Mendès-France was hurling his prophetic warning in the Palais Bourbon. From the moment when the expeditionary corps had been unable to prevent the enemy from establishing a junction with Red China along the Tonkin frontier, it was evident that China would furnish the Viet Minh with support which France, 5,000 miles away, was not in a position to contain alone. Its only chance of doing that was if the United States, considering Indochina as one of the fronts of the Cold War, would supply massive aid and, through unequivocal threats, neutralize all possibility of Chinese intervention.

The Korean War, in drawing the attention of public opinion beyond the Atlantic to the danger of communism's armed expansion in Asia, had pushed Truman to take that position. Forty-eight hours after the Korean War broke out, he had decided to accelerate deliveries of matériel and to send a military mission to Indochina. The volume of American assistance was to continually increase until it reached a total of $785 million in 1954, which covered the bulk of the expenses of the French expeditionary corps. But, in exchange, the United States wanted to have its say. First of all, in order to deprive the Viet Minh of the cooperation it received from very large sections of the population, the United States believed that it had to prove to the Vietnamese that they could enjoy independence without communism. Therefore, it ceaselessly pressured the French Government to immediately grant to Viet Nam, Cambodia and Laos the independence which had been recognized by the Pau Accords of June 1950.

But, obviously, it was not to fight international communism that France had taken arms against Indochina, at a time when the Communists were still part of the government in Paris. It was to maintain, or rather to re-establish, its authority in one of the most beautiful and richest parts of its empire. Who could ask a nation to devote the major part of its military effort to the pacification of a country which it would have to abandon as soon as victory was won? What was then lacking in France, and in the world, was a government leader courageous enough to state clearly the dilemma which General Navarre had perfectly summed up in his *Agony of Indochina*. Either France wanted "to remain," which implied "major sacrifices"—especially a call-up of draftees—which had to be balanced by the United States' noninterference and a limitation of sovereignty for the three associated states within the French Union. Or France—not seeking any advantages for itself—"was only fighting as a participant in an anti-communist league directed by America." In that case, "there would no longer be any reason for France to make the principal military effort and France could demand to be relieved by those whose interests were greater than hers in Southeast Asia." [2]

Outside of those two policies, there was no other conceivable choice than negotiation with the adversary. Because it did not accept to do this while it was still in a position of strength, the Fourth Republic was condemned to do it when, according to the blunt statement by Georges Bidault in Geneva in 1954, it was only holding the "two of clubs and the three of diamonds." [3] In the meantime, all the cards had been played, but one by one and too late.

First a solution had to be sought in the field. The French command believed that if they succeeded in bringing into the open the Viet Minh "main forces"—three divisions—they could crush them easily, inflicting on them, as MacArthur did on the North Koreans after Inchon, a disaster from which the Viet Minh could not recover. This was, among others, the goal of de Lattre's de Tassigny's offensive against the T'ai region which ended, in the fall of 1951, with

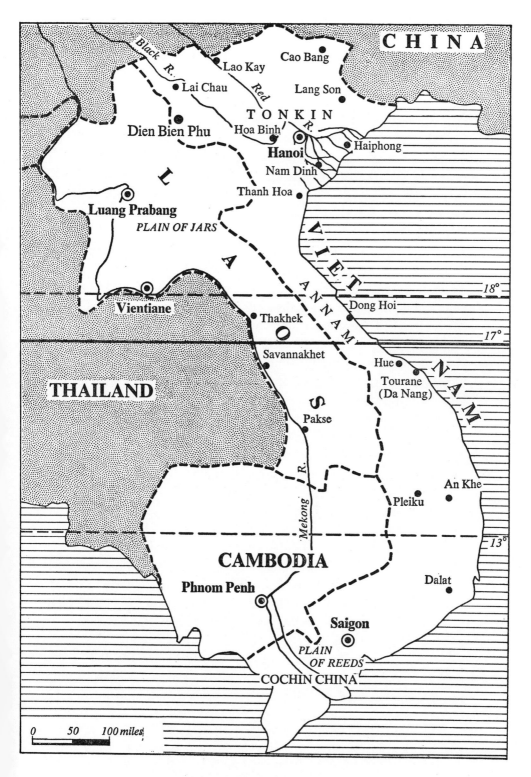

CHINA

Black R.

Lao Kay

Cao Bang

Lai Chau

Red R.

Lang Son

T O N K I N

Dien Bien Phu

Hoa Binh

Hanoi

Haiphong

Nam Dinh

Luang Prabang

Thanh Hoa

PLAIN OF JARS

L

A

O

V I E T

A N N A M

18°

Vientiane

Thakhek

Dong Hoi

17°

Savannakhet

Hue

THAILAND

N

A

M

S

Tourane
(Da Nang)

Pakse

An Khe

Mekong R.

Pleiku

13°

CAMBODIA

Phnom Penh

Dalat

Saigon

*PLAIN
OF REEDS*

COCHIN CHINA

0   50   100 miles

III THE INDOCHINA WAR AND
THE GENEVA ACCORDS

the capture of Hoa Binh. Then victory seemed to smile on the French Army. When, however, after the sudden death of that great soldier, General de Lattre de Tassigny, the French forces had to draw back, it was realized that the enemy had taken advantage of the French advance to consolidate its position behind the lines, thus overrunning from the rear the "de Lattre line": nine hundred small forts established to protect Hanoi and Haiphong, as well as the Red River Delta, Tonkin's rice bowl and as such a prime objective of the "Viets."

A few months later it had to be admitted that far from being "broken" as people were then saying, the Viet Minh's main forces had grown from three divisions to six. And soon the enemy would have to be confronted, not on the plains, but in the jungle, where the French Army, weighed down even more by motorized American equipment, was incapable of catching an adversary living off the country, moving about on foot or on bicycle, and so skillful in the art of camouflage that at the least warning of approaching planes, he literally melted into the landscape.

Those Viet Minh fighters showed a complete willingness to sacrifice themselves and were motivated both by their desire to gain independence and by their certainty of victory. The Americans kept repeating that they could only be overcome by other Vietnamese who would also be inspired by a passion for independence but, at the same time, be convinced that it could be better assured under the flag of liberty than under Stalinist despotism. However, it was only on July 3 that the Laniel government promised to recognize the independence and sovereignty of the associated states, and only on October 28 that it succeeded, after a demand from Bao Dai, in having the National Assembly adopt a resolution approving that promise and recommending the organization of indigenous armies.[4]

By that time the French leaders had lost all hope of victory. Receiving Navarre on May 8, 1953, shortly before the fall of his cabinet, René Mayer told him this explicitly. What we have to look for, he had concluded, is an "honorable way out." [5] However, he himself could not imagine the form it would take.

"If an armistice is signed in Korea," Jean Letourneau, Minister for the Associated States, had said on February 25, 1952, "the government would favor the convocation of an international conference to work out a political settlement of the conflict." [6] While stressing that he would make the first move, he did not dismiss the possibility of a discussion with the Viet Minh; but the French Government's apathy doomed to failure the few contacts that were actually made.

It took the coming to power of the Laniel cabinet in June 1953 for things to begin to change. Before Laniel, Mendès-France had, in spite of the opposition of the Communists, almost been elected; it was a warning. A strong current of public opinion in France pressed for peace, whose chances seemed increased by Stalin's death and the renewal of negotiations at Panmunjom.

The new Prime Minister announced in his ministerial declaration that his cabinet would "work untiringly" in seeking a way to end the war "either through negotiations which would follow the signing of an armistice in Korea or by any other negotiations in agreement with the governments of the Associated States." He admitted that the burden assumed by France in Indochina was "too heavy for France alone" and announced that the situation would be discussed at the "Western summit" in Bermuda.[7] Thus the "honorable way out" mentioned by René Mayer to Navarre was being sought in two directions: negotiations, and the transfer, at least partial, of the responsibilities of the war to both the Americans and the Chinese. The participation of the former would evidently facilitate the participation of the latter.

When the Bermuda Conference opened on December 4, 1953, an event took place which seemed to show that the other side was also looking for a way out. Answering a question asked by Sven Löfgren, Paris correspondent of the Stockholm *Express,* Ho Chi Minh had stated, "if, having learned its lesson from these years of war, the French Government wants to conclude an armistice and resolve the question of Viet Nam through negotiations, the people and the government of the Democratic Republic of Viet Nam are ready to examine the French proposals." [8]

According to Eisenhower's memoirs the presentation that Georges Bidault made in Bermuda did not bring out anything "particularly new," except that although "they were not really hopeful of securing an early and decisive military victory, . . . they were thinking of

winning eventually." [9] It was probably an attempt on his part to convince the United States, which had just greatly increased its aid to
France, not to stop halfway. In any case, the United States was
fully disposed to do it, as much because it dreaded the consequences
of the eventual fall of Indochina on the rest of Southeast Asia as to
facilitate the French ratification of the European Army treaty.
Through personal convictions, Bidault was against negotiations, but
he represented a government whose majority, led by Paul Reynaud,
then Vice President of the Council, was determined to have them.
Opposing Mendès-France, who advocated direct contact with the
adversary, he thought it was possible to arrange an international
conference where, taking advantage of the disarray caused by Stalin's
death in the "socialist camp," he could negotiate under the best
conditions.

The opening of such negotiations presupposed preliminary acceptance by Washington and Moscow, which was not very easy to
get because the Americans did not want to even consider a meeting
with the Chinese Communists, whose presence the Russians thought
indispensable. The Berlin Conference on Germany in February 1954
gave Bidault the occasion he needed to try to find another solution.

Persuaded that the Russians, after the signing of the armistice
at Panmunjom, were having serious difficulties and would seek
to eliminate all situations of external conflict under the best possible
conditions, he awaited a sign from Molotov. It came during the
second session of the conference when the Soviet minister vaguely
intimated that instead of entrusting the task of studying the causes
of international tension in general to the Big Five, as he had untiringly advocated for months, he might accept that the agenda be
limited to specified subjects: Korea and Indochina.

Molotov quickly denied making those statements. Nevertheless
the trial balloon had been sent up and caught in flight. Eden, who
did not hide the fact that he favored a meeting of the Big Five,
agreed with Bidault that such a limitation might make it more easily
acceptable to the United States. But Dulles, to pacify the extreme
right, all ready to label him an "appeaser," had again stated that it
was out of the question for him to discuss problems of world peace
with aggressors who had not made a full apology. Going further, he
opposed any negotiations on Indochina as long as the political

conference on Korea, called for by the armistice agreement, produced no positive results.

The British Foreign Secretary stressed that it was impossible to remain passive in the face of Soviet initiatives. Bidault mentioned the state of mind of the French people: If the United States failed to agree to hold talks, wouldn't they demand negotiations without it? On February 11, Dulles, apparently grateful for the firmness of the former president of the National Council of the Resistance on the German problem, resigned himself to go, as Eden wrote, "as far to meet us as the state of American opinion with regard to China would allow." [10]

The delegation exchanged drafts of communiqués. The discussion bogged down at one point on the distinction between "inviting" powers, among which Molotov wanted to include China—to which Dulles was strongly opposed—and "invited" powers. Molotov accepted the British draft, providing a few changes were made. The next day the Big Four decided to convene on April 26 a conference on Korea at Geneva in which they would participate and which would also be qualified to consider the problem of re-establishing peace in Indochina. To it were invited Red China and the "other interested states," not otherwise specified.

Eden was already beginning to talk of partition, but Bidault nourished other hopes whose visionary character was soon to become evidence. Impressed by the friendliness with which the Russians treated the French delegation each time the Indochinese question was raised, he thought that it was possible, in his own words, "to buy China" which, according to him, "needed everything." In other words, to recognize it, to give it sizable loans, but to exact from it, in return, the abandonment of the Viet Minh. "Ho Chi Minh," he told us one day, "must be the 'Asiatic Markos,' " thus alluding to the chief of the Greek guerrillas sacrificed by Stalin in 1948. "I'm quite willing that he go to Moscow or Peking to teach revolutionary tactics."

Was such bargaining completely unacceptable to the Russians and the Chinese? The Quai d'Orsay and the State Department had paid much attention to a strange speech given at the beginning of March 1954 by Chen Yun, member of the Chinese Politburo. After having exalted the example of the U.S.S.R., which had established socialism "in one country," and denounced the Trotskyite theses, he had stated that the need to maintain peace might lead "to temporary but inevitable setbacks in other countries." And he had recalled that in 1927 many in China had lost courage when Russia concerned itself only with its internal affairs, in the interest of world revolution.[11] Evidently it was tempting to see in this reference to Moscow's abandonment of the Chinese Communists at that particular time, an indication that a new abandonment could be perpetrated.

Unfortunately for Bidault, only the United States could have paid Peking the required thirty pieces of silver, but nothing was further from its intentions. It would have been necessary, to give Bidault's calculations a minimum of probability, for the military situation in Indochina to have been such as to impress the adversary that no idea of a cheap victory could be entertained. But the French command had just made with its own hands the trap into which it would fall.

§   §   §

From a strictly military point of view, the idea of building a fortified camp at Dien Bien Phu was less absurd than it seemed in retrospect. Navarre, to whom Paris had refused any increase in forces, was not at all seeking to win a victory there, but rather to prevent the Viet Minh from swarming over Laos, which was practically within their reach. In de Lattre de Tassigny's time, the tactical use of "porcupines"—strongholds with an airfield permitting the harassment of the enemy—had produced good results. And if Dien Bien Phu was located in a shallow basin exposed to enemy fire, it was because, in that mountainous jungle terrain, it was impossible to build landing strips except on flat land.

Nevertheless, the prospect of approaching negotiations completely changed the situation. Giap, the Viet Minh Commander in Chief, saw the opportunity to win a spectacular victory over the French, who would be obliged to beg for an armistice. All that was necessary, once the supply base was cut off, was to besiege Dien Bien Phu by engaging a large part of its garrison. In that decisive action he could count on the support of the Russians and Chinese, who supplied him with an abundance of trucks and artillery.

On January 1, 1954, Navarre, in a report to Marc Jacquet, Secretary of State in charge of relations with the Associated States, showed that he understood the situation. He singled out the considerable increase in Viet Minh weapons, thanks to Chinese help, and noted: "Everything points to the fact that the enemy is determined to attack in force with considerable matériel. . . . In the face of such reinforcement," he wrote, "I can no longer guarantee success with certainty." [12]

From that report a government which was getting ready to negotiate should have drawn the conclusion that it was more prudent to evacuate the "porcupine." They did not dare. The difficult selection of Vincent Auriol's successor—René Coty—elected only on the thirteenth ballot, had intensified even more quarrels within a cabinet which, besides, could not make the slightest decision, even in the field of military operations, without seeing it immediately reproduced in the newspapers.

That beleaguered government should at least have seized the opportunity offered by Nehru when on February 22, four days after the Berlin Conference, he proposed an immediate cease-fire in Indochina. But the French high command remembered the precedent of the 1946 negotiations, during which the Viet Minh had reinforced their army. It answered that in its opinion the cessation of hostilities ought to crown and not to precede negotiations. On March 4, Laniel made these conditions for a cease-fire: the evacuation by the Viet Minh of Laos, of Cambodia and of the Tonkin Delta, which would be protected by a "no man's land," and the regrouping of its forces in the center of the country. Nevertheless, two days later, against Bidault's advice, Laniel dispatched a young deputy of the socialist left who had also been one of General de Gaulle's early associates, Alain Savary, with the mission of making contact with Ho Chi Minh.

On March 31, Savary came back to Paris without having been able to meet anyone. By then, the long expected attack on Dien Bien Phu had been in progress for eighteen days. On the 16th, the Viet Minh had captured the two advance positions protecting the landing strip, which quickly became useless.

Overnight, the fortress found itself in a desperate situation. There was only one way to help it: the massive bombardment of the assailants. With the means at its disposal, the French Air Force was incapable of proceeding with it. The idea of asking for American help, under such conditions, instantly appealed to a government which didn't want to start the Geneva negotiations with a defeat on its hands.

A first step in that direction had been taken on March 11, or forty-eight hours before the attack on Dien Bien Phu. The Committee on National Defense had asked General Ely, Commander in Chief of the Army, to go to Washington "to acquaint the American Chiefs of Staff with the true military prospects in Indochina," to obtain the assurance of an immediate retaliation by the American Air Force in the event of Chinese air intervention, to inquire into probable reactions should Chinese volunteers arrive and finally, to ask for an increase in American aid to the Vietnamese Army.[13]

Ely met with the highest officials in the United States, among them Eisenhower, who, he wrote, in his presence and without appearing to put "the least restriction," instructed Admiral Radford, Chairman of the Chiefs of Staff, "to give first priority to responding to all French requests for aid to save the fortified camp." The general specified to Dulles that, "in the opinion of the government and the French command, a military solution of the Indochinese conflict does not seem possible under reasonable conditions and at a reasonable price, and that it was advisable to seek a political solution to the problem." [14]

Radford having indicated to him that Paris wanted to be advised on the form that any eventual American assistance would take in the event of Chinese intervention, the Secretary of State moved the discussion to a larger issue. In his eyes the essential problem was to get China to clearly understand that "the free world would intervene in Indochina rather than let the situation deteriorate because of its help to the Viet Minh." He added that if the United States came to the point of committing its own troops, its prestige "would be involved to a point where it would have to obtain victory." [15] Clearly, this seemed to exclude the idea of a temporary helping hand to the French Government simply intended to put it in a better position for negotiating. Nevertheless, Admiral Radford, who had asked Ely to postpone his departure for Paris, made a suggestion: 60 B-29 bombers—the Superfortresses of the Second World War—based in the Philippines and escorted by 150 fighters from the carriers *Essex* and *Boxer* of the Seventh Fleet, could effect a raid on the Viet Minh forces assembled around Dien Bien Phu. It was what would be called "Operation Vulture."

Ely returned to Paris after having signed a protocol concerning the immediate entrance into the war of the American Air Force in the event Chinese Migs intervened. His "very clear impression," [16] which he confided to Laniel, was that if France asked for the execution of Operation Vulture, Radford, who enjoyed Ike's friendship, would convince the American Government to answer in the affirmative. But in reality, the admiral had gone a little too far: Dulles was trying, above all, to intimidate the enemy and he did not conceive of any intervention without moral justification and legal cover. The justification would be "Chinese participation in the Communist aggression," which he denounced in a speech before the Overseas Press Club on March 29, and of which he gave not very convincing proof before the Foreign Affairs Committee on April 5; legal cover was provided by a collective declaration of the United States and of its principal Allies stating that they were acting in the name of Article 51 of the U.N. Charter.

In his speech of March 29 he asserted that "Under present conditions the expansion into Southeast Asia, by any means whatever, of the political system of Communist Russia and of its Chinese ally would present a grave danger for the whole free world community. The United States," he continued, "considers that the possibility of such an expansion cannot be accepted passively, but that it should be met by means of joint action. That can entail grave risks. But those risks would, however, be much less grave than those which we would have to confront in a few years if we did not dare show our resolution today." [17] London was immediately concerned and dispatched Ambassador Rodger Makins to the Secretary of State, with the mission to advocate the partition of Indochina. Dulles answered him categorically that it was imperative to take advantage of the West's temporary military superiority to prevent China from aiding the Viet Minh with the threat of taking direct action.

Thus Dulles envisaged a new plan of action. It was no longer a question of the bombardment of areas surrounding Dien Bien Phu, but of eventual operations against China itself: MacArthur's old idea, which had been reconsidered in the first month of the Republican administration as a means of putting an end to the Korean war, was now revived with the difference that Dulles conceived of it only within the framework of an enterprise in which the principal Allies of the United States were also to participate.

It was on that collective character that the Congressional leaders of the two parties insisted when they met on April 3. After having heard a briefing on the military situation from Admiral Radford which, in his judgment, called for direct intervention in the conflict, they asserted that in their opinion Congress would only authorize it under three conditions: (1) that it be undertaken in the name of a coalition including the "free nations" of Southeast Asia, the Philippines, Great Britain, Australia and New Zealand; (2) that France accelerate the process of granting independence to the Associated States "so there could be no interpretation that United States assistance meant support of French colonialism," and finally, (3) "the French must agree not to pull their forces out of the war if we put our forces in." [18]

By making a prerequisite of collective action—Dulles himself had launched the idea with his speech of March 29—the Congressional leaders found the necessary alibi with which to justify their instinctive prudence. At that point in the crisis they could not ignore the fact that London had decided to do nothing. Besides, their attitude corresponded exactly to Eisenhower's wishes. "There was nothing in these preconditions or in this Congressional viewpoint," he wrote in his memoirs, "with which I could disagree; my judgment entirely coincides with theirs." [19] Truman hadn't had so many scruples in 1950, in intervening in Korea, but it was precisely the memory of the Korean War and the determination not to become enmeshed in a new Asian war which made the leaders of both parties draw back and the President hesitate.

Laniel was in ignorance of their state of mind when, on the evening of April 4, he convened a war council at which were notably present Paul Reynaud, Bidault, Pleven, Juin and Ely. He still thought in terms of the Operation Vulture to be used against Dien Bien Phu's attackers.

A few moments before, Colonel Brohon had come from Hanoi bringing Laniel a message from Navarre, who emphasized the urgency of the operation. Brohon attended the war council. Answering some of the participants who would very much have liked to duck the responsibility of a decision, he made them understand with military bluntness that there was no other way to save the stronghold.

Having obtained approval from the council, Laniel, in the middle of the night, summoned the United States ambassador to hand him an official request for the execution of the proposed raid. The then ambassador was Douglas Dillon, a shy banker of Irish extraction who was very much a Francophile and who would later become Secretary of the Treasury. He was sufficiently aware of what had gone on between Dulles and the Congressional leaders to be able to say immediately that, in his judgment, "Congress ought to be consulted and that the other interested powers should also declare their position." [20] A few hours later an official reply from Washington confirmed that opinion.

§ § §

Thus ended Operation Vulture without ever having begun. In order to understand the hysteria of that period in France, one must recognize the climate of great excitement created by the siege of Dien Bien Phu and how the public's lack of information permitted it to be confused by the wildest rumors.

The proposed raid would probably not have changed the military situation, but neither would it have led to a World War. Far greater were the risks implied by the collective action advocated by Dulles, the necessity of which he had tried for two weeks, with his usual tenacity, to convince the Allies to accept. On April 4, the day when the French request was made, Ike wrote to Churchill: "There is no negotiated solution of the Indochina problem which in its essence would not be either a face-saving device to cover a French surrender or a face-saving device to cover a Communist retirement. The first alternative is too serious in its broad strategic implications for us and for you to be acceptable. . . . Somehow we must contrive to bring about the second alternative. . . ."

After having specified that in his opinion an "appreciable intervention of ground forces," American or British, would not be necessary, he concluded: "We failed to halt Hirohito, Mussolini and Hitler by not acting in unity and in time. . . . May it not be that our nations have learned something from that lesson?" [21]

After formulating its proposals, the American Government would soon present to Paris and London the draft of a joint declaration by the proposed coalition, asserting that the member countries were ready to undertake "Concerted action . . . against continued interference by China in the Indo-China war." [22] When Dulles stated —as he had on April 5—that participation of Chinese Communists in the fighting at Dien Bien Phu "looked very much like direct intervention in the conflict," [23] it appeared that the proposed action was very likely to take place soon. Besides, the warning would have been accompanied by a threat of naval and air action against the Chinese coast and of an active intervention in Indochina proper. Recalling the strange speech given at the beginning of March by Chen Yun, Joseph and Stewart Alsop wrote on April 4 in the *New York Herald Tribune* that it was then believed in Washington that China had hinted that "it might be necessary to abandon the Indo-Chinese to their fate in order to keep the peace in Asia," and also speculated that "the great offensive against Dien Bien Phu was ordered by the Indo-Chinese Communists as a last, desperate effort to win the war before their friends betrayed them." And the two famed commentators pointed out that America could very well find itself quickly involved in the war.

Eden summed up English objections in a note he addressed to his colleagues in the cabinet: "I cannot see what threat would be sufficiently potent to make China swallow so humiliating a rebuff as the abandonment of the Vietminh without any face-saving concession in return. If I am right in the view, the joint warning to China would have no effect, and the coalition would then have to withdraw ignominiously or else embark on warlike action with China." [24] He added that in the opinion of the chiefs of staff a blockade and a bombardment of China would have no military effectiveness, but would supply Peking with a pretext to invoke the Sino-Soviet treaty of assistance. In conclusion, he advocated the search for a negotiated settlement, for example on the basis of a partition, accompanied by a very clear warning against the consequences of any subsequent infringement.

The attitude the French Government adopted on April 6 at a meeting of the cabinet was no less cautious. Taking into account the state of public opinion, it pointed out that the risk of internationalizing the war should only be entertained in the event the Geneva negotiations failed.

When Dulles arrived in London on April 11, to attempt to persuade the British Cabinet to approve the coalition project, he had already abandoned the idea of giving a specific warning to China. In spite of this, he did not succeed in shaking Eden's opposition to any action before the opening of the Geneva Conference. The final communiqué of the talks limited itself to confirming the agreement of the two ministers to "take part, with the other countries principally concerned, in an examination of the possibility of establishing a collective defense, within the framework of the Charter of the United Nations, to assure the peace, security, and freedom of South-East Asia and the Western Pacific." [25] There was no longer any question of giving a legal cover to the impending action but rather of examining the possibility of creating a counterpart of the Atlantic Pact in Asia. Dulles, however, did not despair of promptly bringing his project to fruition. On April 16, Richard Nixon, Vice-President of the United States, asserted before a group of newspaper publishers, "if to avoid further Communist expansion in Asia and Indochina, we must take the risk of putting our boys in, I think the Executive has to take the politically unpopular decision and do it." [26]

This statement had been made, as is said in journalistic parlance, "off the record," in other words, confidentially. As a matter of fact, within twenty-four hours everyone knew its author. Given his position, he could not have launched that "trial balloon" without having been authorized to do so by the President himself.

Such bellicose language was to increase the irritation of the British when they learned that on the twentieth, without having consulted them, Dulles had summoned to Washington the ambassadors of Great Britain, France, Australia, New Zealand, the Philippines, Thailand and the three Associated States of Indochina, for a working session on "the organization of the common defense" of

Southeast Asia. Eden—who wanted to include India in the negotiations both to preserve the unity of the Commonwealth and to let a moderating voice be heard—reacted rather sharply. He finally succeeded in having the purpose of the meeting changed. Officially it would only be a fact-finding conference on the prospects of the negotiations which were to start on the 26th in Geneva. On the 19th, Dulles, following a visit with Eisenhower, reassured public opinion when he qualified as "improbable" the sending of American soldiers to Indochina and added that Nixon had only expressed "a personal opinion, as he had the perfect right to do." [27]

Nevertheless the last trump had not been played. On April 23, Bidault delivered to Dulles, who had come to Paris to meet his Western colleagues on the eve of the Geneva Conference, a message that Laniel had just received from Navarre: The situation at Dien Bien Phu was desperate; the general did not see any solution other than Operation Vulture, the bombing raid against the attacking forces, envisaged by Radford, or a request for a cease-fire. The Secretary of State replied to his colleague that an intervention of B-29's appeared to him to be "out of the question," but that he was going to report to the President.

According to Bidault, he had taken him aside and said: "And if we gave you two atomic bombs?"—the implication being, it would be up to Bidault to use them. To which Bidault answered: "If those bombs are dropped on the Dien Bien Phu region, the defenders will suffer as much as the attackers. If we attack the lines of communication at their source in China, we risk a general war. In both cases, the Dien Bien Phu garrison, far from receiving help, will find itself in a worse situation." [28]

Did the French minister really express himself so clearly? In the message he sent to Ike to report on the conversation, Dulles spoke of Bidault as "a man close to the breaking point," and "confused and rambling." [29] The same day, Eisenhower confirmed that any intervention was impossible. The next day, the Secretary of State met with Eden. In his opinion it was too late to save Dien Bien Phu, but in any case the importance of the fortress had been greatly overestimated. Radford, who was present, believed that an immediate Allied military effort to help the French was imperative.

Dulles pressed Eden to approve a policy of force; it was the only way, he told him, to get approval from Congress. The Englishman began to be seriously worried. On April 25—a Sunday, which underscored the exceptional importance of the occasion—he convened the cabinet to have them ratify a document declaring particularly: "We are not prepared to give any undertaking now, in advance of the Geneva Conference, concerning United Kingdom military action in Indo-China." [30]

As soon as the cabinet session was over, Eden received the French ambassador, René Massigli. Massigli informed him that Washington now proposed that the United States, Great Britain, France, the Philippines, Indochina and the Associated States immediately make public a declaration proclaiming their determination to halt, even eventually by resorting to "military means," the expansion of communism in Southeast Asia. If that declaration were published, the President of the United States would ask authorization from Congress to have American bombers intervene at Dien Bien Phu on the 28th. Another meeting of the British Cabinet was required to reject that plan. The same evening, Eden, en route to Geneva, stopped at Orly and briefed Bidault. On the 27th, Massigli —as Laniel's emissary—approached Churchill directly. The Prime Minister cordially showed him out and went to the Commons to read personally the negative decision adopted by his government on the 25th. Any thought of intervention was now dead.

Washington was quite relieved to put the responsibility on Britain and London boasted of having saved the peace. In reality, it was in the White House that the decision not to act had been taken. Congressional hesitation, as it reflected a public opinion hostile to any repetition of the Korean War, had to be taken into account. Ike himself wrote in his memoirs that the United States could not allow its armed forces to participate unilaterally in the operations in Indochina, "and in a succession of Asian wars," the result of which would be "to drain off our resources and to weaken our over-all defensive position." [31] Therefore, he did not foresee any action except against the "dragon's head," in other words the atomic bombardment of China. But, as in 1950, the simple threat of using "weapons of mass destruction," which could seem appropriate to American military men and politicians who, conscious of the enormous superiority of their arsenal, raised before world opinion the specter of a catastrophe out of all proportion to the stakes of the then present conflict. It could only damage America's moral position and its claims to the leadership of the West.

Having tried a bluff and having ultimately lost, the United States was not in a position to oppose France in seeking an honorable compromise. But all the agitation surrounding the proposed intervention had, at the same time, been an obvious demonstration to the enemy that the West did not want to run major risks in order to keep Indochina. How could the Communist powers help but be encouraged at the time when the Geneva Conference was opening?

Consequently, in the first analysis, the Allies could not have begun negotiations under worse conditions. However one element was in their favor: the fear on the part of the Russians and the Chinese that in the event of the failure of the Geneva Conference, the prime responsibility for the war would pass from France to the United States, something which would certainly restrict the Kremlin's efforts to normalize its relations with the West and to eliminate the risks of a major conflict.

§ § §

From the first, the Russian desire for agreement was evident. Problems of procedure were settled as if by magic, Molotov refraining from raising, as had been feared, the thorny question of the status of Red China. He had two meetings with Bidault which allowed him to finalize the organization of the conference on Indochina, the only one that counted, as everyone knew that the conference on Korea was nothing but empty talk.

By a tragic coincidence, the negotiations on Indochina began on May 8, exactly twenty-four hours after the fall of Dien Bien Phu. At it were represented, in addition to the Big Four and the governments of the three Associated States, Red China and the Viet Minh. While defending in open session the right of the Viet Minh's satellite "governments"—the Pathet Lao and the Khmer Issarak—created in Laos and Cambodia to take part in the discussions, Molotov quickly abandoned that demand. It had been more difficult to persuade Bao Dai—France having finally just given complete independence to his country—to be represented. On May 12 his Foreign Minister offered a draft settlement whose Article 1 implicitly acknowledged his government as the only representative of Viet Nam. It was a claim that no other delegation—except the United States—would dare uphold. And so the discussions were to center around the plans which had been offered, one on May 8, by Bidault, and the other, on the 9th, by the Foreign Minister of the Viet Minh, Pham Van Dong, whose thin and feverish face showed the stigmata of suffering and intense emotion.

The first of these plans entailed principally the regrouping of the regular armies in zones to be determined, the disarming of irregular forces, the evacuation of Laos and Cambodia by the Viet Minh and the immediate cessation of hostilities. The second—the recognition of the independence of the three Indochinese states, the withdrawal, within a period to be determined, of all foreign troops (and, therefore, of the French troops), the holding of elections in the three states under the direction of commissions formed by "the regional administrations in each state" [32] and a cease-fire. It provided that the three states would study the question of their participation in the French Union and would recognize France's economic and cultural interests.

Those two plans had many points in common, and Eden, elected a "co-chairman" with Molotov of the conference, was going, with untiring energy, to bring them out. In successfully doing this, he would benefit from the help of his Soviet colleague who, more than once, seemed to have some difficulty in persuading the Chinese and the Viet Minh to follow him along the path of conciliation. It even happened that the Russian publicly reprimanded Pham Van Dong for having opposed the start of talks between the representative of both commands on military conditions of the armistice, while he himself had agreed with Eden on that point.

On May 14 the members of the conference—the United States being represented by its Under Secretary of State, General Bedell Smith, former ambassador to Moscow, Dulles not wanting to appear to influence the negotiations by his presence—decided to hold sessions behind closed doors. It was a sign that they were beginning to talk seriously. Outside of working sessions the delegations constantly met at all echelons over discreet meals in the villas all around the lake which housed the ministers. It soon appeared that the two principal difficulties to surmount concerned the conditions of regrouping the regular armies and the fate of Laos and Cambodia.

On the first point, two formulas were conceivable: the "leopard skin" formula, and partition. Navarre defined the first, which he and the French Government favored, thus: "In the interior of North Viet Nam, of central Viet Nam and of South Viet Nam each of the adversaries will have to assemble his forces in a certain number of sectors . . . designated by taking into account the military situation on the day of the armistice." [33] Rather difficult to put into effect, it would have led to the maintenance of unity in Viet Nam, its logical outcome being recourse to universal suffrage. The people of Viet Nam would then freely decide, under international control, on the system of government they preferred. At that time, there was no doubt that the people of South Viet Nam would have had no hesitation in choosing the Viet Minh—without which they would not have gained their independence—and not Bao Dai's regime, whose army was in fact nothing but an auxiliary of the French troops. It was for that reason that Eden advocated a partition which would result in cutting losses by establishing a permanent line of demarcation between communism and the West somewhere in the middle of Viet Nam. Bedell Smith quickly joined in sponsoring that proposal. Indeed, even before the opening of the conference, the National Security Council of the United States had conceded, according to Philippe Devillers, that part of Viet Nam had to be sacrificed; but they still believed that it was possible to keep the two deltas—Tonkin and Cochin China.[34]

On April 29, Eisenhower had expressed during a press briefing his hope that it would be possible to reach a *modus vivendi* with the Communists in Indochina, "similar to that in Europe."

Rather curiously, however, it was not from the Western side that the idea of partition was first officially launched, although the newspapers in London, Paris and New York had published enough articles on that subject so that the other bloc might see in it a trial balloon. On May 25, clarifying his conception of the regrouping zones, Pham Van Dong asserted that they had to be "all of one piece" and spoke of the possibility of exchanging territories.

Bidault, rather tempted to "have his cake and eat it too," [36] considered himself bound by his promises to the Vietnamese leaders not to permit the creation of two states "of an international character" on national territory. Therefore, it was only on June 8 that the first direct contact was made to attempt to elucidate the precise significance of Pham Van Dong's overture. Forty-eight hours later, a member of the Viet Minh Government, Ta Quang Buu, met secretly with General Delteil and Colonel de Brébisson and made them understand, his finger on the map, that his friends intended to control at least Tonkin.

But there was more than Viet Nam. On the Communist side they also wanted to divide Laos and Cambodia. But the Americans were not the only ones who would not hear of it. Eden wrote in his memoirs: "The civil war in Vietnam on the one hand, and the direct invasion by the Vietminh of Laos and Cambodia on the other, could not be dealt with on the same basis." [37]

Undoubtedly, those moral considerations were not the only ones involved. The maintenance of South Viet Nam as a buffer state seemed indispensable for the protection of Singapore, the major British base in Southeast Asia, and of Malaysia's rubber and tin; and besides, the two kingdoms had to be protected from Communist domination if Burma and Thailand were to be preserved and beyond them India—an essential part of the Commonwealth, and the only great Asian country besides Japan capable of offering an alternate solution to Bolshevism.

Fearing to see Geneva turn into another Panmunjom, where delegations from the East would try, taking advantage of the progressive deterioration of the French military situation, to nibble away at the West's position, Eden decided to be tough. On June 10, in plenary session he declared that, "if the different positions remain as they are today, it will be the duty of the conference to admit to the world its failure." [38] On the 15th, Bedell Smith, urged by Eisenhower to do all he could to end the conference, persuaded his Western colleagues to immediately suspend negotiations on Korea, using as a pretext the obstinate refusal of the Communists to discuss general elections under U.N. control.

The next day, Chou En-lai showed that he had understood the

importance of the warning by accepting the principle of the with-drawal of all "foreign troops" from Laos and Cambodia, including those of the Viet Minh. Meanwhile, an event had taken place which was going to change the whole course of the Geneva negotiations. On June 12 the Laniel government had fallen because of its policy in Indochina.

However, it was not so much from the Palais Bourbon as from Geneva that the unexpected attack had come. Returning from a brief sojourn in Moscow, Molotov, on June 10, had clearly revealed his intention not to negotiate with Georges Bidault a peace whose terms were, however, gradually emerging from the negotiations. After having denounced those whose intention in taking part in the Geneva Conference was "to prove it was impossible to reach an agreement," the Soviet minister had concluded: "Today we heard the chief of the French delegation say that the conference had already achieved some results on the road to peace. The meaning of that statement will depend on how the French delegation con-forms to it in the future." [39] Why that harshly expressed dismissal? Because, as Jean Lacouture wrote, "Bidault was nothing more in the eyes of the Russians and the Chinese than someone who had wanted to scare them and had not succeeded." [40]

The French minister, who was negotiating under the worst possible conditions, had constantly, in his words, to "change his tactics." That would suppose that he did not have his back to the wall and that there was an alternative to the collapse of French resistance in the event the Geneva Conference failed. To prevent that collapse, the Paris government had sent during May, reinforce-ments to Indochina and called up reserves but, because of public opinion, without daring to take the only measure which would have had real importance: mobilization. And Paris had resumed with Washington the discussions interrupted at the end of April on the modalities of an eventual American participation. The press having noted those talks, Eden demanded an explanation from Bedell Smith, who tried to minimize the significance of the matter. It very quickly became apparent that the United States was hesitating more and more. A poll taken in mid-June showed that 64 percent of Americans were against any idea of "getting involved in fighting in

Indochina." Eisenhower stopped there and wrote his assistant Sherman Adams that he was against "going it alone." He added that he "had a few people to convince." [41] Dulles himself asserted on June 11 that "the work of pacification of Indochina can only be accomplished through a unilateral military intervention." [42]

Bidault, who had gambled everything, if not on the intervention of the United States, at least on the threat of that intervention, found himself once again out on a limb. In France, as well in England, the great majority of public opinion was hostile to him. To the Communists he was an avowed adversary, whom they had every reason to suspect of seeking a truce only to permit final arrangements to be made for the entrance of the United States into the war. His behavior, his apparent revulsion for negotiation with Communists—he waited until the Laniel cabinet had been overthrown before he finally shook Pham Van Dong's hand—his conception of diplomacy which made him yield only little by little, never completely speaking his mind, his taste for colorful expressions for the most part defying translation into Russian or Chinese—all that could only increase the suspicion the Eastern leaders felt toward him.

The man who succeeded him at the head of the French delegation was going to have an entirely different approach to negotiations which were, after all, more advanced than he expected. Pierre Mendès-France was in a better position than anyone to disarm the prejudices of the adversary. For four years he had unceasingly demanded peace in Indochina and on June 18 had been elected Prime Minister with a huge majority (419 votes to 17), including Communists, and on a program which committed him to obtain a cease-fire within four weeks. Actually, the military situation was extremely grave. The Viet Minh's thrust was expected along the Hanoi-Haiphong highway, if not on Hanoi itself, and General Ely, who was sent to the scene, raised the possibility that the native troops now under French command would revolt. It would take two or three months for any reinforcements to arrive from France. Therefore, there was every reason to fear that an adversary, who could not ignore that factor, might drag things out. But the PMF gamble—as it was soon to be called—made Mendès-France act quickly, if he did not want to see, as a result of his failure, the advocates of a hard-line policy return to power and the Americans openly intervene. At the same time he made it difficult for the Viet Minh to launch a new offensive and gave the French troops a chance to catch their breath and regroup.

Mendès-France, whose first objective was to save the expeditionary corps, did not neglect to reinforce his position. He was the only one to publicly consider mobilization. But as one must, in the end, negotiate with the enemy, he didn't waste any time in going to Berne to meet Chou En-lai—a move advised by Eden, with whom he had established a true common front during that arduous month.

The Chinese minister summed up his thoughts, which he had already expressed a few days earlier to Jean Chauvel, ambassador to Berne, and as such number-two man of the French delegation: "In Viet Nam, there are actually two governments; after the armistice free elections will have to reopen the way to unity for that country. . . . In Laos and Cambodia, on the contrary, the royalist governments can be recognized, if that is the wish of their people, on the condition that they achieve national unity by recognition of the existence of national resistance movements in their countries." [43] He did not hide the fact that what he feared most of all was the establishment in those countries of American bases. The head of the French Government immediately reassured him on that point.

The outline of an accord was thus decided upon. There remained little more than two weeks to work out the line of partition and the eventual assignment to the Pathet Lao and to the Khmer Issarak of regrouping zones, to specify the date of elections in Viet Nam and the modalities of a pullback, followed by the withdrawal of the troops of each side.

But that was not all. It was also necessary to persuade the United States to join in the accord, or at least not to oppose it, and to use its influence in overcoming Saigon's inevitable opposition to a solution which would officially divide the country in two; and finally to add international guarantees which would make the armistice more than a deferred capitulation. As in Bidault's time, two simultaneous series of negotiations were then going to take place: one series with the Communists, with the difference that this time open talks would be carried on with China and the Viet Minh, although with repeated appeals to Moscow to exert the necessary pressures; the other series with the United States, with the difference that it would no longer be asked to intervene in the talks in progress with a threat of military action, but rather that it cooperate in creating the groundwork for an agreement.

The first series of negotiations progressed very slowly at first and then more and more quickly as the deadline fixed by Mendès-France approached. On June 28, in response to French delegates who suggested that the demarcation line go through the 18th Parallel, the Viet Minh demanded that it follow the 13th Parallel. It was only on July 20 that Molotov, during a meeting with Mendès-France, Eden, Chou En-lai and Pham Van Dong, arbitrated in favor of the 17th Parallel—a decision which neither side was in a position to reject. The same meeting confirmed the agreement on the deadline by which elections were to take place. Bidault had for all intents and purposes accepted eighteen months. Mendès-France would have liked to leave it unspecified. "Two years?" asked Molotov. They decided on that. As for the time of the withdrawal of French troops, while the Viet Minh would have liked to see it effected in three months, it was finally stretched to ten months.

The United States had had no reason to oppose those conditions, which Eisenhower himself qualified as "the best it [France] could get under the circumstances." [44] Eisenhower and Dulles were rather concerned about what might happen with the coming to power of Mendès-France—across the Atlantic he was generally considered to be a terrible neutralist—and judged the moment opportune to meet with Churchill and Eden, a meeting which had been talked about for several weeks. The talks, which had begun on June 25 in Washington, ended in a joint resolution addressed to the French Government assuring it that the two countries would respect any eventual armistice agreements under the following conditions: if the Viet Minh evacuated Laos, Cambodia and the Vietnamese territory situated south of Donghoi, midway between the 17th and 18th Parallels; if the people wanting to leave the regions abandoned to the Communists could do so; and if effective control of the accords was provided for.

The accords which were concluded at Geneva on the nights of

July 20 and July 21 conformed to those conditions. But the United States refused to join in any document signed by Red China, fearful that it might give the appearance of *de facto* recognition. It took a long interview between Mendès-France and Dulles on July 14 in Paris, and all the head of the government's gift of persuasion, to convince the Secretary of State to send back Bedell Smith, who had left Geneva on June 20, and have him resume the leadership of his delegation. The United States suggested to France that it come to terms with the adversary, as well as with Peking and Moscow, after which it would publish a unilateral declaration precisely stating its position. But Mendès-France especially wanted all the accords to commit the signatories in the same way. It was under those conditions that a complex settlement was reached comprising, first, a bilateral armistice agreement on Viet Nam, Laos and Cambodia, signed by the commander of the French Union forces and that of the Viet Minh; second, two unilateral declarations by the French government and one each from the Laotian and Khmer Governments; and lastly, a "final declaration," whose uniqueness was that it was not signed by anyone, to save the Americans from being soiled by contact with China.

This last text called for "free general elections by secret ballot," to be held in July 1956, under the supervision of representatives of the member states of the control commission (India, Canada and Poland).[45] During the last session of that conference, Bedell Smith took note of the accords, adding that his government "would refrain from threats or the use of threats" to modify them, and that he envisaged "any renewal of aggression in violation of the accords . . . with grave concern and of a nature to seriously threaten peace and international security." He also said: "In the case of nations actually divided against their will we will continue to try to achieve their unification by means of free elections controlled by the U.N. to insure their complete fairness."[46]

That accord, however, still lacked one essential: the approval of the Saigon Government, whose leadership had been assumed a month earlier by a Catholic mandarin, Ngo Dinh Diem, an acknowledged protégé of the United States, where he had lived for a long time. His representative to the conference, Tran Van Do, solemnly protested "against the hasty conclusion of the armistice accord by only the French and Viet Minh high commands when," he said, "the French high command only controls the Vietnamese troops through a delegation of power from the head of the Viet Nam State . . . and against the date fixed by that same high command for future elections, when that is a decision of a political character," in consequence of which the Viet Nam State reserved its freedom of action, only promising "not to use force to oppose the modalities of the cease-fire." [47]

§   §   §

Thus ended, under the least favorable conditions one could have imagined, the second of the "hot wars" related directly to the Cold War. That Molotov had sought the agreement with as much perseverance as Mendès-France, was proved by the concessions he made at the last minute to the obstinate delegate from Cambodia, who refused to deprive his country of the right to seek foreign military aid. The Geneva Accords were indispensable to Soviet diplomacy in continuing the thawing operation it had started after Stalin's death. In other times it would have been unthinkable.

For France, whose Parliament approved the accords on July 22 by 569 votes to 9, Geneva meant a leaf turned and turned quickly. The armistice ended an unpopular war in which the country, although never feeling truly involved, had still lost 92,000 dead, of whom 19,000 were from France, and the equivalent of two classes of army officers. It ended as well the colonial adventure initiated in the Far East under Napoleon III. Diem was only too happy to deal directly with Washington, starting on August 15, concerning the economic aid the United States granted him. As for North Viet Nam, where Jean Sainteny, the negotiator of the 1946 accords, had been sent as a "general delegate" and been received in the beginning with great consideration, it was soon realized by Mendès-France that full diplomatic recognition was the *sine qua non* condition for any close cooperation. But there could be no question of it as it would have meant a complete break with Saigon and compromised the important investments which France preserved in the South.

For the Americans, the armistice was something very different: a battle lost in a Cold War which still continued. On July 21, the day following the conclusion of the accords, Eisenhower during a press conference announced that the U.S. Government "would view any renewal of aggression in violation of the aforesaid agreements with grave concern," [48] and that negotiations to organize Southeast Asian defenses would continue.

On September 8 the United States, Great Britain, France, Australia, New Zealand, Thailand, the Philippines and Pakistan signed in Manila the pact which created the Southeast Asia Treaty Organization (SEATO) inspired by NATO but infinitely less restrictive. The new pact only committed each of its members, in the event of aggression against the territory of one of them or of one of the three former Indochinese states, to act "to meet the common danger in accordance with its constitutional processes." [49] That document, sharply denounced by Communist propaganda, seemed so harmless to Mendès-France that he did not even think it necessary to ask approval from Parliament before signing it.

Did the Eastern countries take it more seriously? Three days before the signing of the pact, the Chinese Communist artillery had begun to bombard the islands of Quemoy and Matsu, occupied by Chiang Kai-Shek's troops. It was the warning signal of a new crisis, which was going to give John Foster Dulles another opportunity to practice "brinkmanship" diplomacy.

BIBLIOGRAPHY AND NOTES

[1] *Journal officiel de la République française*, debates, 1950, p. 700.
[2] Henri Navarre, *Agonie de l'Indochine* (Paris: Plon, 1956), p. 68.
[3] Eden, *op. cit.*, p. 124.
[4] Joseph Laniel, *Le drame indochinois* (Paris: Plon, 1957), p. 11.
[5] Navarre, *op. cit.*, p. 3.
[6] Jean Lacouture and Philippe Devillers, *La fin d'une guerre* (Paris: Editions du Seuil, 1960), p. 35.
[7] Laniel, *op. cit.*, p. 35.
[8] *Ibid.*, p. 9.
[9] Eisenhower, *op. cit.*, p. 246.
[10] Eden, *op. cit.*, p. 99.
[11] *Le Monde*, March 9, 1954.
[12] Jules Roy, *La bataille de Dien-Bien-Phu* (Paris: Julliard, 1963), pp. 440 ff.
[13] Paul Ely, *Mémoires: L'Indochine*

dans la tourmente (Paris: Plon, 1964), p. 59.

14 *Ibid.*, p. 65.

15 *Ibid.*

16 Laniel, *op. cit.*, p. 83.

17 *Le Monde*, March 31, 1954.

18 Eisenhower, *op. cit.*, p. 347.

19 *Ibid.*

20 Laniel, *op. cit.*, p. 86.

21 Eisenhower, *op. cit.*, pp. 346–47.

22 Eden, *op. cit.*, p. 103.

23 *Le Monde*, April 7, 1954.

24 Eden, *op. cit.*, p. 104.

25 *Ibid.*, p. 109.

26 Eisenhower, *op. cit.*, p. 353.

27 *Le Monde*, April 21, 1954.

28 Georges Bidault, *D'une résistance à l'autre* (Paris: Les Presses du Siècle, 1965), p. 198. The reader will find a parallel account in Roscoe Drummond and Gaston Coblentz, *Duel on the Brink* (New York: Doubleday, 1960), pp. 121–22.

29 Eisenhower, *op. cit.*, p. 350.

30 Eden, *op. cit.*, p. 118.

31 Eisenhower, *op. cit.*, p. 354.

32 *Documentation française:* Articles et Documents, No. 064 of June 8, 1954.

33 Navarre, *op. cit.*, p. 304.

34 Lacouture and Devillers, *op. cit.*, p. 131.

35 *Le Monde*, May 2–3, 1954.

36 Lacouture and Devillers, *op. cit.*, p. 190.

37 Eden, *op. cit.*, p. 133.

38 *Ibid.*, pp. 143–44.

39 Lacouture and Devillers, *op. cit.*, p. 204.

40 *Ibid.*, p. 205.

41 Sherman Adams, *First Hand Report: The Story of the Eisenhower Administration* (New York: Harper, 1961), pp. 118–24.

42 *Le Monde*, June 13–14, 1954.

43 Pierre Rouanet, *Mendès-France au pouvoir* (Paris: Robert Laffont, 1965), p. 111.

44 Eisenhower, *op. cit.*, p. 374.

45 *Documentation française:* Notes et études documentaires, No. 1901 of July 30, 1954.

46 *Ibid.*

47 *Ibid.*

48 Keesing's, 13685 A.

49 Keesing's, 13761 A.

· CHAPTER 6 ·

THE SPIRIT OF

GENEVA

What greater victory do you expect than to teach
your enemy that he cannot withstand you?

—Montaigne, *Essays,* III, 8

AT GENEVA, CHOU EN-LAI SPARED NO EFFORT TO
appear, under all circumstances, as a man of conciliation. When he
left the conference in mid-June, it was to go and persuade Ho Chi
Minh to consent to the partition of Viet Nam and to sign in New
Delhi and Rangoon—with the two principal advocates of Asiatic
neutrality, Nehru and U Nu—communiqués exalting the five principles, in Hindi the *Pancha Shila,* of peaceful coexistence: nonaggression, nonintervention, mutual respect, etc. Chou En-lai was received
in triumph everywhere. With heavy flower leis around his neck and
a benign smile on his inscrutable face, he was obviously trying to
give the most reassuring image possible of his country and its policies.

Everything helped: his charm, a skillfullness made up of considerable reserve and prudence and, perhaps even more, the favorable
attitude of the people he spoke to who were only waiting to be convinced. Nevertheless, he had never hidden the fact that even if his
government desired to establish the best possible relations with its
neighbors, whatever their regimes, it did not thereby accept that
Formosa was to remain a lair of hostile forces.

In December 1953, Chiang Kai-shek had expressed his intention of making 1954 "the year of decision," when "the reconquest of the mainland" [1] would be effected, and since that time planes and ships of the two Chinas had been involved in numerous incidents.

On September 3, 1954, at 1:45 A.M., Mao's artillery started a massive bombardment of the islands of Quemoy and Matsu, held by the Nationalists, a few miles outside the large ports of Amoy and Foochow. An attempted landing seemed imminent.

It was apparent that Chiang could not hold the offshore islands without direct American support, but did their strategic value warrant Washington's running the risk of general war to keep them? On September 12, Eisenhower, rejecting the advice of Admiral Radford, who wanted to help the Nationalists bomb the Chinese mainland, endorsed Dulles' position. Dulles wanted to ask the Security Council to order a cease-fire and to maintain the *status quo* in the Formosa Strait. Invited to take part in the debates, China through Chou En-lai refused, pointing out, not without some justification, that it amounted to inadmissible interference in its internal affairs.

Be that as it may, the Council would have been hard put to decide anything, as the U.S.S.R., at that time Peking's faithful ally, had the right of veto. Once more, on February 8, 1955, Molotov took up Mao's arguments before the Supreme Soviet point by point, and asked the U.N. to condemn the aggressive actions of the United States in that area.

The United States had to make its own decision. In November, Senator Knowland, spokesman for the China lobby, had advocated a blockade of the China coast in reprisal against Peking's sentencing to forced labor thirteen Americans accused of espionage. Instead of listening to Knowland, Ike had sent Dulles to sign a treaty of mutual assistance with Chiang's Foreign Minister in December. This treaty was supplemented by an exchange of letters specifying that the use of force to defend areas other than Formosa and the Pescadores—and therefore Quemoy and Matsu—"was determined by mutual agreement." [2] This clearly signified that Taipeh would take no military initiative without Washington's preliminary consent.

On January 18 a contingent of Communist commandos landed

on the island of Ichiang in the Tachens, 220 miles north of Formosa. The same day, Eisenhower stated that "neither Ichiang . . . nor the Tachens . . . were vital to the defense of Formosa and the Pescadores." [3] In the hours that followed, in spite of objections from Admiral Carney, Chief of Naval Operations, it was decided to evacuate the 30,000 civilian and military men in the Tachen Islands. In return a promise to help the Nationalists keep Quemoy and Matsu was made public, and the President sent a message to Congress asking it to authorize him to use the armed forces of the United States if he deemed it necessary for the protection of Formosa and the Pescadores against attack.

In his memoirs Eisenhower asserted that he was primarily guided by the desire to avoid any repetition of miscalculations such as those which had, for example, permitted the outbreak of war in Korea. This time the Chinese Communists were warned unequivocally that the Americans were committed to defend the coastal islands.

However, the message had another purpose. Ike, on January 27, had made it clear that he intended to have sole discretion as to the use of the powers he was asking for. It was a means of reassuring all those who, in the United States and even more abroad, feared that one of the military members of the "war party" might push America and the world into a general conflagration.

In spite of the efforts of the Democratic Senator Lehman, supported by his young colleague John Kennedy, to exclude Quemoy and Matsu from the zone where the use of force would be authorized, Congress adopted the draft resolution almost unanimously. But the reaction from the NATO countries was much less enthusiastic. On March 8, Eden suggested the evacuation of the threatened islands in exchange for a promise from Peking not to attack Formosa and the Pescadores. Similar views were expressed in the press as well as in government circles in France, Belgium, Canada and Australia, not to mention the neutral countries.

§   §   §

The arguments used against American policy were not all equally valid. Some compared the minimal strategic value of the islands to

IV   THE FORMOSA STRAIT

the enormity of the risks incurred in keeping them. They forgot that the same reasoning also applied to the other side. As Dulles untiringly reiterated, if the Communists could be convinced that the United States was ready to go so far as an atomic war to defend those positions, they would not try to seize them. At that time America not only possessed a large margin of superiority in the field of nuclear weapons, but also enjoyed a quasi-monopoly of long-distance bombers. Therefore, the Secretary of State, convinced that a confrontation would have disastrous consequences for the Allies in Asia —he spoke of a tremendous onslaught—did not miss the opportunity to let Peking's leaders know that his government's determination was unshakable. In his opinion, to yield even on a minor point would only serve to encourage the enemy to exert pressure on some other area. "The ability to get to the verge without getting into the war is the necessary art. If you cannot master it, you inevitably get into war. If you try to run away from it, if you are scared to go to the brink, you are lost. . . ." [4]

In that field of elementary strategy, the facts were to prove him right. On the other hand, the political, legal and moral arguments invoked by the opponents of the "Formosa Doctrine" were much more valid. As Walter Lippmann then wrote, in the name of what would the United States assume "a unilateral right to intervene in foreign territory for strategic reasons"? [5] Wasn't the victory of the Chinese Communists over the Nationalist regime, however strongly supported by America, sufficient proof that Chiang had no right to his claim of representing his own people? What did the refusal of any transaction of the kind suggested by Eden lead to? Hadn't Eisenhower himself, following the first bombardment of Quemoy, expressed to his generals, who advocated atomic attacks against China, the hope that the "time would come" when the recognition of the Peking regime could be a "desirable strategic move in the best interests of the United States"? [6]

Tension increased in mid-March with the receipt in Washington of a report from Pacific headquarters, stating that if the Communists in the near future launched an amphibious attack against the islands, it would have a considerable change of success. On the 10th, Dulles had asserted, during a meeting in the White House, that the odds were at least two to one that the United States would find itself in a war between the fall of the islands. On March 23, Carney on his own initiative, invited to dinner several Washington journalists and held forth with the most pessimistic and bellicose views. On the 25th, *The New York Times* announced that Chinese attack on the coastal islands could be expected in April, and that in that event the military chiefs advocated a massive bombardment "to destroy Red China's industrial potential," and thus put an end to its "expansionist tendencies." [7]

This was enough to provoke strong reactions almost everywhere. To the objections of the Allies—notably Canada, whose Foreign Minister, Lester Pearson, had just announced publicly that his countrymen would not fight for the defense of Quemoy—were added those of many famed American columnists and of several Democratic Senators led by the future President, Lyndon Johnson. An opinion poll showed that 90 percent of Americans did not know who held the coastal islands, which made it difficult to pretend that the country was really involved in the affair.

Nevertheless, a détente had already started at the time when tension seemed the greatest. Whether because they were afraid of the rattle of American sabers, or had been influenced by the Russians to employ a prudence conforming to Lenin's teachings, or again because of the proximity of the opening at Bandung, on April 17, of the first Afro-Asian world conference, which had caught the attention of the whole world, the Chinese had decided it was preferable to show their good intentions. Instead of starting the expected attack, they imperceptibly began to decrease their propaganda calling for the liberation of Formosa. And on April 23, at Bandung, Chou Enlai, after having reviewed the situation with the heads of the eight principal delegations, openly stated that the Chinese people "do not want to go to war against the United States," and that his government "was ready to negotiate with it concerning a détente in the Far East and particularly in the region of Formosa." [8]

That change of tone was especially welcomed in Washington where, under pressure from the Allies and the Democratic Left, Ike himself was getting ready to make some concessions. He had just sent Radford to Formosa to urge Chiang to effect a redeployment of forces which, in his own words, would succeed in changing Quemoy and Matsu "from precarious symbols of Chinese Nationalist prestige" into "strongly defended, workable outposts . . ." Quite frankly, it was a matter of persuading the Nationalists to accept a solution "that will neither commit the United States to go to war in defense of the offshore islands, nor will constitute an implied repudiation of the Generalissimo." [9] It was the squaring of the circle. Of course, Chiang did not accept.

On April 26, Dulles, pleased at the "restraint" that the Bandung Conference seemed to have had on China, declared himself ready to discuss with it the terms of a "cease-fire." However, he specified that "we shall not, of course, depart from the path of fidelity and honor toward our ally, the Republic of China." [10]

On May 15, meeting Molotov in Vienna on the occasion of the signing of the Austrian state treaty, the Secretary of State told him that an agreement ought to be reached whereby, as in Germany, Korea and Viet Nam, it would be understood that reunification would not be sought by force. The Russian suggested a Five-Power conference, to which the American replied by demanding the participation of representatives of the Kuomintang. Molotov rejected that suggestion; they stopped at that point. But on May 22 the Communists suspended their operations in the Formosa Strait, and at the end of the month, following the visit to Peking of the Indian minister Krishna Menon, Mao's government announced the release of four Americans. "The peace offensive" which was to result in the "summit" at Geneva was on its way, and it was important that nothing arose in Asia to put it in jeopardy.

§   §   §

On July 21, 1954, following the signing of the Geneva Accords on Indochina, Molotov had told Mendès-France of his desire for a Franco-Soviet rapprochement on Germany. The Prime Minister had made it clear to him that failing a "substantial gesture" from the U.S.S.R. in the field of disarmament or on Austria, it would not be possible to delay rearming yesterday's enemy. In fact, he himself was determined, as he had announced on June 17 in his inaugural speech, to solve as quickly as possible the great problems —besides Indochina—that the preceding governments had left open. The very first priority went to the European Defense Community, "one of the most serious matters of conscience which has ever troubled the country." [11] He knew perfectly well, as he told the Russian minister, that "if France did not act she might soon find herself faced with a decision on the re-establishment of German sovereignty, and subsequently on the future of a German Army over which she could no longer have any control." [12]

Molotov had turned a deaf ear, in the same way as Malenkov, at the same time, was to discourage a confidential overture from Churchill, who had wanted to meet him in Vienna to persuade him to sign the Austrian state treaty. The U.S.S.R. confined itself to asking that a conference examine the proposals which had been made in January, in Berlin, on European security, and to which it had added on March 31 the suggestion that the United States join the European system that it wanted to see organized, declaring itself ready, for its part, to join NATO. But the Kremlin was not so easily discouraged. It brought up again on August 4 its proposal for a European conference, asking this time that the four foreign ministers meet in August or in September to prepare for it.

Did the Soviet Government believe that these diversionary moves would be enough, ultimately, to either avoid German rearmament or to persuade France to quit the Atlantic Alliance? Obviously, it did not ignore the fact that one of the reasons the Gaullists had supported Mendès-France was because they counted on him to bury the E.D.C. But, if such was its reasoning, its error was in not understanding that the French Right and most of the Gaullists objected less to the drafting of German soldiers than to the advent of a European force in the midst of which the French Army would disappear. And that once the E.D.C. was dead, they would easily accept an alternative solution. It remained to be seen if, for the Kremlin, the prospect of a close union of western Europe extended to the military field was not more dangerous than the unilateral rearming of the Federal Republic which would, at least, furnish it with a pretext to continue indefinitely the partition of the old Reich.

Failing to change Molotov's mind, Mendès-France started immediately on the difficult task of getting his colleagues to agree on a compromise capable of winning a majority in Parliament. This could not be expected from the treaty in its original version, even with the few "additional protocols" negotiated so laboriously by Georges Bidault.

In a few weeks a new protocol was worked out. Accepted by all the pro-E.D.C. ministers, it still seemed too "supranational" in the eyes of some of their Gaullist colleagues, who resigned. But when Mendès-France went to Brussels on August 19 to submit a new draft to the foreign ministers of the signatory countries, he found himself facing men who felt that he had succeeded, according to Robert Schuman in "cutting the heart out of the treaty." It was in vain that he brought up the fact that seven parliamentary committees had declared themselves against the E.D.C., and that there was not the slightest chance of obtaining its ratification as it stood. Adenauer and Spaak, on the strength of information provided them by their friends of the M.R.P., socialists and even radicals, were convinced of the contrary; they hardly disguised their doubts as to the good faith of the leader of the French Government.

The American ambassador, David Bruce, who was conducting an indiscreet campaign in the corridors of the conference, delivered a Parthian shot when he brought messages from Dulles to the heads of delegations specifically asking them to avoid any change in the treaty which could either "cause an unacceptable delay," or "seriously damage its supranational characteristics," or yet, "show discrimination against one of its member states." The Secretary of State added that should an agreement fail to be reached in Brussels, Washington would consult on ways of promptly realizing German rearmament with Great Britain and with the countries which had ratified the E.D.C.[13]

If that near-ultimatum resulted in strengthening France's partners in their refusal to accept the compromise which would have saved everything, it also served to reduce still further the minute margin for maneuver that Mendès-France had at his disposal. Therefore, the failure of the conference was inevitable and with it that of the E.D.C., which on August 30 was rejected by the French National Assembly by 319 votes to 264.

Moscow noisily rejoiced, but not for long. On the day of the vote, Eisenhower had asserted that America "has never quit in something that is good for herself or the world." [14] After the rift in

Brussels it took all of London's insistence, and all of Mendès-France's assurances of fidelity to Europe and to NATO which he had lavished on Adenauer and later on Churchill, to convince the United States not to negotiate without France.

In the beginning of September the Allies had informed the U.S.S.R. that they would take part in a conference on European security only if it accepted the Austrian treaty and the principle of free elections in Germany, and Eden visited the capitals of the Six. Mendès-France suggested to him that the framework of the Brussels treaty be utilized to rearm Germany.

At the end of the month a conference in London brought together the interested powers, including the United States and Canada, and adopted a series of drafts calling for the re-establishment of the Federal Republic's sovereignty, its participation in NATO—to which it would supply 12 divisions and 1,000 planes to be placed under the integrated inter-Allied command—and the inclusion of Germany and Italy in the Brussels treaty, duly modified for the occasion. Two solemn pledges had considerably facilitated negotiations: that of Great Britain—taken at the urgent request of Mendès-France and presented by Eden as a "giant step forward" [15] on the part of a country which had always wanted to preserve its total freedom of action—to permanently maintain on the continent forces equivalent to those it kept there at the time; and that of Bonn not to fabricate A.B.C. (atomic, bacteriological, chemical) weapons on its territory.

There was still an obstacle to be surmounted, that of the Saar . . . France made the settlement of that problem the *sine qua non* condition of its consent to the remilitarization of the Federal Republic. On October 22, after a night of heated discussions at the British Embassy in Paris, Mendès-France and Adenauer finally agreed on a proposal for the "Europeanization" of the territory, the matter to be submitted to a referendum. No one then suspected that when it was held, exactly a year later, it would be rejected by 67 percent of the voters, and that in the end, Paris would accept the reunification of the Saar with Germany.

In any case, nothing stood in the way of the signing of the drafts negotiated in London and now finalized on several points—these to be known in history as the Paris Accords. A few days later, Mendès-France had been triumphantly welcomed in Washington, and Dulles, to demonstrate that the dark suspicions he had once harbored against him had disappeared, and to show his admiration for the scope of the results he had already obtained, saluted him with the title of "Superman."

The Kremlin, which might not have been expected to see things turn out this way, started an intensive campaign to persuade the French Parliament to kill this latest version of German rearmament. On October 23, at the time the Allies were signing the Paris Accords, Russia had once again launched its proposal for a Four-Power conference. On November 13 it invited twenty-three countries to take part in a conference on European security scheduled for November 29 in Moscow, or just before the opening of the debates on the ratification of the accords in the British and French parliaments. The United States and China were invited to send observers.

Only eight countries, those of the socialist bloc, accepted the invitation. The conference ended on December 2 after having issued a communiqué announcing that in the event the Paris Accords were implemented, the U.S.S.R. and its allies would take the necessary measures to protect their security. Molotov asserted that ratification of the accords would make talks on German or Austrian problems useless. Finally, in notes of the 16th and the 20th, the Kremlin warned France and Great Britain that it would automatically entail the annulment of bilateral assistance pacts concluded during the war.

Although the French Communists, who had initially supported Mendès's experiment, launched a sizzling attack against the Paris Accords, the head of the government remained as insensitive to threats as to reproaches. On November 22, speaking in New York before the U.N. General Assembly, he categorically brushed aside any idea of negotiations on European security before ratification. Instead, he proposed an East-West conference in May, following that ratification, and suggested that it examine the possibility of an exchange of guarantees between the Western European Union (W.E.U.), to which the agreements had given birth, and a similar organization which could be started in the East. Mendès-France was

the author of a plan for arms control intended to limit Germany's rearmament, and in spite of the skepticism, if not the hostility, of most
of the signers had had it incorporated into the Paris Accords. He
hoped to have it extended to the whole of Europe's armaments, in the
East as well as in the West. The idea was to be taken up again
frequently, but to this day without success.

However, France still had many doubts concerning the Paris
agreements. The alliance of nationalists, leftist-socialists and Communists, which had brought about the rejection of the E.D.C., was
replaced by another which included the same Communists and leftist-
socialists as well as the most dedicated wing of the European partisans of integration, who criticized the new agreements for leading
to a rebirth of German militarism, which E.D.C. had aimed to
prevent. On December 23, 1954, that coalition rejected by 280
votes to 259, Article 1 of a proposed law authorizing ratification.
The Allied capitals were greatly alarmed, especially Bonn, and Adenauer made urgent appeals to the M.R.P. Ultimately, on the 29th,
Mendès-France obtained ratification of the agreements by the National Assembly—by 287 votes to 256. Bidault, with 51 other M.R.P.
deputies, had voted against it, while the principal "European" leaders
—Schuman, René Mayer, Pleven, Pinay, Paul Renaud—abstained.

This project still had to be adopted by the Council of the Republic. In order to disarm a more and more violent opposition—
made up of nostalgic Europeans, of the opponents of German
rearmament and those of the progressive decolonialization to which
Mendès-France henceforth intended to devote himself. On January
5, 1955, he wrote Churchill asking him to accept the proposal for
a Four-Power conference that he had voiced before the U.N. The
answer reached him a week later. Written on thick bristol paper and
sealed like a parchment of the Middle Ages, it contained very friendly
sentiments for the head of the French Government. Nonetheless, it
warned him that if Paris did not proceed with prompt ratification, he,
Churchill, would feel obliged to uphold the policy of the "empty
chair." In other words not to consult with France on the great
decisions of Western policies any longer. "The Soviets," he wrote,
"do not let themselves be seduced by weakness. To mix up the
process of ratification with what might soon follow it, would

detract both from firmness and from conciliation. The sooner we can obtain unanimous ratification the sooner a Four-Power conference at the highest level can take place." [16] He had not always spoken like that. But following events were to prove him right.

That letter was to be one of the last official acts of the Prime Minister. On April 5, conquered by age, he gave up his place to Anthony Eden, without having realized his great dream of going to Moscow to bury the war hatchet. Meanwhile, Pierre Mendès-France had been overthrown by the National Assembly on February 6, 1955, during a session which had all the appearances of an execution. The Assembly had been only too happy to have him to attack the Gordian knots before which the previous regime had retreated. Once those were cut, it did not need him anymore. He even became dangerous as he was getting ready, after granting autonomy to Tunisia, to tackle the colonial problem, whose great urgency had been underlined by the outbreak of the Algerian revolution in November 1954. For years he would have to play the scapegoat and meditate on the fickleness and ingratitude of the masses.

Edgar Faure, who succeeded him, chose as his Foreign Minister, Antoine Pinay, who had abstained during the debate on the ratification of the Paris Accords in the National Assembly. That attitude did not prevent him, once settled at the Quai d'Orsay, from using his influence to persuade the senators to ratify the agreements. The debate started on March 23, in a climate of indifference or general resignation. There were no more than 100 protestors before the Luxembourg Palace when—by 184 votes to 110—the Council of the Republic gave the consent which would permit the implementation of the Accords. On the same day, in the Parc des Princes, 80,000 people attended the game between France and Wales in the finals of the world rugby championship. A comparison of the two figures gives a fairly accurate measure of public feeling!

The way was thus clear for the reopening of the question of European integration. On June 3, at Messina, the foreign ministers of the Six decided "to pursue the establishment of a United Europe through the development of common institutions, the gradual fusion of national economies, the creation of a Common Market and the gradual blending of their social policies." [17] Consequently, after very lengthy negotiations, two treaties were signed in Rome on March 25, 1957, between France, the Federal Republic, Italy and the Benelux countries. They created a "European Economic Community" (E.E.C.) and a "European Atomic Energy Community" (Euratom) —essential elements in the consolidation of Western economies and in "anchoring" Germany in the West.

§ § §

The U.S.S.R. did not waste any time in profiting from the lessons of the ratification of the Paris Accords. As it had intimated, on May 7 it revoked its treaties with Great Britain and with France; on the 14th it formed in Warsaw an organization which was represented as an exact replica of the Atlantic Pact but which, in fact, did not add much to the already very "integrated" character of the network of alliances created in Stalin's time under the close surveillance of the Soviet command.

On one point, however, the Kremlin was to depart completely from the line that it had defined. We have seen that Molotov had stated that ratification of the Paris Accords would render useless any negotiations either on the German problem or on the Austrian problem, as well. But the Austrian state treaty which the Big Four had been vainly debating for ten years was to be signed in Vienna on May 15, 1955, exactly ten days after the start of German rearmament.

The first sign of the Soviet turnabout had coincided with the replacement on February 8, 1955, of Georgi Malenkov, who publicly recognized his "inadequate experience," [18] by Nikolai Bulganin as head of the government. In retrospect, the ouster of the man who had been the closest of Stalin's collaborators was one step in Khrushchev's patient fight to assume complete power. But it is certain that one of the arguments used against him was his excessive softness, his defeatism in respect to the Western Powers, his exaggerated fear of war, which, he had stated a year before, would bring about the ruin of all civilization. Mr. K was to say, much later, that Malenkov, like Beria, had made, "during the first days following Stalin's death, the provocative proposal to eliminate the socialist status of the German Democratic Republic." [19] Was he getting ready to renew that proposal at the time of his disgrace? It is interesting to observe that on February 6, 1955, or forty-eight hours before, a meeting was held in Warsaw for the "peaceful solution of the German problem." On the Soviet side, among others, were the writers Korneichuk and Ehrenburg, both members of the Supreme Soviet, and one of the principal publishers of *Pravda,* Yuri Zhukov. The meeting proposed "the unification of Germany through free controlled elections which would take place on the basis of an electoral law protecting all democratic freedoms as provided for by the plan proposed in Berlin [the preceding year] by Sir Anthony Eden." [20]

The agitation caused by the almost simultaneous fall of Mendès-France and Malenkov probably explained why public opinion paid scant attention to the above text. The absence of reaction from chancelleries is less understandable, unless American pressure for the rearmament of Germany lay behind their silence. It is difficult not to believe that a unique opportunity for getting out of the Cold War once and for all may have been lost at that time. In any case, it is inconceivable that the Russian representatives would have thus committed themselves without authorization, which suggests that a sharp debate on Germany may have taken place within the U.S.S.R.'s highest councils during that period.

Of course, Molotov continued to direct Soviet foreign policy as he had both before and after Malenkov's retirement. But one turnabout more or less hardly fazed him. While—Khrushchev *dixit*—he had fiercely opposed the conclusion of the treaty with Austria, it was he who, in an address given a few hours after Bulganin's promotion, announced the concessions which were going to make it possible. Indeed, it was the first time that he admitted that the Allied troops might evacuate Austria, prior to the signing of the German peace treaty, if "appropriate agreed measures" could be obtained against another *Anschluss.*[21]

As in the same speech he had asserted that the ratification of the Paris Accords "would create a grave danger of *Anschluss* and therefore would threaten the independence of Austria," it was generally concluded by the West that the first of the "appropriate agreed measures" mentioned were precisely the nonratification of those accords.[22]

However, the Soviet minister was to very quickly propose talks with the Vienna Cabinet to determine the chances for an agreement. On April 11, Chancellor Raab arrived in Moscow. Three days later a complete agreement was concluded. The U.S.S.R. accepted the draft worked out by the Austrians, which it had rejected in 1949. Austria agreed to follow policies "free of any" military "alliances" (*Bündnisfrei*), inspired by the examples of Switzerland and Sweden. Detailed instructions settled the fate of "German assets." And it was thus that on May 15, Foster Dulles, Molotov, Pinay, Macmillan, who had become Foreign Minister after Eden's accession as head of the British Government, and Leopold Figl, the Austrian Foreign Minister, put their signatures to the document which, seventeen years after the *Anschluss,* finally restored freedom to Austria. Three months later, there were no longer any foreign soldiers on its national territory. It was the first time, since the evacuation of Iran's Azerbaijan, that the Russians withdrew from an occupied territory. That treaty —which did not prevent the Vienna Government, already a member of the Organization for Economic Development and Cooperation (O.E.D.C.), to make known its adhesion to the principles of Western democracy, to enter the Council of Europe and the European Free Trade Area and to negotiate its association with the Common Market —has been scrupulously respected since then by its four signatories.

In any case, it was too late to prevent the ratification of the Paris Accords. But the U.S.S.R. was probably trying to at least limit their military and political effects. If Austria's occupation had continued, the Western Powers might have been tempted to incorporate their occupation zones into NATO, even into that of the Western European Union (W.E.U.), and even—who knows—to accept their union with the Federal Republic. Neutralization not only eliminated those dangers, but also considerably lengthened the Allied military system's lines of communication between Bavaria and Venetia by breaking their continuity.

Disappointed in their expectation of seeing France prevent German rearmament, the Russians, in playing their Austrian trump, may have attempted to hold out to the German people the possibility of their regaining their freedom provided their government would accept —like the Austrians—perpetual neutrality; and even to persuade the major Allies that since the international climate was so relaxed, it was really unnecessary to recruit divisions on German territory.

On April 18, four days after the agreement had been signed by Chancellor Raab and the Soviet Government, Radio Moscow stated: "If Bonn followed the Austrian example, Germany as a nation would be lastingly won over to world peace." Molotov proposed a Four-Power meeting to the Western Powers which would be principally devoted to the German problem. The *Tägliche Rundschau,* organ of the Soviet command in the German Democratic Republic, wrote: "The way of Austria can also become that of Germany." It was learned that a new contingent of Russian diplomats headed by Ilyichev, who had conducted the U.S.S.R. negotiations on the Austrian treaty, had arrived in East Berlin. On June 4 the Pankow Government sizably reduced the exorbitant tolls established the preceding March 30 on West German vehicles going to Berlin. And on June 7 the Kremlin had a note delivered to Dr. Adenauer inviting him to come to Moscow as quickly as possible to examine with the Soviet leaders means of normalizing relations between the two countries.

But, for an "Austrian" solution to be possible for Germany, it would have been necessary to put Germany in the situation of Austria before the conclusion of the state treaty, that is to say, to let it form, by democratic means, a government that would negotiate peace conditions with the Allies. In Germany's case, such a formula would undoubtedly have led to the disappearance of the Communist regime in the eastern zone. But, without agreeing to give up that essential stake, the Kremlin asked that the Western Powers abandon theirs: the presence of their troops on the soil of the Federal Republic, and its economic and military participation in the collective Western effort. The attempt was doomed to failure. German public opinion understood its significance perfectly and paid only scant attention to the U.S.S.R.'s nudges toward an "Austrian solution."

§   §   §

Moscow was more successful in its efforts to represent the signing of the Austrian treaty as evidence of good will likely to greatly purify the international climate, two years after the Korean armistice and one year after the Indochinese armistice.

When they met in Vienna to sign the state treaty, the foreign ministers of the Four Powers had recognized the usefulness of an East-West conference at the "summit." It opened on July 18 in Geneva in the midst of a great gathering of diplomats and journalists. To increase the impression of détente, the Communist bloc made a series of gestures: reconciliation with Yugoslavia; opening of talks on normalization of relations with Japan; and the expression of regret to the United States for an air incident over the Bering Sea.

Nonetheless, the West had few illusions on the fruitfulness of a meeting limited to a short week because of the obligations of the President of the United States. Ike, on his part, thought above all to utilize it to "detect whether the Soviets really intend to introduce a tactical change that could mean, for the next few years at least, some real easing of tensions." [23] As for Eden, according to his memoirs he attributed to that "summit"—which was in his mind to be the first of a series—a dual objective: "This was to reunify Germany, while giving Russia all the assurances that the consequences of this event would be no threat to her . . ." [24] In that spirit he submitted to his colleagues a project intended to assist in the conclusion of a European security pact, combined with the creation of a narrow demilitarized zone on both sides of the Iron Curtain, and of a controlled limitation on arms for Germany and its neighbors. Edgar Faure, who wanted to believe that the development of the U.N. would gradually surpass the power of the blocs, proposed in the name of France, and against the advice of his Western colleagues, a general reduction of 1 percent in the arms budgets. Bulganin, although also suggesting a European security pact in which he would let the United States participate, did not hide the fact that he wanted to obtain the departure of foreign troops from Europe and the recognition of the two German states. Once more the U.S.S.R. was asking the Western Powers to completely reverse their policy.

Outside of the sessions the Russians took great pains to explain their position to their colleagues. A major V.I.P. had, for the occasion, come out of retirement. Marshal Zhukov—the conqueror of Berlin, whom Stalin, annoyed by his popularity, had relegated to an obscure garrison—had just been named Minister of National Defense. At the end of the war he had established good personal relations with Ike and had sent him several messages in the spring. Therefore, many observers thought that the new Kremlin leaders counted on him to reopen the dialogue with Washington. To be sure, Eisenhower invited him to a small intimate dinner; it was to hear, he wrote in his memoirs, "the same arguments." His old friend seemed to him "devoid of animation, and he never smiled or joked, as he used to do." [25] Bulganin, head of the delegation, seemed much less restricted in his behavior. It was he who confided to Eden during the course of a dinner, "It would really not be possible for his Government to return to Moscow from this Conference if they agreed to the immediate unification of Germany. . . . The people would say that this was something Stalin would never have agreed to." [26]

Everyone wondered at the time who was the "boss"; that bearded personage whose strange stare contradicted the manners of a peaceful tourist, or Nikita Khrushchev, the ebullient First Secretary of the Party, who did not hide his disappointment at being excluded from the group of the Big Four when a final photograph was taken. A curious incident was to reveal the truth.

During a session on July 21, Eisenhower had produced the "bombshell" prepared by Nelson Rockefeller, future Governor of New York State, and Harold Stassen. Recalling that both East and West in the plans they had submitted for years to the U.N. disarmament committees, had recognized the necessity of controls without, however, being able to agree on the modalities of those controls, he suggested that the U.S.S.R. and the United States assign a specified number of planes to the surveillance of their respective military installations. The simplicity of that "open skies" plan gave it a great deal of appeal, and it was wondered whether the U.S.S.R. was going to accept it.

Bulganin, after having heard Ike, did not hesitate to declare that his proposal seemed to have "real merit" and that his government would "give it complete and sympathetic study at once." [27]

A few moments later everything had changed. As the delegates were going to the bar during recess, Khrushchev approached Eisenhower. "I don't agree with the chairman," he said smilingly. "But there was no smile in his voice," wrote the former White House chief: "I saw clearly then, for the first time, the identity of the real boss of the Soviet delegation." [28] All subsequent efforts to convince the First Secretary of the advantages of the American proposals were useless. According to him, it had no other goal but to legalize and intensify espionage against the U.S.S.R.

The failure of the summit was then assured. But world opinion had set its hopes too high to allow them to be disappointed by being told of a break, the responsibility for which, in any case, Soviet propaganda would quickly have attributed to the West. The Big Four, after bitter discussions, succeeded in agreeing on joint directives to be given to their foreign ministers asking them to resume the debate in the fall. That document mostly contained banalities on the necessity of arms limitations, and of the development of contacts between East and West. But the United States had made its signature subject to the insertion of a sentence on the reunification of Germany by means of free elections. The Russians, thinking that the game was worth the candle, finally accepted the following version: "The heads of government, conscious of their joint responsibility concerning the settlement of the German question and the reunification of Germany are agreed that the settlement of the German question and the reunification of Germany by means of free elections will be carried out in conformity with the national interests of the German people and in the interests of European security." [29]

On paper, this represented a threefold success for the Western Powers, who were often to boast about it in the future. The Russians agreed to speak of reunification when they had several times asserted that the ratification of the Paris Accords would render any discussions on that subject useless; they recognized the "joint responsibility" of the Big Four on that problem when they had unceasingly argued that reunification was the affair of the Germans alone, as represented by their two governments; finally, they admitted that that reunification must result from "free elections."

But no one was able to maintain any illusions as to the significance of that formula. On the way home, Khrushchev and Bulganin stopped in East Berlin, and Khrushchev asserted in the quietest possible way that he was convinced that "the working class of the German Democratic Republic would never permit the elimination of all its political and social achievements, the elimination of all its democratic reforms." [30] And Bulganin added on August 6, before the Supreme Soviet: "It would be imperative to consider the situation in Germany where during the last ten years two German states have appeared." [31]

Under those conditions it quickly became apparent that the principal beneficiaries of the conference were the Russians, who duly celebrated the "spirit of Geneva," with the obvious objective of persuading the populations of their satellites that they had to abandon all hope of independence. In fact, if at the beginning of the conference Ike had inserted a little paragraph on the "enslaved nations," he had not insisted on it when, as could be expected, Bulganin had exploded against that interference in the internal affairs of the interested countries and categorically refused to include it in the agenda. A photograph of the Big Four, seated side by side and smilingly chatting like old friends, was extensively circulated behind the Iron Curtain as proof that the Western Powers had definitely renounced any questioning of the *status quo*—in other words the partition of Europe into two.

August still brought some signs of détente: the opening of the Sino-American talks between ambassadors in Geneva on the repatriation of civilians wanting to go back to their own country, as well as on "certain other practical problems"; Russia's return of the naval base at Porkkala to Finland; the reduction of the Red Army by 600,000 men; the exchange of agricultural delegations between the U.S.S.R. and the United States. The Soviet Government had taken its place at the international conference for the peaceful uses of atomic energy, convened at the suggestion of Washington, and the radio war had almost stopped.

But Eisenhower, annoyed at the exploitation of the "spirit of Geneva" by the Russians, asserted that there could be no real peace in the acceptance of a *status quo* in which human beings were being persecuted on a large scale. In the days that followed, Vice President Nixon, then Foster Dulles, strongly condemned the partition of Germany. It was during this period that Adenauer arrived in Moscow on September 9. Whatever his suspicions toward the U.S.S.R., he had not dared refuse its invitation. He did not want his enemies to accuse him of having neglected an opportunity to improve the life of the Democratic Republic's inhabitants, and to obtain the return of thousands of war prisoners that the Russians, in spite of their denials, were supposed to have kept in their country.

He was cordially received and installed in a villa which had belonged to Gorki. But his hosts were insistent and brutally frank when they recalled the sufferings that Germany had brought upon their country. Khrushchev did not let him forget that by participating in NATO, "the Federal Republic had closed the door to any solution of the German problem in the near future," [32] and that, for his part, he would do everything to prevent reunification if it was to lead to the entry of a united Germany into the Atlantic Pact, which would be completely against the interests of the Russian people. As, in his mind, it was too late to question the Federal Republic's participation in the Pact, he proposed, "in order to be realistic," to establish diplomatic relations and to exchange ambassadors between Bonn and Moscow.[33] The Chancellor accepted, in return for the promise of the liberation of a certain number of war prisoners. Curiously enough, during the talks, Mr. K had insisted on talking of the Chinese problem. "China," he said, "already has 600 million inhabitants, who live on a handful of rice. Each year there are 12 million more. How is that going to end?" he had added, folding his hands together . . . "I beg you to help us to resolve our difficulties with China." [34] During the talks he was to return twice more to that subject.

The establishment of diplomatic relations between the two countries represented, on the part of Adenauer, a first step toward the acceptance of the partition of Germany, as the Eastern regime already had an ambassador in Moscow. But until the beginning of 1967, Bonn was to cling to the "Hallstein doctrine," named for its Secretary of State for Foreign Affairs who later became president of the Common Market Commission. According to that doctrine, the recognition of the German Democratic Republic by one country automatically entailed the breaking of its diplomatic relations with the Federal Republic. Two countries, Yugoslavia and Cuba, had tested the validity of that principle. Bonn had immediately closed their embassies and expelled their representatives.

Starting with the Chancellor's trip to Moscow, the "spirit of Geneva" had begun to show its fragility.

September also saw a few skirmishes: especially the vote by the

Soviet delegation in the U.N. for the independence of Algeria, which caused the postponement of a visit to Moscow proposed by Edgar Faure and Antoine Pinay; and a stormy debate in the same precincts on China's representation. If to that was added the heart attack which had put Ike out of circulation for several weeks, leaving to Dulles alone the direction of American foreign policy, without the benefit of Ike's moderating influence, it was understandable that no one dared expect very positive results from the October foreign ministers' conference at Geneva, convened to implement the resolutions of the July "summit."

The conference dragged on for three weeks without achieving anything. In fact, Molotov not only declared that the reunification of Germany could only result from a "gradual rapprochement" of the two German states, but he also brushed aside most of the proposals offered by the Western Powers tending toward increased relations between the two blocs. The "free exchange of ideas," he asserted on November 14, is nothing but "free war propaganda" and something which "the Soviet Union has not granted previously and will not grant in the future." [35] Since then Molotov has lost his place but the Kremlin's position on that point has not changed one iota.

The Big Four separated on November 16 in a climate of bitterness underscored by the biting wind of Geneva. The détente was not completely dead as its fruits remained: the armistices in Korea and Indochina, the Austrian treaty, and the exchange of ambassadors between Bonn and Moscow, but it was clear enough that the harvest was almost all in. Besides, the announcement on September 27 of the agreement for the delivery of Czechoslovakian arms to Egypt had heralded the opening, in the Middle East, of a new front of the Cold War.

BIBLIOGRAPHY AND NOTES

[1] *Le Monde,* December 27–28, 1953.
[2] Keesing's, 14007 C.
[3] Eisenhower, *op. cit.,* p. 466.
[4] Shepley, *op. cit.*
[5] D. F. Fleming, *The Cold War and Its Origins, 1917–1960* (New York: Doubleday, 1961), II, p. 710.

[6] Adams, *op. cit.*, pp. 127–28.

[7] *Ibid.*

[8] Année politique, 1955, p. 386.

[9] Eisenhower, *op. cit.*, p. 481.

[10] Keesing's, 14181 A.

[11] Rouanet, *op. cit.*, pp. 236–37.

[12] Pierre Mendès-France, *Sept mois et dix-sept jours* (Paris Julliard, 1955), p. 22.

[13] Rouanet, *op. cit.*, pp. 265–66.

[14] Eisenhower, *op. cit.*, p. 403.

[15] *Le Monde,* October 1, 1954.

[16] Année politique, 1955, p. 682.

[17] *Ibid.*, p. 718.

[18] Keesing's, 14033 A.

[19] *Khrouchtchev et la culture.* Complete text of speech of March 8, 1963 (Paris: Editions Preuves, n.d.), p. 47.

[20] *Le Monde,* February 10–11, 1955.

[21] Keesing's, 14059 A.

[22] *Ibid.*

[23] Eisenhower, *op. cit.*, p. 506.

[24] Eden, *op. cit.*, p. 323.

[25] Eisenhower, *op. cit.*, p. 524.

[26] Eden, *op. cit.*, p. 334.

[27] Eisenhower, *op. cit.*, p. 521.

[28] *Ibid.*

[29] Année politique, 1955, p. 728.

[30] *Neues Deutschland,* August 28, 1955.

[31] Alfred Grosser, *La situation de l'Allemagne en 1955* (Brussels: Institut des relations internationales, 1955), pp. 105–6.

[32] Konrad Adenauer, "Erinnerungen," 1953–1955, *Neue Zürcher Zeitung,* October 23, 1966.

[33] *Ibid.*

[34] *Ibid., Neue Zürcher Zeitung,* October 27, 1966.

[35] Keesing's, 14537 A.

CHAPTER 7

A WALL

BUILT ON THE SAND

Of all peoples, the Arabs are the least inclined to take orders.

—IBN KHALDUN, Prolegomenes,
1st Book (circa 1375)

HINGE OF TWO SEAS AND THREE CONTINENTS, NURSERY of prophets and warriors, from antiquity the Orient has never ceased to tempt conquerors. But to the traditional fascination of its limitless spaces and its mythical wealth, the contemporary period has added more prosaic attractions. In breaking through the Suez Isthmus in 1869, de Lesseps made it a stop on the road to India.

The First World War had destroyed the Turkish domination of the Middle East, mostly to the benefit of Great Britain. The war which took place there for the second time was as important for the survival of the United Kingdom and the victory of the Allies as the Battle of Britain. After the loss of India, the Attlee government thought that it would be possible to establish an alternate empire there, nicknamed "Bevinistan" after its Minister of Foreign Affairs. For London, it was the only means of ensuring the payment in sterling of its oil supplies, and consequently of maintaining the strength of a currency sorely shaken by the fight against Nazism.

Since Lawrence's time, in order to give stability to their presence, the British had exploited Arab nationalism to the hilt by making some of the outstanding chieftains founders of dynasties, and by opening wide the doors of their colleges and clubs to the ruling classes, whose culture and economic interests could not fail, henceforth, to bind them closely to Britain's destiny.

Going further, Eden in 1941 had stated that the British Government "would view with sympathy any movement by the Arab world toward economic, cultural and political unity." [1] Thus encouraged, Nahas Pasha, whom the British had imposed as Prime Minister to King Farouk in 1942, had taken the initiative of creating a "league of Arab nations." It was organized in March 1945 with the help of men like Abdullah of Transjordan and Nuri es-Said, the dictator of Iraq, who had not hesitated to table their old project of a "greater Syria," which would have made Baghdad rather than Cairo the political center of the Arab world.

The desire to check the spread of Zionism was not the least of the reasons which encouraged the Arab governments of that time to link their destiny to that of Great Britain. In spite of the fact that in 1917 Chaim Weizmann had wrested from the Foreign Office the famous "Balfour Declaration," which promised the Jewish people "a national home" in Palestine, Churchill, then Secretary of State for the Colonies, had clearly indicated in 1922 that Great Britain had no intention of making Palestine, which had been entrusted to its mandate by the League of Nations, a Jewish state. And failing to get the Jewish and Arab representatives to agree on partition, London in 1939 had proposed limiting Zionist immigration to 1,500 people per month. Thus, British troops, which were fighting alongside Jewish volunteers against Hitler, prohibited the wretched people who were fleeing Europe and its gas chambers entrance to the Promised Land—"overpromised," according to the expression of David Catarivas.[2] Ships filled with immigrants were turned back and were wrecked, drowning hundreds of passengers. World opinion was aroused without being able to shake London's determination. The Jewish clandestine army, the Haganah, staged surprise attacks to facilitate clandestine arrivals, not hesitating on occasion to attack the British forces, against which extremist terrorist organizations, such as the Irgun, inflicted particularly spectacular blows. Brutal measures of repression brought about equally brutal reprisals.

Truman sought formulas of conciliation and proposed the lifting of immigration quotas and the creation of a federal state; no one

wanted it. The Attlee government convened a round-table conference; the Arabs refused to sit beside the Jews. In desperation, on
April 2, 1947, Attlee appealed to the United Nations, where the
General Assembly, after a whole series of inquiries, came out on
November 30 in favor of the partition of Palestine into two states,
one Jewish, the other Arab, with "holy places"—that is to say,
Jerusalem and Bethlehem—to be internationalized. The vote, 33 to
13, with 10 abstentions, confirmed the recommendations of a special
committee made up of the United States, the U.S.S.R., Canada and
Guatemala. The Soviet-American cooperation revealed on that occasion was especially remarkable since everywhere else in the world
at that time, Washington and Moscow were engaged in a ruthless
struggle.

If the importance of the Jewish element in the American democratic electorate largely explained the United States' attitude, it is
obvious that the reasons for the attitude of the U.S.S.R. must be
sought elsewhere. In fact, Russia, since 1914, had viewed British
imperialism as its principal rival along its southern flank, and it was
going to confront it in the three great battles of the Cold War in
Iran, Turkey and Greece, following the capitulation of the Reich.[3]

Thanks to the alliance against Nazism, the U.S.S.R. had established diplomatic missions in Cairo and in Beirut, and had installed
top officials, Nikolai Novikov and Daniel Solod, at their head. Many
Russian Moslems were allowed to make pilgrimages to Mecca. The
Orthodox patriarch from Moscow had been received with great pomp
in Jerusalem and in most of the Oriental capitals. After patient
negotiations the Kremlin had obtained restitution of a good many
properties—monasteries, schools, hospitals—which had belonged to
the Eastern Russian Church before 1917.

It would have been surprising if the U.S.S.R. had not tried to
exploit its regained influence to press for the departure of the British
as well as the French. In 1946 and 1947 it supported requests
introduced to that effect in the Security Council, the first time by
Syria and Lebanon, the second time by Egypt. But the local Communist parties personally benefited from the sympathies created by
that attitude, and several cities experienced violent demonstrations
which troubled their governments. Because of them, relations between Moscow and the Arab capitals became strained rather quickly,

and the Soviet press went so far as to denounce the Arab League as "an instrument of the British imperialists to enslave the people of the East." [4]

Evidently, it was with the same concern for defeating British plans in that region that Moscow had supported the United Nations' plan for the partition of Palestine, without taking into account the rancor that decision would certainly earn for Moscow in the Arab states.

The Arab states did not waste any time in broadcasting the fact that they would not implement the U.N. resolution. As for Great Britain, after having reiterated that it would only accept partition if it were accepted by all the interested parties, it announced on December 11, 1947, that, contingent on the consent of the international organization, it would give up its mandate the following May 15. But it hastened to add that until then it intended to exercise it fully.

It is difficult not to speculate that, in so doing, London fully hoped that following its departure, the Arab armies would impose on the Zionist colonies a solution which would, in effect, ensure the stable maintenance of its influence. Actually, as soon as the decision to renounce its Palestinian mandate was announced, Britain concluded a new treaty of alliance with Iraq—the implementation of which was prevented by the Baghdad nationalists—and gave arms to Syria. When its troops began evacuating some strongholds in Palestine at the beginning of April, they did nothing to prevent the commandos of the Arab "Army of Liberation" from immediately taking them over. The Arab legion, throughout the Palestine War, remained under the command of the British military staff headed by the famed Glubb Pasha. The fear of seeing the Arabs and their oil pass into the Soviet camp perhaps explained that attitude; in any case it was shared, according to Truman, by Forrestal, then United States Secretary of Defense, and by the "Department of State's specialists on the Near East [who] were, almost without exception, unfriendly to the idea of a Jewish state." [5]

The President himself, caught between their advice and the pressure from American Jews, tried to get out of the situation by urging moderation on everyone.

It was a difficult task. Following the announcement of the impending expiration of the mandate, violence redoubled in Palestine.

On Christmas Day, 1947, alone, more than one hundred were killed. On March 19 the permanent members of the Security Council— minus Great Britain, which had refused consultations proposed by the United States—observed that once the British were gone, "large-scale fighting between the two communities can be expected." But on the same day the American delegate suggested the provisionary transfer of the administration of Palestine to the Trusteeship Council of the U.N., a body charged to govern the former German, Italian and Japanese colonial possessions while preparing them for their accession to independence. It was enough to make Gromyko explode. He accused the United States of having "killed partition" in putting its "oil and military-strategic interests before the United Nations," and being able to think only of turning Palestine into "an American or American-British military base." [6]

Why did that American reversal come about? Truman would be the first to recognize that in spite of "certain tactical advantages," it was "at odds with my attitude and the policy I had laid down." The former President would put responsibility on the State Department and on some diplomats who "should have known . . . that the Jews would read this proposal as a complete abandonment of the partition plan." [7] As a matter of fact, that is what happened. The Jewish Agency expressed its "regret and astonishment" at the American attitude, and on May 14, a few hours before the expiration of the mandate, the executive head of the Agency, an old militant with a luxuriant mane and indomitable courage, David Ben-Gurion, proclaimed the independence of the state of Israel in Tel Aviv. Eleven minutes later, the United States gave it *de facto* recognition.

The U.S.S.R. followed that example only on May 17, but it lent greater importance to its gesture because it recognized the new state not only *de facto* but *de jure*. Its decision was the more significant since two days before, armies from Egypt, Iraq, Transjordan, Syria and Lebanon had entered Palestine "to put an end to massacres and establish respect for the laws of universal morality and the principles recognized by the United Nations . . ." [8]

The British fleet blockaded the coast. As the United States, in order not to be accused of supporting one side or the other, had put a general embargo on arms deliveries, it could be surmised that Jewish resistance would soon be overcome. But the Haganah possessed three trumps: the courage of its remarkably well-trained troops; Jewish solidarity throughout the world, which made it possible for quantities of arms to pass through the net of the blockade; the discreet support of the U.S.S.R., which, through the intermediacy of Czechoslovakia, organized a more or less clandestine airlift to Israel to bring in artillery and automatic weapons. Glubb, who was accused by some Arabs of not having seriously sought to beat the Zionists, was defeated, and the Egyptian Army was mauled before Jerusalem.

Thanks to the combined efforts of the U.S.S.R., of the United States and of the mediator assigned on May 20 by the U.N., Count Folke Bernadotte, president of the Swedish Red Cross who was later assassinated by Jewish extremists, and of his successor, the Negro American Ralph Bunche, truces—interrupted by many outbreaks of fighting—were agreed upon. They were followed in the first part of 1949 by a series of armistices between Israel and the various Arab governments, with the exception of Iraq, which, of course, had no common frontier with the Zionist state. The line of demarcation which followed the fighting was very different from what had been foreseen by the partition plan. Jerusalem was cut in two, and some 500,000 Palestinian Arabs who had fled their lands before the advance of the Jewish Army were prevented from going back to them. Twenty years later most of them would still be parked, with their innumerable progeny (and with the addition of thousands of new refugees, driven from their homes by the Six-Day War), in camps in Jordan, in Syria, in Gaza and in Lebanon, living on meager subsidies from the U.N., and in sight of the land which they still considered theirs.

The defeat inflicted on them by Israel was to have profound reverberations on the Arab states, instilling in them not only the desire for revenge, but also the conviction that to carry it out they would have to get rid of their weak and corrupt political systems which had been created by foreign will, and which were incapable of galvanizing national energies. It was on his return from Palestine, where he and his troops had been surrounded by the Israelis, that a young officer named Gamal Abdel Nasser founded the secret society of Free Officers, which three years later was to overthrow the Egyptian monarchy. The Middle East thus entered into a period of almost

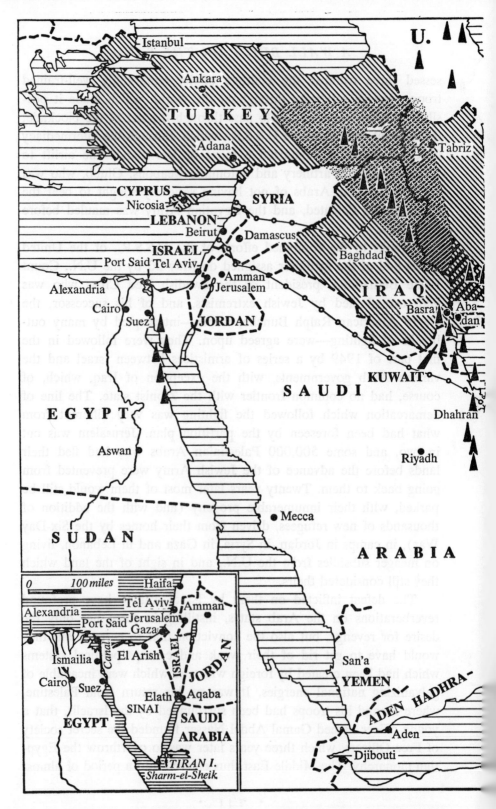

V THE COLD WAR IN

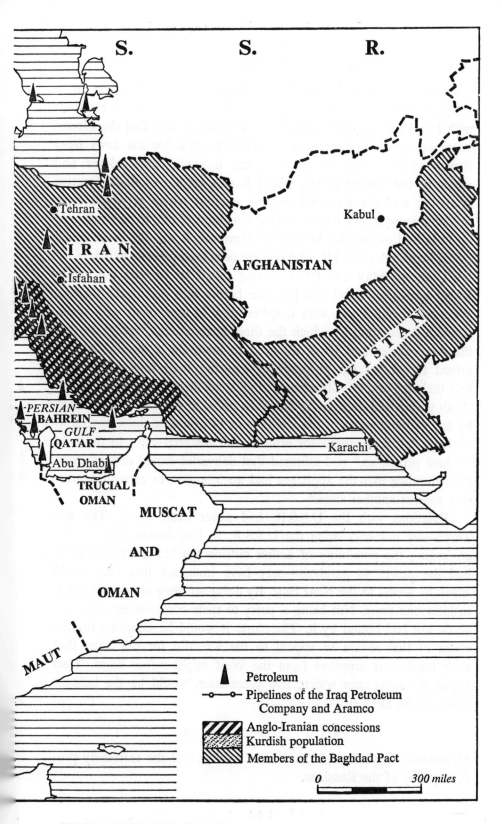

S.   S.   R.

Tehran

IRAN

Isfahan

AFGHANISTAN

Kabul

PAKISTAN

PERSIAN
BAHREIN
GULF
QATAR

Abu Dhabi

TRUCIAL
OMAN

MUSCAT

AND

OMAN

Karachi

MAUT

Petroleum
Pipelines of the Iraq Petroleum
  Company and Aramco
Anglo-Iranian concessions
Kurdish population
Members of the Baghdad Pact

0   300 miles

THE MIDDLE EAST

uninterrupted crises in which the U.S.S.R. would be even more tempted to intervene since, after a brief honeymoon, its relations with Israel had become strained. Outside of the fact that the Zionist state was going to become a powerful magnet for the Jews from Russia and the people's democracies, it would draw closer and closer to the United States, where it was certain of finding active sympathy and the financial support without which it would have been condemned, like the Crusaders' kingdoms of old, to be swallowed up little by little by the Arab sand. However, it was the West which would furnish the U.S.S.R. with reasons or at least pretexts to act.

Thus, on May 25, 1950, having failed to convert the Arab-Israeli armistices concluded the year before into real peace treaties, Washington and Paris, with London, now in agreement with them, issued a declaration by which the three governments "recognize that the Arab States and Israel all need to maintain a certain level of armed forces for the purposes of assuring their internal security and their legitimate self-defense," indicated their intention of acting "both within and outside the U.N." in order to prevent any violation by any of these states of the frontiers or of armistice lines, agreed to evaluate "all applications for arms or war material . . . in the light of these principles," and affirmed that deliveries would depend upon the assurance that the applicant had no intention to commit aggression against another state.[9]

Relations with the U.S.S.R. had never been worse. The Big Three—by not associating the U.S.S.R. in that declaration, and by envisaging the possibility of action outside the U.N., where Russia had the power to paralyze—may have imagined that they could block its access to the Near East. By doing so, they almost invited it to intervene there. Not being a party to their commitment, Moscow could not feel bound by it. Therefore, it would be tempting for the states of that region to appeal to the Kremlin for the arms that their traditional suppliers from the West might refuse them. Thus began the arms race which, five years later, would be the indirect cause of the Suez crisis.

§   §   §

Meanwhile, another crisis gave clear evidence of the extremely prudent policy of the Russians.

In June 1950 the Shah of Iran, convinced as he was of the necessity of radical reforms to pull the empire out of poverty and corruption, had brought to power a strong man, General Ali Razmara. The United States, to which the Shah had just paid a long visit, had promised him its help, knowing very well that if it failed to act, the whole of Asia would soon slide into communism, just as China had done.

One of the first decisions of the new government chief was to open negotiations with the Anglo-Iranian Oil Company, the A.I.O.C. In forty years it had made Iran the principal producer of petroleum on the Persian Gulf and had built in Abadan the largest refinery in the world. In 1949 it had poured into the coffers of the Iranian treasury some 90 million dollars.

That same year the A.I.O.C. had agreed to double the amount of its royalties, but Venezuela, and then Saudi Arabia, had obtained a fifty-fifty division of profits from American companies, and the Iranian pride considered this difference of treatment a real insult. The Majlis, the Teheran Parliament, rejected the agreement, and a strong campaign was started in favor of the nationalization of the company. The wretched masses which formed the largest part of Iran's population imagined that overnight it would transform their lives. More and more violent demonstrations occurred, organized by fanatic Shiite Moslems like the Mollah Kashani, by Communists of the Tudeh, and especially by the National Front led by Mohammed Mossadegh—an extremely colorful individual and a multimillionaire related to the Kajars dynasty, which had been overthrown by the Reza Pahlevi, father of the present Shah Mohammed Reza. Theatrical, a high-flown demagogue, but a stubborn and selfless patriot, Doctor (of laws) Mossadegh was soon to become famous with his striped pajamas, his iron bed and his constant fainting spells—real or simulated.

In 1944 he had played a major part in the defeat of Stalin's claims to Iran's Azerbaijan and the oil fields south of the Caspian Sea, and since then, he had had no other ambition than to defeat Great Britain as well. Obviously, Britain was the target of the resolution Mossadegh induced the Majlis to adopt immediately after it had rejected the treaty giving a concession to the U.S.S.R. The resolution read, in particular: "In cases when the rights of the Nation relating to the natural resources of the soil or the subsoil or others have been infringed upon, particularly relating to the petroleum in the south, the government is ordered to enter into negotiations for the re-establishment of national rights. . . ." [10]

Mossadegh then controlled only a few deputies in the Parliament, and according to Vincent Monteil, those had been elected only by permission of "British Machiavellism . . . as a safety valve." [11]

The pressure of public opinion, disappointed by the small amount of American aid, was such that Mossadegh had been named chairman of the commission charged to decide on the renewal of negotiations with the A.I.O.C. Twice the commission refused to ratify the 1949 accord, while a heated debate began between Mossadegh, who vigorously demanded nationalization, and Razmara, convinced that the country was not capable of exploiting its petroleum resources alone, and who labeled his adversary's plans as "the greatest of treasons." [12]

On March 3, 1951, the Prime Minister asked that experts be allowed to study the problem "calmly . . . realistically." [13] Four days later Razmara was assassinated while leaving the Shah's mosque, and on the 15th the Majlis, "in order to ensure the happiness and prosperity of the Iranian people and to safeguard world peace," decided to nationalize "the petroleum industry throughout its territory without any exception." [14] To make sure of the vote, Mossadegh had told how a white shape had appeared to him during the night and told him: "Stand up . . . go break the chains of the Iranian people!" [15]

On April 28 he was named Prime Minister, and on May 2 the Shah proclaimed the nationalization law. Invoking the petroleum accord of 1933, London proposed arbitration, but Mossadegh objected to the mediator. British technicians refused to work for the new national company, the N.I.O.C., and the Abadan refinery had to shut down. In July the International Court of Justice, on Britain's request, took conservation measures that Teheran refused to observe.

Truman's attempt at conciliation having failed, Great Britain, on September 10, cancelled all the commercial advantages that it had granted Iran until then and ordered its tankers en route to Abadan to return. On the 25th, Mossadegh ordered the expulsion within a week of the British personnel of the refinery, the installations of which were to be occupied forthwith by Persian troops. London feared for its investments and dispatched a cruiser and troops, but did not dare have them land. "The temptation to intervene to reclaim this stolen property must have been strong," wrote Anthony Eden in his memoirs "but pressure from the United States was vigorous against any such action." [16] It is tempting to identify the competition for petroleum, especially fierce in that part of the world, as the prime reason for that pressure. But if, as is probable, it played a part, it only confirmed the White House and the State Department in their personal beliefs. In fact, they were afraid that the U.S.S.R. might invoke the Soviet-Persian treaty of 1921, which gave Russia the right to occupy the northern part of the country in the event of intervention by a third power. They also feared that the eventual failure of the "moderate" nationalists might bring the Communists to power. Besides, the United States had acted in a similar manner in many places where there was no oil.

No longer knowing which way to turn, the Labour government, facing general elections, called on the Security Council to ask Iran to accept the conservation measures adopted in July by the International Court. The debate, in which Mossadegh himself, in spite of all his eccentricities, skillfully presented his country's case, was abruptly cut short. On France's proposal the Council decided to adjourn until the International Court had ruled on its own competence.

Labor having lost by a small margin, Britain had changed governments during the Council session. Eden resumed his post as Foreign Secretary. He had a special interest in Iran since he had learned Persian at Oxford and one of his first duties while he was Under Secretary of State in 1933 had been to resolve the crisis created by the revocation of the agreement with A.I.O.C. by Teheran. A Conservative, a follower of Churchill, who had said one day to Roosevelt that he had not become the King's Prime Minister in order to preside over the liquidation of the British Empire, he had firmly decided to do everything to keep Abadan for the crown, not only because he believed that its loss would jeopardize Britain's oil supplies, but also because he feared that it might quickly bring about the collapse of the whole of the British establishment in the East.

His fear was understandable. On July 20 of that same year,

1951, King Abdullah of Jordan, a British protégé, had been assassinated in Jerusalem. On October 8, exactly one week before the British elections, Nahas Pasha, Egypt's Prime Minister, had unilaterally abrogated the treaty concluded in 1936 which permitted the United Kingdom to station troops in the Suez Canal Zone. Violent anti-British demonstrations took place in Cairo. To show the relation between the two problems, Mossadegh, on his return from New York, stopped on the banks of the Nile where the crowd gave him a delirious welcome.

London having made no response to Nahas' move, snipers started to attack the British, who retaliated on January 25 by attacking the Ismailia police station, killing fifty of its defenders. Popular indignation resulted the next day in rioters' burning four hundred buildings in Cairo. Farouk took that opportunity to get rid of his Prime Minister, whom he suspected of wanting to depose him, but by so doing he hastened his own downfall. On July 22 a group of the Free Officers overthrew the monarchy which had become a symbol of corruption and inefficiency and put at the head of the provisional government one of the heroes of the Palestine War, General Naguib, a big, amiable fellow behind whom the more ambitious shadow of Colonel Nasser would soon be discerned.

Eden's first objective was to convince the United States to give up its neutrality in the oil dispute with Teheran. For him ". . . to come to terms at any price with Mossadegh . . . would be a policy of despair," and he did not believe that "the only choice in Iran lay between Mossadegh and communism." [17]

As long as Truman remained at the helm, his efforts would meet with little success. Naturally, the United States refused the Persian Prime Minister a loan of $120,000,000 that he had personally requested immediately following the debate in the Security Council. But it still sought a solution of conciliation and supported a move, in November, by the World Bank, to grant Iran an emergency loan of $8,750,000. When further negotiations started by the bank failed in March 1952, the American Treasury did not hesitate to grant a direct loan of $23,000,000, accompanied—this may help to explain the loan—by an agreement for military aid.

The Mossadegh government needed that money desperately. Petroleum production had declined precipitously: no one, of course, wanted to take the risk of buying from the new national company, the A.I.O.C. having used the authority granted it by the conservation measures decreed by the Court to let it be known that it considered that the crude oil still belonged to it. On the strength of that claim, the British fleet had imposed a blockade.

Mossadegh, nonetheless, continued to enjoy immense popular support as was shown by the nearly hysterical reception which awaited him on his return from New York. "It is better to be independent and produce only one ton of oil a year," he said, "than to produce thirty-two million tons and be a slave to Britain." [18] Fearing for their lives, the leaders of the opposition took refuge in the Majlis, while the Prime Minister organized new elections at the beginning of 1952. He was given a plebiscite by a crowd who saw in him not only the champion of nationalism, but also that of social justice: in truth, he had pushed through a law for agrarian reform and for the first time in the history of the country someone was seriously fighting corruption. The Communists having aborted an attempt by the palace to replace him with Ghavam Sultaneh—the one who had gotten the best of Stalin in the Azerbaijan affair—he won another victory when, at the end of July, he persuaded the International Court of Justice, before which he pleaded in person, to declare itself incompetent in the petroleum conflict.

In August, at Churchill's request, Truman agreed to join with him in approaching the Iranian Prime Minister. The Court of Justice had to be asked to determine the amount of compensation to be paid to the A.I.O.C. for the nationalization of its installations, and immediate negotiations had to be started on the disposition of the oil stockpile. Mossadegh, who had just obtained full powers from the Majlis, categorically refused. On October 16 he broke off diplomatic relations with Great Britain. But he made the error of wanting to attack the Shah, which made him lose the support of the Army, of religious elements and notably of the followers of Mollah Kashani, elected Speaker of the Parliament. When on February 28, 1953, he persuaded the emperor to abdicate "for reasons of health," Kashani organized a demonstration in favor of the Shah. Mossadegh, still in pajamas, was forced out of his house and had to flee. Finally, the *status quo* was restored. The Prime Minister and the Shah each returned to his own palace and argued all day long, through ministers. But the Prime Minister had saved his post a second time thanks only to the support of the Tudeh Party, whose prisoner he became more and more each day.

However, when at the end of March, Eden visited Eisenhower, newly arrived at the White House, Eisenhower still considered Mossadegh "as the only hope for the West in Iran." He thought "an extension of Russian control of Iran . . . a distinct possibility," which would either bring about the loss of oil supplies from the Middle East or the threat of a world war. For that reason the United States still pursued its efforts at conciliation.[19]

Ambassador Loy Henderson suggested to Teheran the creation of a "consortium of oil companies" which would buy oil from the N.I.O.C. The Prime Minister did not want to hear of it and spoke of "a form of plunder," which did not prevent him from sending a virtual S.O.S. to Ike on May 28, accompanied by a discreet blackmail on the reversal of alliances: "As a result of action taken by the former company, and the British Government, the Iranian nation is now facing great economic and political difficulties. There can be serious consequences, from an international viewpoint as well if this situation is permitted to continue." [20] This time Eisenhower got angry. He answered that "it would not be fair to the American taxpayers for the United States Government to extend any considerable amount of economic aid to Iran so long as Iran could have access to funds derived from the sale of its oil and oil products if a reasonable agreement were reached with regard to compensation." [21]

The end was now in sight. On July 19 the Majlis refused to allow Mossadegh to proclaim himself Commander in Chief of the Army in the Shah's place. The Shah rejected the proposal of dissolution of Parliament announced by the Prime Minister, who called for a referendum forthwith. On the 21st the Tudeh Party organized a vast demonstration in which the names of Mossadegh and the U.S.S.R. were jointly acclaimed. Its entry into the government seemed imminent. When on August 8, Malenkov, then head of the Soviet Government, was reviewing the international situation, he announced that Moscow had initiated negotiations with Iran: "Soviet-Persian relations have therefore such a stable basis as to make possible the solution of problems arising between the two parties to their mutual satisfaction." [22]

But the decision which was going to arrest the process apparently underway had already been taken. Using his constitutional prerogatives, the Shah ousted Mossadegh and replaced him with General Zahedi, whom the Allies had removed in 1941 because of his contacts with the Nazis. But this time the change took place with their complete agreement. Before making his decision, the sovereign had conferred at length with the American General Schwartzkopf, whose membership in the famed Central Intelligence Agency was known to everyone.

The plan of Mohammed Reza and his American advisers was to take Mossadegh by surprise. But Colonel Nazir, who was ordered to inform him, and probably to arrest him, waited two days to get started. When he went to the house of the Prime Minister, who evidently had had ample warning, he himself was apprehended. The sovereign, fearing for his life, immediately flew to Rome via Baghdad, with no hope of returning.

The C.I.A., however, had not yet given up. By a truly remarkable coincidence its chief, Allen Dulles, brother of Foster, Loy Henderson, the United States ambassador to Teheran, and Princess Ashraf, sister of the Shah, met in the same Swiss resort while on alleged vacations. According to the American journalist Andrew Tully,[23] Schwartzkopf spent more than $10 million to engineer an apparently innocent parade which, all of a sudden, became a royalist demonstration. Part of the Army joined the procession, which became larger and larger, and a squad of tanks commanded by Zahedi himself took over the radio station.

The Tudeh asked for arms from the head of the government, who refused, and, to confuse the extreme Left, freed fascist leaders. Twenty-four hours later he was arrested along with the Tudeh leaders although they had taken no part in resisting the *coup d'état*.

The fickle crowd accorded the Shah, who had hastily returned, acclamations as loud as those it had given Mossadegh a few days earlier. The Prime Minister was condemned to three years in prison. He died in March 1967, somewhat forgotten, while the N.I.O.C., the national company which he had founded, continues to exist and prosper, occupying in the center of Teheran a sumptuous marble building which dominates the whole city. In 1954, in fact, an agreement was to be signed between the N.I.O.C. and a consortium in which the Americans held 40 percent, the British 40 percent and France 6 percent, Iran keeping half of the profits. Compared to the 15 percent that the Anglo-Iranian company gave Iran until 1949, it represented a tremendous improvement.

All told, in that affair, whatever goals it had pursued, the major beneficiary was the United States, which was thus installed on an equal basis with its English competitors in what had been for forty years one of John Bull's major fiefs. It had taken great advantage of the passivity of the U.S.S.R., which not only had never made the slightest menacing gesture, but had seemingly intervened, at the time of Mossadegh's fall, to discourage the Tudeh—then practically masters of the situation in the streets—from seizing the power within its reach. Badly burned in 1946 in Azerbaijan, having more oil than it needed in Baku, eager to relax its relations with the West following Stalin's death and, besides, unsure of Mossadegh, it evidently had no reason to provoke an international crisis over Iran in which it would have found itself directly implicated.

Nonetheless, the extreme Left was severely persecuted. Following the arrest in 1954 of a Communist officer at whose house a list of his fellow party members was found, more than 600 soldiers were apprehended and 25 of them shot. In a clandestine brochure cited by Edouard Sablier, the Tudeh's central committee, appropriating sins that it had not committed alone, confessed its "opportunism," and a "false analysis of its forces," which had "prevented it from cooperating with the other anti-imperialist forces." [24]

§   §   §

Quieta non movere. "Don't disturb what is quiet." Foster Dulles and Anthony Eden were to ignore that Latin proverb as soon as Mossadegh had fallen and begin a campaign for the conclusion of a Middle East Defense Treaty, supplementing NATO and very likely to displease the U.S.S.R., as several of its eventual signers were in Russia's immediate proximity. This meant—at a time far removed from

intercontinental missiles—bases for United States planes, radio transmitters for its propaganda and opportunities for its agents to influence
the Moslem populations in the southern regions of the Soviet empire.

We must be fair to the diplomacy of the Fourth Republic, so often
criticized under the Fifth for its alleged servility toward the United
States, for it consistently warned the United States and its British
friends against the inevitable results of the policy summed up in the
formula of the Baghdad Pact.

If London had gotten what it wanted, it would have been called
the "Cairo Pact." The British Labour Party's leaders, who had
foreseen the revocation of the 1936 Anglo-Egyptian Alliance Treaty
understood perfectly well that they could only maintain a military
presence at Suez, which they considered essential, within a framework devoid of any colonial character.

In September 1951 the British had succeeded in persuading
Washington and Paris to join with Ankara in proposing the creation
of a Middle East command, in which Egypt would participate as a
founding member. In the event of a positive response, the British
base at Suez would be turned over to the Cairo Government and
would become an Allied base. British troops not assigned to that
command by mutual accord would be pulled out of Egypt. But
Nahas Pasha had answered on October 8 by abrogating the 1936
treaty and stating that he would sign no other until Great Britain
had evacuated Suez and the Sudan.

The Middle East command was thus created without Egypt, on
November 11, 1951, and established in Ankara. Its four founders
had proposed that Egypt, Syria, Lebanon, Iraq, Israel, Yemen, Saudi
Arabia and Jordan join them, which had immediately led to an
exchange of acrimonious notes with the U.S.S.R.

At the beginning of 1953, Eden formulated a new plan for a
defensive organization which Egypt, the United States and France
would be invited to join, and which would entail at the same time a
gradual withdrawal of British troops from Egypt and the maintenance
in peacetime in the Canal Zone of "a military base . . . under
conditions which would enable us and our allies to have immediate
use of it in war." [25] He personally submitted his plan to Eisenhower,
who agreed to it in principle, on condition that Naguib, who mean-

while had become head of the Cairo Government, officially express his desire for United States participation.

But that wasn't at all what Naguib wanted. As he wrote to Ike, he wanted first to eliminate "the moral and physical barriers and obstacles besetting it, most conspicuous and most serious of which is the destructively persistent stationing of British armed forces on Egyptian territory." [26] Refusing to associate himself, as Churchill would have wanted, in an overture to the Egyptian Government, the President sent Foster Dulles on a tour of the Middle East, including Israel. That was enough for the new Egyptian leaders, who until then had not hidden their sympathies for America, to give Dulles the cold shoulder. But, on the very day of the Secretary of State's arrival in Egypt, the British Prime Minister felt the need of asserting in Commons that "The most important factor in the Middle East is the State of Israel," and that, for his part, he had always been a "faithful supporter of the Zionist cause." [27]

Instantly, Mahmoud Aboul Fath, standard-bearer of the Egyptian press and at the time an unofficial spokesman of the regime, published in his newspaper *Al Misri* an open letter to the Secretary of State literally telling him: "We hate you. . . . We do not ignore, and neither do you, that London and Tel Aviv are accomplices. . . . Arabs do not want to be taken in tow either by the British or the Turks or NATO or any Balkan organization." [28] The colt brought by Dulles as a personal gift from Ike was not sufficient to mollify Naguib, and Dulles left Cairo convinced that there was not much to expect from the Egyptians, more preoccupied with getting rid of the British than with protecting themselves from a distant Soviet danger.

He heard the same refrain in the other Arab capitals. Therefore, when he returned to Washington, he admitted in a speech that he had only met a "vague desire" to organize a system of collective security. No such system, he realistically continued, "could be imposed . . . by the Western Powers, and little could be done in this direction until the Arab states and Israel settled their differences." [29] But those differences were still grave, as the increasing number of frontier incidents showed. The United States tried to intervene by entrusting the study of a project for the utilization of

Jordan—intended to facilitate the resettlement of Arab refugees—to a special ambassador, Eric Johnston, who promptly put together a very ingenious plan. But the Arab states rejected it because it involved a collaboration with Israel which they could not consider until the refugees had been either repatriated or compensated.

In Ankara, however, Dulles had found people like the President of the Republic, Celal Bayar, and the President of the Council, Adnan Mendérès, extremely prejudiced against the Russians; they had not forgotten the fruitless attempts made by the Russians in 1945–1946 to get control of Kars and Ardahan and the straits, and for that reason they wanted to extend the Atlantic Pact to the East. In January 1954, Bayar on a trip to Washington obtained Eisenhower's consent to a proposed alliance with Pakistan, which would be finalized in February during a visit of Mendérès to Karachi and signed on April 2, in spite of all the warnings from the U.S.S.R. and protests from India, which was engaged in an insoluble dispute with Pakistan over Kashmir.

Meanwhile, important events had taken place in Syria, where the fall of the pro-French government of Colonel Shishekly had brought to power a group friendly to Baghdad and London, and especially to Egypt. After a long struggle with Naguib, Colonel Nasser had become Prime Minister in March 1954, in practice assuming all powers and confining the general, who would be ousted at the end of the year, to a purely honorific role. But Nasser, an emotional and intransigent patriot, whose will to ensure the independence of his country and to wipe out past humiliations was reminiscent of Gaullist psychology, was determined to obtain the departure of the British. For that he would pay whatever price was necessary. The United States helped when it promised Cairo sizable economic aid, contingent on an agreement. A settlement was finally worked out on October 19, 1954. London agreed to withdraw all its troops within twenty months. In return, Egypt guaranteed freedom of navigation on the Suez Canal and pledged itself to "grant the United Kingdom every facility needed for placing the base on a warlike footing, and operating it effectively . . . in the event of an armed attack by a power outside the Middle East, against any country which, at the date of the present agreement, is a signatory of the treaty of mutual defense between the Arab States, signed in Cairo in 1950, or against Turkey." [30] In mentioning Turkey, that document fulfilled London's old dream of including the defense of Egypt in NATO. By implicitly excluding Israel from the list of aggressors against which the pact could take effect, it prevented the British from using the renewal of the Judeo-Arab conflict as a pretext for moving again in Suez. Even before the final conclusion of that agreement, Nuri es-Said, who, as soon as he came back to power, had established a harsh dictatorship in Iraq, had written to his king on August 4, 1954, that "The Turkish-Pakistani pact and the Anglo-Egyptian agreement had brought about a political situation to which Iraq could not remain indifferent." [31] He had then undertaken trips to Turkey, England and Egypt, and asserted in Istanbul on October 19, the day of the signing of the agreement for the evacuation of the Suez Canal Zone that "The Arab nations were ready to collaborate with the West when the Suez and Palestine questions had been solved." [32] He had increased anti-Communist measures, going so far as to break diplomatic relations with Moscow on January 3, 1955. On the 13th, following a visit from Mendérès, Iraq and Turkey announced their intention to increase their cooperation in working for the stability and security of the Middle East, and invited the other states of the region to join them.

For Cairo, which for ten years has tried to assemble around Egypt the whole Arab nation, that news rang out like a challenge. Instantly, Nasser saw in it an attempt by London to reassert itself in the Near East through its faithful Nuri es-Said, advocate of the Fertile Crescent, in other words of an empire gathering all the Arab countries of the Near East under the Hashemite crown. He immediately called for the convocation of the Arab League to condemn Iraq, guilty in his eyes of having broken Arab solidarity. He expressed his displeasure to Eden, who was passing through Cairo on February 19, and asserted that the Turkish-Iraqi agreement had "seriously set back the development of effective collaboration with the West by Arab states," although "his interest and sympathy were with the West." [33]

That sharp reaction did not prevent the formal conclusion on February 24 in Baghdad of the Turkish-Iraqi treaty, which the United Kingdom joined on April 4, Pakistan on September 23, and

Iran on November 3. The United States pretended to be out of it, but in reality was present in the major organizations stemming from the Baghdad Pact. The West, or rather America and England—since France, distrusted by all the Arab states because of the war in Algeria, had not even been consulted—could believe that it had won a great diplomatic victory complementing the one obtained through Mossadegh's fall. In reality, it had simply extended the Cold War to the Middle East, toward which the U.S.S.R., since its Iranian and Turkish disappointments of 1947, had behaved with the greatest circumspection.

The Egyptian counterattack quickly gained momentum. On March 6, Cairo joined Syria and Saudi Arabia in proposing to the other Arab states a treaty creating a common military and economic organization which, in the end, medieval Yemen would join.

On March 20, Salah Salem, the colorful Egyptian Minister of National Orientation—in other words of propaganda—famed for his oratorical capers, stated that his government had no territorial ambitions, but that he would like a territorial bond with Jordan. Consequently, he proposed that Jordan be given the whole southern part of Israel, extending from Gaza to Beersheba and Aqaba on the Red Sea, and asserted that his plan represented the "price" that the Western Powers had to pay if they wanted to cooperate with Egypt. Jerusalem immediately rejected that "blackmail." Was Cairo's proposal serious? Henceforth, Nasser seemed to have decided in favor of nonalignment: its two principal leaders, Tito and Nehru, had just conferred at length in New Delhi, where they had condemned the bloc policy. Going home, the Yugoslav marshal stopped in Alexandria, where he met Nasser, still suffering from the emotional shock caused by the signing of the Baghdad Pact. It was the beginning of a friendship which would continue growing, with Tito, the model of patriotism and courage in the eyes of the Egyptian colonel, dispensing advice which would be followed more than once.

Then it was Nehru's turn to visit Cairo. There he signed a communiqué with Nasser according to which "Military alliances and power entanglements which increase tension and rivalry in armaments do not add to the security of a country," [34] and which soon led to the conclusion of a treaty of friendship.

In April, Nasser returned his visit and with him attended the

Afro-Asian Bandung Conference, where he received a triumphal welcome, met Chou En-lai, Sukarno, and discovered the strength of what was soon to be called the "third world" and the leading role it was ready to confer on him.

Unanimously, less Burma's vote, the conference decided "to support the rights of the Arab people of Palestine." [35] It was a great victory for the "Bikbachi" ("Colonel" in the Egyptian Army), as he was then called, and he returned to Cairo crowned with the victor's laurels, and convinced, at the same time, that he had nothing more to expect from the West, which was guilty, in his eyes, of preferring not only Iraq but Israel to him.

Israeli-Egyptian relations had never been good since the armistice of 1949 had not put an end to the state of war. Cairo prevented Israel's ships, or those chartered by Israel, from using the Suez Canal, and Arab snipers operated in Jewish territory. The Jerusalem Government, under pressure of public opinion, had decided to strike back. On February 28 a column of tanks had penetrated the Gaza Strip and slain about sixty Arabs, of whom several were civilians. The brutality of that operation provoked sharp indignation in the West, and it was on the joint initiative of the United States, Great Britain and France that the Security Council had unanimously condemned it. But Nasser could not believe that Israel had acted without the consent of the Americans on whom it closely depended for the realization of its economic plans. Jean Lacouture reported the confidence that Nasser gave to a Western ambassador at that time: "As you know, until last month I was a sincere friend of the West. From now on, don't count on me." [36] Another incident was to convince him of the evil intentions of the capitalist countries. An indiscreet confidential bulletin published in Paris revealed that Israel had concluded an arms transaction with France which included the delivery of tanks and planes, among other weapons. At the same time, because of the escalation of the war in Algeria, Paris had cancelled a delivery of arms promised to Egypt.

However, Nasser's turnabout could not have taken place if the U.S.S.R. had not undergone a complete change after Stalin's death. During the last years of what was subsequently called the "cult of personality," the official doctrine agreed with Zhdanov, that those who were not unconditionally for the Soviet Union were, in fact, against it. The Soviet encyclopedia still, in 1952, described Nehru's Indian Congress party as ". . . obedient executors of the will of the British-American imperialists," and the authors of the Egyptian *coup d'état* as a "group of reactionary officers connected with the United States, with General Naguib at the head." [37] In 1954 the attentions shown to Nehru, the tour of India by Chou En-lai, the active participation of China in the preparation of the Bandung Conference, the elevation to the rank of embassies of Soviet legations in Cairo and Tel Aviv, everything showed that the attitude had totally changed. Now Moscow and Peking were going to do everything to convince the nonengaged countries, without bothering with their internal regimes, that it was in their interest to appeal to them to stimulate "decolonization" and to oppose "imperialism"—typical Leninist expressions which were going to be found more and more frequently on the lips of African and Asian leaders. With a rare gift for the inappropriate, Dulles, who did not, however, hesitate to visit Tito and to praise him, still found it possible to declare in 1956 that "except under very exceptional circumstances, neutrality is an immoral and short-sighted conception." [38]

A few hours before the Bandung Conference, the U.S.S.R. had published a statement denouncing the attempts of the West to marshal the countries of the Near and Middle East into military groups which had been created as an extension of the North Atlantic bloc. It concluded that "if the policy of pressure and threats against those countries continued, the question would have to be examined by the United Nations. The Soviet Government, safeguarding peace, will defend the freedom, the independence and the principle of non-interference in the internal affairs of the Near and Middle East."[39]

Western chancelleries chose to see in this document a gesture primarily intended to sway Arab sympathies toward the Kremlin. In reality there was much more at stake. Five years after publication of the Franco-Anglo-American declaration on the maintenance of the *status quo* in the Middle East, the Kremlin warned the Allies that that region was henceforth no longer their preserve.

BIBLIOGRAPHY AND NOTES

[1] Michel Laissy, *Du panarabisme à la ligue arabe* (Paris: Maisonneuve, 1948), p. 101.

[2] David Catarivas. *Israël* (Paris: Editions du Seuil, 1957), p. 94.

[3] See first volume of this book, Chapter 14, "Block to the South."

[4] *Krasnaia Zviezda*, April 29, 1950.

[5] Truman, *op. cit.*, II, p. 162.

[6] Keesing's, 9237 A.

[7] Truman, *op. cit.*, II, p. 163.

[8] Keesing's, 9243 A.

[9] *Ibid.*, 10405 A.

[10] Suzanne Normand and Jean Acker, *La Route du pétrole au Moyen-Orient* (Paris: Horizons de France, 1956), p. 143.

[11] Vincent Monteil, *Iran* (Paris: Editions du Seuil, 1962), p. 33.

[12] Freidoune Sahebjam, *L'Iran des Pahlavis* (Paris: Berger-Levrault, 1966), pp. 230–31.

[13] *Ibid.*

[14] J. Benoist-Mechin, *Le roi Saud* (Paris: Albin Michel, 1960), p. 119.

[15] Inge Morath and Edouard Sablier, *From Persia to Iran* (London: Thames & Hudson, 1960), p. 56.

[16] Eden, *op. cit.*, pp. 216–17.

[17] *Ibid.*, p. 219.

[18] Eisenhower, *op. cit.*, p. 159.

[19] Eden, *op. cit.*, p. 235.

[20] Eisenhower, *op. cit.*, p. 161.

[21] *Ibid.*, p. 162.

[22] Keesing's, 13097 A.

[23] Andrew Tully, *C.I.A.: The Inside Story* (New York: Morrow, 1962), p. 95.

[24] Edouard Sablier, *De l'Oural à l'Atlantique* (Paris: Fayard, 1963), p. 228.

[25] Eden, *op. cit.*, p. 274.

[26] Eisenhower, *op. cit.*, p. 155.

[27] Keesing's, 12909 A.

[28] Pierre Rossi, *L'Irak des révoltes* (Paris: Editions du Seuil, 1962), p. 184.

[29] Keesing's, 12957 B.

[30] Jean and Simone Lacouture, *Egypt in Transition* (New York: Criterion Books, n.d.,), p. 207.

[31] Central Office of Information, Reference Division, Note R 3287, London, March 8, 1956.

[32] Keesing's, 13854 C.

[33] Eden, *op. cit.*, p. 245.

[34] Keesing's, 14160 A.

[35] *Ibid.*, 14181 A.

[36] Jean and Simonne Lacouture, *op. cit.*, pp. 222–23.

[37] David Dallin, *Soviet Foreign Policy After Stalin* (Philadelphia: Lippincott, 1961), p. 293.

[38] Peter Lyon, *Neutralism* (Leicester, England: Leicester University Press, 1963), p. 107.

[39] *Le Monde*, April 19, 1955.

· CHAPTER 8 ·

THE MIRAGE

A divided isthmus becomes a strait—in other words
a battleground. Until now, one Bosphorus was
enough for the troubled affairs of the world; you
have created another.

—Ernest Renan, address on the
reception of Ferdinand de Lesseps
into the French Academy, 1895

IN MAY 1955, NASSER WAS ATTENDING A DIPLOMATIC
reception when suddenly Daniel Solod took him by the arm. The
Soviet Ambassador drew him into a corner and asked him point-
blank if Egypt would like to buy arms from the U.S.S.R. In the
event of an affirmative response he would inform Moscow. "I
answered," the colonel himself relates, "that I was ready to begin
talks with that end in view." [1] On June 9, pointing to the recent
deliveries of French military matériel to the Jewish state and to the
openly expansionist statements made by some Israeli extremists, he
asked Henry Byroade, the United States ambassador, for armaments and told him that if he were refused, he would appeal to the
other side of the Iron Curtain. However, he made no mention of
the Kremlin's offer.

Ever since the visit to Paris in 1954 of Moshe Dayan, the hand-
some Commander in Chief of the Zionist Army, whose eyepatch
would soon make him famous, France had in fact begun to supply
tanks, planes, land missiles and radar equipment to the Jerusalem
Government—which lived in fear of the war of revenge daily proclaimed by the Arab leaders. It is quite possible that there were a
few political overtones in the French coming to this decision at a

time when the Maghreb was in ferment, but they were not a determining factor. "I said to myself," subsequently declared Diomède Catroux, Secretary of State for Air in the Mendès-France government, "that we could not become accomplices in a new massacre by refusing to help the people of Israel defend themselves." [2]

The memory of the gas chambers was still very vivid, and more than one Frenchman must have felt some remorse at not having done more to save the Jews from them. To this was added a genuine admiration for the magnificent work accomplished by the restorers of the Hebrew state. Thus, in the crisis about to develop, we will see suspicion engender suspicion, reinforcing the antagonists' belief in the justice of their respective causes, and creating around them emotional reactions of solidarity as noble as they were dangerous.

The Americans, reluctant to support an enemy of the Baghdad Pact, evaded Nasser's request by demanding payment in cash, obviously inconceivable for a country as poor as Egypt.

On July 26, Dimitri Shepilov, *Pravda*'s editor in chief, arrived in Cairo to attend the anniversary celebration of the revolution. No one paid any attention to his presence. Nonetheless, he had come to conclude the transaction which, on September 26, Nasser announced to his countrymen. Following the failure of his successive attempts to obtain arms from the Western countries, he said that he had negotiated an agreement with Czechoslovakia, which would supply them in exchange for cotton and rice.

The news of this transaction did not take the Western Powers entirely by surprise. Ever since August 31, Dulles had prepared them for it. Caught between contradictory advice, he decided, in spite of the extremely cool welcome extended to his envoy George Allen by the colonel, to follow the counsels of moderation which Henry Byroade, a strong advocate of American support for Arab nationalism, was dispensing from Cairo. On the occasion of the conference on Germany in Geneva, he broached the question of the Middle East to Molotov, who dismissed any idea of reconsidering an agreement which was of a purely commercial nature in his eyes. Nevertheless, Dulles, on November 9, had Eisenhower approve a declaration affirming his intention to stay out of an arms race in the Middle East which could profit no one. Dulles resisted entreaties from Eden, who would have liked the United States to officially join the Baghdad Pact. He pressured France not to deliver to Israel the Mystère IV planes promised in October by the head of the government, Edgar Faure, to his Israeli colleague, Moshe Sharett. Finally, he decided to help Cairo achieve the most ambitious enterprise of the regime—the construction of the High Dam at Aswan.

Based on favorable geological conditions, the plan was to flood some 10,000 kilometers of land and to transform the arid and grandiose mountain range of ancient Nubia into an enormous lake, thus increasing Egypt's cultivable land by one third, and its installed electric power by one half. For that country, whose 30 million inhabitants had no other fertile land at their disposal besides the delta and a thin strip along the Nile, it was a matter of life or death. But the cost of the High Dam, which had been under consideration since 1924, was extremely high: approximately $1 billion, with at least one-third in hard currency.

The decision to carry out this enterprise had been one of the first that Nasser made when he came to power. Not having sufficient capital, Nasser turned to the International Bank for Reconstruction and Development—better known as the World Bank. After going through various ups and downs in the negotiations, on September 26, 1955, he applied for a loan of $240 million.

According to its regulations, loans from the World Bank are dependent on strict controls as to their use, and on firm guarantees of repayment from the borrower state. But, due to its meager resources, the arms purchase represented a considerable burden on the Cairo Government, and, as the construction of the dam was to result in the flooding of part of the Sudan, it was indispensable to obtain the prior consent of the Khartoum Government, which naturally intended to take advantage of the situation by imposing its own conditions. Finally, the Bank required that the borrowing country's loan transactions with any third party be subject to its preliminary approval.

Nasser, unfamiliar with problems of high finance and of international law, saw in the Bank's demands an infringement of the sovereignty of his country—a subject on which he, as the hero of national independence, could only be intransigent. It was then that the

U.S.S.R. stated its willingness to grant Egypt a loan of $200 million to be repaid over thirty years in cotton and rice, and at an interest rate of only 2 percent. Coming after the arms purchase from Prague, this move greatly disturbed Dulles. "Egypt was far from becoming a tool of the Soviets," he told the leaders of the two great parties, "but it could drift that way if we did nothing to prevent it." [3] To that end he persuaded Eden to join the United States in offering to the Cairo Government—as required by the World Bank as a condition for granting the requested loan—a gift of $70 million, of which $54 million would be provided by America, intended to cover the first stage of construction.

The proposal was not received by Arab public opinion with the enthusiasm Washington expected. The press denounced at length the insulting character of the conditions stipulated by the Bank, and Nasser took his time to give an answer—obviously waiting for a definite offer from Moscow.

"To break out of the ring," [4] as Eden writes in his memoirs, he had, on November 9, proposed a realignment of Arab-Israeli frontiers, following which the United States, Great Britain and eventually other powers would give their territorial guarantee to all the states of the region. But that proposal had been rejected by all parties concerned. It had been the same with an overture made by Antoine Pinay, at the time Foreign Minister, who, very reasonably, tried to get the U.S.S.R. to join in the tripartite declaration of 1950 on the maintenance of the balance of power in the Middle East and to proclaim a general embargo on the delivery of arms to that part of the world. Soon, in retaliation for the increasing wave of terrorist attacks on its territory, Israel launched heavy reprisal raids against the neighboring states.

The British Prime Minister was quite humiliated by the failure of his plan for a Palestinian settlement and was tempted to impute to the U.S.S.R. the principal responsibility for it. He also suspected the U.S.S.R. of encouraging the agitation which was developing in Cyprus, as well as the repeated incidents between the British garrisons on the Persian Gulf and the South Arabian troops. More than ever, Eden put his hopes in the Baghdad Pact and entrusted General Templer, Chief of the Imperial General Staff, to go to Amman at the beginning of December to convince the King of Jordan to join it.

Radio Cairo, and the Palestinian portion of Jordan's population, almost unanimously in favor of Nasser's policies, violently opposed that move. On December 13, Jordan's Government had to resign. It was the beginning of an uninterrupted series of ministerial crises interspersed with violent demonstrations against the pact.

On January 9 the situation became so tense that Great Britain's ambassador cabled London asking that two brigades be sent there, while the King spoke of appealing to his cousin in Baghdad for troops. Nuri es-Said replied that such an intervention could succeed only if it was "in sufficient quantities to make success certain." In his judgment the roots of the evil were in Egypt, and Americans would be well advised "to bring the sternest possible pressure on Egypt to cease her activities in Jordan." To that end he suggested that Nasser be notified that the Allies "would no longer consider the protection afforded by the Tripartite Declaration as applying to Egypt." [5]

Eden dispatched reinforcements to Jordan and Cyprus and sent a personal message to Nasser to ask him—naturally in vain—to moderate the attacks of his radio against the Amman regime. In any case, the Egyptian President was less disposed than ever to listen to a Prime Minister who had, according to him, promised him the preceding year that he would not seek to include Jordan in the Baghdad Pact.

Sir Anthony then took the boat to Washington, to attempt to win over Eisenhower, slowly recuperating from his heart attack, to the forceful policy that he advocated. He found his partner quite reserved, and in any case, unwilling to support the London Government in its quarrel with Saudi Arabia, in which he detected too many "colonialist" interests.

Finally, it was decided to evaluate Egypt's intentions in the light of Nasser's forthcoming talks with the president of the World Bank and to proceed with a general review of the situation with the French Government, which, in a memorandum dated January 17, 1956, had expressed surprise at not having been invited to take part in the Washington talks.

That memorandum had been prepared by the Quai d'Orsay at a time when—because of the January 2 elections—the Faure-Pinay cabinet was on the verge of changing hands, but there was nevertheless no disagreement between the major parties on France's policy in the Near East. In a general way, Paris admitted that the danger of Soviet economic penetration was much greater than that of a military penetration. The Baghdad Pact was not considered an effective parry to that danger, and it was thought that the West should also employ essentially economic means.

Guy Mollet, who became Prime Minister on January 29, believed even more strongly in the wisdom of that analysis, which reflected the opinion of most of the diplomats stationed in the Middle East, because he had been brought to power by voters tired of the war in Algeria, and also because he was getting ready to start secret negotiations with the National Liberation Front (N.L.F.), whose good relations with Cairo he did not ignore. Meanwhile, because Nasser on February 9 had concluded an agreement in principle with Eugene Black, president of the World Bank, whereby Egypt would be granted a loan of $200 million at 3½ percent interest to be repaid in twenty years, a brief wave of optimism appeared on the horizon of Middle Eastern affairs. The British Foreign Minister, Selwyn Lloyd, decided to take advantage of it by going there. It would have been better had he stayed home.

He was dining with Nasser when a message was brought to him announcing that Glubb Pasha, the British Commander in Chief of the Arab Legion, had been ousted by King Hussein. The colonel believed that the decision had been taken in London and saw it as a good turn for which he thanked his guest. In reality, the young sovereign had made that concession to popular outrage without consulting the British, and Selwyn Lloyd interpreted Nasser's felicitations as an insult. Under those conditions the conversations could only be fruitless, and when the Foreign Secretary was asked his impressions of the Egyptian dictator on his return to London he had only one word: "Mussolini!" [6] The proposal, made to Jordan a few days later by Egypt, Syria and Saudi Arabia, that they replace Great Britain by supplying it with an annual grant of $60 million, obviously did not improve conditions. In the future, Lloyd would join Eden as a determined advocate of a hard line with Cairo. The French leaders would shortly come around to their point of view.

Christian Pineau, the new French socialist Foreign Minister, had also believed that it was possible to alter the course of events. On March 2, before the Anglo-American press in Paris, he asserted that he "profoundly disagreed with the policy followed by the Western countries during the last years. We have made an enormous error," he continued, "in determining that the problems of security were the only international problems with which we had to concern ourselves . . . the policy of war has been excluded from consideration . . . now it is time to follow a policy of peace in order to bring about the triumph of our common ideals of justice, equality and liberty. . . ." [7]

This said, the minister, who, a few hours before, had announced that he and Guy Mollet would go to Moscow in the spring, flew off to Karachi, where the Council of the Manila Pact was meeting. On that occasion he reasserted to Dulles the position he had taken in his speech, and then went on to see Nehru, who, impressed by the somewhat "neutralist" tone of his statements, gave him a warm welcome. While France, Pineau declared, was seeking a peaceful solution in Algeria, it could not tolerate Egypt's support for a revolutionary action there. Therefore, the Indian Prime Minister suggested that he visit Nasser in Cairo on his way back. Pineau agreed at once.

Before Pineau's arrival, the colonel had conferred with King Saud and the President of the Syrian republic, both of whom also met with the French minister. The three published a statement asking Paris to recognize the legitimate rights of the peoples of North Africa. Pineau had no lack of arguments to counter with, as Morocco's independence had been recognized March 2 and Tunisia's would be on the 20th. And two envoys from Guy Mollet were getting ready to meet secretly, in Cairo as well, with one of the leaders of the N.L.F., Mohammed Khider.

Pineau could therefore reaffirm his government's liberal intentions, while carefully stating that while France was ready to "give the Moslems a superior status" to the one they had, as well as "rights in Algerian political life," his "firm resolve" was not to abandon

Algeria. But, according to the statement he made on March 15, on his return to Paris, "Colonel Nasser seemed to understand the difference between Algeria, which has never been anything else but a part of the French state, and Morocco and Tunisia, which were, after all, sovereign states. I believe him quite eager," the minister added, "to seek with us a peaceful solution to the problem." [8] The next day, one of Cairo's most important newspapers published a very favorable article about France.

A few months later, Pineau related his talks with Nasser to the National Assembly. According to his account, Nasser told him that he was in favor of peaceful relations with Israel, but that, unfortunately, he could not "acknowledge this publicly, because it would considerably embarrass him in the eyes of the Arab countries." He also revealed a marked "anticommunism and anti-Sovietism." [9]

In the version of that interview which he himself gave to the B.B.C., Nasser did not, naturally, repeat those opinions; but, in all other respects, the two versions agree: "I told him [Pineau]: 'It is our responsibility to help our Arab brothers everywhere. . . . There are no Egyptians fighting with the Algerians; the Algerians are fighting alone. . . .' There were no Algerians at that time in our country for training as soldiers." [10]

In any case, the French minister felt justified in counseling against the use of threats in dealing with Cairo, and in advocating the summoning of an international conference on the Middle East. However, on March 29 any illusions some people might have entertained on Cairo's disinterestedness toward the Algerian revolution were dispelled when the Council of the Arab League adopted a resolution asserting that the member states "will provide assistance to the weak and unarmed Algerian people by all the means at their disposal in order to fight a cruel war being waged against them without any justification whatsoever." [11]

At this, Paris let loose an attack against the ambitions of Nasser —whose word of honor Pineau had invoked. Besides, Mollet was strongly encouraged to act by Eden, with whom he had spent a weekend at Chequers, on March 11 and 12. He found him a man exhausted by the attacks made against him by the right wing of the Conservative Party, which held him responsible for the abandonment of Egypt, and he had decided to accept the challenge of those who dared him to prove that "he had a real mustache." [12] The Prime Minister, obsessed by the precedent of Munich, kept saying that it was imperative to take action at the right time. But he saw perils increasing on every side. Glubb's dismissal had been followed by an offer of assistance from the U.S.S.R. to Jordan. Khrushchev and Bulganin, during a visit to India, had unleashed violent tirades against imperialism—which Eden would sharply reproach them with when, the following month, they went to London. He did not hesitate to tell them that if need be, Britain would fight to assure the freedom of its oil supplies. The Greek Cypriot nationalists had started guerrilla warfare against the British occupying forces, to the point where London had decided to arrest and to deport their undisputed leader, Archbishop Makarios, to the Seychelles Islands.

Mollet, in turn, explained to the Prime Minister his desire to find an honorable solution in Algeria so that the rebels would not be able to boast of having "booted us out." He voiced his concern on the subject of Israel and implied, as he had already written to Ben-Gurion, that France would not desert it. To his surprise, Eden, until then fairly hostile to Zionism, stated that he agreed with him completely: ". . . for the first time in twenty years there was little difference in the attitudes of their respective countries toward the Middle East. Eden's only reservation was to ask Mollet not to undertake any major action in North Africa or the Middle East without first attempting to persuade 'our American allies to bring their policies into line with ours. . . .' " [13] That last sentence is revealing. All along, during the crisis that was soon to erupt, Eden believed he could depend on Washington's understanding. But Ike and Dulles did not want, under any circumstances, a war in which they would appear to be allies of "European colonialism."

Having apparently understood—in this month of March 1956 —the disadvantages of the Baghdad Pact, Ike and Dulles tried to persuade the U.S.S.R. to join them in a general pacification of the region. They obtained initial success in having the Security Council entrust the U.N. Secretary General, Dag Hammarskjöld, with a mission of conciliation. That initiative succeeded, in effect, in reintroducing the Soviet Union into the discussion of the problems of that region, whereas the famous tripartite declaration of 1950 had specifically aimed at keeping them out of it. France, which for months had been advocating an overture toward Moscow, heartily applauded. London may have been vexed, but could not say no. And the U.S.S.R., on April 17, announced that it would give its support to measures taken by the U.N. to strengthen peace in Palestine.

The next day saw a new victory. Thanks to pressure from Dag Hammarskjöld, Egypt and Israel concluded a cease-fire; another was concluded between the Jewish state and Syria. On their trip to Moscow, Mollet and Pineau signed a communiqué on May 16 with the Soviet leaders in which they reaffirmed their support of the United Nations and their desire to "ensure a peaceful settlement of problems in dispute between the Arab states and Israel on a basis acceptable to the interested parties." [14]

Nevertheless, when the Security Council on June 2 unanimously adopted Hammarskjöld's recommendations, the Soviet delegate opposed a British amendment which used, almost word for word, the phrases which had appeared in the communiqué issued by Bulganin and Khrushchev on April 25, following their official visit to London.

How can this reversal be explained? Perhaps the U.S.S.R. was already apprehensive of being outflanked on its left. As a matter of fact, on May 16, Egypt had recognized Red China and announced that it was sending to Peking a military mission headed by Marshal Amer, head of the army and number-two man of the regime. On the 27th, Nasser's spokesman had announced that his government could obtain from Communist China "all the arms they needed . . . even if the United Nations imposed an embargo on weapons to the Middle East." [15] At the time, this seemed to be proof of Moscow's double game, as it was not yet suspected that Peking could act independently. In the light of what has happened since, it was more probable that it constituted one of the first public manifestations of the conflict which was to bring the two great Communist countries to the brink of a complete break a few years later. China was deliberately adding fuel to the flames at a moment when the U.S.S.R., reluctant to be implicated in a major conflict, was seeking to have prevail those peaceful solutions which implied a minimum of connivance with "imperialism." If, in effect, the Soviet Government sometimes felt itself obliged to loudly and publicly support the cause of Arab nationalism, it knew how to quietly deflect its warlike impulses. This was soon to become apparent.

On June 8, Dimitri Shepilov became Foreign Minister of the U.S.S.R., replacing the old-timer Molotov, who had been sacrificed to the reconciliation with Tito and to destalinization. A year before, Shepilov had negotiated the arms agreement with Egypt. As soon as he took office he went to Cairo to attend the celebration organized on the occasion of the departure of the last British soldier. This seemed proof of the reorientation of Russian policy. But far from encouraging Nasser's intransigence. Shepilov stated before a group of fellahin: "The Soviet Union does not intend to encourage the hostility of Arab peoples against any of the Western Powers. . . . We will do everything possible to bring about an international détente in this part of the world." [16] According to the colonel himself, Shepilov told him, "The U.S.S.R. does not want to come between the West and Egypt." [17] He only spoke of unconditional long-term loans. In any case, on July 1, Khrushchev, speaking with a special correspondent of the Cairo newspaper *Al Ahram,* declared that a war between Israel and the Arabs would "trigger a third world war." He even invited the Arabs "to work toward securing peace for the Middle East . . . after having been victorious in the first encounter by having the whole world recognize their wisdom."

The day following Shepilov's visit, Nasser received the president of the World Bank and told him that he was ready to negotiate on the basis of the same conditions previously formulated by the Bank. Nevertheless, a rumor that the Soviet minister had proposed to the colonel that his country completely finance the Aswan project was started and spread widely by Cairo correspondents of the international press.

Dulles was probably influenced by that "news" when he told the Egyptian ambassador, Ahmed Hussein, that "the Western Powers had long interpreted Egyptian silence and their unacceptable counterproposals as a lack of interest in our offer and considered it withdrawn." [18] The diplomat did his best to correct this impression and left for Cairo to try to convince the colonel of the gravity of the situation. As the American fiscal year ended on July 1, aid credits not utilized before that date had to be returned to the Treasury, which necessitated a second Congressional vote in the event the United States wanted to use them again. But the new foreign aid bill stipulated that 80 percent of the loans granted had to be repaid, while the World Bank made the American and British grants the condition for extending its own loan. It estimated that without them the Egyptian Government, already in debt beyond reasonable limits, could not live up to its obligations.

To add further to the difficulties, the Senate Finance Committee, furious because after a bitter debate, Dulles had just won from it the renewal of loans to Tito, forbade the use of any funds to help in the construction of the Aswan Dam without the Senate's special authorization. The Secretary of State tried to remove that restriction, but in vain. American political circles, already strongly influenced by the Israeli "lobby," had been greatly annoyed by Cairo's flirtation with Moscow and its recognition of Red China. Eden, for his part, unceasingly warned Eisenhower against the machinations of the colonel, and Pineau, who in June had made a trip to Washington, boasted on his return of having "enlightened Mr. Dulles about Nasser." [19] In the meantime, Nasser had become convinced that the United States "did not have the least intention of aiding in the development" of Egypt. [20] However, he let his ambassador to Washington convince him to accept the American conditions, while saying that he was "ready to wager a hundred to one that they would never give him one cent." [21]

On July 17, alighting from his plane in Washington, Ahmed Hussein told the press that he had instructions to accept the Anglo-American offer. But Dulles made him wait forty-eight hours before receiving him. As soon as the diplomat was ushered into his office, Dulles delivered a violent indictment of Cairo's policies, and handed him a note stating that it was no longer possible for the United States to take part in the construction of the dam, as "the ability of Egypt to devote adequate resources to assure the project's success has become more uncertain than when the offer was made." [22] On arriving home, the ambassador learned that the State Department had already released that text to the press. The insult was deliberate. The proposal to discuss "at the request of the riparian states . . . a more effective utilization of the water resources of the Nile," [23] seemed a semantic device—even, as Nasser quickly pointed out, an attempt to exploit differences between Egypt and the Sudan.

In London, although he had only been "informed and not consulted," Eden gloated. The Foreign Office published a similar communiqué, which he only handed to the Egyptian ambassador three hours later. The president of the World Bank, "particularly distressed," [24] according to Robert Murphy—at that time Dulles' closest associate—made it known that the offer of the loan no longer held, now that the United States and Great Britain had withdrawn their offer to make the payments which were its prerequisite.

At the time, Dulles could believe that his gamble, based on the conviction that Moscow was incapable of financing the dam, had succeeded. On July 22, to be sure, Shepilov stated that the question of the dam was not urgent, since there were many other issues no less vital for the Egyptian economy—particularly those concerned with industrialization. As for Nasser, on the 24th he made a violent attack against the United States, asserting that he "would not allow the dollar to rule Egypt," but he did not announce any measures of reprisal.

In reality, he had made his decision the day before—after having carefully weighed it, first alone, pen in hand, and then with members of his military staff. He was going to proceed with the immediate nationalization of the Suez Canal, executing a plan he had begun to formulate in the spring, when he became convinced that Washington would not help with Aswan, and whose modalities he had asked a trusted confidant, Mahmoud Younes, to study secretly. He believed that the French were too occupied in Algeria to intervene, and he did not think that the British would resort to force because, "by allying themselves with the Israelis for such an enterprise, they would compromise all their interests in the Middle East." In any event, according to his appraisal of the British military position, it would take London two months to prepare an expedition, "which would allow the time necessary to reach a diplomatic agreement." [25]

He waited to announce the nationalization until the anniversary of the revolution—July 26. On that day he spoke from the balcony of the Alexandria Stock Exchange to a crowd massed in Liberation

Square—a vast rectangle planted with peaceful palm trees and seldom a witness to such harangues. After having simply and colorfully outlined an indictment of "imperialism," he became more and more incensed, shouting above the truly hysterical clamor of the crowd: "The Suez Canal . . . has become a state within the State . . . an Egyptian company from which England has stolen 44 percent of its shares. . . . The earnings of the company for 1955 have reached $100 million, and we who gave 120,000 dead [sic] during the construction of the canal, will only have $3 million. . . . Do you know the amount of aid which America and Great Britain want to allot us in five years? $70 million. . . . We will never let the past repeat itself. On the contrary, we will destroy the past by regaining our rights to the Suez Canal. . . . We will succeed in building the High Dam and we will enjoy again our plundered rights." [26] And then he read the law his government had just approved which called for the immediate nationalization of the Canal Company.

At that very moment a "Canal Authority" took possession of the company's installations and ordered the personnel to continue its operation under police protection. Nasser's return to Cairo assumed the dimensions of an apotheosis.

The news burst like a thunderbolt on Paris as well as London and provoked the most intemperate statements. In the emotional climate of the time, their author's sincerity could not, in a general way, be questioned. But the colonel's initiative gave the British and French leaders the opportunity they had dreamed of to send an ultimatum to Egypt, the acceptance of which would deliver a fatal blow to the dictator's prestige, and the refusal of which would justify armed intervention, which at that time was thought to amount to little more than a parade drill.

Forgetting the exorbitant—in relation to Egyptian poverty— profits which the company made from the canal, forgetting that Nasser had promised to indemnify the stockholders and that, in any case, the concession was due to expire twelve years later, Eden chose only to remember the "theft," [27] and the French Government a "gross violation of agreements." [28] The large number of stockholders and the generous dividends which the company paid were enough to provide that language with a widespread echo.

Added to this were, in France, the increasing anxiety created by the war in Algeria—which a large body of public opinion naively attributed in great part to Cairo's propaganda—and, in both England and France, the conviction that they were dealing with an "apprentice dictator." Guy Mollet did not hesitate, despite warnings from Pineau, to compare the very elementary *Philosophy of Revolution* to *Mein Kampf,* showing that he had failed to read at least one of those works.

Eden learned of the seizure of the canal while he was attending a dinner in honor of the King of Iraq at Buckingham Palace. "It is necessary to strike and to strike hard," [29] Nuri es-Said told him immediately. Churchill's successor summoned his principal civil and military advisers in the middle of the night, as well as the French ambassador, the United States chargé d'affaires, and the director general of the Suez Canal Company, Jacques Georges-Picot, who was passing through London. Most of the people present were convinced of the necessity of a recourse to force, and the Prime Minister advised Eisenhower of the consensus, suggesting in addition that talks begin without delay between the United States, France and Great Britain.

But the American public, which included few Suez stockholders, hardly felt the same indignation as the French or British public over the nationalization of the canal. American traffic through the canal was much less than British traffic. Furthermore, the Presidential election was only four months away, and it was never advisable for a Presidential candidate seeking re-election to show himself to be warlike.

Because Dulles was then in Lima, Ike asked Murphy to go to London to meet with Eden, Selwyn Lloyd and Christian Pineau on Sunday, July 29. The day before, Admiral Nomy, Chief of the French Navy, had gone secretly to meet the British leaders and to tell them that Paris had decided to intervene militarily, even if Britain stood aside.

The number-two man in the State Department dined with Macmillan, then the Chancellor of the Exchequer, and with Field Marshal Earl Alexander. "If Britain did not accept Egypt's challenge," said Macmillan, "Britain would become another Netherlands . . . Nasser has to be chased out of Egypt." [30] And Eden told

Murphy the next day that "there was no thought of asking the United States for anything, 'but we do hope you take care of the Bear.' " [31] Conscious of the danger that Nasser might solicit help from the U.S.S.R., they believed the United States would neutralize any attempt at intervention on Russia's part. But Washington had never given the British any real assurance in that respect. On the contrary, America's behavior in the past should have convinced them that nothing could be expected from it which seemed to support, in any way whatsoever, a "colonialist" policy.

After having listened to Eden and especially Pineau, with whom he had a violent argument, Murphy, convinced of the strength of the Anglo-French determination, alerted Eisenhower. Eisenhower dispatched Dulles to London, with the mission of making the Allies understand that any military operation such as the one they were contemplating would show "the injustice of insisting on these principles in the case of smaller countries if we were willing to wink at violations by greater powers." [32] To gain time, and to at least obtain the postponement of the expedition the French and the British were talking of launching shortly, Dulles proposed to convene all the users of the canal in a vast international conference to examine the situation.

On his first meeting with his British and French colleagues, the Secretary of State, who had devoted a great deal of his life to international law, insisted on the necessity of acting only on an indisputably legal basis. Rather than tackle the issue of nationalization proper, which related to Egyptian sovereignty, he suggested that the discussions deal with the problem of free passage through the canal. This had been guaranteed by the Convention of Constantinople in 1888, and violated by the Cairo Government even before the company's nationalization, when, in defiance of a Security Council vote, it had refused to let ships chartered by the Israeli Government go through. The Secretary of State was afraid that any other approach might be extended to the Panama Canal, leased in perpetuity to the United States, and which the Americans did not for a moment consider abandoning. He advised against having recourse to the Security Council, where the U.S.S.R. had unlimited opportunities for obstruction. He added that, lacking a satisfactory juridical basis for the conference's resolutions, it would be impossible to obtain the indispensable approval from Congress in the event military measures became inevitable.

Ever since the days of the Geneva Conference on Indochina, Eden and Dulles had gotten along like cat and dog. In 1954 the Englishman advocated conciliation, and the American firmness. This time, the situation was exactly reversed, and communication was therefore difficult. The former Prime Minister maintained in his memoirs—which, on the subject of the Suez affair, are too much like a *pro domo* plea and contain too many omissions to be entirely accepted —that he saw an "encouraging" sign in the fact that the United States "did not exclude the use of force if all other methods failed." [33] He asserted that Dulles said, during the course of a meeting, that Nasser had to be made to "disgorge," [34] a statement Murphy did not deny. But it seems difficult to draw from that brutal remark, and from a few others the conclusion that the Secretary of State was encouraging the warlike plans of Paris and London. Perhaps he feared to push his partners too far if he advocated too openly a position diametrically opposed to their own views. Even if he stated the United States "did not exclude the use of force," it was only "if all other means failed," and after having said that it should be able "to create a world opinion so adverse to Nasser that he would be isolated," [35] in the rather naive hope that he could thus be brought into line.

Dulles sought—and succeeded in convincing his partners of the need for—a long delay before the meeting of the international conference. They had wanted it to take place immediately; finally they agreed on the date of August 16.

On returning to Washington, Dulles did not attempt to hide his anxiety from the Australian Prime Minister, Sir Robert Menzies, who had just arrived from Ottawa, or from the Canadian ambassador. Bob Murphy even visited the latter to tell him: "Perhaps you people in Canada can do something to urge caution on them [the British]." [36] The advice was duly heeded. Throughout the crisis, the chief Canadian diplomat, the future Prime Minister Lester Pearson, interceded untiringly in an attempt to have compromise solutions prevail, and he also played a leading role in stationing the famous "blue helmets" of the U.N. in Egypt.

Before leaving London, Dulles had signed with Pineau and

Lloyd, on August 2, a tripartite declaration stating that the national-ization decree "menaced the freedom and security of the canal," and that the means employed to put it into effect would constitute "a violation of the fundamental rights of man." This document assigned to the London conference the following goal: "To establish under an international control a method of operation designed to permanently ensure the functioning of the canal . . . taking into account the legiti-mate Egyptian interests." [73] This evidently reopened the issue of nationalization.

The French and British immediately tried to outdo each other in showing firmness. Listen to Christian Pineau, August 3, in the Na-tional Assembly: "Either Colonel Nasser will yield and will revoke all the measures he has taken—thus admitting his error—or he will not yield. In that event, in our judgment, all measures ought to be taken to oblige him to submit." [38] And to Eden, August 8, on the B.B.C.: "With dictators one is always forced to pay a higher price as time goes on . . . the appetite grows on what it feeds on. . . . We run too great a risk in not taking precautions. We have taken them. . . . We cannot permit an act of plunder to be allowed to succeed." [39]

From that moment on, military talks were actively pursued by the two countries. Following Libya's refusal to allow the use of its terri-tory, where one British division still remained, to launch an operation against Egypt, an amphibious landing had to be planned. Consider-ing the few military resources available, this required a delay of sev-eral weeks—something Nasser had well appreciated. This delay—categorically demanded by the British Chiefs of Staff—made it easier for Mollet to accept the principle of the conference proposed by Dulles. In response to the criticism of those who, like Michel Debré, spoke of "criminal impotence," [40] he stated that the conference would not represent "the suffocation, the miring of the French will." [41]

The conference, however, could not go very far. Nasser refused to participate and rejected as "a clear intervention in the internal af-fairs of Egypt" [42] any idea of creating an international authority for the canal. As for the Soviet Union, it agreed to be represented in Lon-don by Shepilov and, according to Eden, during an exchange of diplomatic views it recognized the existence of British special inter-ests in the Middle East. Nonetheless, the U.S.S.R., in a declaration of

August 9, underscored the legitimacy of nationalization and denounced as "totally unacceptable" and constituting a "menace to peace" the measures taken by the British and French governments.[43] At the same time it indicated that it would not join in any solution which would not be acceptable to Egypt.

Dulles submitted a plan to the conference designed to ensure "the permanent functioning of the canal by means of an international system which would keep it open to all those who, in the course of events, wanted to use it"—namely, "to provide the canal with a non-political administration in order to assure its functioning." [44] A resolution to that effect was adopted by eighteen of the twenty-two participants in the conference, and a delegation headed by Prime Minister Menzies was sent to Nasser to try to persuade him to accept it.

Negotiations opened on September 3. On the 9th, Nasser delivered the text of his reply, according to which the resolution of the Eighteen had no other aim than to "remove the Suez Canal from Egyptian hands and put it back into other hands," and that it was "difficult to imagine anything more provocative for the Egyptian people." [45]

To Menzies, the man most responsible for Nasser's refusal was Eisenhower. The head of the Australian Government had had the impression that Nasser had taken Eisenhower's warning seriously. Hadn't he told him on the 5th: "Frankness as between two heads of Government requires me to offer my personal opinion that you are not facing a bluff but a stark condition of fact which your country should not ignore."? [46] To which the colonel had answered that he had fully understood it. But a few hours later, during a press conference, Ike was to state, "We are determined to exhaust every feasible method of peaceful settlement," going so far as to say that the position of the United States, although favoring the proposals of the Eighteen, "is not to give up, even if we do run into obstacles." [47] And certainly it was not the American ambassador to Cairo, a staunch supporter of Nasser, who would have spoken to him any differently. Under those conditions, it would have been a miracle if Nasser had yielded anything.

The failure of the Menzies mission was not too painful to the British and French leaders. The Egyptian dictator's refusal came at a time when preparations for the landing were almost completed, to the point where the date of September 15 had been tentatively chosen as D-day. To give a judicial justification to the intervention, it had been decided to present the Security Council with a draft resolution quoting the text of the Eighteen. It was thought that a clear majority of members would favor it, but that it would be blocked by a Soviet veto. Citing the impotence of the U.N., Paris and London would then publish a declaration announcing their intention to assure the canal's freedom of navigation by their own means.

But Ike was following the troop movements of the two countries with increasing anxiety: Frenchmen were arriving daily in Cyprus. On September 3 he had sent Eden, who chose to see in it a reversal of policy, a message warning him against a recourse to force which, he said, could not have the support of American public opinion.

The Prime Minister still hoped to influence the President. He answered him on the 6th: ". . . I can assure you that we are conscious of the burdens and perils attending military intervention. But if our assessment is correct, and if the only alternative is to allow Nasser's plans quietly to develop until this country and all Western Europe are held to ransom by Egypt acting at Russia's behest, it seems to us that our duty is plain. We have many times led Europe in the fight for freedom. It would be an ignoble end to our long history if we accepted to perish by degrees." [48]

But in vain. On the 7th, the day the failure of the Menzies mission was learned, Dulles summoned the ambassador of Great Britain to tell him that Washington would support neither the draft resolution nor the appeal to the Security Council. The next day, Selwyn Lloyd stated to his American interlocutors that "Our two countries . . . seemed farther apart in their thinking than at any time since the crisis began." [49]

On the 10th, Mollet and Pineau arrived in London, eager to take action. Eden was almost ready to give final approval for the landing to take place on September 15. But Washington was watchful and urged the Prime Minister to consider an idea that Dulles had had a few days previously, while duck hunting on the banks of Lake Ontario. The Secretary of State had already proposed his plan to the British ambassador: Let's form an association of users of the canal, he had said in effect. It would ensure pilot service and it would collect the tolls, which would prevent Nasser from enjoying the benefits of nationalization. "Prepared to lean over backwards," as he had written in his memoirs, to have the "means of working with the United States," [50] Eden intended to take advantage of Nasser's probable refusal to deal with the users' association. In that event, he told the Commons on September 12, Nasser would violate once again the Treaty of Constantinople and "Her Majesty's Government and other governments will be free to take such measures as will seem necessary to assert their rights." [51]

It is with such arguments that he had succeeded in convincing Mollet, the day before, to postpone the landing planned for the 15th, and to lend his support to the users' association project. The President of the French Council had been hard to convince. His military advisers were unanimous in criticizing the decision, taken in August, to place the expeditionary corps commanded by General Beaufre, under the command of the English General Keightley, with Admiral Barjot as his adjutant. They also considered appalling a plan which had been imposed on them by Eden. It consisted of a minimum of ten days of "aeropsychological" warfare,[52] during which an attempt would be made to convince the Egyptians to end all resistance by limited bombing of military objectives, the dropping of leaflets, and radio broadcasts. The same thinking resulted in the decision not to land in Alexandria, but in Port Said, to show that the operation was aimed only at ensuring freedom of passage in the canal.

Mollet agreed to this only when a suggestion from which he expected great things was accepted: the recall of the company's pilots. They had requested repatriation the day following nationalization and had been asked to remain temporarily on the job. Without them it was thought impossible for Egypt to operate the canal, and this would offer a splendid pretext for intervention. And since Nasser was supposed to be, according to Pineau, a man who was "neither master of his actions nor of his nerves," [53] it was hoped that when the pilots were recalled, he would make some stupid move which would damage him in the eyes of the world.

But if the colonel, in July, had freely expressed his feelings of wounded self-esteem, he had since then, perhaps under the influence of his excellent Yugoslav, Russian and Indian advisers, given repeated proof of self-control. He had declared that he was ready to negotiate on revisions of the Treaty of Constantinople and to discuss with the users of the canal all points relating to freedom and security of navigation, the development of the canal, and tolls. He had halted guerrilla attacks against Israel and postponed the trials of the British agents arrested in Cairo. He let British and French ships through the canal although they had, since nationalization, paid their tolls into a blocked account, from which the Egyptian authorities could not obtain a red cent. Curiously enough, the Western Powers who had, nevertheless, achieved a not inconsiderable victory through this device, took care not to exploit it.

In any case, the departure of the pilots on September 15 took place without interference. Nasser, who had anticipated their recall, had hired technicians to take their places, and traffic moved through the canal as before. In a single stroke, the users' association, which one thought would have had a monopoly on pilots, lost one of its reasons for being. It was imperative to find another pretext to achieve the aim which Guy Mollet summarized at the time to Halvard Lange, the Norwegian Foreign Minister and a fellow socialist: ". . . more important, we think it desirable that a defeat should be inflicted upon Nasser which will result in his disappearance so that other Arab States will have a chance of withdrawing from Egyptian hegemony." [54]

But John Foster Dulles had taken it upon himself, during a press conference, to define his concept of the canal users' association in a way which amounted to a complete disavowal of the belligerent proposals Eden had made to the Commons on the 22nd: "If we are opposed by force," Dulles said, "and we cannot pass through without shooting, we have no intention of shooting. We then plan to send our ships around the Cape." Questioned about what he thought of the declarations of the Prime Minister, he continued: "I think that each nation has to decide for itself what action it will have to take . . . I do not get the impression that there was any undertaking or pledge given by him [Eden] . . . to shoot their way through. . . ." Later, the Prime Minister was to write that these words were "an advertisement to Nasser that he could reject the project with impunity." [55] He reiterated in the Commons, nevertheless, that he could not, for his part, pledge himself not to have recourse to force, and he obtained a majority of 70 votes. On the 14th, invitations were sent out for a meeting of the users of the canal intended to create the association proposed by Dulles.

The debates at that conference confirmed, if there was any need to, that the proposed association would possess nothing of the war machine imagined by Eden. Several of the governments represented —the Scandinavian, the Italian, the Spanish, the Pakistani, and the Iranian—very clearly showed their interest in a peaceful solution. Dulles, who on his departure from Washington had spoken to the new French ambassador, Hervé Alphand, in unusually forceful language, was quickly taken in hand again by the advocates of conciliation. Soon everyone got into the act. Not satisfied with having sent a particularly urgent "personal" message to Eden, signed by Bulganin, the Kremlin submitted to the Security Council a note categorizing the constitution of the association as a "dangerous provocation." India threatened to withdraw from the Commonwealth. The British Defense Minister, Sir Walter Monckton, who was to resign a few days later, told Lester Pearson that he approved of Canada's sensible urgings upon us in London and elsewhere." [56] The result of all this was that when the association was created on September 21, it did not impose any obligations on its members.

In Paris, Parliament, from the radicals to the Gaullists, gave increasing indications of impatience, questioning the genuineness of their government's resolve, although it actually needed little encouragement to act. On the 22nd, Mollet affirmed that he was keeping his "freedom of action" and that he did not intend "to accept any negotiation on the principle of international control of the canal.[57] The day before, tired of waiting for London to decide to act, he had taken a major decision in the greatest secrecy. Two high national defense officials had gone to Jerusalem to inform the Government of Israel that France was ready to undertake joint action against Egypt. Mollet had no way of knowing that at the moment it would begin, a revolution, provoked by destalinization, would erupt in Budapest and that together the two crises were to lead to one of the most dramatic renewals of a Cold War which, a few weeks before, one could have believed permanently quieted.

BIBLIOGRAPHY AND NOTES

[1] Jean and Simonne Lacouture, *op. cit.*, pp. 226–27.

[2] Michel Bar-Zohar, *Suez ultra-secret* (Paris: Fayard, 1964), p. 75.

[3] Adams, *op. cit.*, p. 248.

[4] Eden, *op. cit.*, p. 368.

[5] *Ibid.*, p. 386.

[6] Terence Robertson, *Crisis: The Inside Story of the Suez Conspiracy* (New York: Atheneum, 1965), p. 46.

[7] *Le Monde*, March 4, 1956.

[8] *Ibid.*, March 17, 1956.

[9] *Orient*, January 1957, p. 89.

[10] Anthony Moncrieff (ed.), *Suez: Ten Years After* (New York: Pantheon Books, 1967), p. 37.

[11] *Année politique*, 1956, p. 280.

[12] Remark of a Conservative Member of Parliament, reported by Hugh Thomas, "The Suez Report," *The Sunday Times* (London), September 4, 1966.

[13] Robertson, *op. cit.*, p. 70.

[14] *Année politique*, 1956, p. 304.

[15] *The New York Times*, May 28, 1956.

[16] *Le Monde*, June 20, 1956.

[17] Speech of July 20, 1956, reprinted in *Orient* (Paris), January 1957, p. 56.

[18] Dwight D. Eisenhower, *Waging Peace, 1956–1961* (New York: Doubleday, 1965), pp. 32–33.

[19] Jean and Simonne Lacouture, *op. cit.*, p. 469.

[20] Moncrieff, *op. cit.*, p. 37.

[21] Kenneth Love, interview with Nasser, in *Le Nouvel Observateur*, July 20, 1966.

[22] Keesing's, 14991 A.

[23] *Ibid.*

[24] Robert Murphy, *Diplomat Among Warriors* (New York: Doubleday, 1964), p. 377.

[25] Love, *op. cit.*

[26] *Orient*, January 1957, p. 56.

[27] Eden, *op. cit.*, p. 467.

[28] *Le Monde*, July 31, 1956.

[29] Henri Azeau, *Le piège de Suez* (Paris: Robert Laffont, 1964), p. 121.

[30] Murphy, *op. cit.*, p. 380.

[31] *Ibid.*, p. 381.

[32] *Ibid.*, p. 383.

[33] Eden, *op. cit.*, p. 487.

[34] *Ibid.*

[35] *Ibid.*

[36] Robertson, *op. cit.*, p. 82.

[37] *Orient*, January 1957, p. 81.

[38] *Ibid.*, p. 93.

[39] *Ibid.*, pp. 86–87.

[40] Azeau, *op. cit.*, p. 135.

[41] *Année politique*, 1956, p. 341.

[42] *Orient*, January 1957, p. 121.

[43] *Ibid.*, p. 103.

[44] *Ibid.*, p. 145.

[45] *Ibid.*, pp. 170–71.

[46] Murphy, *op. cit.*, p. 387.

[47] Eden, *op. cit.*, p. 524.

[48] *Ibid,.* p. 521.

[49] *Ibid.*, p. 531.

[50] *Ibid.*, p. 534.

[51] *Orient*, January 1957, p. 206.

[52] Interview with General Beaufre, *Paris-Match*, November 5, 1966.

[53] *Année politique*, 1956, p. 341.

[54] Robertson, *op. cit.*, pp. 120–21.

[55] Eden, *op. cit.*, p. 539.

[56] Robertson, *op. cit.*, p. 124.

[57] *Orient*, January 1957, p. 219.

· CHAPTER 9 ·

SPRING IN

OCTOBER

Night and day the portals of gloomy Dis stand wide:
but to recall thy step and issue to the upper air—
there is the toil and there the task!

—Virgil, *Aeneid*, VI, 126

FEW MEN COULD BOAST OF HAVING SO QUICKLY AND
so well foreseen the consequences of Stalin's death as Marshal Tito.
Three weeks after the disappearance of his principal enemy, on his
return from a trip to England, where he had been the official guest
of Queen Elizabeth and Churchill, Tito stated: "We were convinced
that as long as Stalin lived, he would not begin a new war that might
trigger a world conflict. . . . Will Malenkov and the others who are
now in power, younger and more headstrong, make thoughtless
moves? I don't think they will. I think . . . that they are trying to find
some solution to the impasse to which their international policy
brought them after the war. We, in Yugoslavia, would be happy if
one day they recognized that they had been wrong toward our country . . . we will wait and see. . . . I can say that I don't believe they
will end the Cold War very soon. It is likely that they will still continue it. . . . I believe that one day when the balance of armed
power is established . . . and it is almost established today . . . the men
in the East will understand that and will seek to get out of the impasse where they now find themselves." [1]

The new Soviet leaders evidently singled out from that speech
the cautious overture that was made to them. They did not delay in

answering it. In May, Molotov proposed to the Yugoslav chargé d'affaires the re-establishment of normal diplomatic relations and willingly recognized, during the talks that followed, that his country had been "unjustly treated" [2] in 1948. The tone of anti-Titoist propaganda softened, and agreements were concluded between Yugoslavia and its neighbors for the settlement of frontier incidents, navigation on the Danube and the liberation of Yugoslav prisoners —in return, however, for the thousands of "Cominformists" imprisoned in Belgrade . . .

However, that amelioration was limited to relations between states. It was part of the "peaceful initiative" of the U.S.S.R. that Khrushchev was to summarize in these words in his progress report to the Twentieth Congress of the Soviet Communist Party on February 14, 1956: "(1) Improve relations between the Great Powers; (2) put an end to the hotbeds of war in the East and prevent the birth of new hotbeds and of conflicts in Europe and in Asia; (3) normalize our relations with different states for the purpose of reducing tension in Europe (normalization of relations with the brother country of Yugoslavia, conclusion of a state treaty with Austria, establishment of diplomatic relations between the U.S.S.R. and the Federal Republic [and so forth]). . . ." [3] But that report did not mention the reason for the 1948 break: the relations between the various Communist parties. However, on July 4, 1953, an event occurred in Hungary which led Tito to believe that there, also, a change was to take place: the nomination to the head of the Hungarian Government of Imre Nagy—an old-time Bolshevik who, like Tito, had discovered communism while he was a prisoner in Russia, and who had been eliminated from ruling circles at the time of the 1948 purges for having voiced his opposition to the forced collectivization of agriculture.

Considering the part taken by Rakosi, the Hungarian dictator, in the campaign launched against Tito—according to some information Rakosi had even thought of going to war against Yugoslavia [4]—Tito could justifiably see there a first sacrifice made to the cause of reconciliation. In fact, Nagy felt toward Titoism a sympathy which he was henceforth to show constantly, and for more than a year before the Budapest uprising he was to advocate that Hungary "avoid becoming an active participant in any of the clashes between power groups" [5] and that it follow a policy of "neutrality or active coexistence," taking advantage of its "geographic location" between "neutral Austria, and countries building socialism, among them the Soviet Union and neighboring Yugoslavia, which stands on the principle of active coexistence." [6]

In any case, Tito in an interview on July 4 thought that he could interpret Imre Nagy's nomination as proof that the Soviet leaders had understood that they had to "take another road." He asserted that he saw there a "change in tactical policy, if not in actual aims." [7]

In reality, it was not a question either of a change or of new tactics. Hungary was in a disastrous economic condition, and the Kremlin's leaders feared that the agitation which had been apparent at the time of the East Berlin uprising (June 17, 1953) in the Csepel factories might rapidly degenerate into a serious situation.

Responsibility for the situation fell mostly on the U.S.S.R., but also on Rakosi and on the three leaders who made up with him the "quadriga." A long-standing militant, Rakosi—having lived four years in Moscow in the shadow of Stalin—had such admiration for his methods that he tried to copy them down to the smallest details.

Rakosi, like Stalin, was driven by egomania and a persecution mania, and he served them both with the same cruelty as his master. Because Stalin had made of his famous subway one of Moscow's greatest showplaces, he stubbornly had one built in Budapest, although every engineer had explained to him that the soil in the city was too friable and therefore boring would be extremely difficult. The result was the useless investment of millions. Because rapid industrialization was the leitmotif of Stalin's teaching, Rakosi had no peace until his country's rate of industrialization was higher than the rate of all other people's democracies. Because Stalin took pride in the complete collectivization of agriculture in the U.S.S.R., he wanted 100 percent collectivization in Hungary. The result was that industrial production doubled in four years, which, at first, might seem wonderful, but it didn't help the population in any way because the proportion of articles assigned to domestic consumption was no more than a third, and because articles intended for export cost so much to produce that they had to be sold with heavy subsidies. As to the yield of collective farms, it decreased steadily, to the point that in 1953 one-tenth of the land lay fallow.

Obviously, the situation could not fail to alarm the new Soviet leaders, once the shadow that crushed them had disappeared and they were free to examine the situations that prevailed in the diverse provinces of their empire with the eyes of reason. In May 1953, Malenkov summoned Rakosi to Moscow. He suggested that in order to align Hungary with the new Soviet model, the functions of the First Secretary of the party be separated from those of the Prime Minister, which post he had occupied since August 1952. Rakosi agreed in principle but made objections to all the names suggested.

Immediately after the East Berlin uprising, he was again summoned to the Kremlin in company with a team chosen by the Soviets: the Chief of State, Istvan Dobi; Rakosi's alter ego, Erno Gerö, the Defense Minister, Mihaly Farkas; a young member of the Secretariat . . . and Imre Nagy, whose return to the scene had been skillfully prepared by his reception into the Academy of Science, an occasion for him to deliver an unqualified eulogy of Stalin.

The delegation appeared before the complete Presidium of the Soviet party, including Beria, who did not expect his downfall to come a few hours later. Tibor Meray, Nagy's friend who described the scene based on Nagy's confidences, reported that they were made to feel "as though they were standing before a tribunal rather than being gathered at a friendly meeting held between the leaders of brother parties on a basis of equality." [8] The Magyars were shown a document prepared by Soviet experts which described the catastrophic predicament of their economy, as well as many of the quadriga's abuses of power. The Russians, and notably Beria, stressed the folly which had made Rakosi surround himself only with Jews, in spite of the persistence of anti-Semitic prejudice in Hungary. Khrushchev warned him that "They [the Hungarian people] will chase you with pitchforks" [9] and Molotov asked him to "finally understand that you cannot eternally govern with the support of Soviet bayonets." [10]

Following these words the Soviet Presidium announced its decision. Rakosi had to get rid of two members of the quadriga: Farkas and Joszef Revai, the tsar of cultural life, considered half-mad by

Rakosi himself. Rakosi would remain as the head of the party in order to have the opportunity to redeem his sins, but he had to give up the direction of the government. Malenkov, Molotov and Khrushchev each in turn supported the candidacy of Imre Nagy. They were aware of his popularity with the peasants as the man who had carried out land distribution while he was Minister of Agriculture in 1944, and who, four years later, had lost all political power because he had warned his comrades against the consequences of hell-for-leather collectivization.

The man whom Mr. K was to confine to some dark jail of the socialist paradise four years later became, for the first time and through Moscow's favor, head of the Budapest Government. Evidently the Central Committee of the Hungarian Workers' Party, convened on June 28, could only say amen.

On July 4, Nagy gave his inaugural speech before Parliament and some of his statements created a sensation. "Nothing justifies excessive industrialization. . . . Excessive industrialization has hindered the normal development of agriculture. . . . Cooperatives will be allowed to disband if a majority of their members wishes to do so. . . ." He announced "greater tolerance in religious matters" and that as "the Government . . . bases itself on the legal order . . . and faces important tasks bearing on the correction of errors committed in the past," it was "introducing a bill providing for the release of all those whose crimes are not too heinous, and whose freedom will not imperil the security of the state." [11] That program could best be compared to the N.E.P., the New Economic Policy decreed in 1921 by Lenin to pull the U.S.S.R. out of the abyss where it found itself following the civil war.

It was about that time that the news of Beria's fall burst like a thunderbolt. Somewhat paradoxically it comforted Rakosi. In the Kremlin's discussions the overlord of the Soviet police had been one of his most sarcastic accusers. Hadn't he reproached him for having sought to become the "Jewish king" of Hungary? [12] In any case, his elimination proved that there existed in the Kremlin a conflict over policy, and probably even more a conflict of men, from which he would hope to profit. On the 11th, Rakosi made a speech which was an obvious answer to Nagy's. "Only the lazy and the good-for-nothings want to leave the kolkhozes . . . we will not accept that the results already attained within the framework of rural socialization be brought to naught. . . ." [13]

That controversy was to continue for eighteen months with the Central Committee, divided between the two philosophies, arbitrating the debate after a fashion. But on October 31, 1954, after having heard a particularly pressing appeal from Nagy, it endorsed his policies all along the line noting that "the policy of out-and-out industrialization has not been completely liquidated . . . and the . . . total level of industrial production has scarcely been raised." [14] This was a way of criticizing the unwillingness of the apparatus to implement government directives.

At that moment it appeared that Nagy had definitely won out over Rakosi, who went to hide his discomfiture in a Soviet sanitarium which he only left two months later. But it was not from Budapest that Hungary was then being governed, as Nagy was soon to find out to his sorrow.

On January 7, 1955, the Magyar leaders, who in June 1953 had appeared before the Soviet Presidium, were again summoned to the Kremlin to hear, as on the previous occasion, that their country was on the verge of bankruptcy. But this time, criticism was directed against Nagy and no longer against Rakosi. Backed by excerpts from speeches or articles, Malenkov undertook to prove that Nagy had slandered the party and shown signs of chauvinism and *petit bourgeois* demagogy, [15] concluding that that was not what he was asked to do. The accused was not allowed to say much. The verdict was the same as the one that had once been pronounced against Rakosi: no dismissal, provided he admit his errors and rectify them.

Nagy took up his functions again, but at the end of January a heart attack obliged him to abandon them temporarily. Believing that henceforth he could count on Moscow's support, Rakosi, on March 9, before the Central Committee, condemned the "rightist" and "anti-Marxist" [16] attitude of his rival, who, on April 14, was to be dismissed from his offices, not only as head of the government, but also as member of the Politburo and Central Committee.

What had happened? At the time, Nagy's ouster was interpreted as the consequence of the dismissal on February 8 of Malenkov, who was said to be his protector and who, like him, had insisted on the development of consumer goods. Public opinion considered the removal of the Soviet Chairman of the Council a victory for those who wanted to give priority to heavy industry, and therefore a victory of the enemies of international détente. Under those conditions it seemed perfectly natural that the dismissal of Imre Nagy followed that of Malenkov. At the time it could not have been known that Malenkov had been Nagy's principal accuser a month before.

In any case, events which followed were to show the oversimplification of that interpretation. Not only was Malenkov named Vice Chairman of the Council and Minister of the Electric Industry, but he remained on the Presidium of the Central Committee, a post which in the Soviet hierarchy is as important, certainly in matters of foreign policy, as that of the head of the government, and the détente begun under his reign was continuing as before.

No peremptory explanation has yet been given for the dismissal of the man whom everyone saw, two years before, as Stalin's heir. With information available now, however, it can be speculated that his fall, as well as Nagy's, was the result of the trip Khrushchev made to Peking, from September 29 to October 12, 1954, on the occasion of the fifth anniversary of the proclamation of the Chinese People's Republic. He was accompanied by two members of the Presidium of the Central Committee, Marshal Bulganin and Anastas Mikoyan, by a substitute member, Shepilov, and by Mme Furtseva, whose destiny was henceforth rumored to be closely bound to Mr. K's, although it did not prevent her from keeping her post as Minister of Culture after Khrushchev's disgrace.

The official result of that trip was the signing of new agreements between the U.S.S.R. and China, much more favorable to China than those Mao had obtained from Stalin on February 14, 1950, at the end of his two-month stay in Moscow. In effect, Peking secured the immediate dissolution of Soviet-Chinese societies which had been imposed on it in 1950 and whose hyphenated name poorly hid their essentially Russian character, the promise of evacuation of Dairen and Port Arthur on the following May 14, the delivery of fifteen complete factories, and a loan of 520 million rubles, or almost double the amount that had been granted by the Kremlin in 1950.

In spite of the Russians' refusal to discuss the Mongolian problem, these were sizable gifts, happily complementing those which, immediately following the Georgian's death, the new Soviet leaders had wanted to present to their Chinese comrades: eulogies in the newspapers, simultaneous publication in Peking and Moscow of the latest volume of Mao's works, and the delivery of one hundred factories. Apparently, there had been additional gifts, principally the green light given to the Chinese to try their luck in the Formosa Strait, for it was a few days later that the first crisis over Quemoy and Matsu was to begin. It can also be noted that this was the time they began talk of nuclear aid from the U.S.S.R. to China. Its subsequent suspension played no small part in unleashing the attacks of Peking's leaders against their Kremlin "comrades."

Was there a reason behind such generosity? Stalin's successors may have felt a moral obligation to make amends for the utter selfishness he had shown, during his entire reign, toward the Chinese Communists, who had been sacrificed on several occasions to the search for an agreement first with Chiang and then with the Japanese. Khrushchev, in the key post of the Soviet system, needed all possible cooperation to consolidate his position against men like Malenkov or Molotov, who could use their long collaboration with Stalin as a weapon against him. Nothing could equal cooperation from the second greatest socialist power in the world, whose prestige among colored peoples was immense, as Chou En-lai's triumphant tour of Southeast Asia in June had shown, and as the Bandung Conference in the spring of 1955 was to show even more.

But it stood to reason that the Chinese would only give their support to a man if they approved of the strategy he used in his relations with the outside world, and that strategy may have been the cause of the fundamental divergence between Khrushchev and Malenkov, which enabled the former to obtain the support of the Chinese against the latter.

In principle, Marxist-Leninists are optimists, believing they have discovered the true meaning of history, which can only lead to their ultimate triumph. Still today, when so many Communists are ready to recognize the scope of the illusions on the nature of man which, in Rousseau's footsteps, they have nourished, that faith in the meaning of history is very often the essential motivation of their commitment.

That long-term general optimism permits them to assume all attitudes in respect to short-term prospects. Always fearing the possibility of a backfire, they can give priority to the consolidation of socialist countries. Besides, they can think that this consolidation, by destroying the unity of the world market, will render inevitable the crisis of the capitalist system announced by Marx. They can also project that henceforth the socialist bloc would be sufficiently strong, and its ideas sufficiently widespread, for it to practice an active strategy which, although not provoking armed conflicts, would hasten the ruin of the adversary. To that end it would extend a hand to all those who, throughout the world, wanted to destroy an "order" too unjust to be borne.

Stalin, suspicious by nature, obviously belonged to the first school. His lieutenants, Malenkov and Molotov, even if they deplored *in petto* the criminal madness to which his paranoia had brought him, could not fail to more or less share his way of thinking. After his death, both of them were also concerned primarily with consolidating the Soviet regime. But they advocated different means. Malenkov had clearly shown his fear of war, stating on March 12, 1954, that ". . . given modern methods of warfare, [war] means the destruction of world civilization." [17] Until that time the orthodox doctrine—from which, however, he was to depart in a speech on April 26 of the same year—maintained that a third world war would certainly sound the death knell of capitalism, as Peking still contends. He was therefore advocating concessions externally, including those on the German problem, as well as internally, within the socialist bloc. The riots that broke out soon after his coming to power—not only in East Berlin but also in Pilsen and in Ostrava, in Czechoslovakia, and even in the prison city of Vorkuta, in the Soviet far north—as well as the agitation in Hungary, confirmed him in that belief. This was shown by his speech of August 8, 1953, in which he said: "Over a long period of time we have directed our capital investment mainly toward the development of heavy industry and transport. . . . The Government and Party consider it essential to increase investment considerably for the development of light industry . . . and agriculture. . . ." [18]

This explained Rakosi's replacement by Nagy at the head of the Hungarian Government. Molotov, who of all Stalin's aides was the closest to his master, was hostile in principle to all concessions, thinking that they would only strengthen the enemies of the Soviet camp internally as well as externally.

Facing those two aspects of the same prudence, the robust and jovial Khrushchev was the very image of optimism. A man of the people who remained very close to them, no one was more convinced than he of the rightness of the Communist cause, no one believed more than he in its inevitable triumph. "Whether you like it or not, history is moving in our favor, and it is we who will bury you," he very sweetly declared to the "capitalist gentlemen and their representatives here present," [19] during a Kremlin reception in November 1956. This provoked an outcry of indignation in the United States, where, rather naively, his words were taken literally. One day, while fingering a globe, he would show Lester Pearson, the Canadian Foreign Minister, the way by which, according to him, the revolution would win over the whole world. Subsequently, his trip to America, during which he would discover the power of a reputedly moribund capitalism, his failures in Berlin, in Cuba, his conflict with China, and the bankruptcy of his thousand and one attempts to reform agriculture would cause him to modify a number of the postulates by which he lived. But they would not succeed in completely destroying his optimism; there is no other explanation for the fact that he let himself be so easily eliminated—he was convinced of his own impunity. Had he not told a bench minister, whom he received a few hours before his downfall, evidently alluding as much to himself as to General de Gaulle: "In our time, a true statesman dies in office." [20]

In the fall of 1954 that revolutionary optimism echoed the designs of Peking's leaders, who had continually suffered from Stalin's excessive prudence and from his increasing tendency to behave as the heir of the tsars rather than of Karl Marx. A clear reflection of these grievances can be found in the long article, quite forgotten since then, that the Peking *People's Daily* devoted to Stalin's merits and faults on April 5, 1956, following the Twentieth Congress of the Soviet Communist Party. The scope of the economic aid offered China implied the mobilization of the bloc's resources, which ran directly counter to the priority given by Malenkov to the production of consumer goods and even more to Nagy's N.E.P. Therefore, it was natural that Nagy became the first victim of the Khrushchev-Mao accord of 1954, and Malenkov the second. Although no written document on the Peking talks is available in the West, the message addressed by Mao Tse-tung on February 9, 1956, to the Twentieth Congress of the C.P.S.U. established without any doubt whatever that complete accord had then been reached on a certain number of essential points. In effect, that document recognized again and again the "right direction" taken by the Soviet party; it congratulated it on the whole of its diplomatic initiatives during the year 1955 and asserted that the C.P.S.U. "had been, remained, and will be a worthy example for the Communist parties of all the countries of the world" and saluted the place of the U.S.S.R. "at the head" of the socialist bloc.[21]

§   §   §

One of the initiatives for which Mao especially wanted to congratulate the C.P.S.U. was the normalization of Soviet-Yugoslav relations, which had been followed by a parallel normalization of Sino-Yugoslav relations. This is amusing to note because at that time Peking was ranting against "revisionism" from Belgrade and Moscow. Normalization was not viewed quite similarly by the two interested parties. Obviously Khrushchev considered as an error—it was one of his principal complaints against Stalin in his secret report to the Twentieth Congress—the exclusion of the Yugoslav Communist Party from the Cominform and he firmly hoped, in return for some concessions, that it would return to the bosom of the "bloc." Tito not only intended to jealously preserve the independence of his country, but also to have the other people's democracies, and consequently Yugoslavia itself, benefit as much as possible from his victorious resistance.

As soon as Khrushchev returned from Peking, the climate changed rapidly. On October 20, 1954, *Pravda* used the occasion of the tenth anniversary of the junction of the Red Army and Yugoslav partisans to celebrate their heroism "under the leadership of Marshal Tito." On November 6, Saburov, a member of the Presidium of the Central Committee of the C.P.S.U. recalled in a speech the common struggle of the two countries and a dispute which had only benefited their common enemy. The same month, Malenkov, Khrushchev, and even Molotov, personally went to the Yugoslav Embassy in honor of the national holiday, to toast the health of Tito who had become again, for the occasion, "comrade" Tito.

According to Richard Lowenthal, the Russians then suggested that the two parties admit that each of them had a share of the responsibility for the break and that the Russians assign the major share of theirs to Beria, who could be accused of everything as long as he was dead, and the Yugoslavs to Milovan Djilas, who had just resigned from the Communist Party after having been Tito's trusted aide for years and even, according to some, his heir apparent. An admirer of Stalin, about whom he had even written in 1942 that he was "the only chief of state with an altruistic conscience," [22] he had brought back from his wartime and postwar meetings with his idol a disillusionment which was going, in time, to turn into a fierce hatred. From criticism of Stalinism he had gone to criticism of communism and had not hesitated in January 1954, when he had just been elected President of Parliament, to contend that the Yugoslav party represented an obsolete concept and to outline an indictment of what he would later call the "new ruling class." Deprived of all his posts, he had confessed his sins but then had changed his mind and turned in his membership card. No revolt could have affected Tito more than that of the man he loved like his own son. Whether or not the Russians actually proposed such a deal to him, it was a foregone conclusion that he could not accept it anyway. He replied to the Kremlin's overtures that the reparation to which he was entitled did not require any equivalent action on his part.

Moscow's first reaction was cool. Molotov stated on January 9, 1955, following Malenkov's fall, that the normalization of relations between the U.S.S.R. and Yugoslavia depended as much on one as on the other, while noting that the Belgrade regime had "apparently departed in some degree from the course she embarked upon after the war." [23]

Was Molotov expressing only his personal point of view? It was likely, because one of the reasons for his condemnation in June 1957 was his constant opposition to any détente with Belgrade. In any case,

Pravda reproduced entirely the rather sharp reply Tito sent to the chief Soviet diplomat on March 7. On May 14 the TASS and Tanjug agencies announced that the two governments had decided to arrange a meeting in Belgrade "at the highest level." Twelve days later, Khrushchev landed at the Belgrade airport, accompanied by a delegation almost identical to the one he had led to Peking in September, with the difference that meanwhile Bulganin had become head of the government.

As soon as he emerged from the plane, Nikita put on his round spectacles and pulled a paper out of his pocket that he began to read. This time, the Soviet party had decided to go to Canossa: "We sincerely regret [what has happened]," he said "and we resolutely sweep aside all the bitterness of that period. . . . We have thoroughly investigated the materials on which the grave accusations against, and insults to, the leaders of Yugoslavia were based at the time. The facts indicate that those materials were fabricated by enemies of the people, the contemptible agents of imperialism who had fraudulently wormed their way into the ranks of our party." [24] Tito ought to have been delighted. But his surly expression was obvious to everyone. It was because Mr. K—despite Belgrade's previous refusal to put the blame for the affair on scapegoats—had not hesitated to mention the *provocateur* role played in the relations between the two countries by the "exposed enemies of the people, Beria, Abakumov [the last Minister of State Security in Beria's time, who was executed in December 1954], and others." [25]

This showed great audacity on Khrushchev's part, if we recall that one of the major complaints against Beria, during the secret session of the Cominform when explanations were given to foreign leaders on the reasons for his fall, had been precisely that of wanting to negotiate with Yugoslavia!

As soon as they were far from inquisitive ears, the new master of the U.S.S.R. leaned toward Tito: "Without you, during the dark years, we would have lost all courage . . . naturally, when I said Beria, I meant Stalin." [26] But the marshal was not at all ready to be pacified with words. The last thing in the world he wanted was to rejoin the "socialist camp," which was exactly what Khrushchev wanted. Throughout the talks, Belgrade's press continually attacked the noxious influence of "military" or "ideological" blocs and insisted on the necessity for cooperation between all countries, whatever their regimes.

In the end, Tito obtained full satisfaction. The joint declaration published on June 2 not only recognized that "the policy of military blocs increases international tension" and that the "development of peaceful coexistence implies cooperation from all the states without taking into consideration ideological and social differences," but also proclaimed that "the questions of internal organization, of differences of social systems and of different forms of socialist development concerned only the peoples of the different countries." [27] As reparation for wrongs inflicted, Khrushchev waived repayment of $90 million in credits granted to Yugoslavia by the U.S.S.R. prior to 1948.

Of course, the "noninterference" in the affairs of "brother countries" and the complete equality of rights between them belonged to the traditional vocabulary of international communism. But we have seen how in Budapest, for example, the Soviet leaders conceived the application of that noble principle. By signing with Tito, the champion of national independence, a document which recognized the validity of his position, Khrushchev had dropped a real bombshell on the long-established "monolithic" edifice of the Soviet bloc.

This was enough to alarm all the "little" Stalins who, two years after the tyrant's death, continued to govern the people's democracies and who well knew that the maintenance of their authority depended primarily on the Kremlin's good will. To reassure them, Mr. K stopped in Sofia and then in Bucharest, where he met the Bulgarian, Rumanian, Hungarian and Czechoslavakian leaders, who had all, in turn, called the Yugoslav marshal a "Hitlerian" and a "Trotskyite" and sent to the gibbet or to the firing squad blameless veterans of the workers' movement for the crime of Titoism. What he told them was never published, but the rumor started that he had made only a "tactical concession" in Belgrade and that so far as he was concerned, he did not plan to have the passage from his speech concerning the free choice of the best way to socialism apply to other countries in the "bloc."

Tito did not hear it that way. On July 28 at Karlovac, in a speech otherwise very favorable to the new orientation of the U.S.S.R., he took sharply to task those who "say what has happened is only a manoeuvre . . . especially in Hungary." [28]

He had no peace until Moscow had dismissed the leaders who were most compromised in the affair and let its satellites renew relations directly with Belgrade. This was accomplished a year later, not without difficulty, and when the Twentieth Congress of the Soviet party had, in the meantime, completely changed the climate of relations between the different members of the socialist bloc.

§   §   §

According to its constitution, the Congress, the supreme legal instrument of the C.P.S.U., meets every four years. The Twentieth Congress opened on February 14, 1956, and ended on the 25th. The public reports which were presented illustrated a radical transformation of the orators' language, which, after the fetishistic excesses of Stalin's era, was becoming somewhat secularized. One after another they condemned, in greater or less degree, the "dogmatism" and the "cult of personality," emphasized with Suslov the "successful re-establishment of the principle of collective direction on every level of the party," [29] deplored the split between ideological efforts and life, insisted with Khrushchev on the existence of more and more varied forms in the march toward socialism, and on the possibility that under certain conditions the working classes might win "a solid majority in parliaments and thus be able to transform those organisms of bourgeois democracy into an instrument of the true popular will" [30]; this was what the Social Democrats had continually maintained and which had earned them, for thirty years, the harshest accusations of collaboration first with fascism and then with imperialism. No surprise then if a hand was being extended to them, and several of them—led by Guy Mollet—were seen following each other to the Kremlin. These sensational developments were only small change compared to the report that Khrushchev was to read in great secrecy to the flabbergasted delegates on the closing day.

That document, which the *New York Times* correspondent in Moscow got wind of three weeks later, fell into the hands of the C.I.A. and was published on June 4 by the American State Department. It is too well known to require analysis here. It painted a picture of a Stalin who was "morbidly suspicious" and who took advantage of his "unlimited power" to "annihilate people morally and physically," resorting to torture and to all "violations of legality" to make those he had baptized "enemies of the people" confess their alleged crimes. A complete indictment was made of his behavior before and after Hitler's invasion, which he had not been capable of foreseeing and during which he revealed himself a pitiful organizer and pitiful stragetist.

Then followed the list of the massive deportations embracing whole nationalities which he had effected, and the evocation of the climate around him in the last years of his existence when everyone was fearful, from morning till night, for his own life. One trait was cited as particularly characteristic; in his 1940 "abridged biography" he had himself added the following passage: "Stalin is devoid of all vanity, pretension or desire for personal glorification." [31]

The report has never been published in the U.S.S.R. and was only read during gatherings of militants. Although it provoked an expected emotional reaction among some old Bolsheviks, and although it deeply affected their reverence for an office which was gradually divesting itself of its supernatural, sacramental aspects—directly inherited from Byzantium—the extraordinary passivity of the Russian people softened the shock. In any case, the West had no knowledge of any real difficulties except in Georgia, the birthplace of the fallen idol, where on March 9 a demonstration triggered by Stalinist elements turned into a riot, nationalists having taken advantage of the situation to violently manifest their sentiments. In the end about a hundred people were supposed to have been killed.

Generally speaking, the leaders in the people's democracies gave the least possible publicity to the secret report, but in Poland the press made more than transparent allusions to it, and it became rapidly known to an "intelligentsia" which had already been in ferment for a long time. It saw in it confirmation of the revelations, widely broadcast in Polish by the Western radio, made by Joseph Swiatlo, one of the chiefs of the secret police, who had defected to the West to avoid Beria's fate. For a long time he had been Beria's executioner in his own country. Long before the Congress of the Soviet Communist Party, Bierut, the number-one man in the Polish

Workers' Party, had had to make a complete confession to the Central
Committee which had been convened on January 25, 1955. This was
a prelude to a complete reorganization of the security services and to
the arrest of several of their officials for breach of duty. The session
had been the occasion for several committee members to sharply express their opposition to the leadership of the party and of the country. Their indignation was echoed in newspapers whose writers were
expressing themselves with increasing boldness. This can be judged
from this "poem for adults" by Adam Wazyk, published on August
21, 1955, in *Nowa Kultura*:

> They said:
> In the socialist system
> A finger which is cut does not hurt.
> They cut their fingers,
> They had pain,
> They had doubts.
>
> . . . .
>
> We demand clear verities,
>   the wheat of liberty,
>   blazing reason.[32]

Naturally, sanctions were taken against the editor in chief of that
weekly. But criticism was mounting from all sides, encouraged by the
numerous rehabilitations of militants, persecuted under Stalin, and
by the Soviet-Yugoslav declaration, which, at least in Warsaw, was
taken seriously by anyone who had eyes to read with.

The Twentieth Congress was going to accelerate this tendency,
since on February 19, 1956, it had published a communiqué signed
by representatives of several Communist parties stating that the dissolution of the Polish Communist Party in 1938 had been unjustified
and attributing responsibility for that decision to *"agents provocateurs."* [33] The formula reminds one of the tactic employed by
Khrushchev during his visit to Belgrade, when he had put off on
Beria the responsibility for the exclusion of Yugoslavia from the
Cominform. The communiqué took care not to recall that most of the
Polish Communist leaders who had been accused of deviationism had
then been quite simply massacred.

On February 29, Radio Warsaw exclaimed that now "each person can realize that he has not only the right but the duty to express his opinions." [34] Twelve days later, Bierut, who had fallen ill in Moscow, died. This was a beautiful occasion for the Poles "to think for themselves," but Khrushchev invited himself to the meeting of the Central Committee which had been convened on March 20 to name a new First Secretary. He opposed the nomination—supported by the majority—of Roman Zambrowski, Minister of State Control, on the pretext that his being a Jew might create difficulties with the population. In fact, what created difficulties was Khrushchev's very intervention in Polish affairs less than six months after he had promised in Belgrade to recognize the right of all socialist countries to choose their own way, and also the frankly anti-Semitic tone of his remarks, which were immediately reported by some members of the Central Committee who, carried away by the excitement, had become as talkative as bourgeois politicians.

The Central Committee finally agreed on Edward Ochab, director of political education in the Army since 1950, an old-time Communist, who had stayed out of the turmoil of the last months. On April 6 he announced a sensational decision: the freeing of Gomulka, First Secretary of the party, who had been arrested in 1950 because of his sympathy for Tito and never been tried, probably because of his great popularity. Ochab admitted that the security police had arrested many party members.

Henceforth, good news came rapidly: the rehabilitation, unfortunately posthumous, of the Bulgarian Kostov and the Hungarian Rajk, who had been sacrificed in 1949 to the Stalinist Moloch; the denunciation of the cult of personality, not only Stalin's, which the press had everywhere criticized in sharper and sharper terms, but also his followers' (the Czechoslovak Gottwald, who died in 1953, and the Bulgarian Chervenkov, who had to surrender his post as chief of the government, while remaining Vice President of the Council and member of the Politburo); the elimination of several leaders, among whom were General Cepicka, Minister of Defense in the Prague Government; and, above all, the dissolution on April 17 of the Cominform, whose notoriety was connected with the condemnation of Titoism and the preachings of Zhdanov on the theme that "those who are not with us are against us."

It was in Poland that the campaign went farthest. Some 30,000 prisoners, of whom 4,500 were political, were released, and 70,000 others had their penalties reduced. Indemnities were promised to those who had been unjustly arrested. The Minister of Justice and general military and civil prosecutors were dismissed. Jacob Berman, who had long been Bierut's right arm, resigned from the Politburo. On May 6 the Prime Minister, Cyrankiewicz, asserted before Parliament, whose role he was determined to upgrade, "We are undoubtedly at the threshold of a new historical process of democratization of our political and economic life. . . ." [35] A few days later he agreed that numerous injustices had been committed against members of the Polish clandestine army—Armija Krajowa, or A.K.—the non-Communist Resistance organization which paid allegiance to the exiled government in London during the war. The fact that the Central Committee was divided into several factions was discussed everywhere and everyone knew it. One group favored Gomulka's return to power, while the "Natolin" group—which took its name from the Warsaw suburb where it met—blindly followed the concepts of the most extreme Stalinism.

No one can say how things would have turned out if, on the morning of June 28, the 15,000 workers in the Poznan railroad rolling-stock factory had not revolted with cries of "Give us bread," "Down with communism," "Throw the Russkies out," "We want liberty!" Forming a procession, they went to the headquarters of the Workers' Party where an official who tried to talk to them was beaten up. From there they went to the prison, where they freed the prisoners, vainly tried to enter the radio station and then fired on the main police headquarters. The first troops sent to the scene fraternized with the rioters. When order had been restored, *manu militari*, in the evening, the count was 53 killed, among them 44 demonstrators, and more than 300 wounded; 323 persons were arrested.

The situation was made even more serious for the Polish regime because it had been impossible to hide it from foreign observers. The uprising had taken place at the time when the traditional international fair had brought hundreds of visitors to Poznan. Scores among them had witnessed the incidents which they did not hesitate to describe for their countries' newspapers.

The immediate cause of the riot was apparently a false rumor that a delegation which had been sent to Warsaw to demand better working conditions had been arrested. But the riot would not have broken out if the Poznan workers, like those of East Berlin three years earlier, or like the Kronstadt sailors in 1921, had not been driven to despair by a poverty made more unbearable because the regime continually claimed "spectacular" successes in raising the standard of living and, by definition, claimed to be acting only for the good of the people.

Cyrankiewicz, who hastened to Poznan, put responsibility for the incidents on "provocateurs . . . organizing a demonstration which had been prepared for a long time," [36] without denying that existing economic difficulties had made their task easier. *Pravda* developed in detail the thesis of Western intervention, while *L'Humanité* scornfully labeled the workers of Poznan who had revolted "Chouans," although many were members of the Communist Party. But Jerzy Morawski, in *Trybuna Ludu,* the organ of the Polish Communist Party, insisted that responsibility lay above all with the bureaucrats who had proved incapable of satisfying the workers' aspirations.

Advocates of concession and those of the hard line clashed daily. On July 18 the Central Committee met in plenary session. The marshals Bulganin and Zhukov were in Warsaw on the occasion of the national holiday, and the former did not fail to criticize the excessive freedom of the Polish press. So that their presence should not influence the deliberations of the Committee, they were asked to go on a tour of the provinces.

A number of speakers demanded the immediate reinstatement of Gomulka in the Politburo because he was the most popular man in the country. A Resistance fighter, a Stalin victim, "Wladyslaw," who had championed national communism and opposed hasty land collectivization, was likely to become a hero symbol once the Polish people recovered, no matter how limitedly, the means of expressing their opinions. On the other hand, General Witaszewski, head of the political department of the army, uttered a warning against "defeatism" in terms suggesting that he had been assured of some support from Moscow.

In his report to the committee, Ochab had expressed his sympathy for the liberal trend. About the riots, he said, "it would be an error to concentrate attention on the machinations of provocateurs and agents of imperialism." He recognized that bonds between the party and the workers had been "seriously disturbed." In any case, he concluded, the riots "should not serve as the justification for any attempt to turn aside the process of democratization." The party had to abandon its role of "director and manager" to become a "guide and educator." [37]

That effort to rally public opinion proved decisive. On July 28, three liberals joined the Politburo and on August 5, Gomulka and his friends who had been arrested at the same time—General Spychalski, former Minister of Defense, and Kliszko, former Secretary of State for Justice—were given back their party membership cards. During the session it had been secretly decided that negotiations begin on Gomulka's conditions for returning to the center of power in the party. Solemn homage had been paid to the non-Communist Resistance and on August 24, General Komar, a veteran of the Spanish Civil War who had been imprisoned and tortured under Stalin on the pretext of Titoism, was placed at the head of internal security.

Such a nomination illustrated the gravity of the crisis whose end was in sight. It would soon be necessary to choose between "liberals" and "hard-liners," and at the time of decision, control of the police would be of critical importance. Besides, Gomulka was rejecting the compromise solutions suggested to him; he intended to retake his place in the heart of the Politburo only if the Stalinists, now become "Natolinians," were purged from it. And while the latter were plotting in Moscow, those who wanted change were organizing almost everywhere, particularly in the universities and the large factories.

Gomulka and his adherents were encouraged by the trend of events in neighboring countries. In June, Tito had made a triumphal tour of the U.S.S.R., following which Khrushchev and he had reaffirmed their commitment to the 1955 Belgrade declaration regarding the right of each country to choose its own road to socialism. He had obtained satisfaction on a point he considered essential: the reestablishment of direct relations, without going through Moscow, between the Yugoslav Communist Party and other communist parties. Palmiro Togliatti, chief of the Italian Communist Party, had not awaited that authorization to go and confer with Tito at the end of May, and he stated on his return: "Following the Soviet model no longer can and no longer must be considered obligatory. . . . The whole system is in the process of becoming polycentric, and even in the Communist movement itself we cannot speak of a single guide." And he continued by asserting that criticism of Stalinism required that within the whole movement each party, in its own way, work out means of protection "against stagnation and bureaucratization . . . of mutually resolving problems of freedom and of social justice for the working classes." [38] Finally, Rakosi, *bête noire* of the Yugoslav marshal, had to give up the leadership of the Hungarian Communist Party on July 18.

From Poland itself came news of the resignation of Hilary Minc, the economic tsar, and the dismissal of the Minister of Industry, Fidelski, who had told a delegation of the city's workers that he received on the eve of the Poznan riots: "I am not afraid of your strike. If you take to the streets, we'll send tanks." [39] There was also the granting of a loan of 100 million rubles from the U.S.S.R., and the liberation of half the Poznan demonstrators with only the most seriously implicated being finally brought to justice. The trial, in the words of a publication as outspokenly anti-Communist as *Est et Ouest,* "astonished everyone by the frankness of the statements of the accused, the integrity of the lawyers, the moderateness of the verdicts." [40]

It was to the Central Committee, to the executive machinery of the party and to the state that the responsibility for finding a solution to the crisis belonged. It was convened for October 18, on Ochab's return from Peking, where he had attended the Congress of the Chinese Communist Party, whose leaders, it is now known, urged him to resign in favor of Gomulka.

A few hours before the plenary session, Ochab announced to the members of the Politburo that it had been agreed with Gomulka that the latter would present the report to the Central Commitee in his place. The Natolinians were enraged and one of their important members, Mazur, then in Moscow, was directed to alert Molotov, who found the incident a good pretext for denouncing the perils of destalinization before the Presidium of the Soviet party. Khrushchev, for his part, believed he had been tricked. During Tito's visit he had agreed with him on the step-by-step progress of liberalization, and especially on Ochab's retention of power in Warsaw, even at the price of making a place for Gomulka at his side. He did not waste any time. Soviet troops based in Poland began moving toward the major cities, and he himself took a plane to Warsaw. He arrived there in the morning, flanked by Molotov, Mikoyan and Kaganovich, as well as by Marshal Koniev, Commander in Chief of the armed forces of the Warsaw Pact, and a dozen generals in full dress uniform, their chests covered with decorations.

The plane had hardly landed at the capital's airport, to which the whole Polish party's leadership had come to welcome him, when Khrushchev exploded: "We have shed our blood for this country and now they want to sell it to the Americans." A voice was raised: "We have shed more blood than you, and we are not selling anything at all." "Who is that one?" Mr. K asked Ochab. The object of the question answered for himself: "I am the former secretary general of the party, whom Stalin and you yourself threw into prison. My name is Gomulka." Mr. K turned his back on him. "What is he doing here?" he asked Ochab, who threw down the gauntlet: "He is here because we have decided to elect him secretary general of the party." [41]

"Treason!" cried Nikita Sergeyevich, more and more furious, and he ordered his chauffeur to take him to the Central Committee. But the Poles were firm: the Russians had to go to the Belvedere Castle, the residence of official guests. However, the proceedings of the plenary session were interrupted to permit an explanation to be given to the Russians.

Khrushchev calmed down only when he was warned that if he continued in the same vein, Gomulka would go on the radio to explain to his countrymen Moscow's conception of "friendship between peoples and of Polish-Soviet relations." [42] A discussion that got down to brass tacks ensued, the Russians making much of the numerous articles which had appeared in the Polish press to prove that Warsaw was in the process of turning its back on socialism. Mr. K even contended that Tito agreed that the counterrevolution should be halted; something Tito himself would deny a few hours later. But it was in vain that Khrushchev tried to obtain some token concession from his hosts. He had to go back after having signed an innocuous communiqué and be satisfied with muttering to himself, *"Qui vivra verra."* [43]

In the evening of the 19th, while Russian tanks were still rolling toward Warsaw, the workers put themselves on the alert, and 30,000 young men, assembled in the auditorium of the Polytechnic School and around it, cheered liberal speakers.

On the morning of the 20th, Marshal Rokossovski, Minister of Defense and a member of the Polish Politburo although a Soviet citizen, was asked by the Central Committee to explain the deployment of the Russian troops. He stated that he had requested Koniev to order the troops to return to their bases. Then Gomulka spoke. His speech was broadcast over the radio: "Blood would not have flowed in Poznan," he cried, "if the party, that is to say its leaders, had told the truth." Then, after criticizing the "cult of personality," he continued: "The essence of socialism comes down to the elimination of the exploitation of man by man . . . The model of socialism can vary. It can be the kind created in the U.S.S.R.; it can be organized in the manner we witness in Yugoslavia; it can even be different." [44] The next day, by a margin of 74 votes, Gomulka was elected a member of the Politburo, and by acclamation, First Secretary. No Natolinian was elected and Rokossovski got only 23 votes.

Khrushchev waited forty-eight hours before telephoning his congratulations to the winner, who, through a strange turnabout of events was to become his very close friend, and even the Russians' accomplice in the invasion of Czechoslovakia. On the same occasion he announced the pullback of Soviet troops to their bases. It can be surmised that the delay had been devoted to a lengthy examination of the situation by the Soviet "collective leadership."

From one end of the country to the other, huge meetings celebrated what Radio Warsaw was to call "spring in October." Poland, even at the cost of putting some water in its wine, would henceforth know how to preserve the essential elements of that peaceful revolution, but two unfortunate battles, in Budapest and at Suez, were soon going to make other peoples forget the promises of that late spring.

BIBLIOGRAPHY AND NOTES

1 *Nouvelles yougoslaves,* Paris, April 1953.
2 "President Tito addresses the Indian Parliament," *Yugoslav Review,* Vol. IV, No. 1 (January 1955), p. 12.
3 *XXe Congrès du parti communiste de l'Union Soviétique* (hereinafter referred to as *XXe Congrès*) (Paris: Les Cahiers du Communisme, 1956), p. 36.
4 Confidential communication from Fierlinger, the President of the Czechoslovakian Council, to Konni Zilliacus, the British radical, quoted in Robert Conquest, *Russia After Khrushchev* (New York: Praeger, 1965), p. 239.
5 Imre Nagy, *Imre Nagy on Communism* (London: Thames and Hudson, 1957), p. 32.
6 *Ibid.,* p. 33.
7 *The New York Times,* July 18, 1953.
8 Tibor Meray, *Thirteen Days That Shook the Kremlin* (New York: Praeger, 1959), p. 4.
9 *Ibid.,* p. 6.
10 *Ibid.,* p. 7.
11 François Fetjö, *Behind the Rape of Hungary* (New York: David McKay Co., 1957), pp. 97–100.
12 Meray, *op. cit.,* p. 7.
13 *Est et Ouest,* No. 168 (February 1957), p. 51.
14 Fetjö, *op. cit.,* p. 106.
15 Meray, *op. cit.,* pp. 22–26.
16 *Ibid.,* pp. 126–33.
17 J. M. Mackintosh, *Strategy and Tactics of Soviet Foreign Policy*
(London: Oxford University Press, 1962), p. 95.
18 Keesing's, 10396 A.
19 Année Politique, 1956, p. 407.
20 Author's personal notes.
21 *XXe Congrès, op. cit.,* p. 439.
22 Cited by Kotcha Kristitch in the preface to Milovan Djilas, *L'Exécution* (Paris: Calmann-Lévy, 1966).
23 Keesing's, 10459 A.
24 *Ibid.,* 14265 A.
25 *Ibid.*
26 Author's personal notes.
27 Keesing's, 14265 A.
28 Keesing's, 14358 A.
29 *XXe Congrès, op. cit.,* p. 235.
30 *Ibid.,* pp. 45–46.
31 Full text of the report in *Le Monde,* June 6–19, 1956.
32 Translated into French and published in *Les Temps Modernes,* February–March 1957.
33 Keesing's, 14817 A.
34 *Ibid.*
35 Keesing's, 14880 A.
36 Keesing's, 14967 A.
37 Keesing's, 15033 A.
38 Interview in *Nuovi Argumenti* (Rome), June 16, 1956.
39 *Le Monde,* June 30, 1956.
40 *Est et Ouest,* No. 168 (February 1957), p. 154.
41 K. S. Karol, *Visa for Poland* (London: MacGibbon & Kee, 1959), p. 143.
42 *Ibid.,* pp. 145–46.
43 *Ibid.,* p. 147.
44 Documentation française, Notes et études documentaires, No. 2232.

· CHAPTER 10 ·

THE FIRST "WEEK
OF TRUTH"
—BUDAPEST

The mob were marching to break that fine statue of
the Prince in the gardens of the court . . .

—Stendhal, *The Charterhouse of Parma*
(Translated by C. K. Scott Moncrieff)

IT COULD HAVE BEEN HOPED, DURING THE TWENTIETH
Soviet Congress, in February 1956, that the liberal trends beginning
to appear in Poland would also become apparent in Hungary. The
rehabilitation of the Polish Communist Party, destroyed by Stalin
in 1938, and of Bela Kun, founder of the ephemeral Hungarian
Soviet Republic in 1919, announced one after the other, seemed more
than a coincidence. The latter had mysteriously disappeared in the
U.S.S.R. during the thirties, and since then, no Communist would have
dared pronounce his name. But, of all the leaders of eastern Europe,
Rakosi—who had installed a mere nonentity, Andras Hegedüs, as
head of the government to replace Nagy—was certainly the most
determined to oppose any true reform, and, in any event, to preserve
power in his own hands. After all, in the U.S.S.R. the process of
"destalinization" was being run by Stalinists. Why wouldn't he have
tried to do the same?

On March 15 he stated before the Central Committee that the
cult of personality had led to serious political and ideological errors

in Hungary—without, of course, mentioning that he had organized the cult of his own personality—and that it was necessary to "consolidate collective leadership." [1] When, on the 27th, he decided to announce the rehabilitation of Laszlo Rajk, the Minister of the Interior—who had been hanged in 1949 under the accusation of Titoism, he placed the responsibility for the whole affair on Beria and on his Magyar rival Gabor Peter, condemned in 1954 to life imprisonment for "violations of legality."

Far from appeasing popular discontent, Rajk's rehabilitation only exacerbated it. On March 30 a young critic, Sandor Lukocsi, accused Rakosi himself of having been responsible for his death. Rakosi would not have been so bold if he had not felt he had the support of a large part of the intelligentsia. Had not sixty-seven writers and artists dared send the Central Committee, in October 1955, a petition against "arbitrary interventions by the bureaucracy" which "make impossible the creation of a climate of liberty, of honesty, of health" indispensable to remedy the "unhealthy signs" appearing in the nation's cultural life? [2]

Sanctions taken against members of the party who had signed the petition did not shake their resolution in any way. The Petöfi Circle, founded the previous year by a group of young intellectuals, was the scene of debates which became increasingly impassioned, while visits multiplied to the house of Imre Nagy, who, every time he went forth, was the object of discreet demonstrations of sympathy along his route. On his birthday, June 19, a crowd, among which could be recognized a member of the government, filled his small villa on Orso Street.

The same day, Laszlo Rajk's widow, before the Petöfi Circle, requested that the men responsible for her husband's death be ousted from power. Now, on May 18, Rakosi had admitted that he was partially culpable. "If these illegal acts were possible here among us," he stated to a group of militants gathered at the Sports Palace, "I am at fault myself, since I hold the most important post in the party. But the other leaders of the party are also in some measure at fault." [3] Madame Rajk's appeal was heard: on June 27, thousands of people were at the Circle to hear several speakers. Among them was Tibor Dery, the greatest Hungarian writer, a militant Communist from way back, who called for Rakosi's dismissal and Nagy's return. The chairman of the meeting, a friend of the dictator, was booed, lost control of it and had to give the floor to whoever wanted it. Far into the night, the audience shouted slogans hostile to the regime and loudly acclaimed the journalist Horvath when he demanded that the implementation of the principles adopted by the Twentieth Soviet Congress be determined not in Moscow or Budapest, but by the Hungarian nation.

The next day came the news of the Poznan uprising. Rakosi felt the ground sinking under his feet. On the 30th he got the Central Committee to condemn the "antiparty activity" of the Nagy group and to oust Tibor Dery and his friend Tibor Tardos, another speaker at the June 27 meeting, from the Communist Party. According to Tibor Meray, he had also decided to arrest four hundred persons, headed by Nagy himself.[4] But he had overestimated his strength. The Soviet leaders who, during Tito's visit to Moscow a few days before, had again taken up Rakosi's defense against Tito, saying that he was "an old revolutionary, and honest," [5] had finally understood the necessity of sacrificing him. But they insisted that he should be replaced by Erno Gerö, his deputy and accomplice, who was not much better.

This time the Hungarian leaders were not summoned to the U.S.S.R. Mikoyan himself came to Budapest with Suslov, at the beginning of July, and informed the Politburo that they would have to carry out his orders. That was decided on July 18. In his letter of resignation, Rakosi mentioned his age and his poor health but admitted that his errors "in the areas of the cult of personality and the violation of socialist legality" had been greater than he had thought at first. He beat his breast for the slowness with which those errors had begun to be corrected.[6] A few hours later he left for the U.S.S.R., without expecting to return. Actually, he was to end his days at Alma-Ata, in Turkestan, which had been Trotsky's place of exile for a time.

A ghost from the past, Janos Kadar, was named Gerö's deputy in the Secretariat. A former Minister of the Interior, he had been released after five years of imprisonment for Titoism. During that time he had been tortured personally by the son of General Farkas, the Minister of Defense, who went so far as to urinate on his face, and he quickly took his revenge. On July 22, Farkas was ousted from the party and demoted, accused of violating socialist legality, unjustified persecution of the party's leading officials, etc.

As Ochab, in Warsaw, after Gomulka's liberation, had warned his countrymen against Gomulka's "errors," Gerö thought he could still throw barbs at the "deviationism of the right—a deviationism represented, above all, by Imre Nagy." [7] In Kadar's presence he summoned Nagy to try to persuade him to make his confession. But once more, the Russians were ahead of the Hungarian leaders. Mikoyan returned and between flights told Nagy that Moscow had, at the time, criticized his exclusion from the party and that he hoped he would cooperate in the search for a solution.

After long hesitation and many consultations, the former Prime Minister, who feared a catastrophe for his country, decided on October 4 to ask for his reinstatement in the party. On the 10th the Politburo considered his request and proposed to the Central Committee that a debate be opened on "the precise mistakes committed by Imre Nagy, as well as the excesses of the erroneous statements excluding him from the Party." [8] Meanwhile, on the 6th the Central Committee had decided to hold a solemn funeral for Rajk and his alleged "accomplices." All the leaders were there, grouped around Mme Rajk and Imre Nagy. Three hundred thousand people, whose emotions could not be doubted, huddled tensely in a cold rain. One important person was absent from the ceremony: Erno Gerö. He had been summoned to the Crimea by the vacationing Soviet leaders, not only to be properly scolded but also because they wanted to persuade Tito to make peace with him.

Khrushchev, who had come to the Dalmatian coast in September for a few days rest, had invited the marshal and two of his top aides to continue, at Yalta, the talks begun during their June visit to Moscow. When the Yugoslavs arrived on the shores of the Black Sea, Gerö "happened" to be there. According to Tito, he had "heaped ashes on his head and had promised to correct his previous mistakes." [9] In return, the President of Yugoslavia agreed to receive a Hungarian delegation led by Gerö in Belgrade a few days later. Gerö saw this as a great victory, considering the sympathy that, until then, Tito was supposed to have had for Imre Nagy.

But his visit only raised again the hopes of the partisans of liberalization. On Sunday, October 21, in Györ, one of the principal provincial cities, the dramatist Gyula Hay, winner of the Kossuth literature prize, presided at a meeting which had been called to ask for the withdrawal of the Russian troops. This request was repeated the next day by 4,000 students gathered at the Vocational School in the capital. The same day the Petöfi Circle demanded the convening of the Central Committee to restore to Nagy and his comrades "a place worthy of them in the leadership of the party and the government," to publicly examine the "most delicate questions," including foreign trade reports and plans for the exploitation of Hungarian uranium, and finally, to establish "still closer relations with the Soviet party, the Soviet state and the Soviet people, on the basis of the Leninist principle of complete equality." [10]

It was in this supercharged atmosphere that the news of Gomulka's victory in Warsaw was announced. The students immediately decided to organize for the next day, Tuesday, October 23, a "silent demonstration to express their profound solidarity and their support of developments in Poland." [11] The demonstration, at first forbidden, was finally authorized. The radio announced at the same time that Gerö, back from Belgrade, would address the people at 8 P.M. He did not imagine what that demonstration was going to become.

Only a few hundred young people had assembled in the early afternoon, before Petöfi's statue, where a famous actor read his poem:

> Before God on high, we swear it.
> Nevermore will we be slaves,
> Nevermore . . .

But the crowd numbered 50,000—a mixture of students, workmen and soldiers—when it arrived before the statue of General Bem, the Polish hero of the 1848 revolution. Carrying Hungarian and Polish flags and portraits of Lenin, the crowd sang Kossuth's anthem, the *Marseillaise*—like the Bolsheviks in 1917—and the *Internationale*. After having cheered a list of claims presented by the students of the Technological University, the demonstrators went to the vast square before the Parliament building, a large, Neo-Gothic and vaguely Westminster-inspired palace on the shores of the Danube.

They asked for Nagy, whom a delegation went to fetch at his home. After having long hesitated, for he was increasingly fearful of becoming involved in events he would not be able to control, he let himself be pushed onto the balcony.

"Comrades!" he cried. The crowd, now swelled to nearly 200,000 people, interrupted him: "We are not comrades!" Nagy could see the flags brandished by the demonstrators had holes in the center where the Communist emblems had been torn from them and that the Red Star, a replica of the Kremlin's, which shone atop the Parliament building, had been turned off. The organizers of the demonstration, "revisionist" Communists, were visibly no longer in control: the Hungarian people now wanted to be rid of a regime which had been oppressing them for ten years in the name of freedom.

Nagy did not know what to do except to counsel prudence, which left his audience unsatisfied. Then he asked them to join him in singing the national anthem, which they all did.

It was at that point that Gerö began to speak. His speech showed the extent of his blindness. The few concessions, the promises of democratization were completely lost alongside of his unconditional praise of the U.S.S.R., "which has concluded agreements with us on the basis of complete equality," and his diatribe against "chauvinism," against "the people who want to set proletarian internationalism and Hungarian patriotism against each other." [12]

These words, transmitted by loudspeaker, had a provocative effect. Some demonstrators who were vainly demanding the airing of their views tried to enter the radio building to seize a microphone. It was there that the first shots were fired around 9 P.M. Half an hour later, shooting was raging in many places, while a truck dragged Stalin's statue from its pedestal amid general enthusiasm. Meanwhile, insurgents had taken over Debrecen, the country's third-largest city, and the call for a general strike spread like a trail of gunpowder.

The Central Committee, which had been convened for the 31st only, met immediately. Imre Nagy, who had just had a stormy meeting with Gerö, was also there. Partisans of the hard line and those of liberalization confronted each other, and some speakers advocated that Soviet troops be called in. They finally agreed on the nomination of Nagy to the presidency of the Council. Several "hard-liners" were ousted from the Politburo, and two "liberals" joined Kadar in the Secretariat. But Gerö remained as First Secretary and Hegedüs as First Vice Chairman of the Council. It would take more than that to calm a population which, far from having absolute confidence in Nagy, was inclined to see him as a hostage of the regime whose reassuring name would be used to cloak the repressions it had decided to launch.

To be sure, as soon as the reshuffle of the government and the Secretariat had been made public, the radio broadcast two communiqués on Wednesday at 9 A.M. which were going to raise public indignation to fever pitch. The first, signed by Nagy, announced the adoption of a "summary process to punish—by death —acts aimed at overthrowing the people's republic." [13] The second, unsigned—but who noticed it then?—revealed that the government, "in conformity with the Warsaw Pact," had decided "to call on the Soviet troops stationed in Hungary," to meet the "extremely grave situation" created by the "ignoble armed attacks by counterrevolutionary groups" that "the government was not prepared to repulse." [14] Needless to say, the pact in question, an Eastern replica of the Atlantic Pact, did not contain any sort of clause which called for assistance to be given to a government threatened with a revolution. In fact, the Russians had already begun to move without asking permission from anyone. The Hungarian soldiers, and even some of the police, stayed out of the fighting when they did not make common cause with the rioters.

Soon after, Nagy spoke on the radio. He announced a "greater democratization of public life . . . respect and fulfillment for the national Hungarian personality in the building of socialism," [15] and stated that those who laid down their arms before 2 P.M. would not be subject to martial law. He said nothing about calling for Soviet troops, who, in fact, seemed reluctant to intervene. In several places, the Russian soldiers fraternized with the demonstrators, who climbed on their tanks, waving flags.

At 2 P.M., fighting had not subsided at all, and a delay of four hours was given to the insurgents to surrender. A Soviet tank stopped in front of the Central Committee headquarters. Anastas Mikoyan and Mikhail Suslov emerged from it. They had come to fire Gerö, against whom they made a violent accusation, naturally omitting to recall that it was the Soviet party which had required that he succeed Rakosi three months earlier. It was Kadar who was now to take over the leadership of the party, and it was he who addressed the radio listeners in its name. He spoke only of repression and praised the assistance of "our brothers and allies, the Soviet soldiers." [16]

The comparison of his speech with Nagy's is revealing: it announced the break and the final tragedy. Those two old militants who had suffered, and, in Kadar's case, suffered physically, from the horrors of Rakosi-ism, were drawn into the conflict between communism and the great majority of the Hungarian nation—which the Polish newspapers of October 28, described as "completely on the side of the insurgents"—in two different ways. Imre Nagy, correctly described by François Fetjö as a "reformer lost in the Bolshevist jungle," [17] let the current of public opinion carry him much further than he might have wanted. Kadar, a simple man of good will, frightened by the backlash of "fascism" and aware of the limitations the U.S.S.R. imposed on the emancipation of its satellites, followed the "people" only within Moscow's abstract concept. For one as for the other, the choice was the culmination of a real personal tragedy, and like the amputation of half of themselves. Nagy died of it. As for Kadar, he already suffered frightful remorse. He was Minister of the Interior when Rajk, his old friend, whose wife had saved his life during the war, was arrested. Rajk stubbornly refused to confess to the imaginary crimes he was accused of. To make him do it, Rakosi thought of a device, which gave a measure of his baseness. He directed Kadar to promise Rajk a safe life in the Crimea—after a fictitious death sentence—if he admitted his guilt. The unfortunate man finally confessed and was hanged.

When Kadar himself regained his freedom, he called on Rajk's widow to ask if she forgave him. Her answer was worthy of a classical heroine: "I forgive you. My husband would have been murdered anyway . . . But can you forgive yourself? . . . If you want to live as a decent person, you should inform all Hungary, and the whole world, about the secret of the Rajk trial and about your part in it." [18] To this day, Kadar has kept silent.

Such an ordeal might have been enough to scar a soul forever. But Janos Kadar was to go on to sanction even the crushing of his countrymen by foreign troops and the execution of Imre Nagy and Pal Maleter, the insurgents' commander in chief, to whom he had also personally promised leniency.

It is easy to condemn this man, when one has not been faced with the obligation of making tragic choices. And considering the better life now enjoyed by Hungary, which in large part is owed to him, one can also think that he acted in the name of a certain conception of his duty. That all these trials had marked him to the depth of his soul, I myself cannot doubt, after speaking with him for two hours and seeing suddenly in his eyes the fleeting reflection of immense distress.

When Kadar, on the 25th at 12:30 P.M., was officially installed as First Secretary of the party, the situation had worsened. The strike was almost general throughout the country. Revolutionary committees which, in remembrance of the 1919 revolution, had taken the name of "councils" (soviets) had seized power in the large cities. Over the radio they demanded the departure of the Russians and of all those who had had dealings with them. Even in Budapest, in midmorning, there was bloodshed in Parliament Square. When gunshots broke out, the Russians, who had been quietly chatting with a large group of young men, apparently thinking they had fallen into a trap, reacted violently, killing scores of people. The news went around the city, and the people's anger was unleashed against members of the security police, the A.V.H., many of whom were shot down or lynched without further ado.

As soon as he had been named First Secretary, Kadar made another speech. He spoke again of the necessity of "repulsing by every means the armed attack against the government of the people's republic," but now he advocated "negotiations with the Soviet Government in a spirit of complete equality . . . in order to reach a just and equitable settlement." [19] Nagy, who followed him on the radio, went further: "Under my direction," he declared, "the new leadership of the party and the government are determined to learn a great lesson from these tragic events. As soon as order is restored, the National Assembly will convene. At that session I shall present a vast program of legitimate reforms. That program will deal with all major problems of our national life." He continued by announcing the complete reorganization of the government along the lines of a new national Popular Front "comprising the greatest democratic forces of the nation." He promised to take the initiative in starting negotiations between Hungary and the U.S.S.R., "especially in the matter of the withdrawal of Soviet troops." [20]

The last two promises were promptly kept. On Saturday the 27th, a new cabinet was formed, comprising representatives of two old parties—the peasants' and the smallholders', which had been dissolved by Rakosi—as well as the Marxist philosopher Georges Luckacs, the Stalinists' *bête noire*. The Social Democrats, however, had refused to participate.

On Sunday the 28th, at 5:25 P.M., while fighting was going on everywhere in Budapest, the insurgents, who controlled all the provinces, threatened to march on the capital. Imre Nagy ordered the government forces to cease fire, and announced an agreement with the Kremlin, whose troops were gradually to leave the city as new security forces were being organized. In that same speech, taking the opposite position from the one he had expressed three days earlier, he "rejected the opinion that the present formidable popular movement is a counterrevolution." In reality, he said, it "embraces and unifies the whole nation," and "its aim is to ensure our national independence and sovereignty and to further the democratization of our social, political and economic life. It is the grave crimes of the preceding era which have triggered that great movement." [21]

The revolution, therefore, had attained the major part of its objectives. Wisdom, for the Hungarian people, would be found in resting content, as Gomulka and Tito counseled in urgent personal messages to Nagy. But how was it possible to make a whole nation in revolt comprehend that the tyranny which taught it a horror of communism, was not inherent in communism? How could it be persuaded not to go the whole way, when it had made the Hungarian Government yield and held the Red Army in check? Wasn't it encouraged by the innumerable signs of sympathy which poured in from the whole world and by the belief that those signs would be translated into concrete aid if necessary?

On October 25, Eisenhower declared: "I feel with the Hungarian people." [22] The following day, Washington persuaded London and Paris to ask the Security Council to make an investigation. On the 27th, in a Dallas speech, Dulles saluted the "challenge hurled by the heroic people of Hungary against the murderous fire of the Red Army's tanks," as well as the fight of the Polish people "to loosen the Soviet grip on their beloved country." While he did not consider those countries as "eventual military allies," he affirmed that the wish of the United States was to see them "endowed with freely chosen governments" and promised them "generous economic aid" [23] in the event they succeeded in liberating themselves.

When the Security Council met on October 28, at 9 P.M. (European time), Imre Nagy had already announced the agreement with the U.S.S.R. for the evacuation of Budapest. The Western Powers paid no heed and insisted on having put on the agenda the examination of "the situation created in Hungary by the action of foreign military forces which, by using violence, have disregarded the rights of the Hungarian people guaranteed by the peace treaty to which the Hungarian Government and the joint Allied Powers are parties." [24] The Allied request was unanimously approved, without the U.S.S.R., which voted against a move which its representative Sobolev qualified as "provocative" and conceived for the purpose of "spawning criminal activities in Hungary and inflaming the international situation." [25] Yugoslavia abstained, its spokesman affirming his conviction that "the Hungarian Government and the people of Hungary will find a solution to the present difficulties in conformity with their best interests." [26]

As for Radio Free Europe, whose broadcasts were lapped up by the Hungarians, its military expert declared on October 29: "Imre Nagy and his followers want to revise and modernize the Trojan Horse episode. They need a cease-fire so that the present government in power in Budapest can maintain its position as long as possible. Those who are fighting for liberty must not lose sight even for a minute of the plans of the government opposing them." [27]

If a compromise had been possible, it was obvious that such a campaign—to say the least—was not the kind to facilitate it. It could only stir up natural Russian anxieties over the consequences that an emancipation of Hungary would have. But it was on the same day that the Israeli troops launched their assault against Egypt. Following the script decided on a few days before, Paris and London delivered an ultimatum to Tel Aviv and Cairo on October 30, "directing them to withdraw 17 kilometers on both sides of the canal and to allow the deployment of Franco-British troops at Port Said, Ismailia and Suez." If those demands were not complied with within twelve hours, Mollet and Eden specified before their respective parliaments, the Franco-British troops "would temporarily occupy key positions along the canal, to ensure free passage of ships from all countries." [28]

How could the Kremlin and the countries of the third world help but believe in the complete hypocrisy of the protest over Soviet intervention in Hungarian internal affairs sent to the Security Council by the two capitals?

It was easier for the U.S.S.R. to pose as the only true defender of law and justice before the Afro-Asian peoples, outraged by the Israeli attack and the Franco-British ultimatum, because on October 30 it had made final peace with the Hungarian insurgents and recognized, once and for all, the right of self-determination for the peoples of its bloc.

To be sure, Radio Moscow, in the evening, broadcast a long declaration in which the Soviet Government admitted that "violations" and "mistakes" had "demeaned the principle of equal rights in the relations between socialist states." It recognized the just and progressive character of the workers' movement which had "raised the questions of the need for furthering the battle against bureaucratic excesses in the state apparatus," while it denounced the forces of reaction and counterrevolution which were involved in it. It announced, above all, that, having noted that "the continued presence of Soviet units in Hungary could be used as a pretext for further aggravating the situation," it "had given instructions to its military commanders to withdraw their troops from the city of Budapest as soon as the Hungarian Government feels they can be dispensed with." At the same time, it declared itself "prepared to engage in negotiations with the Hungarian People's Government and the other signatories of the Warsaw Pact, regarding the presence of Soviet troops elsewhere on the territory of Hungary."

But the declaration was not limited to Soviet-Magyar relations. It affirmed that the people of the socialist countries could only base their relations on the principles of complete equality of rights, with respect to territorial integrity, political independence and sovereignty, and nonintervention in the internal affairs of all. That did not exclude but, on the contrary, supposed close fraternal cooperation and mutual assistance. And the Soviet Government said that it was ready to examine, with the other socialist states, the means of suppressing any possibility of endangering those principles, as well as recalling its economic and military consultants, and, if need be, its troops.[29]

That text was remarkable in many ways, but especially because, for the first time, it specified the composition of what could be a "commonwealth" of socialist countries (in Russian, *Sodrujestvo,* a word derived from *drujba*—"friendship"—which literally means "cofriendship").

This explained why it had such a resounding reception, especially in China, where the tendency of the Russian Big Brother to behave as a protector as much as a self-interested exploiter had always been greatly resented. It was also striking that the declaration appropriated the famous "Five Principles" of international cooperation adopted by the Asiatic states on the eve of the Bandung Conference. Imre Nagy, in fact, had taken his inspiration from them in an *aide-mémoire* addressed to his party's Central Committee at the beginning of January 1956, and intended to define the basis of relations between socialist countries.

But publication of the Soviet declaration probably came too late. The whole day had been marked by events which proved that Imre Nagy was moving farther and farther away from the Kremlin.

Early in the morning the insurgents had seized, after a three-hour seige, the building of the Greater Budapest Communist Federation and massacred its occupants. Among them was the Federation secretary, Imre Mezö—one of the most faithful supporters of the new Prime Minister—two colonels who had come to discuss with him the organization of workers' militias, and forty-five young men who had been forcibly incorporated into the A.V.H. Some of them had been burned alive. The savagery of the incident and Mezö's death had deeply affected Nagy and made him understand to what lengths the popular furor could lead if it were not promptly cooled off by substantive concessions. He had therefore decided to announce the end of the one-party system and the formation of a new government "on the basis existing in 1945, during the regime of the democratic parties' coalition." [30] An extraordinary cabinet was formed in which Bela Kovacs, once arrested and indicated for espionage by the Russians, represented the smallholders. Political parties reopened their offices and published newspapers. Cardinal Mindszenty, Primate of Hungary, condemned for high treason and sentenced to forced labor for life in 1949, was freed and spoke in public. Negotiations were started with the various insurgent groups. The radio broadcast a communiqué asserting that the call for Soviet troops on October 24 had been made by Gerö and Hegedüs, and not by Imre Nagy.

Mikoyan and Suslov returned that night to Moscow, all smiles, after having met with Nagy, Kadar and Tildy. They had without difficulty agreed on everything, while the Soviet press published almost enthusiastic articles on the situation in Hungary. For *Pravda,* for example, there was no doubt that the Nagy government "had obtained the people's support." Such appreciation was the equivalent of recognition.

Was Mikoyan sincere? At the time, his interlocutors did not doubt it. But did he have the power to confirm decisions which meant the end of the "proletariat dictatorship," an essential part of a socialist regime? A mere member of the Presidium of the Central Committee, had he been authorized to accept in principle a decision as grave as the withdrawal of Hungary from the Warsaw Pact, which Tildy had openly mentioned to him?

A passage—not sufficiently noticed at the time—from the October 30 Soviet declaration justifies at least posing the question: "The defense of socialist gains in the Hungarian People's Government is at the moment the primary and sacred task of the workers, the peasants, the intellectuals, and all the working people of Hungary. The Soviet Government expresses its conviction that the peoples of the socialist countries will not allow reactionary forces, whether foreign or domestic, to undermine those foundations of the democratic People's Government. . . ." [31] The warning was clear: if the foundations were shaken, "the peoples of the socialist countries" would set things to right.

Nothing proves that Nagy did not understand the warning. He had not deliberately thrown himself into a venture which represented a real provocation for the U.S.S.R.; it was rather because he could not resist a tide of popular feeling which—unlike what had happened in Poland—demanded not only the "liberalization" of the regime, but its destruction and a break with the U.S.S.R. It may also be because he overestimated the support he could hope to obtain from those who, from the outside, unreservedly encouraged the Hungarians' intransigence. Let us listen to Radio Free Europe on October 31: "The Ministry of Defense and the Ministry of the Interior are still in Communist hands. Do not let this continue, Freedom Fighters. Do not hang your weapons on the wall. . . . This little government offers no guarantee. The actual situation is such that it must not be accepted even on a provisional basis. It is urgent, as the free radios have demanded, that a new National Provisional Government, capable of facing the situation, be formed immediately." [32]

The population did not need such encouragement: "No one, at home, wants communism. From the youngest child to the oldest man, no one wants communism. We have had enough of it, forever," an old gentleman told the special representative of Warsaw's *Nowa Kultura,* who had asked the meaning of the expression *"Nem Kell Kummunizmus,"* written across a document.

At Györ, a national revolutionary committee which controlled a radio and rebroadcast programs from Free Europe refused to recognize the Budapest cabinet. It demanded a provisional government and free elections. At Miskolc, the President of the revolutionary Council informed Nagy that unless he secured the departure of Russian troops he would cease recognizing his authority. Even in Budapest a sizable group of insurgents, headed by Jozsef Dudas, a long-time Communist who had become a Deputy of the smallholders before he was thrown into prison by Rakosi, had seized the building of the Communist Party's newspaper and refused to lay down their arms. The C.P. itself had practically ceased to exist when Janos Kadar announced on the radio on November 1 that "the Communists who have fought against Rakosi's communism" have decided to organize a new party, the "party of Hungarian socialist workers," which, "on the basis of national independence . . . will defend the gains of the Hungarian revolution . . . the cause of democracy and socialism."

Part of that speech also ought to have attracted attention. In effect, it complemented the warning given by the October 30 Soviet declaration and clarified Kadar's subsequent behavior: "We are speaking to you frankly. The people's uprising has come to a crossroads: either the Hungarian democratic parties have enough strength to be able to maintain our gains, or we must face an open counterrevolution . . . either the insurrection will ensure our people the essential benefits of democracy . . . or then we will fall back into foreign slavery. There exists a grave and alarming danger: an armed foreign intervention could bring to our country the tragic fate of Korea. Our anxiety over the future of the country compels us to do the impossible to avert that grave danger." [33]

The arrival of Soviet reinforcements had been reported the day before from several points throughout the country, and the capital, although it had been evacuated, found itself practically surrounded. At 11 A.M., Nagy, on the same November 1, summoned the Soviet ambassador, Andropov, to ask him for an explanation. Without batting an eye, the diplomat answered that it was being done only to ensure that there would be no incidents over the departure of the regular units. Nagy did not believe a word of it. An ultimatum could have permitted negotiations, but a barefaced lie could signify only one thing: drastic moves were underway. Only one solution was left, a desperate solution: a headlong flight forward.

He then got the party leadership and the Council of Ministers to approve the principle of a declaration of neutrality to be immediately brought before the United Nations. The declaration was based on the fact that by bringing in reinforcements the U.S.S.R. had violated the Warsaw Pact and its own October 30 declaration.

Kadar attended those two meetings and made no objection to the decisions taken. In fact, when Andropov was summoned again in the afternoon to be told of the measures decided upon and of the request for immediate negotiations, he intervened after Nagy: "If your tanks enter Budapest," he told the ambassador, "I shall go down into the street and fight against you with my bare hands." [34]

Less than three days later, the tanks had entered Budapest, perhaps not on Kadar's request—something he has ceaselessly denied since that time—but, in any case, with his approval. Had he been playing a part before Nagy on that November 1, before or had he been taken in hand again by the Russians only a little later? No evidence, at the present time, permits one to decide with certainty between the two explanations.

In any case, Nagy did not know that Kadar had already reached Ujgorod, a town in Soviet territory, at the time when he broadcast the declaration by which his government "proclaimed the neutrality of the People's Republic of Hungary" and affirmed its intention "to have relations of true friendship with its neighbors, the Soviet Union and all the peoples of the world, based on independence and equality, and in conformity with the spirit of the United Nations Charter." [35] The following day, November 2, he cabled Hammarskjöld to ask the Great Powers to recognize the neutrality of his country. He protested again the movements of Soviet troops and proposed the opening of negotiations, in Poland, for their withdrawal and on the measures to be taken for the renunciation of the Warsaw Pact by Hungary.

On the 3rd, Andropov went to Nagy to inform him that the U.S.S.R. accepted immediate negotiations on the first point, although it had not been able to select the delegation to discuss Hungary's withdrawal from the Warsaw Pact.

The parley started at noon between, on one side, three Russian generals and, on the other, Colonel Pal Maleter, a veteran of the Spanish War, parachuted by the Russians into Transylvania in 1944, and a hero of the insurrection, who that morning had been made Minister of National Defense, and General Kovacs, army Chief of Staff. It progressed rapidly, the Russians insisting on such details as the reconstruction of monuments to the glory of the Red Army which had been destroyed by the insurgents, or honors to be rendered to the troops at the time of their departure, so, that their interlocutors were convinced of their good faith. The meeting was adjourned in the afternoon, to be resumed at 10 P.M. at the Russian Army's headquarters on Csepel Island, in the southern part of Budapest.

Maleter and the others did not suspect anything. They were seated at the table with Malinin, the Soviet Commander in Chief in Hungary, when at midnight an individual without any insignia of rank and surrounded by several armed officials burst into the banquet

room and announced that he had come to arrest the Hungarian negotiators. An oath burst from Malinin's lips. The civilian, who was
none other than General Serov, chief of the U.S.S.R. security police,
cautioned him to keep quiet. Maleter was not seen again. He was
executed along with Imre Nagy, and the news was only made public
on June 17, 1958.

This was, at any rate, the version of the facts given by the special
U.N. committee on the Hungarian question based on the testimony
of Erdei, one of Maleter's assistants who had witnessed the scene.[36]
The "white paper" published by the Kadar government [37] differed on
only two points: (1) The Soviet authorities had refused to negotiate
with Maleter—but why then would he have put himself into the
lion's mouth?—and (2) the Hungarian authorities made the arrest.
The difference was minimal and the ambush indisputable. Had Stalin
influenced his heirs to such a point that three years after his death,
and having more than profusely denounced his crimes, they chose,
like him, to add a gratuitous ignominy to the cruelty of decisions
imposed on them by reasons of state!

"We would have accepted another Finland," Khrushchev was
subsequently to tell a neutral ambassador, "but the Hungarians were
in the process of bringing back fascism." [38] In the eyes of the Russians one is easily a fascist. But it was understandable that they
could not have accepted the establishment of a regime in Budapest
which was more and more turning its back upon that "people's democracy" which Nagy on October 28 described as being "reborn."

On November 3 he had made another reorganization, giving
eight of the ten ministerial posts to non-Communists. And yet, one of
the portfolios had been assigned to Kadar, whose advice had certainly not been sought as he had disappeared two days previously.

If that government had been preserved, there would have been
free elections. As to the number of votes the Communists could have
won in them, Tibor Meray, Nagy's friend and confidant, had no
illusions: no more than 6 to 8 percent. As in 1945 the smallholders'
Christian Democratic Party would have become again, in all probability, the dominant element in the political life of the majority of
the population, and the Catholic Church in its social and intellectual
life. Anti-Semitism, which had often manifested itself, both before

and during the war, had a greater chance of flourishing again because Rakosi and his lieutenants were Jews and many people were inclined to see a relationship between their crimes and their race. Already, in several places, mistreatment of Jews had been reported.

To be sure it could be expected that a government born of free elections would have respected the essential achievements of the revolution: land reform, nationalization of heavy industry, social security. But it would have abandoned agrarian collectivization and restored a large private sector in commerce, handicrafts, small industry. And, most of all, it would have ceased to draw its intellectual inspiration from Moscow and instead have sought enlightenment, less grandiose but more comfortable, from the West. In a word, it is certain that the "foundations of the people's democracy" that, according to the October 30 Soviet declaration, the "peoples of the socialist countries" were determined to protect would have essentially disappeared.

If Hungary had been the only country involved, the Kremlin might, however, have compromised. But if Nagy had finally won, its example would undoubtedly have been an almost irresistible encouragement to counterrevolution in other socialist countries, beginning with Poland, where the Budapest outbreaks had inspired many manifestations of solidarity. In that respect, it is characteristic that Gomulka, Tito and Mao, who had saluted the Hungarian Revolution and had more or less openly condemned, depending on the case, the first Russian intervention, were unanimous in viewing the second as a necessary evil.

Today, however, there is no longer any doubt that the Soviet leaders hesitated a long time before resigning themselves to intervene. It is not only the Peking *People's Daily* which, in one of its endless indictments of the U.S.S.R., wrote on September 5, 1963: "At the critical moment when the Hungarian counterrevolutionaries were in control of Budapest, the leadership of the Soviet party had, for some time, the intention of continuing its policy of capitulation and of abandoning Hungary to the counterrevolution," while, according to it, the Chinese party had "formulated correct proposals" that "the Soviet leadership had finally accepted." Khrushchev himself had recalled those discussions, saying that his own determination had never varied, but had met with some opposition. Speaking to the workers of the Mavag factory in Budapest on December 2, 1959, he declared: "Between ourselves, we have also made statements like these: Will the Hungarian comrades correctly understand us if we give them assistance, inasmuch as some workers, misled by the revolution, are standing by the fascist rebels?" [39] Guiseppe Boffa, who was then the Moscow correspondent of the Italian Communist newspaper *L'Unita,* reported the "perplexity" of the Russian leaders, some of whom wanted to "let the Hungarian people take care of the conflict." [40]

Once the decision was made, however, the operation was briskly handled. On November 4, a few hours after Maleter's arrest, the inhabitants of Budapest, getting ready to enjoy their first quiet Sunday, were awakened at dawn by a cannonade. At 5:05 A.M. an unidentified radio station broadcast an "open letter to the working people of Hungary." It was signed by four of Nagy's former ministers, Kadar among them, and stated that they had understood on November 1 that they could do nothing against the "counterrevolutionary danger" [41] while they remained in the government. They had therefore decided to form a "worker and peasant revolutionary government," whose composition Kadar himself made public an hour later. He announced at the same time that this government had asked the commander of the Soviet Army to "help our nation to crush the sinister forces of reaction and to restore order and calm in the country." He added that once this was accomplished, the Hungarian Government "would begin negotiations with the Soviet Government and other parties to the Warsaw Pact, regarding the evacuation of Hungary by Soviet troops." [42] Thirteen years later, they are still there.

Nagy, speaking in public for the last time, a few moments before Kadar, had declared: "At daybreak, Soviet forces started an attack against our capital, obviously with the intention to overthrow the legal Hungarian democratic government. Our troops are fighting. The government is in its place. I notify the people of our country and the entire world of this fact." [43]

The Russians attacked with hundreds of tanks, both systematically and brutally, not hesitating, for example, to rake with machine-gun fire a queue of housewives before a food store. In a few hours they were in control of the bridges and the principal public buildings, notably the radio station and the War Ministry, whose last defenders were shot down on the spot. But the insurgents still controlled radio transmitters in the provinces, amateur radio stations and the Associated Press wires. Until the last minute, while thousands of combatants were fighting an unequal struggle with small machine guns and Molotov cocktails, and tens of thousands of men and women of all ages were taking the road to exile, Nagy and his supporters would beg the outside world to come to their assistance.

But nothing came, beyond platonic gestures intended to cheaply appease the scruples of leaders aware of their impotence. Eisenhower wrote to Bulganin, asking him to withdraw his troops. Nagy had appealed to the Security Council to instruct the governments of Budapest and Moscow to open immediate negotiations for the withdrawal of Russian forces. Following the announcement of the second Soviet intervention, the Council met in emergency session on Sunday, November 4. By 9 votes to 1, Yugoslavia abstaining, it asked Moscow to recall its troops without delay. But the negative vote was that of the U.S.S.R. and was the equivalent of a veto. The United States was then able to obtain, this time with Yugoslavia's support, the convocation of an extraordinary session of the General Assembly, the second in that eventful day, as there had already been one in the morning to adopt a draft resolution for the creation of an emergency force in the Middle East.

By 50 votes to 8 (the Soviet bloc), with 15 abstentions (among which were India, Yugoslavia and the Arab countries), it adopted a long resolution authored by Cabot Lodge which once more asked the Kremlin to withdraw its troops from Hungary, affirmed the right of the Magyar people to independence and asked the Soviet and the Budapest governments to allow U.N. observers into Hungary.

The debate was the occasion of a beautiful display of eloquence, and no one envied Sobolev, who was called upon to defend the totally indefensible—morally and legally—position of the Soviet Government before the international organization. But the noble words which had been spoken could not change in any way the fate of the Hungarian people. On the 9th, although the general strike was still in effect, all armed resistance had practically ceased. As for Nagy, he had sought refuge in the Yugoslav Embassy with a group of faithful supporters.

What could the West have done to prevent this denouement? Intervene militarily? They did not consider it for one moment, despite all the appeals for help they received, as it would have meant a head-on confrontation with the Soviet Government and the risk of a nuclear war. The error was to have let the insurgents believe in the possibility of intervention. In reality, the only trump they could have played, without in the least being certain of its effectiveness, was political. It might have been possible to propose a neutralization of central Europe, including at least a part of German territory, to ensure a balance of concessions from the two camps. For the Allies to reach agreement on such a bold initiative, in such a short time, it would have been necessary for their entente to be complete and their hands clean; in other words, they should not have been violently opposing each other over Suez, giving the U.S.S.R. the opportunity of having its own wrongs ignored while it was righting the wrongs of others.

BIBLIOGRAPHY AND NOTES

[1] Keesing's, 14827 A.
[2] Est et Ouest, No. 181, p. 80.
[3] Meray, op. cit., pp. 49–50.
[4] Ibid., p. 53.
[5] Tito's speech at Pula, November 11, 1956, reported in Keesing's, 15258 A.
[6] La révolution hongroise. Documents of the "Tribune Libre" (Paris: Plon, 1957), pp. 7–8.
[7] Meray, op. cit., pp. 53–54.
[8] Ibid., p. 59.
[9] Keesing's, 15258 A.
[10] La révolution hongroise, op. cit., p. 23.
[11] Ibid.
[12] Ibid., pp. 28–29.
[13] Est et Ouest, No. 181, p. 109.
[14] La révolution hongroise, op. cit., p. 36.
[15] Ibid., pp. 36–37.
[16] Ibid., p. 47.
[17] François Fejtö, preface to French edition of Imre Nagy on Communism, op. cit., p. 5.
[18] Georges Paloczi-Horvath, The Un-

defeated (London: Secker & Warburg, 1959), p. 259.

19 *La révolution hongroise, op. cit.,* p. 55.

20 *Ibid.*

21 *Ibid.,* p. 101.

22 *Le Monde,* October 27, 1956.

23 *La révolution hongroise, op. cit.,* p. 109.

24 Année politique, 1956, p. 373.

25 *La révolution hongroise, op. cit.,* p. 108.

26 *Ibid.*

27 Meray, *op. cit.,* p. 140.

28 Année politique, 1956, p. 382.

29 Meray, *op. cit.,* pp. 144–48.

30 *Est et Ouest,* No. 181, p. 127.

31 Meray, *op. cit.,* pp. 188–92.

32 *Ibid.,* p. 169.

33 *Est et Ouest,* No. 181, p. 132.

34 Meray, *op. cit.,* p. 194.

35 *Est et Ouest,* No. 181, p. 130.

36 *The Truth About the Nagy Affair* (London: Secker & Warburg, for the Congress of Cultural Freedom, 1959), pp. 10–11.

87 *The Counterrevolutionary Conspiracy of Imre Nagy and His Accomplices.* Publication of the information office of the Council of Ministers of the Hungarian People's Republic (Budapest, 1958).

38 Author's personal notes.

39 *Pravda,* December 3, 1959.

40 Giuseppe Boffa, *Inside the Khrushchev Era* (New York: Marzani and Munsell, 1959), p. 105.

41 *Est et Ouest,* No. 181, p. 121.

42 *Ibid.,* p. 136.

48 *The Truth About the Nagy Affair, op. cit.,* p. 105.

CHAPTER 11

THE FIRST "WEEK

OF TRUTH" — SUEZ

Now to engage in a combat wherein you risk your
whole fortunes without putting forth your entire
strength is, as I observed before, . . . an utterly
foolhardy course.

> —Machiavelli, *Reflections on the
> First Decade of the History of
> Titus Livius, III,* 37 (Translated
> by Ninian Smart)

AN ARMISTICE IS NOT PEACE. THIS BECAME APPARENT
shortly after the failure of the secret attempts of Abdullah of Jordan
to bring about a lasting settlement between the Jews and Arabs in the
years 1949–1950. The continual influx of immigrants into Israel convinced the Cairo leaders that not only would Tel Aviv never agree to
the repatriation of the Palestinian refugees, but that it would be even
more tempted to carry out the plans of the right-wing Zionist irreden-
tists. They therefore set out to try and prevent the Hebrew state from
consolidating itself by prohibiting ships headed for its ports from using
the Suez Canal and the Strait of Tiran, which commanded the entrance
to Elath, the only Israeli port on the Red Sea. It was in vain that the
Security Council enjoined them, on September 1, 1951, to let the ships
pass; three years later a Soviet veto blocked a new Israeli move to
that effect. In order to sound out the intentions of the Great Powers, an Israeli cargo ship, the *Bat Galim,* steamed into Port Said; it
was seized and its crew detained for three months without the international organization's doing very much about it.

This inaction was all the more bitterly resented by Jewish public opinion because, at the same time, after the signing of the evacuation agreement, British troops were to withdraw from Egypt over a twenty-month period. For the Jews it marked the loss of their last chance of obtaining the re-establishment of free passage through the canal and the Red Sea.

A new threat was soon added to these disturbing events. The Israeli raid against Gaza in February 1955, led to an increase of guerrillas, or terrorists, operating from the Palestinian territory occupied by the Egyptian Army. Discontented with a government which was unable to stop them, the Israeli voters sent to the Knesset, their Parliament, a majority of confirmed advocates of the hard line in dealing with the Arabs.

A few weeks later, the signing of the Czech-Egyptian agreement on arms deliveries was made known, and Jerusalem came to the conclusion that Nasser would proceed to attack after the departure of the British and as soon as his troops were sufficiently well equipped.

In September the President of the Council, Moshe Sharett, issued an appeal "to all Israeli citizens, to the dispersed Jewish people, and to the whole world," [1] for arms to be supplied to the Hebrew state. He went to Paris, London and Geneva to meet with the Western leaders, going so far as to use the expression "preventive war." [2] But that phrase hardly reflected his thinking. Considered too soft, he was forced to yield his post on November 2 to David Ben-Gurion, whose resolve had been further strengthened by a long retreat in a *kibbutz*. In his inauguration speech he warned the Powers that "the people of Israel will not be led like cattle to the slaughter. . . ." And although he reaffirmed his desire to respect the armistice agreements "meticulously," he also added that he would take effective measures to ensure the safety of the settlements located in the frontier regions.[3]

He soon translated words into action. The next day a unit of the Israeli Army attacked the Egyptian positions in the theoretically demilitarized territory of El Auja, on the edge of the Sinai Desert. Other incidents occurred in the next few days at different points on the Arab-Israeli borders. On December 11, following a burst of Syrian artillery fire, an Israeli commando unit crossed Lake Tiberias, killed about fifty soldiers and civilians, and returned with some thirty prisoners. On January 18, 1956, the Security Council unanimously condemned this "flagrant violation" [4] of the armistice.

Ben-Gurion did not expect to achieve any lasting solution from these raids. In November 1955, after the failure of the United States' mediation attempts, Ben-Gurion had ordered Dayan, head of the Army, to study plans for an invasion of the Sinai Peninsula, to destroy the terrorist bases and to open up access to Elath. But he lacked the weapons to launch such an invasion, and as soon as Guy Mollet was installed at the head of the French Government, in January, he had turned to him invoking socialist solidarity. This was an approach which could not fail to move Mollet, Secretary General of the S.F.I.O., the French section of the Workers' International, and a man whose entire career was so closely identified with his party. Mollet wasted no time in informing Jerusalem's leaders that he would not abandon them and would, moreover, with Washington's permission, fulfill the promise of an arms delivery made by Edgar Faure to Sharett.

However, although those deliveries very quickly exceeded the amount initially foreseen, Paris did not inform the tripartite body created by the French-Anglo-American declaration of 1950 to watch over the maintenance of the *status quo* in the Near East. The increased shipments were the result of patient negotiations by Shimon Pérès, the Israeli Secretary of State for Defense, with the French Minister of War, Bourgès Manoury. Sharett took offense at these negotiations, conducted without his participation and which he regarded as dangerous. In June 1956 he resigned in favor of the energetic Golda Meir, who had been Israel's first ambassador to Moscow.

In this climate the nationalization of the Suez Canal on July 26, and the violent reaction it provoked in Paris and London, could only be considered as an unexpected windfall by the Jewish Government. Some of those in Bourgès-Manoury's entourage immediately talked about a joint action against Egypt. Pérès, who had rushed to Paris, was asked how much time it would take Israel to reach the shores of the canal. His answer was one week. When a top-level officer asked him whether the Jewish state would be willing to join France if it were to engage in a war against Nasser, Pérès replied in the affirmative.[5] No other proposal could have been more pleasing to Jerusalem's leaders, who were far from possessing the air cover needed to launch an attack against the Egyptians—well supplied with Soviet planes.

At that time, however, plans did not go any further, except for an additional speed-up in the delivery of French weapons to the Hebrew state. Paris was, in effect, involved in preparations for a joint operation with the British, although the attitude of the latter tended to disprove the proverb according to which the friends of our friends are also our friends. Eden naturally wanted to get rid of Nasser, but on no account did he want a dispute with the rest of the Arabs, something which, in his opinion, was bound to happen if the least indication of a deal with Israel were to become known.

Moreover, it seemed that Jordan, the traditional bridgehead of British influence in the Middle East, was in grave danger of falling under Cairo's authority, as the pro-Nasser faction, which was very strong among the Palestinian refugees, gave every indication of winning the general elections to be held on October 21. In order to avoid this unpleasant eventuality, the London Government spoke once again of sending an Iraqi division to Jordan, and it used every opportunity to underscore the viability of its treaty of alliance with Amman. Evidently, it was trying to gain popular favor at a time when border incidents with the Jewish state were increasing. Ben-Gurion, however, whom experience had taught to be extremely wary of the British, was convinced, not without some cause, that King Hussein of Jordan was personally encouraging the terrorists. On September 24, in the wake of three particularly daring attacks, he got his cabinet to approve reprisals against Jordan's Arab Legion in spite of his desire "not to give the British a pretext to condemn Israel and thereby cover up their own ineffectiveness in the Suez affair," wrote Dayan.[6] In the same way, it was decided, should Iraqi troops enter Jordan, to have Israeli troops occupy that part of the country which prior to 1947 had belonged to Palestine.

On October 10, implementing this decision, the Israeli Army carried out a lightning operation against the Jordanian village of Qalqilya, shooting about a hundred civilians and soldiers. On the 12th the British chargé d'affaires in Tel Aviv warned Ben-Gurion that the Iraqi division was about to enter Jordan and that London would come to the aid of the Hashemite kingdom if Israel were to invade it. The Prime Minister replied in the same tone that, were this to happen, he would preserve his freedom of action. Public declarations on both sides strengthened the determination of both governments. The spokesman for the Foreign Office approved an interview in which Nuri es-Said, the Iraqi Prime Minister, suggested the settlement of the Arab-Israeli conflict on the basis of the 1947 partition plan. He referred to Eden's November speech on the frontier revisions, which had been so poorly received by Jewish public opinion. Tension mounted rapidly on both sides. A conflict seemed imminent, to the extent that when President Eisenhower, on October 27, sent an urgent message to Ben-Gurion asking him to abstain from the military action which preparations by the Israeli Army had seemed to indicate was forthcoming, he still thought that the latter was going to attack Jordan.

Two important things, however, were about to enlighten him: the victory of the pro-Nasser faction in the Jordanian elections of October 21, immediately interpreted in Israel to mean that the danger of an Iraqi intervention had passed, since Nasser and Nuri es-Said were at sword's point; and especially the speech which Ben-Gurion gave before the Knesset October 17 in which he declared that "the greatest danger still is threatened from the Egyptian dictator, who dominates the other Arab states and never tires of proclaiming his intention to destroy Israel." [7]

While an outbreak of hostilities between the Jewish state and the Hashemite kingdom seemed imminent, this sudden attack against Nasser provoked general surprise. In order to explain that speech, one would have to know about the secret negotiations, which remain controversial to this day, that led Paris and Jerusalem to agree in principle, at the end of September, on joint action against Egypt. On the 26th, Pineau informed the British leaders, for the first time, of Ben-Gurion's intention to attack the Sinai Peninsula. He expressed his desire to see France and Great Britain support that operation, in the event that the complaint which they had just made to the Security Council, against the advice of the United States, was not, as seemed probable, to be acted upon.

On October 3, Eden informed the British Government of this proposal. He, as well as his colleagues, were still under the shock of Dulles' declaration that it was not a matter "of sharpening the teeth" of the canal-users' association, as he did not believe the latter had any.[8] On the same day, Eden handed Pineau, who was passing through London, an agreement in principle.

The French Government agreed to try to persuade Jerusalem's leaders to stop being concerned with Jordan and to reserve all their energies for Egypt; while Selwyn Lloyd and Pineau, having gone to New York, met outside the Security Council meetings with their Egyptian colleague Mahmud Fawzi. On the 5th the French minister told Dulles that "he did not believe that any peaceful way existed"[9]; due to the efforts of Hammarskjöld, however, the Three-Power negotiations were proceeding quite rapidly, based on a list of six principles drawn up by Selwyn Lloyd. Despite the fact that Cairo refused to permit the free passage of Israeli ships and that on the 13th a Soviet veto put an end to the Security Council debates, Washington believed that negotiations would be resumed and that the crisis was over. "A very great crisis is behind us,"[10] President Eisenhower naively declared. But shortly after, there was again some measure of anxiety in the State Department, Eden having completely neglected to inform the Americans of the conversations he had had in Paris on October 16. "It is very strange," Dulles said to his aides, "that we have heard nothing from the British for ten days. We must try to find out what they and the French are up to."[11]

What they were up to became known a few days later. At the request of the British, a script of such bad faith was worked out that it seemed almost naive. It was understood that when the Israelis attacked Egypt, France and Great Britain were to use the excuse that the security of the canal was in danger to deliver an ultimatum to the two belligerents asking them to withdraw their troops, or else they would occupy the Canal Zone. This was the first time in history that a country was threatened, in the event that it did not comply with an ultimatum, with the invasion of the territory—of its enemy. But Eden, in his quite vain desire not to cut his ties with the Arabs, stuck firmly to that pitiful tactic, the complete hypocrisy of which would become self-evident when it became known

—only in 1964—that Selwyn Lloyd had secretly met with Ben-Gurion near Paris on October 22, in Pineau's presence, in order to finalize details of the operation.

They decided that Israel would attack on October 29 in the direction of the canal; that the Anglo-French ultimatum would be delivered on the 30th to give the Israeli soldiers sufficient time to arrive within the proximity of the canal; that Ben-Gurion would accept the terms of that ultimatum by withdrawing his troops fifteen kilometers; that the R.A.F. and the French Air Force were to pound the Egyptian airfields beginning on the 31st; and that the expeditionary corps was to land on November 6, the same day the American Presidential elections were being held.

In the beginning everything went according to plan, except for the British Air Force, which only went into action after some delay. Complete surprise was achieved even in France and in England, where very few people shared in the secret, for fear that some indiscretion would lead to a new dilatory action by the United States. Even the Secretary General of the Quai d'Orsay and the French ambassadors in Washington and London were themselves unaware of what was being hatched.

In Cairo, Nasser had taken seriously the agreement in principle, presented a few days earlier by Pineau and Selwyn Lloyd, for "exploratory talks" with Egypt—something which had been suggested by Dulles and Hammarskjöld—and Nasser's Foreign Minister had drafted an acceptance telegram a few hours before the onslaught of the first Israeli paratroopers. Even after the ultimatum had been handed to him, he at first refused to believe the evidence. In an interview with the weekly journal *Akher Saa* on December 5, 1956, he was to relate that in trying to put himself in Eden's place, he thought at the time that "The aim of the ultimatum was simply to intimidate Egypt and to make it fear an Anglo-French landing in order to induce it to maintain the bulk of its forces in the delta and thus to prevent it from using its entire forces against Israel."

§   §   §

Ike, at the time of the Israeli attack, was making a tour of the South. The impending Presidential elections would have been enough to make him consider this action very untimely. Added to this was his conviction that in this day and age no one any longer possessed the right to mete out justice by himself. Finally, he could not fail to see the serious damage which this resort to arms did to the West, at the very moment when the Hungarian uprising was so glaringly pointing up the Soviet failure to win the hearts of the people within its sphere. Hence the violence of his reaction; in the words of *The New York Times* of November 4, 1956, "the White House rang with barracks-room language that had not been heard at 1600 Pennsylvania Avenue since the days of General Grant."

Did this mean that no one really suspected anything in Washington? Foster Dulles affirmed it more than once. But his brother Allen, seven years later, wrote that "intelligence was well alerted to both the possibility and later the probability of the actions taken by Israel and then by Britain and France" and that they "had kept the Government informed." [12] It is necessary therefore to conclude, as some imaginative minds have insisted, that the United States had set up a trap for its Allies by letting them act, and even discreetly encouraging them in order to more successively substitute its own imperialism for theirs. This is a rather farfetched hypothesis which no one, not even the French or British leaders most harshly critical of the American attitude, would have dared to offer as their own. More prosaically, the explanation of Andrew Tully—the author of the book, already cited, on the C.I.A.—is probably much closer to the truth: ". . . although the United States had been informed of the attack in advance," he wrote, "it had decided there was nothing we could do to dissuade the attackers." [13] Another explanation springs to mind: that is, that the warning was simply not taken seriously.

In any case, even before the Franco-British ultimatum was known, Ike sent a message to Ben-Gurion asking him to withdraw his troops from the Sinai Peninsula, now that Israel had obtained its objective —the destruction of the terrorist bases—and assured him that in the event this request was heeded, he would personally and publicly express his approval. He sent the Sixth Fleet to the eastern Mediterranean under the pretext of protecting American nationals. He requested the Allies to demand an immediate reconvening of the Security Council in order to condemn Israel. Eden, who was conferring with Mollet in London had replied that while he was all for submitting it to the Council, "Experience, however, shows that its procedure is unlikely to be either rapid or effective," and "We feel that decisive action should be taken at once to stop hostilities." [14]

The Council met on the 30th at 4 P.M. (9 P.M. Paris time), at the very same moment that Eden and Mollet were having their parliaments approve the terms of the ultimatum. Cabot Lodge, Permanent Representative of the United States, managed to have a request for adjournment introduced by France and Great Britain brushed aside, and presented a draft resolution expressing the "deep concern" of the Council with regard to the violation of the armistice by Israel and requesting it "to immediately withdraw its armed forces inside the armistice line to be established." The member states were requested to abstain from using force or threats and not to give any military, economic or financial assistance to the Jewish state as long as it had not complied with the Council's recommendations.[15]

The French and British veto having blocked this resolution and a similar Soviet proposal, the General Assembly met in a special session, on the initiative of Yugoslavia. It adopted, on November 2, by 64 votes to 5 (Australia, France, Israel, New Zealand and Great Britain), with 6 abstentions, a resolution introduced by Foster Dulles and employing the same terminology as Cabot Lodge has used in the Security Council.

The Israeli troops, who had halted their advance sixteen kilometers from the Suez Canal in accordance with the Franco-British ultimatum, were nevertheless proceeding systematically with the conquest of the Sinai Peninsula, seizing the stronghold of Rafah and the Palestinian territory of Gaza, which had been occupied by Egypt since 1948 and was the jumping-off point for the terrorist raids. On November 5 the base of Sharm-el-Sheik, in the far south of the peninsula, from which Egyptian batteries were blocking the Strait of Tiran, fell into their hands.

The Egyptian Army, retreating in order to avoid being surrounded, left 1,000 dead on the field and lost 4,000 prisoners, almost 100 tanks and 300 pieces of artillery, 1,500 automatic weapons and as many trucks to Dayan's soldiers. Jordan and Syria, which had promised help, had refrained from joining the battle.

However, if the private statement of several leaders from Amman and Damascus can be believed, it was Marshal Amer, the U.A.R. Commander in Chief, who reportedly asked them not to move; one of them supposedly told Hussein: "If you attack Israel when Egypt itself is asking you to do nothing, it will be thought that you are doing it on purpose to expose your Arab front to an inevitable defeat." [16]

§   §   §

In any case, the Arab states were doing Nasser a double favor by giving asylum to his planes and by sabotaging the oil pipelines of the Iraqi Petroleum Company. For their part, the Egyptians—far from panicking—showed their support for their government and enlisted in the hastily assembled militias, sinking ships weighted with cement in the Suez Canal, and completely obstructing it. Thus, instead of ensuring the freedom of west European oil supplies, as was its official aim, the Anglo-French-Israeli action had the initial effect of abruptly interrupting them. The call for American oil reserves and the rerouting around the Cape of tankers coming from the Persian Gulf were insufficient to maintain France and Great Britain's supplies at a sufficiently high level, and rationing had to be instituted for several months.

In Paris the news of the ultimatum had been enthusiastically received. Public opinion, which still remembered Nasser's "word of honor," which Pineau had cited when he came back from Cairo, was outraged to learn of the seizure, a few days earlier, of Egyptian arms intended for the Algerian rebellion, on board the yacht *Athos* II. It had approved the decision by Paris to break off pending negotiations with Morocco, as a result of the official reception given by Mohammed V to the leaders of the F.L.N., and when the latter, upon their return to Rabat, had been intercepted aboard a Moroccan plane, most people had applauded this evidence of firmness, without being overly concerned by the violation of sovereignty which it implied or with the reaction it might provoke in the third world.

Henceforth, there no longer seemed any doubt that it would finally be possible to get revenge for all the humiliations suffered for twenty years. Only the Communists and some nonconformists, including Pierre Mendès-France once again, publicly dared to disassociate themselves from the general chorus. It was in vain that, behind the scenes, Jean Monnet, although he was the official mentor of the Fourth Republic, and other diplomats predicted catastrophes if this policy of force was stubbornly continued. Mollet and Pineau were convinced that the Russians, occupied with Hungary, would not make a move and that the Americans, once the elections were over, would fly to the aid of the victors. However, it was necessary to act quickly since each delay might be interpreted as evidence of misgivings and would only reinforce the tide of indignation rising from one end of the globe to the other, even in pacific Switzerland. This could lead to a situation in which, once Cairo had accepted the resolution voted by the U.N., the famous ultimatum of October 30, and thereby the Anglo-French intervention, would have lost any purpose.

With the support of Hammarskjöld, the Canadian Foreign Minister, Lester Pearson, tried to find a peaceful solution to the crisis. On November 2, intervening after the vote of the U.N. General Assembly which requested that Israel withdraw its troops and that the parties in question seek a cease-fire, he explained his delegation's abstention. "This resolution," he said, "does provide for a cease-fire . . . it does not provide for any steps to be taken by the United Nations for a peace settlement. . . . The armed forces of Israel and Egypt are to withdraw or . . . return to the armistice lines, where presumably . . . they will face each other in fear and hatred. What then? . . . Are we to go through all this again? . . .

"I would like to see a provision in this resolution . . . authorizing the Secretary General to begin making arrangements with Member States for a United Nations force large enough to keep these borders at peace while a political settlement is being worked out. . . ." [17]

Pearson had already explained this idea to Dulles prior to the session, saying that his goal was to avoid having France and Great Britain lose too much face. But the Secretary of State, whom Eisenhower had charged to "stop them [the bombings of Egypt]—fast," [18] replied that this was not possible for the time being. Therefore, the Canadian minister was surprised to hear Dulles, before the General Assembly, agree with him on his proposal, specify that Eisenhower shared his feelings, and invite the Ottawa Government to submit a resolution to that effect.

Pearson and Dulles offered an out to Eden, who the previous day, under pressure from the Opposition, had raised before the House of Commons the possibility of replacing the Franco-British force with a U.N. force.

Unlike Mollet, Eden was faced in his own country with a real revolt against what Hugh Gaitskell, leader of the Labour Party had described, during a debate in Commons on October 31, as "an act of disastrous folly, whose tragic consequences we shall regret for many years, because it will have done irreparable harm to the prestige and reputation of our country." [19] A Conservative peer, Lord Altrincham, accused the Prime Minister of "leading his country into disaster," whereas the Archbishop of Canterbury declared that the British action "violates the spirit and the letter of the United Nations Charter." [20] The Queen herself is said to have criticized the cabinet decision, while Nehru threatened to take India out of the Commonwealth.

In these circumstances it was essential that Eden stick to the indefensible fiction, the basis of the double ultimatum of October 30, according to which the aim of the Anglo-French intervention was to separate the Israeli and Egyptian belligerents, since Paris and London "had available forces," whereas the U.N. "was not yet the international equivalent of our own legal system and of the rule of the law." [21] This explained his determination to avoid anything which might resemble "collusion" with the Israeli forces, which naturally only served to complicate operations, even though the French, luckily for Ben-Gurion, did not have the same scruples. Murphy correctly wrote that Eden's greatest miscalculation was that "he was unable to enlist the support of Eisenhower." [22]

While the Hungarians were being abandoned to their fate, a real race against time then began. It was between Jerusalem and Paris on the one hand, who were urging the British to hasten their landing, originally planned for November 6, and, on the other, Washington, Ottawa and Hammarskjöld, speaking for the great majority in the U.N., who were trying to work out a solution as quickly as possible to prevent this landing.

At Cairo's request the U.N. General Assembly reconvened once again in an emergency session. By a vote of 57 to nil, with 19 abstentions, it adopted, on the 4th, the Canadian resolution which used the terms of the proposal for a U.N. emergency force initiated the day before by Lester Pearson. The General Assembly then approved an Afro-Asian resolution requesting the Secretary General to report within twelve hours on the execution of the cease-fire ordered on November 2.

At that very moment the ships of the Anglo-French expeditionary force were heading for Port Said, which the paratroopers were preparing to occupy at dawn. Eden began by promising the Canadian High Commissioner in London that the landing would be postponed for twenty-four hours. But he was brought back into line by Pineau and Bourgès-Manoury, who had come expressly to see him, and also by General Keightley, commander in chief of the operation, in whose opinion any delay in execution would be disastrous. He cabled Eisenhower, "If we draw back now chaos will not be avoided. Everything will go up in flames in the Middle East. You will realize, with all your experience, that we cannot have a military vacuum while a United Nations force is being constituted and is being transported to the spot. That is why we feel we must go on to hold the position until we can hand over responsibility to the United Nations." [23] At the same time, Paris and London replied to Hammarskjöld that they still considered that "it is necessary to interpose an international force to prevent the continuance of hostilities between Egypt and Israel, to secure the speedy withdrawal of the Israeli forces." [24] Although no "new expression of British hypocrisy" could surprise him, wrote Dayan, Ben-Gurion cabled Paris to express his "astonishment" at seeing his "friends in France" associate themselves with such a proposal,[25] which evidently showed that the operation was doomed.

The Russians, whose tanks had been engaged in crushing Budapest since that morning, knew it. On the 5th, at 3 P.M., or seven hours after the arrival of the first British paratroopers, the Egyptian commander of Port Said proposed to discuss its surrender with the allies. The French occupied Port Fuad, on the other bank of the canal. At 7 P.M. the defenders laid down their arms. But an hour and a half later the picture had completely changed. All the dispatches which passed over the wires of the press agencies gave proof to Nasser that his country had only to endure a few more bad moments and he could then fearlessly follow, if need be, the counsel of firmness which the Soviet diplomats were showering upon him.

At 12:15 P.M. on that same November 5, the U.N. General Assembly had approved another resolution authorizing the Canadian General Burns, appointed as head of the international force, to recruit his personnel without delay, it being understood that it was not to consist of troops from the permanent members of the Security Council. This resolution had the advantage of excluding both the United States and the U.S.S.R., but had the disadvantage for France and Great Britain of dispelling what hopes they had had of incorporating their expeditionary force into it. However, they did not dare to vote against it and contented themselves with abstaining.

In the evening the Soviet Union laid down its cards. Up to that point it had, as usual, acted with extreme prudence, going so far as to scatter the airplanes which it had supplied to Egypt on friendly airbases, rather than have them engage the aggressors. Many of the planes still had their Russian crews. The Soviet Union had also requested all of its technicians to go to the Sudan, and the resolution which Sobolev had submitted to the Security Council on October 30, after Cabot Lodge's resolution had been blocked by the Anglo-French veto, made no mention of the role of Paris and London. Subsequently, the Soviet Union had been content to go along with developments in the U.N. General Assembly, while abstaining from voting on the emergency force, but not without emphasizing the role of the Security Council where the veto could at any time paralyze it —a fact they knew better than anyone else (having used it and abused it). The U.S.S.R. had also proposed, in vain however, that India and Indonesia organize another Bandung Conference to consider the Egyptian problem. In order to measure the completely platonic character of that move, one only has to imagine the time it would have taken to convene such a conference, and the little effective help that it could have given Cairo's resistance.

The reasons for this passivity were clear: the Hungarian Revolution and the Polish crisis were still fresh enough to require dramatic decisions on the part of the Soviet party and the state, and there was also fear of the United States' reaction in the event that the Soviet Union found itself too directly involved against France and Great Britain in Egypt. Naturally, it was difficult for the leaders of the Kremlin to believe that these two countries, both so financially dependent on Washington, could have undertaken such an adventure without its consent.

But on that evening of November 5 it was no longer possible to entertain the slightest doubt as to the real intentions of the United States. At 8 P.M., Sobolev requested an urgent meeting of the Security Council with the aim of inviting Great Britain, France and Israel to end, within twelve hours, the military action taken against Egypt and to withdraw their troops within three days. Should this summons remain unanswered, he proposed that "the members of the U.N., in particular the United States and the U.S.S.R. as permanent members of the Security Council and possessing powerful air and naval forces, provide military aid to the Egyptian Republic." [26] Only two others, the Iranian and Yugoslav delegations, joined the Russians when it came to voting on its inclusion on the agenda. Cabot Lodge aptly summed up the majority opinion in his statement that "One has to be somewhat cynical to present oneself as the defender of a people who are victims of an aggression when at the same time one is in engaged in a massacre in Hungary." [27]

The same tone was used by the White House in replying to Bulganin's message, which he had sent to Eisenhower at the same time to propose a joint military action. It issued a communiqué deploring the fact that the Soviet Union had not voted in favor of the U.N. emergency force and declared that the best service the U.S.S.R. could render in the cause of peace would be to honor the resolution of the General Assembly urging it to stop its intervention in Hungary. Taking note of the fact that the marshal's letter had been released in Moscow before it reached the President, Ike released to the press his own message to Bulganin of the previous day in which he declared himself "inexpressibly shocked" [28] by the events in Budapest.

The Kremlin could hardly have had any illusions as to the results of its twofold move. But it had every reason to believe that so spectacular an initiative would impress the people of the nonaligned countries and conveniently divert attention from what was happening on the shores of the Danube.

Bulganin had not only written to Eisenhower, he had sent impressive personal messages to Ben-Gurion, Mollet and Eden as well. He accused Ben-Gurion of acting "as an instrument of imperialistic forces" and of "playing with the fate of peace and with the fate of its [Israel's] own people." He wrote that he was "sowing hatred of the State of Israel among the Eastern peoples which . . . puts a question mark against the very existence of Israel as a State," and he announced that the Soviet Government was recalling its ambassador and was "taking steps to put an end to the war and to restrain the aggressors." [29]

He expressed himself a little less haughtily but no less threateningly in addressing the leaders of the French and British governments, stressing in Mollet's case—not without reason—that it was difficult to reconcile the socialist ideals he believed in with the "treacherous" and "banditlike" aggression he had perpetrated against Egypt. "What would be the position of France," he asked, "if she were attacked by other States having at their disposal modern and terrible means of destruction?" Knowing that the weakest link of the chain was in Britain, he addressed a letter to Eden which used a similar sentence and an argument meant to be even more disquieting. "There are countries which need not have sent a navy or air force to the coasts of Britain but could have used other means, such as rocket techniques." [30] Both messages ended by raising the risk of a third world war and by pointing out the dire necessity for Paris and London to base their decisions on that possibility.

A careful reading of the content of these letters clearly demonstrates that they were primarily intended to frighten, but that they did not contain any definite threats. Therefore they were calmly received by Eden, who, at 1 A.M. on the 6th, reassured a somewhat alarmed Mollet over the phone. However, they agreed that in order to counteract the maneuver it was necessary to obtain United States guarantees immediately.

Eisenhower himself was convinced that the Russians were bluffing. In his opinion, "Geography makes effective Soviet intervention difficult if not impossible." [31] But he was still determined to stop the

Franco-British expedition. In addition, an emergency operation to remove a cancerous intestinal tumor had been performed on Dulles forty-eight hours previously, and the State Department was in a state of turmoil. The Under Secretary of State, Herbert Hoover, Jr., the interim replacement, was considerably less familiar with the problems involved. As for Cabot Lodge, his role in the United Nations of necessity made him a determined opponent of Franco-British intervention. Although Douglas Dillon, the United States ambassador to Paris, had been authorized to answer Mollet's pointed questions by saying that the United States had no intention of participating in a joint action with the Soviet Union in Egypt and that it would carry out its commitments of assistance in Europe, he left unanswered the question of what would happen if the Franco-British forces were to come up against Soviet "volunteers" in Egypt.

Eden responded sharply to Bulganin, telling him that this was a poorly chosen time for Moscow to speak, as it had, of "barbarous" acts and suggesting instead that it support the proposal for an international force. Mollet expressed himself even more forcefully. Nevertheless, the firmness of tone did not succeed in hiding the clear retreat on the part of the two prime ministers, as they now decided to rally to the projected creation of the emergency force, whereas about twenty-four hours earlier their respective representatives in the United Nations had abstained from taking part in the discussions on that very same proposal. Eden was, in fact, subjected to the strongest pressure from all sides. Not only were some of the Conservatives threatening to vote against him if he did not order a cease-fire, but Washington brutally reminded Great Britain of its financial dependence by selling the pound right and left. This attack developed with such speed that Eden wrote in his memoirs that it "threatened disaster to our whole economic position." [32] In vain, he tried to reach Eisenhower on the telephone. As it was election night, the only information he could obtain from his ambassador in Washington was that should the pound continue to drop, the United Kingdom would be threatened with bankruptcy. The President, however, received Hervé Alphand, the French ambassador, to whom he said, ". . . you must withdraw from Egypt. Our position is that of the United Nations Charter. It is inviolate. . . . Life is a ladder which mounts up to Heaven. I am near the top of that ladder, and I wish to present myself with clean hands before my Creator." [33]

Paris and Jerusalem were still holding fast, but London was obviously weakening. On the 6th, while the Anglo-French forces, having finally landed, were rapidly advancing along the Canal, Ankara reported that jet planes "of unknown nationality" had flown over its territory. The Swiss Federal Council sent an appeal to the Big Four and to India to meet in Geneva in order to save the peace. Nasser invited volunteers from all nations to come and fight for Egypt. The Soviet Union asked Turkey for authorization for its warships to go through the straits.

At the end of the morning, Eden was informed by Washington that a loan of $1 billion would be authorized if he ordered a cease-fire by midnight. The Prime Minister instantly summoned his ministers to inform them of the necessity of stopping hostilities without delay. Then he phoned Mollet to advise him of his decision. The Prime Minister was conferring with Adenauer, who advised him to yield and withdrew after a few moments to let him consult freely with Pineau and Bourgès-Manoury. The two ministers, convinced that Nasser was about to fall and that he would immediately be turned into a hero if hostilities ended, were in favor of continuing without Great Britain. But Mollet, after having gotten Eden to agree that the cease-fire would be postponed five hours, decided with the majority of the government, on the opposite course. At midnight the guns fell silent. A few hours later, Eisenhower's re-election was announced.

Thus ended—to the relief of some and the bitterness of others —a week of anxiety which, in retrospect, appears as the first week of truth of the Cold War. It had brought a twofold warning. To the people of eastern Europe, tempted to revolt against the Soviet Union, it had shown that the West could do nothing for them. To France and Great Britain, it had shown that they were forbidden to act without a green light from the United States. It would take years and another week of truth before a frustrated power, on each side of the Iron Curtain, believed it could seriously challenge what de Gaulle was to call "the double hegemony" of the Soviet Union and the United States.

BIBLIOGRAPHY AND NOTES

[1] Keesing's, 14486 A.

[2] Bar-Zohar, *op. cit.*, p. 100.

[3] Keesing's, 14520 A.

[4] *Ibid.*, 14643 A.

[5] Michel Bar-Zohar, *Ben Gourion, le Prophète armé* (Paris: Fayard, 1966), pp. 286–87.

[6] Moshe Dayan, *Diary of the Sinai Campaign* (Jerusalem: Steimatzky's Agency, 1965), p. 23.

[7] Keesing's, 15149 A.

[8] Azeau, *op. cit.*, p. 226.

[9] Hugh Thomas, "The Suez Crisis," *The Sunday Times* (London), September 11, 1966.

[10] Robertson, *op. cit.*, p. 144.

[11] Murphy, *op. cit.*, p. 388.

[12] David Wise and Thomas B. Ross, *The Invisible Government* (New York: Random House, 1964), p. 118.

[13] Tully, *op. cit.*, p. 110.

[14] Eden, *op. cit.*, pp. 586–87.

[15] Année politique, 1956, p. 522.

[16] Author's personal notes.

[17] Robertson, *op. cit.*, p. 191.

[18] *Ibid.*, p. 171.

[19] Keesing's, 15179 A.

[20] Benoist-Méchin, *op. cit.*, p. 466.

[21] Keesing's, 15173 A.

[22] Murphy, *op. cit.*, p. 392.

[23] Eden, *op. cit.*, p. 617.

[24] Dayan, *op. cit.*, p. 183.

[25] *Ibid.*

[26] Benoist-Méchin, *op. cit.*, p. 491.

[27] *Ibid.*, p. 492.

[28] Keesing's, 15217 A.

[29] Dayan, *op. cit.*, pp. 184–85.

[30] Keesing's, 15218 A.

[31] Murphy, *op. cit.*, p. 390.

[32] Eden, *op. cit.*, p. 622.

[33] Robertson, *op. cit.*, p. 254.

· CHAPTER 12 ·

NO SALVATION

OUTSIDE THE

CHURCH

But the jungle is large and the Cub he is small.
Let him think and be still.

—Rudyard Kipling, *The
First Jungle Book*

ON NOVEMBER 7, 1956, THE MOST DANGEROUS PERIOD
the world had experienced since the Second World War ended. At
zero hour the fighting stopped in Port Said. At 2:53 P.M. that same
day the last radio station in the hands of the Hungarian rebels went
off the air.

The double crisis, however, continued to keep the United Nations
in a state of feverish activity for weeks. Four times, on November 9,
November 21, December 4 and December 12, the General
Assembly, by a large majority, requested that the Soviet Union
cease its intervention in the internal affairs of Hungary. No one had
any illusions as to the practical effect of those resolutions. Kadar
did not even agree to receive the U.N. observers, and after having
consented to a visit by Hammarskjöld, he rejected the date suggested
for it without suggesting another.

The activity resulting from the termination of the Suez crisis was
obviously of a more practical nature. As France, Great Britain and

Israel did not hurry to withdraw their troops, the Kremlin declared on November 10 that if they were not evacuated, "the competent authorities would not be opposed to the departure for Egypt of Soviet civilian volunteers, should they desire to take part in the struggle of the Egyptian people for their independence." [1]

As this warning had set no time limit for the withdrawal, it was taken all the less seriously. It had been mainly intended to protect the backlog of sympathy which the Kremlin had built up in the Arab world as a result of the Suez affair which might have been impaired by the Hungarian tragedy. Paris and London had already clearly indicated that they would recall their soldiers as soon as the international force, whose creation the General Assembly had adopted in principle on November 4, was operative. On December 24 the change-over was accomplished.

The case of Israel was different. Although on January 5, 1957, General Dayan had agreed with the chief of the U.N. force on the withdrawal of his units to the El Arish–Sharm-el-Sheik line, Golda Meir announced on the 8th that Gaza and the islands situated at the entrance to the Strait of Tiran would not be evacuated until the U.N. had formally guaranteed that the terrorist raids would not recur and that Israeli ships would have free access to Elath. Under American pressure, El Arish was finally evacuated on the 15th, but on the 23rd Ben-Gurion had his Parliament endorse his determination not to make any move as long as the requested guarantees had not been obtained.

This was in open defiance of the U.N., which, on the 19th, after a vote of 75 to nil, with 3 abstentions, had asked him to recall all his troops within five days. But he finally won out. While Cairo wanted a buffer force only if it were based on Israeli territory, and Canada had suggested that it be deployed on both sides of the frontier, in the end the blue helmets were stationed entirely on Egyptian soil. In the first few days of March, therefore, the Israeli troops were repatriated amid protests from the Zionist Right. This result was obtained through patient negotiations, the success of which was due as much to the insistence of the United States as to the good offices of France, the resourcefulness of Pearson and Dag Hammarskjöld's exceptional diplomatic gifts.

A man of wide culture, often ignobly slandered, Hammarskjöld was driven by a remorseless consciousness of his responsibilities, which made him a true citizen of the world, to seek a lasting peace settlement on the basis of that compromise. But it was asking too much. The best that could be obtained was an armistice which, through a curious paradox, benefited both Israel and Egypt. Israel was freed not only from the threat of the terrorist raids, but also from the threat of Egyptian aggression, and was able to use the port of Elath at will. Egypt had forced the world to accept as a *fait accompli* the nationalization of the canal; it was reopened in March and would soon become one of Egypt's principal sources of revenue.

For Great Britain and France it marked the end of their illusions. Most of the Arab countries broke off relations with them, seized their property and educational establishments and expelled their nationals. It was the beginning of the agony of the French Fourth Republic. For Great Britain it meant the loss of its traditional status. Nasser not only denounced the treaty he had concluded with Great Britain in 1954, but Iraq declared that it no longer wanted to cooperate with Great Britain within the Baghdad Pact, and Jordan extracted a promise for the withdrawal of its troops. Great Britain also became involved in a conflict with Yemen on the matter of the oil sheikdoms of the Persian Gulf and was confronted with new outbreaks in Cyprus which threatened to transform the island into another Algeria.

For the United States the temptation was strong to fill the "vacuum" that had been created. Why not benefit from the position it had taken during the Suez crisis and from the isolation of the U.S.S.R. in the wake of the Hungarian crisis in order to finally recruit the Middle East on its side, thus ensuring that the region's oil did not fall into the hands of hostile powers? It was encouraged in this endeavor by Great Britain, which, immediately following the cease-fire at Port Said, had decided to return to its traditional policy and—having resigned itself to its growing dependency on the United States—to try to become again its "privileged" ally, hoping thereby to influence American decisions from within.

Forgetting the disappointments which the politics of the Baghdad Pact had brought him, Ike proposed to Congress on January 5,

1957, what was later to be called the Eisenhower Doctrine. After having sharply denounced Russia's ambitions in the Middle East, he requested authorization to "give economic and military assistance to all countries or groups of countries in that region wishing to benefit from it, it being understood that this assistance could include the use of American forces." [2] It was during the course of the rather stormy debate which ensued in the Senate that Foster Dulles, replying to the nonconformist Wayne Morse, who wanted to associate France and Great Britain in this project so that "American boys won't have to fight alone," made the famous remark, "If I were an American boy, as you term it, I'd rather not have a French and a British soldier beside me, one on my right and one on my left." [3]

Paris and London refrained from reacting. Mollet and Pineau were too much in need of Washington's support in the difficult debate on Algeria which was to begin in February in the U.N. General Assembly and which ended, mainly through the efforts of Cabot Lodge, with an almost unanimous vote in favor of an innocuous resolution. Because of illness, Eden—on January 9, four days after the proclamation of the Eisenhower Doctrine—relinquished his seat to an old stalwart of the Conservative party, Harold Macmillan. Macmillan had an American mother and, for that reason perhaps, was even less disposed than anyone else to pick a quarrel with the United States, with which he had maintained relations of friendly trust since the war.

The acceptance of the Eisenhower Doctrine was assured in the beginning of March, despite the Kremlin's efforts against it, notably its repeated feelers in the direction of Great Britain, which Russia probably could not believe would thus let itself be eased out of one of its principal zones of influence.

On February 11 the Soviet Government put before the President of the U.N. General Assembly a request for a debate on the threat to peace which, in its judgment, the Eisenhower Doctrine represented, and delivered the draft proposal of a joint declaration on the Middle East to the ambassadors of the Big Three.

Calmly analyzed today, out of the context of the times, that proposal appears to have been a wise one. It can be summed up in six points, which, if adopted, would have led to the complete neutralization of that part of the world: (1) the solution of pending

HISTORY OF THE COLD WAR

problems only through peaceful means; (2) noninterference in domestic affairs; (3) the renunciation of any attempt to draw the Middle Eastern countries into military blocs; (4) the liquidation of foreign bases and withdrawal of foreign troops; (5) an agreement not to provide arms to the countries of that area; and (6) aid without any political, military or any other condition incompatible with their sovereignty.

But if the resolution text was reasonable, in any event more reasonable than the unfortunate Eisenhower Doctrine, its rejection was inevitable, even if Shepilov had not described the doctrine as an instrument through which the U.S.A. "intends to cover the area with a network of atomic bases and at the first opportunity, to launch from the area a war of aggression," and asserted that the American leaders pointed out "a vacuum . . . every time American leaders intend to ensconce themselves in some part of the world." [4] Since its intervention in Budapest, the U.S.S.R. was disqualified in the eyes of Western public opinion from playing the role of defender of the peace. Great Britain was busy completing its reconciliation with the United States. On March 21 and March 23, Ike and Macmillan had concluded agreements in Bermuda by which Washington was to supply the United Kingdom with guided missiles. This would, a few days later, permit Britain to substantially reduce the burden of its conventional weapons, in order to improve the position of the pound. Mollet himself was received by Ike in Washington at the end of February and signed a joint communiqué stressing, among other things, the necessity of "jointly settling the problems raised by the threat of Communist imperialism." [5]

On March 11, therefore, the three Western Powers rejected the Kremlin's proposal and held the U.S.S.R. responsible for the tension in the Middle East because of its arms deliveries to several states in the region; they also compared its conduct in Hungary to its protestations in favor of nonintervention in the affairs of other countries. This rebuff, however, did not discourage the U.S.S.R.; for several months it continued to harp on this theme in innumerable notes and messages it exchanged with the other "great powers."

The several capitals involved did not wait so long to consider what to do about the Eisenhower Doctrine, whose author made his first mistake when he forgot that nothing is as disagreeable to an Arab as the idea that foreigners are trying to enlist him in a struggle against other Arabs. As early as January 9 an unofficial spokesman for Nasser declared that "Egypt would not permit Franco-British influence to be replaced by the influence of another power, either Western or Eastern" and qualified the Doctrine as a "corollary of the Franco-British policy of aggression." [6] The Syrian Government, which had just brought to trial a number of politicians and diplomats accused of having attempted to incite an armed revolt, adopted the same position.

Eight days later, the head of the Damascus Government conferred in Cairo not only with his friend Nasser, but with two kings whose regimes and backgrounds should have cast them as the opponents of the Syrian and the Egyptian. It is difficult to imagine two men as different as little Hussein, the British-educated youth, and Saud, the cynical and pleasure-seeking giant, who kept his people in the twelfth century while he lived like a prince out of *The Thousand and One Nights,* thanks to the royalties of the Arabian-American Oil Company. The Four flatly declared that they did not see any "vacuum" to be filled in the Near East. But since the King of Arabia—whom Dulles had decided to make the pillar of American penetration in the Middle East—had been invited to Washington to negotiate a renewal of the agreement on the use of the Dhahran base by the Strategic Air Command, it was decided that another meeting would take place upon his return to hear the explanations he might have received.

Saud landed in Manhattan on the 30th, with an impressive retinue of emirs, sheiks and bearded janissaries draped in their black *abayas,* wives and concubines making a more discreet entrance. The democratic municipality of New York, so as not to alienate its numerous Jewish voters, refused to welcome a "character who says," the Mayor declared, "that slavery is legal." [7] But Washington showered him with attentions. He departed with a loan of $250 million and the promise of sizable deliveries of weapons, including jets, whose pilots would be trained in the United States. In exchange he renewed the treaty on Dhahran for five years—not without having received a promise from the United States, which swallowed its pride, to send no Jewish airmen—and before the press he let fall from his royal mouth the few words which were expected of him: "The Eisenhower Doctrine is good and deserves a favorable reception." [8] That, of course, did not mean that he planned to accept it for his own country.

On February 24 he met again with his Arab partners in Cairo. In spite of the "explanations" from the President of the United States which he emphasized to them, the communiqué issued by the Four on the 27th reaffirmed their determination to "protect the Arab world from the harm of the 'cold war' and to abide by the policy of 'positive neutrality.' " [9]

Lebanon, on the other hand, unwisely breaking with the neutral stand which was indispensable to the maintenance of its precarious internal balances, had on January 6 accepted the principles of the Doctrine, which had been accepted not only by Pakistan, Iraq, Turkey and Greece—traditional allies of the West—but also by Afghanistan, Libya, Tunisia and Morocco. The Sudan, however, after some hesitation had turned it down.

In Jordan, the situation was less calm. Hussein had only repudiated the English alliance under pressure from the Palestinians, the most restless element in his fragile kingdom, which through Nabulsi controlled the government and through General Nuwar the armed forces. At the end of February, Nabulsi and Nuwar agreed to accept economic aid under the Eisenhower Doctrine, but on the condition that it would not lead to any interference in the affairs of the country.

The United States, concerned about Amman's shift toward the Left, illustrated by the establishment of diplomatic relations with the U.S.S.R., urged Hussein to resist. The King of Jordan, without consulting his Prime Minister, gave orders to the army and proposed another meeting of the Arab heads of state. On April 10, Nabulsi, having threatened to resign, dismissed twenty high officials well known for their pro-Western sympathies and dispatched tanks to the capital. Hussein, who knew that he could count on Saud, and if need be, on the Americans, pressed him to resign.

Nabulsi gave up, but the young monarch could not find a successor and continued to purge the administration, while strikes and demonstrations multiplied throughout the Palestinian section of the state.

On April 14, fighting broke out near Zerka—where the Syrian troops were stationed—between a loyalist regiment and soldiers who had mutinied on orders from their officers, following the announcement of the false news of the King's death. Hussein rushed to the spot, identified himself to his supporters and crossed over the barricades to reach the rebels. The Arabs have more respect for physical courage than anything else, and they stopped fighting each other and cheered him. General Nuwar, who had been involved in the affair, fled to Syria to escape arrest.

The next day, Hussein succeeded in forming a coalition government in which Nabulsi took over foreign affairs. But the reconciliation did not last very long. General Hayali, who had been appointed Chief of Staff in place of Nuwar, also turned up in Damascus, where he declared that he had fled "because the Palace was plotting against Jordan's independence together with foreign military attachés." [10]

Radio Cairo was denouncing with growing vehemence the collusion between the monarch and the West. Strikes and demonstrations in the streets were assuming a clearly insurrectional character. Once again, Hussein acted swiftly. He proclaimed martial law and formed a cabinet composed of long-time servants of the dynasty, dissolved the political parties and requested the immediate departure of the Syrian troops. Eisenhower, for his part, dispatched the Sixth Fleet to the eastern Mediterranean, and Iraq declared that its troops would move into Jordan if the monarchy were overthrown.

The U.S.S.R. contented itself with verbal protests and the Hashemite kingdom was saved without American marines' having to fire a single shot. A few days later, Washington granted Jordan a loan of $10 million, the first in a long series of loans, thereby assuring the survival of a throne whose stability, one month earlier, no one would have dared to bet on.

This first success of the Eisenhower Doctrine was followed by another. In June, elections were to take place in Lebanon. President Chamoun, who made no secret of his pro-Western sympathies, rejected an ultimatum by the pro-Nasser opposition which demanded that the elections be supervised by a neutral committee. Disorders broke out in Beirut but did not shake Chamoun's resolve, and the United States, at the risk of being accused by Moscow of intervention in Lebanese internal affairs, released a chunk of economic aid twenty-four hours before the second round of consultations had taken place. This represented a triumph for Chamoun.

Egypt and Syria, fearing, not without some justification, that they might be the next targets of the American counteroffensive, sent urgent calls for help to the U.S.S.R. It increased its economic assistance to those two countries, sent them technicians in increasing numbers and, at the end of June, announced the sale of three submarines to Cairo. The net result of all this was that the United States had to take a much more clear-cut position not only in favor of Israel, which after much hesitation decided to accept the Eisenhower Doctrine, but also on the question of freedom of navigation in the Gulf of Aqaba.

During July, a Syrian delegation left for Moscow. It was headed by the Defense Minister, Khaled el Azm. A multimillionaire, former Prime Minister in the time of Vichy, he had never hidden his pro-French feelings. The Quai d'Orsay had, however, made the mistake of not supporting him in the race for the presidency of the republic against the pro-Nasser Shukri el-Kuwatly, and since that time he had been looking for a way to get revenge. He apparently thought he had found it when the Soviet leaders, thumbing their noses at the Eisenhower Doctrine, concluded an agreement with him, the terms of which were not made public, causing Washington all the more anxiety since, on August 5, the Syrian ambassador to the Kremlin had declared that he was "in a position to state that Syria's military requirements will be fulfilled." [11] The U.S.S.R. promised to participate in the construction of railroads, roads, dams and hydro-electric plants and sent an economic delegation to Damascus.

The treaty was presented as being devoid of any political taint. On August 13, Damascus announced the uncovering of an American plot against the regime and brought before the Security Council this threat to the peace. According to the Syrians it was led by Shishekly, former dictator of the country, who had been condemned to death *in absentia* a few months earlier and had long been generally considered to be an agent of the French secret service. Two diplomats and a United States military attaché were expelled and the Chief of Staff was replaced by General Bizri, who was commonly supposed to have belonged in his youth to the French Communist Party.

Soviet officers arrived in the country to train the troops in the use of Russian weapons.

These developments came as a complete surprise to the Americans. Turks and Iranians portrayed the situation in the worst light and Wall Street had one of its worst days. Ike refused to contemplate any military action. He contented himself with declaring the Syrian ambassador *persona non grata* and charged the Assistant Secretary of State for the Middle East, Loy Henderson, to head up a fact-finding mission on the spot.

Henderson first went to Turkey, where he met not only with Mendérès, but with the kings of Iraq and Jordan; then he left for Lebanon. But he did not go to Damascus, and this naturally reinforced the Syrians in their belief that Washington was plotting against them. Upon his return to the United States he declared that the situation in Syria was "extremely serious," and could affect "the security of the whole free world." On September 7, Dulles made public a communiqué stressing that there was "deep concern at the apparently growing Soviet Communist domination of Syria." Ike ordered the speed-up of arms deliveries to Jordan, Lebanon and Iraq, while Turkey called up some of its reserves and started holding maneuvers along the Syrian frontier. On the 9th Nasser declared in *Al Ahram* that Syria's only crime "was . . . that she did not . . . obey American orders," and that the United States had invented the Communist threat in order to smash the movement of Arab nationalism. He assured Syria of his complete support.[12]

On the 10th, Gromyko who in February had become Foreign Minister, replacing Shepilov, held a press conference in Moscow to denounce American, British and Turkish "provocations." On that same day, Bulganin addressed a message to the head of the Ankara Government, warning him against any attempts to participate in an aggression against Syria, in a tone which was reminiscent of his correspondence during the Suez crisis.

On the 19th, Dulles declared in the U.N. that Turkey "now faces growing military danger from the major build-up of Soviet arms in Syria." [13] On the 21st, Russian warships were anchored in the port of Latakia, where the population, led by Kuwatly, welcomed them enthusiastically. Leaves were cancelled in the Syrian Army.

It was Saud who saved the day. Interrupting his vacation in

Germany, he landed in Damascus on the 25th, after having conferred in Beirut with President Chamoun. While one of his ministers stated that he had not "seen any sign that Syria was drifting toward communism," [14] he promised Syria his support "against any aggression" and publicly declared that Syria could not constitute a danger to any of its neighbors.[15] Finally, by playing the trump card of Arab solidarity for all it was worth, he managed to bring to Damascus the Iraqi Prime Minister—the champion of Western policy, the perennial enemy whom Damascus suspected of having the worst annexationist designs in the name of the old dream of the "Fertile Crescent"—and got him and the Syrian President to join hands. Immediately, Bitar, the Syrian Foreign Minister, offered to meet with Foster Dulles.

Nasser also cooperated. In an interview he declared himself ready to discuss the problems of the Middle East with Eisenhower and made use of that opportunity to express his gratification at the good will shown by Great Britain and France in the negotiations just started for the settlement of the Suez problem and the resumption of economic relations. Mendérès had the wisdom to reply to Bulganin, on September 30, that he had never had any aggressive intentions toward Syria.

The crisis seemed to have been weathered when, on October 9, Khrushchev accused Foster Dulles of pushing Turkey into a war with Syria, coupling this accusation with a strong threat, "If war breaks out, we are near Turkey and you are not. When the guns begin to fire, the rockets can begin flying, and then it will be too late to think about it." [16] Dulles responded in a hardly less brutal manner. For three weeks the Kremlin was to continue in that tone. Marshal Rokossovski, who had once more become a Soviet citizen after Gomulka had dismissed him, had been appointed Commander in Chief of the troops in the Caucasus region, and maneuvers were being held there, as well as in Bulgaria.

Doubtless, there is more than one explanation for this turnabout, ranging from the nearness of the Turkish legislative elections to the launching of the first Sputnik three days earlier, which might have made Khrushchev want to test his powers of intimidation. But it can also be wondered whether the Kremlin might not, in fact, have been alarmed at the designs against Syria which it attributed to Washington and Ankara as a result of confidential United States documents which had fallen into its hands. Receiving the British Labour Party leader Aneurin Bevan on September 17, Khrushchev had made much of a plot against Syria, assuring him that he had ample proof for these assertions and that he would produce it "at the right time," [17] which, however, he never did.

Did he base his accusation on documents found in a briefcase which, as was then rumored, Henderson had lost on a Bosphorus ferry? Washington as well as Ankara denied it vehemently. Nevertheless, there must have been some fire behind the smoke, if only because general staffs are in the habit of foreseeing every eventuality on paper, and the secret services, especially in the East, are always trying to get hold of their plans.

On October 18, TASS published a violent declaration relating, in its own way, Henderson's efforts to persuade Syria's neighbors to take part in an attack against the Syrian's regime. For his part, Gromyko asked the U.N. to send a fact-finding commission to the Syrian-Turkish border, to which, incidentally, Ankara agreed. Saud again proposed to play the role of mediator. But while the debates in the General Assembly became more acrimonious and the United States sent warships to Turkey, the Secretary General of the Foreign Ministry in Ankara, the wise Selim Sarper, held frequent talks with his Syrian colleague behind the scenes and succeeded in convincing him of his government's good intentions. He had the same moderating influence on the Prime Minister, Mendérès, whose optimism had returned with his electoral triumph of the 27th.

On the 29th, Khrushchev created a sensation among the diplomatic corps when he attended a reception given by the Turkish ambassador in honor of the Turkish national holiday. He was all smiles, drank one toast after another to peace and exclaimed: "Let him be damned who wants war! Let him fight alone! But why talk about war anyway—there will be no war." Asked about the talk of war over Syria, Mr. Khrushchev replied, "The more talk there is of war, the less likely war becomes." [18]

The danger had passed. Soon Mr. K was to hold Marshal Zhukov responsible for the entire affair. One month later he had Bulganin

send a note to Mendérès asserting that the U.S.S.R. "sincerely de-
sires the establishment of improved and friendly relations with
Turkey." [19] This wish was to be granted: A few years later the heads
of government of the two countries exchanged official visits and
the U.S.S.R. took part in the financing of the Turkish Five-Year
Plan.

But it would still take more than a year, after some dramatic
turns, for the Middle East crisis to end. In the way it developed, it
was one of the most typical Cold War crises and can be explained,
above all, by the extreme distrust that each side harbored against
the other. The Americans saw Moscow's hand everywhere. The Arab
nationalists interpreted the Eisenhower Doctrine as another manifes-
tation of Western colonialism and, in order to resist it, drew closer
to the U.S.S.R., thus justifying Washington's apprehensions after all.
As for the Soviets, they were only too happy to be asked for help,
on condition that they did not have to take any risk at a moment
when they were busy erasing the aftereffects of the Hungarian affair.

§   §   §

The military success which the U.S.S.R. had achieved in Budapest
was unable to hide the very serious blow dealt to its prestige.

Although they had already been curiously shaken by Mr. K's revelations of Stalin's crimes, the intelligentsia of the extreme Left
throughout the world showed how deeply they had been affected. On
November 8, *France Observateur* published a letter signed by well-
known intellectuals, three of whom were Communists, protesting
against "the use of cannons and tanks to break the revolt of the
Hungarian people." Sartre, in his serial article in the *Temps Modernes*
of January 1957, broke with the French Communist Party, which
he coarsely accused, by its complaisance toward neo-Stalinist crimes,
"of having given syphilis to the entire Left."

Many members of the World Council of Peace also protested
and with them the secretary general of the Italian trade unions, di
Vittorio, and the president of the Italian Socialist Party, Pietro Nenni,
who sent back to Moscow the Stalin Prize which he had received a
few years before as a result of his unconditional alliance with the
Italian Communist Party. Nehru also condemned the Soviet policy,

which no longer had a single defender in the United Nations outside of the socialist camp. On the diplomatic level the Soviet policy had resulted in bankruptcy and reduced to zero the gains made by the patient efforts and the numerous concessions which had followed Stalin's death.

Everything pointed to the fact that within the Communist world, and to begin with, even in Moscow, Khrushchev was strongly blamed. The nomination on November 20, 1956, of Molotov, known for his approval of Stalin's firmness, to the position of Minister of State Control, which gave him the right to look into everything, was one of Khrushchev's first setbacks. On December 31, at the end of the traditional reception at the Kremlin, Mr. K felt obliged to prostrate himself before the statue which, less than a year earlier, he had wanted to pull from its pedestal. "Stalin," he declared, "was a great Marxist. He made mistakes but we all are responsible for the mistakes which were made at that time. . . . Personally, I grew up under Stalin. We may be proud of having participated in the struggle against our enemies, for the progress of our great cause. From that point of view, I am proud that we are Stalinists." [20] On the 17th, at the Chinese embassy, the First Secretary outdid himself: "I wish that God [*sic*] would help every Communist to fight like Stalin." [21]

From that period on, probably, some people tried to eliminate him. The Central Committee, taking note of the failure of the Five-Year Plan, created an economic commission, headed by Pervukhin, who in fact removed a large part of Khrushchev's powers. When in February 1957, Khrushchev expounded his theories on industrial decentralization, not one member of the Presidium, as Bernard Feron remarked,[22] publicly supported them.

In June, on a visit to Finland with Bulganin, the opposition thought that the time to act had come. Khrushchev had barely returned from Helsinki, on the 18th, when he failed to win a majority in the Presidium. But he appealed that vote to the Central Committee.

The members of the Central Committee were brought to Moscow posthaste. Almost half of its members had been elected for the first time at the Twentieth Congress, thanks to Khrushchev, and they declared themselves overwhelmingly in his favor. On June 29 the principal architects of the conspiracy—Malenkov, Molotov and Kaganovich—were accused of having formed an "anti-Party group." They were expelled from the Central Committee and a great number of Mr. K's supporters entered the Presidium with General Zhukov, without whom he probably would have lost the battle. It was, in fact, Soviet military planes which, on orders from the Minister of Defense, had flown to the provinces and even to the foreign capitals, where some of them were ambassadors, to bring back the members of the Central Committee who reversed the decision of the Presidium. But if Stalin's teachings had not been sufficient, experience had taught mistrust to the day's winner: among dictators, ingratitude is one of the elementary forms of prudence. At the end of October, Zhukov would be relieved of his duties as Defense Minister and, three days later, expelled from the Presidium and the Central Committee after being accused of dabbling in "adventurism"—an allusion to the Turkish affair—and in the cult of his own personality.

But Khrushchev would not stop there. In March 1958, Bulganin would be forced to turn over to him the presidency of the Council, before being expelled from the Presidium; it became known at the end of the year that during the famous June 1957 vote, he had sided with Mr. K's opponents. As for old Marshal Voroshilov, President of the Presidium of the Supreme Soviet, in other words head of the Soviet state, on whose initiative Nikita Sergeyevich had been asked to assume the leadership of both the party and the government, he would be thanked by being relieved of all his duties in October 1961. He would even, on a national holiday, be denied access to the official reviewing stand on Red Square. Thus, eight years after Stalin's death, only two of the ten members who had then composed the Presidium would remain in office: Khrushchev and Mikoyan.

§   §   §

The reorganization which Khrushchev brought about in the socialist camp was no less remarkable, although he resorted to more brutal methods. First, Hungary—the weakest link of the chain—where, according to all witnesses, the entire population was in open rebellion against the regime and the foreign power which was its secular arm.

The cessation of fighting by no means had meant a return to normalcy, and 200,000 persons had fled the country. There was a general strike; there no longer existed either army, police or Communist Party. Kadar could not count either on Rakosi supporters or on those of Imre Nagy. With the few militants who remained faithful to him, Kadar at first tried to reassure the population and get them to return to work. "The government," he declared on November 6, 1956, "approves of the evacuation of Hungary by the Soviet troops, but only when order and peace have been restored; it then will begin negotiations to that end." [23] On the 14th, he received a delegation from the Central Workers' Council of Greater Budapest, which had been formed during the revolution. They assured him that the council "strictly adhered to the principles of socialism, and especially to the nationalization of the means of production." But they asked that several socialist parties be allowed to function, that Imre Nagy be recalled to power and that elections take place within a certain time limit.

Kadar replied that "if Nagy were to leave his extraterritorial location"—namely, the Yugoslav Embassy where he had found refuge —"it would be possible to consult him and to come to an agreement with him." And according to the version of the interview published on November 15, in the newspaper of his party, *Nepszabadsag*, he "confirmed unequivocally that nobody would be punished for having participated in the great popular movement of the last weeks." [24]

Negotiations with Belgrade had already been under way for several days so that Nagy and several dozen of his friends could leave the Yugoslav Embassy where they were housed. On November 21, Kadar, in a note to Marshal Tito's government, "reiterated," according to him, that the Hungarian Government "has no desire to punish Imre Nagy and the members of his group in any way for their past activities." They expected that "the asylum granted by the Yugoslav embassy to this group . . . be withdrawn, and that its members . . . return to their homes." [25]

The next day, Nagy and his companions left the embassy in a bus placed at their disposal by the Hungarian authorities. But the vehicle was intercepted a few moments later by two Soviet tanks. In the evening, Radio Budapest announced that the former Prime

Minister and his friends, having requested the privilege of asylum in another socialist country, had left for Rumania.

On the 25th, Kadar stated on Radio Budapest: "We have promised that we will not take legal action against Imre Nagy and his friends for their past crimes—even if they admit them themselves. We will keep our promises." And he affirmed to the members of a delegation that it was to ensure their safety that the travelers in the bus were not brought home. According to him, in fact, "the government had good reasons to suspect that counterrevolutionary elements . . . might resort to an act of provocation, murdering Nagy or one of his collaborators and trying to fix the responsibility before the public upon the Hungarian government." [26] As for the Rumanian delegate to the U.N., he declared on December 3, 1956, that "all necessary steps would be taken to guarantee the safety of Mr. Nagy and his friends." And he added that the attitude of the latter was "marked by a spirit of understanding and good humor." [27]

And thus, everything was done to calm the legitimate apprehensions of public opinion with regard to the circumstances in which Nagy had been abducted. On December 8, 1956, the provisional Central Committee of the new Hungarian Socialist Workers' Party, founded by Kadar during the revolution as a substitute for the defunct Communist Party, published a manifesto which recognized that the Workers' Councils were "important organs of the working class, and also will be in the future"; it spoke of making room for individual initiative and of assuring a greater possibility of development in the private sector. It admitted the need for freedom of discussion between Communist and non-Communist scientists and for trips abroad.[28]

However, either Kadar deliberately wanted to betray his compatriots, or his hand was later forced by the Soviets, but most of his promises remained mere words. On December 9 the government dissolved the Regional Workers' Councils, including the one of Greater Budapest, whose leaders were arrested, the arrests provoking work stoppages everywhere. On January 8, 1957, the elections which had been promised by the Trade Unions leadership were adjourned *sine die*. On the 13th, a strike call was made punishable by death.

Repression also fell on the intellectuals who, on November 17, had issued a manifesto affirming their solidarity "with the heroes of the struggle for freedom" and protesting the deportations of insurgents to the U.S.S.R. Several of them were arrested, along with the Marxist philosopher, Georges Lukacs, Imre Nagy's former Minister of National Education, who, on November 18, had left of his own accord the Yugoslav Embassy where he had sought refuge. On January 17 the Writers' Union was dissolved. Two great trials of intellectuals took place in 1957.

The Minister of Justice declared, on February 23, that forty death sentences had been pronounced. In June, the prosecutor having appealed *a minima* against their short prison sentences, the two founders of the clandestine newspaper *Elunk* were condemned to death. Their lives were spared only because the news evoked such violent reactions throughout the world and because numerous Communists, headed by Picasso, intervened in their behalf.

But naturally, it was Nagy's case which gave rise to the greatest anxiety, followed by indignation. We have already seen the numerous statements made by Kadar promising him immunity. But on January 6, 1957, the Hungarian Government, after having conferred with Khrushchev, Malenkov and the representatives of the Bulgarian, Rumanian and Czech Communist parties in Budapest, made a public declaration accusing the former President of the Council of having, through his treason, "opened the way to the fascist counterrevolution." [29] On March 7, Revai, one of Rakosi's former ministers, asked that Nagy be condemned "without restriction or appeal." [30] The party's newspaper, on April 7, published "admissions" from Colonel Kopacsi, Maleter's former deputy, which seemed to indicate that a trial was being prepared. On June 2, Thomas Schreiber wrote in *Le Monde:* "A public trial, if it were conducted according to legal procedures, would turn against the regime. A conviction behind closed doors of Messrs. Nagy, Losonczy, Maleter, etc., would be more convenient. That is what may finally happen."

In fact, on June 17, 1958, the Hungarian Minister of Justice issued a communiqué announcing, without giving any details as to the place or date of the trial, that Nagy, Maleter, Gimes and Szilagyi had been condemned to death and immediately executed; that Geza Losonczy had succumbed to illness during his detention; and that five other defendants had been condemned to sentences ranging from five years to life imprisonment. The accusations were, according to the case, plotting against the legal order, high treason and mutiny. Nagy and his principal lieutenants were accused of having organized, starting in December 1955, a plot to overthrow the people's republic.[31]

This news, coming as it did almost two years after the crushing of the Hungarian revolt and at a time when Kadar's authority seemed well established, caused indignation everywhere. Mauriac summarized the general public opinion when he wrote: "This political crime . . . does more than kill innocent people, it kills the hope which had been born in all the satellite peoples of Russia, when, following the death of Stalin, his methods had been publicly condemned and branded." [32]

Even today, no convincing reason has been given for the execution of the man whose name, like Gomulka's and later Dubček's, had briefly symbolized the hope that communism would finally live happily with liberty. It was as if Khrushchev, accused of sympathy toward imperialism—by the Chinese?—had wanted to prove that he had nothing in common with the *bourgeoisie* or with the morality to which it claimed allegiance.

Naturally, one of the sharpest reactions to Nagy's execution came from Belgrade. For *Politika,* the capital's principal daily newspaper, "the execution was necessary as a terrible warning to all those who resist the present resurrection of Stalinist policies. But it was also necessary as a factor in the worsening of relations with a socialist nation such as ours." [33]

The Soviet-Yugoslav reconciliation did not last long after the Hungarian Revolution. Tito, after having criticized the first Soviet intervention, had said of the second, in Pula on November 11, 1956, that if it was an "error" and an "evil," it was, however, preferable to "chaos, civil war, counterrevolution and world war." And he had ordered the arrest of Djilas, guilty of having sent an article to the *New Leader* in New York, in which he said that "the Hungarian Revolution was the sign of the end of communism in general."

In that same speech, Tito had placed responsibility for the events in Budapest, which some people might be tempted to blame on Yugo-slavia, on the Soviet leaders, who had been wrong in attacking the "cult of personality" and not the "system which made it possible." And he had launched into a violent criticism of "Stalinism's left-overs." [34]

Pravda, on the 19th, criticized Tito's "tendency to meddle in the internal affairs of other countries." *Borba* replied in the same tone. Meanwhile, Nagy's abduction further increased tension. For their part, the Albanian leaders—whom Tito, in Pula, had excoriated, calling Enver Hodja a "pseudo-Marxist, who only knows the word Marxism-Leninism and nothing else" [33]—reacted sharply. In the be-ginning of January they expelled a Yugoslav diplomat from Tirana.

Suddenly, tension relaxed. On April 18, after Mr. K had proposed to bury the war hatchet, all polemics between Belgrade and Mos-cow stopped. The elimination of the "anti-Party group," in June, helped matters, since Molotov, one of its principal members, had constantly appeared as one of the most determined opponents of Yugoslav revisionism. However, in Prague on June 11, Khrushchev made a speech hardly flattering to the "Yugoslav way." "The Work-ers' Councils are all very well," he said, "on condition that one receives American wheat and American meat . . . if the Yugoslavs contend that their form of socialism is the best, that, frankly, is ridiculous. If they do not fear men when they affirm that, they should at least fear God." [35]

The Belgrade press took it rather badly, but on the 18th, Mr. K brought together, near Moscow, Rankovich and Kardelj, and dele-gations from Albania and Bulgaria, which on January 30 had issued a joint declaration strongly criticizing Yugoslavia. Mr. K thus showed his intention of playing the role of mediator between the different members of the "socialist family." He himself met with Tito, on August 1 and 2, in Bucharest. The communiqué issued at the end of these talks gave some satisfaction to the Yugoslavs, since it made special reference to the Belgrade declaration of "noninter-ference" in the internal affairs of other socialist states. But the mar-shal was to give him much greater satisfaction when, a few days later, he recognized East Germany, which led Bonn to immediately break off relations with Belgrade.

Poland, which, in the wake of the Hungarian revolt, had had

the fleeting idea of finding inspiration in Yugoslav neutralism, had been very quickly brought back into line. In truth, during the Budapest fighting, Poland had displayed a cautiousness hardly in keeping with its temperament, which inspired the Warsaw urchins to wisecrack: "The Hungarians behaved like Poles, the Poles like Czechs and the Czechs like pigs . . ." Whereas most newspapers had published reports favorable to the insurgents, the Central Committee had made appeals to the nation, beginning on November 2, which, while encouraging those who were fighting for "socialist democratization" against those who wanted to maintain the "old system of government hated by the people," noted that the reactionaries were gaining ground. They warned against any anti-Soviet propaganda and, in particular, against any request for the departure of Soviet troops.[36] Cardinal Wyszynski, who had been released from prison a few days earlier, was not the least to preach along similar lines. In his first sermon, given on the day of the second Soviet intervention in Budapest, he had declared: "It is easier to die in glory than to live in the midst of hardship and sacrifice. This is why the latter heroism is far the greater." [37]

It seemed as if Gomulka—perfectly aware of the limitations imposed on Poland by its geographical location between the Soviet giant and a Germany eager to recover its unity and its former frontiers—had limited his ambition to obtaining, within the socialist camp, the maximum internal autonomy and the best possible treatment from the U.S.S.R. As of November, in any case, he had been promised 1,400,000 tons of wheat and a loan of 700 million rubles. He had also succeeded in getting rid of Rokossovski and his thirty Soviet generals who, from within, controlled the Polish Army.

Despite the fact that the government was progressively curbing the freedom of expression of journalists and writers, the Polish people let themselves be easily convinced that they could hardly hope for better conditions. And when, on January 20, 1957, the Poles voted in free elections for the first time in more than ten years, they declared themselves almost unanimously in favor of the slates sponsored by Gomulka, as, indeed, the Cardinal had expressly advised. Gomulka had clearly explained the significance of the ballot by declaring that "to rule out the names of the Communists would mean erasing Poland from the map of Europe." [38] The Hungarian tragedy was still close enough for everyone to understand the significance of that warning.

Though Moscow was forced to accept the existence of a Polish way toward socialism, it became very clear, in 1957, that Poland, like Yugoslavia, was forbidden to serve as an example. The young philosopher Harich was arrested in East Berlin for having advocated the extension of "Gomulkaism" to East Germany. In April, *Kommunist,* the ideological spokesman for the Soviet party, declared that the tendency to oppose an "individual path" to the experience of other socialist countries "was equivalent to the rejection of the international teachings of Marxism-Leninism." "National communism," it wrote, "is only bourgeois nationalism . . . the experience of the U.S.S.R. . . . is the common highway which must be taken by the proletariat of all countries in order to gain victory."

§   §   §

Beginning in the summer of 1957, therefore, at the cost of a few nonessential concessions and promises of economic assistance, which resulted in a quite sizable improvement in the general standard of living, Khrushchev had reunified the socialist bloc. It must be said that Mao helped him considerably in this.

But this support was not unconditional. The qualifications of the parvenu peasant Khrushchev were very meager when compared to those of a man like Mao Tse-tung, a thinker, poet and man of action, a veteran of the workers' movement, who, starting from nothing and despite Stalin's ill will, to put it mildly, and the declared hostility of the United States, had established socialism in China. Therefore, Mao expected Mr. K to consider his advice—but not to imagine that the U.S.S.R.'s acknowledged leadership of the "camp" required its members to servilely follow its example and carry out its directives.

The way in which the Twentieth Congress of the Soviet Communist Party had criticized Stalin had been judged by Peking to be "in error from the standpoint of principle as well as of method," and the Peking press had published, in April 1956, an article titled "On the Historical Experience of the Dictatorship of the Proletariat." While admitting that the Georgian had made certain mistakes—of which the Chinese Communists, more than anyone else, had often had occasion to complain—it praised him for having followed the Leninist line in the industrialization of the U.S.S.R. and in the collectivization of agriculture. The article concluded that his name was covered "quite rightly, with immense glory throughout the world." [39] While receiving Mikoyan during that same period, Mao had told him that "Stalin's merits were greater than his errors," [40] and he and his lieutenants had taken up this theme again in subsequent talks with the Russian ambassador or the Soviet leaders.

The October crisis had given rise to new anxieties in Peking, where great pains had been taken to persuade Khrushchev to reach an understanding with Gomulka and to intervene in Hungary. In any case, in the face of danger, it was necessary to close ranks. Therefore, on November 4 the *People's Daily* hailed the return of the Russian tanks to Budapest as "a great victory for the Hungarian people" and on the 14th asserted that the U.S.S.R. had neither violated its October 30 declaration on the equality between socialist countries nor the five principles of peaceful coexistence. On the 28th, Chou went to New Delhi, where he tried to convince Nehru of the propriety of the Russian action in Hungary. On the 15th, however, India had signed a declaration along with Indonesia, Burma and Ceylon, asking that the "Soviet forces be withdrawn from Hungary and that the Hungarian people be left free to decide their own destiny and to form a government." [41] Then Chou went on to make the same statement in different Asiatic capitals, from Hanoi to Colombo and Karachi.

On December 29 the *People's Daily,* in one of those interminable articles for which it has a unique talent, analyzed the problems of the Communist world. After having admitted that the U.S.S.R. had made mistakes and had let itself fall into "Great-Power chauvinism" in its relations with the east European countries, the newspaper of the Chinese Communist Party affirmed that the latter, for their part, had ventured into "excessive nationalism." But in any event, these contradictions were "not fundamental" and the Yugoslavs were wrong to consider them fundamental—for fundamental differences could exist only between the two blocs. The U.S.S.R., the author of the article continued, had now corrected its errors and therefore remained "the center and the heart of the movement." *Pravda* reprinted the entire article on the following day.

On January 7, 1957, Chou En-lai arrived in Moscow, where he met with the Soviet leaders and Kadar before going on to Warsaw and Budapest. On his return to the U.S.S.R. on January 17, he made the most unconditionally pro-Russian speech ever heard from the mouth of a Peking leader: "The Chinese people," he said, "are fully conscious of the fact that our gains are inseparable from the support and assistance of the Soviet Government and people . . . a unified and strong socialist camp, headed by the Soviet Union, represents the most important fortress for the cause of peace in the world and for the progress of humanity." [42]

Why was such a categorical position taken? Like their Soviet comrades, the Chinese Communists are Leninists—that is to say, men who think in terms of strategy and weigh the pros and cons before acting. In the light of what has taken place since then, it is possible to see that Mao was, at that period, motivated by several considerations. First it was necessary to reunify the socialist camp at any price, confronting the American "imperialists" who were openly congratulating themselves on its divisions and who were taking the offensive in the Middle East. Moreover, he was able to put Khrushchev somewhat more in his debt. The calculation did not prove false, for on October 15 of that same year, 1957, the U.S.S.R. concluded a bilateral treaty on the "new techniques of national defense," in other words, on nuclear cooperation, the existence of which the Chinese would reveal six years later.

§ § §

Nonetheless, in the summer of 1956, China had not escaped the backlash that was rocking central Europe. Here, as elsewhere, workers and students were growing restless, creating unions other than official organizations and even resorting to strikes in order to attain an easier life and more freedom. To channel this agitation the head of the propaganda department had declared in May 1956, "To artists and writers we say: 'Let flowers of many kinds blossom.' To scientists we say: 'Let diverse schools of thought contend.' " [43] On February 27, 1957, Mao intervened in his turn, in a speech which was not to be published until June of that year, in a considerably revised form—after experience had failed to justify his expectations. Returning to the theme already developed by the *People's Daily* on December 29, he compared the contradictions between the Communists and their enemies, which "are antagonistic ones" and can only be resolved through revolution, with the contradictions "among the working people," which are "not antagonistic" because of the people's similar interests and can "be resolved . . . by the Socialist system itself."

In the socialist society, Mao continued, "the growth of new things can also be hindered. . . . That is why we should take a cautious attitude in regard to questions of right and wrong in the arts and sciences, encourage free discussion, and avoid hasty conclusions . . . Plants raised in hothouses are not likely to be robust. Carrying out the policy of letting a hundred flowers blossom and a hundred schools of thought contend will not weaken but strengthen the leading position of Marxism in the ideological field." [44]

The campaign of the "hundred flowers"—just like destalinization in eastern Europe the preceding year—took on dimensions which had not been foreseen by its initiators. Journalists demanded freedom of the press and the creation of a coalition government, and students organized street demonstrations. The walls of the universities were covered with slogans which condemned not only the abuses of the bureaucracy and of dogmatism, but also the regime itself. In Peking, for example, one could read, "Communist society makes human beings inhuman," and in Tientsin, "Capitalism is more democratic than socialism." [45]

In the middle of May a halt was called and a "rectification campaign" was started, as happened each time the party had made a wrong move. A sharp offensive was declared against the "right-wingers," aimed at bringing the intellectuals into line. The students were deprived of their vacations and invited to make self-critical confessions. Large numbers of them were subsequently sent out into the fields. The party and the administration were harshly purged, and 300,000 functionaries were "transferred to productive work." Several ministers made public confessions of guilt. The authorities, in their national mania for quantifying everything, announced the uncovering, between July 24 and August 19, of 13 conspiracies, and the arrest, since July 1955, of 81,000 reactionaries.

On May 5, 1958, the Congress of the Chinese Communist Party was convened in extraordinary session to hear Liu Shao-chi give a report on the "general theme" that the masses were "full of confidence in the forward leap in production" and were "eager to remove the obstacles placed in their way by technical and cultural backwardness." Using again the old Trotskyite slogan of the "uninterrupted revolution," he told his listeners "this is . . . the first of three years' hard struggle"; for the speed with which work is done "has been the most important question confronting us since the victory of the socialist revolution." [46] And he set the goal for steel production for that year at 7.1 million tons, as against 6.2 million tons which had been fixed three months earlier. In July it was raised to 10 million tons and based on anticipated production from the greater number of "small blast furnaces" in the villages.

The emphasis having thereby been put on industrial progress, the policy was to depopulate the countryside, but there too the party was to demand a superhuman effort, setting fantastic goals for irrigation and agricultural production. To reach this objective, the "people's communes" movement, originating in Hunan in April 1958, tried simultaneously to effect a total permanent mobilization of the agricultural workers and to liberate men and women from household chores and the care of children. During August 1958 the Central Committee enthusiastically hailed the success of the communes, declaring with a straight face that "the quantity of agricultural products had doubled or increased several times over and even, in some cases, more than tenfold" and that "the realization of communism in China was no longer to be relegated to some far-off future." [47]

By the end of 1958 the Chinese leaders had to admit that sights had been set too high and—under the condescending smiles of the Soviet technicians, who had warned the Chinese leaders against their statistical mania—had to return to notably more modest objectives, abandoning their small blast furnaces and encouraging production in the individual plots of the peasants.

When Mao left for Moscow in October 1957 to assist at the

celebrations of the fortieth anniversary of the October Revolution, he was not aware of the resistance which human nature would set in the path of his ambition. Convinced by the success of Sputnik that the socialist camp had already won, and disappointed at failing to find, from the American side, any echo to his speeches on peaceful coexistence, he had decided to preach before Khrushchev and the other leaders of the socialist world the message of a fight to the finish, both internally and externally, against all who dared oppose the irresistible march toward communism.

BIBLIOGRAPHY AND NOTES

[1] Année politique, 1956, p. 402.
[2] U.S.A., Bulletin of the U.S. Information Service in Paris, No. 1988, January 6, 1957.
[3] Sherman Adams, op. cit., p. 274.
[4] Keesing's, 15370 A.
[5] Année politique, 1957, p. 298.
[6] Le Monde, January 11, 1957.
[7] Ibid., January 30, 1957.
[8] Ibid., February 8, 1957.
[9] Keesing's, 15504 B.
[10] Le Monde, April 23, 1957.
[11] Mackintosh, op. cit., p. 224.
[12] Keesing's, 15745 A.
[13] Fleming, op. cit., II, p. 889.
[14] Le Monde, September 27, 1957.
[15] Ibid., September 28, 1957.
[16] Interview with James Reston, The New York Times, October 10, 1957.
[17] Année politique, 1957, p. 455.
[18] Keesing's, 15920 A.
[19] Année politique, 1957, p. 466.
[20] Le Monde, January 3, 1957.
[21] Ibid., January 19, 1957.
[22] Bernard Féron, L'U.R.S.S. sans idole (Paris: Casterman, 1966), p. 39.
[23] La révolution hongroise, op. cit., p. 257.
[24] Ibid., pp. 264–65.
[25] The Truth About the Nagy Affair, op. cit., p. 15.
[26] Ibid., pp. 14–15.
[27] Ibid., pp. 21–22.
[28] François Fejtö, "Hungarian Communism," in Griffith, Communism in Europe (Cambridge, Mass.: M.I.T. Press, 1964), pp. 219–23.
[29] Thomas Schreiber, L'évolution politique et économique de la Hongrie 1956–1966. Documentation française. Notes et études documentaires, No. 3335, November 8, 1966, p. 9.
[30] Fejtö, in Griffith, op. cit., p. 227.
[31] The Truth About the Nagy Affair, op. cit., pp. 36–41.
[32] Le Figaro Littéraire, June 28, 1957.
[33] Keesing's, 15258 A.
[34] Ibid.
[35] Le Monde, July 13, 1957.
[36] Keesing's, 15379 B.
[37] Karol, op. cit., p. 161.

[38] *Ibid.*

[39] "The Divergences Between the Conduct of the C.P.S.U. and Ourselves," *People's Daily,* September 6, 1963. Documentation française. Notes et études documentaires, No. 3092, May 22, 1964.

[40] *Ibid.*

[41] Année politique, 1956, p. 405.

[42] *Izvestia,* January 18, 1957.

[43] Klaus Mehnert, *Peking and Moscow* (New York: Putnam, 1963), p. 184.

[44] Mao Tse-tung, *People's China, op. cit.,* p. 4.

[45] Mehnert, *op. cit.,* p. 198.

[46] *Peking Review,* June 3, 1958, No. 14, p. 14.

[47] René Dumont, *La Chine surpeuplée* (Paris: Editions du Seuil, 1966), pp. 65–67.

PART TWO

CHINA TAKES
UP THE TORCH

*The two great dangers which threaten the existence
of religion are schism and indifference.*

—De Tocqueville, *Democracy in America*

· CHAPTER 13 ·

HIS MAJESTY

SPUTNIK

M. de Conty spoke like a man who wanted war, and
acted like a man who wanted peace.

—Cardinal de Retz, *Mémoires*, Book II

ON AUGUST 26, 1957, TASS ANNOUNCED A SERIES OF
nuclear and thermonuclear explosions as well as the launching of
an "intercontinental ballistic supermissile in several stages," in other
words, a weapon capable of reaching American soil without a moment's warning.

At the time many Western "experts" believed that Khrushchev
was bluffing. On October 4 they had to change their opinion: the
U.S.S.R. had put its first Sputnik in orbit. It was a sphere weighing
116 pounds with a diameter of 22 inches whose *beep-beep,*
breaking the eternal silence of space, filled it with the glory of
Russia and of Marxism-Leninism. On the 8th, Radio Cairo expressed
the near unanimity of the third world when it proclaimed: "The
planetary era rings the death knell of colonialism; the American policy
of encirclement of the Soviet Union has pitifully failed." On the
same day, Moscow announced the test of a hydrogen bomb "of
great power and of a new design." On November 3 another Sputnik was
launched: it weighed six times more and contained a dog, a fact which
horrified animal lovers, especially in Britain.

The first United States reaction to that technological leap forward was ridiculous. "The Sputnik has no military value," stated
Ike, whose Secretary of Defense, Charles Wilson, affirmed that "It's

only a scientific gimmick which won't disturb anyone's sleep." [1] It
was a total misconception. If the Russians had been able to launch
an artificial satellite, it was thanks to an extremely powerful missile;
therefore it was quite probable that they had an intercontinental
weapon. Immediately following victory over the Reich and Japan,
the United States, with the cooperation of German specialists, had
started work on missile projects, with the notorious V-2 as the starting point. But the Pentagon's absolute confidence in its strategic
bombers and the Defense Secretary's passion for economies had
resulted in a slowing down of the development programs demanded
by the most dynamic of the young generals. It was only in 1958
and after many failures that the United States would make successful
tests of the prototype of the intermediate-range missile (I.R.B.M.)
Jupiter and of the intercontinental weapon (I.C.B.M.) Atlas.

While waiting for the Atlas to become, in military parlance,
"operational," all the strategic concepts of Soviet-American competition had to be revised. United States territory had ceased to be an
inviolable "sanctuary." Very quickly, however, the administration
realized its error and understood that both the prestige and the
security of the United States were at stake. "The Sputnik," said
Paul-Henri Spaak, Secretary General of NATO since May 16, 1957,
"may be the event that will awaken us." [2] On October 23, Eisenhower and Macmillan issued a declaration in which they affirmed
their conviction that "despotisms have often been able to produce
spectacular monuments," but their "price has been heavy . . . if
the free nations are steadfast and if they utilize their resources in
harmonious cooperation, the totalitarian menace that now confronts
them will in time recede." [3]

So the hour of "interdependence" had struck. To study the
means of implementing it, they proposed to their Allies the convening
of a NATO summit conference in Paris, in December. When it
opened, America's prestige was at a low point; the space administration, Wernher von Braun's NASA, had vainly tried to orbit a
minute copy of Sputnik, the "grapefruit." Its failure, after publicized
preparations, provoked laughter throughout the world, while the
Communist press took up again the theme developed by Khrushchev
before two Brazilian newsmen: "The sputniks prove that socialism
has won the competition between Socialist and capitalist countries

. . . that the economy, science, culture, and the creative genius of the people in all spheres of life develop better and faster under socialism." [4]

It was only in February 1958, that the Americans succeeded in putting a very small Explorer into orbit. Three months later the Russians launched a Sputnik 125 times heavier.

One year after Budapest, optimism reigned in Moscow when the fortieth anniversary of the October Revolution brought there the leaders of all the Communist parties of the world, including Mao, for whom it would be the final trip to Russia. The leaders of the twelve countries in which Communist parties were in power conferred for several days behind closed doors. On November 22 they published a long declaration stating that Communists, "in spite of the absurd imperialist assertions about an alleged Communist crisis," would know how "to deal with the attempts of the imperialist reactionary forces to impede the march of society toward a new era by a further strengthening of their unity and their solidarity." [5]

At the time, that document had the effect on the West of a new declaration of war, or at least of a cold war, a reaffirmation of the Communists' conviction that the course of history was in their favor and that "imperialism" should not try to benefit from the coexistence it proposed by thwarting their march toward universal victory. However, this meeting, one year after the crisis which had so greatly shaken the Communist movement, was above all an attempt to end an increasingly evident divergence now that the despot, whose iron will had maintained the cohesion of the "socialist camp" as long as he was alive, was dead and removed from his pedestal.

At that time the Chinese were still determined to gamble on Khrushchev. To the twelve leaders gathered behind closed doors, Mao stated that the line he represented "was more correct and that objecting to that line was an error." [6] For him "the distinctive aspect of the present situation was that the wind from the East was overcoming the wind from the West, which meant that the socialist forces had acquired a crushing superiority over the imperialist forces."

From it he concluded that the latter would not start a war. However, he added, "If the imperialists are determined to wage war, we can do nothing else but to resign ourselves to fighting the enemy."

He continued, "I had a discussion with a foreign political figure"—
Nehru, according to the Soviet version of that speech—"on that
subject. In his judgment, should an atomic war break out, man
would be exterminated. I said that if, at worst, half of the world's
population was utterly annihilated, the other half would still remain.
But then imperialism would be liquidated and the whole world would
become socialist." [7]

In the same speech, Mao called "the supposedly powerful reactionaries paper tigers—to be scorned from a strategic viewpoint"
because "Marx and Engels have declared that capitalism would be
overthrown throughout the entire world." But he added, "In respect
to practical questions . . . if we do not take the enemy into account,
we would fall into the error of adventurism." [8]

Nevertheless, still in the same speech, he blamed those who
"are continually fearing war." [9] Evidently he meant the Russians,
because a month later the Chinese magazine *World Culture* calmly
wrote: "The Soviet intercontinental ballistic missiles can not only
reach any military base in Central Europe, Asia or Africa, but
can also force the United States, for the first time in history, into a
position from which neither escape nor the power to strike back is
possible." [10]

The Russians might have been able to do that, but they certainly
didn't want to, and it is now known that the insertion of the most
militant passages in the declaration from the twelve Communist parties was due to China's insistence. The same is true of the simultaneous condemnation of revisionism and dogmatism, the latter
being considered less dangerous than the former, and of the belated
recognition of the U.S.S.R.'s role as leader of the Communist bloc,
which Khrushchev did not want publicized at all. He had no greater
desire than to bring Yugoslavia back to the socialist bosom. But
Yugoslavia could not sign a declaration which both condemned
revisionism—a synonym for Titoism—and underscored the necessity
of reinforcing the bloc; Yugoslavia had been calling for the dissolution of blocs, believing that the universal advent of socialism was
the result not of war, hot or cold, but of its intrinsic superiority and
when conditions were ripe, of its triumph in different countries.

However, the situation did not deteriorate quickly. Kardelj,
who represented Tito at the Moscow festivities, signed the document,

a long series of platitudes adopted by the delegates of the sixty-four invited parties. In April, at Ljubljana, the Yugoslav Communist Congress approved another platform which, among other heresies, proclaimed that "Socialist thinking should no longer primarily be concerned with questions relating to the overthrow of capitalism" and that it was "theoretically wrong" and "harmful in practice" to maintain that Communist parties have a monopoly over every step of society's movement toward socialism. It also affirmed that, "in consequence of the hegemonistic position it has acquired for one reason or another," it is possible even for a socialist state "to resort in one form or another to economic exploitation of the other country." [11]

On April 19 the Moscow *Kommunist* denounced revisionism as guilty of putting "on the same footing the pacifist policy of socialist states and the aggressive policy of the ruling circles of imperialist states." On May 5 the Peking *People's Daily* declared that the Yugoslav program "conforms to the wishes of American imperialists." *Pravda* reproduced that article in its entirety and on the 9th itself attacked the Belgrade theses. On the 29th the U.S.S.R. postponed for five years the granting of credits promised to Belgrade in 1956 for the implementation of its Five-Year Plan.

On June 15 the Hungarian Communist paper *Nepszabadsag* published an extensive article in which a denunciation of Yugoslav deviationism was sprinkled with frequent mentions of Imre Nagy's name. Two days later, a communiqué from the Budapest Minister of Justice announced the execution of the former Prime Minister and stated that he had "found support" from the Yugoslav Embassy.[12] Belgrade replied, expressing its "profound indignation" at the news of the execution and denying as "invented from beginning to end" the Hungarian assertions concerning the contacts with the Resistance made by Nagy and his friends during the time when they had sought asylum in the Yugoslav Embassy.[13] The Kadar government answered in the same tone and the Communist press of the whole world showered insults on Tito. Gomulka himself, returning from Hungary, declared in Gdansk, "Nothing, absolutely nothing, justifies their [the Yugoslavs'] stand in the present conflict, which is different from 1948–1950. Today the blame is on Yugoslavia." [14]

The West, ignorant at that time of the Sino-Russian disagreements, was tempted to see in the ebullient Nikita—now that he had re-established order in the "camp," liquidated his adversaries in the Soviet Government, and established the power and prestige of the U.S.S.R. on Sputniks and intercontinental missiles—a reincarnation of Stalin. Hence, the declaration adopted by the Atlantic summit itself in Paris on December 19, 1957, denounced the Twelve's reaffirmation in the Moscow document of "their determination to gain domination over the whole world, if possible through subversion, and if need be, through violence." [15]

This declaration was coupled with a communiqué whose signatories, while stating their desire to negotiate disarmament with the U.S.S.R., expressed their determination to give to the Western defense the "maximum efficiency in keeping with the latest technical progresses," [16] in other words, to find a means of warding off the menace to American territory created by the Soviet's intercontinental weapons.

Already, during the days following the launching of the first Sputnik, the Strategic Air Command had decided to keep a certain number of its planes continually in the air so that in the event their bases were destroyed by a surprise attack, they could nevertheless execute their missions of reprisal. But the installation in Europe of launching pads of intermediate range weapons would constitute a more effective protection, and from November 1957, conversations on that subject were started between the United States and some of its allies: Great Britain, Turkey and Italy, which promptly accepted in principle.

The eventuality of those installations naturally prompted a heated debate in a public rather tempted to think that, in the event of a conflict, its primary effect would be to attract lightning. Khrushchev didn't neglect to kindle those anxieties; in his colorful language he declared to the Greek ambassador that in case of war he could expect destruction of the Parthenon, at the same time evoking for the Italians' benefit the havoc to be suffered by the orange groves among which, according to their press, Jupiters would be hidden.

§   §   §

Naturally, these apprehensions influenced an attempt to renew the disarmament negotiations which since 1946 had not made much progress; in the final analysis the problem of controls was always the stumbling block: the suspicious West did not want to reduce its forces without knowing exactly what the U.S.S.R. would be left with. Russia, unwilling to facilitate the work of the capitalists' spies, did not accept any controls over its resources until general disarmament had been achieved. Besides, Moscow in its claims had given priority to the renunciation of atomic weapons, whose possession represented for the United States the only way of counterbalancing Russia's superiority, at the time a crushing one, in the conventional means of waging war.

For that reason there was almost general skepticism among the leaders of both sides on the possibility of reaching an appreciable agreement in that area. To Foster Dulles, Sherman Adams wrote, "it was a problem that had never seemed to get out of the laboratory where it had been ever since he had become familiar with it in the Wilson administration." [17] However, for Ike, disarmament "was a real and urgent necessity of today, the only means of gaining peace and security," [18] and he had entrusted the responsibility of those questions to a supreme optimist, Harold Stassen, unsuccessful candidate for the Republican nomination in the 1948 Presidential election. A former Governor of Minnesota, he was convinced that all the problems were soluble, provided they were attacked with energy and good will, and he constantly pointed out the advantages that the American economy would reap from an effective disarmament.

Stassen, an author of the "open skies" plan already submitted by Eisenhower in 1955 at the Geneva summit conference, was in London during March 1956, at the time of the B and K visit, and they invited him to talk with them. Khrushchev attacked the aerial inspection plan as an attempt by the imperialists to know everything by "peeking into other peoples' bedrooms and gardens." He said that he was convinced that the time for disarmament had not come, while adding that the U.S.S.R. would patiently wait for it. In conclusion, he suggested that the Americans begin by reducing their forces in Germany, promising to follow their example if they did.[19]

At Lancaster House, a few steps away from Claridge's Hotel, where this encounter took place, the meeting which had brought Stassen to the British capital was being held. It was that of the disarmament subcommittee, created in 1954 in the climate of détente following the Korean armistice and to which only the United States, Great Britain, the U.S.S.R., France and Canada belonged.

Chaired by men like Stassen or Jules Moch, who had both the will to achieve substantial agreements and a thorough knowledge of a still astonishingly complex dossier, those deliberations were being held in a constructive spirit. Yet whatever way they approached the problem, it always ended up facing the same crucial difficulty: verification. In the "open skies" plan the Russians had opposed the idea of a control exercised at railroads and road junctions, at airfields and ports. On March 21, Stassen suggested the creation of limited zones in the United States and the U.S.S.R. where the methods of control proposed by the two countries would be tested. But the Russians would not hear of it. When, on March 27, they reversed their traditional position and said that they would be satisfied, in the beginning, with a reduction of conventional arms, it was seen as a maneuver which presented, as a conciliatory gesture, a measure aimed essentially at enabling the Russian economy to profit from the progress of military technology. In fact, on May 14, the Kremlin decided on a unilateral reduction of the Red Army.

However, on November 17 the U.S.S.R. accepted an aerial inspection area limited to 500 miles on each side of the Iron Curtain. The purpose of the declaration in which this suggestion was made, along with extremely offensive remarks about England and France, was above all to propose a Five-Power summit conference. Given the date of its publication, it looked too much like a spectacular peace initiative by the Kremlin to disarm the reprobation it had earned for its intervention against the Hungarian rebels thirteen days before.

On March 20, 1957, the Soviet Union went a step further in proposing a ban on nuclear tests; this measure had been suggested by Nehru on March 31, 1954, in the wake of some particularly spectacular experiments at Bikini. The Moscow Government had claimed it as its own, but it was the first time that it presented it as a separate measure which could be adopted independently of any other steps taken toward disarmament.

The Anglo-Saxons approved when Jules Moch declared that France would not feel bound by such an accord if it were not ac-

companied by a halt in the production of fissionable materials for
military use. However, on August 21, after lengthy discussions, the
West proposed to suspend the tests for two years, it being understood that each side would be free to resume tests at the expiration
of that period if no satisfactory system of controls had been implemented during the interval. On the 27th, a few hours after the
announcement of the launching of a Russian intercontinental missile,
Zorin, the U.S.S.R. delegate to the London subcommittee, rejected
that offer in terms intimating the future withdrawal of his government
from disarmament agencies. This, in fact, was announced by Kuznetsov
on November 4 at the U.N.; he added that in the future he
would participate only in negotiations in which all the U.N. members
took part. On being asked to reconsider its position, the Soviet Union
repeated that henceforth it would sit only in a body where East and
West were equally represented.

His withdrawal caused consternation. Although *Life* on December 16 published an article in which Foster Dulles denounced the
futility and the risks of any discussions "with the malignant forces
of evil," a number of delegates to the December Atlantic summit,
including Adenauer, pointed out that it would be difficult to make
European public opinion accept the measures of rearmament necessitated by the development of Russian intercontinental weapons if it
were not convinced beforehand that all possibilities of disarmament
had been exhausted.

But the Eastern countries had just presented, through a speech by
the Polish Foreign Minister before the General Assembly on October
2, a new idea which was soon to take his name and become the
Rapacki Plan. In January 1956 the U.S.S.R. had proposed to "de-
nuclearize" Germany and its neighbors, in other words, to prohibit
the production and the stockpiling of atomic weapons on their soil.
At the time, the Warsaw Government expressed its willingness to
make such a commitment if the two German states were, in fact,
denuclearized. Czechoslovakia had made a similar declaration, and
Bulganin had presented the same idea again in messages addressed
to the government heads of NATO prior to the meeting of the Atlantic Council.

Other formulas for "disengagement" had been put forward by

several influential people in the West, such as the former American diplomat George Kennan, the German Social Democratic leader Fritz Erler, English Labourites like Hugh Gaitskell and Denis Healey, etc. The Western press had commented on those proposals at length. The Danish and Norwegian prime ministers and the Canadian Foreign Minister requested the Council "to evaluate whether such ideas contained elements which might be utilized in a constructive peace policy." [20]

Naturally, the Great Powers of the Alliance saw a triple danger in the Rapacki Plan: it froze the European *status quo*, by implying a *de facto* recognition of East Germany; by discriminating against the Federal Republic, it might encourage German public opinion to seek a direct accord with the Russians; finally, it complicated the defense of Europe. But it would permit the implementing of a system of controls—provided it functioned satisfactorily—likely to serve as a model for a more comprehensive formula; it would lead to a loosening of the Soviet hold on Poland and Czechoslovakia; finally, by eliminating, for the Russians, the major danger that the participation of a united Germany in an "atomic" alliance would represent, it would facilitate German reunification.

No one doubted that the Rapacki Plan was going to be one of the important questions discussed at the next summit conference, suggested by the new French Prime Minister, Felix Gaillard, in an interview in the *U.S. News and World Report* in December 1957. The last of the government heads of the Fourth Republic, he was caught in the throes of the Algerian drama which, a few months later, was to cause the downfall of his regime, and was evidently trying to reinforce his very modest authority at home by a spectacular gesture in the international arena.

On both sides the first reactions were positive, but the Russians' refusal to mention Germany's reunification was a stumbling block. Preparations for a summit which seemed so difficult to organize that no truly important results could be expected from it would soon yield priority to other events: the Algiers coup on May 13, followed, on the 29th, by General de Gaulle's return to power, the deterioration of the Middle Eastern situation, and lastly, on June 17, the announcement of the execution of Imre Nagy and Pal Maleter, which again greatly tended to increase tensions between East and West.

The day before, the Kremlin had judged the moment opportune to publish unilaterally several confidential documents on East-West negotiations, "because of personal indiscretions which could give a distorted idea of Soviet principles." [21] The painstaking work of diplomats to adjust the contradictions of draft communiqués was brought to naught.

Khrushchev continued to bombard the West with letters urging a prompt meeting of the conference. In July he even suggested a treaty of friendship and cooperation between all the European states, open to the United States. But when a meeting of heads of government was seriously considered, it would be in a completely different perspective and with another agenda.

As for the discussions on disarmament, they had been reactivated by Gromyko's announcement before the Supreme Soviet that the U.S.S.R. was suspending its atomic experiments, that it invited the other interested powers to do as much, but that it would resume them should its example not be followed. The moment was well chosen: the Russians had just completed a series of about fifty tests, while the United States and Great Britain were preparing to undertake some in the Pacific. Dulles' first impulse was to say that it was primarily a propaganda gesture, but Eisenhower proposed that scientists from the interested countries gather to study the possibility of developing effective controls in case of an eventual cessation of tests. Mr. K having accepted, a conference of Russian, American, British and French scientists opened on July 2 in Geneva. The "fraternity of scientists" made a good show, and on August 21 they separated after having issued a communiqué enumerating the different possible tests and the probabilities of their detection. In conclusion, they advocated the establishment of 180 control stations on all continents under the direction of an international organization, and, in the event of a suspected explosion, the sending of observers to the spot.

The unexpected rapidity of the accord created a favorable climate for the opening of political discussions. Eisenhower suggested the calling of a conference on the basis of the scientists' report: if the

U.S.S.R. agreed and abstained from making new tests, the United States itself was ready to observe a renewable moratorium of one year.

The British joined in that suggestion. The U.S.S.R. replied that it could only accede to a final cessation of tests. On October 2 it announced that in view of the numerous tests made by the United States and Great Britain, it was renewing its own tests. Nevertheless, the conference opened on the appointed date, October 31, in Geneva, the United States and Great Britain having suspended their own tests twenty-four hours earlier. It would take five years to complete the drafting of the treaty in which Maurice Couve de Murville, de Gaulle's Foreign Minister, had, from the beginning, intimated that France would not join, stating before the U.N. General Assembly that "the cessation of nuclear tests was only conceivable within the framework of effective nuclear disarmament," and that France considered the Geneva Conference useless unless it proceeded without delay to "the study of means to control the cessation of atomic production for military uses." [22]

On November 10, 1958, a few days after the beginning of the conference on the cessation of nuclear tests, another conference was opening in Geneva to study the means of preventing surprise attacks. Khrushchev deserved credit for this, as he had proposed, the preceding July 2, that this problem be tackled by a meeting of experts such as that used to deal with atomic tests.

The appearance of long-range missiles on the scene had created a real obsession with the kind of attacks which, without a declaration of war, would utterly destroy all ability to resist in the country attacked. Therefore, a discussion of this point was likely to reassure the potential adversaries as to their mutual intentions. However, when the conference convened—on the parity basis asked for by the U.S.S.R.—it was quickly apparent that both sides envisaged the negotiations in an entirely different way. The delegates from the West wanted them to be confined to technological considerations, and the Russians and their allies wanted to discuss concrete measures such as the installation of ground-control stations, the determination of an aerial zone and the Rapacki Plan. As the United States and Great Britain had finally categorically rejected the latter at the beginning of May, the Russians must have had few illusions as to their proposal's chances of success.

The conference on surprise attacks stagnated until the end of December 1958, when it adjourned *sine die*. When Moscow, on January 10, 1959, requested a resumption of negotiations, Washington answered that "more significant progress not having been made . . . it behooved the two powers most interested to smooth over their differences . . . before meeting again." [23]

In the meantime, Khrushchev had issued his first ultimatum on Berlin, reopening the Cold War, which had been strongly primed in the summer by two serious crises in the Middle East and in Asia.

§   §   §

On January 31, 1958, Egypt and Syria decided to form a single state, the United Arab Republic. That long-expected decision was primarily an answer to the fear expressed by the Syrian ruling class, headed by the President, Kuwatly, of being unable to check the growth of communism, whose chief, Khaled Bakhdash, a skilled and courageous Druse, had been elected to the legislature the previous summer.

On February 6, Bakhdash fled to Prague, while Khaled el Azm and General Bizri, the two pro-Soviet leaders, were removed from office. Soon the Communist Party was dissolved, along with all the other political parties, and Serraj, Nasser's proconsul in Damascus, tortured and jailed the militants of the extreme Left.

At first the U.S.S.R. accepted the *fait accompli* with good grace. It was the first power to recognize the U.A.R. and gave Nasser a triumphant welcome when he came on an official visit to Moscow, after having settled the Suez litigation with the West on terms very satisfactory to him, thanks to American pressure.

Khrushchev went so far as to tell him that in assuming power, he had "changed the course of history" and that he hoped "to see Arab unity achieved under his leadership." [24] In spite of it, Nasser did not align himself with the Kremlin. On his return to Cairo on May 16 he declared that the United States had let him know that they respected the neutrality of the U.A.R. and that the Soviet leaders had told him the same thing. On the basis of these statements he claimed the triumph of the policy "for which he and his friends had fought: an uncommitted policy, an independent policy, a policy of positive neutrality." [25] In September the Kremlin supplied him with an atomic reactor. On October 23, Mr. K announced, in the presence of Lieutenant General Amer, the number-two man in the Cairo regime, that the Soviet Union had decided to grant a loan of 400 million rubles to the U.A.R. for the construction of the Aswan Dam, and to put the necessary technicians at its disposal.

At first, Arab public opinion—loudly expressed in the streets of Baghdad—saw in the creation of the U.A.R. an answer to the imperialists' machinations, and the sign that the day was near when the Arab nation, triumphant over all those who stood in its way, would at last achieve unity. In retaliation, Iraq and Jordan on February 14 decided to organize among themselves an "Arab Union" presided over by the King of Iraq and, in his absence, by his cousin from Jordan. The two armies were to merge.

At the time, Nasser applauded an action which, he wrote in a message of felicitation to Feisal, "brought the Arab nation closer to the great day of general union." [26] But he soon changed his mind, and Cairo Radio launched attacks against a regrouping which had been too openly encouraged by the West. In Baghdad there were repeated demonstrations against a union with Jordan. In the face of a worsening situation, Feisal, on March 3, recalled to power Nuri es-Said, the British protégé. On the 5th, Serraj stated that Saud had given him £22 million to have Nasser assassinated and to prevent the Syrian-Egyptian union. Saud denied it, but at the end of the month he was obliged to turn over the Prime Minister's post to his brother Feisal, a man much more open to the outside world, and who was even said to be sympathetic to Nasser.

In May a new fire broke out in that overcharged region. A large part of the Lebanese population, including many Christians, were alarmed by the expressed intention of the pro-Western President, Camille Chamoun, to have his hand-picked Parliament, elected the year before, amend the constitution so he could seek a second term. On May 8 the editor in chief of one of the opposition's important newspapers was assassinated. Nasser's supporters imputed responsibility for the crime to the government, and started a general strike which, in Beirut and Tripoli, turned into a riot. Many important figures, headed by the Maronite Patriarch, urged the chief of state to renounce a policy which ran the risk of disturbing the delicate religious balance on which the country rested. In fact, fighting spread, without, however, taking the form of a real civil war because everyone realized that Lebanon's independence and its exceptional prosperity would not survive it. Everything seemed to show that each side wanted above all to prove that the other was not capable of imposing its rule: the pro-Westerners, that the pro-Nasser elements were incapable of forcing allegiance to the U.A.R.; and the pro-Nasser elements, that the pro-Westerners could not maintain the allegiance imprudently given to the Eisenhower Doctrine.

The army—whose unanimously respected chief, General Chehab, was a member of one of the oldest families in the country—was profoundly conscious of its mission as guardian of the national unity. It intervened only to keep the rebellion divided by preventing its diverse elements from forming a united front and from moving too close to Syria, from which it could receive massive aid.

On May 13, Chamoun asked France, Great Britain and the United States for their help against what he called an "external aggression against Lebanon." On the 20th he appealed to the Security Council, which decided on June 11 to send a group of observers to the scene. On the 17th, Dag Hammarskjöld himself went to Beirut, then to Jerusalem and Cairo. His avowed objective was to reduce the tension, following which a discussion between the interested parties could be envisioned. Besides, the observers' report, while admitting that it was possible for them to investigate only a small part of the Lebanese territory, had stated that they had no definite proof of foreign intervention.

Chamoun, who felt he was losing control of the situation, made more appeals to Washington, even requesting, according to Bob Murphy, the Under Secretary of State, that "tanks be airlifted" to him. But the Americans, who were again beginning to see in Nasser a counterweight to communism, doubted that Cairo's intervention had the importance given it by Lebanon's President. They had little desire to stick their noses into the hornets' nest of a civil war, dreading to incite the Kremlin to intervene in its turn—a possibility raised by TASS on June 24.

Chamoun only obtained the assurance that the United States

would "help Lebanon, if necessary." [27] Disappointed, he turned to Nuri es-Said, who was in London at the time, and who returned to Baghdad on July 3, having given *The Times* an interview in which he openly advocated Turkey and Iraq's intervention in Lebanon, the latter via Jordan.

The Moslem leaders of the Baghdad Pact decided to meet in Istanbul, without the presence of the Anglo-Saxons, whose prudence —excessive in their eyes—they probably dreaded. The Western press was filled with dispatches according to which they were getting ready to supply help to President Chamoun's government.

In vain, Turks and Iranians waited in Istanbul for Nuri, King Feisal and the ex-regent, Abdul Illah, who had remained his mentor. The last two had been shot down by a group of Free Officers led by Colonel Aref and General Kassem, who had taken advantage of a troop movement apparently designed to prepare for intervention in Lebanon. As for the old Pasha, who had escaped, he was found the next day disguised as a woman and hacked to pieces by a frenzied crowd.

The coup did not meet with any resistance. The guards of the royal palace quickly joined the insurgents, and it was Nuri's own aide-de-camp who, perhaps out of compassion, gave him the *coup de grâce*. The dynasty, and the Anglo-Saxons who had unwisely backed it, were thus recompensed for thirty years of a police regime and for the shameful exploitation of a wretched proletariat.

The coup was greeted with enthusiasm in Moscow and Cairo and with consternation in Washington and London. The first thought in the West was to intervene. In order to give legal justification to an armed intervention against Baghdad, the King of Jordan, urged on by Ankara, Teheran and Beirut, invoked the accord concluded with Feisal in February to proclaim himself head of the Arab Union.

But that intervention would not take place. With the death of Nuri es-Said and Abdul Illah, there was no longer anyone in Iraq to whom the West could give its backing. The absence of any resistance was proof enough that the revolution was approved by almost the entire population; to intervene under those conditions would be to trample underfoot, two years after Budapest, the exalted principle of self-determination. No one knew what the U.S.S.R. would do.

Finally, Britain, fearful for its oil interests, sought to establish immediate contact with the new Baghdad regime.

Baghdad itself was eager to reassure its allies. On July 18, Kassem declared that he would honor the oil agreements concluded by the previous governments. The Iraqi representative to the U.N. even affirmed that his country had not abandoned the Baghdad Pact. In August, on the occasion of a visit by Murphy, Kassem told him that "he had not risked revolution for the purpose of handing Iraq to the Soviet Union." [28]

As soon as he heard of the Baghdad *coup d'état*, Chamoun reminded Eisenhower and Dulles of the commitment they had made, fifteen days earlier, to "help Lebanon." Ike immediately summoned the leaders of the two parties, to whom Dulles said that the time had come "to bring a halt to the deterioriation in our position in the Middle East." [29] Accordingly, the President decided to send 10,000 men—or more than the whole Lebanese Army—to Beirut. He explained to Murphy, who had been sent to the scene to try to find a political solution to the Lebanese imbroglio, that if America stood by, doing nothing, it would suffer "irreparable losses in Lebanon and in that area generally," and that it must prove that it was "capable of supporting its friends." [30]

Washington did not find time to consult with its allies. De Gaulle took it rather badly, especially since Lebanon had long been under French influence and Dulles, received by him a few days before, had promised him that Americans would not take any important decision without consulting him. That certainly was one of the reasons that impelled the general, two months later, to demand of Ike and Macmillan—although in vain—that a tripartite body be formed to coordinate the West's global military and political strategy.

The British had only been informed at the last minute of the American decision. But they rejoiced in it, especially since Hussein of Jordan, fearing that his turn might come soon, was also calling for help. On the morning of the 17th, 2,500 paratroopers, the famous "Red Devils," landed in Amman.

Nasser had just left Tito when the crisis broke out. He turned around and secretly hurried to Moscow aboard the private plane of the Marshal, who had counseled prudence. He met with Khrushchev

for eight hours then went to Damascus, where, on the 17th, he proclaimed that the "flag of liberty will soon be raised in Algiers as in
Beirut and Amman." [31]

The same day, TASS broadcast a statement from the Soviet Union
demanding that the United States stop "instantly" its "armed intervention in the internal affairs of Arab countries." [32] The warning was
repeated the next day for the benefit of Great Britain, while large-
scale maneuvers began in the south of the U.S.S.R. and Bulgaria.

Khrushchev was determined not to add fuel to the flames and
not to lift a finger, except in the event of Western intervention in
Iraq. For his part, Nasser had no desire to see the Russians establish
themselves in Syria or anywhere else.

The socialist countries, nevertheless, started a violent propaganda
campaign against the United States, accompanied by enormous street
demonstrations, especially in Moscow and Peking. At the Security
Council, Sobolev vetoed a United States proposal to organize the
replacement, with a unit of "blue helmets," of the American contingent which had landed in Lebanon. He had no interest in facilitating
a détente, which would have deprived Khrushchev of the opportunity
offered by the crises to renew his proposal for a summit meeting.

On the 19th, Khrushchev sent Eisenhower, de Gaulle, Macmillan
and Nehru messages in which he asserted that the world was placed
"on the brink of a military catastrophe" and that "the slighest impru-
dent move could have irreparable consequences." After having compared the Anglo-American intervention in Jordan and Lebanon to
Nazi aggressions and to the Suez expedition, he asked that the states-
men seek a "solution based on calm and reason and not on the
exacerbation of warlike passions," and that the heads of government
to whom he was writing meet with Hammarskjöld as soon as possible, "to take the necessary measures for the cessation of the armed
conflict." [33] Nehru stated that he was willing, on condition that the
other interested parties were also willing. Although they spoke in
different terms, the Western leaders mentioned the competence of
the Security Council—de Gaulle accepting a summit if the U.N.
failed in its efforts to restore peace, and Macmillan suggesting that
the Council meet at the level of chiefs of state and government
heads, without taking a vote. On July 28, to everyone's surprise,

Khrushchev accepted the British proposal and suggested that the meetings be held in New York, on July 28, it "being understood that the governments of the involved Arab states would be invited." [34] Ike, who did not expect such a positive answer, replied in an embarrassed tone that the date of the 28th was premature and that the members of the Security Council must first determine among themselves whether everyone fully approved of such a meeting. De Gaulle took advantage of this occasion to show his independence by saying that what he had accepted was a summit meeting of the Five Powers "in a climate of calm and reason," and not a special session of the Security Council in which would participate, besides its eleven members, India, the interested Arab states, and other countries, such as Iran, Israel and Turkey, "which must also be invited." He stated that, for his part, he favored the original project, insisting that the meeting take place in Europe.[35]

On the 28th, Khrushchev, coming back to his original idea, wrote Eisenhower: "We would like to receive a clear answer to the following question: When will the United States be ready to take part in the conference of the Five Powers' government heads?" [36] De Gaulle proposed that it take place at Geneva, and that it discuss the "continual state of crisis which prevents the Middle East from living its life and developing under normal conditions." [37] But Macmillan and Ike, only too pleased at the turn taken by the discussion, held to the idea of a summit Security Council meeting.

Meanwhile, to everyone's surprise it was announced that the Soviet leader had suddenly left for Peking. It was clear that the worst of the Middle East crisis was over. Not only was any idea of Anglo-American intervention in Iraq abandoned, but thanks to the efforts of Murphy, whom Eisenhower had sent to Beirut along with the marines, Chamoun had given up his intention of seeking a second term in office. The American expeditionary force had so well succeeded in remaining completely uninvolved in active operations that its three months' presence resulted in only one dead soldier. And General Chehab had, almost unanimously, just been elected President of the Republic, under the banner of national reconciliation and noninvolvement. Lebanon had gone back to normal and the civil war was ended.

It may have been a success for the United States, but it was a success obtained at the price of renouncing the objective it had at the beginning of the crisis: to try to enlist Lebanon in a coalition against other Arab states.

Under those conditions, and given the overt disagreement between de Gaulle and the Anglo-Saxons, the summit meeting on the Middle East became every day less necessary and less probable. It was doubtful that Mr. K had traveled to Peking just because Mao was furious that he had accepted Macmillan's suggestion for a top-level Security Council meeting, which contained the risk of bringing together Chiang Kai-shek and the First Secretary of the Communist Party of the U.S.S.R. The possibility of a visit to Peking by the head of the Soviet Government had been rumored in East Germany and Moscow since the beginning of July, and a dispatch from A.F.P. had echoed it. It is true that on his return, Mr. K was to use the Chinese argument, among many others, to definitely reject the idea of a Security Council meeting. But when he had first accepted it, the *People's Daily* did not hesitate to rejoice over "that important step in the cause of peace."

It is nonetheless true that the crisis had, for the first time, brought to light a divergence between China and the U.S.S.R., China having advocated sending volunteers to the Arab countries, while Khrushchev himself had declared that such a move would increase the risk of a real war. In general, the tone of the Chinese press was more violent than that of its Russian counterpart. It was imperative to hasten to the aid of Iraqi revolutionaries and of Lebanon and Jordan's anti-imperialists, "without being stopped by the threat of a new world war." [38]

It can thus be surmised that during the meeting this view led to an exchange of recriminations and that the same applied to the subject of Formosa, which certainly dominated the talks. Mr. K also expressed to Mao his "doubts" about the people's communes and other "innovations." [39] Even discounting the unrealistic character of the Chinese economy, whose inflexible objectives had already prompted numerous admonitions from Russian technicians, there was an evidently unbearable wound to the Kremlin leaders' pride in Peking's pretension to achieve communism by methods more direct than those followed by Moscow.

In any case, on his return from Peking on August 5, Khrushchev sent messages to Eisenhower and Macmillan deploring their refusal to participate in a Five-Power summit meeting and declaring that the United States was trying to make the Security Council, where China's seat was occupied by the representative of a "political corpse," into "an auxiliary service of the State Department." He continued with warm praise of Red China which could continue to be ignored only through "lack of judgment," and concluded with a proposal for a meeting of the U.N. General Assembly in extraordinary session.[40]

This last suggestion was perfectly acceptable to the United States, as it had already made it as early as July 18. On August 13, Eisenhower addressed the delegates in person, asking first that the U.N. watch over Lebanon and Jordan by means of a permanent peace force, and then for the end of subversion and hostile propaganda and of the armaments race. He also proposed the adoption of a plan for regional economic development. Gromyko counterattacked by declaring that the principal question to be settled was the immediate withdrawal of foreign troops.[41]

No one knew how to break the deadlock, when, on August 21, all the Arab League members succeeded in agreeing on a resolution which was accepted unanimously the same day, including Israel's vote. The resolution was a polite invitation to the West and the East to please keep the Middle East out of their quarrels. It made no reference whatever to the creation of a U.N. force and requested Hammarskjöld to take the "necessary practical measures" to facilitate the early removal of foreign troops from Jordan and Lebanon.[42]

The Arabs' general reconciliation, which permitted this unhoped-for result, did not survive it for long. Not only did tensions continue between Cairo and Amman, punctuated by various incidents—such as the one on November 10, 1958, when an attempt was made by two Migs to intercept King Hussein's plane over Syrian territory—but the break between the two leaders of the Baghdad putsch brought about the rapid deterioration of Iraqi-Egyptian relations. While Aref hoped that Iraq would become, like Syria, a U.A.R. province under Nasser's authority, Kassem was determined to maintain its independence. On October 1, Kassem exiled his lieutenant, who, on November 4, attempted a return from Elba. Condemned to death with four other "Unionists," he was pardoned by Kassem. Five years later he showed his gratitude by killing Kassem with his own hands.

Meanwhile, in order to fight the U.A.R. backers, the Iraqi chief was obliged to lean not only on the Shiite Moslems, traditionally hostile to the Sunnites, who were in the majority on the Mediterranean coast, but on the Kurds, whose leader, Barzani, had returned from his long exile in Moscow, and on the Communists. The latter, whose courage and resolution had been strengthened by Nuri es-Said's fierce repression, were, like their brothers in Syria, naturally hostile to a U.A.R. where the Communist Party was outlawed.

Obviously, in that situation the U.S.S.R. was inclined to support Kassem rather than Nasser, who, on December 23 at Port Said, had vigorously denounced the "collusion of imperialists, Communists and Zionists" against Arab unity. On January 27, 1959, at the Twentieth Congress of the C.P.S.U., Khrushchev replied that it was "unjust to accuse the Communists of standing against Arabs' interests" and that it was "naive to put on the same level communism and Zionism." [43] The Cairo press became more vituperative, and on February 22 in Damascus, Nasser conjured up the "Red Terror" which would reign under Kassem.[44]

On March 8 a group of officers from the Mosul garrison revolted against the regime. The uprising was a bloody one, and Iraq, publicly vilified by the U.A.R., was moving each day a little nearer to the U.S.S.R., which kept Cairo at a distance. The death under torture in a Syrian prison of the Lebanese Communist Party Secretary Farajallah Hélou, kidnapped by Serraj's police, raised in all countries and from all Communist parties a unanimous wave of protests against Nasser, and at one point even Moscow cut off its aid to Egypt. Washington, however, had the wisdom to try not to exploit the situation by renewing its attempts at enrollment. In that perspective it can be said that the vote on the August 21 resolution by the General Assembly had confirmed the tacit acceptance—albeit without great enthusiasm —of a certain "disengagement" by the United States and the U.S.S.R. in that part of the world.

§   §   §

Twenty-four hours after that vote, which singularly improved the international climate, another crisis broke out, this one in the Far

East. During the night of August 22–23, Chinese Communist artillery began a massive shelling of Quemoy, which, in the winter of 1954–1955, had been a pawn in a long test of strength, and where Chiang Kai-shek, ignoring Washington's counsel for prudence, had massed about 75,000 men.

The resumption of hostilities represented a turning point in Chinese policy. In 1956–1957, Peking had made numerous overtures to the Kuomintang, Chou En-lai going so far as to tell American journalists during a trip to Cambodia: "The peaceful solution of the Formosa problem would be the return of Generalissimo Chiang Kai-shek to the continent in a post higher than that of a minister." [45] But Chiang had ignored those overtures. He would periodically repeat his determination to liberate his country; and on May 7, 1957, he concluded an accord with Washington for the installation on Formosa of Matador missiles, with nuclear warheads easily capable of reaching the mainland. The Nationalists were always inclined to suspect the United States of wanting to deal with Peking behind their backs. In order to mollify them, the United States had, in December 1957, reduced the level of its representation in the bilateral parleys agreed upon by the Geneva summit, which led Red China to withdraw from them. American diplomacy was mobilized in an effort to prevent the admission of the Peking Government to the U.N. Everything pointed to the fact that Mao's good behavior left Dulles completely cold, and it is quite possible that its ineffectiveness was a contributing factor in the sudden hardening of the Chinese position at the conference of the twelve Communist parties at Moscow in November 1957.

But a stiffening in external policy could also seem necessary at that time, when China, under the policies of the "leap forward" and the people's communes, was going to throw itself into an unprecedented effort which required the mobilization of every moment. It was also possible that Mao, fearful that Chiang might take advantage of the unrest certain to be created by the implementation of those policies, had decided that it was better to be the one to shoot first.

At the close of a military conference held between May 27 and July 27, 1958, the Chinese Communist Party announced its determination to liberate Formosa at any time. The date of Khrushchev's visit suggested that he knew or guessed the plans being hatched, which explained the scornful comments made by the *People's Daily* immediately after Khrushchev's departure: "Oversensitive people, frightened by imperialists who make them believe that the only choice they have is between submission and war. . . . Others wrongly conclude that peace can only be preserved on condition that no armed struggle, no stubborn resistance, be made against imperialistic attacks." It doesn't require much imagination to believe that these remarks were addressed to Mr. K.

There can be no certainty, at this time, as to what took place during the talks between Khrushchev and Mao except that specific military problems were discussed, as the two Defense Ministers, Malinovski and P'eng Teh-huai, took part in the meetings. It may have been at that time that Moscow presented what the *People's Daily* called an "unacceptable demand aimed at placing China under its military control," which "met the Chinese Government's legitimate and categorical rejection," this having taken place in 1958, according to the newspaper.

Was it a question of bringing China into the Warsaw Pact? Or of the creation of a unified command in the Pacific? In any case, the purpose was clear and the Kremlin's intention of preventing China from undertaking rash ventures was only too manifest.

What was said about Formosa? All suppositions are permitted, including the one that Mao did not reveal his intentions to Mr. K, since the latter stated at Smolensk, "Apparently there is no cloud which could produce lightning." [46] But then how can the *People's Daily*'s veiled criticism of the Soviet leader's faintheartedness be explained? It is more probable that he tried either to dissuade his Chinese comrades from taking any action or, in the event that Mao had harbored greater ambitions, to persuade him to be content with an operation against Quemoy. This operation seemed to entail only limited risks, especially now that the international press was filled with dispatches saying that Washington was trying to get Chiang to evacuate the coastal islands.

In any case, when the bombardment began, the Russians remained silent for a week, which is generally a sign of embarrassment. But there was no question of their showing the least sign of disapproval of Peking. When *Pravda* commented on the event—under the byline the "Observer," reserved for important occasions—it was to warn the United States not to "play with fire" and to "stop trying the Chinese people's patience." The liberation of Formosa and of all the coastal islands belonging to China, affirmed the party newspaper, only concerned the Chinese people: "In the fight against all the maneuvers of the enemies of peace, the U.S.S.R. will grant the People's Republic all necessary moral and material help in her just struggle."

On that date the American position had not been clearly defined. However, the State Department had affirmed that "if the Communists attacked or tried to seize the islands, it would be extremely dangerous for anyone to suppose that it would be a limited operation." [47] Dulles declared that the President "has not yet made any finding under that resolution that the employment of U.S. armed forces is required or appropriate in ensuing the defense of Formosa. The President would not, however, hesitate to make such a finding if he judges that the circumstances made this necessary to accomplish the purposes of the joint resolution." [48] But at the same time he asked that the Chinese Communists resume the Geneva negotiations in order to seek a peaceful solution to the crisis. On September 6, Chou En-lai, while holding the United States responsible for their past failure, declared himself ready to resume the negotiations. The same day the White House announced that the American ambassador in Warsaw was prepared to meet as soon as possible with his Chinese counterpart.

As the danger seemed to have passed, Khrushchev could afford to raise his voice. On September 8, in a letter to Ike, he demanded the withdrawal of American forces from Formosa and declared that an attack against China would be considered an attack against the U.S.S.R. Moscow had never gone so far, as the 1950 alliance had been concluded only against Japan and its eventual allies. Eisenhower replied by asking Mr. K to use his influence to hasten the meeting of the American and Chinese ambassadors in Warsaw. The conference opened on September 15, but on the 19th, Khrushchev climbed another step in the "verbal" escalation, stating that if the Chinese People's Republic "falls victim to such an attack the aggressor will at once suffer an attack by the same means." [49]

This was coupled with such violent attacks on American policy that Washington decided to return the message to its author as "unacceptable under established diplomatic practice." At the same time, it was learned that the United States had sent atomic weapons to Quemoy and had increased their number in Formosa. On the 22nd, Chiang's Prime Minister, Ch'en Ch'en, declared that the Nationalists "might launch attacks against Communist shore batteries unless the bombardment eased within two weeks." [50]

On the 30th, however, Dulles considerably softened his position. He said that in the event of a cease-fire, the United States would be in favor of at least a partial withdrawal of the troops stationed in Quemoy. In any case, it had no more intention than before of committing itself to the defense of the islands. Dulles himself said that he was ready, if it would be useful, to meet with Chou En-lai. Finally, he said he did not believe in the possibility of the reconquest of the mainland by the Nationalists. As could be expected, these comments caused some nervousness in Taipeh. Ike and Nixon again made much more warlike statements.

Faced with such abrupt changes of temperature, Khrushchev probably did not quite know where he stood. Nonetheless, on October 5, or twenty-four hours before the expiration of the deadline fixed by the Nationalist Prime Minister, Khrushchev had TASS publish a notable rectification. "The U.S.S.R. will come to her aid . . . if China is attacked by the United States . . . but as for the civil war that the Chinese are waging against Chiang Kai-shek's clique, we did not get mixed up in it and have no intention of doing so." [51] In other words, if Chiang carried out his threat to bombard the Communist shore batteries, let Mao not count on us.

One may wonder whether he had ever counted on them much. Moscow boasted subsequently that it had "thrown in the balance, without hesitation, all its international prestige, its military power, to stop the hand of the aggressor." Peking replied that, at the time, "there was nothing to indicate the possibility of a nuclear war. Therefore, it was not necessary to help China with nuclear weapons. And so it was in full knowledge of the facts that the Soviet leaders publicized their support of China." That did not prevent Mao on October 15, 1958, from addressing a letter to the Soviet Central

Committee, expressing his "cordial gratitude" and his certainty that, in the event of a Sino-American war, the U.S.S.R. "would certainly" give Peking "all possible aid." [52]

In fact, Mao had also judged it more prudent not to give the Nationalists an opportunity of showing whether they meant what they said. On October 6 his Defense Minister, P'eng Teh-huai, announced that the bombardment would be stopped for a week to allow the defenders, which he predicted sooner or later would be abandoned by the United States, to receive food supplies on condition that the American convoys be halted during that time. A week later the truce was extended for two more weeks. A White House spokesman hailed this "good news" as an opportunity for reaching a negotiated settlement.

But on the 20th the bombardment resumed, apparently in honor of Dulles' expected arrival on Formosa the next day. In spite of it, Dulles persuaded Chiang to sign a communiqué recalling the "defensive" character of the treaty between Washington and Taipeh, and asserting that the Nationalist Government's "sacred mission" was "the re-establishment of liberty for its people on the continent" and that it should not rely "on the use of force." Forty-eight hours later, Peking announced that the bombardments would be halted . . . every other day and offered food to the Quemoy inhabitants, to whom P'eng addressed these typically Chinese counsels: "We do not advise you to break off immediately with the Americans. That would not be realistic. We only hope . . . that you will not yield to their sudden changes of mood, that you will not lose your sovereign rights only to be deprived of a shelter on land and be thrown into the sea. These words are . . . in good faith. In time, you will realize it. . . ." [53]

Meantime, the danger had passed. But, once more, the world breathed too soon. On November 10, Khrushchev, breaking the Big Four protocols on Berlin's status, triggered the gravest crisis of the Cold War, and one which was to last for four years.

BIBLIOGRAPHY AND NOTES

[1] Année politique, 1957, p. 446.

[2] *Ibid.*, p. 467.

[3] Keesing's, 15823 A.

[4] Dallin, *op. cit.*, p. 454.

[5] Documentation française. Notes et études documentaires, No. 2950, December 31, 1962.

[6] Cited by Suslov in his report to the Central Committee on February 14, 1964. Supplement to *Etudes soviétiques,* No. 193, April 1964.

[7] Cited in the declaration of the Chinese Government of September 1, 1963. Documentation française. Notes et études documentaires, No. 3089, May 12, 1964.

[8] Cited in an editorial in the *People's Daily* on "The divergences Between Comrade Togliatti and Us." *Chine Nouvelle,* December, 31, 1962.

[9] Documentation française. Notes et études documentaires, No. 3089, of May 12, 1964.

[10] Edward Crankshaw, *The New Cold War: Moscow v. Peking* (Harmondsworth: Penguin Books, 1963), p. 73.

[11] Keesing's, 16171 A.

[12] *The Truth About the Nagy Affair, op. cit.*, p. 146.

[13] *Ibid.*

[14] Dallin, *op. cit.*, p. 487.

[15] *Le Monde,* December 21, 1957.

[16] *Ibid.*

[17] Sherman Adams, *op. cit.*, pp. 317–18.

[18] *Ibid.*

[19] *Ibid.*, p. 321.

[20] Année politique, 1957, p. 490.

[21] Année politique, 1958, p. 364.

[22] *Le Monde,* September 26, 1958.

[23] Jean Klein, *L'Entreprise du désarmement* (Paris: Cujas, 1964), p. 195.

[24] Année politique, 1958, p. 353.

[25] *Orient,* No. 6, p. 162.

[26] Année politique, 1958, p. 311.

[27] Murphy, *op. cit.*, p. 397.

[28] *Ibid.*, p. 414.

[29] Sherman Adams, *op. cit.*, p. 291.

[30] Murphy, *op. cit.*, p. 398.

[31] *Le Monde,* July 18, 1958.

[32] *Orient,* No. 7, p. 8.

[33] *Le Monde,* July 22, 1958.

[34] *Ibid.*, July 25, 1958.

[35] *Ibid.*, July 29, 1958.

[36] *Ibid.*, July 30, 1958.

[37] *Ibid.*, August 2, 1958.

[38] Tibor Meray, *La rupture Moscou-Pékin* (Paris: Robert Laffont, 1966), p. 57.

[39] Declaration of the Soviet Government of September 21, 1963. Supplement to *Etudes soviétiques,* No. 186, September, 1963.

[40] *Le Monde,* August 7, 1958.

[41] *Ibid.*, August 15–16, 1958.

[42] *Orient,* No. 7, p. 190.

[43] *Ibid.*, No. 9, p. 124.

[44] *Ibid.*, No. 9, p. 19.

[45] Roger Lévy, *La Chine* (Paris: Presses Universitaires de France, 1964), p. 154.

[46] *Le Monde,* August 26, 1958.

[47] Année politique, 1958, p. 410.

[48] Keesing's, 16388 A.

[49] *Ibid.*, 16472 A.

[50] Tang Tsou, "The Quemoy Imbroglio: Chiang Kai-shek and the United States." *The Western Political Quarterly,* XII, No. 4 (December 1959), p. 1084.

[51] Année politique, 1958, p. 441.

[52] Documentation française. Notes et études documentaires, No. 3089, May 12, 1964.

[53] Année politique, 1958, pp. 444–45.

· CHAPTER 14 ·

THE

CANCEROUS TUMOR

> Personal feelings play in all big world events a part
> that can never be discerned to its full extent. The fact
> that a state of friendship exists or doesn't exist be-
> tween two men, or two groups of men, can in certain
> cases prove decisive for the destiny of the human
> race.
>
> —Simone Weil, *The Need for Roots*

BERLIN AT THE CLOSE OF 1958 WAS BOTH AN OASIS IN
the Cold War and the one place in the world where the Cold War
was most evident.

In East Berlin, along streets empty of cars, ruins were only slowly
being rebuilt. When night came, inadequate lighting gave them a
sinister aspect which was reinforced by the long red and blue stream-
ers which, with complete disregard of esthetics, bore the heavy-
handed slogans of a regime which had concentrated all its efforts on
a gigantic plan of industrialization. In West Berlin the industrious-
ness of the people and the financial aid provided through the Marshall
Plan and the Federal government had given rise to a city of light,
brightly glowing in the middle of the Red night. Wealth was reflected
from the shop windows, the glass and steel buildings, the Kurfürsten-
damm palaces, and the night clubs which provided all the refinements
and all the obscenities of decadence.

Everywhere else the two worlds were separated by an iron or
bamboo curtain which could be crossed with only rarely granted

visas, or lacking those, at the risk of one's life. But in Berlin any man could, if he pleased, go from East to West, on foot or by subway, ten times a day.

West and East Berliners alike used and abused that freedom. The former took advantage of the ridiculously low exchange rate of the East German mark to raid the meager stocks of the "H.O.," the unattractive cooperative stores of the Soviet sector. On the eastern side this unusual opening gave the nationals of the German Democratic Republic, when the regime's austerity and discipline became unbearable, an easy way to "choose freedom." In ten years, close to 3 million people had bolted Walter Ulbricht's regime, and he anxiously watched his technicians, his professors and his students leaving en masse for a more hospitable state where they could talk, act, read and move as they pleased. The population of the G.D.R. was steadily decreasing—at a time when the whole world was undergoing a demographic "boom"—and thereby putting in jeopardy the execution of the Five-Year Plan.

Understandably, the Pankow leaders were anxious to find the means to correct the situation. Even if they had succeeded in imposing tight control over the population's mobility, West Berlin would have remained a challenge and a source of defiance, with its numerous anti-Communist organs of propaganda, notably the powerful American radio station, Radio Rias. Sooner or later, once the power of Stalin's successor was established, it was inevitable that the Kremlin would be tempted to eliminate that provocative example of capitalism's prosperity.

On September 20, 1955, in response to the Paris agreements which restored full sovereignty to the Federal Republic, the Russians took a similar decision toward the rival Democratic Republic. They specified that, only temporarily, they were keeping control over military convoys bound for the old capital. This led the Allies to remind the Kremlin that its agreement with Pankow could not in any way free it from its obligations toward them. *Neues Deutschland,* Ulbricht's newspaper, nevertheless stated on December 1 that the Four-Power status of Berlin "was without any foundation."

The years 1956 and 1957, with the backlash produced by destalinization and by the Polish and Hungarian uprisings, were not ostensibly propitious for an initiative from East Germany. But a move may have seemed more urgent to its leaders, inasmuch as the Federal Republic did not neglect any opportunity to affirm its sovereignty over West Berlin, where, in 1954, Professor Heuss had been elected chief of state, and where, the following year, the Bundestag had begun to meet periodically.

Minor incidents, public statements and significant articles followed each other until March 1958, when it appeared that, after serious preliminary deliberations, the leaders of East Germany and Russia had begun their offensive. On March 14 the Munich *Süddeutsche Zeitung* published an interview in which Ebert, Mayor of East Berlin, said that "the situation was too complicated to allow for a separate settlement on the Berlin question before the whole German problem had been clarified." Waldemar Schmidt, his assistant, had stated the next day that the Western Powers had "lost any right to the maintenance of garrisons in Berlin." [1]

Other events—the Algiers coup of May 13 and the affairs of the Near East and Quemoy—were soon to engage world public attention. It was only once all that activity had subsided that Walter Ulbricht, speaking in Berlin, returned to the theme developed by Waldemar Schmidt, adding to it arguments which were soon to become the leitmotif of Soviet diplomacy.

His thesis was based on two points: "When the different zones of occupation were established in 1945," he said, "Berlin did not become a fifth zone . . . all of Berlin is located within the territory of the G.D.R." As for the participation of the Western Powers in the administration and occupation of the city, "it was based on the Potsdam Agreement." From which he deduced that, as they had violated that agreement by rearming the Federal Republic, they no longer had any right to be in Berlin. [2]

Obviously, that thesis made light of Article 1 of the Anglo-Soviet-American protocol of September 12, 1944, confirmed at Yalta—hence long before Potsdam—and amended on July 26, 1945, to include France, and worded thus: "Germany, within its December 1937 frontiers—and to serve the needs of the occupier—will be divided into three zones, each of which will be allotted to one of the Three Powers, and a special Berlin zone created which will be placed under the joint occupation of the Three Powers." [3]

In spite of a clear warning from Dulles, Khrushchev used the same arguments on November 10, in Moscow's Lenin Stadium, in Gomulka's presence. "The time has evidently come for the Powers which signed the Potsdam Agreement to abandon the remnants of the occupation regime in Berlin and thus make it possible to create a normal atmosphere in the capital of the German Democratic Republic. The Soviet Union, for its part, will hand over to the sovereign German Democratic Republic those functions which are still wielded by Soviet organs. Let the United States, France, and Britain form their own relations with the German Democratic Republic and come to an agreement with it, if they are interested in certain questions relating to Berlin. . . .

"Should any aggressive forces attack the German Democratic Republic," he continued, "we will consider it as an attack on the Soviet Union and on all parties to the Warsaw Treaty." [4]

On November 27, disregarding a warning from Eisenhower, the U.S.S.R. informed the Western Powers in a 9,600-word note that it considered the agreement on the Berlin occupation obsolete and that it would start "at the appropriate time, negotiations with the G.D.R. Government for the transfer to it of functions that Russian bodies have provisionally exercised on the basis of the said agreement." The note continued that "the most just and natural solution" would be the return of West Berlin to the G.D.R. But, foreseeing the "difficulty that the Western Powers would have in accepting such a solution," it proposed that West Berlin be made "into an independent political entity, into a free city, in whose affairs no state, including the two existing German states, would interfere." That free city would be self-governing and demilitarized. The Big Four would be bound to respect its status, which would be comparable to that of Austria, and the U.N. could participate "equally, under one form or another, in the safeguarding" of that status. An agreement would have to be concluded with the G.D.R., concerning the "guarantee of the city's freedom of access."

The Kremlin proposed to open negotiations on that subject with the West. But, it added, if within six months they had not reached a "suitable agreement, the Soviet Union would put the above-mentioned measures into effect by means of an accord with the G.D.R." And it brought again to the attention of those who would have liked to use the language of "brute force" that "threats and intimidation have no effect on the Soviet people," and any violation of the frontiers of the G.D.R. would be considered as an act of aggression against all the members of the Warsaw Pact.[5]

Khrushchev, who the same day, in the Kremlin, had been initiated into the difficult art of the press conference, declared that West Berlin had become "a sort of cancerous tumor," and for that reason the U.S.S.R. had decided to perform a "surgical operation." He also said, "We are not posing the question as an ultimatum," adding that if the United States did not accept his proposals, "he would be sorry," but it would not stop him from putting them into effect.

Annoyed by the existence of a hotbed of provocation and by Ulbricht's incessant demands for its suppression, and criticized by the Chinese for his faintheartedness, he probably thought that his proposal for a free city would be acceptable to the West. In any case, the start of his moves coincided with measures of decentralization in Russia, notably the abolition of the Ministry of the Interior, which did not seem to fit in with preparations for war. But, knowing the natural passivity of Western diplomacy, he thought that mentioning the threat of the danger it risked by saying no, would be the best way of getting it to act.

Whatever his intentions, however, his proposals contained nothing capable of seducing the Western Powers. Contrary to all the laws of "the balance of terror," he was asking them to surrender, without any compensation, an outpost for whose maintenance they had already been willing to run grave risks nine years earlier, at the time of the blockade. The guarantees offered—outside of vague U.N. participation, not otherwise specified—were limited to the word of the Moscow Government, whose value, at a time when that very government was breaking the most solemn contracts, could be doubted.

As a certain number of pledges were required from the future free city, notably to abstain from any "undermining action" against the Communist regime, one wonders if the U.S.S.R. had not already chosen the excuse that it might one day invoke to grab West Berlin. Finally, it seemed logical that the first thing it would demand from the new free city would be that it stop serving as a bolthole for the East Germans wanting a change of air.

In any case, in a country that remembered the precedent of Danzig, the idea of a free city would not be popular. The West Berliners very quickly had the opportunity to show what they thought of it, as on December 7, municipal elections were held in the city. The S.E.D. (United Socialist Party, in other words, the Communist Party), the only one in favor of Khrushchev's proposal, obtained 1.9 percent of the votes against 2.7 percent in 1954.

The Western reaction to the Soviet move was sharp. The German and British newspapers *Die Welt* and the *Manchester Guardian*, usually advocates of conciliation, joined with Foster Dulles, de Gaulle and Adenauer in declaring that under no conditions could the West abandon the 2½ million Berliners who trusted in it.

But the threat was followed by a long delay of six months, and delay in a democracy always means a crumbling of determination. One stands right up to an immediate challenge; one does not fight a war of erosion so well.

In mid-December, despite the curtness of their official communiqués, the Western Powers admitted among themselves that sooner or later they would have to resign themselves to a conference of foreign ministers. The Atlantic Council, gathered in Paris from December 14–16, stated that the U.S.S.R. would be held "responsible for any action aimed at interfering with" the presence of the Big Three in West Berlin and the freedom of access to it. But it added that the Berlin question could be resolved only "within the framework of an agreement with the U.S.S.R. on the whole German problem," and that the Western Powers "are always ready to discuss that problem, as well as those of disarmament and European security." [6] However, that was not enough for Gromyko, who on the 25th, before the Supreme Soviet, expressed surprise that the Allies had not yet officially replied to the Russian proposal. He talked of a "second Sarajevo" and evoked in melodramatic terms what would happen if the Western Powers seriously considered using arms to clear a path to Berlin, "as some generals and journalists" were inciting them to do. [7]

When the Big Three finally decided to reply to the Kremlin,

on the 31st, it was in the same tone. The French text, in which General de Gaulle's hand could be detected, was particularly curt. He did not hesitate to say of the long historical arguments which prefaced the Russian note of November 27: "The best that can be said about them is that they don't conform to reality." He mentioned the German-Soviet 1939–1941 collaboration and concluded that he was not "disposed to negotiate under threat of an ultimatum," but if "such is not the aim" of the Russian note, he was "always ready to discuss the Berlin question in the framework of negotiations for the solution of the German problem and that of European security." [8]

§   §   §

Thus ended in anxiety a year filled with all sorts of crises. It had witnessed the death of Pius XII and de Gaulle's return to power and had just been marked, on December 16, by an unexpected event: the resignation of Mao Tse-tung from the presidency of the Chinese People's Republic, which was to lead, several years later, to the so-called cultural revolution.

On the other hand, there were as few in the East as in the West who grasped the significance of the first "flash" sent over the press agencies' teletypes on the first day of the new year: the seizure of power in Cuba by a handful of students and bearded peasants—led by a young, passionate and romantic lawyer, Fidel Castro—at the end of a two-year guerrilla war fought against the despicable dictatorship of the ex-sergeant Batista.

The whole world had its eyes fixed on Berlin and wondered if 1959 would not be the year of that third world war whose shadow had so often hovered on the horizon during the past twelve years. But suddenly the skies cleared: Mikoyan, the great fence-mender of Soviet diplomacy, landed in the United States on January 4, supposedly on a vacation. The next day he met with Dulles, to whom he said that the Soviet proposals were not at all an ultimatum, that the six-month deadline was just a suggestion, but that, nevertheless, the Western Powers could not stand by and do nothing. He even intimated that their right of access could be maintained and guaranteed, based on a formula to be worked out. All the officials he met received the impression that he was seeking conciliation. As for Ulbricht, the East

German leader denied the threatening remarks he had made in Warsaw.

On January 10 the Kremlin sent the Allies another message. Khrushchev's tone was appreciably less rough. Not only did he describe himself as "naturally far from considering that his proposal on the free city of West Berlin would exclude all counterproposals and amendments" and omit any reference to the notorious six-month deadline mentioned on November 27, but he submitted to all the countries that had been at war with the Reich the draft of a peace treaty with Germany and declared himself ready to start "a preliminary exchange of views" with the West on its contents.

That document comprised forty-eight articles, stating in particular that Germany could not join any military alliance, would renounce any territorial claims beyond the Oder-Neisse line, would neither possess nor manufacture atomic, bacteriological, or chemical weapons, bombers or submarines etc. "The right of the German people to the re-establishment of Germany's unity" was recognized by Article 22, which anticipated that the Allies "will give their complete cooperation toward that goal, through the rapprochement of the two German states." Until the re-establishment of that unity, West Berlin would remain a "demilitarized free city." [9]

Several times in the past, and especially in 1954, the U.S.S.R. had already submitted proposals for a peace treaty. But it was the first time it suggested that it be concluded with the two republics and not with a reunited Germany. That was sufficient reason for the West, which for more than ten years had consistently maintained that the problem of reunification had priority over that of the peace treaty, to reject this new initiative.

Before replying to the Soviet proposal, Dulles decided to go to Europe. In London, his first stop, he found his interlocutors filled with anxiety because the Russians had just immobilized an American convoy on the Berlin highway for several hours. They were determined not to take any steps that would leave the Allies no choice but to bypass Mr. K's Caudine Forks and force the blockade. Macmillan, who was himself getting ready to leave for Moscow on an exploratory trip, pressed for a new summit meeting.

In Paris the picture was altogether different. De Gaulle summed up the situation by saying that if the Russians wanted war, it was not by yielding on Berlin that it would be avoided, and if they didn't want it, there was no reason to make concessions to them. As usual, his *sang-froid* was total. A little later, when the Soviet ambassador made threatening statements to his face, he answered, "Well, Mr. Ambassador, we will die together!" [10] He was certain that Mr. K was bluffing. This was involuntarily confirmed, at the same time, by a Russian diplomat in Paris, in speaking to a high official of the Quai d'Orsay: "We are determined to go very far," he said.—"Then you want to make war?"—"Of course not." "In that case," answered the Frenchman, "we too shall go as far as you like. . . ." [10]

But the aged and gravely ill Dulles, who in the past, at Quemoy and elsewhere, had so fearlessly played his famous games of brinkmanship, now preached conciliation. As soon as he returned to Washington, after a last meeting with his old friend Adenauer, he was hospitalized. A hernia was mentioned, but three days later it was admitted that he had cancer, and his assistant, Christian Herter, was designated as a temporary replacement. He was an affable and calm gentleman without any experience of Soviet methods and totally incapable of replying to Gromyko's sneering remarks in kind.

On February 16 the Big Three replied to the Soviet note. While reserving for themselves the right to ensure "by all appropriate means" their freedom of access to Berlin, they declared that they were ready to participate in a foreign ministers' conference which "should deal with the problem of Germany in all its aspects and implications." Finally, they suggested that "consultants" representing the two parts of Germany be invited.[11] When the same idea had been proposed a few years earlier by Molotov, it had been curtly rejected. It was Bonn, curiously enough, which had suggested that it be reconsidered. Naturally, the British had vigorously supported it. The Americans had joined them. And France, after having strongly opposed it, had finally bowed to the other three.

For a moment it was feared that that concession, far from mollifying Khrushchev, would only encourage him to make further demands. To be sure, the next day, after having declared that the Soviet troops were not in Germany to "play skittles," he aired for the first time the threat of signing a separate peace with the G.D.R. —in the event the Allies rejected the proposed treaty—which would transfer to it the exclusive control of access to West Berlin.

The next day, Eisenhower accused Mr. K of putting the cart before the horse. If the Western Powers were prevented from going to Berlin, he said, it would be "somebody else using force." [12]

It was in that climate that Macmillan arrived in Moscow on February 21. He was affably welcomed, but on the 24th, while his guest was visiting the Dubna nuclear research institute, Mr. K, during an electoral meeting in Moscow, launched a violent attack against the Allies and declared that the proposed meeting of foreign ministers would be only a "waste of time." He asked for a meeting of government heads with "full powers to make decisions." [13] The luncheon Macmillan hosted the next day for his Soviet colleague was a rather chilly affair.

Meanwhile, it was announced that the chief of the Soviet Government, suffering from a violent toothache, would not be able to accompany his British guests to Kiev, as he had planned to do. A deliberate insult? That was the way it was generally interpreted. Mikoyan put balm on the wound by unexpectedly going to Leningrad to welcome Macmillan on his return from the Ukraine. The talks ended in a cordial atmosphere. The communiqué published on March 3 mentioned continuing disagreements over Berlin and the peace treaty, but recognized the necessity of urgently studying the possibility of limiting the armed forces and both conventional and nuclear weapons in a specified part of Europe "with an appropriate system of inspection." [14] The day before, the Soviet Government, reversing Mr. K's refusal, had given the Allies its consent to a meeting of ministers to discuss the peace treaty and Berlin, on the condition that not only would the two Germanies be represented, as they proposed, but also Poland and Czechoslovakia. This unreasonable new demand would soon be abandoned. On March 9, Mr. K envisaged the possibility of having the security of the West Berlin free city guaranteed either by armed contingents supplied by the four victors over the Reich—which would allow the maintenance of Allied troops, on condition, of course, that the Russians had access to the Western sectors—or by neutrals, with U.N. participation. Soon, Moscow accepted the May 11 date suggested by the West for a foreign ministers' conference.

Before that conference officially opened, many speeches were heard, including one by de Gaulle at a press conference on March

25, the first since his election to the presidency of the Republic on the preceding December 21. He assured his listeners that he would not lend himself to "anything which might bring despair to the German people." There was no question of recognizing the Pankow plan, "for it exists only by reason of the Soviet occupation, and, if I dare say, by virtue of an implacable dictatorship," nor of delivering Berlin to it. He further affirmed that if the Atlantic Alliance did not exist, "nothing could prevent the Soviet dictatorship and the Soviet nation from spreading over all Europe and over all Africa and from there to cover the whole world." He contrasted the "dangerous news coming from West Berlin, from the G.D.R. and from the German disengagement" with the "only worthwhile quarrel, that of man," in other words, aid to the underdeveloped world, "a major subject" that, for his part, he would like to see put "on the agenda of future East-West conferences." [15]

§   §   §

On May 11, then, everything was prepared to welcome Gromyko, Couve de Murville, Herter and Selwyn Lloyd to the Geneva Palais des Nations, in the chamber where, in 1955, Dulles, Molotov, Macmillan and Pinay—after their superiors' promising summit meeting —had separated without being able to agree on the future of Germany.

However, it took three hours for the ministers to decide to begin the session. An earnest debate opposed East to West on the issue of seating the "consultants" from the two Germanies. Gromyko wanted to make sure that the conference table, instead of being square as usual, would be round so that the Germans from the two parishes would be seated on the same basis as the Big Four. Finally, it was decided that the Germans would not sit at the round table, but behind it at small rectangular tables, which however, would only be a few centimeters from the main table. That distance gave a fair measure of the pretended "retreat" of the Soviet delegation. Had they not, in fact, obtained almost everything they wanted? Dr. Bolz, Foreign Minister of the German Democratic Republic, the existence of which the Western Powers persisted in denying, was in the room, and he was able to speak at any time he wished.

As soon as the session began, the Allies offered a "European peace plan," whose principal thrust was the creation of a pan-German committee to develop contacts between the two rival republics and at the same time to work out an electoral law for the election of the Parliament of a unified Germany. For the rest, that "package deal," which was made up of diverse and theoretically inseparable elements, was in fact a new version of the Eden plan proposed in 1954. It provided for reunification following free elections, combined with all imaginable guarantees to protect the Kremlin against any rebirth of German militarism, and was to be put into effect in four stages.[16]

The whole proposal was not without ingenuity and its intellectual qualities might have impressed collaborators less prejudiced than the Russians. But it was of such complexity that its own authors, after months of assiduous labor, did not conceal their skepticism about its future. It was completely impossible to sell it to the public, and Selwyn Lloyd openly deplored its "lack of sex appeal."

What was expected to happen, happened. On May 18, Gromyko declared that the Western proposals were "clearly unacceptable" and "totally unrealistic."[17] However, he was quick to single out and retain as definitive two or three clauses which agreed with his viewpoint. The next day, he got tit for tat, when he was told that there was no question of signing a peace treaty as long as Germany was not reunified, or of consenting to any surrender of rights over Berlin.

The conference had made no progress whatsoever, when on the 24th the news of Dulles' death was announced. Immediately, the four ministers flew off to attend his funeral, a curious ceremony seemingly devoid of any trace of emotion except on the part of the relatives of the deceased and the nearly disconsolate President. However, the next day, Ike had recovered his smile and entertained at luncheon the fifteen foreign ministers who had come in a motorcade of two hundred Cadillacs to accompany the man who had been the most famous American diplomat to his final resting place. Their jovial expressions, as fixed for posterity in the photograph taken in front of the White House, seemed somewhat unusual, if not indecent. But Gromyko was part of this "Areopagus": he returned the same night to Geneva in Herter's plane, accompanied by Couve de Murville and Selwyn Lloyd, and their good humor appeared to be a favorable omen.

The Western Powers gave up the idea of their package deal and declared themselves ready to seek a provisional agreement on Berlin. There was no point in having repeated a hundred times that they would never agree to separate the settlement of the old capital's future from the settlement of the whole German problem.

At first, the Russians seemed cooperative, but controversy broke out again on June 9, after Gromyko had made new "proposals" which were, in fact, a new ultimatum. At the last minute the collapse of the talks was avoided thanks to a new Russian plan which, for the first time, contained no threat of a separate peace. But tensions were too great and the protagonists took a few weeks off for reflection.

§   §   §

The conference reopened on July 13, but the day before the White House had made a decision which amounted to its burial: Frol Koslov, a member of the Presidium who had gone to New York to open an exhibition of Soviet industrial products, had been asked confidentially to extend an invitation to Khrushchev to visit the United States in September, provided that Eisenhower returned his visit in the fall.

The idea came from the State Department, which saw the advantages that the United States could obtain from a tour of the U.S.S.R. by a man like Ike—the glamorous general of the common war against the Axis, a man whose popularity in Russia could not be doubted. It was also a means of resolving the impasse in which the Geneva Conference had bogged down. For Khrushchev, who for years had been seeking a summit meeting, there could have been no better news. But it was quite evident that he would now wait for the results of his talks in Washington before making, if need be, a new concession or proposal. Therefore, the Geneva Conference dragged on until August 3, when the exchange of visits, news of which had begun to leak out a few days before, was announced. Forty-eight hours later, the conference adjourned *sine die,* the particularly brief final communiqué mentioning only a rapprochement of positions "on certain unspecified points." [18]

As a prelude to the meeting, Vice President Nixon himself had gone to the U.S.S.R. to open the American exposition, counterpart of the one opened by Koslov in New York the preceding month. Crowds of Muscovites attended it to discover with astonishment the latest gadgets of the consumers' paradise which for years they had heard described as the kingdom of inefficiency and poverty. Mr. K, who was present at the ceremony, confessed that he admired the displays with a "feeling both of satisfaction and of a certain envy," but affirmed his conviction that the day was not far off when the U.S.S.R. would catch up with and surpass America.[19] A sharp yet courteous controversy then followed. Shown on TV, it gave millions of Russians the opportunity of hearing the Vice President of the United States proclaim, not without some presumption, that his country, "the world's largest capitalist country has, from the standpoint of the distribution of wealth, come closest to the ideal of prosperity for all in a classless society."

Asserting that "we had arrived at a point in world history when the Scriptural warning 'He who lives by the sword will perish by the sword', could be taken literally," he said that he eagerly welcomed the idea of a peaceful competition between the two systems, such as Mr. K had extolled on several occasions.[20]

August was occupied with preparations for the great meeting. Khrushchev went to Poland and then conferred at Yalta with leaders of Czechoslovakia and the G.D.R. Ike, on his part, paid a quick visit to Europe to reassure the Germans and the French, who were somewhat concerned over the possible results of the Russian-American dialogue which was about to begin. Eisenhower, acclaimed by large crowds in Bonn, solemnly reaffirmed his determination to ensure the freedom of Berlin. In Paris he skillfully found words which allayed the suspicions of the President of the Republic, whom he praised for "his enthusiasm and resolute courage" and for "his dogged determination in the cause of justice and of peace." [21] The meeting was the occasion for the American general and President to promise his French counterpart, toward whom he had always acknowledged a feeling of warm personal admiration, that he would consult with him freely on all great world problems. Not to be outdone, de Gaulle revealed to his illustrious visitor, who was delighted and honored by this confidence, that he was at last ready to recognize the right of the Algerian people to self-determination.

On September 15, under a sun as bright as his smile, Khrushchev landed near Washington. Although he was only President of the Council, he was given, at his request, the welcome which, according to protocol, was reserved for chiefs of state. Forty-eight hours before, in an attempt to fire the world's imagination, a Soviet rocket had planted the red flag and the U.S.S.R. state shield on the moon. Khrushchev, bursting with pride, expounded at length on this exploit in his answer to the speech of welcome from Eisenhower, who had forgotten to mention it. At the great formal banquet in the White House the toasts were most cordial. "In two world wars," said Ike, "we have been allies. . . . Because of our power, because of our importance in the world, it is imperative that we understand each other better. . . . Facts and truth must be the basis for that understanding." And the Russian answered: "We believe that our system is the best—and you think that yours is the best. But, of course, we cannot let that difference of opinion turn into an open fight . . . if we quarrel, not only will our countries suffer colossal losses, but other countries will also be swept away in the annihilation of the world." [22]

The next day did not go so well. While the street crowds showed more curiosity than sympathy or hostility toward Mr. K, he also faced the traditional National Press Club luncheon. Touchy questions were fired at him—on Hungary, on what the chief of the Soviet Government was doing "while Stalin was committing his crimes." He became flushed, refused to answer that "provocation" and asserted with unfailing conviction that "communism is a science." Soon, he concluded, "we will surpass you." [23]

The tour of the country abounded in picturesque incidents. In Los Angeles, the Mayor having reproached him for his famous statement "We will bury all of you," Nikita took umbrage. "If you want to compete with us in the sphere of armaments, then, that's too bad . . . if I have been invited just to be shown the strength of the United States, I can go back as quickly as I came." [24] In Hollywood he embraced his host, Spyros Skouras, the president of Twentieth Century-Fox, whom he called "his brother in Jesus Christ," in deference to his Greek origin. Then he proudly compared his own career to that of that self-made man, who had taken the liberty of praising the American system, in which every man had a chance to get ahead.[25] In San Francisco, where the welcome was much less warm than elsewhere and where, for the first time, he mingled with the crowd, he argued with union leaders, at one point denouncing as "immoral" the French can-can spectacle which the day before he had apparently watched without too much displeasure in Hollywood.

In Iowa, where he was received by his friend Garst, who had organized an exchange of visits between Russian and American farmers, he did not conceal his admiration for the remarkable results obtained in the cultivation of corn, whose champion he was in the U.S.S.R. He praised American supermarkets and snack bars, and after chatting with the personnel of a factory canteen, he publicly admonished his ambassador, the smiling Menshikov, for having giving him false information on the Americans' standard of living. In Pittsburgh, after having visited the steel mills, whose workers were then on strike, he declared, "I have come to see how the slaves of capitalism live. Well, I must say that they don't live too badly." [26]

If, in the end, America impressed him, Eisenhower—with whom he spent two days tête-à-tête at Camp David—seemed to have really charmed him. On his return to Moscow he described him to a cheering crowd as a man "who enjoys the complete confidence of his people" and who "sincerely wants, like us, to end the Cold War." [27]

The contrast may seem surprising between that enthusiastic speech—ending with the cry of "Long live Russian-American friendship!"—and the completely noncommittal communiqué which followed the conclusion of the talks, and in which the only specific point was the postponement of Ike's visit to the U.S.S.R. until the spring. However, Eisenhower had made two major concessions which were revealed in his September 28 press conference: he had promised Khrushchev he would intervene with de Gaulle and Macmillan for a prompt arrangement of a summit conference; he had also recognized the "abnormal" character of the Berlin situation, adding that it was necessary to seek "a solution which would safeguard the legitimate interests of the Russians, of the East Germans, of the West Germans, and above all, those of the West." For his part, Mr.

K abandoned any deadline for the solution of the Berlin question, "without, however," specified Eisenhower, on Khrushchev's request, "allowing those negotiations to be indefinitely prolonged." [28]

The people of Moscow, who desired peace more than anything else, gave their leader a triumphant welcome. But Khrushchev still had another trip to make: to Peking, where he arrived on September 30 to take part in the celebrations of the tenth anniversary of the founding of the Chinese People's Republic.

§ § §

There were fewer smiles there. The Chinese leaders had all sorts of grievances against Khrushchev, who had dared criticize the people's communes they were so proud of, and had, worst of all, done it in front of Senator Humphrey, an American. Behind the scenes, in East Germany, in Bulgaria and in Poland, he had discouraged those who were tempted to follow the Chinese example. It seemed that he had influenced P'eng Teh-huai, the Chinese Defense Minister—whom he had met in April during a visit to Albania and who was to be ousted soon after his return—to take a position against the communes.

But there were more serious complaints. Not only had Mr. K said before the Twenty-first Congress of the C.P.S.U. on January 30 that ". . . even before the complete victory of socialism on earth, while capitalism still remains in parts of the world, there will be an actual possibility of excluding world war from the life of society . . ." [29] which went directly counter to the classic Leninist thesis put forth again by Mao at the 1957 twelve parties' conference, but on June 20 he had denounced the atomic agreement he had made with Peking in October 1957, refusing to deliver the prototype of the bomb promised to them. The Chinese were to reveal this four years later. His trip to the United States, his praise of Eisenhower—in Chinese eyes the principal champion of imperialism—could only add to that climate of extreme suspicion. Although the Chinese press had approved Mr. K's visit to the United States to preserve the unity of the socialist bloc, as early as May, Mao had made a revealing statement on "some people who have described Eisenhower as a man who loves peace," hoping that they would "find the road back to reality." [30] The conflict between India and China over Tibet revealed the extent of the Sino-Soviet split to the Western world, which, as a matter of fact, had actually begun to guess it.

The status of Tibet, that vast territory lying mostly at an altitude of more than 12,000 feet and governed by a unique type of theocracy, had never ceased to be a bone of contention since 1912, when its divine ruler, the 13th Dalai Lama, had proclaimed the country's independence, thanks to the anarchy prevailing in the Middle Kingdom at that time. In 1914 an agreement between London, Peking and Tibet had recognized Tibet's autonomy, under the sovereignty of China. But China having dismissed its plenipotentiary, the treaty was reduced to an Anglo-Tibetan bilateral accord, which remained in force until the 1947 proclamation of the independence of India which inherited the British privileges. Although China had several times reaffirmed its sovereignty over the country, during all that time the Dalai Lama—whose troops had had to repulse attacks from the Kuomintang's forces on several occasions—enjoyed a *de facto* sovereignty. It settled its affairs with London, notably the demarcation of its frontiers, without interference from the Chinese Government.

On January 1, 1950, Mao, who had moved his government to Peking three months earlier, gave orders to the People's Army to liberate Tibet. This was done at the request of the Panchen Lama, a thirteen-year-old boy whose spiritual authority extended over part of the country. In the summer of the same year, talks opened in New Delhi between representatives of Lhasa and of the People's Republic. While they were dragging on, the army of liberation invaded the country. On November 7 the Dalai Lama appealed to the U.N., but at the request of London and New Delhi the assembly adjourned its debate *sine die* in order to facilitate a peaceful solution.

In effect, on May 23, 1951, a "seventeen-point agreement on procedures for the liberation of Tibet" was signed in Peking. According to its terms the central authorities would alter neither the political system then in use "nor the established status, the functions and the powers of the Dalai Lama as well as those of the Panchen Lama." In return, Tibet "returned to the great family of the fatherland, its forces to be integrated into the Chinese Army," and a Chinese "military and administrative committee" was set up in Lhasa.[31] India accepted that arrangement and in its agreement with

Peking on April 29, 1954, recognized that Tibet "was henceforth only the Tibetan region of China." [32]

At that time, Chou En-lai was saying: "It is simply impossible to establish communism or socialism in Tibet. That may be possible in fifty or a hundred years." [33] Nevertheless, during the years that followed, Peking's leaders attempted to make Tibet gradually develop a way of life more consistent with Mao's teachings. Apparently encouraged by the monks, the population had shown signs of resistance on numerous occasions. On March 10, 1959, the local government—fearful that the Dalai Lama might be kidnaped—persuaded him to reject an invitation from the Chinese forces' commander, then broke the 1951 agreement, proclaimed the country's independence and asked for the withdrawal of Chinese troops. On the 17th an armed revolt broke out which the Chinese ruthlessly suppressed. But they could not prevent the flight of the Dalai Lama. who arrived in India on the 31st, with his mother, his younger brother, his sister, three of his ministers and his personal astrologer. Nehru had dispatched a contingent of troops and a high official to welcome him.

This put a full stop to the Sino-Indian romance. Peking asserted that the rebellion had been directed from the Indian city of Kalimpong. On April 2, Nehru denounced that allegation as completely false. On the 18th the Dalai Lama held a press conference, in which, as is proper for a living God, he spoke of himself in the third person, and affirmed that, contrary to Chinese propaganda, he had left his country of his own free will. He also accused Peking of having violated the 1951 agreements by destroying monasteries, killing some lamas and obliging others to work on highway construction projects.

At this point the *People's Daily* wrote on the 23rd that "the zeal shown by certain political circles in India for interference in the internal affairs of Tibet goes well beyond the support of a friendly and forbearing neighbor." The next day, Nehru met with the Dalai Lama for four hours. On the 27th, before Parliament, he accused the Chinese leaders "of using the language of the Cold War regardless of truth and propriety." [34]

Things got worse following a meeting held at Lhasa on July 17, at which speakers demanded the "liberation" of Sikkim and Bhutan,

India's Himalayan protectorates, as well as of Ladakh, a territory on the Kashmir-Tibetan border. In August there were clashes on the frontier which obliged the Indian garrisons to evacuate some posts and which were characterized by Nehru as a "clear case of aggression." [35] Soon after, New Delhi made public an exchange of notes with Chou En-lai begun in December 1958. From this, it appeared that Peking in fact claimed certain territories south of the line of demarcation fixed by the 1914 Anglo-Tibetan agreement. On the 12th, Nehru represented those claims as "absurd, fantastic," concluding that it was impossible for India to accept them, whatever the consequences.[36]

On September 6 the Chinese Government had confidentially asked the Soviet chargé d'affaires "not to fall into the trap set by Nehru, who was trying to use the U.S.S.R. to bring pressure on China" [37] But TASS published a statement in which the "Soviet leadership," without taking one side or the other, "expressed the certainty that China and India would settle their misunderstandings to their mutual benefit." On the 12th the Kremlin signed an agreement with India by which it was to grant a loan of 1.5 billion rubles to help India achieve its fifth Five-Year Plan. China had never obtained so much from the U.S.S.R. Mr. K, who had been wildly acclaimed during a visit to India and had established excellent relations with Nehru, was apparently little disposed to compromise for Mao's sake the enormous investment he had made in India.

It was in that climate that the Sino-Soviet talks opened on September 30. To set the tone, Khrushchev stated during a banquet for 5,000 people in honor of the tenth anniversary of the People's Republic: "We must think as realists and clearly understand the present situation. The fact that we are as strong as we are does not at all mean that we should test the stability of the capitalist regime by force . . . I had the impression that the President of the United States understands the necessity of reducing international tensions. Even a regime as noble and progressive as socialism cannot be imposed by force of arms, when the people do not want it." Naturally, following the speech, Chou En-lai congratulated the speaker on the success of his trip to the United States "made as a messenger of peace," [38] but the Chinese leaders' frozen faces were obvious proof that their hearts were not in it. Besides, Khrushchev left four days

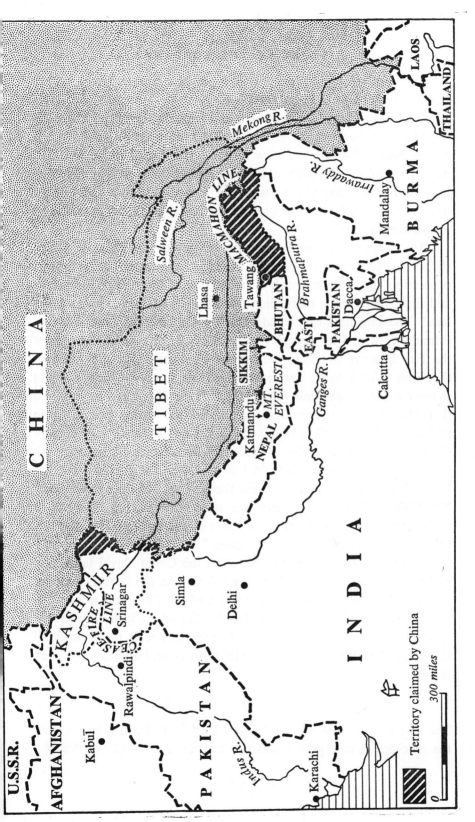

U.S.S.R.

AFGHANISTAN

Kabul•

PAKISTAN

Rawalpindi•

Karachi•

Indus R.

KASHMIR

Srinagar•

CEASE FIRE LINE

Simla•

Delhi•

I N D I A

C H I N A

T I B E T

Lhasa•

Salween R.

Mekong R.

Katmandu•

NEPAL

MT. EVEREST

SIKKIM

Tawang•

MACMAHON LINE

BHUTAN

Brahmaputra R.

Ganges R.

EAST PAKISTAN

Dacca•

Calcutta•

Irrawaddy R.

B U R M A

Mandalay•

LAOS

THAILAND

Territory claimed by China

300 miles

0

VI THE HIMALAYAN CONFLICT

later without releasing a communiqué, as was customary, or crowds being mobilized to bid him good-bye.

Obviously, everything that Mao and Khrushchev talked about did not filter out. However, it is known that Mao tried at length to win Mr. K over to his point of view on the quarrel with India, but that, according to the *People's Daily,* the latter "was not in the least interested in learning about the situation or about the authors of the provocation, and he only insisted on the fact that, in any case, killing people was wrong." [39]

Always according to Peking, on the matter of Formosa Khrushchev declared it was imperative to seek to eliminate that "source of contention" in order to reach a "relaxation of international tension" and that "there exists more than one solution to any complex problem." The one he strongly advocated resembled the "two Chinas" formula advanced by American liberal circles. He cited the case of the Far Eastern Republic created in Vladivostok in the wake of the First World War, and recognized by Lenin—which did not prevent it later from joining the U.S.S.R. [40] Finally, it can be surmised that Mr. K on that occasion expounded the theme according to which "the Chinese Communist Party did not know how to classify their problems in the order of their real importance—something the Communists of the U.S.S.R. had to do after the forced peace of Brest-Litovsk, which had despoiled them of part of their territories." The Chinese Communist Party was wrong "in placing Formosa in the center of all its preoccupations without concern for the development of the international situation." [41]

In a word, Nikita Sergeyevich, after the Camp David talks, had real hope of reaching a satisfactory solution to the Berlin question, thus opening the way to the recognition of the European *status quo,* and he was determined not to let the Sino-American dispute endanger that opportunity. Peking's leaders had well understood all this before his visit, and nothing he told them could appreciably shake them.

§   §   §

The first man on this side of the Iron Curtain to learn a lesson from the Sino-Soviet divergences was General de Gaulle, who in his November 10 press conference was pleased to note from the Soviet world "a few signs of détente . . . after years of international tension," and "guessed" that the reason for it was "perhaps Russia . . . admits that a conflict, from whatever side it comes, would end in general annihilation and that failing to wage war, peace would have to be made. . . . Perhaps Soviet Russia . . . realizes that nothing can make it be anything but Russia, a white nation in part of Asia, and on the whole well endowed with land, factories and wealth, facing China—with its yellow multitudes, innumerable and poor, indestructible and ambitious—building, through a trial of strength, a power that cannot be measured, and looking at the wide spaces over which one day it will have to spread." Giving credit to the present head of Soviet Russia for a "determining role in the beginning of a new orientation," he announced that Khrushchev had agreed to make a visit to France on March 15, 1960.[42] De Gaulle, the only one of the three great Western leaders who had never met Mr. K, except in 1944 in Stalin's shadow, wanted to talk with him privately before the summit meeting. For that reason he had succeeded in having it postponed to May 16 of the same year, and in having it held in Paris.

At no time did the events which followed contradict the fact that Moscow and Peking were no longer on the same wavelength. Chinese commentaries on the anniversary of Stalin's birth maintained that his merits were much greater than his faults. On January 1 an article in Peking's *Red Flag* asserted that the change of United States policy was only tactical, and that its objective remained the destruction of socialism through war. On January 14, before the Supreme Soviet, Khrushchev revealed that a "fantastic" weapon was being perfected and stated that therefore there was no other solution but peaceful coexistence. As evidence of good will he announced that the Soviet armed forces were going to be reduced by one-third and that the U.S.S.R. would not resume its nuclear tests as long as the Western Powers didn't resume theirs. He asserted that "all international problems could be solved given the good will of both sides." [43] Eight days later, Foreign Minister Chen Yi declared that an accord on disarmament which was concluded "without the participation of the Chinese People's Republic and the signature of its delegates cannot have any binding force on China." [44] On January 31 the U.S.S.R., co-president of the International Control Commission for Laos, agreed to its adjournment *sine die*, disregarding a request from Peking, supported by Hanoi. On February 6 the Central Committee of the C.P.S.U. accused China, in a confidential verbal note, of "narrow nationalism"; it stated that the idea that a weak country such as India could attack China could not be considered "at all seriously," and reproached China, because of its disagreement with New Delhi, with having "shackled the U.S.S.R.'s peace-seeking activities" on the eve of Khrushchev's visit to the United States.[45]

When Mr. K himself went to India a few days later, he was able to measure the damage caused to Soviet prestige by the Himalayan conflict. The welcome he received was not in any way comparable to the indescribable enthusiasm which had greeted him four years earlier, or to the very warm reception Eisenhower had received in December. Nevertheless, the final communiqué affirmed that "Soviet-Indian relations have never been based on a more friendly or understanding attitude." [46] It was a slap at Peking, whose press kept completely silent on that tour.

Then came March 15, the projected date for the journey of the chief of the Soviet Government to Paris. At the last minute he begged off, pleading an attack of flu. Some thought it was only a pretext; but a week later, de Gaulle, as regal as usual, greeted a thinner, tired, but beaming Khrushchev, flanked by every member of his family and by Gromyko and Kosygin, then president of Gosplan, the planning committee. The "blood flag" which Lamartine had persuaded the Second Republic to renounce in 1848, waved over Paris for the first time.

Mr. K, Lenin and Stalin's heir, stayed at the Quai d'Orsay in the royal apartment. It was apparent that he was not insensitive to the pomp of the welcome. At the Elysée banquet, de Gaulle toasted "two very old and very young countries, daughters of the same mother, Europe," and Khrushchev stated that he was convinced that it "could and must become an area of peaceful and fruitful coexistence." He approved of the general's statements on Algerian self-determination but revealed that he had not abandoned his objectives when, before the diplomatic press, he renewed his threat to sign a separate peace treaty with the G.D.R., "if our efforts remain in vain." [47]

In the provinces, where he undertook an extensive tour, he discovered with apparent surprise that his harangues on the German peril carried little weight, to the point that he let himself be persuaded to tone them down. On his return he had several talks with de Gaulle. The communiqué did not bring out anything new. Nonetheless, Khrushchev was pleased to have met one Western leader who had finally accepted the Oder-Neisse frontier and who seemed not to have the slightest illusion on the chances of Germany's reunification. Jules Moch's idea for an agreement on the prohibition of "vectors" of nuclear weapons, in other words, missiles and strategic bombers, was taken up again by the general and undeniably appealed to him. But de Gaulle, who very nearly thought of communism as a dead idea, was surprised, it was said, by the manner in which his guest asserted, in private as well as in public, the depth of his Marxist convictions, saying of himself that he was a "hopeless case." [48] "At heart, he is a Communist," the general later was to confide to a visitor, somewhat dreamily.[49]

On his return to Moscow on April 4, the Communist in question reported to the crowds, as he had done following his trip to Washington, in the most jovial manner, affirming that on the problem of disarmament the positions of the two countries were in agreement, and speaking warmly of de Gaulle. The détente promised to have a long future. Three weeks later, however, a small cloud appeared on the horizon, whose warning of a heavy storm was not heeded quickly enough.

BIBLIOGRAPHY AND NOTES

[1] *Neue Zürcher Zeitung*, March 18, 1958.
[2] *Neues Deutschland*, October 28, 1958.
[3] *Le Monde*, August 4, 1961.
[4] Keesing's, 16505 A.
[5] Supplement to *Etudes soviétiques*, No. 130.
[6] *Le Monde*, December 18, 1958.
[7] Questions on International Policy to the Supreme Soviet of the U.S.S.R., Supplement to *Etudes soviétiques*, No. 131.
[8] Documentation française. Articles et documents, No. 0750, January 25, 1959.

9 The Soviet Union's Proposals on the German Problem. Supplement to *Etudes soviétiques*, No. 131.

10 Author's personal notes.

11 Keesing's, 16707 A.

12 *Ibid.*

13 *Ibid.*, 16719 A.

14 *Ibid.*, 16721.

15 Année politique, 1959, pp. 615–17.

16 Documents on Geneva. American Information Service, 1959, pp. 51–55.

17 Keesing's, 16889 A.

18 Documents on Geneva, *op. cit.*, p. 62.

19 Keesing's, 16933 A.

20 Année politique, 1959, p. 450.

21 *Ibid.*, p. 482.

22 *Le Monde*, September 17, 1959.

23 *Ibid.*, September 18, 1959.

24 *Ibid.*, September 22, 1959.

25 *Ibid.*, September 18, 1959.

26 K. S. Karol, *Khrouchtchev et l'Occident* (Paris: Julliard, 1960), p. 100.

27 *U.R.S.S.*—Bulletin of the Soviet Information Bureau in Paris, No. 1802, September 29, 1959.

28 *Le Monde*, September 30, 1959.

29 Hudson, Lowenthal, MacFarquhar, *The Sino-Soviet Dispute* (New York: Praeger, 1961), p. 57.

30 Tibor Meray, *La rupture Moscou-Pékin, op. cit.*, p. 73.

31 "Le Tibet et la République populaire de Chine." Commission internationale des juristes, Geneva, 1960, pp. 226–29.

32 *Ibid.*, p. 171.

33 Heinrich Bechtoldt, *Indien oder China* (Stuttgart: Deutscher Verlags Anstalt, 1961), p. 308.

34 Keesing's, 16797 A.

35 *Ibid.*, 17116.

36 *Ibid.*, 17119.

37 Documentation française. Documents sur les relations sino-soviétiques en 1963, II, p. 59.

38 *Le Monde*, October 2, 1959.

39 Documents sur les relations sino-soviétiques, *op. cit.*, II, p. 60

40 *Ibid.*, p. 33.

41 "Pour l'unité idéologique du mouvement communiste mondial," anonymous brochure attributed to the C.P.S.U. and reproduced in *La Voix Communiste*, June–July 1961.

42 *Le Monde*, November 1–2, 1959.

43 Keesing's, 17250 A.

44 *Ibid.*, 17344 C.

45 Documents sur les relations sino-soviétiques, *op. cit.*, II, p. 60.

46 *Le Monde*, March 25, 1960.

47 *Ibid.*, March 27–28, 1960.

48 *Ibid.*

49 Author's personal notes.

CHAPTER 15

THE SHOE ON

THE TABLE

Talk, talk, that's all you can do.

—Raymond Queneau, *Zazie*

A MONTH BEFORE THE PLANNED SUMMIT MEETING IN Paris on May 16, 1960, the Western bloc was in a state of general euphoria. When de Gaulle made a triumphal tour in the United States at the end of April, which repaid him for many humiliations, he agreed with Eisenhower that Khrushchev was not going to pull any surprises. As he said on April 23, it was essential to create a "new climate" from which "solutions, at the moment impossible, may emerge. That is particularly true of disarmament, the German problems, and aid to underdeveloped countries." [1]

The State Department itself had published a large selection of documents, with an introduction in which the following thought stands out: "It would be unrealistic to expect the settlement of outstanding problems to result from a single conference of heads of governments. The road to peace is long and arduous." [2]

Herter nevertheless declared on April 20 that the success of the conference depended on the Russians.

That statement did not please Khrushchev who, three days later in Baku, warned those who expected concessions from the U.S.S.R. that "they will be disappointed." And he reiterated that, after the signing of a peace treaty, the G.D.R. would have the right to bar access to West Berlin to the Western Powers if they refused to participate in it. But he also said that the Soviet Government would "spare no efforts to ensure the success of the meeting." [3] Because of that last sentence, the warning was hardly noticed.

He returned to the same subject on May 4, speaking before the Supreme Soviet. While saying that he was convinced of "President Eisenhower's desire to further the cause of peace," he was obliged to declare that "some American circles can prevent him from doing it." And he cited among disturbing signs the fact that two American planes, one of which had been shot down on May 1, had violated the Soviet frontier.[4]

His pessimism was surprising since no one could believe that, within sight of the summit he had worked so hard to bring about, Mr. K would suddenly give up the whole business. But Washington's attitude was not going to facilitate matters. Soon after Khrushchev's speech, the NASA spokesman stated that a U-2 plane, "used to study meteorological conditions at high altitude," had been missing since the first of May. The State Department itself said that the missing plane might be the one shot down, but that there "was absolutely no deliberate attempt to violate Soviet airspace and never has been," and added that Eisenhower, who had had no knowledge of that flight, had ordered an investigation.[5]

In reality, Ike knew perfectly well what it was all about. It was with his consent that U-2 planes had been systematically taking pictures of Soviet territory for the last four years. All those who shared the secret felt smugly secure, as these planes flew at an altitude of 75,000 feet, which was believed to put them outside the range of Russian fighters and missiles. In the event of any malfunction, the pilot was under orders to trigger a mechanism which would cause the plane to disintegrate, thus making its identification impossible.

However, those missions were everybody's secret. In 1958 and 1959 the magazine *Soviet Aviation* had several times denounced the American spy flights. In June 1959 the French review *Science et Vie* had devoted to them an extremely well-documented article. It was even said that during his meeting with Eisenhower at Camp David, Khrushchev had complained of those repeated flights.

Russian military engineers were relentless in trying to perfect a weapon capable of intercepting them. On May 1 the fruit of their research, the SAM 2, made a hit for the first time, a U-2 having lost altitude due to engine trouble. Marshal Verchinin, Air Force Commander in Chief, rushed to bring the news to Khrushchev at the Red Square stand where he was reviewing the traditional parade. The pilot, Gary Powers, had fallen into Russian hands, carrying the whole James Bond paraphernalia, from the revolver with silencer to the poisoned hypodermic needle—not to mention a small fortune in rubles, gold pieces, and watches intended to buy the silence of any people he might run into. It was rather difficult for him to deny the evidence, because he had been unable to operate the destructive mechanism, and the Russians had found, in the wreckage of the plane, soon to be exhibited in Moscow, all the proof they could ask for.

Khrushchev was very careful not to reveal the news of his prize catch. It was only on May 7, after NASA and the State Department had been trapped in their lies, that he revealed the truth to the world. While attacking "the militarists in the Pentagon" who "seem unable to call a halt in their war effort," he stated that "he was quite willing to grant that the President knew nothing about the plane having been sent into the Soviet Union. But," he said, "this must alert us even more." [6]

Nothing irremediable had happened—yet. Verchinin had just confirmed that he was soon going to the United States. The State Department published the following explanation: "U-2 aircraft have made flights along the frontiers of the free world for the past four years as a precaution against surprise attacks. . . . There was no authorization for such flights as described by Mr. Khrushchev." [7]

Therefore, Mr. K could believe that Washington was going along with him, and on the 9th, during a reception at the Czechoslovakian Embassy, he appeared cordial and relaxed, asking that the people he talked to refrain from making deductions which could complicate the situation. A few hours later, however, another communiqué from the State Department reopened the whole business. Eisenhower's advisers had decided that his prestige would be hurt by the implication contained in the first explanation—that is, that he was in ignorance of Powers' flight. This time, Herter put his foot in his mouth in a way that placed Khrushchev in an impossible situation:

"The Soviet leaders have almost complete access to the open societies of the free world and supplement this with vast espionage networks. . . . The Government of the United States would be derelict to its responsibility, not only to the American people but to free peoples everywhere, if it did not, in the absence of Soviet cooperation, take such measures as are possible unilaterally to lessen and overcome this danger of surprise attack."

Admitting that unarmed civilian planes were undertaking missions of intensive surveillance, "normally of a peripheral character but on occasion by penetration," he pointed out that since, apparently, the Soviet leaders were aware of the fact, it could be wondered what their objective was in seeking to "exploit the present incident as a propaganda battle in the Cold War." [8]

What could Khrushchev do? For months, he had been telling the Chinese and their followers in the socialist bloc that the United States had changed, that Eisenhower truly wanted peace, that he was ready to make concessions in order to "normalize" the Berlin situation. And now, after de Gaulle's and Herter's statements, he was not only sure that he would obtain nothing from them in that area, but on top of that the Americans claimed the right to quietly violate Russian territory in order to make sure of his good intentions. His only chance to save face was to obtain apologies from Eisenhower and to exact from him, as from a child caught in a mischievous act, the promise that he wouldn't do it again. If he succeeded in thus humiliating the head of the greatest power in the world, he would have no trouble in convincing his critics that the Peking *Red Flag* was wrong when on April 16 it took him to task, without naming him: "There are some who are not revisionists, but well-intentioned people who want to be Marxists, but who derive certain incorrect ideas from various new historical phenomena which baffle them." [9]

And so, on May 11, he declared that Herter had "taken off all the veils and removed all the paint which was used to camouflage, embellish and 'make up,' as it were, the policy of the U.S. imperialists," [10] and that the hopes he had for Ike were somewhat shattered, thus intimating that his visit to the U.S.S.R. might well be compromised. However, he did not seem to challenge the principle of a summit meeting, since, on the contrary, he announced that he intended to arrive in Paris one or two days earlier, "to get acclimatized a little." On Saturday the 14th, he landed smiling at Orly and declared that the Soviet Government "will do everything in its power for the success of the conference." [11] Then he went sightseeing.

On Sunday morning he called on de Gaulle and gave him a message, euphemistically called "oral," informing him of the three conditions which he expected to present to the United States President as prerequisites for the summit conference: an apology for the U-2 affair; the severe punishment of the culprits; and an announcement that the flights would stop. The general was dismayed. He told his visitor that if he made those conditions in plenary session, the conference was doomed in advance.

To no avail. When, at lunchtime, Mr. K left his office, de Gaulle did not doubt for a moment that this had been a decision taken by the Kremlin and completely irrevocable. He did not believe that the United States would make the slightest concession and, besides, he hoped it wouldn't. That was what he said, a few moments later, to Eisenhower and Macmillan. Both were completely flabbergasted and refused to believe that conciliation was impossible.

The British Prime Minister then met with Khrushchev. The morning's scenario was repeated word for word, with the difference that the Englishman became emotional and begged his Soviet colleague to be reasonable. He himself promised to urge Ike to compromise.

On Monday morning, at breakfast, Eisenhower showed Macmillan the declaration he intended to make, which, for the first time, included a promise of renunciation of the U-2 flights. Macmillan, relieved, thought that negotiations could be opened on that basis.

When the four met at the Elysée Palace, Khrushchev immediately asked to speak. He read the document seen the day before by Eisenhower and Macmillan. Then he added to that harsh but understandable statement an insulting item directed at Eisenhower: a proposal to adjourn the conference from six to eight months. In passing, he called on Marshal Malinovski to verify his statements on the Soviet Union's air power and the extent of the punishment it could, if necessary, inflict on aggressors.

What could Ike say in the face of that well-planned attack, whose virulence might be explained by the fact that the Russians, having already learned from the British that Ike had canceled the U-2 flights, hoped to exploit the advantage thus obtained? Dismayed but calm, he read the paper he had shown to Macmillan that morning. Mr. K asked only one question: "How long will the flights' suspension be valid?" [12] "As long as I am President," replied Eisenhower, who constitutionally could not say anything else. Khrushchev snickered.

General de Gaulle suggested that airspace be one of the questions considered by the conference and vainly attempted to make Khrushchev give up the publication of his note. Macmillan literally pleaded with the head of the Soviet Government, who was adamant. Even more: he demanded that the President's reply be made public.

Therefore, the two documents were delivered to the newspapers. They were a bombshell. In his speech Khrushchev had declared that "since the United States does not wish to reach an agreement . . . the conference would be a useless loss of time and a betrayal of public opinion in all countries."

Consequently, he considered it proper to postpone Ike's visit to the U.S.S.R. Eisenhower had replied that the U-2 flights "canceled in the wake of the recent incident, would not be resumed" and that "therefore, the Soviet argument did not hold up." But Khrushchev had "swept aside all reasonable arguments. . . . Hence it appeared that he was determined to torpedo the Paris conference." [13]

It was with the greatest skepticism that General de Gaulle let the British Prime Minister counsel the two principal antagonists to make a last effort at conciliation. Far from joining him, he firmly upheld the determination of the President of the United States, who saw the collapse of years of effort for peace. If another man had led France, one of his advisers was to tell us a few days later, Ike might have given in to British pressure. Be that as it may, he stood his ground, convinced that a conference which would begin with a capitulation would necessarily lead to other capitulations.

The split seemed final. Khrushchev stated that he was going back to Moscow via Berlin, and he scheduled a press conference. Suddenly, it was canceled and it was learned that he had decided to go to Sézanne to meditate at the places where Malinovski had fought during the First World War as a member of the tsarist expeditionary corps.

Why this diversion? It is probable that by using the threat of his departure and then by delaying it, he hoped to give his protagonists enough time for reflection to enable them to change their attitude. Wouldn't Ike's pacifism, Macmillan's inexhaustible good will, and fear of the reaction of disappointed public opinion induce them to make another attempt at conciliation? A sentence used in the press conference supported that hypothesis: "If the President of France and the Prime Minister of Great Britain had taken a completely objective attitude in the examination of facts, if they had not let themselves be carried away by their relationship as allies, if they had shown greater determination, it is possible that the leaders of the United States would have been brought to condemn their acts of aggression." [14] This opinion was also expressed in a confidence from Mikoyan, a month later, during a trip to Norway: "Macmillan sincerely wanted the conference to succeed, but he did not dare oppose President Eisenhower." [15]

But above all, what leads one to believe that Mr. K still hoped for an apology from Ike was his reaction when an official motorcyclist brought him, in the village of Feurs, a message from de Gaulle asking him to come to the Elysée at 3 o'clock to "see if it is possible for the summit conference to begin to examine the questions which we had agreed would be debated." [16] The journalists who had followed him on his pilgrimage over the battlefields saw his face light up. He ordered a return to Paris at full speed.

If he believed that Ike was getting ready to go to Canossa, he was mistaken. The invitation from the general was part of a scenario which he had sold to his American and British counterparts that morning. If the Soviet leader did not come to the meeting, his absence would be noted. If he came, there would be no discussion on the conditions he had made.

On arriving at his embassy, Khrushchev was brought back to earth. Officials showed him a new statement from the United States Embassy, according to which his participation in the meeting would signify that he had abandoned his conditions. A telephone call to the Elysée stripped away his last illusion. At 5 o'clock the three Western leaders separated after having released an official report taking note of his absence.

On Wednesday he followed protocol by paying good-bye calls to de Gaulle and Macmillan, then demonstrated, in an unforgettable press conference, the full range of his talents. The atmosphere was rather like that of a political rally. The already large crowd of journalists was swollen with a few hundred invited guests, a mixture of Communists, policemen and well-connected curiosity-seekers. The steaming heat in the immense hall caused the men to take their coats off, and there was a queue for beer and Coca-Cola. When Mr. K arrived, his admirers' wild applause provoked protests. Soon he would take the authors of those protests to task: "If the rest of the fascist invaders who have survived start to boo us as did Hitler's brigades, if they prepare another attack against the Soviet Union and other so-cialist countries, we will boo them right out of their skins." [17] New waves of applause, new vociferations. Khrushchev continued intermi-nably in the same vein, finally exhausting the patience of his listeners who slipped away one by one. Those who remained until the end saw him, before he sat down, turn toward Malinovski in a self-satisfied way, as if expecting praise for the way in which he had cut the lackeys of imperialism to ribbons. The master comedian had made a magnificent show of anger, which was the only role available, but it was only an act. There was no reason to be concerned about the immediate consequences of the break. When the next day I happened to meet the head of his press services in the street, he was completely calm; the only worry he had was learning which records he could bring back to his family from his too brief excursion to Paris.

In the course of his press conference, Mr. K, besides, showed his true colors: "The Soviet Union stands firmly for peaceful coexistence, for talks, and for agreements based on common sense and which are mutually acceptable. It is toward that end that we are going to work. We would like to believe that it is toward that end that the leaders of the Western Powers will also work and that within six to eight months we will meet again with our partners, under new and more favorable conditions, to examine and resolve overdue inter-national problems." [18]

Why that delay? Because before that time expired, the United States would have a new President, and the young Senator Kennedy, who had won all the primaries for the nomination of the Democratic candidate for the White House had declared on May 18: "I would certainly express [if I were President] regret at the timing and give assurances that it would not happen again." [19]

When Mr. K, on his return from Paris, stopped in East Berlin, it was to quiet Ulbricht's impatience. "It makes sense," he said, "to wait a little while longer and to attempt by a joint effort of the four powers who have defeated Hitler's forces, to find a solution to the problem of the signing of a peace treaty with the two German states which actually exist." He added that neither the U.S.S.R. nor the G.D.R. had any intention of allowing the occupation of West Berlin to drag on. But he also said, no less forcefully, that the socialist countries "will never engage in a policy of adventurism . . . will never undertake anything which would bring the world back to the unhappy period of the Cold War." [20]

Welcomed with relief in the West, that speech was obviously not the kind that would satisfy those in Peking who had anxiously followed the preparations for the summit meeting and organized a demonstration of a million and a half people, on May 20, against its "sabotage by the imperialists." For the *People's Daily* of the same day, in fact, that failure was hardly surprising to "those who looked at the world situation from the standpoint of class struggle and do not let themselves be deceived by certain superficial developments."

But, what do Mr. K's declarations prove if not that the U-2 affair had been insufficient to clearly enlighten him on American intentions, and rather than finally recognizing that he had no chance to make the imperialists see reason, he preferred to incriminate a minority and even a man incapable of controlling it. But the Chinese leaders judged all that agitation worthless, and the moment had come to try to ask the brother parties to bring pressure on Mr. K to make him change his attitude.

The kickoff to their campaign was given on June 8 in Peking, on the occasion of the meeting of the council of the World Federation of Trade Unions. Liu Chang-sheng, vice president of the All-China Federation of Trade Unions, declared: "It is entirely wrong to believe that war can be eliminated forever while imperialism still exists. The spreading of such illusions . . . will lead to evil consequences of a serious nature and, in fact, we can already see such consequences at present." [21] Forty-eight hours later, the *Sovietskaia Rossiya* newspaper, soon echoed by *Pravda,* used the pretext of the fortieth anniversary of the publication of Lenin's famous work on "communism's childhood sickness," to recall that that expression meant the "communism of the Left"—guilty of rejecting any compromise with the *bourgeoisie*.

It was soon learned through the Italian delegates to the Peking meeting that a sharp and impassioned debate, which lasted several days, had started over the report of the secretary general of the World Trade Unions Federation, Louis Saillant. The Chinese particularly criticized his insistence on disarmament, and on the necessity of turning over to the underdeveloped countries the money thus saved.

A few days more and no one could any longer ignore the existence of a real split between the Big Two of the socialist bloc. Following a Soviet proposal, it had been decided to take advantage of the Third Congress of the Rumanian Workers' Party in Bucharest to exchange ideas on the international situation between representatives of the various Communist parties. On the opening day, June 21, Khrushchev asserted: "Lenin's propositions about imperialism remain in force. . . . But it should not be forgotten that [they] were advanced and developed tens of years ago, when the world did not know many things that are now decisive for historical development. . . ." One cannot ignore "the specific situation, the changes in the correlation of forces in the world," or merely "repeat what the great Lenin said in quite different historical conditions . . . If we act like children who, studying the alphabet, compile words from letters, we shall not go very far." [22]

That statement smells of revisionism. Until then, no one in the socialist world had dared to affirm that Lenin could be surpassed in any way whatever. Its full significance could be evaluated if one noted that two months earlier, Peking's *Red Flag,* celebrating the ninetieth anniversary of Lenin's birth, had published under the title "Long Live Leninism!" a series of three articles which contained the following highlights: "We believe in the absolute correctness of Lenin's thinking; war is an inevitable outcome of the systems of exploitation, and the source of modern wars is the imperialist system. Until the imperialist system and the exploiting classes come to an end, wars of one kind or another will always occur." [23]

P'eng Chen, Mayor of Peking, who was later to fall victim to the "cultural revolution," represented China in the Rumanian Congress and answered Mr. K that "the aggressive and predatory nature of imperialism will never change," and that "American imperialism is the arch-enemy of world peace." [24] The Russians circulated among the delegations an informative paper sharply denouncing the Chinese dogmas. Mr. K took these up again in private sessions, denouncing the "madness" and the "Trotskyism" of Mao's party, accused among other things of wanting to "trigger a war" and to "take up the banner of the monopolistic *bourgeoisie.*" [25] According to Peking, "someone waved a wand and the Chinese Communist Party was encircled on all sides and subjected to a violent surprise attack." [26] The Albanian delegation was the only one to categorically defend the Chinese position.

On June 26 the Chinese presented to the other delegations a declaration asserting that Khrushchev had, during the meeting, "completely violated the principle of the settlement of common problems through consultation between brother parties," that he had also adopted an attitude "patriarchal, arbitrary and despotic," and that there existed between Khrushchev and the Chinese Communists "differences relating to a number of fundamental principles of Marxism-Leninism." However, they believed that those differences "are only partial in nature" and that it was possible to "talk calmly and in friendship in order to eliminate them." [27]

The repercussions from that altercation spread rapidly, although the Bucharest communiqué made no allusion to it. But, for a moment, it could be believed, seeing the growing ruthlessness of Soviet diplomacy—if it can be called that—that Mr. K must have made some concessions to Chinese demands.

The Kremlin engaged in a campaign of vituperation. The Soviet press, which for eight months had eulogized the friendship between the U.S.S.R. and the United States, accused the "Pentagon militarists" of preparing for a bacteriological war and of seeking to emulate the Hitlerian sadists. American citizens in the U.S.S.R. were subjected to various harassments. The B.B.C. and the Voice of America, which had been heard freely since the fall of 1959, were again jammed. Trips between the two countries were canceled. Warnings and threats filled the air. Khrushchev used the most outrageous language toward Eisenhower, saying that it was "dangerous to let such a man govern a nation because he could do things that it would be hard to undo," adding that when he left the White House, he could safely be given a job "as head of a kindergarten." [28]

On June 27 the Eastern countries' representatives withdrew from the Ten-Power Committee on disarmament which had been set up on a fifty-fifty basis during the Geneva Conference on the Berlin problem and which, in the fall of 1959 and in the climate of détente created by Mr. K's visit to the United States, had been considering the Soviet and British plans for complete and general disarmament in three stages. According to Zorin, chief of the Soviet delegation, a continuation of those deliberations "could only disorient world public opinion." [29]

On July 1 an American plane was shot down over the Barents Sea. In its note, Moscow spoke of a gross violation of its frontiers, while Washington maintained that the attack took place over international waters. Kuznetsov unleashed an attack against the United States in the Security Council. The crises which were erupting in Cuba and in the Congo, and which we will consider in the next chapter, were also the occasion of an outburst of verbal violence. On July 19, Macmillan wrote Mr. K to express "his deep concern over what now appears to be a new trend in the conduct of Soviet foreign policy" and to confess that "I simply do not understand what your purpose is today." [30]

Khrushchev replied in a long *pro domo* indictment interspersed with sharp criticisms of British colonialism and assured the Prime Minister that if after the American elections, obstacles were again put in the way of a settlement of the problem in litigation, the U.S.S.R. would conclude a peace treaty with the G.D.R.

He bitterly reproached de Gaulle for having changed his mind since their talks at Rambouillet and for having made Jules Moch support "the line of the American representative, or more exactly, of the Pentagon" in the Disarmament Commission.[31] Whereas, until now, he had adopted an attitude of prudent reserve toward the Algerian question, in contrast to the unconditional support given by Peking to the provisional government of Algiers, he now invited the Algerian President, Ferhat Abbas, to Moscow and on October 7 declared that "our meetings and conversations with the representatives of the Algerian Provisional Government constitute *de facto* recognition of that Government." [32] However, he watered down the significance of his declaration by adding that after all, General de Gaulle had done as much, since official emissaries of the N.L.F. had been received at Melun in June.

It was in New York that Mr. K made those statements. In New York, where he returned—no longer a guest of Eisenhower as in the year before, but in his role as chief of the Soviet delegation to the U.N.—accompanied by his principal satellites, from Gomulka to Kadar and Fidel Castro, as well as by numerous leaders from the uncommitted world, headed by Tito, Nasser and Nehru.

His reception by the American authorities was quite cool, and they asked him not to leave the island of Manhattan. As soon as he arrived, numerous demonstrations took place in both the neighborhood of the U.S.S.R. delegation's headquarters on Park Avenue and in that of the U.N. headquarters. On September 23, Nikita Sergeyevich ascended the rostrum of the General Assembly to intervene in the general debate which was traditionally held at the opening of each session. The United States had "attempted to supplant international law with piracy, and honest negotiations between sovereign equal states with perfidy." [33]

Hammarskjöld was accused of having become the tool of the colonial powers in the Congo, from which Mr. K concluded it was necessary to abolish the post of Secretary General of the U.N. and to substitute for it an "executive body" composed of three persons representing the three groups of states—Western, socialist and neutral—which would be called the "troika." As for the seat of the international organization, it should be moved outside the United States. He also offered a draft resolution immediately granting to all the territories that were not self-administered "full independence" and "full liberty," as well as a proposed general and complete disarmament treaty.[34]

Macmillan followed him to the rostrum, and it was in vain that

Khrushchev became agitated, interrupted him from his seat, and in a lowered tone of voice asked Hammarskjöld, after having insulted him, to demonstrate his "chivalrous spirit" by resigning. When the Secretary General himself intervened on October 3, to let the General Assembly judge his case, an immense ovation greeted him such as had never before been heard in that hall. Furious, Khrushchev pounded his desk with his fists while his friends, obviously embarrassed, followed his example.

That was not his only failure. Outside of the Soviet bloc, only three delegations, on October 11, approved the suggestion from the U.S.S.R. that the disarmament question be taken up by the General Assembly itself, as much as possible on the level of heads of government. "We know committees," he had said, "we know what they are . . . stinking stables . . . if you want to compete with us in the field of armaments, we will beat you. Our economy is flourishing, we are producing missiles like a chain of sausages—the arms race is going to come to a head and in that war we will crush you." [35] The following day went better for Mr. K. In spite of the fact that the Organization Committee of the General Assembly had tabled the Soviet draft resolution on the immediate emancipation of all the remaining dependent territories, numerous speakers declared themselves in favor of Moscow's proposal, and were finally joined by the United States.

But its spokesman explained that, in his opinion, the debate ought to cover the self-determination of all the peoples, including those behind the Iron Curtain. Those words, echoed by the Philippines' delegate, provoked vehement protests from Khrushchev, who, in order to be better heard, was seen removing from his foot a resplendent light-tan shoe with which he began pounding his desk in rhythm. The assembly hall of the East River building had never seen such a spectacle. Trying to restore order, the Irishman Boland, who was presiding, pounded his gavel with such force that he broke it. "How shaky the United Nations is," the Russian jubilantly cried before returning to Moscow a few hours later, "it's the beginning of the end." [36]

A hard task awaited him there. During the June Bucharest meeting, at the request of the Chinese, it had been decided to hold—on the occasion of the Bolshevik Revolution's anniversary celebrations in the Soviet capital in November—a general conference of all the world's Communist parties for the purpose of outlining a common ideological platform, in other words, to arbitrate the dispute between the Chinese and the U.S.S.R. For Khrushchev, who hoped to resume the aborted negotiations started with Ike with the new President of the U.S., whose election was to take place on November 8, it was imperative to obtain from this conference massive approval of his policies. It was obviously with that goal in mind that he had so noisily fought in the U.N., acting in front of the whole world as the spokesman for the peoples of the underdeveloped countries. But, in the final analysis, his only success in New York had been the vote on the resolution for the liquidation of colonial regimes. For critics as determined as the Chinese, who were skillful at uncovering the snares hidden in words, there was nothing in it which could shake their conviction that Khrushchev was betraying the world revolution.

He had only two arguments to counter them with. He ceaselessly expressed his faith in the inevitable victory of the U.S.S.R. in economic competition with the capitalist world. For example, on October 22 he told the Cuban journalist Carlos Franqui: "According to our calculations, we will surpass the United States in the vital contest of per capita production in 1970, that is to say, in ten years. According to the economists' calculations, in 1980 we will produce much more per capita than the United States of America. In 1965 we will produce per capita as much and even more consumer goods than the European countries." [37]

The events to follow showed that such a statement contained quite a few illusions, but at the time that affirmation was taken seriously by many people who were not Communists. Even more impressive was the seizing of power in Cuba and in several African countries by men who seemed inclined to follow the Soviet example. Khrushchev could point to those successes in support of his thesis, according to which coexistence did not help strengthen imperialism, but rather extended socialism. But a few years later, that thesis would also have to be seriously modified, following the counterrevolutions in Brazil and Indonesia, the American intervention in the

Dominican Republic, and a succession of *coups d'état* in Africa.

Neither Peking nor Moscow made any conciliatory gestures in preparation for the November confrontation. As soon as the Bucharest conference ended, the *People's Daily* and *Pravda* published on the same day, June 29, completely divergent commentaries on the final communiqué. One after the other, the leaders of the major communist parties made declarations supporting the Soviet viewpoint.

Soon all sorts of news leaked out which illustrated the growing deterioration of relations between the two Meccas of socialism. Resorting, although with no more success, to the methods of brutal coercion formerly employed by Stalin toward Yugoslavia, Khrushchev ordered the recall of Soviet technicians and the massive reduction of supplies to China. Those measures were deeply resented at a time when China was facing enormous economic difficulties, caused by the excesses of "the great leap forward," by the people's communes and by particularly unfavorable weather conditions. A report was widely circulated during meetings held behind closed doors which informed the "activists" of the C.P.S.U. of the deterioration of relations between the Soviet and Chinese parties.

On August 7 *Pravda* openly attacked the "dogmatists" who "affirm that imperialism will never lose its savage aggressiveness, and that, under those conditions, it is only up to the imperialists to trigger or not to trigger a war. If that was the case," continued the author of the article, "our struggle for peace, would lose all its *raison d'être*. Besides, the rebirth of leftist sectarianism would have a demoralizing effect upon the builders of the new society. Indeed, what would be the use of creating, of building, of planning for the future if it were known in advance that the fruits of that labor would be destroyed by the cyclone of war?" [38]

The same *Pravda* took the credit for condemning the book in which Kardelj, Tito's lieutenant, had just criticized—dotting all the *i*'s—the orientation of Chinese policy, which "gives rise to a lack of confidence . . . in the ranks of the working-class of other countries," and tends "to subordinate the interests and views of world socialism to her own interests and views." [39] It was especially important for the Soviets to try to demonstrate that, although opposing Mao's "dogmatism," they did not thereby lean toward "revisionism," which, according to the 1957 resolution of the twelve Communist parties, was a worse danger.

During September, while Chinese and Russian delegations conferred in the greatest secrecy and without the slightest success, the controversy was continued in the Communist papers. It had not yet reached the point where it specified that "modern revisionists" or "Yugoslavs" in reality meant "Russians," and that "dogmatists" or "leftist deviationists" meant "Chinese." But no one was any longer in doubt.

On November 6 the Chinese Communist Party's delegation arrived in Moscow. On both sides the anniversary of the October Revolution was the occasion for proclamations on the unfailing character of the friendship between the two countries. While most of the eighty other Communist parties represented had sent their top men as delegates, Mao was absent, as well as Chou En-lai, at that time generally considered the number-two man of the regime. Liu Shao-chi, who headed the delegation, had succeeded Mao to the presidency of the Republic a few months earlier, and was surrounded by five members of the Politburo, among them P'eng Chen, who had been on the receiving end of Khrushchev's attack in Bucharest. The conference, whose existence was officially revealed only after everybody had gone home, apparently lasted at least two weeks. What transpired would only gradually become known following the growing controversy between Peking and the "revisionist" Communist parties, especially the French party.

The departure of Enver Hodja and other Albanian leaders for Tirana, while all the other parties' delegates remained in the Soviet capital, attracted attention, especially since the Albanian national holiday gave Chou En-lai the opportunity of warmly praising that country.

Furious at seeing the Albanian party siding with the Chinese in Bucharest, Khrushchev had nevertheless proposed talks in August, in order to smooth over their differences. But Tirana had refused, arguing that it would mean "holding discussions behind the back of a third party on questions which concerned it." [40]

Enver Hodja himself, before the eighty-one parties' conference, attacked Mr. K's denunciation of the cult of personality, his rapprochement with Yugoslavia and his behavior toward the Albanian party. In fact, the first two grievances explained everything. Having selected "the party and government cadres," according to a Soviet brochure, "not according to the men's value and experience, but according to their blood ties, their origin, or their friendship with the ruling circles," [41] Hodja feared that Tito, conscious that criticism of Stalin's cult of personality might reflect on his own, had never conceded the fact that his complete reconciliation with the Kremlin depended on the liquidation of his Albanian adversaries.

Mr. K was quite willing to offer that gift to the Yugoslav marshal, and in order to make the Tirana leaders repent, until he could attempt to organize a putsch, he had used techniques of economic pressure. But they had no other effect than to drive the Albanians into the arms of Mao, who was only too happy to keep that mosquito on the flank of the revisionist bear. The dispute would break into the open during the Twenty-second Congress of the C.P.S.U. in October 1961, and would lead the same year to the breaking of diplomatic relations between Moscow and Tirana and to the *de facto* exclusion of Albania from the Warsaw Pact.

§   §   §

As Ulbricht was to reveal very quickly, "the most burning question of our time, that of war and peace" dominated the debates of the conference of the Eighty-One, and all the speakers took a position on it.[42] Before its opening, the delegates, through the good offices of the C.P.S.U. had been handed a long philippic against the Chinese party of such unprecedented violence that it brought the emotions of the participants to fever pitch.

The delegates had to consider a draft resolution prepared by the organizational committee made up of representatives from twenty-six parties and in which certain portions had remained blank because the Russians and Chinese could not agree.

The tone of the debates could be judged from that of the interventions which were published. As an example, the Italian Luigi Longo declared as "unjust and even libelous, completely devoid of foundation and going beyond the acceptable limits of criticism," the

Chinese thesis according to which the Soviet Central Committee had deviated from Marxism-Leninism, and "as inadmissible . . . the Albanians' attempt to raise again the issue of the condemnation of Stalin's cult of personality." Enver Hodja was reproached for having made a gesture "so much more despicable because he had tried to hide, behind shameful protestations of friendship and brotherhood, words and sentences which could only be intended for a class enemy." Dolores Ibarruri, La Pasionaria—spokesman for the Spanish Communist Party—qualified Hodja's intervention as "inconceivable provocation from the mouth of a militant proletarian." [43]

Maurice Thorez, after having mentioned in passing the criticism heaped on the French Communist Party by the Yugoslavs, at the time the Cominform was created in 1947, because it had been in favor of the "parliamentary process," declared: "We do not understand the Chinese comrades' statements on the 'paper tiger' which ought to be mastered strategically and considered seriously, tactically speaking. A reasoning so confused cannot enlighten the peoples on the state of imperialist forces and on the means of combating them." [44]

Under those conditions, the passage of a joint resolution adopted on December 1 by the eighty-one parties, according to which "the speculations of imperialists, renegades and revisionists on the possibility of a schism in the midst of the socialist bloc are built on sand and doomed to failure" was obviously not without irony.[45]

The interminable document developed from a proposal by Suslov's pen, showed, from beginning to end, signs of laborious compromises. The Chinese themselves admitted that the conference was, from first to last, "a struggle between the two trends existing within the international communist movement and it almost ended in a break." [46] For their part, the Russians would very much have liked to have Mao's dogmas condemned by the whole movement. But most of the parties represented feared the consequences of such a decision on the very prestige of the Communist philosophy in the world, and their delegates tried to persuade both sides to make concessions so as to maintain a façade of unity.

The Chinese finally resigned themselves to leaving, in that joint declaration, a reference to the Twentieth Congress of the C.P.S.U., although they considered it the source of all deviations. For the rest, they had to content themselves with adding statements to the formulas of the Soviet proposals which watered them down, when they did not actually contradict them. Thus the adhesion to the principle of peaceful coexistence was weakened by the assurance that it "implied the strengthening of the class struggle." The declaration proclaimed at the same time that "the aggressive nature of imperialism has not changed" (Peking's thesis) and that "war is not inevitable" (Moscow's thesis).

But the passage according to which the complete failure of colonialism was inevitable, was especially noted: "The collapse of the system of colonial slavery under the impetus of the national liberation movements is a phenomenon which, because of its historical significance," the declaration affirmed, "ranks immediately after the formation of the system of world socialism. . . . The face of Asia has completely changed, the colonial regimes are crumbling in Africa. An active fighting front has been opened against imperialism in Latin America." And in the declaration could be seen the renewed optimism given to the world Communist movement by the violent collapse of colonial empires, which Lenin had long ago identified as the very source of imperialism's power. Didn't the militants, gathered in Moscow, witness the fulfillment of the 1923 prophesy, according to which "the outcome of the struggle as a whole can be forecast only because in the long run capitalism itself is educating and training the vast majority of the population of the globe for the struggle. In the last analysis, the outcome of the struggle will be determined by the fact that Russia, India, China, etc., account for the overwhelming majority of the population of the globe"? [47]

Vladimir Ilyich had come to that conclusion only after the failure of his dream of the widespread outbreak of revolutions in Europe. Curiously enough, his 1960 epigoni also looked to the colonial countries after the failure of their expectation of seeing the capitalist system in the developed countries crumble by itself. It is time to examine more closely the source of their confidence.

BIBLIOGRAPHY AND NOTES

1 *Le Monde,* April 26, 1960.
2 *Ibid.,* April 13, 1960.
3 *Ibid.,* April 26, 1960.
4 *Ibid.,* May 6, 1950. Keesing's, 17425 A.
5 Keesing's, 17427.
6 *Ibid.*
7 *Ibid.*
8 *Ibid.*
9 *Red Flag* (Peking), April 16, 1960.
10 Keesing's, 17429.
11 *Le Monde,* May 15–16, 1960.
12 Author's personal notes.
13 Nikita Khrushchev, press conference. Supplement to *Etudes Soviétiques,* No. 146.
14 *Ibid.*
15 *Le Monde,* June 28, 1960.
16 *Ibid.,* May 18, 1960.
17 Khrushchev, press conference, *op. cit.*
18 *Ibid.*
19 Fleming, *op. cit.,* II, p. 1015.
20 *Le Monde,* May 22–23, 1960.
21 *Peking Review,* No. 24, June 1960.
22 Hudson *et al., The Sino-Soviet Dispute, op. cit.,* pp. 132–39.
23 *Ibid.,* pp. 82–112.
24 *Ibid.,* p. 139.
25 *Pékin Information,* September 15, 1963.
26 *People's Daily,* February 27, 1963.
27 *Ibid.*
28 Dallin, *op. cit.,* pp. 514–15.
29 Keesing's, 17601 A.
30 *Ibid.,* 17549 A.

31 *Le Monde,* July 28, 1960.
32 Keesing's, 17832 A.
33 *The New York Times,* September 24, 1960.
34 *U.R.S.S.,* Bulletin of the Soviet Information Bureau in Paris, No. 2111, September 27, 1960.
35 *Le Monde,* October 5, 1960.
36 *The New York Times,* October 13, 1960.
37 *Le Monde,* October 13, 1960.
38 *Pravda,* October 31, 1960.
39 Edward Kardelj, *War and Socialism* (Belgrade), pp. 196, 200.
40 *Zeri i Populit,* February 7, 1963.
41 *Voix Communiste,* No. 23, June–July 1961.
42 *Neues Deutschland,* December 18, 1960.
43 "Interventi della Delegazione del P.C.I. alla conferenza degli 81 partiti communisti e operai." Rome, Sezione centrale di stampa e propaganda della direzione del P.C.I., 1962.
44 "Contribution de la délégation française à la conférence des partis communistes et ouvriers." (Paris: Editions du P.C.F., 1961).
45 *L'Humanité,* December 6, 1960.
46 *Pékin Information,* September 16, 1963.
47 "Better Fewer, but Better," *Pravda,* March 4, 1923.

· CHAPTER 16 ·

THE COLD WAR

IN THE TROPICS

"Well, the long and the short of it is this: I won't
have folk look down on me."

—André Malraux, *L'Espoir*

THE YEAR OF THE SUMMIT *MANQUÉ* AND THE BEGIN-
ning of the Sino-Soviet dispute, 1960 will also go down in history
as the year of the decolonization of Africa. On February 8, at the
end of an extensive tour of the English-speaking countries of the
dark continent, a speech given by Macmillan before the South African
Parliament reaffirmed Great Britain's decision to set down the white
man's burden which for centuries it had been proud to bear. "The
wind of change is blowing through the continent. . . . Whether we
like it or not . . . we must all accept it as a fact." [1]

In June, on television, de Gaulle also alluded to "the liberation
movement which sweeps along the peoples of the whole world," and
which had led France to recognize in those who were dependent on
it "the right of self-determination." [2] By November 28 all French
possessions in Africa, as well as Madagascar, would have proclaimed
their independence, with the exception only of the Somaliland coast
and temporarily of Algeria.

The evolution had been rapid since the return to power of the
man who, in 1945, had sent troops back to Indochina and sternly
crushed the Kabyle rebellion, on the very day that victory was won
in Europe. Although the decolonization of Africa had already been
primed with the proclamation in 1956 of the independence of the
Sudan, Morocco and Tunisia, and in 1957 of that of Ghana, the

former British Gold Coast, de Gaulle believed, in 1958, that he could still propose to the Africans living under the Tricolor "a community along Federal lines with separate estates and a common estate." [3] When he declared at Brazzaville, "Whoever wants independence can take it immediately," by voting "No" to the constitutional referendum of September 28, he did not conceal the fact that he did not believe any of the countries involved would be crazy enough to choose what he preferred to call "secession."

However, Guinea followed its chief, Sékou Touré, when after a stormy discussion with the President of the Republic, Touré asked him to agree to his country's immediate independence. De Gaulle took it very badly. Not only did he refuse recognition until the new state had proved its capability for self-rule, but he set about liquidating all French presence in that country within the space of three months, thus creating a complete administrative and economic vacuum which the U.S.S.R. could not help but be tempted to fill.

Until that date the Russian role in African affairs had been insignificant. In spite of the traditional Marxist position in favor of the emancipation of colonized peoples, and of the active support the Comintern and the French Communist Party had given to the revolt of Abd el Krim in the Moroccan Rif in 1924, the few Communist parties in that vast continent had, on the eve of the Second World War, no more than 5,000 adherents—and these were Europeans, Arabs or Asiatics rather than Africans. It is only thanks to the war that the Communist parties of Algeria, Tunisia and Morocco seceded from the French party and that the first Russian diplomatic mission arrived in what was then de Gaulle's Algeria, as well as in Ethiopia and in Egypt, which, with Liberia, were then the only independent states in Africa.

After the Allied victory, Molotov tried in vain to put all of the "dependent" territories under U.N. trusteeship. He did not even succeed in obtaining for his country the trusteeship of Tripoli, taken from Italy. Until 1957 this was almost the extent of Russian activity in Africa, at a time when the United States vastly increased its investments and missions of all kinds, not to mention the bases that its Strategic Air Command had obtained in Morocco and Libya.

Many factors, besides distance, explain the hesitancy the Soviets felt toward a part of the world which they still, to judge by the

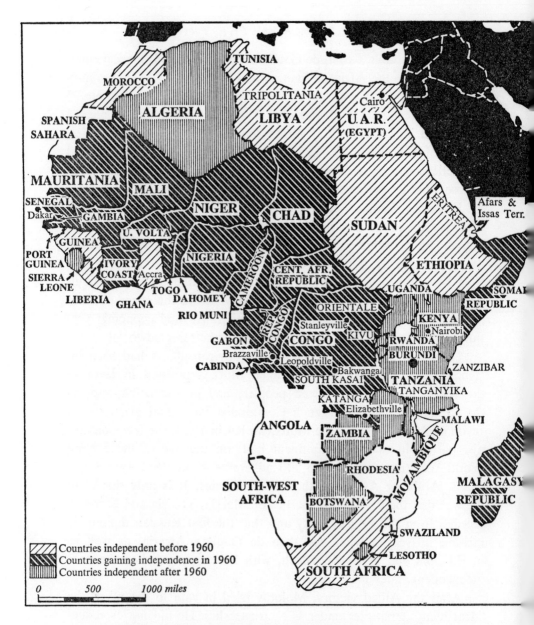

0   500   1000 miles

VII   THE STRUGGLE FOR AFRICA

failures they have suffered there, have some trouble understanding. Since 1933 the necessity of developing a common front with Paris and London against Nazi Germany had led them to put a damper on their anticolonialist propaganda. When, after 1945, the anti-Nazi coalition had broken, they attempted to appeal to the overseas peoples: across a large area of Asia, guerrilla groups, dominated by Communists, were formed. However, Stalin's despotism and pathological suspicion could not accept nationalists who did not completely follow his instructions, and only after his death did the U.S.S.R. consent to modify its attitude.

Except on the Mediterranean shores and in the far south, local conditions in Africa were not favorable to the propagation of Communist ideas: weak urban concentrations; low educational levels; social structures fragmented into castes, age groups and tribes; the persistence of Islamic or fetishistic beliefs completely alien to the very notion of economic and social progress; and finally, the attachment of the Africans to a civilization which taught, according to Senghor's beautiful formula, "the loving abandon to nature," [4] and thus stood at the very opposite pole from Marxism-Leninism, whose ambition was precisely to control it.

The two world wars had played an essential part in creating the turmoil in a continent which had only feebly resisted its colonization, except for a few glorious exceptions; a continent which the Great Powers had divided up among themselves like a pie in Berlin in 1885, and which since then had been exploited, under the alleged best motives, in a spirit of permanent paternalism. The hundreds of thousands of African soldiers who had come to Europe to shed their blood in a crusade for democracy and freedom could not help but ask themselves, once they had returned home, why that democracy and that freedom did not extend to the territories where they were born—although, at this point, they were asking only for equality of rights through assimilation. In 1912, following the institution of military service for the Moslems, the Algerian nationalist newspaper *Djidjelli* wrote: "Our sons are ready to serve France, but they will serve her only on one condition: that in exchange for years spent under the flag they be given the right to be French." [5] It is because that right was never granted to the Algerians or to the Africans —except the Senegalese—despite a thousand promises, that one by one they ended by claiming and obtaining independence.

Independence, for so long inconceivable, had slowly become a more and more attractive goal. In 1919 the League of Nations had "provisionally" recognized "the existence as independent nations" of "certain areas which had previously belonged to the Ottoman

Empire," and directed the powers which were taking them under their "mandate" to "supervise their administration until such time as they would be able to conduct their own affairs." [6] The trend thus started was continued, after the Second World War, with the former Italian possessions.

In 1949 it was decided that Libya would achieve independence in two years, although it was from every point of view an under-developed country. How then was it supposed that neighboring Tunisia and Morocco, disregarding the protectorate treaties and still run under a direct administrative system, which did not hesitate to depose their rulers, would not claim the same privileges? And that once the two neighboring peoples were emancipated, 10 million Algerians would be willing to see themselves forever treated as second-class citizens in the midst of a community which denied them the essential rights granted to a European minority? And that the African possessions would quietly remain under French domination once the Maghreb had seceded?

Many other factors were thus working toward emancipation: the loss of prestige suffered by France following its occupation, the determined anticolonialism on the part of Roosevelt and most of his countrymen, who had learned in school that the American nation was born of a revolt against foreign domination and who never hesitated to encourage the nationalism of the people in the liberated territories. The Indochinese war, which demonstrated to the Algerians and Africans fighting under the French flag that a people determined to achieve their freedom could defeat a power a thousand times better armed. The inability of a large part of the French population to understand in time that only a total commitment to equality and to respect for the dignity of every man could save, while transforming, the structure of what had been the empire. The gradual development, since 1949, of the Afro-Asian movement, culminating, at the Bandung Conference in 1955, in the proclamation of the peoples' right to self-determination and the duty of the countries already liberated to help the others gain independence. The autonomous intelligentsia, which had been attracted by Marxism, whose studies enabled them to evaluate the profits which the white powers had obtained from the economic exploitation of their colonies and the small amounts that trickled down to the native populations. And, finally, the decision taken by Britain's Labour Government to facilitate the gradual change to autonomy for the colonies within the framework of the Commonwealth, culminating, in 1951, in the installation of the nationalist leader Kwame Nkrumah, released from prison for the event, as the head of the Government of the Gold Coast. Seven years later, the Gold Coast, now Ghana, achieved complete independence, and the Duchess of Kent danced in the arms of Nkrumah at a great ball given on that occasion. It was unthinkable that a movement thus begun would not continue to spread and that the Francophone countries would not listen to the inflammatory speeches of Nkrumah on the theme of a United States of Africa.

In April 1958, Accra, the capital of Ghana, was the seat of the first conference of the independent African states, followed in December by the first conference of African peoples, which issued a call for general liberation. In April 1957, Richard Nixon, then Vice President of the United States, brought back from a tour of the dark continent the conviction that it was "that part of the world which is, actually, being transformed the fastest. Its evolution, while its inhabitants liberate themselves from colonial status or assume the responsibilities of independence," he wrote, "could well represent the decisive factor in the conflict between the forces of freedom and international communism." [7]

The first conclusion drawn by the American leaders from that evaluation was that it was more than ever fitting for the United States, which had already extended the benefits of the Marshall Plan to the African colonies and help under Point Four to the independent countries, to exercise its influence, as the House of Representatives had asked on June 23, 1955, to support "the other peoples in their efforts in attaining autonomy or independence, in order that they may reach a state of equality among the free nations of the world." [8]

In November 1957, Washington gave a clear example of that attitude by deciding to sell to Tunisia, where the Algerian insurgents had an important base, the light arms which they had tried in vain to buy from Paris. French public opinion was aroused, but it was the Americans' turn to protest when, a few months later, the French forces in Algeria, invoking a "right of retaliation" that no international convention had ever recognized, bombarded the Tunisian village of Sakhiet Sidi Youssef where N.L.F. artillery was positioned. America did not anticipate that a few years later, in Viet Nam, its air force would daily commit tens if not thousands of Sakhiets, without arousing its indignation.

Tunis, then Paris, appealed to the Security Council, but Washington, joined by London, persuaded them to accept their good offices. Bourguiba made the withdrawal of the French troops from Tunisia the condition for any settlement, and the Gaillard government, under strong pressure from Eisenhower, agreed in principle, on condition that it could keep the base at Bizerte. A courageous speech by the Prime Minister on the dangers of chauvinism did not save his cabinet, which, accused by the Gaullist Soustelle of taking orders from Washington, was overthrown by a large majority on April 15. The opponents were convinced that in the event that the United States succeeded in having its views prevail, it would not be long before it had set itself up as intermediary in the Algerian conflict. Had not Dulles said at a press conference on February 11 that even though this was "an internal French problem, juridical considerations would not stop him if an examination of that problem, in the framework of the Atlantic organization or of another organization, would bring about an amelioration of the situation"? [9] No wonder, under those conditions, that the putsch of May 13, 1958, in Algiers, had started with the sacking of the offices of the United States Information Service.

In the face of that quasi-overt pressure from the United States —comparable to that which it had exerted on the Netherlands and on Great Britain to make them give up their possessions in the Middle and Far East—the role of the Soviet Union seemed astonishingly cautious. Clearly fearing that the eviction of France from the Maghreb would result in the United States' moving into that strategic region, Russia was careful not to recognize the provisional Algerian government. After Guy Mollet's visit to Moscow in May 1956, Khrushchev had merely expressed the hope that "working in the liberal spirit that animates it, the French Government will know how to find the solution for this most important problem, which is appropriate to the spirit of our times and in the interest of the people." [10] On the return flight, Sergei Vinogradov, then Russian ambassador to Paris, was to tell me: "You have seen what we have done in Armenia. Why don't you attempt the same thing in Algeria?" In spite of the fact that the French Communist Party had been the only one, on December 9, 1954, the day following the insurrection, to dare demand "an Algerian republic with its own parliament," [11] it had not hesitated, on March 12, 1956, to vote for "special powers" for Guy Mollet's government, which had promised nothing more than recognition of the "Algerian personality." [12]

Furthermore, in the autumn of 1959, Khrushchev congratulated de Gaulle for having recognized the right of self-determination for the Algerian people. After the failure of the East-West summit in 1960, Gromyko denounced the war that France, supported by her NATO Allies, had been waging for more than six years against the Algerian people as "one of the most shameful manifestations of the policies of colonialism in our time," and compared the atrocities committed by the French troops in Algeria to those of the Nazis.[13] But the U.S.S.R. would wait for the Evian Accords, in 1962, to recognize the Algerian Government, and it was somewhat surprised by the reaction from the Elysée, when France, considering that Russia was thus prejudging the results of the referendum provided for by these accords, asked for the recall of ambassadors.

Thanks in great part to de Gaulle—who, after the tragedy of the war and the departure of the *pieds noirs,* had maintained close cooperation with Algeria—it had not been up to now a battlefield in the Cold War. The same thing can be said of the only other African nation whose emancipation resulted from a long armed struggle: Kenya. Its mild climate had induced a large English population to settle there after the Second World War. One would look in vain for any sizable trace of Communist influence in the Mau Mau revolt, begun in 1952, although its leader, Jomo Kenyatta, had lived in Moscow. Once he had finally obtained independence for his country in 1963, he revealed himself to be the most moderate of men, not hesitating to appeal for English troops to put down the mutiny of the Kenya Rifles.

The only test of strength which pitted the Americans and Russians against each other on the dark continent was played out in the Congo, which the Berlin treaty of 1885 had made a nominally independent state under the Belgian crown. But the Congo had been subjected to such brutal exploitation that Belgian public opinion had been aroused and a commission of inquiry was sent to the scene in 1905. The result had been that the pseudo-state had been transformed into a colony pure and simple, whose copper and uranium were largely responsible for saving Belgium, in the aftermath of its defeat by the Reich, from the lean years then experienced by France, Italy, Germany and England.

Firmly held in hand by a *force publique* which absorbed 17 percent of the country's budget, it had been exploited in a very businesslike way. The Congolese were, on the whole, well treated but systematically kept out of the posts of responsibility and practically deprived of all possibilities of gaining a higher education. It was only in the last few years of the Belgian presence that the Lovanium University was created for Africans. At the time of independence it had granted only about ten diplomas.

There existed in Belgium, as everywhere else, a segment of the population which recognized the need for fundamental changes. However, even after the triumphal trip of Belgium's King Baudouin through the Congo in 1955, during which he announced the first series of reforms, no one believed that it could be rapidly emancipated. The publication that same year of a plan by Professor Van Bilsen, providing for a delay of thirty years, provoked a storm of protest. Everything points to the fact that independence would not have been proclaimed in 1960 if the example of the neighboring French possessions had not stimulated the nationalists.

Guinea's refusal in 1958 to remain in the "French community" certainly played a decisive role. Immediately recognized by sixty capitals, the new republic was admitted to the U.N. in December 1958. France, the only one to vote against its admission, had to resign itself to recognizing its independence in January 1959 and signed treaties of mutual economic, monetary and cultural cooperation. Sékou Touré had already concluded economic agreements with Czechoslovakia and East Germany and, with Nkrumah, had published a joint declaration by the terms of which Guinea and Ghana, following the example of the thirteen rebellious American colonies in 1776, decided to form the "core of the West African United States," open to other states.[14] In May 1959, on the occasion of a visit by Nkrumah to Conakry, a "Union of African Independent States" was created, which Mali (the former French Sudan) would later join.

That "core"—whose very existence convinced the Africans that, contrary to what the colonists were constantly telling them, they were able to govern themselves—proved to be considerably attractive to the countries which had chosen to belong to the French community. At its head was the President of the Republic, whose authority embraced "foreign policy, defense, currency, economic and financial common policies, as well as policies relating to strategic raw materials," [15] such retention of these essential powers making most theoretical the recognition of equal rights for the community's members.

That paternalistic system obviously could not last very long. The French community ceased to exist before it had actually begun to function, and the constitution was modified in 1960 to permit its members to acquire international sovereignty.

As British Africa was also moving step by step toward independence, without too many difficulties, it is impossible to see by what miracle 14 million Congolese would have been satisfied to remain *ad vitam aeternam* the subjects of the King of the Belgians.

Nothing in the colonists' behavior indicated that they had the slightest intention of showing in their daily contacts with the Africans "the greatest mutual understanding" which had been urged on them by Baudouin during his 1955 trip.[16] They even openly sabotaged the modest reforms introduced by public officials aimed at achieving the official goal of partnership between the two races.

In December 1957 the results of the first municipal elections in the three principal cities should have served as a warning. Joseph Kasavubu, the future President of the Republic, was elected mayor of a suburb of Leopoldville, and he demanded "universal suffrage, general elections and internal autonomy." [17] At the end of 1958, while political parties were emerging—which, unfortunately, usually expressed only tribal rivalries—Congolese delegates took part in the Congress of African Peoples, in Accra. On January 4, 1959, the police having prohibited their holding a meeting to report on their trip, a riot erupted in Leopoldville which resulted in one hundred deaths. Kasavubu was arrested and his party was dissolved, but on the 13th, the King outlined a program for the Congo's gradual accession to independence.

A round-table conference opened in Brussels in 1960. The Congolese answered the Belgian proposals to shorten the steps by asking for immediate independence. To have denied it would probably have provoked an angry explosion in the colony and risked an endless wave of disturbances. Besides, the Belgians were not in any way inclined to support an Algerian-style war. Parliament adopted a law recognizing the independence of the Congo as of June 30, general elections to take place in the meantime to provide the new state with its own administration.

But the Congo was an immense territory, peopled with scattered and often hostile tribes and races, which had owed its unity only to the presence of the colonizers. It was believed that to preserve it, it would only be necessary to divide the powers of the President of the Republic and the President of the Council between the federalist Kasavubu, chief of the Abako Party and representing the ethnic Bakongo group, which was predominant in the capital and the surrounding country, and the unitarian Lumumba, whose Congolese National Movement, C.N.M., was the only one that sought to function in every part of the country. The maintenance of order would, as in the past, be in the hands of the *force publique*—25,000 carefully screened natives, none above the rank of warrant officer, under the command of white officers. Its commander, General Janssens, affirmed on July 5 that he was "absolutely sure of his men," to whom he blindly declared: "Independence is good for civilians. For the military, there is only discipline. Before June 30 you had white officers. After June 30 you will still have white officers . . . nothing is changed. . . ." [18]

This is not the way the Africans understood emancipation. As Lumumba had not hesitated to say on June 30, before Baudouin, who had come to assist at the independence ceremonies, emancipation had been "won through a day-by-day struggle . . . a struggle of tears, of fire and of blood . . . to put an end to the humiliating slavery that had been imposed on us by force." [19]

For the first time, in that land, a black had dared to say to a white, and a king at that, what was in his heart. The contrast between that statement and the exhortation of the commander of the *force publique* was too glaring. A few hours after the issuing of his order of the day, a group of soldiers met at Camp Leopold II, on the outskirts of the capital, demanded the dismissal of Janssens and the Africanization of the army, and seized the camp armory. At Thysville, 200 kilometers from Leopoldville, the garrison imprisoned its officers.

Lumumba went to Camp Leopold to order the soldiers to obey their officers, white or black; they threatened him and he had to flee hurriedly. The next day he announced Janssens' removal and the promotion to a higher rank of all the members of the *force publique*. President Kasavubu was named Commander in Chief, and First Sergeant Lundula, the uncle of the head of the government, was instantly promoted to lieutenant general. His chief of staff was Sergeant Mobutu, future dictator of the Congo.

But it was too late to correct the situation. The mutineers took to the streets, firing their rifles in the air, and occupied the government palace from which they had chased the white personnel. Panic seized the Europeans, among whom the most fantastic rumors spread, including one of the arrival of Russian planes to aid the "Communists." They fled by the thousands, Janssens at their head, abandoning all their possessions. The mutiny spread rapidly, the central government apparently having neither the experience nor the necessary means to deal with the situation.

Belgian public opinion was inflamed on hearing the greatly exaggerated reports by the refugees of the rapes and atrocities, alas undeniable, but which were far from being as extensive as could have been feared. On July 8 the Brussels Government dispatched paratroopers to the scene to guarantee the safety of its nationals. The Congolese interpreted this move as an attempt to jeopardize their independence. To further complicate matters, the president of the regional government of Elizabethville, Moise Tshombe, whose close relationship with the Union Minière had given him the nickname "Mr. Strongbox," proclaimed the independence of Katanga on July 11. Lumumba and Kasavubu wanted to go there to persuade him to give up his project, which would have deprived the Congo of its principal source of wealth and which would, in all probability, have condemned it to rapid dismemberment; but the control tower of the Elizabethville airport was in the hands of the Belgians who refused to give their plane, Belgian as well, it goes without saying, permission to land.

For Lumumba, this was proof of Brussels' treachery. In his rage he ordered his pilot to head for Moscow. It was with the greatest difficulty that he was made to understand that the plane was far too small to undertake such a flight. He told the Belgian general who welcomed him at the Leopoldville airport and who offered him an escort, "You are here illegally and we have no need of your protection." [20] He rushed toward Parliament, where he described the Belgians as "serpents" and announced that they had, by their actions, torn up the treaty of friendship and assistance which they had concluded with the Congo.

While order was quickly re-established in Katanga, to which the Belgian Government sent a permanent representative without having gone through the formal process of recognition, confusion reigned over the rest of the Congo, where the worst could now be feared.

One man, who was to lose his life there, had foreseen these developments: Dag Hammarskjöld. Receiving me in New York in April 1960, he had voiced his apprehensions over the sudden emancipation of a country which, in every respect, was so badly prepared for it. He had asked his first assistant, the American Negro Ralph Bunche, winner of the Nobel Peace Prize, to represent him at the independence ceremonies and to closely follow developments.

On July 11, Lumumba sent Bunche, who had remained there, an urgent request for U.N. military specialists to help in the reorganization of the Congolese armed forces; the next day, while the Prime Minister was away from the capital, his government asked the American ambassador for 3,000 soldiers "to help establish order in the Bas-Congo." [21] The United States decided that a unilateral intervention was contraindicated and they made this known to Hammarskjöld.

On July 13, Kasavubu and Lumumba denied having asked for American assistance; what they wanted, they said, was help from the small U.N. countries in expelling the Belgians. But the Brussels Government, far from recalling its troops, immediately dispatched three additional companies while supporting the request made to the United Nations by Leopoldville for military assistance.

The Security Council met during the evening, while Gromyko delivered notes to the Western governments protesting their "aggression" in the Congo and demanding an immediate halt to it,[22] but containing no threats. The Tunisian, Mongi Slim, acting with Hammarskjöld's approval, presented a resolution asking Belgium to recall its soldiers and authorizing the Secretary General to provide all necessary military assistance to the Congolese Government. This resolution was adopted unanimously, with three abstentions: Great Britain, Nationalist China and France. A little later, General de Gaulle would say that it would have been better for the United States, Great Britain and France to have "coordinated their policies," to encourage Belgians and Congolese "to establish their relationship under realistic and reasonable conditions and to guarantee the independence of the new state." [23]

The next day, Tshombe announced that he would not allow U.N. troops, which had started to arrive in the Congo, to enter Katanga, while Lumumba broke off diplomatic relations with Belgium and wrote Khrushchev that he might be "obliged to ask for the intervention of the Soviet Union unless the Western Powers halted their aggression." [24]

On the 15th he gave the Belgians twelve hours to get out of the country, and Khrushchev replied "What the U.S.S.R. asks is simple: 'Hands off the Congo!' . . . The Soviet Government will give the Congo Republic all necessary assistance for the triumph of your just cause." This prompted the State Department to deplore Mr. K's declaration as "excessive, misleading and irresponsible." [25]

However, on the 19th, Bunche got the Belgians to agree to evacuate Leopoldville before the 23rd. That was not enough for Lumumba, who announced on the 20th that he had decided to appeal for Russian troops or for those of any Afro-Asian nation, but that he would wait for the results of the Security Council's meeting before acting. At the same time he announced his intention of going to New York himself.

The Council was the scene of a verbal duel between Kuznetsov and Cabot Lodge. Kuznetsov declared that "in the event that the aggression continues, both the U.N. and the peace-loving countries which sympathize with the Congolese cause will face the question of the necessity to take more effective measures." Cabot Lodge accused the U.S.S.R. of "trying to bring the Cold War into the heart of Africa." [26] In spite of this exchange a resolution was unanimously passed which expressed confidence in Dag Hammarskjöld and asked the Belgians to hasten the withdrawal of their forces.

Lumumba said he was satisfied. Before his departure for New York he declared that "the reason which had led him to appeal to the Russians no longer existed" [27] and signed an agreement with an American businessman, Detwiler, which was to shower riches on the Congo. Unfortunately, Detwiler was only a dreamer or an adventurer, and the agreement would never even come close to being carried out. That brief episode was enough to upset Belgian financial circles and to make the unstable Lumumba once more consider cooperation with the West. Besides, he was received in Washington with all honors due to his rank, sleeping at Blair House.

Belgian public opinion was outraged, especially since Lumumba calmly denied that there had ever been the least violence against the whites in the Congo. *La Libre Belgique* certainly expressed a widely held sentiment when on July 27 it contrasted Lumumba—that "savage crook" wallowing "in the sheets used by the King of the Belgians, Charles de Gaulle and Khrushchev"—with the "millions of black Americans" who are "confined to the back of buses, behind the color line, under pretext that they smell."

There was good reason to think that this journey—Lumumba then visited Ottawa, Tunis and Rabat—had somewhat inflated his ego. Meanwhile, on August 5, he learned that Hammarskjöld, then in Leopoldville, had canceled the order, given to the U.N. soldiers on the 2nd, to enter Katanga on the 6th. Hammarskjöld explained his decision by the fact that Tshombe's government had expressed its intention to use force to oppose the execution of the Security Council's resolution, which had not authorized the "blue helmets" to use force.

During another meeting of the Council, on August 8 and 9, Kuznetsov sharply criticized the Secretary General and offered a resolution requesting him not to hesitate "to use any means for the immediate removal of the Belgian troops." [28] But he abandoned the request for a vote after the adoption of a resolution stating (1) that the international force must enter Katanga and (2) that it must not involve itself in any internal conflict, constitutional or otherwise.

Lumumba chose to see the vote of the Council as a "great victory" for the Congolese people. [29] But he would quickly change his tune. Hammarskjöld, who went to Elizabethville on August 12, stated that he had no intention of utilizing the U.N. forces to oblige Tshombe to accept the authority of the central government. Then the chief of the Balubas of South Kasai, Albert Kalondji, quietly proclaimed himself "emperor and king" of a "mining state," covering approximately one-third of that rich province. Finally, the Abako Party of the President of the Republic insistently urged that the Congo be turned into a confederation.

Lumumba, who felt that he was losing control of the situation, announced that "Those who confuse subversive maneuvers with freedom . . . will soon be judged by the people." [30] Asserting that he had "lost confidence in the Secretary General," he asked, on the 15th, that a group of Afro-Asian observers be sent to the Congo to assure the execution of the decisions of the Security Council.[31] On the same day he secretly wrote to Khrushchev, asking him to specify "the immediate aid that he could directly supply him with . . . in order to permit the government of the Republic of the Congo to assure the integrity of a dangerously threatened territory." [32]

On August 20, while various incidents occurred between the "blue helmets" and Congolese soldiers, the Kremlin issued a statement supporting all of Lumumba's positions and asserting that "if the aggressors do not leave the Congo and do not renounce their plans for its dismemberment, the peace-loving nations will be obliged to consider the necessity of taking other measures." [33] On the 21st the Security Council met without being able to agree on the text of a resolution. On the 26th, Lumumba's troops captured Bakwanga, capital of the mining state of Kasai and penetrated the north of Katanga. On September 2, the first of fifteen planes supplied by the U.S.S.R. landed in Leopoldville, with a large contingent of Soviet technicians.

But that help, which arrived too late to save Lumumba, was going to contribute to his downfall. In a country where most of the leaders were members of a church, the idea of appealing to Moscow was bound to provoke reactions made even stronger by the Prime Minister's attacks against the church and by the news that Lumumba's partisans had perpetrated a veritable massacre of the Balubas in Kasai. To which was added the fact that the disturbances had created an economic crisis throughout the whole country, with the exception of Katanga, which U.N. subsidies had been insufficient to alleviate. In Leopoldville the unemployed were legion, and those lucky enough to be working were unable to get their pay.

Several demonstrations revealed Lumumba's unpopularity in the capital. Kasavubu, who enjoyed the confidence of the Bakongo population, felt that the time had come to act. On September 5, having forewarned Van Bilsen, the Belgian adviser whom he always kept beside him, that he was going to "throw out the rabble," he went to the radio station and interrupted the broadcasts to announce that he had dissolved the government, "Lumumba's presence constituting a threat to national unity," that in his place he nominated the President of the Senate, Joseph Ileo, and that he demanded the U.N. guarantee the order and security of the country.[34] But Lumumba himself rushed to the radio station, where a contingent of U.N. soldiers, alerted by Kasavubu, vainly attempted to deny him access. He declared that the President of the Republic, having joined the imperialist plot, had lost all right to govern the state and that there remained only a people's government.

For eight days these two men, each claiming to represent a different yet equally nonexistent "authority," were to defy each other. On the 14th the Army Chief of Staff, Joseph Mobutu, took it upon himself to reconcile the President of the Republic and the two rival prime ministers by dismissing them. "I run a peaceful revolution," he said, "in order to give everyone time for reflection and calm." He gave the two politicians until December 31 to agree and announced that until then he would appeal to Congolese technicians and foreign specialists to save the country from chaos.[35]

No one expected such a sudden turn of events. Mobutu, a former sergeant in the militia and sometime newspaperman, had, prior to independence, represented Lumumba's Congolese National Movement in Brussels. He gave the impression of being a rather weak man and everyone knew that for a time he had served as an informer for the Belgian police. According to Andrew Tully it was the C.I.A. which had pulled him out of its sleeve at the opportune moment.[36] According to other testimony,[37] and in spite of the fact that at that time Rabat was openly flirting with Moscow, the principal ringleader of the operation was supposed to have been General Kettani, the commander of the Moroccan U.N. contingent and a former major in the French Army. In any case, it was he who had selected the 2,000 "paracommandos" whom Mobutu had made his praetorian guard and his principal Congolese instrument of power.

After a period of discouragement, Lumumba nevertheless attempted to turn the situation to his advantage. Besides, Ghana still continued to recognize no other authority but his. But the U.N. command decided to send home the Ghanaian "blue helmets" and Lumumba thus lost precious support. Furthermore, the Soviet and Czechoslovakian diplomats and advisers let themselves be expelled without resistance after Mobutu had denounced their interference in Congolese affairs.

In the fall of 1960, however, Mr K could still believe that the game was not completely lost. One of Lumumba's lieutenants, Antoine Gizenga, succeeded in seizing power in Stanleyville, capital of the Eastern Province, where, on November 23, he created a government which claimed to have the sole authority to represent the Congo and which received the support of the "progressive" states of Africa and of the Eastern countries. On January 2, 1961, another leftist leader, Kashamura, seized power in Kivu. The country was thus torn asunder, without any indication of who might be able to pull it out of anarchy. It faced the danger that the Russians and Americans would increasingly intervene in support of various protégés who lacked both experience and cadres and who were completely incapable of dealing with the problems confronting their unfortunate country.

§   §   §

Thousands of kilometers from the Congo, another new theater in the Cold War had just opened. Fidel Castro, master of Cuba since January 1, 1959, aligned himself with Moscow, which promised him its support, while the United States was more or less openly preparing the overthrow of his regime.

Cuba was not the first cause for alarm in that part of the world, where, long before the First World War, Marxist ideas had enjoyed a certain success under the influence of European political refugees. By 1922 there already were Communist parties in Mexico, Brazil, Argentina, Uruguay and Chile. Another was founded in Cuba in 1925 and still others, after the great convulsion of 1929, in several countries of Central and South America. They attacked the major American corporations as the principal champions of a vile social order and of a political system which too often culminated in ferocious struggles between little clans for the prize of a dictatorship conceived of essentially as a way to line the pockets.

This did not take into account the petty tyrants whose power depended entirely on the bounty of the United States and even, as was the case in Nicaragua until 1934, on the presence of U.S. marines.

Before the First World War, guerrillas had attempted to overthrow the established authority in several places, but the only violent action which claimed to be Communist was the promptly crushed putsch organized by a Brazilian officer, Luis Carlos Prestes, on his return from Moscow in 1935. The consequence of that rash action was the banning of the party and the sentencing of its leader to forty-six years in prison.

The United Front strategy decided upon by the Internationale in that same year, 1935, was going to produce better results. In 1938 the Popular Front candidate won the presidential election in Chile, and in 1946 three Communists held posts in the government. In 1940, during his first presidency, Sergeant Batista, who was later to become one of the bloodiest dictators in the Caribbean, gave portfolios to two Communists, one of whom, Carlos Rafael Rodriguez, was later to be in charge of agrarian reform under Fidel Castro.

Batista, defeated in the elections of 1944, bowed to the popular will. As for the Chilean Communists, in spite of their electoral success they soon had to leave the government; their party was outlawed in 1948. In Argentina the majority of the working classes had rallied behind the leftist fascism of Juan Perón. At the time of Stalin's death only five of the twenty Communist parties in Latin

America could function legally, and the U.S.S.R. maintained diplomatic relations only with Argentina, Uruguay and Mexico.

No one has ever been able to prove that Colonel Arbenz, who at thirty-seven was elected President of Guatemala in 1951, was himself a Communist, as Washington was to maintain. There were, however, Communists in his entourage, and, above all, he committed the crime of wanting to expropriate 200,000 acres of undeveloped land belonging to the American firm, the United Fruit Company, the world's leading banana trust, to effect a program of agrarian reform. United Fruit immediately unleashed a violent campaign against his government, which John Moors Cabot, Assistant Secretary of State for Inter-American affairs, accused in October 1953 of "openly playing the Communist game."[38] As a matter of fact, the attacks by United Fruit had provoked popular demonstrations, during which the far Left had won applause by harshly criticizing American intervention in Korea and the "dirty war" in Indochina.

It was about this time that a new ambassador, John E. Peurifoy, was appointed to Guatemala City. His service in Greece in 1947 had convinced him that one had to use the hard line in opposing the advance of communism. For a six-hour interview with Arbenz, during which he asked all sorts of questions on the political attitudes of some of his collaborators and the reasons for the trips they had taken behind the Iron Curtain, he brought back "the impression of a man who thought like a Communist, and talked like a Communist, and if not actually one, would do until one came along." In his report to Dulles he expressed the opinion that "unless the Communist influences in Guatemala were contracted, Guatemala would within six months fall completely under Communist control."[39]

From that moment on, Washington decided to seek ways to overthrow Arbenz. Miguel Ydigoras Fuentes, future President of Guatemala, personally recounted that at the beginning of 1954, when he was exiled in Salvador, he was visited by a former director of United Fruit and two men introduced as C.I.A. agents. They proposed to help him overthrow Arbenz and, in return, asked him to grant special privileges to United Fruit, to destroy the labor-union movement, and to reimburse "every cent that was invested in the undertaking."[40]

Fuentes having refused, the C.I.A. approached Colonel Castillo

Armas, who had fled Guatemala in 1950 after an abortive attempt at a *coup d'état*. Arbenz succeeded in intercepting correspondence between Armas and Fuentes which proved the existence of a plot and published it. He accused Nicaragua of allowing emigré commandos to train on its soil, which was completely true, but which the State Department chose to deride. American diplomacy then sought to persuade the other Latin American governments to give their blessing to an action destined to " 'protect their political independence against' such intervention," which the implanting of international communism in the hemisphere would represent.[41] Arbenz, sensing that time was getting short, looked for arms wherever he could find them. Soon the C.I.A. learned that a Swedish freighter had taken on 2,000 tons of light arms from Czechoslovakia, destined for Guatemala. Dulles revealed that fact during a press conference on May 17. A week later the United States sent the first shipment of 50 tons of weapons to Nicaragua by air.

On the 24th Ike announced that he had decided to prevent any further arms deliveries to Central America by stopping and inspecting suspect ships sailing under foreign flags. Finally, on June 18, Castillo Armas crossed the frontier of Guatemala, while Thunderbolts piloted by C.I.A. men neutralized the small government air force. This did not prevent Cabot Lodge from maintaining before the Security Council, which had been convened on Arbenz's request, that it was solely a matter of a "revolt of Guatemalans against Guatemalans." [42]

The protestations of the U.S.S.R. having remained ineffectual and the Security Council being satisfied to ask for an inquiry by the Council of the Organization of American States, Castillo Armas landed in Guatemala City on July 2, in Peurifoy's plane. Forty-eight hours earlier, Dulles had the audacity to declare on the radio, "Now the future of Guatemala lies with the Guatemalan people themselves." [43]

§   §   §

Arbenz fled to Czechoslovakia, and for the next five years communism would no longer be considered a serious problem in South America. When, on January 8, Fidel Castro Ruz made his triumphal entry into Havana, at the head of the guerrillas who had put the dictator Batista to flight after a two-year struggle, no one guessed that within a few months he would transform his country into an outpost of the socialist bloc. Indeed, in the program which he presented in April he declared: "Capitalism destroys man. The Communist state, in its totalitarian concept, sacrifices the rights of man. That's why we do not agree with either one or the other . . . This revolution is not red, but olive-green" (the color of the rebel army's uniforms).[44]

He appeared to all his partisans as a man who was going to restore liberty to his country and achieve the program of radical reforms which Batista had promised at the time of his 1952 *coup d'état,* and which he had turned away from little by little, thinking only of protecting—through terror and torture—the power which was slipping from his grasp.

As Claude Julien reported, returning from a Cuban trip, it was not an easy task to put back on its feet an economy which had been subjected to "pillage." [45] The courage and faith which animated Fidel and his companions was evidently insufficient to accomplish the task. Their intentions may have seemed no more than common sense: to achieve agrarian reform; to put an end to the disparity existing between the modern cities and the poverty of primitive villages; to industrialize the country so as to combat unemployment and give Cuba the means of achieving its independence; and finally, to pull it out of its total subjection to the United States. In reality, as Cuba's resources were almost entirely limited to sugar-cane production, its fate depended entirely on the quantity of sugar that the United States would buy from it and on the price it would pay—as it had been agreed upon that the price was that prevailing in the domestic American market and not in the world market. But it was inevitable that in attacking that policy, the new government would come into conflict with the all-powerful sugar interests in Washington, and, almost as inevitable, that those interests would also pressure Cuba to show more flexibility by threatening it with import cuts.

But economic blackmail is the one kind to which a proud people are least likely to submit. In Cuba's case there was also the fact that while Batista was in power, the United States had been very careful not to resort to those methods in order to make his regime change in a direction a little less contrary to the ideals of American democracy. Finally, national dignity had been quite rightly outraged by the behavior of American tourists. No one has described this better than Arthur M. Schlesinger, John Kennedy's adviser and the authorized chronicler of his Presidency. Mentioning a convention he had attended in 1950, he wrote "I was enchanted by Havana—and appalled by the way that lovely city was being debased into a giant casino and brothel for American businessmen over for a big weekend from Miami. My fellow countrymen reeled through the streets, picking up fourteen-year-old Cuban girls and tossing coins to make men scramble in the gutter. One wondered how any Cuban—on the basis of this evidence—could regard the United States with anything but hatred." [46] There is, in the life of each people, a moment when the need for dignity comes before that of bread; nine times out of ten that is what explains revolutions. The United States was soon to discover this to its sorrow.

From the start, the new regime's relations with Washington had turned sour. The American press had been outraged by the execution of two hundred of Batista's followers who had been denounced as "war criminals," and on January 14, Fidel Castro replied: "The assassins will be shot to the last man. . . . The United States should have been concerned about the executions which took place when the tyrant was in power—with its support. . . ." [47] That was enough for people to begin talking about the "Red peril."

In April Castro went to the United States to address the Association of Newspaper Publishers, in the hope, he said, that the American people "will better understand the people of Cuba," and that he himself "will better understand the people of the United States." [48] Before the press he appealed for increased private investment but only in industry, which until then had been rather neglected by Wall Street. In Central Park on April 24, in front of a huge crowd made up mostly of Latin Americans, he delivered this manifesto: "No bread without freedom, no freedom without bread . . . no dictatorship of one man, no dictatorship of one class . . . freedom with bread, without terror, that is humanism!" [49]

Such language only convinced a small minority of Americans.

Vice President Nixon, who received Castro, wrote in a memorandum that Castro was not a Communist but a "captive of the Communists," which, according to him, was even more dangerous. And Nixon advocated the training of commando groups of exiles to overthrow him.[50] Fidel himself, by forbidding his advisers to discuss economic and financial aid with Americans, did not make things any better. "We are not here to ask for money," [51] he had told the newspaper publishers, not wanting to put himself in the humiliating position of a beggar.

In reality, what he wanted was to move away from the framework of bilateral aid and to have the U.S. set up another Marshall Plan—this time for Latin America. He made this point crystal clear on May 2 in Buenos Aires, during the meeting of the Economic Council of twenty-one American republics. "Within ten years $30 billion will be needed for the full economic development of South America. . . . How can we get those funds? Under the form of public loans, since other methods face almost insurmountable difficulties, which is the procedure the United States has used in dealing with European and Middle Eastern countries." [52]

Ignoring exact figures, this was the idea which would be brought to life in the Alliance for Progress, launched two years later by Kennedy. But the Republican administration was incapable of envisioning such a bold enterprise. It saw, above all, despite the enthusiasm generated by Fidel's speech among many of his listeners, the little interest he himself had shown for talks with American diplomats, and, since the summer of 1959, the increasing role played in his regime by Communists who had, nonetheless, carefully avoided joining the armed opposition to Batista. At the end of the year, several of his close associates broke with Castro, who appointed to the head of the National Bank Ernesto Che Guevara, born in Argentina and one of the confirmed Marxists among his early companions. Hubert Matos, military commander of the province of Camagüey, who had opposed these changes, was condemned to twenty years in prison. On October 23, two civilian planes piloted by anti-Fidelists had bombed the capital and thus created an emotional climate which the authorities fully exploited.

On January 1, 1960, Mikoyan himself came to Havana to inaugurate a Soviet exposition and to sign a commercial treaty, according to which the U.S.S.R. agreed to buy one-fifth of Cuba's sugar production for five years and to lend Cuba $200 million at 2½ percent interest. Washington, completely involved in détente and in preparations for the summit meeting, was less alarmed than could have been expected. On February 20 the State Department stated that it was ready, as suggested by Castro, to begin discussions with him on the resolution of bilateral problems. On March 4 a French freighter loaded with Belgian arms exploded in the port of Havana. The next day, in a violent speech, Castro, without naming it, blamed the American Government.

On the 7th, Herter summoned the Cuban chargé d'affaires to ask him to retract the accusations made by Castro, whose behavior he qualified as irresponsible, adding: "More and more the United States finds itself obliged to question the Cuban Government's good faith when it expresses the desire to improve relations between the two countries." [53] On the 15th, on his return from South America, Ike secretly gave the C.I.A. the green light for the training and equipping of anti-Fidelists. A base with a landing strip for heavy planes was hastily built in Guatemala, while Cuban exiles were recruited in Miami.

The failure of the Paris summit could not fail to aggravate Cuban-American relations: Washington cut off economic aid; Khrushchev and Castro announced that they would exchange visits; Havana seized three refineries which had refused to process the crude oil bought from the U.S.S.R.; Ike lowered the ceiling on Cuban sugar imports by one-quarter, and Castro accused him of having committed "a blind, stupid act" designed to reduce the Cuban people to "hunger and ruin." [54]

On July 10, Khrushchev announced that he was ready to buy the 700,000 tons of sugar from Cuba that Washington no longer wanted. The day before, he had declared "figuratively speaking, [sic] in case of necessity Soviet artillery can support the Cuban people, with their rocket fire, if aggressive forces in the Pentagon dare to start an intervention against Cuba." [55] Immediate reply from Eisenhower: "The United States will not permit the installation in Cuba of a regime dominated by international communism." [56]

Kennedy, on the point of obtaining the nomination of the Democratic Party for the November Presidential election, declared that it was a question "of the first violation of the Monroe Doctrine in a century." [57] However, the future occupant of the White House knew enough history to know that that Doctrine was reciprocal, including the noninvolvement of the United States in Old World affairs. On the 12th, Khrushchev asserted that the said Doctrine had "died a natural death," and that it was proper that "the remains of this doctrine should be buried." [58]

A violent debate broke out in the Security Council. It did not prevent the escalation of measures and countermeasures, while inside Cuba the Catholic hierarchy showed concern with the progress of communism and defections among the Fidelist old guard multiplied. On August 7 all the large American enterprises were nationalized. The shareholders were advised that they would be compensated with state bonds payable in fifty years, but on condition that the United States restore its sugar quota to the 1959 level and pay a price close to the world rate. On August 28 the conference of foreign ministers of the O.A.S. gathered at San José in Costa Rica and—without explicitly mentioning Cuba, whose representative, Raul Roa, had delivered a violent indictment of the United States—unanimously condemned "any intervention or threat of intervention, even conditional, by overseas powers in the affairs of the American republics." [59]

Roa stormed out and returned to Cuba where, on September 2, before an enthusiastic crowd of 300,000 people, Fidel answered the San José declaration with the "Havana Declaration," in which "the National Assembly of the Cuban people is convinced that Latin America will soon go forward, united and victorious, freed of the ties which make of its economy a prey handed over to American imperialism." [60]

Then Fidel left for New York, on the same ship bringing Khrushchev to the U.N. He chose to stay in a hotel in Harlem, a fact which provoked easily imagined excitement. On the 26th, in battle dress, he occupied the General Assembly rostrum for four and a half hours after having, in his opening remarks, promised to be brief. On all issues he aligned himself with the position taken by the

U.S.S.R., whose disinterestedness he contrasted with the perfidious actions of American imperialism.

Soon, Washington decreed a general embargo on exports to Cuba, and Che Guevera toured the Eastern countries before concluding, in Moscow on December 19, an accord by which the U.S.S.R. promised to buy half of Cuba's sugar production. Anti-Fidelist Maquis were formed here and there on the island, while gradually a number of essential state posts passed into Communist hands. The press was filled with stories on the training of Cuban exiles as commandos. When, in November 1960, Kennedy was elected President of the United States, the test of strength appeared imminent.

§   §   §

As if it wasn't enough to have added a Cuban confrontation to the pressing problems of Berlin and the Congo which were waiting for the President in the White House, an untimely intervention of the C.I.A. in Laos had just reactivated another theater of the Cold, or better, lukewarm, War.

The 1954 armistice had provided that the two battalions of the Communist forces—the Pathet Lao—which occupied the two provinces adjoining Viet Nam would be integrated into the royal army. After interminable discussions on the methods of that integration, an accord had finally been reached. At the last minute the Pathet Lao demanded more than it had been promised. The royalist forces attempted to disarm its troops, which succeeded in escaping and were joined, a little later, by two hundred officers and soldiers from the regular army. Sporadic fighting took place, and the American press was filled with the most fanciful reports on the massive participation of North Viet Nam in operations which, however, never involved more than very limited forces. On December 31, amid general confusion, General Phoumi Nosavan took power in Vientiane, the capital, with the blessings and dollars of the C.I.A., thus establishing an openly pro-Western regime and organizing rigged elections in which his opponents had no chance.

On August 9, 1960, thanks to another *coup d'état*, a twenty-six-year-old captain, Kong-Le, seized Vientiane. He announced his intention to consolidate "the nation, religion, throne, and constitution" [61] and to maintain the neutrality of Laos, and he appealed to Prince Souvanna Phouma, the former Prime Minister and President of the National Assembly, to help him.

In a country so peace-loving that its soldiers were said to habitually shoot too high so as not to risk hitting the enemy, the team of Kong-Le–Souvanna Phouma seemed well chosen. Winthrop Brown, the United States ambassador, fully concurred in that opinion. But the C.I.A. believed that Kong-Le was a secret Communist and persuaded General Phoumi to reject his proposals of collaboration, which had the effect of pushing Souvanna Phouma further toward the arms of the Pathet Lao. On December 9, 1960, General Phoumi started a campaign against the neutralists, leading Souvanna Phouma to turn to the Russians. Only too happy to insinuate themselves into a country then the private property of the Americans and Chinese, the Russians organized an airlift in record time. It did not prevent Vientiane's fall on the 18th, but it did permit Kong-Le and the Pathet Lao, which he had joined, to seize several important areas, notably the crucial Plain of Jars. In order to conceal its difficulties, the government appointed by General Phoumi asserted, on December 31, that the country had been the object of aggression from "seven battalions of North Vietnamese troops." [62]

When, on January 19, 1961, Eisenhower briefed his successor on the Laos situation, he apologized for leaving him such a "mess." [63] The word could have applied to all the problems which the new President had to tackle as quickly as possible.

BIBLIOGRAPHY AND NOTES

[1] Keesing's, 17267 A.
[2] Le Monde, June 16, 1960.
[3] Alfred Grosser, La politique extérieure de la Ve République (Paris: Editions du Seuil, 1965), p. 69.
[4] Leopold Sedar Senghor, Négritude et Humanisme (Paris: Editions du Seuil, 1964), p. 125.
[5] Charles-Henri Favrod, La révolution algérienne (Paris: Librairie Plon, 1959), p. 144.
[6] Petit manuel de la Société des Nations, Geneva. Section d'information de la S. D. N., 1938, p. 36.

7 Charles-Henri Favrod, *Le Poids de l'Afrique* (Paris: Editions du Seuil, 1958), p. 407.

8 Henri Grimal, *La décolonisation* (Paris: Armand Colin, 1959), p. 175.

9 *Année, politique*, 1958, p. 313.

10 *Ibid.*, 1956, p. 304.

11 Jacques Fauvet, *Histoire du parti communiste français* (Paris: Fayard, 1965), II, p. 273.

12 *Ibid.*, p. 276.

13 *U.R.S.S.*, Bulletin of the Soviet Information Bureau in Paris, No. 2163, December 24, 1960.

14 Text of the declaration in B. Ameillon, *La Guinée, bilan d'une indépendance* (Paris: Maspero, 1964), p. 137.

15 *Année politique*, 1958, pp. 553–61.

16 Grimal, *op. cit.*, p. 316.

17 *Ibid.*, p. 317.

18 Marcel Niedergang, *Tempête sur le Congo* (Paris: Plon, 1960), p. 5.

19 Pierre de Vos, *Vie et mort de Lumumba* (Paris: Calmann-Lévy, 1961), p. 195.

20 *Ibid.*, p. 214.

21 Keesing's, 17639 A, 17641.

22 *Le Monde*, September 7, 1960.

23 De Vos, *op. cit.*, p. 220.

24 *Le Monde*, September 7, 1960.

25 *Ibid.*

26 *Ibid.*

27 *Ibid.*

28 Keesing's, 17753 A.

29 *Ibid.*, 17777 A.

30 *Ibid.*, 17760.

31 *Ibid.*, 17777 A.

32 *Est et Ouest*, December 16–31, 1960.

33 *Ibid.*

34 De Vos, *op. cit.*, p. 235

35 *Ibid.*, p. 239.

36 Tully, *op. cit.*, pp. 206–9.

37 De Vos, *op. cit.*, p. 239. Michel

Merlier, *Le Congo de la colonisation à l'Indépendance* (Paris: Maspero, 1962), p. 323.

38 Eisenhower, *Mandate for Change*, p. 422.

39 *Ibid.*, pp. 421–22.

40 Wise and Ross, *op. cit.*, p. 171.

41 Eisenhower, *op. cit.*, p. 423.

42 Wise and Ross, *op. cit.*, pp. 177–78.

43 Eisenhower, *op. cit.*, p. 427.

44 Marcel Niedergang, *Les vingt Amériques latines* (Paris: Plon, 1962), p. 553.

45 Claude Julien, *La révolution cubaine* (Paris: Julliard, 1961), p. 47.

46 Arthur M. Schlesinger, Jr., *A Thousand Days: Kennedy in the White House* (Boston: Houghton Mifflin, 1965), pp. 172–73.

47 Jacques Grignon-Dumoulin, *Fidel Castro parle* (Paris: Maspero, 1961), p. 76.

48 Julien, *op. cit.*, p. 108.

49 Grignon-Dumoulin, *op. cit.*, p. 89.

50 Theodore Draper, *Castro's Revolution: Myths and Realities* (New York: Praeger, 1962), p. 62.

51 Grignon-Dumoulin, *op. cit.*, p. 100.

52 *Ibid.*

53 *Ibid.*, p. 150.

54 Keesing's, 17538 A, 17542.

55 *Ibid.*, 17590.

56 Grignon-Dumoulin, *op. cit.*, p. 186.

57 *Ibid.*

58 Keesing's, 17590 A.

59 Grignon-Dumoulin, *op. cit.*, p. 199.

60 *Ibid.*, pp. 202–7.

61 Keesing's, 17719 A.

62 Bernard Fall, *Street Without Joy* (Harrisburg, Pa.: Stackpole, 1963), p. 329.

63 Wise and Ross, *op. cit.*, p. 170.

· CHAPTER 17 ·

THE COUNTER-

OFFENSIVE

For, although one may be very strong in armed
forces, yet in entering a province one has always need
of the good will of the natives.

—Machiavelli, *The Prince*, III

PROBABLY NEVER HAS A PRESIDENT OF THE UNITED
States been better prepared to conduct its international affairs than
the tall, slightly stooped young man who on the first Tuesday of
November 1960 was chosen by his countrymen to succeed Dwight
Eisenhower. That he had won by only less than 120,000 votes over
his Republican rival, Richard Nixon, out of a total of 69 million
votes cast, says a great deal for the electorate's ability to put aside
party loyalty or religious prejudice and give recognition to native
gifts and character.

In a society dominated by the pursuit of profits, it is not unusual
to find the most selfless idealism among the sons of well-to-do families
who, having no material cares, have been able to carry on extended
studies and to discover, by traveling throughout the world, the
stupidity of parochial thinking. But a sheltered childhood seldom
prepares a man for great deeds. If John Fitzgerald Kennedy was a
man of courage and decisiveness, it was not only because he had had
the opportunity to see at first hand, at the side of his father, ambassador to London in 1939, the perils faced by a country which had
gone soft. The war, in which he lost his elder brother, and personal
illness had brought him face to face with death more than once.

Reflection and experience had taught him that the true statesman must aim far less at being the interpreter of the popular will—too easily swayed by glibness if not by cowardice—than at leading his people, at showing them the way toward a more equitable and rational future, without allowing them to ignore the sacrifices of all kinds that it demands. That is what was represented by the slogan "New Frontier," on which he had been elected, and which summoned the American nation, like its pioneers of bygone days, to advance beyond the "frontier" of self-satisfaction and the materialistic euphoria in which it had merely existed under Eisenhower.

Before his election, Kennedy had described, in *The Strategy of Peace,* a small, meaty book filled with historical parallels, his conception of foreign policy, which of all subjects interested him the most. One sentence summarizes rather well the book's spirit: "It is time to stop reacting to our adversary's moves, and to start acting like the bold, hopeful, inventive people that we are born to be, ready to build and begin anew, ready to make a reality of man's oldest dream, peace." [1]

He was going to act often and in all areas at the same time, not without being mistaken and sometimes grossly mistaken. It is, however, difficult to deny that he greatly advanced the cause of peace, at least between the two superpowers whose confrontation had produced the Cold War which, once again, under his government, was going to threaten to degenerate into a world catastrophe.

The State of the Union message in which the new President presented his program to Congress on January 30, 1961, was written in Churchillian style. After having enumerated all the factors which, from Asia to Europe and from Africa to Latin America, brought the United States "each day nearer the hour of maximum danger," he continued by asking that the nation not be "lulled into believing" that the U.S.S.R. or China "has yielded its ambition for world domination." But he challenged the Soviet leaders "to demonstrate that beneficial relations are possible even with those with whom we most deeply disagree." And to that end he suggested renewal of negotiations on the cessation of nuclear tests, and Soviet-American collaboration for the exploration of space and in providing assistance to the third world. And he concluded, "There will be further setbacks before the tide is turned. But turn it we must." [2]

According to him the first condition for achieving a stable peace was to persuade the Communist countries that "aggression and subversion will not be profitable routes" to reach their ends.[3]

First, the prevention of aggression. To accomplish this, the President ordered a spectacular missile development program, which was going to show rapid progress. When he took power, the core of America's deterrent capability was still represented by the 2,000 bombers of the Strategic Air Command, whose death sentence would soon be pronounced by the rapid development of the Soviet surface-to-air missiles. Intermediate-range missiles based in England, Italy and Turkey were also doomed because of the vulnerability of their surface installations and the slowness of their firing. There remained about 30 land-based intercontinental missiles and two Polaris submarines capable of launching their sixteen missiles from the bottom of the sea against any Soviet city. In 1969 that arsenal comprises more than 1,000 intercontinental missiles buried in their concrete silos where they could be destroyed only by a direct hit, and about 40 submarines armed with Polaris missiles, which are to be replaced by multiple-warhead missiles, the Poseidons, even more difficult to intercept. No longer is any attack capable of destroying in one strike the American capacity for reprisal, and therefore the possibility of practicing atomic blackmail on the United States no longer exists. The total impunity now actually enjoyed by America, and from which it greatly benefited in Viet Nam, is, in large part, due to Kennedy and his Defense Secretary, the energetic McNamara, the champion of method and organization.

The fight against subversion, against the emergence in underdeveloped countries of armed revolutionary movements, was more difficult. As a good American liberal, Kennedy attributed their primary causes to poverty and ignorance, and he maintained that communism was only trying to turn inevitable revolutionary conditions to its own advantage. Hence he thought that the only means to contain them was to attack the causes themselves, through massive aid in a spirit of brotherhood. This led him, on January 30, to announce "a new and more effective program for assisting the economic, educational, and social development of other countries and continents." [4] If a struggle against the causes was not sufficient, however, he believed himself justified to fight, by every means possible, against the effects. Hadn't Khrushchev announced "unlimited support" to "the peoples fighting for their liberation," in a speech he gave on January 6, 1961, before officials of the Soviet Communist Party? Hadn't he defined peaceful coexistence as a "form of intensive struggle, economic as well as political and ideological, between the proletariat and the aggressive forces of imperialism," and unhesitatingly characterized as "just" only the so-called wars of liberation and not the world wars, or the regional wars which could lead to a world war? [5] The new Secretary of State, Dean Rusk, who had been Acheson's assistant during the Korean War, was to offer the following interpretation of Khrushchev's thought on December 30, in the same year: "Behind this concept [of the wars of liberation] is the notion that the safest way to extend Communist power and influence is to exploit the inevitable turbulence which accompanies the revolutionary movement towards modernization. . . . This method, from the Communist point of view, is designed to bypass American nuclear strength and bypass the conventional strength that we have helped to build with our allies, and to tear down institutions not under their own control." [6] The economist Walt Rostow—author of a non-Communist manifesto in which he had set against the classical concept of Marxism-Leninism a brilliant theory of development by stages—was to specify on May 21, 1962, with his authority as special consultant to the White House and later as head of the planning board of the State Department: "The entire government under the direction of the President has addressed itself with extraordinary energy to the problem of learning how to prevent or confront the techniques of subversion and guerrilla warfare on which the international Communist movement places so much hope for the sixties. The most brilliant minds of the government, civilian as well as military, are now attacking that problem which for a long time received only relatively low priority." [7]

During the first weeks of his Presidency, Kennedy revealed his determination to put into effect this dual plan of economic aid and, if it came too late or was not sufficient, of direct political and, if need be, military intervention.

Latin America—in which Khrushchev, in his speech of January 6, 1961, had been pleased to discern "the opening of a new front against United States imperialism" [8]—was his first concern. On March 15, Kennedy assembled the ambassadors of all the countries in that part of the world, and said: "I have called on all people of the hemisphere to join in a new Alliance for Progress . . . a vast cooperative effort, . . . to satisfy the basic needs of the American people for homes, work and land, health and schools—*techo, trabajo y tierra, salud y escuela.*" [9] The following day he announced he would ask Congress to vote an appropriation of $500 million and advocated the preparation of a ten-year plan for Latin America, as well as the encouragement of various projects aiming at the economic integration of the continent.

The new language—"We have not heard such words since Franklin Roosevelt," [10] said the Venezuelan ambassador—helped to create an extraordinary feeling of optimism around the young President. Enthusiasm and faith had entered the White House and the State Department, where conformity and disenchantment had reigned for too long. "The future of the hemisphere did seem bright with hope," [11] wrote Arthur Schlesinger.

However, reality was less bright. Although all the other Latin American governments supported J.F.K.—with the exception of Brazil, where the recently elected leftist President, Janio Quadros, only succeeded in "agreeing" with Adolf Berle, the representative of the State Department, "on their disagreement," [12]—relations with Cuba were deteriorating. A few days before leaving office, Eisenhower had decided to break off diplomatic relations. The new President, who had canceled all purchases of sugar from Havana, had declared in his State of the Union message that "Communist domination in this hemisphere can never be negotiated." [13]

The C.I.A. was actively preparing an operation designed to overthrow Castro's regime and Kennedy, briefed on it at the end of November, did nothing to prevent it. In spite of strong opposition from the Under Secretary of State, Chester Bowles, from Schlesinger and from Senator Fulbright, the chairman of the Foreign Relations Committee, certain arguments influenced his final decision in favor of an invasion. "Are you going to tell this group of fine young men," Allen Dulles, the chief of the C.I.A., told him, "who asked nothing better than the opportunity to restore a free government in their country . . . ready to risk their lives . . . that they would get no sympathy, no support, no aid from the United States?" [14]

It had also been pointed out to him that it was necessary to act without delay, as the imminent return to Cuba of pilots trained in the Soviet Union to fly the Migs which it had supplied was going to be a major factor in quickly reinforcing the island's defensive potential. Finally, on April 14 a marine colonel who had just come from inspecting the brigade of 1,400 Cuban exiles assembled in Guatemala sent an enthusiastic report: "They say they know their own people and believe that after they have inflicted one serious defeat upon the opposition forces, the latter will melt away from Castro . . . they have supreme confidence they will win . . . I share their confidence." [15] That message, which reached Kennedy a few hours before the expected start of the operation, resolved any lingering doubts. But, as he had publicly committed himself to do during the press conference of the 12th, he gave the order that under no circumstances were American forces to take part in the action.

Therefore, on Saturday the 15th, eight B-26 bombers left Nicaragua with Cuban crews and attacked the island's three major airports. The arrival of two of them in Miami immediately provoked questions, which Adlai Stevenson, the former Democratic candidate for President whom Kennedy had appointed United States representative to the United Nations, answered in all good faith by saying that they were deserters.

The next day the curiosity of the American journalists, which had long been aroused by the concentration of exiles in Guatemala, made short work of that story. An outraged Stevenson persuaded Dean Rusk, in order to avoid international complications, to suggest to Kennedy a halt to raids originating in Nicaragua. The President, after much hesitancy, decided to give an order to that effect. According to Arthur Schlesinger, he was visibly "worried" and asked himself "what would go wrong next." [16]

General Cabell, in charge of the operation, personally tried to persuade Rusk to get the President to reconsider his decision. The first attack against the Cuban bases had, in fact, only destroyed five of Castro's planes. But the Secretary of State would not discuss it with him. In the end, eight planes of the invasion force were shot down at dawn on April 17, the very moment when the brigade of exiles was establishing a beachhead in the Bay of Pigs. At 9 o'clock that morning the ship *Houston,* in which the invaders had made the crossing, received a direct hit and went aground on a reef, thus depriving them of all their supplies.

When the White House decided to authorize another bombardment, which in any case was rendered difficult by poor weather conditions, it was too late. The operation had failed and the boastful proclamations of the Cuban Revolutionary Council, according to which "Before dawn Cuban patriots in the cities and hills began the battle to liberate our homeland," [17] could not alter the fact. In three days the Fidelists would kill two or three hundred of their adversaries and would take 1,113 prisoners, who much later, and after protracted negotiations, would be exchanged for medical supplies and tractors.

Kennedy could have tried to rectify the situation by directly committing the United States to the hostilities, as the Chiefs of Staff urged him to do, but without hesitation he refused. This is not what he had wanted, and he thought that his country would gain nothing on a moral level by forcibly imposing a puppet regime on Cuba. Although he was furious with the C.I.A., which had dragged him into the mess, he courageously assumed the whole burden of the enormous fiasco. It was a rude awakening for a promising Presidency. "Victory has a hundred fathers and defeat is an orphan," he was going to say later. "I am the responsible officer of the government. . . ." [18]

On an international level the affair was to have disastrous effects. In the General Assembly of the U.N., which was in session, the Cuban Foreign Minister, Raul Roa, had no difficulty in embarrassing the unfortunate Stevenson, who had become entangled in his own lies. The support of the Latin American bloc and the NATO countries was the only thing that saved the United States from a major condemnation. On the 18th, Khrushchev sent a message to Kennedy, asserting that the U.S.S.R. would "render the Cuban people and their Government all necessary assistance in beating back the armed attack on Cuba." [19] The President replied rather curtly that the United States had no intention of intervening militarily in Cuba, but it would not accept any military intervention by an outside power and that if "what the Soviet Government did at home concerned only it, what it did abroad concerned the entire world. In the history of humanity," he concluded, "the great revolution is the revolution of those who are determined to be free." [20] The failure of the operation quickly put an end to this exchange of amenities, but from every corner of the third world messages of sympathy came to Fidel Castro, whose prestige had never been higher.

§   §   §

Kennedy was to be luckier in the Congo. A few weeks after he came into office the situation had shown a dramatic turnabout, with the assassination, announced on February 14, 1961, of the unfortunate Patrice Lumumba, who had not deserved such an ignominious death. Arrested as he was attempting to rejoin, at Stanleyville, his lieutenant, Gizenga—who had set up in his name a government which was thus recognized by the socialist countries and the progressive African states—he had been turned over to Tshombe by Mobutu, whose scruples later would not prevent him from dedicating a statue to Lumumba. Tortured in the plane by his guards, Lumumba was shot almost as soon as he arrived in Katanga during an alleged attempt to escape.

In an exceptionally violent statement the U.S.S.R. declared that this murder was "the crowning achievement of Hammarskjöld's criminal activities" and it demanded his immediate removal. It asked for the condemnation of Belgium, the arrest of Tshombe and Mobutu by the U.N. troops and the subsequent withdrawal of the latter within one month. Finally, it characterized as "a sacred duty for all the freedom-loving states" the granting to "the legal government of the Congo"—that is to say, in its view, Gizenga's government—that help he had requested "from all countries." [21] However, in the end that language found only a weak echo in the U.N., and the Soviet delegate did not dare to veto an infinitely more moderate resolution passed by the Security Council.

An attack by Gizenga's troops on North Katanga having failed, diplomacy returned to the scene. In the middle of the year, and after many trials, the U.N. succeeded in having the Central Parliament convene. It designated a government in which Gizenga was given the vice presidency of the Council. Negotiations were started with Tshombe, who was, for the moment, the prisoner of Mobutu's troops. To gain his freedom he signed whatever they asked him to sign, but as soon as he was safe, he reneged on all his commitments.

Gizenga ordered the head of the new government, Cyrille Adoula, to crush the secession, but the Congolese Army comprised only a few thousand men, and was incapable of successfully opposing the Katangese gendarmerie, trained and led by well-disciplined white mercenaries. Adoula had no other recourse but to appeal to the U.N., France, Belgium and England vainly opposing it. In September, Hammarskjöld decided, in order to implement several resolutions of the General Assembly, to send the "blue helmets" into Elizabethville.

The operation failed lamentably. The Secretary General of the United Nations, deeply affected by the Congolese tragedy, was in the process of losing both his composure and his awareness of the limitations of his office. On September 17, the day before the opening of the annual session of the Assembly and while on his way to Rhodesia to negotiate a cease-fire, he met his death in an airplane accident, even now not clearly explained. His successor, the Burmese U Thant, appointed after weeks of arduous negotiations between Americans and Russians, was to personally take charge of the affair in December, still with the support of Washington, which supplied the U.N. force with the dollars without which they would have been immobilized. In the meantime, Stevenson had not been able to prevent the vote by the Security Council on a motion which ordered the "blue helmets" to subdue Katanga's separatism, while ignoring the quasi-rebellion of Gizenga, who had once again established himself in Stanleyville.

In mid-December, Tshombe wrote Kennedy asking him to set up a meeting with Adoula. This took place in Kitona, a former Belgian base, with the very active participation of the American ambassador, Edmund Gullion. An agreement was signed by which the Katangese leader recognized the authority of the central government. But as soon as he got home, he repeated the performance of the preceding summer and reneged. The United States continued to bring pressure on him. After having seemed to accept "with enthusiasm" [22] a plan worked out by U Thant and supported by Washington, London, Brussels, Bonn and Rome, which provided for the transformation of the Congo into a federation of which Katanga would become one of the members, he rejected it as he had the others. Then he prepared to fight, reinforcing his army, buying planes abroad and brushing aside all the counsels of prudence showered on him by Kennedy's envoy, McGhee. On Christmas Eve, incidents broke out between the U.N. troops stationed in Elizabethville and the Katangese gendarmerie. But, in the beginning of January 1963, Tshombe abruptly gave up the game.

Arthur Schlesinger wrote that Kennedy had decided to lend American planes if necessary to the U.N. forces.[23] The United States followed up that success by granting massive aid in money, military equipment and Cuban exile pilots to the Congolese Central Government, which Tshombe himself, through a strange twist of events, briefly headed. Gizenga's government gradually crumbled, as did the progressivist guerrillas dispersed to the four corners of that vast country, and whose leaders did not have at their disposal either the organization or the outside support needed to overcome Mobutu's army, reinforced by thousands of white mercenaries. In September 1964, Belgians and Americans would not hesitate to intervene directly at Stanleyville to free whites taken as hostages by the rebels. That action sounded the death knell of organized revolt.

§   §   §

The "mess," in his own word, that President Eisenhower had left in Laos demanded equally urgent decisions from John Kennedy. Disagreeing with the C.I.A., the results of whose unfortunate interventions in that peaceful kingdom we have already seen, he did not think that Laos "deserved the attention of the great powers." [24] In his judgment, which was shared by Paris and London, the wisest course was not to make it move toward the West, which would inevitably bring about a reaction from the Eastern countries, but to neutralize it. That is the substance of what he stated during his first press conference after taking office. The proposal made by the

U.S.S.R. in December to reconvene the Geneva Conference on Indo-china, of which it was co-chairman with Great Britain, could provide a perfect framework for negotiations along that line.

A fruitless offensive by the pro-Western troops of General Phoumi at the beginning of February served to convince the President that Washington had been wrong to back him. But he had to overcome a great deal of resistance to win over the State Department to Prince Souvanna Phouma, the neutralist, a Paris favorite whom Washington persisted in considering a crypto-Communist. Neither Phoumi nor the Communist Pathet Lao, each believing itself able to completely eliminate the other, showed much cooperation. In the middle of March an attempt at conciliation between the three Laotian factions aborted while the Pathet Lao forces, although much fewer in number, won a series of victories, threatening Vientiane and Luang Prabang, the country's two major cities.

The situation seemed so serious and Soviet aid had so increased that the National Security Council of the United States was convened to study the possibility of a limited intervention; but it was strongly opposed by the Chiefs of Staff, who, because of the doctrine of "massive reprisal" favored under Eisenhower and Dulles, could only dispose of a very small number of fighting units which they feared they might very soon need in Berlin. Finally it was decided to get tough, to try to persuade the Russians that a choice had to be made between an escalation of the conflict and neutralization of the country. At a press conference on February 23, J.F.K. announced that he agreed with Great Britain's reply to the Soviet proposal for another meeting of the 1954 Geneva Conference on Indochina, on condition that there be a preliminary cease-fire, as he feared that the Communists might use their military advantage to control the negotiations. "The United States," he said, ". . . strongly and unreservedly supports the goal of a neutral and independent Laos." But, he added, if "the present armed attacks by externally supported" Communists did not stop, the members of SEATO would "have to consider their response." [25] At the same time, obvious military precautions were taken in Southeast Asia.

Kennedy himself received Gromyko, who was in New York for the U.N. session, and warned him against "miscalculation," his favorite term. He wrote to de Gaulle, who counseled him against any military engagement in China, but he obtained only lukewarm support from Macmillan. In contrast, the other SEATO members praised him.

On March 27, *Pravda* wrote that "any use of force by SEATO would bring about retaliation." But on April 1 the Kremlin accepted the London proposal for a joint appeal for a cease-fire and the convocation of an international conference. Finally, hostilities ended at the beginning of May, and on the 16th a conference including the five Great Powers, the three members of the international control commission (India, Canada, Poland), the countries adjoining Laos and the three political factions of the kingdom met in Geneva. But the conference quickly bogged down in a controversy over the verification of the cease-fire. And it was only on July 22, 1962, that the treaty neutralizing Laos, under the authority of a government made up of representatives from the three parties, was concluded.

§　　§　　§

In order to implement the treaty, it would have been necessary for the civil war in neighboring Viet Nam to have stopped, and for the northeast provinces controlled by the Pathet Lao not to be utilized for communications between the guerrillas in South Viet Nam and the North Vietnamese Government; in other words, that Kennedy attempt to extend the Laotian settlement to Viet Nam instead of being drawn into a policy of intervention whose illusory character he had so clearly recognized when France pursued it eight years earlier.

"I am frankly of the belief," he had said on April 6, 1954, from the rostrum of the Senate, "that no amount of American military assistance in Indochina can conquer . . . 'an enemy of the people' which has the sympathy and the hidden support of the people." [26] Better still, the following was his common-sense reply to his unlucky rival, Richard Nixon, who in the spring of 1961 advocated intervention by the American Air Force: "I just don't think we ought to get involved in Laos, particularly where we might find ourselves fighting millions of Chinese troops in the jungles. In any event, I don't see how we can make any move in Laos, which is 5,000 miles away, if we don't make a move in Cuba, which is only 90 miles away." [27]

In fact, Kennedy had inherited in Viet Nam, as he had in many other places, a situation which it was not in his power to magically remedy. The 1954 accords, which had put an end to the Indochinese War, contained in their "final declaration" an Article 7 according to which "general free elections by secret ballot" [28] would take place two years later for the purpose of reunifying the country, under the control of an international commission, and under conditions which were not otherwise specified. But the Saigon Government, headed since mid-June by the Catholic Ngo Dinh Diem, had officially protested the accords, adding at the outset that they did not obligate it in any way. As for the United States, it had been satisfied to promise that it would use neither force nor threats in order to modify them.

Naturally, the legitimacy of the commitment made by the French high command concerning the elections could be contested, as it had to do with a political clause which undeniably exceeded its authority and, besides, was opposed by the government of a country whose complete independence had just been recognized. But it must be conceded, as well, that the promise was the *sine qua non* condition of the accords, that without their ratification the French troops would have found themselves in a critical situation, and that Diem, therefore, would have been incapable of exercising an authority which, without their bayonets, would have crumbled within an hour.

The juridical basis of Diem's "power" was itself most questionable. It had been practically imposed by Foster Dulles—following the advice of the American Colonel Lansdale, the great authority on the Philippine guerrilla war—on the former Emperor, Bao Dai, who had again become chief of state only through France's favor and who was so unsure of his subjects' loyalty that he spent most of his time in Cannes.

At the time of the signing of the Geneva Accords, the United States had only one goal in Viet Nam: to consolidate the South Vietnamese regime at all costs, to prevent it from falling within the Communist orbit, and to begin to put it in a position to resist an eventual aggression from the North. In fact it was doubted in Washington that the Viet Minh would accept free elections under international control. Hadn't the Communist governments of East Germany and North Korea both refused to have recourse to free elections in order to permit reunification of their fatherlands? Didn't the arrival in the south of close to a million Annamites and Tonkinese—fleeing a collectivist regime, as they were allowed to do by the accords—demonstrate that Hanoi was far from being able to pretend that it spoke in the name of the whole population?

It was in that perspective that the Americans had insisted, along with their allies in SEATO, on including South Viet Nam, Laos and Cambodia in a protective zone. This had immediately provoked protests from the Communist members of the Geneva Conference. Didn't the accord on the cessation of hostilities in Viet Nam state that it could not "belong to any military alliance?" [29]

The United States also wanted to strengthen Diem's internal position as well as the army at his disposal. But in that area it met a major obstacle. Articles 16 and 17 of the accords prohibited "the importation into Indochina of new military aid." [30] As Dulles himself was to admit, "the U.S.A. can't increase the number of its military advisers"—a total of 225 officers and 60 soldiers at the time of the armistice—and this, he added, "places a strong dependence on France." [31]

At the time, two tendencies were apparent in the policy to be followed in Viet Nam by the Mendès-France government. First, it veered toward a policy of balance between north and south, illustrated by dispatching to Hanoi a general delegate, Jean Sainteny, who in 1945 had negotiated with Ho Chi Minh. The advocates of that policy were certain that the Viet Minh would win the election and that therefore France had an interest in protecting its future by being actively represented in the north. But General Ely, France's High Commissioner in Saigon, was categorically opposed to that initiative, thinking that it would have the effect of demoralizing the anti-Communist elements in the south. He obtained from Mendès-France the pledge that the Sainteny mission would be devoid of all political character and in an interview on August 31, 1954, he set forth the principles of a policy of "complete support" of the Vietnamese national government, in other words, the government of the south, to put it in a position to win the anticipated elections of 1956. This, in his judgment, required that "the elections be free and that in particular they not be altered by any Viet Minh subversive action" south of the demarcation line, and that "the Vietnamese Government be in a position to exploit the considerable advantages of a free regime and of the aid of the free world which is bound to increase general prosperity." [32]

At first sight such a policy should have been able to fully satisfy the Americans, especially since Paris made repeated gestures to demonstrate the reality of Vietnamese independence. But Congress, dominated by a spirit of anticolonialism and suspicion toward France, urged the administration to deal directly with Saigon. On August 17, Eisenhower gave the order that "aid to Indochina henceforth be given directly to the Associated States rather than through France." [33]

Diem's authoritarian temperament was to complicate matters further. Like the American ambassador, Heath, Ely thought that the only way to consolidate the South Vietnamese regime was to broaden the base of its government by bringing into it especially the representatives of the large "sects," the feudal religious groups, or illegal trading associations which controlled the largest part of the country. But the Prime Minister did not intend to share his power with anyone. Very quickly he got into conflict with the army—exiling its Commander in Chief, General Hinh, Bao Dai's henchman—then with the sects, and especially with the Binh Xuyen, which controlled the police and all the shady commerce in Saigon and was also faithful to the former Emperor. Bao Dai, sensing danger, tried to replace Diem with the Binh Xuyen chief, "General" Le Van Vien, who liked to receive his visitors with a python wrapped around his neck. Washington, in the name of outraged virtue, threw all its weight on the balance scales. Without notifying Paris, Eisenhower wrote a beautiful letter to Diem on October 27, assuring him of his complete support on condition that he begin a policy of economic and social development and also replace Heath by General Lawton Collins, who, however, was quick to adopt the French concepts.

At that time the Mendès-France government was not in a position to give priority to Indochinese affairs. Its last weeks in power were spent in a crossfire from the Left, furious over Germany's rearmament; the "Europeans," who didn't forgive him for the burial of the European Defense Community; and the Right, which accused him of wanting to sell off Africa after he had sold off the Middle East. Public opinion did not understand why a powerful expeditionary corps was stubbornly kept in Viet Nam, when the situation in Morocco and Algeria was becoming more and more critical. Therefore Mendès-France sought formulas of conciliation designed to protect what seemed to him to be essential, namely the maintenance of the very important French economic interests in Saigon.

On December 13, Ely was authorized to conclude with Collins a secret accord, which transferred to the chief of the American military mission, under the nominal authority of the French command, responsibility for the aid to be given to Saigon for the organization and training of its army, with the participation of American military personnel. In June 1955, Paris agreed to transfer to Diem the broadcasting station and the control of American aid, and then, in February, the command of the army.

In the beginning of March the sects formed a united front with various nationalist parties which, on the 21st, appealed to the President of the Council, asking him to create a coalition cabinet within five days. He replied by sending armored cars against the Binh Xuyen. Ely and Collins succeeded in negotiating a truce but Lansdale alerted Washington, which disavowed its ambassador, and on April 28 Diem began an attack against the sect, which was promptly crushed. With the candid dualism which characterized so many of his compatriots, Senator Mansfield declared: "The struggle now taking place is a test of strength between two elements, one personified by Mr. Diem, who represents an honest and sincere government, the other resting on those who mock integrity and sincerity or ignore what they mean." [34]

Bao Dai summoned the head of the government to Cannes. Diem replied that he was too busy and had him removed on April 30 by a "general assembly of revolutionary forces" whose legitimacy was somewhat doubtful. It was in vain that Edgar Faure, then Prime

Minister, pleaded with Dulles, who had gone to Paris a few days later, for the need of reaching a compromise with the sects. Although on April 29, Faure had said of his Vietnamese counterpart that his government was "not adapted to its mission," on May 13 he stated that complete agreement had been reached on support for Diem, adding, however, that he would like to see his government made more representative. He announced that, although no official request had been made to him along that line, the French expeditionary corps would be gradually repatriated.[35]

Those statements did not pacify Diem in any way. Anti-French incidents increased and on May 20, Ely asked to be recalled— officially for reasons of health. Negotiations begun in the month of August for the conclusion of a military and cultural accord were broken off in September by the South Vietnamese, who had demanded, among other things, that the expeditionary corps be placed under their command. Soon Viet Nam left the franc zone to enter the dollar zone, and on April 28, 1956, the last French soldier left the country. On February 23, Pineau, now Foreign Minister, had openly denounced before the Council of the Republic "the mistake made by the United States in trying to eliminate France." [36]

In October 1955 a referendum on his regime and Bao Dai's removal was initiated by Diem and gave him 98.2 percent of the votes—a majority obviously too large to be convincing. In March 1956, elections supposedly "free," but in which Communist candidates could not participate, created a National Assembly in which Diem's supporters had an absolute majority. The chief of the government added to his title those of Chief of State and Commander in Chief of the Army. He replaced elected municipal officials with functionaries faithful to him.

From that time on, by hunting down Communists and alleged Communists, he showed what little respect he had for the Geneva Accords, which prohibited all reprisals against combatants and all discrimination. In the first year following the armistice, the international control commission identified in its fourth report "390 incidents leading to loss of human lives," without being able "to specify that, outside of the incidents mentioned, there had not been other reprisals or acts of discrimination." [37] Soon, Saigon would simply refuse demands for inquiries by the commission, whose headquarters were sacked during a demonstration of a very dubious spontaneity. On January 11, 1956, an ordinance permitted the imprisonment of any person "dangerous to national defense and public order." [83] On February 19 another ordinance called for fines or imprisonment for anyone who "propagates, publishes, disseminates, or repeats in any way news or commentaries favorable to Communist or antinationalist activities." [39]

Under those conditions it was not surprising that Diem also refused to implement the clause relative to general elections in the final Geneva declaration. According to the terms of the accords, negotiations were to begin on July 20, 1955, between the two Vietnamese governments on the modalities of their organization. On June 6 and then on July 19, Hanoi asked Saigon to choose its representatives and a meeting place "acceptable to both parties." [40]

Paris and London succeeded in persuading Washington to join them in a move requesting Saigon to reply to the north's overtures. On August 9, Diem, after having recalled that his government had not signed the Geneva Accords, declared that although he "considered the principle of free elections as a peaceful and democratic institution—yet the conditions of freedom of life and of suffrage must be fulfilled beforehand. Nothing constructive in this area will be done," he continued, "as long as the Communist regime will not permit each Vietnamese citizen to enjoy democratic freedoms." [41] Dulles quickly agreed with him and joined him in "noting that conditions existing in North Viet Nam were not then propitious for elections in the whole of Viet Nam." [42] Under those circumstances the French Government bore a serious responsibility in withdrawing its expeditionary corps a few weeks before the election date specified by the Geneva Accords: that is what Pham Van Dong, head of the Hanoi Government, wrote to Pineau on April 12, 1956. But it would take more than a letter for the consultation to take place, and the deadline for the July meeting came and went without the least attempt being made in that direction.

Western chancelleries were briefly concerned about possible reactions from Moscow, Peking and Hanoi, which in the end were extremely weak. Didn't the U.S.S.R. and Great Britain, as early as April 1956, jointly admit that the holding of elections was less important than the maintenance of peace? Even the Kremlin would propose, at the beginning of 1957, the simultaneous admission of the two Viet Nams to the U.N., as if it had finally accepted the permament division of the country.

The passivity of the Communists was attributed to the desire of the Kremlin, then in crisis over destalinization, not to create international tension and to the relative prosperity enjoyed by South Viet Nam. After fifteen years of war, North Viet Nam was only recuperating very slowly. The food situation was very difficult. The agrarian reforms had been carried out with such brutality that in September 1956, they provoked a peasant uprising in that same Nghe An region where, twenty-six years earlier, the first Indochinese soviets had been proclaimed. Giap had to recognize in a ringing speech that "grave" and "widespread" errors had been made.[43] In a secret and free vote, unexpected results might have come out of the ballot boxes. In any case the Suez crisis and then the Hungarian Revolution were to promptly divert attention from what was happening in Indochina.

In March, and again in December, 1958, the North Vietnamese Government proposed to the South Vietnamese Government that, in the absence of reunification, the relations between the two zones be established. Through Diem's will they had remained completely nonexistent to the point where it was impossible to send a letter from one zone to the other. Saigon did not even reply.

At that time large numbers of the Viet Minh's former combatants had stayed in the south, where they had buried large quantities of arms at the time of the armistice. They had begun to use the same methods which had permitted their control of the north: systematic recruitment among the population, physical elimination of village chiefs appointed by the Saigon authorities and generally very unpopular with the people of their districts, and containing extension of guerrilla activity. This was considerably facilitated by the worsening of Diem's dictatorship, which placed members of his family or intolerant Catholics in all key posts and gave land and special, much-sought-after privileges to refugees from the north. Finally, the police, under the orders of the pitiless Ngo Dinh Nhu, brother of the President, multiplied their extortions, especially against the Buddhists, who revolted several times.

As early as December 1954 a Viet Minh officer had told Max Clos, the *Le Monde* correspondent in Saigon: "The United States wants to start the war again. We know that their goal, like Diem's, is to prevent at all costs the 1956 election which would give us certain victory. However we are not worried. The wheel of history cannot be stopped, and in the end we shall have victory even if to obtain it the war has to be started again." [44]

The head of the South Vietnamese Government had been quite wrong in boasting on January 31, 1957, of having "crushed the feudal rebels, stopped Communist subversion in the villages and restored peace and security to the whole country." In the beginning of 1959 he had to recognize that "Viet Nam was in a state of war." [45] At that time an average of one village chief disappeared every day. This did not prevent General Williams, chief of the American military mission, from asserting that guerrillas "had ceased to be a major menace to the government." [46]

By the end of the year the number of daily assassinations reached ten and then in 1960, twenty-five. The South Vietnamese Army, which had been reorganized into large units, following American advice, in order to be able to cope with an eventual Korean-style frontal attack from the north, couldn't do much to prevent the spreading of civil war. This led to the decision, borrowed from French strategy in Algeria, to regroup rural populations into fortified villages, named "prosperity centers," in order to protect them from armed attacks and from contagious, subversive ideas.

These uprootings, going against the traditional social structures and way of life of the Vietnamese peasant, had exactly the opposite effect, depriving Diem of a large part of the support he could still count on. Desertions abounded in the army. In April 1960, eighteen former close collaborators of the chief of state, among them ten former ministers, published a manifesto asserting that "truth will burst in waves of hate from a people long subjected to terrible sufferings and rising up to break the chains that bind them." [47] The American press, which had so highly praised the head of the Saigon Government, began to be concerned about the intolerably Catholic and nepotistic character which his dictatorship revealed more clearly every day, and about growing corruption in the power structure. Washington discreetly advised him to slow down.

On November 11, 1960, three battalions of paratroopers, apparently encouraged by some American agent, seized most of Saigon's public buildings. Their leader made the mistake of entering into negotiations with Diem, who promised everything, especially the formation of a provisional government in which the army would participate. As soon as a secretly gathered loyalist regiment had encircled the presidential palace, Diem reneged on his commitments. The organizers of the putsch did not dare pit army against army and fled.

Diem was going to remain in power for three more years; but, from that moment, it was clear that he could no longer count on the unconditional support of the military and that his popularity had sunk as low in the capital as it had in the villages. This was the time chosen by some hundred important anti-Diem individuals, who favored the strict implementation of the Geneva Accords, to secretly form on December 20, 1960, a National Liberation Front. They named to the presidency a Saigon lawyer, Nguyen Huu Tho, at that time detained by the Diem authorities but able to escape a year later through the efforts of his friends. In its manifesto the front proposed to bring about "the unification of all economic levels of the population, all classes, all nationalities, all parties, all organizations, all religions, and of all patriotic individuals of South Viet Nam, without distinction as to political tendencies, in the fight to throw off the American imperialist yoke and that of all their puppets in South Viet Nam, in order to achieve independence, democracy, the raising of the people's standard of living, peace, South Viet Nam's neutrality and progress toward the peaceful reunification of the fatherland."

Then followed a ten-point program notably calling for the creation of a "national and democratic coalition government," and "progress" toward the "settlement of the land problem, that is, distributing the land to those who cultivate it," and a "foreign policy of peace and neutrality." [48]

The relative moderation of that program should not hide the true significance of the front: it was a declaration of war against Diem and the Americans who supported him.

Moreover, the event took place three months after the Third Congress of the North Vietnamese Communist Party, the Lao Dong, which, in its final resolution, had called for the liberation of the south and nominated to the post of First Secretary one of the organizers of the armed struggle in Cochin China as late as 1954, Le Duan. In its report the congress had advocated the formation of a united front in the south.

§   §   §

Not without reason, Schlesinger imputes responsibility for the deterioration of the situation to Dulles' "moralistic" and "abstract" analysis and to the fact that no one had seriously studied the actual situation in Viet Nam. If that had been done, he wrote, "a more discriminating view might have regarded Ho Chi Minh . . . less as the obedient servant of a homogeneous Sino-Soviet bloc than as a leader of nationalist communism, historically distrustful of the Chinese and eager to preserve his own freedom of action." [49] Was Kennedy better informed? That is to be doubted considering the information on which he based his action in Cuba or in reading in Schlesinger, for example, that the South Vietnamese guerrillas had named themselves "Viet Cong," while actually the term, which simply means "Vietnamese Communists," had been invented by Diem's propaganda machine with the aim of providing a pejorative simplification.

In April 1961, the month of the Bay of Pigs, Diem asked for an increase in American aid, which since the Geneva Accords had already reached the sum of $460 million, $73 million of which were for 1960 alone. On May 4, Rusk replied favorably, and the next day it was learned that Vice President Johnson himself was going to Saigon, in the course of a vast Southeast Asian tour, essentially aimed at persuading the allies of the United States that it did not intend to abandon them in spite of the neutralization of Laos.

The future President laid it on pretty thick. He did not hesitate to call Diem "a Churchill of the decade who had to fight on the beaches and in the streets against tyranny." [50] Chiang Kai-shek would get the same treatment a few days later.

Before leaving Saigon, the Vice President signed with Diem a communiqué asserting that "the independence and territorial integrity of South Viet Nam are being brutally and systematically violated by Communist agents and troops from the north."

Thus took root the thesis which was soon to become the leitmotif of American diplomacy: that the sovereign and peaceful state of South Viet Nam had been the object of aggression from another state, that of North Viet Nam. The thesis is legally indefensible: the Geneva Accords had stated that the demarcation line on the 17th Parallel should not "in any way be interpreted as constituting political or territorial frontiers." It prohibited any entry of foreign troops or matériel and, in the event of armistice violations, offered no other recourse than an appeal to the international control commission created by the Geneva Conference, or, should agreement fail, to the Conference itself.[51] If from the legal level one goes to the factual level, it is disturbing, to say the least, to note that in its extensive report published on February 27, 1965, on "The Aggression of North Vietnam against South Vietnam," the State Department, which cited a number of examples of infiltration of North Vietnamese into the South, did not represent any of these as having occurred before the summer of 1961, later than the publication of the Johnson-Diem communiqué, which emphasized the violation of the territorial integrity of South Viet Nam by the "forces of the north." No specific details of any kind were given as to the identity of the "1,800 men and probably 2,700 others" who had allegedly crossed into the south from 1959 to 1960, and of the "minimum of 3,700" who followed them in 1961.[52] It was only in June 1962 that the Indian and Canadian members of the international control commission admitted that there existed "sufficient proof beyond reasonable doubt to establish" [53] that Hanoi had sent arms and men into the south, which the North Vietnamese Government continued to deny in spite of the evidence.

On his return to Washington, Johnson asked that the U.S.A. "move forward promptly with a major effort to help these countries help themselves." [54] His reports were so pessimistic that Kennedy, in complete disregard of the Geneva Accords, decided to send to Diem's army, in addition to great amounts of matériel, American instructors and even military advisers who were directed to supervise operations. A little later, in spite of the hostility of the people, the creation of fortified villages, abandoned awhile, would be resumed in an attempt to build actual "agrovilles."

In September 1961 the situation had again deteriorated. "It is," said Diem on October 2, "a real war waged by an enemy who is seeking a strategic decision in Southeast Asia in conformity with the orders of the Comintern." [55]

Kennedy reviewed the problem with his advisers. He dismissed the only reasonable idea which had been advanced by the Under Secretary of State, Chester Bowles, who wanted to create a belt of neutral states, on the model adopted by Laos, under the guarantee of the U.S.S.R., China, Japan, India and the SEATO countries. He sent to Saigon his military adviser, General Maxwell Taylor, together with Walt Rostow, to determine what form the "major effort" demanded by Johnson should take.

The report they presented a few weeks later deliberately stressed military aspects. It asked for a limited intervention by American troops, while pointing out that "if the infiltration from the north continued there would be no end to the war." [56] Taylor and Rostow did not hesitate, in that event, to advocate a policy of reprisals against the north. Kennedy hesitated for some time; then at the end of December he made his decision, raising to 15,000 the number of American military men in Viet Nam. That decision seemed at the time to boost the morale of the government troops, and at the beginning of January 1962 things appeared favorable enough to the President for him to say, "The spearpoint of aggression has been blunted." [57] He had never been more grossly mistaken in any area. His error was the more unforgivable in that he had just reiterated that the "war in Vietnam can only be won if it remains a war for the Vietnamese. Otherwise," he added, "if it becomes a white man's war, we will lose it as the French did before." [58]

Everything points to the conclusion that Schlesinger was right when he said that that fateful decision could in great part be explained by the climate created by the Berlin crisis brought to its height by the erection of the Wall, by the renewal of Soviet nuclear tests, and by Kennedy's conviction that, "an American retreat in Asia might upset the whole world balance." [59]

BIBLIOGRAPHY AND NOTES

[1] John F. Kennedy, *The Strategy of Peace* (New York: Harper, 1960), p. 30.

[2] U.S.A., documents, January 31, 1961.

[3] *Ibid.*

[4] *Ibid.*

[5] *Nouvelle revue internationale,* January 1961.

[6] D. C. Watt, *Survey of International Affairs, 1961* (London: Oxford University Press, 1965), p. 350.

[7] *Le Monde,* May 31, 1962.

[8] *Ibid.*

[9] Schlesinger, *op. cit.,* pp. 204–5.

[10] *Ibid.*

[11] *Ibid.,* p. 205.

[12] Grignon-Dumoulin, *op. cit.,* p. 242.

[13] U.S.A., documents, January 31, 1961.

[14] Theodore Sorensen, *Kennedy* (New York: Harper, 1965), pp. 295–96.

[15] Schlesinger, *op. cit.,* p. 267.

[16] *Ibid.,* p. 273.

[17] Wise and Ross, *op. cit.,* p. 52.

[18] Sorensen, *op. cit.,* p. 308.

[19] Keesing's, 18151 A.

[20] TASS dispatch of February 14, 1961.

[21] *Ibid.*

[22] Année politique, 1962, p. 514.

[23] Schlesinger, *op. cit.,* p. 578.

[24] *Ibid.,* p. 329.

[25] Keesing's, 18561 A.

[26] Schlesinger, *op. cit.,* p. 322.

[27] *Ibid.,* pp. 336–37.

[28] Documentation française. Notes et études documentaires, No. 1901, July 30, 1952, p. 4.

[29] *Ibid.,* No. 1909, August 18, 1954, p. 4.

[30] *Ibid.,* p. 5.

[31] C. L. Sulzberger, in *The New York Times,* June 3, 1964.

[32] Ely, *op. cit.,* p. 241.

[33] Eisenhower, *Mandate for Change* p. 371.

[34] Nguyen Kien, *Le Sud Viet-Nam depuis Dien Bien Phu* (Paris: Maspero, 1963), p. 64.

[35] Keesing's, 14949 A.

[36] Nguyen Kien, *op. cit.,* p. 68.

[37] *Ibid.,* p. 111.

[38] *Ibid.,* p. 104.

[39] *Ibid.,* p. 105.

[40] Georges Chaffard, *Indochine, dix ans d'indépendance* (Paris: Calmann-Lévy, 1964), p. 95.

[41] *Ibid.,* p. 98.

[42] *Ibid.*

[43] *Ibid.,* p. 144.

[44] *Le Monde,* December 16, 1954.

[45] Nguyen Kien, *op. cit.,* p. 203.

[46] Fall, *op. cit.,* p. 334.

[47] Chaffard, *op. cit.,* p. 176.

[48] Bulletin of Viet Nam, No. 56, July 20, 1965.

[49] Schlesinger, *op. cit.,* p. 536–37.

[50] *Daily Telegraph* (London), May 13, 1961.

[51] Documentation française. Notes et études documentaires, No. 1901, July 30, 1954, pp. 3, 4.

[52] U.S.A., documents, No. 2166, March 3, 1965.

[53] *Ibid.*

[54] Schlesinger, *op. cit.,* p. 542.

[55] *The Times* (London), October 3, 1961.

[56] Schlesinger, *op. cit.,* p. 546.

[57] *Ibid.,* p. 550.

[58] *Ibid.,* p. 546.

[59] *Ibid.,* p. 548.

· CHAPTER 18 ·

THE WALL

Peace cannot be bought, for the one who has sold
it is thereby in a better position to sell it again.

—Montesquieu, *Grandeur and
Decadence of the Romans*

IN THE BEGINNING, MOSCOW FAVORED KENNEDY, FOR
it remembered he had said that if he had been in Eisenhower's place,
he would have apologized for the U-2 affair. Therefore, Khrushchev
quickly congratulated him on his election, expressing the hope that
during his Presidency "relations between the two countries would
again become what they had been in Franklin Roosevelt's time." [1]
The new President followed suit in the first of his speeches, with an
elegance and strength which were to be, for two and a half years, the
hallmark of his office and were to set its style. On January 21 he said,
"So let us begin anew—remembering on both sides that civility is
not a sign of weakness, and sincerity is always subject to proof. Let
us never negotiate out of fear. But let us never fear to negotiate." [2]

Overnight, the Kremlin ceased the violent campaign it had begun
after the summit failure. As if by magic, Americans ceased to be de-
generates, warmongers, and colonialists spurred on by whisky, gold
and the taste of blood to commit the most abominable crimes. In
Krokodil there were no more caricatures of death in the company of
Yankee soldiers with sinister countenances and pockets bursting with
atomic bombs. In rapid succession, Khrushchev announced the withdrawal of his complaints to the U.N. on the U-2 affair and the release
of the two survivors of the American plane shot down, the preceding
July 1, over the Barents Sea.

Nonetheless, in his speech of January 6, 1961, he renewed his threats against Berlin, asserting that if the imperialists refused "to take into consideration the true situation," the U.S.S.R. "would take firm measures and would sign a peace treaty with the German Democratic Republic." [3] In other words: Agree to our terms, or we'll know how to force you to.

It was in that spirit that he informed the United States ambassador to Moscow that he would like to meet Kennedy as soon as possible, without disguising the fact that he intended, above all, to discuss Berlin. In mid-February, the President agreed in principle.

The misadventure of the Bay of Pigs seemed to bury the project. From Kennedy's behavior in that situation, Khrushchev got the impression he was dealing with an inexperienced and faint-hearted opponent and that clearly the future was in his own hands. Therefore, he wrote him on May 12 to tell him that his invitation was still open and the meeting was set for June 3 in Vienna.

J.F.K. first stopped in Paris to meet de Gaulle, whose personality fascinated him. The capital, always ready to get worked up over crowned heads and movie stars, gave a triumphant reception to the Presidential couple, whose youth and energy seemed to promise a new beginning to the United States and to the West. The meeting with the chief of state, in spite of his well-known prejudices against America, was an equal success. The two men competed in showing consideration for each other, and the conversation of Jackie Kennedy, carried on in impeccable French, prompted the general to tell his delighted guest that few Frenchwomen knew the history of France as well as she did.

The discussion on both sides was frank and in depth. De Gaulle was convinced that Khrushchev would do nothing in Berlin, if it were made apparent to him that any unilateral initiative ran the risk of general war. He asked that preparations for a new airlift be made: if a plane were shot down, the issue would be clear. A little later he warned Kennedy that once the Berlin crisis was over, he would pull France out of NATO—in his eyes an outmoded organization— while remaining in the Atlantic Alliance. He believed that the United States would have recourse to nuclear weapons only if its own territory were threatened, and therefore it was important that France be able to defend itself on its own. The President's assurances did not make him change his mind. Although they disagreed on that issue, as well as on the eventual entrance of Britain into the Common Market and on American chances in Viet Nam, they separated delighted with each other. "Never had the common destinies of the two nations been closer," [4] wrote Schlesinger. In the days that followed, all who visited the Elysée could confirm that opinion. The general, who may have expected to receive a youngster—J.F.K. looked much younger than his forty-four years—had quickly recognized in him the makings of a statesman of the first order. A confidence to the British ambassador the day after the Dallas tragedy probably summed up his feelings: "At heart, he was a European." [5] Coming from de Gaulle, there could have been no greater compliment.

In Vienna, no time was lost in superfluous amenities. We want peace, said Khrushchev, in effect, but America must understand that communism has earned the right to grow and develop and he expounded on the scientific reasons he had for believing in communism's inevitable triumph. Kennedy answered by explaining the American conception of the self-determination of peoples. In any case, said Khrushchev, the U.S.S.R. will never impose its ideas through war. " 'My ambition,' the President replied 'is to secure peace.' The greatest danger was the miscalculation by one power of the interests and policy of another."

The Russian got angry. "Did he mean that communism should exist only in countries already Communist and that, if it developed elsewhere, the United States would be in conflict with the Soviet Union?" It suggested to him that "America wanted the Soviet Union to sit like a schoolboy with hands on top of the table. . . . Ideas did not belong to one nation. . . . No immunization was possible against them. . . . The Soviet Union was going to defend its vital interests whether the United States regarded such acts as miscalculations. . . ." [6]

Kennedy explained that by that expression he had meant the difficulty of foreseeing the intentions of others and, citing the Bay of Pigs, he said that he himself had been mistaken in his calculations. What had to be done was to reduce the margin of uncertainty. Agreed, said Khrushchev . . . then adopt the Soviet policy of non-interference! But then, retorted Kennedy, what does your speech of

January 6 mean in promising support to wars of national liberation? Khrushchev repeated that it was "a sacred duty." The President warned him against any modification of the balance of power. The conversation then got embroiled in an argument over the degree of true democracy in elections in Poland and in the United States.

However, the argument had to come to an end. At Kennedy's suggestion they spoke of Laos, on which the two K's were already practically in agreement—and this gave the communiqué of their meeting its only positive element. Then they came to the treaty on the cessation of nuclear tests designed to improve the international climate, which the President was quite hopeful of being able to conclude. But Khrushchev proved intractable, despite the fact that on March 21 the American and British delegations to the disarmament conference had made concessions to the Soviet viewpoint. They had proposed a less rigid control system and the extension to three years of the moratorium on nondetectable tests, which as such were excluded from the treaty's implementation provisions. But the Russian delegate, Tsarapkin, had replied by introducing a new demand: the replacement of the single administrator of the control body, which the Kremlin had previously accepted, by a "troika" (one Western, one neutral and one Communist member) on the model Khrushchev had suggested for the office of Secretary General of the U.N.

In Vienna, Khrushchev insisted on that provision, asserting that the experience of the Congo had taught him that no true neutrality existed. He refused to authorize more than three inspections a year—the West demanded at least twelve—stating that to accept more would be to accede to the Pentagon's desire for espionage which had already been revealed in the famous Eisenhower "open skies" plan. Vainly, Kennedy tried to show him that a troika would automatically be paralyzed by a veto. Khrushchev told him there was a very simple means of reaching agreement: general disarmament—because a treaty prohibiting only nuclear tests would be of little importance. Thus they went around and around until they finally came to the principal problem—Berlin.

The Russian said that the situation had become intolerable and that with or without an agreement with the United States, he had decided to sign a treaty with the German Democratic Republic before the end of the year. The American replied that his country had a vital interest in Berlin and that should it let itself be driven out, from then on its commitments would be worthless scraps of paper. Khrushchev retorted that only German militarists and warmongers had a stake in preventing the settlement of that problem. If the United States wanted to fight for Berlin, he could do nothing about it. But madmen who sought war deserved only strait jackets.

During the luncheon which followed this sparring match, the two K's tried to joke, but the tone remained grave. When Kennedy mentioned the union leader Walter Reuther—who had had an argument with Khrushchev during his visit to San Francisco in 1959—the head of the Soviet party declared unsmilingly, "Yes, I met him. We hung the likes of Reuther in Russia in 1917." [7] He also said that after reflection he thought it better to abandon the project of a joint United States–Soviet expedition to the moon which J.F.K. had outlined the day before and which he had not then rejected. The only positive note of the meeting came when Khrushchev said he would not be the first to resume atomic tests. In less than three months he would forget that promise.

During the last private meeting, initiated by him, Kennedy made a new effort to dissuade Khrushchev from acting in Berlin. It was useless. " 'I want peace,' Khrushchev told him, 'but if you want war that is your problem.' The treaty decision was irrevocable. He would sign in December." [8] " 'It will be a cold winter,' JFK said taking leave of him." [9]

World opinion was quickly able to measure the gravity of the situation. Moscow published the two *aide-mémoire* delivered in Vienna to the President of the United States by the head of the Soviet Government. The first, dealing with nuclear tests, adding nothing new, but the second publicly renewed Soviet claims on Berlin: "If the United States does not show an understanding of the necessity for concluding a peace treaty, we shall regret this, since we would have to sign a peace treaty, which it would be impossible and dangerous to delay further, not with all States, but only with those that want to sign it." [10] However, contrary to the statement made by Khrushchev to Kennedy, the note did not set any time limit.

Khrushchev returned to that subject in an address he gave to

officers graduating from military academies in which he announced
the suspension of any reductions in the armed forces and a one-third
increase in the military budget: "Comrades, you are military men
and will perfectly understand the significance of delaying the conclusion of a peace treaty and of trying to violate the German Democratic Republic's sovereignty. Many of you are going to serve with
the troops which, according to the Warsaw Treaty, are stationed on
the soil of the German Democratic Republic; therefore you will have
to deal with the aggressive forces should they attempt by force of
arms to foil a peaceful settlement." [11]

On June 12, Gromyko told the German ambassador, Hans Kroll,
that the day the peace treaty was signed Soviet troops would be deployed along the demarcation line. "Then we shall see," he added
"whether the Western Powers will make war." [12]

On the 17th, the United States and its allies answered that "There
is no reason for a crisis in Berlin. If a crisis develops it is because
the U.S.S.R. is attempting to attack the basic rights of others." [13]

On the 25th, Kennedy addressed his countrymen on radio and
television. "If war breaks out," he said, "it will have started in Moscow and not in Berlin. . . . . Only the Soviet Government can use the
Berlin frontier as a pretext for war." [14] In order to cope with the
situation, he asked Congress to approve a series of measures:
authorization of an additional $3,247,000,000 for the armed forces,
raising the ceiling on combat effective troops, doubling and then
tripling draft calls, calling up the reserves, and reconditioning planes
and ships which had been put in "mothballs."

While declaring that the freedom of Berlin "was not negotia-
ble," he stated nevertheless that "he was willing to consider any
arrangement or treaty regarding Germany which would be com-
patible with the maintenance of peace and freedom and the legitimate
security interests of all countries." [15]

"Three times, in the course of my life," he continued, "our country and Europe have been involved in great wars. In each case, serious
errors of judgment were made on each side concerning the intentions
of the other—errors which brought about great devastation. Now,
in the nuclear age, any miscalculation made by one of the parties
regarding the intentions of the other, could, in a few hours, create

more devastation that there has ever been in all the wars of history." [16]

This position was the outcome of lengthy discussions during which, once again, the advocates of force and those of conciliation opposed each other. The first group was led by Dean Acheson, whom Kennedy had named to head a task force on the Berlin question.

In the judgment of Truman's Secretary of State, the Russians were not seeking a settlement of the problem, but rather to make the West surrender. Any sign of willingness to negotiate would be interpreted by the Kremlin as proof of anxiousness or of weakness. Therefore, American forces, both atomic and conventional, must be rapidly strengthened and, in the event that Khrushchev signed his peace treaty, an airlift had to be started. If the airlift could not be maintained, a division should advance along the Autobahn to clearly demonstrate to Moscow the Allies' determination. Rusk and McNamara, and also de Gaulle, as we have seen, favored this policy. The ambassador to Moscow, Llewelyn Thompson; his predecessors, Averell Harriman and Charles Bohlen; the majority leader of the Senate, Mike Mansfield; and the chairman of the Foreign Affairs Committee, along with the British, asked that priority be given to diplomatic measures in any case.

In the end, Kennedy adopted this approach, deciding to use firm language, supported by limited military measures, and leaving the door open to negotiations—rather than declaring the state of emergency advocated by Acheson with the support of Vice President Johnson. It was Kennedy's conviction that the Russians might take an atomic threat as a bluff and if they replied in the same spirit, the United States would soon find itself in an impasse. But the President was not too sure of himself and feared that Khrushchev, as he told an editor of the *New York Post,* "wants to rub my nose in the dirt," in which case "it's all over." [17]

The next day, Khrushchev received John McCloy, the former American high commissioner to Bonn, at Sochi on the Black Sea, where he had come to discuss disarmament. Khrushchev told him that Kennedy had issued an ultimatum and that if there was war he would be the last President of the United States.

On August 1 he reiterated all his arguments, without yielding an inch, to the Italian Prime Minister, Fanfani, who was visibly impressed. On the 7th, he mentioned the possibility of calling up the reserves to meet the "mobilization measures" taken by the U.S. which "threatened to trigger a war," asserting that "the barring of access to West Berlin, the blockade of West Berlin, is entirely out of the question." He declared that if he abandoned his plans to sign his treaty, the West would see in it a "strategic breakthrough" and would immediately widen the scope of their demands: "They would advance their main claim—the abolition of the Socialist camp. . . ." He asked, however, "Let us honestly meet around the conference table, let us not create war hysteria, let us clear the atmosphere, let us rely on reason and not on the power of thermonuclear weapons." [18]

At that time, Rusk was in Paris where he had been trying to work out a proposal for negotiations with the Soviets with his Western colleagues. The British were entirely in favor of it, and the Germans, who were going to have general elections on September 17, were less hostile to it than Adenauer's usual rigidity would indicate. But de Gaulle was convinced that the opening of negotiations could only lead to surrender in the end and wrote to Kennedy to that effect, thus blocking any Western initiative.

A crisis, therefore, seemed imminent. But it did not take the form which had been expected. On August 13, at 12:30 A.M. the Vopos, the East German police, put barbed wire entanglements along the 30-mile line dividing the two Berlins. At 1:00 A.M. the press service of the German Democratic Republic announced that the frontier would remain closed until the peace treaty was signed. Soon it was learned that Marshal Koniev, who sixteen years before had conquered the capital for Stalin, had again taken command of the Soviet forces stationed in Germany.

The motives behind the Kremlin's action were clear. The aggravation of international tension and the fear of Moscow's signing a separate peace treaty with the German Democratic Republic had recently hastened the exodus of East Germans into the Western sectors. The number of crossings had reached 15,000 between August 1 and August 10. On the 12th alone—the day before the demarcation line was sealed off—more than 4,000 refugees had been counted. Among them were many technicians, physicians, students and skilled workers. If that hemorrhaging continued, all of Walter Ulbricht's five-year plan would get nowhere. "Man is the most precious capital," Stalin had said once. East Germany was on the point of losing that capital.

Already, several times, the possibility of closing the frontier between the two Berlins had been mentioned. In the beginning of August, Kennedy discussed it with Walt Rostow, adding that if Khrushchev took such a decision, he did not see what he could do to stop him. On July 30, Senator Fulbright had gone so far as to declare, during a televised interview, "I don't understand why the East Germans don't close their border, because I think they have a right to close it." [19]

These extremely thoughtless words were comparable to Acheson's famous declaration in 1950 that Korea was not in the defensive perimeter of the U.S.—a statement which had certainly contributed to the starting of the war. The Russians' limited understanding of the workings of the Western democracies made it difficult for them to really believe that the chairman of the Senate Foreign Relations Committee could speak idly and express only his own opinion. It wouldn't be surprising if they saw his words as a kind of trial balloon, even an invitation to act—in which case Fulbright would bear some responsibility for the erection of the Wall.

However, it seemed that the Russians were groping their way, keeping open the possibility of an orderly retreat if things turned out badly. The date chosen was significant: Sunday, August 13—in the middle of the longest weekend of the year, the one during which ministries are run by department heads and embassies by attachés and, therefore, a time when the great democracies, whose swiftness of response is not their principal characteristic, would be least likely to react. As an added precaution the people's police were not armed, and the East Berlin newspapers were forbidden to report the news. They would only mention it three days later when it was quite clear that the Allies were not going to do anything.

When, a few days earlier, the Allied foreign ministers had confered in Paris to consider all the forms that a Soviet initiative could take, they had deliberately avoided that one, as no one dared assume responsibility for advising an attack on the Wall. On the 13th Willy

Brandt, Mayor of West Berlin, tried to calm his countrymen who wanted to go *en masse* to the Brandenburg Gate; the West Berlin police intervened and scattered demonstrators who were trying to get through the barbed wire. Adenauer discouraged the fanatics. Neither the sharpness of the Allied protests nor Kennedy's decision to dispatch Vice President Johnson and General Clay—the man behind the 1948 airlift—along with a reinforcement of 1,500 GI's to Berlin, could hide the fact that the West was bowing before a *fait accompli*.

Following their initial move, the Russians were tempted to take additional steps. They transformed the barbed wire barricade that a few hundred brave souls had still been able to cross into a real wall of brick and cement. On August 22 all the crossing points were closed to the Allies, with the exception of one where the East German authorities insisted on inspecting soldiers' papers; they forbade any approach to the Wall closer than 100 meters; the Kremlin dispatched notes to Paris, Bonn and Washington formally demanding that the West German leaders be prevented from using their planes to enter Berlin. The next day the Soviet ambassador to Bonn, Seminov, declared that civilian flights to the former capital "must be subjected as quickly as possible" to East German control, preferably by their use of the Schönefeld airfield located in the eastern sector.[20] This time the West got angry. Under orders, four American soldiers refused to show their papers to the Vopos, who arrested and later released them. Allied tanks patrolled the wall within the area Pankow maintained was out of bounds. While Paris called the note on the flights to Berlin *"un élément . . . particulièrement grave,"* [21] the White House stated that any interference by the Soviet Government or by the East German regime with free access to Berlin was "an aggressive act for the consequences of which the Soviet Union would bear full responsibility." [22] And on the 26th the three powers formally answered the Kremlin to that effect.

While new incidents were reported in Berlin—the East Germans always, however, finally surrendering before the Allies' determination—Khrushchev on the 27th wrote to Fanfani, who had said he favored negotiations, that he himself was quite ready to negotiate. The same day, Kennedy, who one week earlier had informed Rusk of his decision to begin negotiations on September 1 with or without the

Allies, wrote in vain to de Gaulle, while the American press widely publicized his intentions.

Khrushchev, in order to bring things to a head, struck another great blow. On August 29 the Soviet Government announced that "in the face of the threat by the leaders of the United States and Allied countries to take up arms and to start a war in response to the conclusion of the peace treaty with the German Democratic Republic," it had decided to resume nuclear tests which had been interrupted since the fall of 1958. The statement mentioned Soviet projects to fabricate a series of bombs of 20, 30, 50 and 100 megatons.[23]

On September 3 he repeated his formal demand that the Allies prohibit the Bonn leaders from using their planes. "They are bent on scaring the world to death before they begin negotiating," said Kennedy to the Secretary of State, "and they haven't quite brought the pot to boil. Not enough people are frightened. . . ."[24] The same day he ordered resumption of underground nuclear tests and de Gaulle held a press conference during which he declared that "against an ambitious imperialism, any retreat only serves to excite the aggressor—there is in that welter of insults and demands hurled by the Soviets something so arbitrary and so artificial that one is led to attribute it either to a premeditated unleashing of frenzied ambition, or to a need to escape from great difficulties." Choosing the second explanation as the most "plausible" he dwelt on the Soviet regime's "omissions, weaknesses, international failures" and "above all, on its characteristic inhuman repression."[25]

On September 8, with a very curt refusal—which represented the climax of the crisis—the Allies answered the Kremlin's claims to control flights to Berlin. This time Khrushchev understood that it was time to back down if he wanted to take advantage of Kennedy's good will. "I have been a steel worker," he had said a few weeks earlier. "I know how to cool red-hot metal. . . ."[26]

The Western note would remain unanswered for a long time. When the answer came, it would be couched in very moderate terms and apparently be without any other objective than that of depriving the adversary of the last word.

In the meantime Mr. K, after a fruitless attempt to use the

Italians' good offices, conveyed to Spaak, once again the Belgian Foreign Minister and champion of a conciliatory line in the Atlantic Council, that he would like to see him.

The former Secretary General of NATO arrived in Moscow on September 19. His host expressed himself very frankly. "I realize," he told him in effect, "that contrary to what I had hoped the Western Powers will not sign the peace treaty. I also realize that it will be difficult for us to conclude an accord with the German Democratic Republic, because that would imply its *de jure* recognition which the West does not want. Sooner or later," he continued, "you will come around to it because you are not sincere when you speak of reunification. But I realize that today it would be very difficult for you to do it. And I'm not trying to put you in an impossible situation; I know very well that you can't let yourself be stepped on."

When the Belgian minister alluded to the grave incidents which could arise from the harassment to which the Russians subjected the West—ranging from the flight of fighter planes in the air corridors, to the halting of military convoys on the road to Berlin—Khrushchev told the following anecdote: In Russia a fisherman was being tried for having stolen spikes from the railroad ties. "I only wanted," he said, "to use the spikes as ballast for my nets. . . ." "But didn't you understand that you could derail the trains?" "I left enough spikes so that they would not derail. . . ."

That said, Khrushchev declared that he was "forced" to sign the treaty which would put an end to the occupation status. But before the signing of the treaty he was prepared to negotiate another protocol, and incorporate it into the treaty, by which East Germany would, in effect, be party to the granting to the West of every guarantee of access to Berlin that they could wish. All he asked from them was that they agree with the GDR on conditions of flights over its territory, "in the same way that the U.S.S.R. has an accord with Denmark for its Moscow-Paris route."

"You know," he continued, "Berlin is not such a big problem for me. What are two million people among a billion Communists!" A few days earlier, he had been speaking again about a "cancerous tumor," about a "bone stuck in the throat" which had to be quickly removed, about a "Sarajevo" likely to lead to another world war. "In any event," he continued, "I'm not bound by any deadline"—to Kennedy he had insisted "by the end of the year"—"but I cannot let the negotiations drag on indefinitely. Besides, we could examine other problems at the same time—disarmament, European security and even reunification." Finally, questioned on the resumption of nuclear tests, he maintained that the military had forced him to resume them.[27]

The meaning of his words was clear. Khrushchev was no longer at all sure that the Allies would yield before his attempts at intimidation. Having built his Wall, which very adequately protected Ulbricht's regime, he tried to obtain concessions from the West which would have allowed him to save face. On his part, Spaak was quite ready to help him do it, and he didn't lose any time in briefing the NATO members and in advising them to negotiate.

As Kennedy himself was inclined to negotiate, it had already been agreed that Rusk would meet with Gromyko at the meeting of the U.N. General Assembly. However, in order to make allowance for the objections raised by de Gaulle, who increasingly doubted America's determination, it was decided that no actual negotiations would be started; only "exploratory talks to see whether serious negotiations could be undertaken." [28]

As it happened, Rusk spoke to Gromyko quite sternly, telling him that the crisis was entirely a Soviet creation, and that the signing of a separate peace treaty would constitute a threat to the vital interests of the United States. He added, reaffirming a formula which J.F.K. had offered a few weeks earlier to Kekkonen, President of the Finnish Republic on a visit to Washington, that the United States was not ready to make concessions in order to keep what it already had. It would be, he told him, like "buying the same horse twice." [29]

The Russians made several gestures calculated to improve the international climate. Moscow's press reprinted an article in which the American journalist James Wechsler had written that Kennedy "had achieved a certain composure about the brutal nature of the choice he may have to face in the solitude of some ghastly night," and if Khrushchev truly believed the President was an imperialist, it proved "he is mad and we are all doomed." [30] The Kremlin agreed to submit to the U.N. a joint declaration with Washington on the principles of disarmament. Finally, presenting his report on October 17 to the Twenty-second Congress of the C.P.S.U., Khrushchev declared, "The Western Powers are showing some understanding of the situation and are inclined to seek a solution to the German problem and the issue of West Berlin."

"If this is so," he continued, "we shall not insist on signing a peace treaty absolutely before December 31, 1961." [31]

In spite of that, the crisis was not yet over. Minor incidents occurred in Berlin during the last days of October, and the U.S.S.R., indifferent to the emotions provoked by the resumption of nuclear tests among the uncommitted nations gathered in a summit meeting in September in Belgrade, went ahead with explosions of unprecedented magnitude, one of which surpassed 50 megatons, or equivalent to more than 3,500 Hiroshima-type bombs. On November 25, Kennedy took a conciliatory step by declaring, in an interview given to Adjubei: "All we wish is to maintain a very limited—and they are very limited—number of troops of the Three Powers in West Berlin and to have, for example, an international administration on the *autobahn* so that goods and people can move freely in and out." [32]

But *Izvestia* and later Ulbricht categorically rejected that trial balloon, and Gomulka even stated that if negotiations on Berlin did not begin before the end of the year the Soviet bloc would have to return to its original position on the peace treaty. In that climate the NATO ministerial council gathered in Paris in mid-December almost unanimously agreed with Rusk in advocating another Four-Power conference. But de Gaulle would not hear of it, in spite of a telephone call from Kennedy. Speaking to me eighteen months later on means of reopening contact with the French chief of state, Kennedy had such an unpleasant memory of that call that he declared: "In any case, I will not telephone him for anything in the world."

Unable to negotiate, the Americans continued to send out feelers as to the intentions of the U.S.S.R., which periodically continued to disrupt communications with the former capital. In April 1962 the Americans went so far as to confidentially propose to Moscow the creation of an international control authority to assure freedom of access to Berlin and on which would sit representatives from the two rival republics as well as from neutral countries. To the accord would be added a treaty of nonaggression between the NATO countries and the members of the Warsaw Pact, and a commitment from the three nuclear powers not to assist the other nations, in any way, in acquiring nuclear weapons. But that suggestion was to be rejected by everyone. Bonn objected to East German participation and the Kremlin to West German participation, while most of the members of the Atlantic Alliance were concerned with the effects a nonaggression pact could have on the military efforts which were expected of them. In June new incidents erupted in the former capital, leading to an exchange of the sharpest notes and a new wave of anxiety. It was only the Cuban missile crisis in October which restored calm to the banks of the Spree.

It later became apparent that Khrushchev was not completely in command of the situation throughout this entire affair, and that he had to take into account the often divergent views of his allies in the socialist bloc and the anxieties created among their populations by the mobilization of reserves, which had led individuals to hoard food supplies. This situation was revealed in the reports presented to their respective parties by some foreign Communist Party leaders who attended the Twenty-second Congress of the C.P.S.U. in October 1961 in Moscow.

The most interesting report is certainly that of Todor Zhivkov, First Secretary of the Bulgarian Communist Party. "When the world situation had deteriorated because of the West Berlin question," he declared on November 28, before the Central Committee, "some comrades were perplexed and asked: Aren't we in favor of peaceful coexistence? Why, then, do we arbitrarily insist on signing the treaty before the end of the year?" Then, mentioning the abandonment by Mr. K of the December deadline, he continued, "Other comrades have declared that it was a setback for our cause, that we were losing face, that the prestige of the U.S.S.R. and of the socialist countries was declining. . . . What do those comrades want? That we practice a policy of adventurism, as advocated by the Albanian leaders with criminal thoughtlessness?" [33] On November 22, Gomulka himself spoke in terms which clearly showed his pleasure with the action of the Soviet Congress "in eliminating any trace of a policy by ultimatum." [34]

The documents published by the Twenty-second Congress itself, however, did not show any discussion of the Berlin problem. It was only after it had ended, that Enver Hodja, First Secretary of the Albanian party, openly asked: "Who is afraid of responsibility for the settlement of the German problem? Who is delaying things?" [35]

It must be pointed out that Hodja was not bound by the slightest consideration for Khrushchev, who, during the Congress, and after having tried to organize a putsch against him, had made him the object of a virulent attack declaring in particular, "It is no longer a secret from anyone that the Albanian leaders stay in power through the use of force and despotism." But, he added, "we are certain that the time will come when the Albanian Communists, the Albanian people, will rise to have their say and then the Albanian leaders will have to answer for the damage they have caused their country, their people, and the building of socialism in Albania." [36]

That diatribe, which was going to lead the following December 10 to the breaking of diplomatic relations between the two countries, was especially significant because it followed a public attempt by Chou En-lai, from the rostrum of the Congress, to reconcile the antagonists. "If, unfortunately," he remarked, "discussions and divergences arise between brother parties, it is proper to resolve them with patience and in the spirit of proletarian internationalism, according to the principles of equality of rights and of a common viewpoint achieved through consultations. A public unilateral condemnation . . . does not facilitate the solution of the problem." He had added that, "the great unity and the great friendship existing between the Chinese and Soviet peoples will live on for centuries to come, as the Yang-tse and the Volga will flow on eternally." [37]

It was probably an application of the Coué method. It had already been observed that the Chinese Prime Minister had abstained from making the ritual reference to the teachings of the Congress of the C.P.S.U. on destalinization. On October 21 he had gone to lay a wreath to the glory of "Stalin, the great Marxist-Leninist" at the base of the mausoleum in Red Square. The Congress was going to unanimously vote to remove the dictator's remains from it "because the serious violations of Lenin's precepts by Stalin, the abuses of power, the massive repressions against honest Soviet citizens and other actions during the period of the cult of personality make it impossible to keep his mortal remains in Lenin's mausoleum." [38] Without provoking any smiles, an old militant, Dora Lazourkina, had stated before the Congress that Lenin had appeared to her in a dream and told her: "It is unpleasant for me to be beside Stalin, who has caused the party so much sorrow." [39] The Congress was also going to decide to rebaptize Stalingrad, whose name, in the eyes of the whole world, was the symbol of a decisive victory over the most odious form of totalitarianism. In the meantime, Chou had taken a plane back to Peking and no really convincing explanation for his departure had been offered.

However, it was not only from Albania and China that Khrushchev would receive challenges to his authority. The advocates of the hard line had retained supporters in the very midst of the Soviet party, beginning with Molotov. After the defeat of the anti-Party group in 1957, he had been appointed ambassador to Mongolia—the Dutch Government previously having wittily refused to accept as ambassador a man "who did not enjoy the trust of his government." [40] He had taken advantage of his post to establish contacts with the Chinese. He had later been transferred to a minor post with the international atomic energy agency in Vienna. But he was continually trying to stir up the party against Khrushchev's "revisionism," and even on the eve of the Twenty-second Congress, he had sent another letter to the Central Committee criticizing the party's new program. Among other things, he reproached it for having renounced certain basic principles of the Marxist-Leninist dogma, beginning with the "dictatorship of the proletariat," this no longer being necessary, according to Khrushchev, now that the U.S.S.R. had been transformed into a "state of the entire people," [41] that is to say, a state where there were no longer any social classes.

The attacks to which Molotov was subjected at the Congress dealt mostly with his attitude toward international problems. Mikoyan accused him of "underestimating the power of the socialist bloc," [42] Satiukov, *Pravda*'s editor in chief and Khrushchev's yes-man, of "trying to push us along the road of adventurism, the road to war," [43] and Pospelov, director of the Marxist-Leninist Institute, of asserting that "it is by means of war that we must win over to communism

hundreds of millions of people." [44] The denunciations spread to
other members of the anti-Party group and were particularly interesting in that they revealed divergences not only in the accusations
directed against Stalin's former Prime Minister, but in the sanctions
to be taken against him. They ranged from the "severe condemnation" [45] asked for by the writer Cholokhov to the "just punishment"
demanded by Rodionov, Second Secretary of Kazakhstan, for
"adventurers" who have "dipped their hands in the blood of the best
sons of the people." [46]

That, in the end, Molotov was not the object of any public sanction—his discreet expulsion from the party was to be learned of
only much later—was sufficient to show that Khrushchev's authority,
in that fall of 1961, was not complete—even in the Russian party
whose executive posts he had filled with his minions. Nor could he
depend on strengthening his authority through the unconditional
support of foreign Communists. A sharp controversy erupted between the two greatest parties of the diaspora, the Italian party,
whose chief, Palmiro Togliatti, promoted his ideas on the "polycentrism" of the worker's movement, which he had formulated following the Twentieth Congress, and the French party which, through
Maurice Thorez's voice, attacked a formula aimed at "negating the
universal value of the Marxist-Leninist theory of revolution." [47]
This attack was notable because, a few days before, the Italian party
had carefully specified that by polycentrism it did not mean the
"establishment of specific regional centers of administration" but only
the affirmation of the autonomy of different parties. [48]

In attempting to regain control of the vast empire which Stalin
had turned into a monolithic structure and of the legions it had at its
disposal beyond its frontiers, Khrushchev was almost obliged to seek
a spectacular victory. Another reason may have motivated him: the
consciousness that it was impossible for the Soviet economy to realize
the ambitious program he had planned for it and to "catch up with"
and then to "surpass" the production and consumption levels of the
West.

In fact, the capitalist nations, far from going through the "cy-
clical" crisis constantly predicted for them by Soviet theorists, and
far from suffering the break-up of the world market following the

advent of collectivist socialism on a third of the planet and the loss of their colonies, were breaking all records for production and growth. And Europe was forgetting that fifteen years earlier it had believed that it would never be able to get out of the abyss into which the war had plunged it. As for the United States, under the Presidency of a young, energetic man full of confidence in liberal values, it was rediscovering the dynamism of its pioneers. Its gross national product was twice as great as that of the U.S.S.R., which, spending equal amounts on space programs and the arms race, could not avoid exhausting itself before the U.S. With 6 percent of its working population making their living from agriculture, America was able to dispose of enormous surpluses, while Russia, with more than 30 percent of its inhabitants working on the land, did not produce enough to feed itself.

The two were not equally matched. But this would become apparent only when Khrushchev's imprudence and his determination to engineer a breakthrough, intended to dispose of the resistance of his adversaries as well as of the suspicions of his Chinese allies, inspired him to take a gamble in the Caribbean which was to prove disastrous for him.

BIBLIOGRAPHY AND NOTES

1 *U.R.S.S.*, Bulletin of the Soviet Information Bureau in Paris, November 11, 1960.

2 *The New York Times*, January 21, 1961.

3 *Nouvelle revue internationale*, January 1961.

4 Schlesinger, *op. cit.*, p. 356.

5 Author's personal notes.

6 Schlesinger, *op. cit.*, pp. 360–61.

7 *Ibid.*, p. 373.

8 *Ibid.*

9 *Ibid.*

10 Keesing's, 18163 A.

11 *U.R.S.S.*, No. 2276, July 11, 1961.

12 *New York Herald Tribune*, July 23, 1961.

13 U.S.I.S., Paris. Document published by the Department of State, August 25, 1961.

14 *Ibid.*

15 *Ibid.*

16 *Ibid.*

17 Schlesinger, *op. cit.*, p. 391.

18 Keesing's, 18271 A.

19 Schlesinger, *op. cit.*, p. 394.

20 Watt, *op. cit.*, p. 252.

21 *Le Monde*, August 25, 1961.

22 Watt, *op. cit.*, p. 253.

23 *U.R.S.S.*, No. 2311, August 31, 1961.

24 Schlesinger, *op. cit.*, p. 398.

25 *Le Monde*, September 7, 1961.

26 Author's personal notes.

27 Author's personal notes.
28 Sorensen, *op. cit.*, p. 597.
29 *Ibid.*, pp. 598–99.
30 Schlesinger, *op. cit.*, p. 400.
31 *U.R.S.S.*, No. 2351, October 17, 1961.
32 Keesing's, 18495 A.
33 Todor Zhivkov, *Discours, rapports, articles* (Sofia: Foreign Language Editions, 1962), II, pp. 570–71.
34 *Trybuna Ludu,* November 23, 1961.
35 Keesing's, 18528 A.
36 *U.R.S.S.,* No. 2366, October 27, 1961.

37 Jean Baby, *La grande controverse sino-soviétique* (Paris: Grasset, 1966), p. 98.
38 *U.R.S.S.,* No. 2367, October 29, 1961.
39 *Pravda,* October 31, 1961.
40 Author's personal notes.
41 Baby, *op. cit.,* p. 103.
42 *Pravda,* October 22, 1961.
43 *Ibid.,* October 27, 1961.
44 *Ibid.,* October 28, 1961.
45 *Ibid.,* October 26, 1961.
46 *Ibid.,* October 31, 1961.
47 *Le Monde,* December 1, 1961.
48 *L'Unità,* November 22, 1961.

· CHAPTER 19 ·

THE SECOND "WEEK

OF TRUTH"

History determines the weight of nations.

> —Anatole de Monzie, *In Defense
> of History*

AT THE END OF AUGUST 1962 THE POLICY-PLANNING
council of the State Department, headed by Walt Rostow, estimated
in a report to Kennedy and Rusk that the Soviet leaders were ready
to admit the failure of the great offensive they had triggered after the
launching of the first Sputnik. The council deemed it improbable
that Moscow would passively accept that failure and voiced the
hypothesis that the world might very rapidly see "perhaps the greatest act of risk-taking since the war, in an attempt to retrieve a waning
Communist position." [1]

Indisputably, there was a certain amount of exaggeration in that
diagnosis of the scope of the Soviet failure. The United States was
unconsciously getting entangled in Viet Nam. Nasser, after Syria's
secession—a cruel blow inflicted to his pride at the end of September
1961—was trying to achieve a dramatic rapprochement with Moscow,
which would soon result in his being crowned a "Hero of the Soviet
Union" by Khrushchev himself. The Russian penetration was consolidated in Ghana, which Brezhnev, then President of the Presidium
of the Supreme Soviet, had visited in February 1961, to inaugurate an
"ideological" institute. Nkrumah asserted in all modesty "that
Nkrumah-ism ought to be allied to scientific socialism." [2] A similar
situation was developing in Indonesia, where the Communist element
was each day gaining ground by means of the paradoxical trinity:

nationalism, religion, communism—the "Nasakom" on which Sukarno depended.

It was, nonetheless, obvious that the great attempt of African seduction had not produced the results that Khrushchev had counted on. In September 1961 the twelve members of the Brazzaville bloc, representing the great majority of the Francophone states, had no hesitation in attacking Russian sensibilities by demanding the "decolonization of Soviet Asia." [3] The Soviet venture in the Congo had been liquidated as a complete disaster. On March 19, 1962, the conclusion of the Evian Agreement, after a dramatic challenge by the O.A.S., led to the declaration of Algerian independence on July 3. This denouement, which was going to greatly enhance General de Gaulle's prestige in the third world, had brought about a rapprochement between the progressive African states which, like Guinea and Ghana, had recognized the provisional government of Algeria, and those which had preferred to remain in the French community. A skillful American ambassador, William Attwood, won the ear of Sékou Touré who, in November 1961, had reacted to a somewhat aggressive petition from the teachers' union by arresting its leaders and expelling the Soviet ambassador, Daniel Solod, whom we have already seen at work in the Middle East, under pretext of his complicity in a conspiracy. In April 1962 the President of Guinea promulgated legislation intended to facilitate foreign investments and, the following month, signed with the Senegalese leader Senghor a declaration stating that they were "moving toward African unity through socialism" [4]—a socialism which was evidently not that of Marx and Lenin.

In Latin America as well, the United States was regaining ground. In December 1961, Kennedy and his wife visited Venezuela and Colombia, in order to show support for the reform presidents, Betancourt and Llera Camargo. The enthusiastic reception they received made one forget the tomatoes directed a few months earlier at the then Vice President, Richard Nixon. In the spring of 1961 the assassination of Trujillo, the tyrant who had given himself the title of Benefactor of the Dominican Republic, enabled a more democratic regime to take power. It benefited from the generosity of Washington, which was delighted to be thus able to give evidence of its preferences.

However, J.F.K. did not want to appear too naive. "There are three possibilities," he said to his advisers the day after the murder, "a decent democratic regime, a continuation of the Trujillo regime" [5]—one of whose protégés, Balaguer, had assumed the presidency of the republic and one of his sons the command of the army —"or a Castro regime. We ought to aim at the first, but we really can't renounce the second until we are sure that we can avoid the third. . . ." [6]

In spite of the anticolonialist tradition of the United States, especially strong since the Monroe Doctrine, he had been pressuring Great Britain to postpone the declaration of the independence it had promised its colony of Guiana. Chedi Jagan, the head of the government of Georgetown, did not hide his Marxist sympathies. He went so far as to declare, in August 1962, that "communism was winning throughout the entire world," [7] and Kennedy greatly feared that he would transform his country into a second Cuba. Johnson was guided by this philosophy when, in April 1965, he ordered a massive intervention of marines in the Dominican Republic, following a *coup d'état* which he believed to be Fidelist inspired.

The personal charm of the young President, the halo of liberalism which surrounded his administration, added to the dollars of the Alliance for Progress, and the shadow of the "big stick" dear to Theodore Roosevelt, had unquestionably impressed the Latin American leaders. They had formed a common front against Cuba, which, on January 30, 1962, had been expelled from the Organization of American States by a unanimous vote, less six abstentions, at the close of the Inter-American Conference at Punta del Este, in Uruguay.

In Cuba itself the situation was not very promising. Castro said on December 1, 1961: "The more we face imperialism . . . [and] the reality of a revolution and of class war, the more we are convinced of all the truths written by Marx and Engels and of all the general interpretations of scientific socialism made by Lenin." Even though he had to confess that he had not read *Das Kapital* beyond page 370,[8] he declared he had always been a Marxist-Leninist. The damaging effects of the embargo, extended in February 1962 to all American exports to the island, were added to those of a disastrous economic condition—credited by giving priority to accelerated industrialization while sugar production was falling rapidly. Draconian reform measures were imposed under the direction of an old-time Communist, Carlos Rafael Rodriguez, who had been promoted to the presidency of the National Institute for Agrarian Reform.

On March 26, Fidel made a violent attack against another old-time Communist, Anibal Escalante, guilty of having transformed the single party then being formed, the "Integrated Revolutionary Organization," into an instrument of his own ambitions. Apparently the Russians had been more or less mixed up in the affair, which probably planned to give real power to a man more flexible than Castro and therefore more likely to follow their instructions. In any case the Russian ambassador Kudriavtsev—well known to the Canadian counterespionage service, which had had encounters with him right after the war—was asked to pack his bags as quickly as possible. Although *Pravda*, after two weeks of reflection, decided to approve of Escalante's dismissal, there followed an exchange of recriminations between Havana and Moscow, and in Cuba itself a few outbreaks provoked by the shortage of some products. On the 4th of June, addressing Fidelist students who were going back to their country, Khrushchev advised them to work hard because "arms and heroism" were not enough to solve every difficulty. As an example he cited the New Economic Policy planned by Lenin in 1921 to save the country from the economic catastrophe which threatened it, by means of a partial return to capitalism.[9] In July, Castro denounced the "bourgeois elements of the cities and villages" which were supporting the counterrevolution.[10] In September it was learned that, following the discovery of a conspiracy, a wave of executions had taken place.

The reality of the world picture was obviously very different from the dreams of communism's rapid growth nurtured at the time of the great world conference of Communist parties in November 1960. It was impossible to imagine where the U.S.S.R. could obtain, without running too great a risk, the one spectacular success which would completely disarm Khrushchev's detractors. This is probably what encouraged Khrushchev—in spite of his evident hesitation—to attempt a poker play actually better suited to the American mentality and contrary to the traditions of Lenin and Stalin, who both believed in the prudent strategies of chess.

As early as the summer of 1962 a crisis was felt to be imminent, despite the relief created by the termination of the Algerian drama and by the signing, on July 23, of the treaty on the neutralization of Laos. The Soviets had answered the February 7 resumption of nuclear tests by the West with a series of tests of their own, each more terrifying than the last. The Geneva meeting of the foreign ministers of America, Russia and Britain in April, on the resumption of disarmament talks, yielded no results. All attempts at compromise in Berlin had failed, and the anniversary of the erection of the Wall, in August, had been the occasion of serious incidents and an exchange of acrimonious notes.

Khrushchev was beginning to make it known through his diplomats that his patience was wearing thin. He did not hide from visitors —like the Austrian Vice Chancellor, Bruno Pittermann, and the American poet Robert Frost—his lack of belief in the reality of the oft-repeated "determination" proclaimed by the leaders of the capitalist world to resist communism. On September 6 he sent a confidential message to Kennedy assuring him that "nothing will be undertaken before the American Congressional elections in November that could complicate the international situation." [11] From this it could be deduced, *a contrario,* that he might well undertake something *after* the elections; especially since in that same letter he mentioned the possibility of his coming to the United Nations in the second week of November. It can be surmised that his intention was to meet Kennedy at that time in order to offer him some kind of deal. Hadn't the Chinese ambassador to Moscow confided to one of his neutral colleagues that "this time, he [Khrushchev] had made his decision"? [12]

Gromyko confirmed all these fears when, visiting Kennedy on Thursday, October 18, he declared that after the elections serious negotiations would have to be entered into. Without them the U.S.S.R. would be "obliged" to sign the peace treaty itself, and no threat would be able to shake its determination.[13]

A test of strength seemed imminent. However, it was not in Berlin that it was to take place, but in Cuba—and the first to know it was the President of the United States. For forty-eight hours he had been in possession of photographs irrefutably revealing the presence of Soviet strategic missiles on the island.

§   §   §

To understand how this situation could have developed, it is necessary to refer to the past. After the misadventure of the Bay of Pigs, Castro's regime had every reason to fear that the United States would try to take revenge—a justifiable fear, if only because exiled Cuban commandos were still being trained on U.S. soil, in plain sight of everyone. Besides, Cuba's serious economic and political crisis could strongly tempt the Americans to intervene.

The best way for Cuba to meet that threat lay in the promise of aid from the U.S.S.R. In July 1960, at the height of the crisis provoked by the U-2 affair, Khrushchev had declared that "if necessary, the Soviet armed forces could help the Cuban people with the might of their missiles if the aggressive forces of the Pentagon dared to begin an attack against Cuba." [14]

But he had appreciably reduced the significance of his words by indicating that he only spoke "figuratively" [sic]. Che Guevara, at the time one of Fidel's principal lieutenants, lost no time in translating this commitment correctly: "An invasion of Cuba now," he exclaimed, "would mean that atomic missiles would wipe off the map, once and for all, the country which today represents colonial oppression." [15] But, subsequently, every effort by Havana to get Khrushchev to specify exactly what assistance he had promised only met with evasions.

In April 1961, receiving Walter Lippmann, Khrushchev had actually told him that he would "oppose" any landing of Cuban exiles supported by the United States. But the famous American columnist had added, in reporting these words, "I hope that I was not misled in understanding him to mean that he would oppose us by propaganda and diplomacy, and that he did not have in mind military intervention. I would, in fact, go a bit farther," he continued, "based not on what he said but by the general tone of his remarks, that, in his book, it is normal for a great power to undermine an unfriendly government within its own sphere of interest." [16] Khrushchev's behavior in the affair of the Bay of Pigs a few days later does not refute that interpretation. Once again in a message to Kennedy, he invoked the specter of a "world . . . catastrophe," but he promised Cuba nothing more than the "necessary assistance" to resist aggression. [17] In any case he was very careful not to mention the missiles which he had been ready to utilize "in the figurative sense" the preceding year. And four days later he dispatched a new message to J.F.K. in which he affirmed that the U.S.S.R. "had no bases in Cuba and did not intend to establish any." [18]

At what point did Khrushchev change his mind? No one knows exactly. What is known, however, through Castro's confidences to Jean Daniel, is that in January 1962, Castro had received alarming news from Moscow. It concerned a report of a conversation which had taken place a few days earlier at Hyannisport—the vacation home of the Kennedys—between the President and Alexei Adjubei, an ambitious and ruthlessly cynical man entrusted more and more frequently with confidential missions by his father-in-law, Khrushchev.

According to Fidel's statements to Daniel, J.F.K. had told his visitor that the American Government had decided to no longer tolerate the presence of a Communist regime in Cuba. He further asserted that the Soviet influence in Cuba was destroying the agreed-upon balance of power and he reminded the Russian that the United States had not intervened in Hungary. This was obviously, according to Castro, a means of exacting a pledge of Russian nonintervention at the time of the projected invasion. In the weeks which followed, added the Cuban leader, "they received considerable information" on the preparations being made by the C.I.A. for another invasion. Having compared the data which they both possessed, the Russians and the Cubans concluded that a landing could take place at any time, and they discussed means of opposing it.

Pierre Salinger, at that time Kennedy's spokesman, categorically denied those statements. As the Russians have revealed nothing about their transactions with the Cubans, Castro, who has often discussed them, represents the only source of information. Unfortunately, he has given very different versions. To several American journalists he said that he himself had asked for the installation of strategic missiles. He let Daniel understand that he would have preferred the conclusion of an alliance, but that the Russians emphasized that the missile installation would be the best means of discouraging the Americans from invading Cuba. They allegedly said they had a double objective: "To save the Cuban revolution—that is to say the success of socialism in the world—and at the same time to avoid a world conflict. According to the Russians, if Cuba had been satisfied with conventional weapons, the United States would not have hesitated to invade. In that event, Russia would have had to reply and a world war would have been inevitable." [19]

This explanation would have been more convincing if the decision had been made public at the time. But the communiqué issued on September 3, after Che Guevara's trip to Moscow, announcing that the U.S.S.R. had agreed to furnish Cuba with arms and technicians to enable it to meet "threats from imperialist quarters," [20] was silent on the nature of those arms. Again, when Kennedy had declared, on the 4th, that to his knowledge there were no offensive weapons in Cuba, but if there were some "the gravest issues would arise," [21] the Kremlin felt obliged to declare, on the 11th: "Our nuclear weapons are so powerful, and the Soviet Union has such powerful rockets to carry these nuclear warheads that there is no need to search for sites for them beyond the boundaries of the Soviet Union." [22]

Why broadcast that unadulterated lie if Khrushchev did not someday intend to confront Kennedy with the *fait accompli* of the presence of missiles in Cuba? Wasn't it Castro himself, who, in an interview with Claude Julien which he never actually denied, declared: "We had debated among ourselves the idea of asking the U.S.S.R. to supply us with missiles, but we had reached no decision when Moscow proposed sending them to us. They explained that in accepting them we would reinforce the socialist bloc on a global level. And because we were receiving substantial aid from the socialist bloc, we decided that we could not refuse. . . . This is the truth, even if other explanations are given elsewhere." [23] If this version is accepted, we can even ask whether Adjubei had not somewhat padded the story of his meeting with Kennedy in order to influence Castro to agree to an arrangement which had, after all, as many chances of drawing lightning to Cuba as of protecting it.

§   §   §

Ever since the beginning of August the C.I.A. had received many reports of the arrival in Cuba of a large quantity of military supplies and Soviet technicians. On the 22nd, the head of the agency, John

A. McCone, advised Kennedy that according to the photographs brought back by the U-2 spy planes which were flying over Cuba twice a month, surface-to-air missiles (SAMs) were being installed. In his judgment, such a move was meaningless unless the Russians also intended to deploy strategic missiles which the SAMs could protect. But no one believed him, and he did not think it necessary to cancel his wedding trip to Europe which was to begin the following day. He did send a series of warnings from Cap Ferrat, where he was spending his honeymoon, but his subordinates did not forward them either to the President or to his close advisers, who, in any case, did not want to believe that the U.S.S.R. would run the enormous risk of installing in Cuba weapons capable of threatening the soil of the United States.

Nevertheless, on September 13, Kennedy renewed his admonition of the 4th to Khrushchev, declaring that even if, according to the information he had at hand, the arms delivered to Cuba "did not represent any serious danger for the Western Hemisphere . . . the United States would take appropriate measures in the event that one day Communist installations in Cuba would threaten its security. However," he added, "under the actual circumstances, a unilateral military intervention cannot be necessary or justified." [24] On the 14th he obtained from Congress special powers to call up 150,000 reservists if the need should arise during the Congressional recess.

Meanwhile, the number of U-2 overflights was increased around the world. But because one of those planes had been shot down over China by a SAM, the pilots were asked to prevent an international incident by not venturing too often through Cuban skies. It took urgent requests from McCone, who had returned from France on September 26, for Kennedy to decide, only on October 9, to order reconnaissance flights over the western part of the island. In the meantime, persistent rumors reached the ears of the American leaders as well as of some congressmen such as Senator Keating, who did not hesitate to exploit them, that strategic missiles were actually being installed.

On September 21 the C.I.A. had, in point of fact, detected a missile "larger than the others." However, as reported by Elie Abel in his exciting book on the crisis, the C.I.A. believed that two enormous Soviet freighters built for the transport of lumber, which had arrived in Havana riding high in the water as if only half full, could be explained by "the shortage of cargoes" from which it seemed the U.S.S.R. suffered. Naturally, in retrospect their draft can be explained by the presence of the precious missiles in their holds." [25] Abel also reported that a Castro pilot had said, after a few drinks in a bar, that now Cuba possessed strategic missiles. In addition, one of the leaders of the revolution had told Henry Brandon, the Washington correspondent of *The Sunday Times,* who was visiting the island: "Cuba is not as defenseless as you may think. We now have missiles on Cuban territory whose range is good enough to hit the United States. . . . We will not use them for aggressive purposes. . . . But obviously if you want to defend yourself it is first of all not enough these days to intercept ships and planes at fifty miles range. And . . . you must also be able to hit an attacker's territory if necessary." [26]

Because of unfavorable weather the U-2 missions could not be resumed until October 14. On the 15th the photographs brought back were minutely studied by specialists. They were revealing: here were long mobile missiles such as were seen during the May 1 parades in Moscow . . . there was the location of a launching pad of an intermediate-range missile with its bunkers, its radar and, in a corner protected by a grove of trees, a silo with a metal roof situated between mounds of earth on freshly cleared ground which had all the appearance of a storehouse for nuclear warheads.

This documentation was brought to the President while he was eating his breakfast, on Tuesday the 16th, by his special assistant on matters of national security, McGeorge Bundy. Kennedy did not hide his surprise but preserved perfect composure and, in order to cover up, performed the major part of the public duties scheduled for that day, beginning with the reception for the astronaut Walter Schirra at the White House. At 11:45 that morning he convened a war council, made up of some fifteen men he had selected himself, among whom were Johnson, Rusk, McNamara, Robert Kennedy, Bundy and Maxwell Taylor. This group, which met secretly two or three times a day until the end of the crisis, was named the Executive Committee of the National Security Council, in abbreviated form, the Ex-Com.

During that first meeting, on October 16, Kennedy directed that as much proof as possible be assembled, to make sure that there was no question of a hoax. He also asked that no word of this matter leak out until the United States had determined the modalities of its reaction, in order to avoid either a Soviet initiative which would be difficult to check, or a reaction of panic in America. For that reason it was decided not to inform the Allies. Several interpretations of the Soviet intentions were offered, and several countermeasures suggested. Discussions on both subjects continued during the following days.

According to Sorensen, who took part in all these meetings, five explanations for Khrushchev's decision were considered. For his part, Kennedy was tempted to think that Khrushchev wanted to test American determination, and if, as he hoped, it weakened, he would move forward in Berlin. Others thought that he wanted to provoke the United States into attacking Cuba, expecting that such action would result in a wave of indignation against the United States of which he would take advantage in order to grab Berlin. Others formulated more reassuring hypotheses: Khrushchev was simply seeking to regain a nuclear advantage jeopardized by the spectacular advances in American missiles—the weapons launched from Cuba could reach American soil so quickly that the bombers of the Strategic Air Command would not have the time to take off—or that he was preparing a Cuba-Berlin deal; or even that he only intended to reinforce the defenses of the island.

Any possible course of action had to be determined on the basis of an evaluation of Khrushchev's declaration of September 11 in which he had affirmed that the Soviet Government had no plans to deploy nuclear arms in Cuba, but had added that any attack against Cuba would mean the "beginning of the unleashing of war." Khrushchev had raised the specter of an atomic conflict and recalled, evoking Hitler's fate, that "he who sows the wind, will reap the whirlwind." [27] There was certainly not in that document any firm commitment from the U.S.S.R. to resort to its nuclear arsenal to support the Havana regime. But Kennedy had been sufficiently impressed with it to tell his advisers that, whatever action was taken, it "raised the prospect that it might escalate the Soviet Union into a nuclear war." [28] The fact that Khrushchev had committed an error in be-

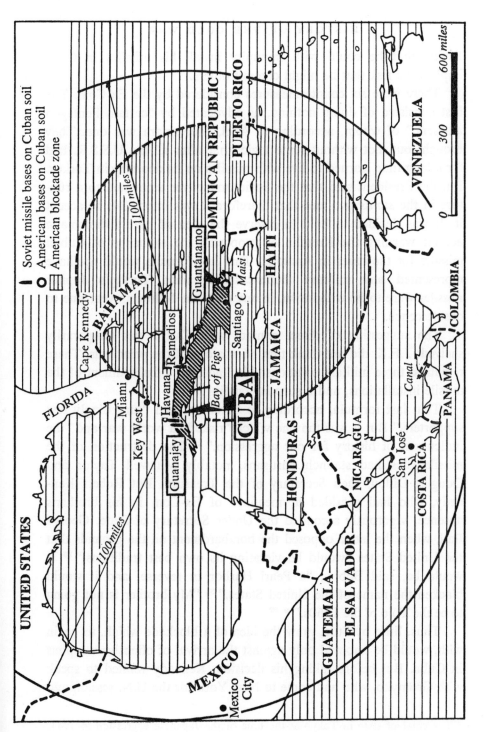

VIII THE CARIBBEAN REGION

Soviet missile bases on Cuban soil
American bases on Cuban soil
American blockade zone

UNITED STATES

FLORIDA

Miami

Key West

Cape Kennedy

BAHAMAS

Guanajay

Havana Remedios

Bay of Pigs

CUBA

Santiago C. Maisí

Guantánamo

DOMINICAN REPUBLIC

PUERTO RICO

HAITI

JAMAICA

Mexico City

MEXICO

GUATEMALA

EL SALVADOR

HONDURAS

NICARAGUA

San José

COSTA RICA

Canal

PANAMA

COLOMBIA

VENEZUELA

1100 miles

1100 miles

0   300   600 miles

lieving that he could with impunity install his missiles in Cuba implied the risk that he might commit others.

There were six countermeasures considered by the Ex-Com. The first consisted of doing nothing, as advocated by "certain Pentagon advisers," of whom, according to Abel, McNamara was one. They brought out, not without some logic, that after all the U.S.S.R. had for a long time learned to live with missiles on its doorstep in Turkey. But the President said that the Soviet maneuver amounted to a rupture in the *status quo* and that therefore it was impossible to accept it. It was decided to hold in reserve the idea of purely diplomatic action: warning the Kremlin or proposing the exchange of Cuban missiles for the bases in Anatolia. That last formula would not have represented any military inconvenience, since Turkey's Jupiter missiles were to be withdrawn, in any case, the following year due to obsolescence.

The suggestion of direct contact with Castro was temporarily shelved: J.F.K. did not think that he was one of the principals. There remained three military solutions: blockade, the bombardment of the missile installations, and a surprise landing.

That last formula, according to Sorensen, had "surprisingly few supporters." But it was the one which "risked" a world war and "the indictment of history for our aggression." [29] The destruction of the missile sites had staunch partisans, notably Maxwell Taylor and Douglas Dillon, then Secretary of the Treasury. But Robert Kennedy, who had presided at meetings of Ex-Com in his brother's absence, vigorously seconded the Under Secretary of State, George Ball, when the latter opposed the bombardment on the grounds that the United States "would be violating its own best traditions." [30] It would be, said Bobby, "a Pearl Harbor in reverse, and it would blacken the name of the United States." [31] "My brother is not going to be the Tojo of the 1960s." *[32]

Thus, little by little, grew the idea of a blockade which, to begin with, would be imposed only against the arrival of offensive weapons in Cuba. But before taking his decision, Kennedy wanted to speak with Gromyko, who had come to New York for the U.N. session and

* The chief of state in Tokyo at the time of the Japanese aggression in 1941.

had asked to meet him. The audience had been set for a long time for the afternoon of Thursday, October 18.

When the Soviet minister, after having reiterated his threats on Berlin, complained about the United States' anti-Cuban campaign, Kennedy warned him, without mentioning the pictures taken by the U-2's, against any future establishment by the U.S.S.R. of strategic bases on the island.

Looking him straight in the eye, the Russian replied that the U.S.S.R. had no other intention than to contribute "to the defense capabilities of Cuba; if otherwise," the Russian continued, "the Soviet Government would never become involved in rendering such assistance." [33]

A few hours later, while Rusk was entertaining his Kremlin colleague at dinner, the Ex-Com gathered at the White House under President Kennedy and weighed once more the relative advantages of blockade versus bombardment. The President, who, more and more, favored the first solution, permitted himself to quip: "Whatever you fellows are recommending, you will be sorry about a week from now." [34]

The next day, as if nothing were happening, Kennedy took a plane for the Middle West, where the Congressional electoral campaigns required his presence. At 1:20 P.M. the commanders in chief of the American forces in the Atlantic and in the Caribbean areas received the order to be ready for any eventuality. The comings and goings of officials had begun to arouse the curiosity of the press and, even more, of the British Embassy, which had almost discovered the secret. The Pentagon categorically denied that it had any information on the presence of offensive weapons in Cuba and therefore that it had ordered emergency measures. During that time, the members of the Ex-Com continued to vacillate between blockade and the destruction of the missile sites, and Sorensen was writing the speech in which Kennedy was going to announce his decision to the world.

The next day, at 8 o'clock in the morning, the President asked Pierre Salinger, his official spokesman, to come and see him in the hotel where he was staying in Chicago. He gave him a communiqué he had written himself: "Slight respiratory [infection], 1 degree temperature. Weather raw and rainy. Recommended return to Washington." [35] Once in the White House, the President asked him to "stick around," because something was going to happen. "If you know nothing about it," he told him, "you're lucky." [36]

A few moments later he announced to the Ex-Com that he had definitely decided to begin with a limited action—the blockade of offensive arms, it being understood that if this was not effective, it might be necessary to have recourse to bombardment. He brushed aside a suggestion from Stevenson—his delegate to the U.N.—who wanted to offer the Russians either the evacuation of Guantánamo or the withdrawal of the Jupiter missiles from Turkey, in exchange for the removal of Russian missiles, saying that the only result of that policy would be to undermine any confidence that its Allies had in the United States.

It was more and more difficult to hide the reality of the situation. On Saturday evening, James Reston, the famed *New York Times* reporter, was able to write an article describing the precautionary measures taken in the Caribbean area, and come to the conclusion that the Russians must have finally installed strategic missiles in Cuba. To satisfy his conscience, he submitted it to the White House before publishing it. The President himself telephoned the editor in chief of the newspaper to urgently request him to sacrifice the scoop in the interests of national security. Otherwise, he added, we will have an ultimatum from Moscow before we are able to take action.

The article was withdrawn, but the capital was buzzing with rumors which were echoed in the Sunday papers and even more in the Monday morning newspapers. It was on that day, October 22, following a script carefully worked over during the weekend, that Kennedy was to reveal the situation and the measures he intended to take to meet it.

Abroad, Macmillan and de Gaulle were the first ones to be notified. Kennedy had asked Dean Acheson to cross the Atlantic to inform de Gaulle and at the same time the NATO Council. As could have been expected, the President of the Republic was equal to the occasion. "Are you consulting or informing me?" was the first question he asked the former Secretary of State, before stating that he understood perfectly why the United States had made its decision without consulting its Allies. Brushing aside the clichés that Acheson was offering, he said that he was convinced that Kennedy had acted knowing what he was doing. According to him, the Russians would not react—either in Berlin or in Turkey. "You can tell your President," he concluded, "that France will support him. . . . I think that under the circumstances President Kennedy had no other choice. This is his national prerogative and France understands." It was only then that he asked to see the photographs, which he examined closely with a large magnifying glass. *"C'est formidable,"* he said, when it was explained to him that they had been taken at an altitude of 72,000 feet.[37]

In the afternoon, at the White House, J.F.K. summoned the Ex-Com, then the Cabinet, several members of which knew nothing, and finally the Congressional leaders, some of whom, particularly Fulbright, who was usually more of a pacifist, were surprised that he had not decided on an immediate invasion. At 6 o'clock a smiling Soviet ambassador Dobrynin came to see Rusk. He emerged twenty-five minutes later, visibly shaken, with a copy of the speech that Kennedy was getting ready to make. The Latin American diplomats were briefed by the Under Secretary of State.

Finally, at 7 o'clock, the President addressed his countrymen on television. First he told them that "unmistakable evidence" had established the presence in Cuba of bases for missiles which could reach "Washington, D.C., the Panama Canal and Mexico City," that bases for intermediate-range ballistic missiles "capable of travelling more than twice as far . . . and ranging from as far north as Hudson's Bay and as far south as Lima, Peru," appeared to be in the process of installation, and that bombers capable of carrying nuclear weapons were actually being "uncrated." He saw in this "an explicit threat to the peace and security of all the Americas. . . . This action also contradicts the repeated assurances of Soviet spokesmen. . . . Neither the United States of America nor the world community of nations can tolerate deliberate deception . . . a deliberately provocative and unjustified change in the status quo. . . ."

"The nineteen-thirties," he continued, "taught us a clear lesson. Aggressive conduct, if allowed to go unchecked and unchallenged, ultimately leads to war. . . . Our policy has been one of patience and restraint. . . . We will not risk prematurely or unnecessarily the course of world-wide nuclear war . . . but neither will we shrink from that risk at any time it must be faced."

In view of this, he said, he had ordered a "strict quarantine" —that word had been chosen in preference to the more alarming "blockade"—of all offensive military equipment en route to Cuba, to be followed, if need be, by stronger measures. "It shall be the policy of this nation to regard any nuclear missile launched from Cuba against any nation in the Western Hemisphere as an attack by the Soviet Union on the United States, requiring a full retaliatory response upon the Soviet Union." He asked that the Council of the Organization of American States and the U.N. Security Council be convened. Finally, he asked Khrushchev to abandon "this course of world domination and to join in an historic effort to end the perilous arms race and to transform the history of man. . . . The cost of freedom is always high, but Americans have always paid it." [38]

The dice had been cast in the most important "brinkmanship" gamble the Cold War had known. As soon as they became convinced of the reality of the presence of Soviet missiles in Cuba, Kennedy's strong language earned him the unanimous support of his Allies, including the members of the Rio Pact, who were not always unquestioningly on the side of the United States. They had probably recognized the magnitude of the threat against their collective security. On Tuesday, at 4:45 P.M., the Council of the O.A.S. voted 19 to nil, with one abstention—that of Uruguay, whose delegate had not received instructions—a resolution recommending that the nations of the western hemisphere "intensify individual and collective surveillance of the delivery of arms and implements of war and all other items of strategic importance to the Communist regime in Cuba, in order to prevent the secret accumulation in the island of arms that can be used for offensive purposes against the hemisphere." [39] Two hours later, Kennedy signed the proclamation establishing the quarantine, which was to go into effect the next day, October 24, at 10 A.M. Nineteen warships of the Second Fleet were positioned to implement it along the arc of a 500-mile radius around the eastern tip of Cuba.

Until that moment the Kremlin had not yet reacted, except verbally. Thirteen hours after Kennedy's speech, TASS had published a declaration "warning the government of the U.S.A. of the grave responsibility that it assumed for the destinies of the world in carrying out the measures announced by President Kennedy." It asserted that the arms furnished to Cuba were intended "exclusively for defensive purposes," and that "no state which cherishes its independence" could bow before the claim of the United States "to insist that the war matériel necessary for the self-defense of Cuba be removed from its territory . . . The Soviet Government resolutely rejects," the declaration continued, "the claims of the Government of the U.S.A.," when it "assumes the right to oblige countries to report on the organization of their defenses and to apprise it of what they transport in their ships on the high seas." In cognizance of this, the Soviet Government informed the Security Council of the violation of the Charter and of the threat to peace represented by Washington, which it accused of not hesitating to do anything, even risking the "cataclysm of a military catastrophe," in its efforts "to stifle a sovereign state, a member of the U.N." [40]

This is approximately the same language that Zorin was going to use before the Security Council, in reply to Stevenson's indictment of the policy followed by the U.S.S.R. since the beginning of the Cold War, and of Castro, accused of having betrayed the revolution which brought him to power. "If we do not stand firm here," concluded Ike's old Presidential rival, "our adversaries may think we will stand firm nowhere. . . ." [41] After the delegate from Cuba had identified the American measures as "an act of war" and affirmed that there was no other base on the island save the one maintained by the United States at Guantánamo, the Soviet speaker attacked the "big stick" policy of Washington toward Latin America and its ambition to play the "world gendarme." He declared that Stevenson's speech was "false from beginning to end" and that the United States "was introducing the law of the jungle into international relations." [42]

While the debate continued, Radio Havana announced that "combat units, put back on a war footing, had been sent to their respective bases," and that, "hundreds of thousands of men had been assembled in a few hours." [43] Castro himself characterized Kennedy's speech as the declaration of a pirate and the Soviet reaction as firm, calm and exemplary, and he asserted that anyone attempting to inspect Cuba would have to go ready for battle.[44] Finally, it was learned that twenty-six Soviet ships were en route to Cuba. However, no irretrievable steps had been taken.

§ § §

On October 24, at 10 A.M., the American quarantine was put into effect. Kennedy's declaration specified that any ship headed toward Cuba would receive an order to submit to an inspection and that if it did not comply it could "be interned, force being used only when absolutely necessary." [45]

It was soon learned that the Kremlin had rejected as unacceptable the text of the declaration which had been sent to it. Then Khrushchev, in response to a telegram from the British pacifist-philosopher Bertrand Russell which beseeched him not to be "provoked by the unjustifiable measures taken by the United States in Cuba and to abstain from any rash action," had assured him that the Soviet Government "would do everything to eliminate a situation, fraught with irreparable consequences, which was created following the aggression of the United States Government," but that if it "carried out the programs of piracy which it had planned, we would be obliged to take defense measures against the aggressor. . . . It is necessary," he added, "to deal forcefully with the brigand in order to prevent the law of the jungle from regulating relations between states and civilized peoples." In conclusion, however, he did not dismiss the possibility of a summit meeting.[46]

That discreet hint was accompanied by a few other gestures calculated to show that the Kremlin did not intend to burn its bridges. Surprisingly, Khrushchev, who, it might be thought, had other things to do, had attended a recital by the American singer Jerome Hines the evening before. On Wednesday he asked the president of Westinghouse, William Knox, who was then passing through Moscow, to come and see him. For three full hours he recounted all his grievances against the U.S. and asked Knox to explain to Kennedy that if American ships tried to stop Russian freighters, his submarines would be obliged to sink them. But he assured him that he had no aggressive intentions. "If I aim a revolver at you," he said, "it is an offensive weapon, but if I only do it to prevent you from shooting me, it is a defensive weapon. Isn't this so?" [47] Thus he implicitly admitted that he had in fact supplied Cuba with strategic missiles. Also, on October 24 the Soviet naval attaché in London, Ivanov, lunching with the soon-to-be famous Dr. Stephen Ward, told him that only the British, by taking the initiative of calling a summit, could save the peace.

In the afternoon, U Thant read the Security Council an appeal that he had just sent to the two Ks at the request of many member countries: "It is important that time should be given to enable the parties concerned to get together with a view to resolving the present crisis peacefully and normalizing the situation in the Caribbean.

"This involves, on the one hand, the voluntary suspension of all arms shipments to Cuba, and also the voluntary suspension of the quarantine measures applied, involving the search of ships bound for Cuba." [48] He suggested that voluntary suspension last two or three weeks, and he offered his good offices.

Kennedy took his time before answering. He had just learned that a dozen of the twenty-five Russian ships en route to Cuba had either stopped or turned around. "We're eyeball to eyeball," declared Rusk to McGeorge Bundy, "and I think the other fellow just blinked." [49] Nevertheless, the Pentagon wondered if those ships were not simply going to rendezvous with the submarines which had been spotted in the vicinity. In his uncertainty the President ordered the suspension of the order to stop any ships entering the blockade zone and that, for the moment, it was sufficient to follow them. Obeying those instructions, the United States let the Soviet tanker *Bucharest* go through without inspecting it. On being questioned, its commander politely answered that he was only carrying oil. Due to the high level of the water line and the fact that he had left the U.S.S.R. before Kennedy's speech—which seemed to exclude the hypothesis of a complicated camouflage—the Americans accepted those verbal assurances.

In the evening, Harriman telephoned Schlesinger that, in his opinion, Khrushchev was seeking a way out, and if one could be skillfully shown to him, the U.S.A. could "downgrade the tough group in the Soviet Union which persuaded him to do this." [50] If not, in his opinion, it would be an escalation toward nuclear war. Kennedy received him on Thursday the 25th, before replying to U Thant that he did not reject any solution: "Last night, you made certain suggestions and proposed preliminary talks in order to see if satisfactory arrangements could be made. Ambassador Stevenson is ready to promptly discuss those arrangements with you." [51]

Khrushchev himself had simply accepted the truce of two or three weeks suggested by the Secretary General of the U.N. But Kennedy feared that if he did the same, it might give the Russians time to expedite the installation of their missiles, and therefore in his reply he reiterated that he intended to have them removed.

The crisis was far from over. Besides, the Security Council was that same day the scene of a violent battle of wits. Zorin stated that the proofs on which Washington had relied to decree the Cuba blockade were "faked." Stevenson, raring to go, said to him, "Let me ask you one single question: Do you, Ambassador Zorin, deny that the U.S.S.R. has placed and is placing medium and intermediate-range missiles and sites in Cuba? Yes or No? [Mr. Zorin refused to answer.] I am prepared to wait for my answer until hell freezes over." Zorin burst into a nervous laugh which spread to his colleagues and answered: "We are not in an American court: you are not a prosecutor and I am not going to reply to your questions." Stevenson had easels brought in on which were displayed enlargements of the photos taken by the U-2. With the help of an expert, he analyzed that documentation before concluding, "Our job here is not to score debating points. Our job, Mr. Zorin, is to save the peace. And if you are ready to try, we are." [52]

It was on the next day, Friday, that the crisis began to be resolved. At 7 o'clock in the morning, the destroyer *Joseph P. Kennedy Jr.* —named for the President's elder brother who had been killed in the war during a mission over Germany—intercepted, according to explicit instructions from J.F.K., a neutral steamer chartered by the U.S.S.R., which unresistingly let itself be inspected from top to bottom. As it did not contain any cargo prohibited by the blockade proclamation, it was allowed to continue on its course.

Obviously, this was meant to show Mr. K—without taking major risks—that the United States was not weakening in its determination.

But the American reconnaissance planes, now authorized by the Pentagon to fly over Cuba at low altitudes, brought back photos showing that the missile installations were being accelerated. Kennedy, while putting aside the immediate bombardment of the sites which had been suggested by some officials, endeavored, through a brilliantly organized "saturation" campaign to convince the interested parties that he would not refrain from making such a decision if the U.S.S.R. did not promptly dismantle the bases. Almost everywhere new military measures were being taken without the slightest attempt at secrecy. The crews of the bombers of the Strategic Air Command, openly known to be loaded with nuclear bombs, exchanged clear, apocalyptic messages. Because the press services of the White House had spread more alarming news than they had been authorized to, the newspapers appeared with headlines announcing an imminent catastrophe.

Kennedy was furious, but the maneuver was successful. A little before noon, a Soviet Embassy official, Alexander Fomin, generally thought to be the chief of Russian intelligence in the United States, asked a reporter from A.B.C., John Scali, whom he knew fairly well, to have lunch with him immediately. Right off, he asked him if the State Department would be willing to settle the affair under three conditions: (1) the return of the missiles to the U.S.S.R. under U.N. control; (2) a commitment on Castro's part not to accept any more offensive weapons, and (3) a commitment from the U.S. not to invade Cuba. A few hours later, Rusk himself dictated to Scali the text of the reply which he communicated to Fomin the same night: "I have reason to believe that the U.S.G. [United States Government] sees real possibilities in this and supposes that representatives of the two governments could work this matter out with U Thant and with each other. My impression is, however, that time is very urgent." [53]

Fomin's move was apparently intended to reinforce Khrushchev's own. During the same evening the American Embassy in Moscow relayed to Kennedy a confidential message from Khrushchev. That document has never been made public, and several rumors circulated as to its tone. "Rambling" and "obviously composed under the stress of great emotion," according to newsmen James Daniel and

John Hubbell [54]; "the nightmare outcry of a frightened man," according to Elie Abel [55]; "not . . . hysterical," but "gave the impression of having been written in deep emotion," [56] for Schlesinger, who surely had read it. "Full of polemics . . . but appearing to contain a germ of a reasonable settlement," [57] for Sorensen, who had also read it. In any case, its essential elements are known.

Repeating the arguments he had developed before the president of Westinghouse, Khrushchev, while admitting that he had deployed strategic missiles in Cuba, argued that a weapon is offensive not from its nature, but from the use that can be made of it. He added that the missiles had already arrived, and that it was therefore completely useless to try to search the Russian ships. He was ready to solemnly affirm this and asked Kennedy to pledge himself not to attack Cuba. In that event, he said, the problem of "weapons called offensive would appear under another light." In conclusion, he asked the President to stop, as he himself was ready to do, "pulling on the rope" and to try "to undo the knot" which was tightening in the middle.

In spite of skepticism from Acheson, who did not believe that the Russians would carry out the arrangement they proposed, the Ex-Com decided on Friday night to treat the letter "as a move in good faith." Then everyone went to bed, obviously reassured.

Unfortunately, the next day, the tune had to be changed. Radio Moscow broadcast another message from Khrushchev to Kennedy, this one public, proposing the simultaneous removal of missiles from Cuba and Turkey, under control of the U.N. On a military level Washington had everything to gain from such an exchange, because, as already mentioned, the Jupiters in Turkey were pretty obsolete. But when, in the spring, Rusk had conveyed to the Ankara Government the United States' desire to remove them, its Foreign Minister, Selim Sarper had opposed it, stating that their presence represented an indispensable token of Allied solidarity. It can also be stated that if the affair had been settled this way, it would have represented a political gain for the Soviets since—in relation to the situation prevailing two months earlier—only the Americans would have made a concession.

Without hesitation, Kennedy decided to reject the deal proposed to him, although he did not thoroughly understand the reasons why Khrushchev had reversed his position of the day before. Perhaps Khrushchev believed that a suggestion to that effect from Walter Lippmann had been inspired by the White House—the Russians have never completely understood that an independent journalist could suggest ideas without being a spokesman of the government or of a group of vested interests. Another explanation, which tends to corroborate the study of that period made by Michel Tatu,[58] is that the Soviet hierarchy was in a state of turmoil and that the advice that prevailed at noon might very well not be acceptable at 5 o'clock. On October 29, a few hours after Khrushchev had made his missile trade proposal, *Izvestia* rejected similar suggestions made by some American commentators, declaring that they only reflected "the guilty conscience of their authors." Such a contradiction was without precedent in the Soviet press.

Two hours and fifteen minutes after the publication of the Soviet note, the White House released a communiqué according to which "the preliminary condition to any consideration of proposals is that work on the Cuban bases must stop. Offensive weapons must be neutralized and the sending of offensive weapons to Cuba must stop. All this must take place within the framework of effective international verification." [59]

Scali was asked to renew contact as soon as possible with his man at the Soviet Embassy to ask him for explanations. Embarrassed, Fomin declared that Khrushchev's second letter must have been written before his report had reached Moscow. Scali, repeating the message entrusted to him, said that he did not believe a word of it and that it was an "ignoble, put-up job." If that was the case, he continued, the Russians were about to commit one of the most colossal miscalculations in history. And he assured him that, under no conditions and at no time, would Kennedy accept a deal on the bases. The diplomat replied that he would convey that warning and that there would soon be an answer.

In the meantime, it was announced to Kennedy that a U-2 had lost its way over Soviet territory, despite all instructions that had been given to avoid anything that could resemble a provocative act, and that Russian fighters had taken off to intercept it. Fortunately, it had succeeded in escaping by the time Washington swore to the Kremlin that it was an unintentional error. However, when all is said and done, it may be that this untimely flight helped convince the leaders of the U.S.S.R. of America's determination. In any case, they were very careful at the time not to mention the incident.

Then, another U-2 was reported missing. This one had been shot down over Cuba, and Radio Havana warned that "Any military plane which invades Cuban air space does so at the risk of being fired at by the D.C.A."

Until then, the aviators who flew over the island did not encounter any resistance. Thus, a major step had been taken toward escalation. Most informed officials in Washington now believed that the missile installations would be attacked within forty-eight hours. But Robert Kennedy had an idea. He suggested to his brother that he answer not the second letter from Khrushchev, the one which had been published, but rather the confidential message of the day before. And as the drafts submitted to Robert Kennedy did not satisfy him, he and Ted Sorensen wrote the letter which was sent to the Soviet council during the evening of October 27.

"As I read this letter," he has J.F.K. saying, it contains elements "generally acceptable, as I understand them," [60] and which he enumerates as: elimination, under control, of the missiles from Cuba, then a lifting of the blockade and a promise from the United States not to invade the island. Twenty minutes before, U Thant had written Castro, somewhat ignored throughout this affair, asking him to make "a significant contribution to the peace of the world" in ordering the suspension of the construction of missile bases while negotiations were in progress.

Fidel's reply was prompt and negative. Let the U.S. begin by lifting the blockade. "Cuba has not violated any international law." [61] Khrushchev's reply was longer in coming, and the early hours of Sunday, the 27th, were filled with alarming news: recall to active duty of 24 squadrons and 14,000 reservists; mobilization in Venezuela. But at 10:30 A.M. Washington time, the crackling teletypes of the press agencies sent out the most sensational "flash": Khrushchev had agreed to remove the missiles!

This time, Khrushchev did not bother with preambles: "I understand perfectly your anxiety," he wrote Kennedy. "In order to re-solve as quickly as possible a dangerous conflict . . . and to reassure the American people . . . the Soviet Government, supple-menting the instructions previously given concerning the cessation of further work of construction on bases for the installation of weapons, has given a new order to the effect that the weapons you call offensive are to be dismantled and brought back to the Soviet Union."

After mentioning the continued threat which weighed over Cuba and reiterating that he only wanted to supply it with means of defense against aggression, Khrushchev stated that he had "respect and confidence" in the statement contained in Kennedy's message of October 27—according to which there would be no invasion of Cuba either by the U.S. or by other American countries. The reasons which had made him grant aid to the island having thus vanished, the dismantling of the bases became possible and he was quite ready to have U.N. representatives control it.[62] A few hours later, Fomin saw Scali once more: "I have been instructed," he said, "to thank you and to tell you that the information you supplied was very valuable to the Chairman in helping him to make up his mind quickly. And," he added, "that includes your 'explosion' Saturday!"[63]

§   §   §

The Verdun of the Cold War had just ended with a victory which only cost the United States the lives of five men: the U-2 pilot shot down over Cuba and the four crew members of a bomber which had exploded on takeoff. But, whatever their relief and exultation, the American leaders had the wisdom not to exploit their adversary's admission of defeat. Rusk received diplomatic reporters and told them: "If there is a debate, a rivalry, a contest going on in the Krem-lin over how to play this situation, we don't want the word 'capitu-lation' used or any gloating in Washington to strengthen the hands of those in Moscow who wanted to play this another way."[64]

For his part, Kennedy lost no time in hailing that decision as "worthy of a statesman" and to reply to Khrushchev that his message made "an important contribution to peace."[65] Expressing his regrets for the incident of the U-2 which had, twenty-four hours earlier, flown over Russian territory and of which Khrushchev had complained, he advocated prompt action against proliferation of nuclear arms and for the cessation of tests.

Cuba, however, refused to participate in the general euphoria. Three hours after the publication of Khrushchev's letter to Kennedy, Fidel Castro, who obviously had not been advised by Moscow, published a declaration according to which the "guarantees against an aggression aimed at Cuba" mentioned by Kennedy, would not exist as long as the U.S. would not put an end to their harsh economic measures against the island, to their subversive activities, to their violations of Cuba's airspace, and would not evacuate Guantánamo. The Cuban populace, which throughout the crisis had demonstrated extraordinary discipline, encouraged him to hold fast, singing:

> *"Nikita, Nikita,*
> *Lo que se da no se quita . . ."* *

Forty-eight hours later, Fidel reiterated the five conditions to U Thant, who had come to see him to work out the control by U.N. observers of the dismantling of missile bases, promised by Mr. K to Kennedy. He added, that "the inspection request was intended to humiliate his country once more, and for that reason, he would not accept it." [66] But, in the same speech where he reported this conversation to his countrymen, Castro asserted that he would continue to have confidence in the "principles of the Soviet Union's policy" and its "leadership" and that he did not intend to let his enemies take advantage of the "differences which had arisen" between Moscow and Havana by discussing them publicly. In any case, he would not oppose the removal of the Soviet strategic weapons.[67]

Much later, he was to open his heart to Claude Julien: "Khrushchev ought not to have removed his missiles without consulting us. Cuba does not want to be a pawn on the world chess board . . . we are not a satellite. . . . Khrushchev avoided war, but he did not achieve peace. No one has the right to dispose of Cuban sovereignty. . . . The Cuban people were very hostile to Khrushchev's decision. Their anger was very natural and I understood that I would have to appease popular wrath by expressing publicly what everyone was

* "Nikita, Nikita, that which is given is not taken back." (Abel, *op. cit.*, p. 213.)

thinking . . . yielding before imperialism encourages it to be more demanding." [68]

As there was evidently no question of Kennedy's accepting Castro's conditions, two problems remained unsolved: the control of the dismantling of the missiles and the removal of the bombers supplied to Cuba by the U.S.S.R. In fact, the United States considered them to be weapons as strategic as the missiles, while Castro, pointing out that they had been delivered to his air force, intended to keep them. It took all the diplomatic patience of Mikoyan, "the man who could sell refrigerators to Eskimos," sent by Khrushchev to Havana on November 2, to find a solution. Mikoyan stayed twenty-four days in Havana without even returning to Moscow for the funeral of his wife, who had died in the meantime. Finally, Kennedy was able to announce on November 20, that Khrushchev had promised to remove the bombers within thirty days—agreeing that they would be "observed and counted" on departure. Consequently, he had ordered the lifting of the blockade of offensive arms and given assurances of the United States' intention not to invade Cuba. [69] It was already quite a while since the missiles had returned to the U.S.S.R. on board freighters amply photographed by American planes and that the U-2's, in place of U.N. observers, had brought back photographs confirming the destruction of the sites.

Receiving me a few days later in Paris, Walt Rostow said, with all the self-assurance of a victor: "As things now stand the Russians can try to take their revenge by attempting to catch up with us in the arms race. There is every chance that they will get winded doing it. They can also try to make peace. We are ready for both eventualities." It was soon to become evident that they had chosen the second.

BIBLIOGRAPHY AND NOTES

[1] W. W. Rostow, *View from the Seventh Floor* (New York: Harper, 1966), p. 9.

[2] *Est et Ouest*, No. 367, July 16–31, 1966.

[3] Vincent Monteil, *L'Islam Noir* (Paris: Editions du Seuil, 1964), p. 316.

[4] Ameillon, *op. cit.*, p. 191.

[5] *Ibid.*

[6] Schlesinger, *op. cit.*, p. 769.
[7] *The Sunday Times* (London), May 13, 1963.
[8] *Le Monde*, January 3, 1962.
[9] Draper, *op. cit.*, p. 227.
[10] *Le Monde*, July 18, 1962.
[11] Sorensen, *op. cit.*, p. 667.
[12] Schlesinger, *op. cit.*, p. 804.
[13] Draper, *op. cit.*, p. 82.
[14] *Ibid.*
[15] *Ibid.*
[16] Walter Lippmann, "What Khrushchev Told an American Writer," *U.S. News and World Report*, May 1, 1961.
[17] Keesing's, 18151 A, 18152.
[18] *Ibid.*, 18185.
[19] *L'Express*, December 6, 1963.
[20] Keesing's, 19057 A.
[21] *Ibid.*
[22] *Ibid.*, 19058.
[23] *Le Monde*, March 22, 1963.
[24] *Ibid.*, September 15, 1962.
[25] Elie Abel, *The Missile Crisis* (Philadelphia: Lippincott, 1966), pp. 41–42.
[26] *The Sunday Times* (London), October 28, 1962.
[27] Keesing's, 19058.
[28] Sorensen, *op. cit.*, pp. 680–81.
[29] *Ibid.*, p. 683.
[30] Abel, *op. cit.*, pp. 63–64.
[31] Sorensen, *op. cit.*, p. 683.
[32] Abel, *op. cit.*, pp. 63–64.
[33] Schlesinger, *op. cit.*, p. 805.
[34] *Ibid.*
[35] Abel, *op. cit.*, pp. 91–92.
[36] *Ibid.*
[37] *Ibid.*, pp. 112–13.
[38] *The New York Times*, October 23, 1962.
[39] Keesing's, 19057 A.
[40] *U.R.S.S.*, No. 2688, October 23, 1963.
[41] Keesing's, 19059 A, 19060.
[42] *Ibid.*
[43] *Le Monde*, October 24, 1962.
[44] Draper, *op. cit.*, pp. 240–41.
[45] *Le Monde*, October 25, 1962.
[46] *Ibid.*, October 26, 1962.
[47] *Ibid.*
[48] Abel, *op. cit.*, pp. 149–50.
[49] *Ibid.*, p. 153.
[50] Schlesinger, *op. cit.*, p. 821.
[51] *Le Monde*, October 27, 1962.
[52] Sorensen, *op. cit.*, pp. 706–7; Schlesinger, *op. cit.*, p. 824.
[53] Abel, *op. cit.*, p. 179.
[54] James Daniel and John G. Hubbell, *Strike in the West* (Paris: Robert Laffont, 1963), p. 150.
[55] Abel, *op. cit.*, p. 180.
[56] Schlesinger, *op. cit.*, pp. 826–27.
[57] Sorensen, *op. cit.*, p. 712.
[58] Michel Tatu, *Le pouvoir en U.R.S.S.* (Paris: Grasset, 1967), pp. 281–320.
[59] *Le Monde*, October 30, 1962.
[60] *Ibid.*
[61] *Ibid.*
[62] *Ibid.*
[63] Roger Hilsman, *To Move a Nation* (New York: Doubleday, 1967), p. 224.
[64] Abel, *op. cit.*, p. 207.
[65] Tatu, *op. cit.*, pp. 281–320.
[66] Hilsman, *op. cit.*, p. 224.
[67] Merlier, *op. cit.*, p. 210.
[68] *Le Monde*, March 22, 1963.
[69] *The New York Times*, November 21, 1962.

· CHAPTER 20 ·

THE ARMISTICE

Peace is a gift from heaven; but as with other gifts
it can only bear fruit if it is cared for.

—Victor de Mirabeau, *The Friend of
Man, or a Treatise on Populations* (1756)

WHEN THE CUBAN MISSILE CRISIS ERUPTED, MANY
people—especially Kennedy—expected a Soviet move against Berlin.
Nothing happened, but it could still be wondered if, once Khrushchev
had removed his weapons, he was not going to attempt to take his
revenge one way or another. The opposite occurred. Tension rapidly
diminished in the old capital and gradually silence surrounded the
problem which Khrushchev had contended for four years contained
the explosive elements of a new Sarajevo, and which had to be
resolved promptly if a new world war was to be avoided.

On November 2, just five days after the announcement of the
removal of missiles from Cuba, Khrushchev received Ulbricht and
the other G.D.R. leaders. It was probably to advise them that the
signing of the peace treaty had been postponed until better days. In
any case, the TASS dispatch did not make the slightest reference to
the treaty. Soon there were no more incidents in the city, on the
Autobahn or in the air lanes. On December 1, Ulbricht declared
that the signing of a treaty was dependent on the development of a
long-term policy of accommodation, and that solving economic problems was much more important. He did not say one word about a
separate peace.

In the major speech he made on September 12 before the Supreme Soviet concerning the budget, Khrushchev returned to the
familiar theme that his patience was not limitless, but he only spent

three minutes on it in a presentation lasting three hours. As he had said somewhere else that ". . . imperialism . . . if it is now a 'paper tiger' [a phrase frequently used in Chinese propaganda] . . . has atomic teeth. It can use them and must not be treated lightly. . . ." [1] It is very clear that he had learned his lesson from the failure of his attempts at intimidation. Besides, Novotny, President of the Czechoslovakian Republic, had declared a week earlier to the Congress of his country's Communist Party, "The time has not yet come to consider imperialism a harmless old man who makes threats which he has not the strength to carry out." [2] The harsh tone of the note the Kremlin sent Adenauer at the end of the year could not, under those conditions, either deceive or upset anyone. Furthermore, on January 15, 1963, Khrushchev declared in East Berlin, before the Congress of the United Socialist Party, that the construction of the wall had made a peace treaty less urgent. By this time the crisis which had so often kept the world in suspense was over—completely over.

If, as there was every reason to believe, the offensive started by the Kremlin in Berlin and then in Cuba had, among other goals, that of disarming Chinese criticisms it was evident that the double setback could only revive them. A week after the Soviets' decision to remove the missiles, the Peking *People's Daily* wrote that "to negotiate a compromise with Kennedy or to accept his brutal demands can only encourage the aggressor." On the 15th it attacked, without naming them, "modern revisionists" who "submit to imperialistic pressure," thus tending to "encourage imperialism to increase its aggression and its war policies." On December 31, in a long article devoted to the "differences between Togliatti and us," it specified that China had neither requested the installation of missiles in Cuba nor objected to their withdrawal, but that it was firmly opposed "to the sacrifice of the sovereignty of another country as a means of reaching a compromise with imperialism." Such a compromise being "simply another Munich." Finally, on March 4 it mentioned "several persons who had committed first the error of adventurism and then that of capitulationism, asking the Cuban people to accept humiliating conditions which would have meant the sacrifice of their country's sovereignty."

The Soviet retreat before imperialism was not the only reason for the recent deterioration of relations between Peking and Moscow. In the spring of 1962, as would be learned later, trouble had broken out in Sinkiang, Chinese Turkestan, a vast, half-desert territory on the distant borders of the U.S.S.R. and China, which contained China's nuclear plants. According to Chou En-lai, "At the instigation and under direct orders from abroad the most reactionary elements of local chauvinism in Sinkiang, traitors to the fatherland, have started a counterrevolutionary armed rebellion, inciting and organizing the flight abroad of many inhabitants of the border regions." [3] In any event, Kazakh Moslems had crossed into the U.S.S.R. where the press was later to publish the story of their persecution at the hands of the Chinese authorities. Soviet consulates in Sinkiang had been closed in July 1962.

At the same time, Sino-Indian relations, strained since the 1959 incidents in the contested frontier region of the Himalayas, were going through a period of great tension. Peking and New Delhi bombarded each other with notes—the total reached four hundred —to reaffirm their claims. On July 9, the *People's Daily* had urged India to control itself "if it wanted to avoid falling into the abyss."

On July 21 a brief skirmish resulted in one death. The Indian press urged Nehru not to permit the nation's sovereignty to be mocked any longer.

At the beginning of October the Indian leaders, completely misunderstanding the actual military situation, began to use a language that could only appear to the Chinese leaders as either a provocation or at least as an attempt to increase the difficulties they faced in Sinkiang and Tibet, both provinces touching on disputed regions. Krishna Menon, the Indian Defense Minister, gave orders to the troops "to open fire if necessary." His colleague, the Minister of the Interior, stated that there was no other alternative but to "drive out the Chinese aggressors," and Nehru declared that troops had been sent to the frontier to occupy "battle positions." [4]

On October 12, after another incident, the Prime Minister ordered his troops to "liberate the territory to the northeast frontiers" [5] and Menon, on the 14th, announced that his countrymen would "fight to the last man, the last gun." [6] Peking reacted quickly and on the

20th, the day on which Kennedy decided to enforce the Cuban blockade, started a general offensive against the Indian positions. Apparently no one in New Delhi had any idea that the Chinese were capable of transporting tens of thousands of men, well equipped and perfectly trained to fight in the snow, along wretched roads, at an altitude of 13,000 feet.

In spite of their gallantry the Indians were rapidly overwhelmed and India appealed for American and British aid in the form of loans and arms. The next day, Chinese advance units were within sight of the Assam Plains where there were no longer any natural obstacles to stop them, and within 95 miles of the oil fields which might have been the prime objective of their leaders. But once more China chose to upset the world's expectations. On the 20th, probably believing that the Indians had been taught a severe enough lesson—they suffered the loss of some 6,000 men killed and missing—China's leaders ordered a cease-fire and withdrew its troops to a frontline 12 miles behind the line which, in fact, had separated Chinese and Indians in October 1959. At the same time, Peking clearly demonstrated its good will in negotiations undertaken with Pakistan for the peaceful demarcation of their common frontiers, including Kashmir which was claimed by New Delhi.

Through its swift action China had scored several successes. It had humiliated India and considerably weakened its prestige in the nonaligned world whose leader it had seemed to be for so many years; it had obliged India to turn again for help to the Anglo-Saxons, thus demonstrating the weaknesses of neutralism and its *de facto* "collusion" with "imperialism"; finally, it had greatly embarrassed the U.S.S.R.

In the beginning, Khrushchev, in any case preoccupied with the Cuban crisis, had had *Pravda,* on October 25, approve as "constructive" an appeal from Peking, which New Delhi imprudently rejected, proposing an immediate cease-fire, a meeting between Nehru and Chou En-lai and the withdrawal of troops 16 miles behind either side of the "line of actual control." [7] But that approval was not sufficient for the Chinese, who, by transparent allusions appearing in the *People's Daily* of October 27, asked the Russians to openly side with them. It was the day of truth for Khrushchev in the Cuban crisis, when he had to decide between accepting Kennedy's conditions or risking a bombardment of the island. It was a bad time for him, while he was trying to disentangle himself from one perilous adventure, to begin another.

Pravda waited until November 5 to publish an article advocating unconditional negotiations which were, in fact, more favorable to China than to India. On November 12, Khrushchev, during his presentation to the Supreme Soviet, congratulated Peking for withdrawing its troops, but added that it would have been much better for a "fraternal" country and "our friend the Indian Republic" not to have had to fight each other. He showed where his heart was when he said that if India had taken over *manu militari* the Portuguese enclave of Goa, while the Chinese were tolerating Macao and Hong Kong, it was because India probably had good reasons.[8]

In the same speech he castigated the Albanian leaders: "Someone has taught them foul language, and they go about and use it against the Soviet Communist Party. And yet it is their mother.
. . ."[9] A week earlier at the Congress of the Italian Communist Party one of the principal executives, Giancarlo Pajetta, had for the first time called a spade a spade. "A party like ours," he stated, "has no need to say Albania when it means China."[10] No one was deceived any longer.

In November, Khrushchev's direct intervention had brought about the failure of a pro-Chinese *coup d'état* organized in Sophia by the president of the council, Anton Yugov. Then Tito was invited to the U.S.S.R., where he was shown the greatest consideration. Khrushchev, in his presence, said that "dogmatism" (China) and no longer "revisionism" (Yugoslavia) had become the principal danger, and Tito wholeheartedly supported "the Soviet representatives—Comrade Khrushchev at their head—who are now engaged in an attempt to reduce international tensions."[11] Then a courtly controversy broke out between the Italian and Chinese Communist parties on the orientation to be given to the international workers' movement, while Peking campaigned for another world Communist conference.

On January 7, 1963, *Pravda* approved the idea for "a collective discussion of problems in dispute," and, on the 16th Khrushchev made the idea his own while speaking in Berlin before the Congress of the East German United Socialist Party. The Chinese representative, reproaching the pro-Soviet parties from that same rostrum for having violated the declarations of 1957 and of 1960, was interrupted by boos. The following day, in spite of an impassioned appeal by Fidel Castro for unity in the socialist bloc, the controversy was renewed on all sides more vigorously than ever.

On February 15, Khrushchev took advantage of a reception to offer the Chinese ambassador an accolade which immediately made headlines in all the newspapers, and to toast the friendship of the two giants of the Communist world. That gesture led to another: a letter of February 21 from the Soviet Central Committee to the Chinese Communist Party proposing to put an end to the public debate and to organize bilateral talks, "in order to strengthen our friendship and to reach a better understanding," and to "create a favorable climate for the preparation of a conference of Marxist-Leninist parties." [12] Peking accepted on March 9, suggesting that Khrushchev take advantage of a trip he was soon to make to Cambodia to stop in China. Khrushchev answered on the 30th that he would be pleased to visit China, but that it was Breshnev, not he, who planned to go to Phnom Penh. The letter recalled that in 1960, Mao had agreed to vacation in the U.S.S.R., and suggested that he carry through that old plan. If not, a meeting in Moscow could be arranged. Then followed a lengthy review of the U.S.S.R.'s well-known position in the ideological dispute, reinforced with praise of Yugoslavia, which "the Communist Party of the Soviet Union considers to be a socialist country, in spite of serious divergences." In conclusion he declared, "If we do not reply to the gratuitous attacks recently published in the Chinese press, it is only because we do not want to give the enemies of the Communist movement cause to rejoice." [13]

If the Chinese had believed that the Russians sought a reconciliation, they were now disabused. The paragraph on Yugoslavia alone sounded like a provocation. Hostilities were about to break into the open, and the Sino-Soviet meeting, finally set for July 5, would confirm the split between the two greatest Communist parties in the world.

On June 15 the *People's Daily* published a twenty-five-point reply from the Chinese Central Committee to the Soviet Central Committee: a document of 60,000 ideographs which represented a systematic indictment of the position of the U.S.S.R. on major issues. One sentence sums up its spirit: "It cannot be maintained that with the emergence of nuclear arms the possibility or necessity of undertaking social or national revolutions has disappeared or that the fundamental principles of Marxism-Leninism and, in particular, its theories on the proletariat revolution, on war and peace, have become obsolete and been transformed into useless dogmas."

In every area the Soviet Communist Party was accused of "sliding towards opportunism, degenerating into bourgeois nationalism and becoming an appendage of imperialism," of having recourse to "great power chauvinism," to "sectarianism," to "schismism," and to "subversive activities" in the internal functioning of brother parties. All of Khrushchev's dicta on coexistence, disarmament, compromises with imperialism, possibilities of peaceful transition to socialism, "the state of the whole people," alliances with native bourgeoisie in colonial countries, were each analyzed in turn, without the slightest attempt to hide the deviations. In conclusion, Peking expressed the hope that "the public debate would end," but asserted that "as long as it had been provoked that public debate could only be conducted on a basis of equality between brother parties, on a democratic foundation and proceeding through reason and documentation of facts" and that "in the midst of the international Communist movement, no one has the right, in order to further his own designs, to attack whenever he chooses and to order a 'stop to the public debate' when he wants to prevent the other party from replying." [14]

Although the Soviet Central Committee declared on June 18 that the publication of that paper, which would lead to a "new aggravation of the controversy," was "contraindicated," the Chinese Embassy in Moscow saw to it that it was distributed. On the 27th the U.S.S.R. expelled five Chinese nationals, including three diplomats who had taken care of that job. This provoked a sharp protest from Peking, followed by an explanation from the Kremlin in the same tone.

In such a climate the Moscow bilateral talks could hardly be productive. They were adjourned, *sine die,* on July 20, after publication of a series of polemical statements, notably, on the 14th, a long letter from the Soviet Central Committee "to all the Communists in the U.S.S.R.," answering in detail Peking's "twenty-five points" of June 14. "The Chinese comrades," so identified for the first time, were accused of "beginning to attribute to the Soviet party and to other Marxist-Leninist countries views they had never expressed and which were foreign to them. Then the Chinese comrades, by agreeing verbally with the statements and positions of the Communist movement, attempt to camouflage their false views and their incorrect positions. . . ."

Here are other examples of that rhetoric: "The Chinese comrades evidently underestimate the danger of a thermonuclear war. 'The atomic bomb is a paper tiger; it isn't so frightening,' they pretend. 'Don't we agree that the most important thing is to put an end to imperialism as quickly as possible?' But, how it should be done and at what cost is of secondary concern. One has the right to ask for whom is it secondary? For the hundreds of millions of people who are certain to die in a thermonuclear war? . . . No one, including the Great Powers, has the right to gamble with the destiny of millions of people. . . .

"The leaders of the Chinese Communist Party have assumed the role of defenders of the cult of personality, of advocates of Stalin's erroneous ideas. They try to impose on the other parties the priorities, the ideology, the morality, the forms and methods of leadership which were in effect during the period of the cult of personality. Let's speak frankly: that role is not enviable, it will bring neither honor nor glory. No one will be able to get the Marxist-Leninist, the progressive man, to rally to the defense of the cult of personality . . . the false conceptions of the leaders of the Chinese Communist Party on major questions of the day, both political and theoretical, are unquestionably linked to their practical attempts to undermine the unity of the world socialist bloc and of the international Communist movement." [15]

It was the final break. The "ideological" label with which the quarrel was dressed up could not, in effect, hide the fact that it opposed not only "two revolutions," but also, according to the excellent definition of an expert, Tibor Meray, "two leaders, two empires, two standards of living, and two skin colors." [16]

Even the date of this break served to underline its gravity. It coincided with the opening of negotiations which, a few days later, would lead to the signing in Moscow of a treaty on the cessation of nuclear tests between the three Great Powers, which, in retrospect, assumes the importance of an actual armistice in the East-West Cold War.

§   §   §

In the messages they had exchanged at the end of the Cuban missile crisis, the two Ks had each expressed the desire to renew the talks on disarmament in order to protect humanity from any repetition of such games of chance. In that spirit, the American delegation to the disarmament conference on December 12, 1962, offered a six-point program. It provided for an exchange of information, the creation of inspection systems, and the improvement of techniques of communication in periods of tension. The Kremlin, once again, brushed aside anything related to controls as belonging to the area of espionage, but let it be known that it was interested in improving communications.

It must be said that during the missile affair they had been quite inadequate. The classic method of handling messages to the ambassador demanded considerable time for translation, coding and decoding, and that is probably why the Kremlin had had recourse to the more efficient method of using the good offices of Alexander Formin in making contact with John Scali.

Technical negotiations were started in April 1963. They ended on June 20 with a signing of an agreement for the installation between the White House and the Kremlin of a direct line, which was immediately nicknamed the "hot line."

One could not have found a better symbol for the mutual recognition by the leaders of the United States and the U.S.S.R. of the essential responsibility they had for the maintenance of world peace, and of the tremendous gap existing between the roles allotted to the two superpowers and to the rest of humanity.

However, the installation of the "hot line" implied that all risks of direct confrontation had not disappeared. It only helped to avoid *in extremis* their most unfortunate consequences. Something else was needed to strengthen the lasting détente desired by both sides.

On December 19, 1962, Khrushchev, after having vainly put out feelers for a conference "at the summit," had written Kennedy, "It seems to me . . . the time has come to put an end once and for all to nuclear tests," and said he was ready "to meet you halfway" to reach an agreement, and proposed two or three annual inspections in the regions where atomic explosions took place.[17]

Negotiations were promptly undertaken, but they foundered once more on the problem of control. In the United States the government met opposition from many military men, and from some of the Senate who feared making a bad bargain, which would, in the end, lead to the weakening of national resources. For their part, the Russians refused to discuss methods of inspection so long as the number of inspections could not be agreed upon, and tenaciously held to a maximum of three. Their short-lived rapprochement with the Chinese, whose hostility to any treaty intended to confirm the dominance of the three great nuclear powers was well known, did not make things easier.

In April, Khrushchev complained to an American visitor, Norman Cousins, of having been hoaxed: "So once again I was made to look foolish," he said, because he had guaranteed his comrades that the acceptance of three annual inspections would lead to the signing of a treaty. "If you can go from three to eight," he went on, "we can go from three to zero." [18]

A wave of pessimism engulfed Washington. "If we don't get an agreement this year," Kennedy said in the month of May, ". . . I would think . . . the genie is out of the bottle, and we will never get him back in again. . . ." [19] However, he proposed new talks to Khrushchev and decided that once the series of tests in progress was ended, the United States would not be the first to begin them again. But it was the address he gave on June 10, 1963, at commencement at the American University in Washington, which was suddenly to thaw the atmosphere and to allow the renewal of negotiations, followed by agreement.

Never, perhaps, had his philosophy been more clearly expressed than in this speech, and in the one delivered forty-eight hours later on television which was devoted to the racial problem—"the most formidable of all the ills," de Tocqueville had written in 1835, "which threaten the future existence of the United States." [20] What he asked of his countrymen was that they go beyond their prejudices and admit that Russians and Negroes were human beings like themselves, with whom they had to learn to live.

"I have, therefore, chosen this time and place," he said, "to discuss a topic on which ignorance too often abounds and the truth is too rarely perceived—and that is the most important topic on earth: peace.

"What kind of peace do I mean and what kind of peace do we seek? Not a *Pax Americana* enforced on the world by American weapons of war. Not the peace of the grave or the security of the slave. I am talking about genuine peace—the kind of peace that makes life worth living—and the kind that enables men and nations to grow and to hope and build a better life for their children—not merely peace for Americans but peace for all men and women—not merely peace in our time, but peace in all time. . . ." Then followed a parallel between the United States and the U.S.S.R. demonstrating that "Among the many traits the peoples of our two countries have in common none is stronger than our mutual abhorrence of war," and a moving appeal for a halt to nuclear testing.[21]

Khrushchev, who was going to say to Harriman that it was "the greatest speech by an American President since Roosevelt," [22] caught the ball on the rebound. Although Kennedy had, during a trip to Europe, used very firm language calculated to appease the Germans who were always uneasy about American second thoughts, he suggested on July 2 in Berlin, the signing of a treaty on the cessation of tests limited to those detectable without an on-the-spot inspection. Thanks to the latest scientific progress, this only ruled out weak underground explosions. On the 15th, the day after publication of the Soviet Central Committee's indictment of the Chinese party, negotiations were opened in Moscow on the basis proposed by Russia. But Khrushchev would have liked to conclude a nonaggression pact between the two blocs at the same time. The Western Powers made it dependent on a Russian commitment to respect the freedom of access to West Berlin—a proposal which enraged Nikita. They proposed another treaty, this one on the nondissemination of nuclear arms. Finally, they had to be satisfied with the agreement on the cessation of controllable tests, which was signed on August 5, 1963, at the Kremlin by the foreign ministers of the U.S.S.R., the United States and Great Britain.

Before leaving Moscow, Harriman had a talk with Khrushchev and asked him to persuade China to participate in the treaty. Khrushchev answered that China was a socialist country and that he had no intention of discussing its policies with a capitalist. It was in vain that the American asked him what would happen if France was prevailed upon to sign the treaty.

The disagreeable tone of that discussion could have made one believe that the signing of the treaty which, in any case, had only "a limited practical importance," [23] as de Gaulle was to remark on July 29, did not have much political importance either as the two over-armed powers continued to stare menacingly at each other. However, the truth was quite different and the very sharpness of the reactions from Peking and Paris, displeased by that attempt to strengthen the nuclear club to their detriment, only underlined the historic significance of the first joint decision of the U.S.S.R. and the United States, against the wishes of Russia's principal ally and one of America's principal allies.

If de Gaulle had sought conciliation he could have grasped the chance offered him: Kennedy had confidentially written to him on the 25th proposing to supply France, if it adhered to the treaty, with the technical information France expected to acquire through its own experiments. But the President of the Republic did not want his *force de frappe* to depend on anyone, even technologically. For months now he had been making one gesture after another to show that, as he was to say much later, although his glass was small, it was from that glass and no other he would drink. At the beginning of the year he had haughtily rejected the Nassau Accords hastily improvised by Kennedy and Macmillan, which were intended to give a privileged nuclear position to Great Britain and France within NATO. Then he had slammed the door in the face of the British, who after thirteen years of reflection had decided, under insistent pressure from the United States, to apply for membership in an integrated Europe. In so doing he had checked the "great design" suggested by Kennedy on July 4, 1962, in a speech in Philadelphia: an Atlantic world "interdependent" and founded on the "equal partnership" of America and Europe.

There followed a period of greatly strained relations between Paris and Washington, aggravated by the State Department's plan for a multilateral nuclear force. This was designed to give Germany the satisfaction of participation without bringing it any nearer to the actual possession of atomic weapons, and it would have definitely put Germany on the American bandwagon. What did not help the situation was the signing of the Franco-German treaty of cooperation on January 22, 1963, between General de Gaulle and Adenauer, who was eager to solemnly consecrate the great project of reconciliation between the two peoples before his retirement. The Americans immediately saw this treaty as a war machine directed against them and they had no rest until their many friends in the German political parties had added a preamble reprising all the themes of Atlantic orthodoxy. De Gaulle saw in this, as he told Willy Brandt, who was passing through Paris, a "personal offense" [24] and did not hesitate to openly compare the life span of treaties to that of roses.

Contact between France and the United States had practically ceased, to the point where, when Kennedy was going to Europe in June 1963, he let the President of the Republic know that he was ready to meet with him anywhere; de Gaulle simply ignored his offer. Under those conditions it would have been surprising if the general had been interested in the proposal to share nuclear secrets.

However, there is no comparison between his spirit of independence, of rebellion, which was going to lead to France's withdrawal, not from the Atlantic Alliance but from the military organization to which it gave birth, and the wave which swept China and which would, in a few years, make it the U.S.S.R.'s most determined enemy.

On July 31, 1963, the Peking Government published a long declaration devoted to the treaty on the cessation of nuclear tests, "a great deception" which it intended to "unmask completely and decisively." Quoting Khrushchev, who had stated on September 9, 1961, that an agreement excluding underground tests "would render a disservice to the cause of peace and would only deceive the people," China accused the Soviet Government of having "capitulated" to imperialism, of having "sold out the interests" of its own countrymen, of those in the socialist bloc and of all peace-loving people. For the first time, it asserted that "incontestable facts show that the policy pursued by the Soviet Government was to ally itself with the forces of war in order to oppose the forces of peace; with imperialism in order to oppose socialism; with the United States in order to oppose China." In conclusion, it asked for the immediate destruction of all types of nuclear armaments.[25]

On August 21 the Kremlin replied by denouncing the "anti-Marxist, anti-Leninist and anti-human" character of China's foreign policy. It also wondered if "anyone had asked the Chinese people, who are condemning themselves to death, if they were willing to serve as fuel for the bonfire of a nuclear war ignited by missiles, and if they had empowered the leadership of the People's Republic of China to arrange their funerals in advance." [26]

Thus the two capitals kept insulting each other for months, each attempting to mobilize the Communist parties and the underdeveloped world against the other. They exhumed confidential dossiers from internal debates, they attacked each other as "Hitlerians" and "Trotskyites." Overnight, more and more evidence testified to the fragility of the Marxist claim that the advent of communism would suffice to eliminate the "national contradiction," which was the essential characteristic, according to them, of imperialism. It was relatively easy for "the proletariat of all countries," to whom Marx and Engels had revealed that "they had no fatherland," [27] to unite in order to better their condition. But those among them who had come to power had ceased *ipso facto* to belong to the proletariat.

Neither Moscow's "revisionists" nor Peking's "dogmatists" had yet discovered the way to deny that evidence. They could only do it by denying the sacred egotism which through the ages had generally been the foundation for nationhood. Nothing is more difficult than to be simultaneously the repository of an ethical idea and the master of a temporal empire. Before Marx was born, the history of the Roman Church had already made that abundantly clear.

§ § §

While the Sino-Soviet break was worsening, the détente between the Kremlin and the West was being confirmed. On September 20,

1963, addressing the U.N. General Assembly, Kennedy said "Today we may have reached a pause in the Cold War—but that is not a lasting peace. A test ban treaty is a milestone—but it is not the millennium. We have not been released from our obligations—we have been given an opportunity. And if we fail to augment this . . . then the indictment of posterity will rightly point its finger at us all. But if we stretch this pause into a period of cooperation—if both sides can now gain new confidence and experience in concrete collaborations for peace—then, surely, this first small step can be the start of a long and fruitful journey." [28]

He believed it, and the wonder is that Khrushchev—who had once confronted him in a decisive test and learned to recognize both his determination and his wisdom—also believed it. It is difficult to know what results their mutual understanding, their agreement on "the rules of the game," could have achieved, since two months later John Kennedy was assassinated in Dallas. But Nikita Khrushchev's reaction to the news of that tragedy showed clearly what hopes he had placed in his understanding, one would be tempted to say his connivance, with the young President. He burst into tears, and according to the testimony of a high Soviet official quoted by Pierre Salinger, "He just wandered around his office for several days, like he was in a daze." [29]

As a matter of fact his sorrow was the sorrow of all humanity. With John Kennedy's passing there disappeared a symbol of the triumph of youth. From Peking to Washington the earth was governed by old men, to whom the years had brought many wounds and disillusionments which had hardened their hearts. And then a man had entered the White House who was happy, energetic, confident in the destiny of a society whose members he urged to advance its frontiers, like the pioneers of old. Beyond the expected emotion there were the feelings of personal loss, of the injustice of fate, of the revenge of a blind fatality. And above all, for the first time since the end of the war, the sorrow of the American people was shared by the Russian people, who, thanks to television, had been able to follow the events moment by moment in a way they had never before in history been able to do. Suddenly the world realized how much the mental gap which for decades had separated East from West had diminished. Only the Chinese were an exception to the rule.

A similar coming together had already been noted five months earlier when Pope John XXIII died before he could complete his great work of rejuvenation, of *aggiornamento*, of the Catholic Church —its emergence into the modern world—which he had launched before the Vatican Council was convened. Then also the world had seen the Soviet Union, in the past and still today the citadel of the godless, expressing its regret, while in the temples, the mosques, the synagogues and the churches, the faithful of all religions were praying for the repose of the soul of the Holy Father. Wasn't this a sign that the Cold War, which so many times in the past had been within inches of degenerating into a hot war, was, at least in the hearts of the peoples, virtually ended?

BIBLIOGRAPHY AND NOTES

[1] Keesing's, 19288 A.
[2] *Ibid.*, 19246 A.
[3] Baby, *op. cit.*, p. 113.
[4] N. J. Nanporia, *The Sino-Indian Dispute* (Bombay: Times of India, 1963), p. 1.
[5] Année politique, 1962, p. 563.
[6] *Christian Science Monitor*, October 15, 1962.
[7] Hinton, *op. cit.*, p. 300.
[8] Keesing's, 19288 A.
[9] *Ibid.*
[10] Baby, *op. cit.*, p. 114.
[11] François Fejtö, *Chine-U.R.S.S., le Conflit* (Paris: Plon, 1966), II, p. 208.
[12] Documentation française. Notes et Etudes documentaires, No. 3037, November 12, 1963, p. 8.
[13] *Ibid.*, p. 20.
[14] *Ibid.*, pp. 21–38.
[15] *Ibid.*, pp. 51–71.
[16] Chapter titles of the book by Tibor Meray, *La Rupture Moscou-Pékin* (Paris: Laffont, 1966).
[17] Schlesinger, *op. cit.*, pp. 895–96.
[18] *Ibid.*, p. 897.
[19] Sorensen, *op. cit.*, p. 729.
[20] Alexis de Tocqueville, *Democracy in America* (New York: Pratt, Woodford, 1948), p. 386.
[21] *The New York Times*, June 11, 1963.
[22] Schlesinger, *op. cit.*, p. 904.
[23] *Le Monde*, July 31, 1963.
[24] Author's personal notes.
[25] Documentation française. Notes et Etudes documentaires, No. 3089, May 12, 1964, p. 4.
[26] *Ibid.*, pp. 17–26.
[27] Marx and Engels, *Communist Manifesto*, p. 30.
[28] *The New York Times*, September 21, 1963.
[29] Pierre Salinger, *With Kennedy* (New York: Doubleday, 1966), p. 335.

EPILOGUE

The United States had fought the Cold War because Britain alone was no longer capable of attaining those objectives which had shaped its policies for centuries: namely, ensuring the security of its commerce through the policing of the seas and preventing any European power from establishing hegemony on the continent.

For this reason, the United States had gotten involved in two world wars, and had been their principal victor. Not only had its enemies been crushed, but the immunity enjoyed by its territory, because of its geographical remoteness, had made the United States the arsenal and the banker of two anti-German coalitions, stimulating the expansion of its productive capacity, and vastly increasing its financial resources. These two experiences had yet another result: they fostered among the American people the idea that they were the best, the most capable, and that they had all the qualifications necessary to act as disinterested policemen in a world destined to remain imperfect—a world forced to appeal to them as long as American methods were not followed.

Even if the cost of the third world war, the Cold War, has been high, it has had largely comparable effects. The challenge of the Soviet Union prodded the United States to work twice as hard in the space and strategic arms race. After a few years of anxiety, its fortress has again become impregnable, completely impervious to nuclear blackmail. If the United States encounters too many disappointments, will the consciousness of that security push it one day into a new isolationism?

That has not yet happened. After almost twenty years of rivalry with the U.S.S.R., the Americans still believe, in effect, that they are responsible for universal peace. And since, on occasion, a veto always risks paralyzing the U.N., they must not hesitate to take it upon themselves to have their interests respected, not doubting that these correspond to the general interests.

It is in this spirit that they have pursued in Viet Nam a war which they conceived of as another battle in the "containment" of communism. We will hold on as long as necessary, they said, so that Hanoi's leaders and their supporters will understand, as Khrushchev did, that they will not exhaust our determination. This is the "long haul" tactic whose creator was John Foster Dulles.

For years the Americans always believed that they had arrived at the "final stage" in Viet Nam. A little more patience and the enemy was going to beg for peace. If he made a gesture of conciliation, that was proof that he was in a position of weakness. Therefore, all it took was continued military pressure to convince the enemy to yield still more. And it is thus that Johnson, who replied on October 21, 1964, to the bellicose statements of his Republican opponent, Goldwater, by saying: "We are not going to send American boys 15,000 miles away from their homes to do what Asian boys should do themselves," increased to 500,000 men the expeditionary corps which, at the moment of his predecessor's death, numbered 15,000. And it was Johnson who, on August 29 of the same year, having told those who advocated the bombing of North Viet Nam that he, "had decided not to extend the conflict," ordered the planes and the guns of the Seventh Fleet to pound that country around the clock. All this was done in the name of a South Vietnamese Government whose many troops show less and less desire to fight, and whose legal basis, since the assassination of Ngo Diem a few days before that of Kennedy can be, to put it mildly, questioned.

Dean Rusk contended that the aim of the war in Viet Nam was to "prevent China from establishing its power over the masses of the East." In reply he could have been told that, at the time, there was not the least evidence of Chinese intervention in Viet Nam. And that what was happening there was the nature of a preventive war against a country which might justly remind America that it was only American intervention which prevented the reunification of Formosa to the motherland. In any case, it was one more reason for Peking's leaders, although at other times they have seemed rather inclined to seek conciliation with America, to exploit the opportunity given to them to hold in check the famous "paper tiger" which had become, according to them, the source of all evils. Thus did they encourage the North Vietnamese and the fighting men of the National Liberation Front to hold fast and to confront Washington with equal determination.

Were these encouragements necessary? Ho Chi Minh could not but remember his unfortunate experience with the two negotiations he once agreed to enter into with the capitalist world. The first time, in 1946, France reopened the question of his nation's independence which it had already granted. The second time, in 1954, it was Russian pressure, accompanied by the promise of reunification through elections, which persuaded him to negotiate. That promise has never been kept. It is understandable that this old revolutionary, rather indifferent to the global strategic considerations on which the U.S.S.R. bases its policy of peaceful coexistence, was not very anxious to lose once more at the conference table what had been gained on the battlefield. The decision to partially suspend the bombing of the north, announced by Johnson on March 31, 1968, after the success of the Tet offensive, has shown that Ho Chi Minh was right in thinking that in the struggle between the tiger and the elephant, the United States would be the first to tire. Americans have now to admit that they might have found a better way to reach that *modus vivendi* with China—which has to be reached one day—than an armed intervention which has not only considerably postponed its eventuality, but has also influenced Peking to acquire nuclear weapons in record time.

§   §   §

It was reasonable to believe that the extensive United States intervention in Viet Nam would unite the two great enemy-brothers of the socialist bloc against it. But the contrary happened. The patient attempts of Khrushchev's successors to renew friendly relations with the Chinese have failed, the Chinese letting it clearly be known, after a brief period of expectancy, that reconciliation could only come with the complete capitulation of the revisionists. Today, the two capitals accuse each other of playing Washington's game and some ominous troop movements have taken place along the Sino-Soviet frontier.

It was also reasonable to expect that the extension of the war to

Viet Nam would weaken the position of the United States in relation to the rest of the world. Undoubtedly, it has never been less popular, except in countries relatively close to China such as Australia, where its protection is sought as eagerly as it was in Europe in the fifties. But the time when the United States sought to be loved is over: it is satisfied to be respected. Of course, the United States has the means of gaining this respect, if only because a large part of humanity cannot survive without its supplies of foodstuffs or its financial aid. And the U.S.S.R., with its evident agricultural failure and its grave economic difficulties, has little chance of soon replacing it.

For several years, following the Caribbean crisis, the United States has continued to regain ground. If Cuba, through trial and error, remains the laboratory of an experiment in truly popular democracy probably unique in the world, the Latin American guerrillas, completely abandoned by Moscow, now have only a few thousand combatants, and their most famous leader, Che Guevara, has been caught and killed. The leftist regime of João Goulart in Brazil, who favored Moscow and Castro, has been swept away by a military putsch. In the Dominican Republic, Lyndon Johnson, ignoring the general uproar, did not hesitate to send in 40,000 marines, under the pretext of avoiding the creation of a second Cuba, against a *coup d'état* which had no other ambition than to restore the constitution. The following year, the candidate favored by the United States was legally elected to the presidency.

Ben Bella, the ephemeral "hero of the Soviet Union," Nkrumah and Sukarno, principal champions of anti-imperialism, have fallen. In spite of a remaining "Chinese" beachhead in Tanzania, progressivism has completely lost its momentum in Black Africa, where military *coups d'état* have multiplied. The thrones of Saudi Arabia, Iran and Morocco, apparently built on sand, have been consolidated, whereas the massive aid in military material and credits given by the U.S.S.R. to the U.A.R. and to Syria, did not save them from disaster when, in June 1967, President Nasser imprudently decided to blockade the Israeli port of Elath. In Italy, the "opening to the Left," though temporarily favored both by the Vatican and the White House, has resulted in the isolation of the Communist Party which, when it was allied to Nenni's socialists (today won over to NATO), had seemed on the eve of seizing power. India, a perennial and severe critic of United States policies, is not too displeased to know that nation is containing Chinese power in this part of the world. The astonishing proclamations of the "cultural revolution" launched by Mao Tse-tung have definitely checked the evolution towards neutralism that had begun to be felt in Tokyo, and South Korea did not hesitate to send 40,000 troops to Viet Nam.

As for the U.S.S.R., in the past the standard-bearer for revolutionary forces in all countries, it is hard to believe that as recently as 1962 it was engaged with the United States in the Cold War's most serious test of strength. By approaching the edge of the abyss, its leaders have understood that they can no longer tickle the American superman, surrounded as he is by intercontinental ballistic missiles and Polaris submarines. Today, their desire to dampen the temerity of Soviet intellectuals and artists tired of forty years of conformity, as well as their repeated assertions that coexistence should not extend into ideological areas, cannot hide the affluent society's growing attraction for Eastern European populations.

After decades of travail, the Communist peoples are more interested in better standards of living, in travel, and in cultural freedom, than in winning over the universe to the ideas of Marx and Lenin. The cult of the automobile has replaced that of personality and, for most, faith has degenerated into habit. "As the moral ideas of the revolution weakened, their place was taken by material ideas," noted Barras, a few months before the fall of Robespierre. It is the very nature of industrial civilization, brought to Russia by the Revolution, which demands the replacement of doctrinaires by technocrats. The "*aggiornamento*" of the Communist Church, which has now caused its members to speak less of dogma than of profits, is no less spectacular than that of the Catholic Church. Probably nothing better symbolizes the transformation of both, and their common adjustment to the century, than the fact that Pope Paul VI, at the beginning of 1967, received a visit from Nikolai Podgorny, the head of the Soviet state.

Monolithism, so extolled during the Stalin era, is nothing but a memory. Signs of independence are multiplying, not only in China, the U.S.S.R.'s worst enemy, but also in the countries and parties which have too quickly been identified in the past as "satellites." Cuba, Viet Nam, North Korea and the Italian Communist Party refused to participate in the conference that Moscow has been trying to convene in order to excommunicate Mao Tse-tung, twenty years after the excommunication of "Tito's clique." It is the same with Rumania, which decided to determine its own destiny after being displeased with the essentially agricultural role assigned to it in the plans of the "Council of Mutual Aid" of the Eastern countries, known as Comecon, in the "apportionment of Socialist work." In 1962, Rumania had discreetly let the United States know that in case war erupted over Cuba it did not intend to take any part in it. In the winter of 1966–1967, Rumania did not hesitate to renew official relations not only with Franco's Spain, but, in spite of all the protests from East Berlin and Warsaw, with Federal Germany.

The Albanian mosquito continues to defy the Soviet bear. Yugoslavia, the first to shake off the yoke of Stalinism, is increasingly reluctant to re-enter the Kremlin orbit. Tito has dismissed Rankovitch, his police chief, and freed Djilas, the intransigent champion of liberty; from Slovenia to Macedonia, a complex experiment is in progress, attempting to reconcile central planning and individual initiative, socialism and freedom. Nowhere, however, has the appeal of freedom reached such a climax as in Czechoslovakia, where, after two decades under the sternest of yokes, a group of young Communist leaders, pushed forward by the intelligentsia, managed to fire the old Stalinist team led by Novotny. Twelve years after the Polish "spring in October," the emergence of "spring in Prague" seemed to open new hopes to those who believe in the final merging of socialism and freedom. This unexpected revolt threatened not only Soviet claims to ideological leadership, but perhaps their strategic stand in Central Europe, and after months of disarray the Soviet leadership decided to crush it. For the first time in the history of the Communist movement a socialist country invaded another without being able to quote the name of a single national leader who would have called for their "brotherly help," as they dare say.

The Russians hastened, afterward, to make clear that this move inside their own sphere of influence should not interfere with their policy of coexistence. This was more or less taken for granted by the bourgeois governments of the West, unable to play the slightest role in this tragedy. But the harm it brought to the Communist movement seems almost hopeless. Already shaken by the social and political crisis of May 1968, which had shown it far from ready to take part in any revolution, the French Communist Party for the first time in its fifty-year history dared to criticize its Russian mother and goddess, thus showing the deep disarray of its membership. The Italian Communist Party went further, asking bluntly for removal of the Soviet leaders. Tito pronounced that the only solution was the end of the tyranny of Soviet bureaucracy.

In the long run, this could pave the way to a rapprochement between Social Democrats and Communists of the diaspora on a moderate and reformist platform much closer to the present trends of a working class deeply changed by the many gifts of the affluent society. In this context, the fact that two Communist ministers took secondary posts in 1966 in Finland's Government is probably significant as a symbol and perhaps as a precedent. It has been a long time since the extreme Left made of "participationism" one of its principal grievances against the "social traitors" of the Second International.

§　　　　§　　　　§

"The wind from the East has triumphed over the wind from the West," Mao proudly proclaimed not so long ago. Today, nothing is more problematical. The course of history does not follow a straight line and Communism's appeal to the third world was considerably weakened from the moment when, instead of offering it a unique truth, Peking and Moscow asked it to arbitrate their quarrels.

For a while it looked as if the triumphant wind blew, rather, from America—the new Rome. But soon, from the dollar crisis to the murders of Martin Luther King and Robert Kennedy, in the midst of the profound division created in the public mind by the Vietnamese drama, it became apparent that the country suffered from a major internal crisis, perhaps the gravest since the Civil War, and that anything, including the advent of some kind of fascism, was henceforth possible in America.

For the first time, Americans themselves, at the peak of their military and industrial might, are apparently suffering from self-doubt. How, then, can their admirers abroad not also question the validity of their admiration? Who can follow or recommend as an example a country incapable of preventing the assassinations, less than five years apart, of a liberal President, of his younger brother dedicated to the same faith, and of the apostle of non-violent racial integration? A government incapable of working out, and even more of getting adopted, measures indispensable to the health of its economy? A government which has not known how to convince either the outside world, or a large part of its own electorate, or, above all, the Vietnamese themselves, that it has only intervened in Viet Nam to protect a "freedom" menaced by "subversion"?

Subversion: it is probably not by accident that that word, which has so often appeased the conscience of the West, is today also used by Brezhnev. It is typical of the lexicon of the "easy way," indicating, in the final analysis, a refusal to face reality. If so many values heretofore considered as fundamental within the two blocs are being questioned again today, it is primarily because they have ceased to be true and because the number of those who realize this is growing daily.

In the end the two systems which have divided the world between them have not succeeded in protecting themselves peacefully from each other's influence. The United States can no more prevent revolutionary social ideas from spreading, not only in distant Viet Nam but in South America, among European students, and even in its own universities and black ghettos, than the U.S.S.R. can prevent a reflowering of the old belief in the value of political and intellectual freedom in its sphere of influence and even in the midst of its own intelligentsia.

Does this mean that synthesis is in sight? Even before the invasion of Czechoslovakia it would have been an overoptimistic assessment. The general devaluation of the models heretofore previously approved, notably in Western Europe, has not led to the adoption of a new model, the possibility of which is challenged even before coming into existence: Mao's message, the claims of Black Power, Fidelism, as well as student extremism, are clearly directed against everything which could lead, one day, to a synthesis of

Russian and American dogmas. In fact, the world in which we live is being dismembered more than it is being put together. Besides, the dissociation from creeds is paralleled by the renewed increase of language particularism and the loosening of military alliances.

To deplore an evolution tending toward the relaxing of the often abominable restraints which for years and years have weighed on so many millions of men would be the sign of a singularly saturnine temperament, and we have to hope that, in spite of Czechoslovakia, this evolution will continue. But societies cannot exist for long without order, and that order can only rest on the majority's commitment to a certain number of common values.

Prisoners of a past which has swollen their ambitions and of a present which confines them to pragmatism, the Great Powers, whose intentions will, besides, always be suspect, are probably unable to offer the new models so unquestionably required.

In spite of the "cultural revolution" which France experienced in May 1968, and of the echoes it stirred among students throughout the world, Peking's model, outside of China, has failed to inspire many imitators.

The radicalism of the President of the Chinese Communist Party, the growing excess of the cult of his personality, the matter-of-factness with which he mentions the millions of victims of a possible conflict, frighten the world's pacifists. The proletariats of the developed nations prefer their fate to that proposed for them by Peking, and in the countries of the third world there are many leaders who wonder if Mao's protestations of ideological purity do not conceal, as was the case once in Stalin's Russia, a deliberate national, even racial, pride which seeks to recruit allies rather than to promote emancipation. After all, China showed itself quite capable, when it was in its interest, of closing its eyes to various villainies of imperialism.

The excesses of the Red Guards, the systematic purge of all who had a position of responsibility, and the emergence of the army upon the scene, perplexed those who, throughout the world, rejoiced in seeing an outstanding socialist leader once more seize the torch of world proletarian revolution from the too-well-kept hands of Khrushchev's successors. The influence of China, in spite of its spectacular development—at what cost—of its nuclear weapons, is almost everywhere waning. Indonesia, yesterday its *de facto* ally to the point where it withdrew from the U.N., has changed course, massacring some 400,000 Communists or reputed Communists and making peace with Malaysia, denounced, a little while before, as the fortress of British imperialism in Asia. North Korea has left the Chinese orbit, as has the Japanese Communist Party. In Viet Nam, Soviet influence more and more counterbalances Mao's. Following a short war over Kashmir, Kosygin, at Tashkent in January 1966, succeeded in infuriating Peking by bringing together, at least temporarily, India, despised by the Chinese, and Pakistan, on which they had showered their favors. Albania itself, after a long period of allegiance to the "great helmsman," has decided after the invasion of Czechoslovakia to improve its relations with Yugoslavia, top on the list of the revisionists denounced by Peking. Everything indicates that the great proletarian cultural revolution has cost millions of man hours in lost production, and thus weakened a country that is still only at the dawn of its development.

§   §   §

A contemporary of Mao, General de Gaulle, too, has undertaken to challenge the two superpowers at the same time. But unlike that of the Chinese, his predicament is of a purely national—or nationalistic—nature, without any ideological content—he would rather say "mask." It is the predicament of a man who has not accepted the diminished role of his country in the aftermath of the Second World War; a man who has sworn to restore France to its former rank, which implies its escape from the dual hegemony under which Europe has been placed for twenty years.

This determination explains the general's policies: first, his persistent resistance to the U.S.S.R. when it seemed to menace the whole of Europe; his fruitless attempt in 1958 to participate on an equal footing with the Anglo-Saxons in the direction of the Western world; the achievement of reconciliation with Germany; the progressive withdrawal of France from NATO, finally accomplished in 1967, and the creation of a national *force de frappe;* the veto in 1963 to the entrance into the Common Market of a Britain considered to be nothing but an American Trojan horse; the recognition of Red China in 1964; the rapprochement with the U.S.S.R., crowned in 1966 by a triumphal trip to Moscow; the old dream, evoked a hundred times, of a "Europe from the Atlantic to the Urals"—in other words a continent which would find, between the two superpowers, a prominent place as the champion and arbiter of peace.

Listened to with suspicion, in the western part of Europe, because of de Gaulle's hegemonic behavior, this message has been received, in its eastern part, as one of liberation. The crowds who cheered him, in 1967 in Poland and in 1968 in Rumania, had understood its meaning perfectly. "Independence" and "nation" are words which easily appeal to peoples kept under close protection. But the hopes awakened were bound not to last. When he flew back to Paris from Bucharest, de Gaulle was faced with a moral, social and intellectual crisis of extraordinary scope, one which challenges not only the Elysée's pretensions to be a schoolmaster to the world, but the very type of society that the West was so proud to have begotten.

Once again he faced the danger and won, at the time almost everybody thought he was about to give up. But the price of victory was heavy: a deep bitterness among the defeated students, whose dreams of revenge can lead at any time to new upheavals; the loss, due to the concessions made to workers after a month-long strike and to its impact on exports, of a major asset of his power policy—the huge stockpile of gold, second only to the American one, that he used to fight the dollar's supremacy.

Coming soon afterward, the Czech tragedy ruined, for some time at least, de Gaulle's pretension of overcoming, through détente and common understanding, the division of Europe.

It is possible that Khrushchev had tried, before his ouster, to eliminate that division, or at least to diminish its effect, through direct contact with the Federal Republic. In a note dated December 27, 1961, he called for a rapprochement of "the two most powerful countries of Europe," the U.S.S.R. and Germany. During the summer of 1964, Adjubei traveled throughout the Federal Republic meeting political leaders and Ruhr industrialists and not hesitating to say in private that Ulbricht was suffering from cancer, and that after his approaching demise it would be easy to get together. Khrushchev's sudden visit to Prague in September to meet the Polish, East German and Czechoslovakian foreign ministers, in other words the representatives of the three nations most interested in the German problem, seems to have been intended to chart a new course of action.

A few days later an intelligence officer from Bonn was wounded by a hypodermic injection while he attended Mass in the cathedral in Zagorsk, a holy city of Russia. The *Frankfurter Allgemeine Zeitung*, citing informal sources in Bonn, placed the responsibility for the assault on adversaries of the policy of détente. The very profuse apologies offered by the Kremlin to the Federal authorities seemed to confirm that interpretation. The German problem, according to public statements made by Khrushchev, had played a role in the fall of Beria and later in that of Malenkov. It can be wondered if it had not been the same in his case.

Undoubtedly, many reasons can help explain his sudden dismissal on October 15, 1964, by astonishing coincidence on the eve of the day his enemies in Peking tested their first atomic bomb. He had, in all areas, met with failures which resulted, essentially, from his tendency to rush ahead without worrying too much about what might happen if things did not go according to his expectations whether they had to do with agriculture, Berlin, Cuba or China. It has often been said that in a democratic country, any administration managed in such a way would have been voted out of power several times.

It is quite possible that the straw that broke the camel's back was, as has been rumored, his intention to make Adjubei secretary of the party for agricultural matters, a position to which he had no other claim but his marriage. It is no less true that one of the first effects of the palace revolution of October 15, 1964, was the cancellation of any projected visit to Bonn by the head of the Soviet Government. The invitation immediately addressed by the Federal Republic to Kosygin, Khrushchev's successor to the chairmanship of the government, still remains unanswered at the time of writing.

After a few months' hesitation, the new team—which seemed, until it decided to invade Czechoslovakia, the most reassuring, the wisest, and the most attractive in many ways which has ever governed Russia—has taken up again, in the main, the policy of cooperation with the West initiated by Khrushchev. The Viet Nam war did not prevent the Russian Government, despite what it said, from concluding treaties with the United States for the demilitarization of space and the nonproliferation of nuclear weapons. It even proposed to the Labourite Wilson, who came to power in London the very day of Khrushchev's fall, a treaty of friendship and cooperation, in spite of Wilson's fidelity to NATO and his almost unconditional alignment with United States foreign policy. The new Russian Government actively cooperates with its Japanese, Turkish and Iranian neighbors, all avowed allies of the United States. It works with America, at arm's length, in sustaining the fragile Indian economy. If, in their dispute with Israel, it provides the Arab nations with diplomatic and military support, which certainly encourages them in their refusal to work out a peaceful solution, behind the scenes it discourages any desire on their part to take revenge in the field for the humiliating defeat inflicted on them in June 1967.

Inversely, on the question of Germany, the "troika" of Brezhnev, Kosygin and Podgorny follows a strictly conservative line. All it demands from the Western Powers is that they accept the conditions which the Kremlin has continued to make for years for the settlement of the problem of so-called European security: the recognition of existing frontiers, including those of the German Democratic Republic, and Bonn's renunciation of any kind of nuclear weapon, either individually or collectively owned. In other words, to accept the *status quo* on the basis of the partition of Europe and the maintenance of the Federal Republic in a diminished juridical position.

Will the U.S.S.R., through a détente, obtain what it could not wrest through threats and pressure? In a dramatic fashion, in a speech on October 7, 1966, Lyndon Johnson endorsed the theory which, when coming from General de Gaulle a few months earlier, had still seemed shocking: namely, that the reunification of Germany, and consequently of Europe, could only be the result and not the prerequisite, as good Atlantic orthodoxy would have it, of détente between East and West.

These words from a country which, since the creation of NATO, has based its policy on the reunification of a wholly sovereign Germany by means of free elections, could not fail to create certain doubts in Bonn as to the practical effects of the American alliance. It is not surprising that under those conditions, the government of the dour Erhard, whose Minister of Foreign Affairs, Gerhard Schroeder, had gambled everything on the American horse, gave way to a more enterprising team. It was led by another Christian Democrat, Kurt Kiesinger, himself a former Nazi, flanked by Willy Brandt, an anti-Hitlerian from way back, and the Social-Democratic ex-Mayor of West Berlin, as Minister of Foreign Affairs.

The new government gave priority in its foreign policy to the amelioration of its relations with its neighbors in the East as well as France. In so doing, it followed the only policy which could have a chance to interrupt the dialogue of the two superpowers, in a voice strong enough to have a chance of being heard, especially when de Gaulle will no longer be there. Russia unfortunately never paid any attention to these moves, and finally it decided to block any attempt to establish direct links between the Federal Republic and the people's democracies of eastern Europe. Anyway, the impact of the Czech crisis is bound to ruin for a long time any chance of uniting the two parts of Europe.

Perhaps a strong federation of its western part, including Britain and really free from any American interference, could provide a way to overcome, in the long run, the partition of the old continent. Otherwise, and alas! perhaps, in that case too, the odds are that this partition will be consolidated as long as the peoples of the Russian empire have not succeeded in overthrowing the bureaucracy which has brought a world revolution to a path of the most selfish conservatism. Until that time there is little hope for Europe to regain the role of center of world politics it held for centuries. "Two empires will divide the world between them," wrote Frederick Grimm to Catherine the Great when Louis XVI was still reigning in France, "Russia to the east and America to the west. And we, the peoples between the two, will be too discredited, we will have sunk too low, to know, except through a vague and incoherent tradition, what we once were."

It is quite true that the Europeans have primary responsibility for the wars that have destroyed their influence. It is equally true that, in the past, their example has been far from sufficiently disinterested and virtuous to completely efface the crimes and selfishness of the white race. However, in the era of the superpowers, who except Europe can speak to the world in the language of justice and freedom with enough authority and yet without being suspected of wanting to dominate it? A Europe which would succeed in replacing the rule of force with the rule of law between its members, as most of them have already done within their frontiers. Who can deny that the wane of Europe in the wake of two world wars has been the principal cause of the Cold War? Who can be sure that as long as this condition is not remedied, the Cold War, more or less appeased after half a century, will not someday erupt again more violently than ever?

CHRONOLOGY

1950

January 31: Truman decides to build H-bomb.
February 14: Sino-Soviet Friendship Pact.
May 9: Schuman Plan launched.
May 25: tripartite declaration on maintainance of *status quo* in Middle East.
June 25: start of Korean War.
August 11: Germany joins the Council of Europe. Churchill launches idea of a European Army.
September–October: failure of insurrectional strikes in Austria.
September 26: Atlantic Council agrees on principle of a German contribution to common defense.
October 2: United Nations forces cross 38th Parallel.
October 7: Chinese Communists invade Tibet.
October: fall of Cao Bang and Lang Son in Tonkin.
October 15: Chinese intervention in Korea.
October 21: Pleven Plan for a European Army is launched.
November 5: end of diplomatic boycott of Spain.
December 3: beginning of retreat of U.N. forces in Korea.

1951

March 5–June 21: failure of Four-Power conference in the Pink Palace in Paris.
April 11: MacArthur's dismissal.
April 28: Mossadegh becomes Prime Minister of Iran. Nationalization of petroleum industry.
May 23: Sino-Tibetan treaty.
July 10: beginning of armistice negotiations in Korea.
July 20: assassination of Abdullah of Jordan.
September 8: peace treaty with Japan.
October 7: Churchill returns to power.
October 8: Cairo denounces Anglo-Egyptian treaty.

CHRONOLOGY

1952

February: Atlantic Conference in Lisbon agrees on objectives of Western rearmament. Greece and Turkey join NATO.
March 10: U.S.S.R. proposes neutralization of Germany.
July 21: fall of Egyptian monarchy.
September: Stalin's article on the economic problems of socialism.
October 15: Japan creates a national security corps.
October 16: breaking off of Anglo-Iranian diplomatic relations.
November 1: the first American H-bomb exploded.
November 4: Eisenhower elected President of United States.
December 3: execution of Rudolf Slanski in Prague.

1953

January 13: arrest in Moscow of the "assassins in the white coats."
February 2: deneutralization of Formosa.
February 11: Soviet Union breaks off diplomatic relations with Israel.
March 5: death of Stalin.
March 6: Malenkov becomes Prime Minister.
March 28: amnesty in U.S.S.R.
April 27: resumption of armistice negotiations in Korea.
June 16: East Berlin uprising.
July 4: Imre Nagy becomes head of Hungarian Government.
July 10: Beria's arrest announced.
July 27: armistice in Korea.
August 8: Malenkov announces U.S.S.R. possesses H-bomb.
August 19: fall of Mossadegh.
September 3: Khrushchev becomes First Secretary of C.P.S.U.
December 4–7: Western summit meeting in Bermuda.
December 8: Washington launches "atoms for peace" plan.

1954

January 25–February 18: Four-Power conference in Berlin.
February 25: Nasser assumes power in Cairo.
March 9: creation of Iranian international petroleum consortium.
April 26: opening of Geneva Conference on Korea and Indochina.
April 29: Sino-Indian agreement.
May 7: fall of Dien Bien Phu.
June 16: Ngo Dinh Diem becomes Prime Minister in Viet Nam.
June 18: investiture of Pierre Mendès-France.

June 28: Chou En-lai and Nehru proclaim five principles of peaceful co-existence.

June–July: crisis in Guatemala.

July 20: signing of Indochinese armistice.

August 9: signing of Greco-Turkish-Yugoslav treaty of alliance.

August 19–22: Brussels conference on European Defense Community fails.

August 30: French Parliament rejects European Defense Community.

September 5: beginning of bombardment of Quemoy and Matsu.

September 8: signing of Manila Pact.

September 29: Khrushchev and Bulganin in Peking.

October 3: London agreements on rearmament of Germany.

October 23: Paris agreements on Germany's entry into NATO.

October 27: Eisenhower assures Diem of his complete support.

November 1: beginning of Algerian War.

December 13: Franco-American agreement on military assistance to South Viet Nam.

1955

February 6: fall of Mendès-France. Replaced by Edgar Faure.

February 8: Malenkov replaced by Bulganin; Molotov accepts principle of evacuation of Austria.

February 24: conclusion of Baghdad Pact.

March 9: Hungarian Central Committee condemns Imre Nagy.

March 27: France concludes ratification on Paris Agreements.

April 5: Eden succeeds Churchill.

April 17–24: Afro-Asian Bandung Conference.

May 15: signing of Austrian state treaty.

May 22: cessation of operations in Formosa Strait.

May 26–June 2: Khrushchev in Belgrade.

June 3: Messina Conference decides to create European Economic Community.

July 18: East–West Summit Conference in Geneva. American "open skies" plan.

September 9: Adenauer in Moscow. Establishment of diplomatic relations between U.S.S.R. and West Germany.

September 27: agreement on delivery of Czech arms to Egypt.

October 27–November 16: Geneva Conference of Big Four Foreign Ministers fails.

November 2: Ben-Gurion returns to power in Israel.

November–December: Khrushchev and Bulganin tour Asia.

1956

January 29: Guy Mollet assumes office.

February 14–25: meeting of Twentieth Congress of C.P.S.U. Khrushchev denounces crimes of Stalin.

March 2: independence of Morocco.

March 20: independence of Tunisia.

April 6: Gomulka is freed.

April 17: Cominform is dissolved.

April 28: departure of French expeditionary corps from Indochina.

June 28: Poznan uprising.

July 18: Rakosi resigns from leadership of Hungarian Communist Party.

July 19: withdrawal of American offer to finance Aswan Dam.

July 26: nationalization of Suez Canal.

October 22: Gomulka becomes First Secretary of Polish Communist Party. Secret meeting in Sèvres between Pineau, Ben-Gurion and Selwyn Lloyd.

October 23: beginning of Budapest uprising.

October 24: Imre Nagy becomes Hungarian Prime Minister.

October 25: Kadar becomes First Secretary of Hungarian Communist Party.

October 28: cease-fire in Budapest.

October 29: launching of Israeli offensive in Sinai. Franco-British ultimatum to Egypt and Israel.

October 30: Soviet declaration on equality of rights between socialist countries.

November 4: Soviet intervention in Budapest.

November 5: beginning of Franco-British landing in Port Said.

November 6: Eisenhower is re-elected. Cease-fire in Egypt.

November 20: Molotov becomes Minister of State Control.

November 25: abduction of Imre Nagy.

December 24: Re-embarkation of Franco-British troops in Port Said.

1957

January 5: launching of Eisenhower Doctrine for Middle East.

January 6: Hungarian-Soviet-Rumanian-Czech declaration on Imre Nagy's "treason."

January 17: Chou En-lai in Moscow.

January 20: Gomulka triumphs in Polish elections.

February 11: Soviet proposal for neutralization of Middle East.

February 27: Mao's first "Hundred Flowers" speech.

March 6: independence of Ghana.

March 21: Anglo-American agreement on strategic nuclear missiles.
April 10–17: Jordanian crisis.
End of June: uncovering of "anti-Party group" plot in U.S.S.R.
August 26: firing of first Soviet intercontinental missile.
August-September: Syrian-Turkish crisis.
October 4: launching of first Sputnik.
October 15: conclusion of secret atomic agreement between Peking and Moscow.
October 22: Moscow declaration of twelve Communist and workers' parties.

1958

January 31: Syrian-Egyptian union.
February: launching of American satellite "Explorer."
March 1: Khrushchev becomes Prime Minister, replacing Bulganin.
March 31: U.S.S.R. suspends nuclear tests.
May 1: Nasser makes triumphal journey to Moscow.
May 3: the Chinese "great leap forward."
May 13: Algiers coup.
May 29: de Gaulle becomes Prime Minister.
June 17: execution of Imre Nagy and Pal Maleter.
End of June: civil war in Lebanon.
July 14: American intervention in Lebanon and British intervention in Jordan. Assassination of King Feisal.
July 31: Khrushchev in Peking.
August: spread of "people's communes" in China.
August 21: U.N. vote ends Middle East crisis.
August 22: beginning of bombardment of Quemoy.
October 2: independence of Guinea.
October 22: end of Formosa Strait crisis.
October 31: opening of tripartite conference on cessation of nuclear tests.
November 4: *coup d'état* attempt by Colonel Aref in Iraq. Egypt-Iraq tension. Khrushchev's speech on Berlin.
November 10: opening of conference on prevention of surprise attacks.
November 27: Soviet note on transformation of Berlin into free city.

1959

January 1: victory of Fidel Castro in Cuba.
January 10: U.S.S.R. proposes a German peace treaty.
February 21: Macmillan in Moscow.
March 17: revolt in Tibet.

May 11: opening of conference of foreign ministers in Geneva on Berlin and German problems.
May 24: death of John Foster Dulles.
June 15: Moscow secretly denounces its atomic agreement with Peking.
September 12: Sino-Indian agreement.
September 15: arrival of Khrushchev in United States.
September 16: de Gaulle's speech on self-determination for Algeria.
September 30: Khrushchev's arrival in Peking.

1960

January 1: independence of Cameroon (followed in course of year by most of French-speaking African states).
February 8: Macmillan's "wind of change" speech.
March 23: Khrushchev in Paris.
April 16: publication in Peking of article "Long Live Leninism" criticizing, without naming him, Khrushchev's revisionism.
May 1: Khrushchev announces two American planes have been shot down.
May 16: opening of abortive summit in Paris.
June 8: congress of World Federation of Trade Unions in Peking. First public echos of Sino-Soviet quarrel.
June 21: Congress of Rumanian Communist Party. Controversy between Khrushchev and Chinese.
June 30: independence of Belgian Congo.
July 8: Belgian intervention in Congo.
July 11: secession of Katanga.
July: Security Council decides to send U.N. force to Congo.
August: recall of Soviet technicians from China.
September 5: dismissal of Lumumba.
November 7: Kennedy elected President.
November 11–25: conference of eighty-one parties in Moscow.
December 9: Souvanna Phouma asks for Soviet aid to Laos.
December 20: creation of National Liberation Front in South Viet Nam.

1961

January 3: rupture of diplomatic relations between Cuba and United States.
January 6: Khrushchev's speech on wars of liberation.
February 14: announcement of death of Lumumba.
March 15: launching of Alliance for Progress.
April 17: abortive landing of Cuban exiles in Bay of Pigs.
May 16: opening of Geneva Conference on Laos.
May 30: Kennedy in Paris.
June 3: Kennedy-Khrushchev meeting in Vienna.

August 13: building of Berlin Wall.
August 29: resumption of Soviet nuclear tests.
September 17: death of Dag Hammarskjöld.
September 28: Syrian-Egyptian union dissolved.
October 17–31: Twenty-second Congress of C.P.S.U.
December 10: rupture of Albanian-Soviet relations.
December: Kennedy increases number of American "advisers" in Viet
 Nam to 15,000.

1962

February 7: resumption of English and American nuclear testing.
March 18: Evian Accords.
April 14: Pompidou becomes Prime Minister in place of Michel Debré.
May 4: McNamara sets forth doctrine of "flexible response" at Atlantic
 Conference in Athens.
July 2: Raul Castro's trip to Moscow.
July 3: independence of Algeria.
July 19: first successful testing of an antiballistic missile.
July 23: treaty on neutralization of Laos.
August 15: Dutch-Indonesian treaty on New Guinea.
September 2: Moscow announces increase of military and economic aid to
 Cuba.
September 13: American warning to U.S.S.R. on installation of offensive
 weapons in Cuba.
September 27: beginning of civil war in Yemen.
October 11: opening of Vatican Council II.
October 18: U.S. Air Force reports presence of Soviet missiles in Cuba.
October 20: Chinese offensive in Himalayas.
October 22: United States establishes "quarantine" around Cuba.
October 28: Khrushchev announces withdrawal of missiles from Cuba.
October 31: Castro refuses to admit U.N. observers.
November 5: elimination of pro-Chinese and pro-Stalin Bulgarian leaders.
November 20: removal of Soviet bombers from Cuba. Lifting of quaran-
 tine.
December 21: Nassau agreement between London and Washington on
 nuclear weapons.

1963

January 14: de Gaulle rejects Nassau agreement and denies Great Britain
 entry into Common Market.
January 21: end of Katanga secession.

January 22: Franco-German treaty of cooperation.

February 8: *coup d'état* in Iraq. Assassination of Kassem.

June 10: Kennedy's speech on peace.

June 14: indictment of the C.P.S.U. by Chinese (the "twenty-five points").

June 23–July 3: Kennedy's tour of Europe.

July 14: C.P.S.U. replies to Chinese Communist Party. Ideological split between Peking and Moscow.

July 15: opening of English-Soviet-American negotiations on cessation of nuclear tests.

August 5: signing of Moscow treaty on nuclear tests.

October 9:   resignation of Macmillan and Adenauer.

October 16: Erhard becomes Chancellor of West Germany.

October 19: Douglas Home becomes Prime Minister of Great Britain.

November 1: military *coup d'état* in Saigon. Assassination of Ngo Dinh Diem.

November 22: assassination of Kennedy. Johnson becomes President of United States.

December 5: beginning of leaning to Left in Italy.

December 31: Khrushchev proposes a general agreement on nonrecourse to force in settlement of territorial conflicts.

1964

January 17: cease-fire between Malaysia and Indonesia.

January 27: France recognizes Red China.

March 4: Security Council decides to send an international force to Cyprus.

April 1: military *coup d'état* in Brazil against President Goulart.

April 6: "Molotov group" excluded from C.P.S.U.

April 20: Soviet-British-American agreement on reduction of production of fissionable material for military uses.

April 25: Ben Bella visits Moscow; is made a "Hero of the Soviet Union."

May 6: Khrushchev, while visiting U.A.R., makes Nasser a "Hero of the Soviet Union."

May 8: Peking publishes its secret correspondence with the C.P.S.U. Refuses to participate in a world conference of Communist parties.

May 27: death of Nehru; Shastri becomes Prime Minister of India.

July 6: U.S.S.R. proposes creation of a permanent peace force. Fidel Castro proposes reciprocal cessation of Cuban subversion in Latin America and of American subversion in Cuba.

July 11: death of Thorez.

July 28: Adjubei in Bonn to prepare Khrushchev's visit.

August 10: Moscow convenes a meeting preparatory to world Communist conference.

September 2: *Pravda* scores Chinese territorial claims vis-à-vis U.S.S.R.

October 15: Khrushchev relieved of all posts. Replaced by Brezhnev, as head of party and Kosygin, as head of government.

October 16: Labour Party wins British elections; Harold Wilson becomes Prime Minister.

November 3: explosion of first Chinese nuclear bomb.

November 9: Johnson elected President of United States.

November 23: intervention by Belgian paratroopers in Stanleyville.

1965

January 1: Indonesia leaves U.N.

January 24: death of Churchill.

February 5–6: Kosygin's trip to Peking and Hanoi.

February 7: beginning of United States raids against North Viet Nam.

February 15: Bonn suspends all economic aid to U.A.R.

April 24: "Constitutionalist" putsch in Dominican Republic; massive intervention by United States.

May 12: establishment of diplomatic relations between German Federal Republic and Israel.

June 19: Ben Bella overthrown by Boumedienne; adjournment of Afro-Asian conference in Algiers.

August: serious political crisis in Greece.

August 24: Feisal-Nasser agreement on Yemen.

August 25: Indo-Pakistani war in Kashmir.

September 30: failure of an extreme left-wing *coup d'état* in Indonesia; violent anti-Communist repression.

October 28: Couve de Murville goes to Moscow.

December 19: de Gaulle's re-election to Presidency of Republic.

1966

January 10: Soviet-Indian-Pakistani agreement in Tashkent. Death of Shastri.

February 6: Fidel Castro violently attacks Chinese.

February 24: fall of Nkrumah.

March 7: de Gaulle announces France's withdrawal from NATO.

March 29: Twenty-third Congress of C.P.S.U. Brezhnev, Secretary General.

April 18: beginning of Chinese cultural revolution.

April 21: Pope Paul VI receives Gromyko on visit to Rome.

June 20: de Gaulle visits U.S.S.R.

June 25: signing of agreement between Vatican and Yugoslavia.

July 1: dismissal of Rankovich, number-two man in Yugoslav regime.

August 31: de Gaulle's speech in Phnom Penh asking Americans to agree to leave Viet Nam.

October 7: Johnson's speech on East-West détente.

November 10: Wilson announces he is going to open consultations on Great Britain's eventual joining of Common Market.

November 23: Chinese "Red Guards" attacks against President Liu Chao-chi.

December 1: Kosygin visits France. Resignation of Erhard cabinet, replaced by coalition government of Christian Democrats and Social Democrats.

December 2: U Thant is re-elected Secretary General of U.N.

December 13: Soviet Central Committee scores anti-Leninist policy of Mao Tse-tung's group and requests international Communist conference.

December 21: agreement on stationing of French troops in Germany.

1967

January 24: Paul VI receives Podgorny.

January 27: signing of treaty on demilitarization of space.

January 30: opening of diplomatic relations between Rumania and German Federal Republic.

February 14: signing of treaty on denuclearization of Latin America.

March 12: fall of Sukarno.

April 7: severe Israeli-Syrian air clash.

April 21: military coup in Athens. Svetlana Stalin is granted asylum in the United States.

May 18: on Cairo's request, U.N. troops are withdrawn from Egypt.

May 23: Nasser decides on blockade of Strait of Tiran.

June 5-9: the third Israeli-Arab war.

June 9: Nasser's resignation rejected.

June 17: first Chinese H-Bomb tested.

June 23: Johnson and Kosygin meet at Glassboro, New Jersey.

July 25: de Gaulle, in Montreal, supports French Canadian claims.

September 18: the United States decides to erect a billion-dollar "thin" antiballistic-missile system.

1968

January 3: Dubcek replaces Novotny as First Secretary of the Czechoslovak Communist Party. Beginning of "spring in Prague."

March 31: Johnson orders partial halt of bombing against North Viet Nam and announces he will not run for presidency.

May–June: turmoil in France.
July 15: warning to Czechoslovakia by Russia and four of its partners in the Warsaw Pact.
August 3: agreement between Czechs and the Warsaw Pact.
August 21: invasion of Czechoslovakia.
August 24: first French H-bomb tested.
November 1: total halt of bombing of North Viet Nam.
November 5: Richard M. Nixon elected President of the United States.

THE MAJOR FIGURES

ACHESON, Dean (1893–): lawyer. Under Secretary of the Treasury during the first few months of the Roosevelt administration in 1933; Assistant Secretary of State 1941–1945; Under Secretary of State 1945–1947; Secretary of State 1949–1953. Returned to his law practice after Eisenhower's election; presided over the NATO Advisory Group under Kennedy and Johnson.
Bibliography: *An American Vista, Power and Diplomacy*, etc.

ADENAUER, Konrad (1876–1967): lawyer. Deputy Mayor of Cologne in 1906, then Lord Mayor from 1917 until his dismissal by the National Socialist regime in 1933. Member of the Executive Committee of the "Zentrum" (Catholic Party of the Center) and of the Rhine Diet 1917–1933. Representative of the Center Party in the Prussian State Council 1920–1933. Interned by the Nazis in 1934 and 1944. Reinstated as Lord Mayor of Cologne by the Americans, removed by the British. Cofounder (1945) of the Christian Democratic Union, and its president from 1946 to 1966. Chancellor of the Federal German Republic 1949–1963; and Foreign Minister 1951–1955.
Bibliography: *World Indivisible: Memoirs*.

BEN-GURION, David (1886–): born in Poland under the name of David Grin. A militant member of the Zionist Socialist movement, Poalei Sion. Settled in Palestine in 1906, then studied law in Constantinople 1913–1914. Enlisted in the Jewish Legion of the British Army during World War I. Participated in the creation of the Jewish workers' party, Mapai. Secretary General of the Federation of Unions (Histadruth) 1921–1935. President of the Jewish Agency for Palestine from 1935 to 1948, he battled against the reformism of Chaim Weizmann and for the use of force. President of

the Council of Israel 1948–1953 and 1955–1963. Losing his majority in the Mapai, he founded the Rafi party, which he represented in the Jerusalem Parliament.
Bibliography: *Eretz Israel; The Struggle*, etc.

BULGANIN, Nikolai Aleksandrovich (1895–   ): official of the political police from 1918 to 1922. Held posts in industrial management. Mayor of Moscow 1931–1937; Chairman of the State Bank 1937–1941. Deputy Commissar for Defense (1944), then Minister of Defense (1947) with the title of Marshal. Deputy Chairman of the Council of Ministers from 1949 to 1955, then Prime Minister from 1955 to 1958. Substitute member (1946), then full member of the Politburo (1948). Excluded in 1956. President of the Sovnarkhov of Stavropol 1958–1962.

CASTRO RUZ, Fidel (1926–   ): lawyer. President of the Federation of Cuban Students, organized the unsuccessful attack against the Moncada barracks (1953) hoping to provoke general uprising. Condemned to prison for 15 years. Released under general amnesty in 1956. Went to Mexico. Landed on December 2, 1956, in the province of Oriente with a group of partisans, organized the underground of the Sierra Maestra and led the guerrilla campaign that ousted Batista on January 1, 1959. Prime Minister of Cuba since February 1959, First Secretary of the Unified Party of the Socialist Revolution since 1963.

CHOU EN-LAI (1898–   ): member of a noted Mandarin family. Educated at Nankai University. Founder of radical youth movement and leader of rebellion of 1919. Imprisoned in Tientsin for 1 year. Studied in France 1920–1922; helped found Chinese Communist Party in Paris and became a founder of the organization simultaneously formed in China. Political Director of the Whampoa Military Academy, headed by Chiang Kai-shek, 1924–1936. Directed uprisings of Shanghai and Kiangsi (1927). Participated in the fighting (1927–1933) against Chiang Kai-shek and the Long March of the Communist Army (1934–1935). Negotiated with Chiang from 1936 to 1946. Premier and Foreign Minister of the People's Republic of China 1949. Prime Minister since 1958.

COUVE DE MURVILLE, Maurice (1907–   ): Inspector of Finances. Director of Foreign Finances 1938; dismissed and deprived of French citizenship by Vichy government. Joined Free French government. Secretary General for General Giraud 1943; Commissioner of Finances for the French Committee of National Liberation in Algeria 1943; French Delegate to the Consulting Council for Algeria 1944; Ambassador to Italy for provisional French government 1945; General Director for Political Affairs at the Quai d'Orsay 1945–1950; Ambassador to Cairo 1950–1954; Permanent Representative to NATO 1954; Ambassador to the U.S. 1955–1956; then to Germany 1956–1958. Foreign Minister 1958–1968. Appointed Prime Minister in July 1968.

DULLES, John Foster (1888–1959): lawyer. Member of the American delegations to the Hague Conference (1907); member of Reparations Commission (1919). Advisor to U.S. delegation at San Francisco conference on the U.N. (1945); served as U.S. delegate at various sessions of the U.N. General Assembly. Appointed Senator (1949) to finish unexpired term of Robert F. Wagner of New York. Negotiator of the peace treaty with Japan in 1951. Secretary of State 1953–1959.
Bibliography: *War, Peace, and Change; War or Peace.*

GOMULKA, Wladyslaw (1905–   ): militant Communist before the war of 1939; arrested several times; participated in the founding of the clandestine Polish Workers' Party in 1942, and the Resistance army. Secretary of the Central Committee 1943; first Deputy President of the Council and Minister of Recovered Territories 1945–1949; ousted from cabinet in 1949, then excluded from the party; imprisoned for Titoism from 1951 to 1954. First Secretary of the Party since 1956.

GROMYKO, Andrei Andreyevich (1909–   ): graduate of a teachers' college; former student at the Institute of Agronomy and Institute of Economics; lecturer in Russian universities. Counselor at the Soviet Embassy in Washington 1939–1943; ambassador to the United States 1943–1946; Permanent Representative of the U.S.S.R. to the U.N. 1946–1948; ambassador to Great Britain 1952–1953.

Deputy Foreign Minister 1953–1957; Foreign Minister since 1957. Substitute member (1946), then full member (1956) of the Central Committee.

HAMMARSKJÖLD, Dag (1905–1961): Assistant professor at the University of Stockholm (1933). Under Secretary of Finance 1936–1945; Chairman of the Board of the Bank of Sweden 1941–1948; Under Secretary, then Deputy Foreign Minister 1949–1952; Secretary General of the U.N. 1953–1961.
Bibliography: *Markings.*

HO CHI MINH (1890–   ): fled native Annan at age of 19. Became pastry cook in London; went to France in 1919 and worked as a photo retoucher in Paris; militant member of the Socialist Party and cofounder of the French Communist Party in 1920; founded the *Paria.* Lived in Moscow, then in Canton where he created the first Indochinese Communist organization in 1929. Returned to Viet Nam. Fled after the uprising of Yen Bay to Hong Kong, where he was arrested by the British (1933). Created the Viet Minh in 1943 in China; returned secretly to his country where he organized armed groups and in 1945 proclaimed the Democratic Republic of Viet Nam, over which he has presided ever since.

KENNEDY, John Fitzgerald (1917–1963): naval officer during the Second World War; seriously injured in the Pacific. Journalist in 1945. Member of the House of Representatives 1947–1953; Senator from Massachusetts 1953–1960; President of the U.S. 1961–1963.
Bibliography: *Why England Slept; Profiles in Courage; Strategy of Peace.*

KHRUSHCHEV, Nikita Sergeyevich (1894–   ): worked in plants and mines of the Ukraine; joined Communist Party in 1918. Became a member of the Central Committee of the C.P.S.U. in 1934, and First Secretary of the Moscow city and oblast party organization in 1935. Substitute member (1938) and then full member (1939) of the Politburo. First Secretary of the Ukrainian Communist Party in 1938. Political Commissar in Stalingrad during the Second World War. He then returned to Kiev, where he assumed the dual functions

of Chief of the Party and Chairman of the Council of Ministers. First Secretary of the All-Union Party of the Central Committee, and First Secretary of Moscow Regional Committee, 1949. First Secretary of the Central Committee 1953. Combined these functions from March 1958 with those of head of the government. Removed from all his positions in 1964. Nickname: Mr K.
Bibliography: *Peaceful Coexistence;* numerous collections of his speeches.

MACMILLAN, Harold (1894–   ): publisher. Captain during the First World War. Conservative Member of Parliament 1924–1929, 1931–1945 and 1951–1963; resident Minister, then High Commissioner in Northwest Africa and the Eastern Mediterranean 1942–1945; Minister of Housing 1951–1954; Minister for Defense 1954–1955; Secretary of State for Foreign Affairs 1955; Chancellor of the Exchequer 1955–1957; Prime Minister 1957–1963.
Bibliography: *The Winds of Change,* etc.

MALENKOV, Georgi Maksimilianovich (1902–   ): engineer; official of the Central Committee of the C.P.S.U. from 1934; Secretary of the Central Committee 1939; alternate member (1941) and then full member (1946) of the Politburo. Close collaborator of Stalin from 1948 to 1953. Premier 1953–1955. Excluded from the government and Presidium in 1957, and appointed director of a hydroelectric plant.

MENDÈS-FRANCE, Pierre (1907–   ): lawyer and economist; deputy from the Eure 1932–1940 and 1946–1958. Under Secretary of State to the Treasury 1938. During Second World War, enlisted in the Free French Air Force; Commissioner of Finances for the National Liberation Committee 1943; Minister of the National Economy 1944–1945; French representative on Board of Governors of the International Monetary Fund 1947–1958; Prime Minister and Foreign Minister 1954–1955; Secretary of State 1956; First Vice President of the Radical Party 1955–1957.
Bibliography: *Seven Months and Seventeen Days; To Govern Is To Choose; The Modern Republic,* etc.

MOLLET, Guy (1905–   ): teacher of English. Secretary General

of the "Fédération de l'enseignement" (Socialist teachers trade union) 1939. Secretary of the Committee of Liberation of the Pas-de-Calais; Mayor of Arras since 1945; Secretary General of the French Section of the International Worker's Party and Deputy from the Pas-de-Calais since 1945. Secretary of State 1946–1947 and 1950–1951; Vice President of the Council 1951; Prime Minister 1956–1957; Minister of State 1958–1959.
Bibliography: *Socialist Summing Up and Perspectives.*

NAGY, Imre (1896–1958): became a Communist during his captivity in Russia in 1917–1918; fought in the Red Army. Militant in the secret Hungarian Communist Party between the two world wars. Broadcaster on Radio Moscow from 1942 to 1944. Minister of Agriculture 1952–1953; Prime Minister 1953–1955 and 1956. Executed in 1958.
Bibliography: *A Communism Which Does Not Forget Man*

NASSER, Gamal Abdal (1918–   ): at 16 led a student demonstration in Cairo against British domination in Egypt; career officer; commander during the Palestine War. Founded the secret Society of Free Officers which overthrew the Egyptian monarchy in 1952. Deputy Prime Minister and Minister of the Interior 1952–1954; Prime Minister 1954–1956; President of the Republic since 1956. Nicknames: "the Bikbachi" and "the Rais."
Bibliography: *The Philosophy of the Revolution*

NEHRU, Jawaharlal (1889–1964): lawyer; member (1918), then Secretary General (1929) of the Pan-Indian Committee of the Congress. In 1929 (the first of four times) elected President of the Indian National Congress. President of the All-India States People's Conference 1939; Vice President and Foreign Minister in the provisional government 1946; Prime Minister and Foreign Minister 1947–1964.
Bibliography: *India and the World; Autobiography; Glimpses of World History,* etc.

NGO DINH DIEM (1901–1963): Vietnamese official. Minister of the Interior of Amman in 1933. Retired from politics and went into exile in Europe and the United States until 1954. Prime Minister 1954–1956, then President of the Republic 1956–1963.

RUSK, Dean (1909–   ): assistant professor of government and then dean of the faculty of Mills College (California) from 1934 to 1940. Served in the military from 1940 to 1946. Official in the State Department from 1946 to 1949; in 1950 became Assistant Secretary of State for Far Eastern Affairs. President of the Rockefeller Foundation 1952–1961. Secretary of State 1961–1969.

THANT, U. (1909–   ): Director of Secondary Schools in Burma, then Secretary of the Bureau for Reorganization of Teaching (1942). Director of the Press, then of Radio, 1947–1948; Secretary of State for Information 1949–1957. Representative from Burma to the U.N. 1957–1961; Secretary General of the U.N. since 1961.

The first volume of this work contains biographical notes on the following personalities mentioned in the second: Georges Bidault, Winston Churchill, Anthony Eden (Lord Avon), Dwight D. Eisenhower, Charles de Gaulle, Mao Tse-tung, George Marshall, Vyacheslav Molotov, Joseph Stalin, Chiang Kai-shek, Maurice Thorez, Josip Broz Tito, Harry S Truman.

INDEX

Acheson, Dean, 23–4, 29, 40, 42, 418, 446–7; on "defensive perimeter" of the U.S., 10–11, 56, 420; profile, 503

Adenauer, Konrad, 39–40, 43, 44, 48–9, 69, 72–3, 78, 120–1, 132–3, 473; profile, 503

Adjubei, Alexei, 425, 438, 439, 487–8

Adoula, Cyrille, 395

Afghanistan, 258

Africa, 359–75; *see also individual countries*

African Independent States, Union of, 367

African Peoples, Congress of, 367

Albania, 271, 353–5, 427–8, 465, 482

Algeria, 167–9, 359, 362–5; independence of, 433, 435

Algiers, 300, 364

American Joint Committee, 58

Anglo-Egyptian agreement (1954), 155–6

Anglo-Egyptian Alliance Treaty (1936), 148, 153

Anglo-Iranian Oil Company (A.I.O.C.), 145–7, 149, 152

ANZUS Pact, 37

Aqaba, Gulf of, 260

Arab-Israeli raids, 158, 234–6

Arab nationalism: exploited by the British, 136–7

Arab nations, league of, 137, 139

Arbenz Guzmán, Jacobo, 377–8

Argentina, 376–7

Associated States: *see* Indochina

Aswan Dam, 171–2, 174, 296; U.S. offer of aid, 164; U.S. decision not to aid, 172–3; U.S.S.R. aid, 296

Atlantic Council, 42, 77, 316

Atlantic Pact, 29, 34–6, 39, 41, 45–7, 78, 413, 426, 473; *see also* NATO

Atomic bombs, 33–4, 74, 76, 114, 116; MacArthur's suggestion to use, 26; U.S. controversy, 33; U.S.S.R., 283, 422, 425; Communist China, 488

Atomic Energy, International Agency of, 77

"Atoms for Peace" program, 76–7

Attlee, Clement, 23–5, 40–1, 138

Auriol, Vincent, 40

Austin, Warren, 16; debate with Gromyko, 20

Australia, 18, 37

Austria, 32, 73, 79, 80; state treaty, 125, 127, 129, 186

Baghdad Pact, 153, 156–7, 163–4, 166, 169, 254, 298–9

Balfour Declaration, 137

Balkan Pact, 36

Bandung Conference, 117–18, 158–9, 192, 222, 362

Bao Dai, Emperor, 86, 100, 399, 401–3

Batista, Fulgencio, 376, 379

Baudouin, King, 366–8

Bay of Pigs, 393, 413–14, 437

Bayar, Celal, 155

Belgian Congo: *see* Congo, the

Belgium: the Congo and, 366–75; intervention in the Congo, 369–70

"Benelux" countries, 44

Ben-Gurion, David, 140, 234–7, 239–40, 245, 248, 253; profile, 503–4

Beria, Lavrenti, 58–9, 188, 196–7; fall and execution of, 70–1, 189, 488

Berlin, 311–20, 337, 415–23, 425, 461–2; U.S.S.R. ultimatum on, 314–18; autobahn blockade, 318; proposed airlift for, 418; wall, 419–

51, 236–50, 252–6, 262, 294, 299–300, 397–8, 404–5, 414, 434, 472, 486; on German rearmament, 40–2; in the Middle East, 136–40, 144, 148–50, 153–6, 164–6, 168–9; Iranian petroleum crisis and, 146–9; on Suez Canal, 174–83; Egypt and, 148, 155–6, 221, 236–50; *see also* Churchill; Eden; Lloyd; Macmillan

Greece, 36, 258

Gromyko, Andrei, 18, 38, 63, 140, 261, 263, 316, 321–3, 397, 424, 444–5; debate with Warren Austin, 20; profile, 505–6

Guantanamo, U.S. naval base at, 446, 449, 458

Guatemala, 377–8, 392; arms shipment from Czechoslovakia, 378

Guevara, Ernesto Che, 381, 384, 437, 439, 480

Guinea, 359, 366, 433

Haganah, the, 137, 140–1
Haiphong, 86
Hallstein doctrine, 133
Hammarskjöld, Dag, 64, 169–70, 238–9, 243, 245, 253–4, 297, 349–50, 372–3, 394–5; death of, 395; profile, 506
Hanoi, 32, 86
Harriman, Averell, 35, 451–2, 473
H-bombs: *see* Atomic bombs
Hegedüs, Andras, 210, 216, 223
Henderson, Loy, 150–1, 261, 263
Herter, Christian, 319, 321, 339–40
Ho Chi Minh, 87, 89, 112, 400, 408, 479; profile, 506
Hodge, John R., 15
Hodja, Enver, 353–5, 427
"Hot line" between Kremlin and White House, installation, 469
Hungary, 71–2, 186–90, 211–31, 266–71, 287; U.S.S.R. and, 187–91, 198, 212–31, 253; Budapest uprising, 214 *ff.*; U.S.S.R. intervention, 225–31, 256, 264, 266–70, 274; arrests and executions, 268–70; *see also* Nagy; Rakosi

Hussein I of Jordan, 166, 242, 257–9, 299

Inchon: landing of MacArthur, 19
India, 20, 27, 31, 50, 55, 66, 136, 155, 274, 328, 481; conflicts with China, 328–30, 463–4; loan from U.S.S.R., 330; *see also* Nehru
Indochina, 45, 81, 83–109, 400; U.S. assistance, 83–4, Dien Bien Phu, 90–1, 93, 95–6, 98–9; "Operation Vulture," 92–3, 95, 98; conditions under which Congress would allow U.S. intervention, 93; decision of U.S. and U.K. not to intervene, 99; Geneva conference, 100–9; armistice agreement and declarations, 108
Indonesia, 274, 432, 486
Intercontinental missiles: *see* Missiles
Iran, 145–52, 157, 480; Anglo-Iranian Oil Company, 145–7, 149, 152; nationalization of petroleum industry, 145–9; National Iranian Oil Company, 146, 149–52; Great Britain and, in petroleum crisis, 146–9; *coup d'état*, 151; return of the Shah, 151
Iraq, 137, 139, 153, 156, 236–7, 254, 258, 261–2, 298, 301; proposed merger with Jordan, 296; *coup d'état*, 298–9; Egypt and, 303–4
Iraqi Petroleum Company, 242
Israel, 153–4, 156, 158, 168–70, 221, 233–5, 240–3, 247–8, 252–4, 480; break in relations with U.S.S.R., 58; independence, 140; U.S.S.R. aid, 141; defeat of Arabs by, 141; strained relations with U.S.S.R., 144; barred from Suez Canal, 158; raid against Gaza Strip, 158, 234; arms transaction with France, 158, 161–3, 235–6; appeal for arms, 234; Sinai Peninsula invasion by, 235, 237–41
Italy, 35, 44, 362, 480, 483; return of Trieste to, 36

Japan, 37; peace treaty, 38, 52; rearmament of, 38–9

U.S.S.R., 283, 288, 291; U.S., 284, 389, 481; U.S., expansion of development program, 389; Soviet, in Cuba, 436 ff.

Mobutu, Joseph, 369, 374–5, 394, 396

Moch, Jules, 42, 45–6, 290–1

Mohammed Reza Shah Pahlevi, 145, 149–51

Mollet, Guy, 166–7, 169–70, 175, 178, 180–3, 199, 235, 239–41, 243, 248–50, 255–6, 364–5; profile, 507–8

Molotov, Vyacheslav, 46, 58–9, 64, 66, 71, 78–80, 88–9, 100–1, 104, 107, 109, 113, 118–19, 126, 186, 189, 192–4, 265–6; critical of Khrushchev, 428; denounced at Twenty-second Congress, 428–9

Monnet, Jean, 35, 42–3

Morocco, 258, 359, 362, 480

Mossadegh, Mohammed, 145–51; arrest of, 151

Murphy, Robert, 173, 175–7

Naguib, Mohammed, 148, 153–5

Nagy, Imre, 72, 186–91, 194–5, 210–20, 222–6, 231, 267–9, 287, 508; execution of, 270

Nahas Pasha, 137, 148, 153

Nassau Accords, 472

Nasser, Gamal Abdal, 141, 155–8, 161–8, 171–4, 176, 178–9, 181–2, 254, 257–8, 261–2, 295–6, 299–300, 432, 480; see also Egypt; United Arab Republic

National Iranian Oil Company, 146, 149–52

National Liberation Front, 166

National Security Council of U.S., 11, 18, 19; "N.S.C. 68," 11; Executive Committee of, concerning Cuban missiles (Ex-Com), 441, 444–7, 454

NATO (North Atlantic Treaty Organization), 78–80, 119, 121, 156, 413, 425–6, 472, 480, 486, 489; see also Atlantic Pact

Navarre, General, 84, 86, 90–1, 94, 98

Nehru, Jawaharlal, 19, 31, 91, 112, 157, 167, 244, 264, 274, 300, 463–4; profile, 508

Nenni, Pietro, 264, 480

Netherlands, the, 18

"New Frontier," 388

New Zealand, 18, 37

Ngo Dinh Diem, 108, 399–408, 410; assassination, 478; profile, 508

Nicaragua, 376, 378, 392; U.S. arms shipment to, 378

Nixon, Richard, 97–8, 132, 323–4, 363, 381–2, 433

Nkrumah, Kwame, 363, 366–7, 432, 480

North Korea, 482, 486; invasion of South Korea, 9, 15

North Viet Nam, 102, 384, 404–5, 409

Novotny, Antonin, 462

Nu, U, 112

Nuclear arms, 426, 467–8, 470–3, 479

Nuclear tests, 333; proposal of ban on, 290–1, 293–4, 388, 415; resumption of, 422, 424–5, 436; treaty on cessation of, 469, 471–3

Nuri, es-Said, 137, 156, 237, 296, 298; assassination, 298

Ochab, Edward, 202, 206–7

Oder-Neisse frontier, 48, 318, 335

"Open skies" plan, 130–1, 289–90, 415

Organization of American States (O.A.S.), 383, 433–4, 448

Pakistan, 155, 258, 464

Palestine, 137; limitation of Zionist immigration, 137; see also Israel

Panchon Lama, 328

Pankow Government, 128, 312, 321, 421

Panmunjom peace talks, 29–30, 53–6, 66; prisoners of war issue, 30, 53–4, 55, 66; armistice, 67

Pannikar, Sardar K. M., 20–1

Paris Accords, 122–7, 131, 312

Paris, planned Summit meeting in, 337, 343–4

Pathet Lao, 100, 106, 384–5, 397–8